ACCA

NEW SYLLABUS
PRACTICE & REVISION KIT

Paper 3.5

Strategic Business Planning & Development

BPP Publishing
August 2001

First edition August 2001

ISBN 0 7517 0796 1

British Library Cataloguing-in-Publication Data
A catalogue record for this book
is available from the British Library

Published by

BPP Publishing Limited
Aldine House, Aldine Place
London W12 8AW

www.bpp.com

Printed in Great Britain by W M Print
Frederick Street
Walsall
West Midlands, WS2 9NE

We are grateful to the Association of Chartered Certified Accountants for permission to reproduce past examination questions. The answers to the past examination questions have been prepared by BPP Publishing Limited.

CONTENTS

The headings in this checklist/index indicate the main topics of questions, but questions often cover several different topics.

Preparation questions, listed in italics, provide you with a firm foundation for attempts at exam-standard questions.

Questions preceded by * are **key questions** which we think you must attempt in order to pass the exam. Tick them off on this list as you complete them.

Questions set under the old syllabus *Management and Strategy (M&S)* paper are included because their style and content are similar to those which will appear in the Paper 3.5 exam. The questions have generally been amended to reflect the new syllabus exam format.

MOCK EXAM 1

Questions 51 to 54

MOCK EXAM 2

Questions 55 to 58

global industries. p 199

BPP

TOPIC INDEX

Listed below are the key Paper 3.5 syllabus topics and the numbers of the questions in this Kit covering those topics.

If you need to concentrate your practice and revision on certain topics or if you want to attempt all available questions that refer to a particular subject (be they preparation, exam-standard or case study/scenario-based questions), you will find this index useful.

The New Syllabus *Strategic Business Planning and Development* paper differs from the Old Syllabus *Management and Strategy* in a number of ways. Some of the questions in this kit are on topics which were not covered under the Old Syllabus, and these are marked with an asterisk (*).

RETAKE STUDENTS SHOULD PAY PARTICULAR ATTENTION TO THE QUESTIONS ON THE TOPIC AREAS MARKED WITH A *. THESE ARE BEING EXAMINED FOR THE FIRST TIME UNDER THE NEW SYLLABUS.

	Syllabus topic	Question numbers
	5 Forces	6, 8, 16
	Benchmarking	11
	Core competences	5
	Ethics in business	17, 49
*	Global strategy and operations	39, 40, 41, 45, 48
	HR (including motivation and management)	29, 30, 44
	Learning organisation	37
	Marketing issues	15, 16, 21, 24, 25, 26, 27, 28, 32, 45
	Outsourcing	31
	Performance measures	28, 38, 44
	Porter's diamond	3
	Position audit	7, 10, 44, 46, 49
	Project management	19, 23, 49
	Quality	22
	Stakeholders	42, 47, 48
	Strategy development	5, 13
	Strategy evaluation and selection	14, 18, 43, 46, 47, 48, 49
	Structure and strategy	33, 34, 35, 43, 45, 49
	Sustainable competitive advantage	17, 36

Syllabus topic	**Question numbers**
The nature of strategic management	1, 2, 3, 4, 9, 12, 46, 48
Value chain	9

THE EXAM PAPER

The examination is a **three hour paper** divided into **two sections**. All the questions will require discursive answers. Very little computation will be required.

Section A will consist of one compulsory case study question worth 60 marks. The question setting will include a table of numerical information; this information is likely to include non-financial data. Question 1 is likely to be mainly concerned with the strategic management of the organisation concerned.

Section B will consist of three 20 mark questions; the candidate should answer two of these. These questions are likely to focus more closely on specific topics, though where a question has more than one requirement, it may cover more than one distinct syllabus area.

The Examiner for Paper 3.5 is Geoff Gravil, who was the Examiner for Paper 12 under the old syllabus. His questions require a practical approach, in which theory is used to **support** analysis and proposals rather than as a **substitute** for them.

The Paper 12 examinations displayed a distinct evolution and we can expect the Paper 3.5 examinations to be a continuation of that development to some extent. However, there are important differences.

(a) Question 1 is worth 60 marks rather than 50 and Section B questions are worth 20 marks rather than 25.

(b) Section B questions are likely to have substantial scenarios. This reflects the Examiner's concern that answers should be **practical** rather than mere theory dumps: you will have to **address the scenario** in you answers.

(c) The syllabus is significantly changed. In particular, routine management topics such as communication and human resource management receive far less attention. The focus is on **strategic** aspects of management throughout.

Summary

		Number of marks
Section A	One compulsory question	60
Section B	Choice of 2 questions from 3	40
		100

ANALYSIS OF PILOT PAPER

Section A

1 Analysis of strategic challenges; control of a decentralised conglomerate; disposal of a subsidiary as a strategic option

Section B

2 Launching a new professional partnership; cost-based pricing
3 Commercial priorities and ethics; performance indicators
4 Management style and organisational change

HOW TO PASS PAPER 3.5

Revising with this Kit

A confidence boost

To boost your morale and to give yourself a bit of confidence, **start** your practice and revision with a topic that you find **straightforward.** The **preparation questions** are relatively easy.

Key questions

Then try as many as possible of the **exam-standard questions**. Obviously the more questions you do, the more likely you are to pass the exam. But at the very least you should attempt the **key questions** that are highlighted in the questions and answers checklist/index at the front of the Kit. Even if you are short of time, you must prepare answers to these questions if you want to pass the exam – they incorporate the key techniques and concepts underpinning Strategic Business Planning and Development and they cover the principal areas of the syllabus.

No cheating

Produce **full answers** under **timed conditions**: practising exam technique is just as important as recalling knowledge. Don't cheat by looking at the answer. Look back at your notes or at your BPP Study Text instead. Produce answer plans if you are running short of time.

Imagine you are the marker

It is a good idea to actually **mark your answers**. Don't be tempted to give yourself marks for what you meant to put down, or what you would have put down if you had time. And don't get despondent if you didn't do very well. Refer to the **topic index** and try another question that covers the same or a similar area.

Ignore them at your peril

Always read the **Tutor's hints** in the answers. They are there to help you.

Trial run for the big day

Then, when you think that you can successfully answer questions on the whole syllabus, attempt the **two mock exams** at the end of the Kit. You will get the most benefit by sitting them under strict exam conditions, so that you gain experience of the four vital exam processes.

- Selecting questions
- Deciding on the order in which to attempt them
- Managing your time
- Producing answers

USEFUL WEBSITES

The websites below provide additional sources of information of relevance to your studies for Strategic Business Planning and Development.

- ACCA www.accaglobal.com
- BPP www.bpp.com
- Financial Times www.ft.com
- Wharton Business School http://knowledge.wharton.upem.edu
- The Economist www.economist.com
- Business Strategy Search Specialist www.sookoo.com

SYLLABUS MINDMAP

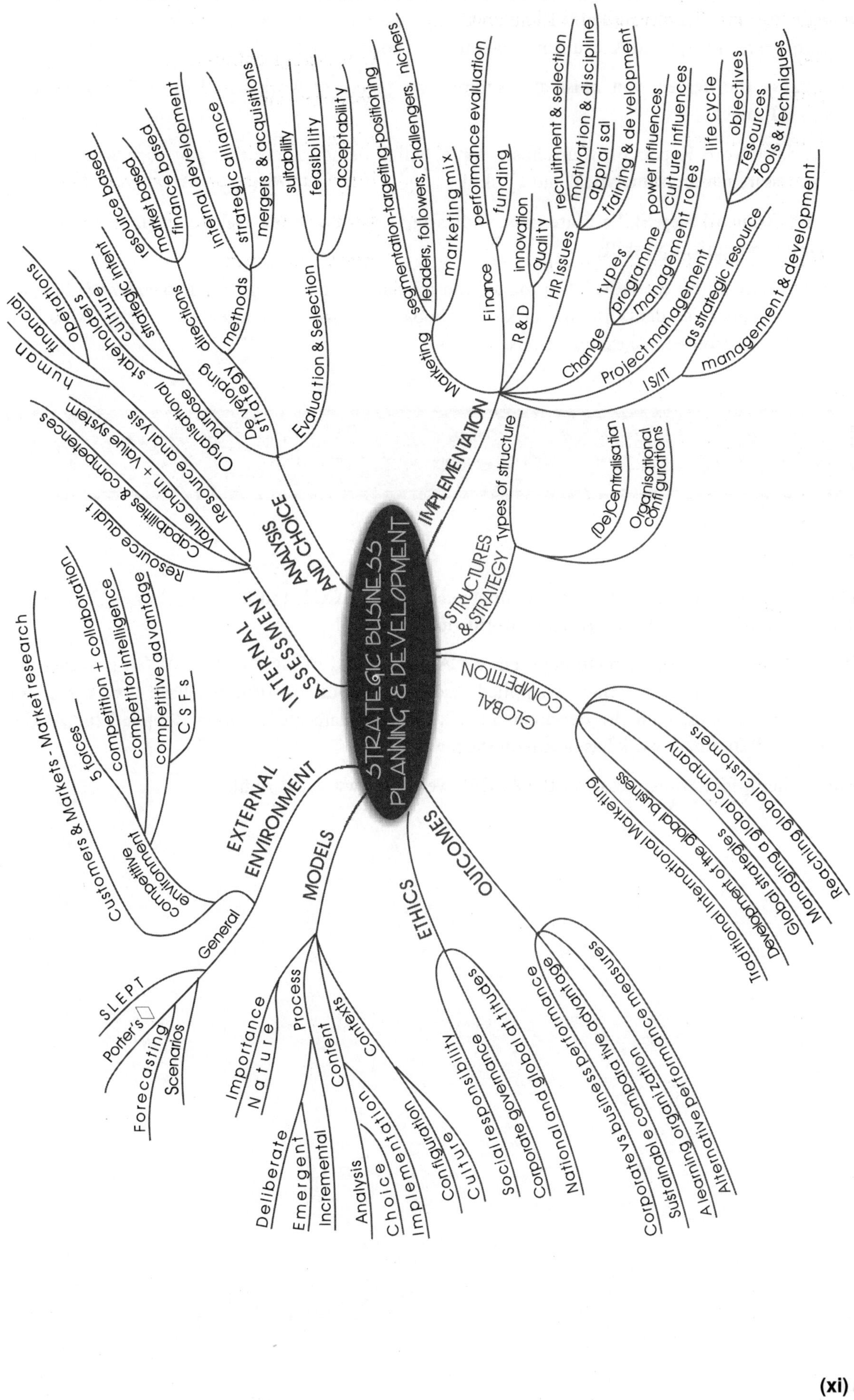

BPP PUBLISHING

OXFORD BROOKES

The standard required of candidates completing Part 2 is that required in the final year of a UK degree. Students completing Parts 1 and 2 will have satisfied the examination requirement for an honours degree in Applied Accounting, awarded by Oxford Brookes University.

To achieve the degree, you must also submit two pieces of work based on a **Research and Analysis Project.**

- A 5,000 word **Report** on your chosen topic, which demonstrates that you have acquired the necessary research, analytical and IT skills.
- A 1,500 word **Key Skills Statement**, indicating how you have developed your interpersonal and communication skills.

BPP was selected by the ACCA to produce the official text *Success in your Research and Analysis Project* to support students in this task. The book pays particular attention to key skills not covered in the professional examinations.

AN ORDER FORM FOR THE NEW SYLLABUS MATERIAL, INCLUDING THE OXFORD BROOKES PROJECT TEXT, CAN BE FOUND AT THE END OF THIS STUDY TEXT.

MBA

Plans for a new joint MBA have been announced by the ACCA and Oxford Brookes University. This new qualification will be available worldwide from 2001.

It follows the existing agreement between ACCA and Oxford Brookes to offer ACCA students the opportunity to qualify for BSc in Applied Accounting. Both institutions have now agreed to strengthen links through the development of a postgraduate qualification designed for ACCA members. Preliminary work has begun on the new MBA.

For further information, please see the ACCA's website: www.acca.org.uk

Questions

MODELS OF STRATEGIC MANAGEMENT

Questions 1 to 5 cover models of Strategic Management, the subject of Part A of the BPP Study Text for Paper 3.5

1 PREPARATION QUESTION: DISTINGUISH

Distinguish between items in the following pairs.

(a) Intended strategy and realised strategy

(b) The rational model of strategy making and the concept of emergent strategies

(c) Strategic and non-strategic decisions

Guidance note

- The items in the above pairs are different, obviously, but they are not necessarily opposites.

2 PREPARATION QUSTION: AURORA LIGHTING PLC

Aurora Lighting plc is a company which designs, manufactures and installs lighting systems for large buildings, such as theatres, hospitals, and scientific laboratories (eg where certain wavelengths of light must be excluded to avoid damage to the experimental process). The business was founded by Dawn and Helmut Wagner in 1985. It has two activities.

(a) Aurora designs and builds bespoke lighting systems to its customers' specifications.

(b) Aurora manufactures standard lighting systems which can be purchased from a catalogue.

For a while, demand grew rapidly. The construction boom in London and London's Docklands, in particular the prestigious Parrot Quay project, meant that the company's products and services were in great demand, and the company's sales revenue grew at a rate of about 20% per annum on average. Profits did not follow this trend. Whilst the company made gross margins of about 30%, net profits increased at a lower rate than sales. This was caused by several factors.

(a) The company's expansion led it to occupy new premises in north London in Haringey Science Park. The factory and the related design centre and offices are modern and ultra-clean. (Dust has a damaging effect on some of the materials used.)

(b) Research and development costs of a new standard range of lighting equipment. The range is called Borealis. Dawn and Helmut have invested a great deal of time and their own money in this range, but it came on stream just as the commercial property market collapsed. The Borealis range is dear to their hearts and is central to their hopes for the future.

(c) The company has recently started to employ qualified architects to assist liaison with developers, architects' practices and contractors, so that lighting considerations can be considered earlier on in the design process. Architects will then be aware of the novel lighting systems the company has to offer.

(d) The company has had to employ more electrical engineers to cope with the demand for specialist lighting systems.

Such was the initial demand in the UK that the company neglected exports. However, Helmut's German roots meant that this option was never abandoned altogether. Helmut had contacts at quite a high level with a number of German construction companies, and he was always careful to design the company's products to take German technical standards into account. The firm was thus able to profit from German unification and has been the preferred supplier of lighting systems. Borealis, however, has been less in demand than the firm's bespoke services, in which products are made strictly to a client's specification.

In the early days of the company, Helmut and Dawn both felt that the firm needed a mission statement, especially as Borealis was only on the drawing board, and Helmut regarded this as the company's raison d'etre. Their *mission* was brief:

> Aurora will develop and market a standard range of high quality, value for money lighting equipment, employing the most advanced materials and using information technology in the product and in the design process.

The strategic plan was first devised in 1989. In it, Helmut charted the company's growth for the next ten years. There have been some revisions: Borealis has been slower to grow than was hoped. It was hoped that a net profit margin of at least 8% will be achieved at all times. The strategic plan did not mention exports, but Borealis was anticipated to win 25% of the UK market by 1997. In fact, it has only gained 10% of the market, at the moment. Competition is severe, and margins are lower than expected, but Helmut believes that the quality of the range will win through in the end.

Helmut feels that events have driven the mission off course a bit, but he still feels that once the European economies have emerged from recession Borealis should be back on course. The managers of the Borealis production line complain about lack of resources. The expansion of the manufacturing division was done at the Borealis production director's insistence.

At the height of the 1980s boom in commercial property, Aurora was floated on the London Unlisted Securities Markets (USM) and subsequently went for a full listing on the Stock Exchange. The firm introduced an employee share option scheme. Dawn and Helmut have retained 51% of the shares, but wish to raise more capital: the share price has been falling recently despite the growth in profits and despite the briefings that Dawn and Helmut are happy to give investment analysts.

After they report their profits for 1996, Helmut is dismayed to read the following in the *Financial News*.

'Shareholders can't really complain. A net profit margin of 15% is high for a firm in this sector, and Aurora's ability to spread its wings in Germany has convinced some wavering sceptics about the firm's strategy in the medium term. But doubts as to whether this results from good management or just good luck continue to depress the share price, especially as Phelps lighting system's division is muscling in on the bespoke market that Aurora has dominated until now.'

Required

(a) Does Aurora Lighting plc have a coherent approach to making strategies?

(b) With reference to appropriate models of strategic management, analyse the strategic management process in Aurora Lighting plc.

(c) What sort of goals and objectives are found in Aurora Lighting plc? How do they relate to the way in which strategy is made and managed?

3 PREPARATION QUESTION: PLANNING COMPONENTS

(a) Describe the different components of strategic planning at its corporate, tactical and operational levels, and show the relationship between these components.

(b)   Distinguish between operational and non-operational goals.

(c)   Briefly explain the segments into which the business environment can be analysed.

Guidance note

- This question identifies the different kinds of goals, some of which can compromise the planning process.

4   INTRODUCING STRATEGIC MANAGEMENT   *36 mins*

N Ltd is a small family-controlled manufacturing company. In its 40-year history, the company has grown to the extent that it now employs 35 staff, producing a wide and diverse range of household goods and utensils. The company has increased in size from its small original base. However, it has never employed a strategic management approach for its development and has relied on operational decision-making to determine priorities. N Ltd has never gathered any information relating to its markets. In recent years, the company has experienced a reduction in turnover and profitability and is assessing how it might redress the situation.

The directors of N Ltd have now decided to introduce a strategic management approach which will assist in the selection of appropriate strategies for future development of the company.

Required

(a)   Explain how strategic management differs from operational management.   (8 marks)

(b)   Discuss the cultural and organisational changes which N Ltd will need to implement in order to successfully introduce strategic management.   (12 marks)

                                                                      (20 marks)

5   ELITE FABRICS → sell fabrics to manufacturing G → now intends to design a *36 mins* product its own "clothes" (end product.

Elite Fabrics (EF) is a medium-sized manufacturer of clothing fabrics. Historically, EF has built up a strong reputation as a quality fabric manufacturer with appealing designs and has concentrated mainly on the women's market, producing fabrics to be made up into dresses and suits. The designs of the fabric are mainly of a traditional nature but the fabrics, almost all woven from synthetic yarns, include all the novel features which the large yarn producers are developing.

Three years ago EF decided that more profit and improved control could be obtained by diversifying through forward integration into designing and manufacturing the end products (ie clothes) in-house rather than by selling its fabrics directly to clothing manufacturing companies.

EF's intention had been to complement its fabric design skills with the skills of both dress design and production. This had been achieved by buying a small but well-known, dress design and manufacturing company specialising in traditional products, targeted mainly at the middle-aged and middle-income markets. This acquisition appears to have been successful, with combined sales turnover during the first two years increasing to £100 million (+ 34%) with a pre-tax profit of £14 million (+ 42%). This increased turnover and profit could be attributed to two main factors: firstly the added value generated by designing and manufacturing end-products and secondly, the increased demand for fabrics as EF was more able to influence their end-users more directly.

In the last financial year, however, EF had experienced a slow down in its level of growth and profitability. EF's penetration of its chosen retail segment - the independent stores specialising in sales to the middle-class market - may well have reached saturation point. The business had also attempted to continue expansion by targeting the large multiple stores which currently dominate the retail fashion sector. Unfortunately the buying power of such stores has forced EF to accept significantly lower, and potentially unacceptable, profit margins. The management team at EF believes that the solution is to integrate even further forward by moving into retailing itself. EF is now considering the purchase of a chain of small, but geographically dispersed, retail fashion stores. At the selling price of £35 million, EF would have to borrow substantially to finance the acquisition.

Required

(a) Consider how the EF strategy of integrating forward into dress manufacturing has affected its ability to compete. Use an accepted model as a framework for analysis.

(10 marks)

(b) EF's potential expansion into retailing presents both advantages and disadvantages to the company. Evaluate the consequences of such a move for the business and assess the change in competences which would be required by the newly expanded business.

(10 marks)

(20 marks)

STRATEGIC ANALYSIS AND OPTIONS

Questions 6 to 18 cover Strategic Analysis and Options, the subject of Part B of the BPP Study Text for Paper 3.5

6   PREPARATION QUESTION: COMPETITIVE FORCES

(a) Briefly describe Michael Porter's model of the five forces in an organisation's competitive environment.

(b) Briefly describe Porter's model of the determinants of the competitive advantage of nations.

Guidance note

- This topic is so basic to the syllabus that if you can't list the factors in the model you have a lot more work to do.

7   PREPARATION QUESTION: IMPERIAL TRADERS PLC

Imperial Traders plc was established in 1785 and its head office has always been in London. Currently, most of its business takes place in and around the 'Pacific Rim', ie in Japan, Korea, Malaysia and Australia.

Required

small nations of Eastern Asia (Pacific ocean)

(a) (i)   Explain what a position audit is.

(ii) Describe the benefits to Imperial Traders plc of conducting such an audit in respect of a possible move of the head office from London to a Pacific Rim country.

(b) Discuss the effects of a relocation to a Pacific Rim country on the various aspects considered by the position audit.

(c) Describe briefly the cultural differences that Imperial Traders plc may encounter in its new domicile.

8   PREPARATION QUESTION: THREAT OF NEW ENTRANTS

In order to achieve sustained profitability, a company engaged in a low-technology industry must continually assess the threat posed by the entry of new competitors.

Required

(a) Explain how new competitors entering a low-technology industry can pose a threat to established companies.

(b) State, with reasons, the information you consider a company in low-technology industry requires to assess the extent of the threat posed by potential new competitors.

(c) Discuss how a company in a low-technology industry can counter the threat posed by the entry of new competitors.

9 PREPARATION QUESTION: CLASSICS ON THE CHEAP

Adapted from Tony James, 'Classics on the Cheap', Air UK Flagship, Issue no 45, August-September 1993, Stansted, Essex

Clive Reynard piles twenty glossy new paperbacks on the desk of his executive office. A year ago, a comparable array of similarly printed paperbacks - Austen, Hardy, Dickens etc - would have cost the reader around £150. But the books on Clive Reynard's desk retail in total for £20.00. Why?

The answer contains one of the most spectacular and audacious success stories in recent British publishing. As hardback sales shrink by around 15% a year and dozens of small firms fall victim to the recession, a publisher employing only ten full-time staff is bucking every trend by selling books by the million.

It was in June last year that Wordsworth editions, started five years earlier as a luxury book publisher, launched twelve classic paperback titles, apparently in headlong collision with market leaders, Penguin, Everyman and Oxford University Press.

Wordsworth sold two million books at £1.00 each, a phenomenal success achieved in a slump market. By the end of its first year in paperbacks, Wordsworth Editions had published nearly sixty classics, each with a minimum initial print run of 75,000. Most go almost immediately into at least one 30,000 reprint, ten of the first twelve titles sold out in a month, and they are best sellers internationally.

'We produce books for hard times,' says Reynard, head-hunted from Oxford University press and now Wordsworth's senior general editor. 'People want to read but increasingly cannot afford to spent the current £6-plus on a paperback. With our books they don't have to.'

All of which begs the question: why not?

Wordsworth's answer was to produce out-of-copyright books in huge quantities. The profit per unit is low, but there are a lot of units. The profit margin on a 1,500 page book selling for £1 is poor, but Wordsworth prove that it's there.

No one denies Wordsworth were in deep trouble two years ago. 'We began selling remainders, other people's mistakes,' remembers Michael Trayler, who started the company in 1987. A move into large colour books started promisingly but with hindsight there was too much dependence on the US market and when this suddenly went soft, the effect was calamitous.

Trayler and editorial director Marcus Clapham returned from America convinced disaster was closing in on Wordsworth unless something drastic was done. One day Mike said: 'Why don't we do classics for £1?' A crucial decision was not to tie products to the UK's price fixing scheme, the *Net Book Agreement*, but to allow shops to price as they pleased. (**Tutor's hint**. The *Net Book Agreement* is now suspended, enabling supermarkets to sell books at discount.) Despite such generosity, few retailers made concessions to Wordsworth's tight budget. W H Smith, the national book-selling chain, a major customer from the start, took between fifty and sixty per cent of every £1.

Smaller retailers are offered books in quantity for around 65p each but still fix their own profit margins. Some stores may offer six books for £5, others have been know to charge as much as £1.99 for the 1,642 page War and Peace or as little as 99p for the 951 pages of Vanity Fair. Paperback wholesalers and freelance sales reps looking for non-traditional markets which would sell a lot of books, suggested a range of supermarkets and service stations.

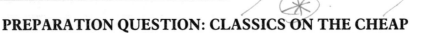

'If you're selling a classic book for about the price of a quality Sunday newspaper there is theoretically no limit to your outlets,' Trayler maintains. 'But without rapid turnover, you're dead.' A shoestring philosophy was essential from the start. Trayler vetoed an advertising budget: 'When you're selling a book at £1 that £1 does the advertising for you.' Staffing was kept to a minimum. Wordsworth's head office is above a shop in Ware, Herts, and executive staff are expected to travel economy class, answer their own phones and type their own letters.

'Our secret is that we're not greedy,' Reynard says. 'This is reflected in the price of our books. We're often asked why we don't double the price to £2 and make a lot more money. The danger is that someone would then come in and undercut us. At the moment no one can produce books any cheaper than we do. It simply wouldn't be worth the effort.'

Cheap or not, titles wouldn't sell unless the quality was good. Most of the books are printed and bound in Britain and the text is not abridged. But it is the ingenious legal manipulation of the copyright laws which keeps Wordsworth editions alive and viable. 'We give daily thanks for the two words "public domain",' Trayler says.

In most countries, copyright expires fifty years after an author's death, and the work moves into the public domain, anyone can reproduce it for nothing. 'Selling books for £1 we simply could not afford an author's royalty,' says Reynard. 'When you are dealing with margins like ours there is a magnifying effect which would transform, say, 1p royalty per copy into an enormous percentage of our unit cost.' 'We don't see ourselves in direct competition with Penguin Classics or Oxford University Press,' says Reynard. 'Our editions are not for schools and universities but for people who wish to read the classics inexpensively.'

Required

(a) Describe Wordsworth's *current* competitive strategy.

(b) Undertake a value chain analysis and identify those aspects of Wordsworth's organisation which underpin its success.

10 PREPARATION QUESTION: FAMILY DOCTOR

Conversations with a family doctors' general practice manager

'They felt threatened, I suppose. That's why I was appointed. After years of security and growth the ground had shifted beneath them. Hard work was no longer enough to ensure success. Legislation which created the General Practitioner's Contract of 1990, for example, had reduced the level of capitation fees (and the proportion of a General Practitioner's salary which they represented). At the same time it introduced a payment by results system whereby General Practitioners had to earn additional revenue through attaining target outcomes in problem areas such as cervical smears, childhood immunisation and periodic health checks. Clearly, it was going to pay to be even more customer orientated, and we have a range of customers.

The doctors who are partners in the practice had responded to this new tighter control by the Department of Health through a series of ad hoc initiatives designed to protect and grow their business. The partners had found it difficult, initially, to think about their practice in terms of being a business. I think they realised, however, that a new situation, calling for new project developments and a new professional managerial approach on top of their traditional and heavy workloads, required the introduction of some professional help. That is where I came in.

Their largely unconsidered decisions about the changes they should make to the practice had created some new problems. For example, the support staff were demotivated. They felt as though they were being asked to do a lot of new jobs for the sole benefit of the partners. A 'them and us' atmosphere prevailed. Some of them, I am sure, were passively working against the successful implementation of the new ideas. I have had to work on this problem.

I have also had problems related to the power nuances of the practice. For example, I do not have much power with which to impose my preferred ways of changing the enterprise. Rather, I have to undertake reasoned persuasion. It doesn't always work and I do not always get my own way. Another power problem involved one of the clerical administrators whose positions as the sole expert on our computer system meant that we were too dependent on him.

Also, I have problems because the partners do not share a common vision for the organisation. One of them is ready for retirement and not so interested in the longer term viability of the group. Another, I think, sees this practice as a career stepping stone. The other two, however, are more interested in the longer term success of the practice and I was gratified, recently, to hear one of them talk about the need for us to agree a vision for the practice. He also raised the idea of us going off for a half-day, or so, to undertake some sort of brain-storming session for our future.

Another big problem is information, or to put it more accurately, our lack of it. For example, we have no means for ensuring the success of anti-smoking measures. We don't even know how many of our patients smoke. Neither did anybody realise, until after I'd done some investigations, that the partners' gentlemanly approach to the development of the patient list wasn't being reciprocated by all of our neighbourhood practice colleagues. One of the bigger practices nearby has been actively recruiting our patients.

We do have a number of strengths, however. I do think we have a good reputation as a family practice and our range and locations of health promotion clinics is good. The practice is also learning to learn from initiatives being taken in other areas and is prepared to try out new ideas for the benefit of our clients. A recently introduced Exercise Clinic is one example of the sorts of change taking place in the practice.

Also, unlike many of our competitors we are taking full part in the strategic activity of our Health Authority which, as you know, is an important resources supplier to organisations such as ours. One of our partners is a member of the Authority's Family Health Committee. This keeps us close to an important aspect of our environment and helps to protect us from surprises. Currently we are monitoring developments in the moves to take selected secondary health care activities out of the hospital consultancy services.

Obviously, we need to build on our strengths and develop our weaker points. All in all, this is an exciting and challenging job. I am glad they offered it to me and I am glad that I accepted the post.'

Required

(a) Using appropriate analytical techniques, identify and evaluate the key internal and external issues facing the doctors' practice described above.

(b) Advise the new Practice Manager in her role as an agent of organisational change. Discuss some of the problems she is already facing or is likely to face in her attempts to introduce a more professional approach to the management of the practice and offer advice on how she might address these problems.

11 SALES TEAM BENCHMARKING *36 mins*

A company which manufactures and distributes industrial oils employs a team of regional sales people who work directly from home. All members of the sales team have their own geographical areas to cover and they visit clients on a regular basis.

The sales team staff are each paid a basic monthly salary. Each member of the team is set an identical target for sales to be achieved in the month. A bonus payment in addition to the basic salary is made to any member of the team who exceeds the monthly sales target.

Generally, experience has been that the members of the sales team succeed in improving on their targets each month sufficiently to earn a small bonus. However, the managers are unclear whether all the team members are achieving their maximum potential level of sales. Consequently, the managers are considering introducing a system of benchmarking to measure the performance of the sales team as a whole and its individual members.

Required

(a) Explain the objectives of benchmarking and how it may be used to assist the managers in evaluating operational performance. (8 marks)

(b) Describe how a system of benchmarking could be introduced to measure the performance of the sales team both as a whole and as individuals in comparison with each other. (12 marks)

(20 marks)

12 PREPARATION QUESTION: MISSION, VISION AND STRATEGIC INTENT

Explain what is meant by the three terms *mission, vision* and *strategic intent*.

13 PREPARATION QUESTION: COST LEADERSHIP

(a) What factors are important in achieving 'overall cost leadership'?
(b) Discuss the risks to an organisation of adopting this strategy.
(c) Identify two other generic strategies.

Guidance note

- A choice of competitive strategy cannot be made without considering the choices made by competing organisations.

14 PREPARATION QUESTION: PHARMIA PLC

Pharmia plc is a drugs manufacturing company. It is operating in an intensively competitive market and prices are being forced down all over the world.

To maintain its position, Pharmia plc utilises the concept of the product portfolio. Currently, there are 34 new products in the portfolio, at various stages of development. Pharmia plc cannot predict if any of these will become a major product. However, its belief is that 'There are a number of runners in the race and the more you have the greater the chance there is of picking a winner'.

The company has also stated that it is a 'Research and Development (R&D) driven company'. Therefore Pharmia plc always tries to ensure that there is adequate investment in R&D. The other major aspect of its corporate strategy is a belief in aggressive marketing, occasioned by the circumstances of the global market.

A product manager of Pharmia plc has been unexpectedly given £5 million extra funding and has the following options available.

(i) Tyrix is a drug in the early stages of development. If £5 million is invested now, it will reduce the time required before the drug is ready to be sold.

(ii) Medvac has been successfully introduced into the market. It is having to compete against two rival products. An investment of £5 million would pay for an advertising campaign which it is thought would increase its market share.

(iii) Sonprex is a mature product and is probably going to be superseded in the near future. An investment of £5 million would enable it to be repackaged and allow some promotional activities to be undertaken.

The following information has been provided by the marketing department.

Investment	*Product*	*Outcome*	*Probability*	*Discounted payoff* £ million
£5m	Tyrix	Success	3%	150
		Failure	97%	Nil
		Market share		
£5m	Medvac			
		+30%	1/6	48
		+15%	1/3	27
		+10%	1/2	(10)
£5m	Sonprex	Success	1	14

The options are mutually exclusive and must be undertaken completely or not at all. The payoffs are calculated before the cost of the investment.

Required

(a) Present the expected values of the outcomes of the three options in the form of a decision tree.

(b) Evaluate the appropriateness of the use of expected values and subjective probabilities for this decision.

(c) Advise the product manager as to which drug should receive the investment.

15 PREPARATION QUESTION: CHILDREN'S NOVELTY CONFECTIONERY

ZQ Ltd manufactures a range of children's novelty confectionery. In addition to having to meet the usual competitive pressures, ZQ Ltd experiences sudden changes in demand. These are thought to be due to promotion, both by the company and its competitors, of particular novelty products, any one of which may appeal to consumers for only a very short period of time. ZQ Ltd is always ready to introduce its next available confection into the market at what it believes to be the most appropriate time in order that its total demand remains stable.

The company evaluates each new line developed in its laboratory according to the expected positioning of that line in its product portfolio. The marginal return on marginal investment is related to the perceived risk associated with the new line which is defined after 'panel testing' by local schoolchildren. The new line is accepted if the portfolio including it provides prospects of a higher return at less risk than the previous portfolio which excluded the new product. Where gains are not perceived, or increased risk is apparent, further test marketing, promotion or product launch is suspended.

It is admitted that there have been occasions when new confections, previously rejected as a result of the application of these criteria, have been demanded by consumers and a successful outcome to their marketing experienced by ZQ Ltd. Again, not all the new lines meeting the criteria referred to have been found to be worthwhile.

Required

(a) Explain how the compilation of a product portfolio can assist the marketing function to recognise the most suitable position for its company to adopt with respect to a particular product range.

(b) Argue how valid the testing of a new product geared to children's tastes on a panel, such as a particular school, would be in making judgements as to the likely acceptance of such a product.

(c) Suggest how marketing can differentiate similar products when compatibility within existing production processes is to be maintained.

16 PREPARATION QUESTION: IMPORT CONCERN

BM plc imports and distributes consumer durables such as televisions, stereos, and microwave ovens. BM plc buys its products in Asia, and sells them in Europe. As part of its continual environmental monitoring process, the company has become aware of the following factors that cause it concern.

(a) Predictions of the level of consumer spending show a marked rate of decrease in the next five years.

(b) Some European governments are considering imposing retaliatory import restrictions against Asian products.

(c) Some of BM plc's supplier countries have been criticised by pressure groups because of their poor working conditions and the low pay received by their nationals.

Required

(a) Advise BM plc as to how it should examine and adapt its short-term plans in the light of these factors.

(b) Advise BM plc on the methods of influencing governments' policy in its favour.

(c) Recommend what options are available to a company faced with profitable opportunities that conflict with its corporate culture.

17 LARGE FINANCIAL SERVICES COMPANY *36 mins*

The chairman of a large financial services company, after discussion with the non-executive directors and the Audit Committee, has become concerned that the company is taking too many risks in its business operations.

The company has been very successful and has grown rapidly by being more innovative than its competitors in designing and selling new products. These include investment and savings plans and long-term loans to high-income individuals This has been achieved in a decentralised environment by rewarding product managers with substantial bonuses on current profits earned by products they have designed and for which they are responsible. Sales executives have been rewarded by high commissions on sales. The company has been successful in recruiting and retaining very able staff by providing the highest rewards in the industry. Staff have the maximum freedom to maximise their earnings.

Regulation of the industry has increased considerably, and is expected to increase further. There have been no major problems with the regulatory authorities. However, following a series of minor problems, some products have had to be withdrawn or modified and some sales staff have been disciplined. The company has often been criticised by consumer organisations and journalists for its treatment of customers, and its products appear poor value for money in comparative surveys.

The Chairman is proposing to introduce a company code of conduct with the aims of instilling ethical values and helping the company appear in a better light in newspapers and surveys.

Required

As a consultant, prepare a report on this proposal for the Board. In your report:

(a) Explain the extent to which a code of conduct can help to change organisational culture and encourage ethical behaviour. (10 marks)

(b) Propose any other changes, including possible control systems, that may be needed to achieve the Chairman's aims. (10 marks)

(20 Marks)

18 ACQUISITION *36 mins*

C plc, a quoted chemical manufacturing company, has until recently achieved a steady increase in profitability over a number of years. It faces stern competition and the directors are concerned about the disquiet expressed by major shareholders regarding performance over the last two years. During this period it has consistently increased dividends, but its share price has not grown at the same rate as it did previously.

K plc, a direct competitor, is similarly experiencing a reduction in profitability. Its shareholders are diverse, with the majority being financial institutions. K plc has been criticised for under-investment and has achieved no product development over the last two years. Following a concerted media campaign, K plc is facing prosecution for discharging untreated pollutants into a river.

C plc is seriously considering making a bid to acquire K plc. The directors of C plc, however, are divided as to whether K plc should be closed down or permitted to continue production post-acquisition if a bid is made. In either situation, significant staff redundancies would follow.

Required

(a) State the strategic factors which C plc would need to consider before making a bid to acquire K plc. (8 marks)

(b) What are the social and ethical implications of the acquisition and the environmental issues it raises? (12 marks)

(20 marks)

IMPLEMENTING STRATEGY

Questions 19 to 38 cover Implementing Strategy, the subject of Part C of the BPP Study Text for Paper 3.5.

19 PREPARATION QUESTION: PROJECT MANAGEMENT

An increasingly popular method of ensuring co-ordinated effort towards the introduction of change is to apply the techniques of 'project management'.

(a) List the features (apart from those mentioned in (b) and (c) below) which distinguish project management from 'process' or 'business as usual' management.

(b) Amongst the key requirements for successful project management are:

(i) Clear aims
(ii) A sponsor
(iii) A management structure
(iv) An owner
(v) A project team
(vi) A communication system

Briefly describe these key requirements.

(c) A further key requirement of the project is the project plan. Briefly outline the process of planning a project.

Guidance note

- This question is about the purpose and management environment of project management, not about techniques of project management.

20 PREPARATION QUESTION: RESISTING CHANGE

Discuss the most effective processes for initiating and implementing organisational change and say why individuals and groups tend to resist change.

Guidance note

- The unfreeze-change-refreeze framework describes the change process but does not suggest how you go about it.

21 PREPARATION QUESTION: SEGMENTATION

Describe the likely means of segmentation which would be used by:

(a) A manufacturer of diesel engines
(b) A manufacturer of breakfast cereals

Guidance note

- Again, you are dealing with both consumer and industrial markets.

22 PREPARATION QUESTION: GRENDALL AND FELIX

Grendall and Felix specialise in the design and manufacture of industrial valves. Grendalls (as they are usually known) enjoy an excellent reputation, their valves are found in oil refineries, chemical plants, food processing factories and other processing plants in Europe,

North America the East Asia. Such valves must be of high quality as they are located at the heart of the plant and must go on working for many years without interruption.

Yesterday, Grendalls received a letter from Barnhams, one of their most important customers. The production manager was particularly upset when he read the letter. 'I can't understand it', he said, 'we have been supplying Barnhams for years and we've never had any complaints. Now they send us a threatening letter like this. We've argued over price in the past but never over quality.'

Gradually a clearer picture begins to emerge. Barnhams have recently gained accreditation from the British Standards Institution. Their letter invites Grendalls to apply for similar accreditation under BS EN ISO 9000. Barnham's letter states that if Grendalls does not achieve BS EN ISO 9000 status then their supply relationship will be under review.

Grendalls does not have a specific job of 'quality manager' and therefore as head of internal audit you have been asked to speak to Barnhams and to provide a briefing paper for management on the implications of the Barnham letter.

Required

Provide a briefing paper for the management at Grendalls. Specifically, management have asked that you cover the following points in your paper.

(a) Why have Barnhams asked Grendalls to apply for accreditation?

(b) What are the advantages of accreditation to Grendalls? Are there any disadvantages? If so, what are they?

(c) How do accreditation procedures, such as BS EN ISO 9000, relate to other approaches to quality, for example Total Quality Management?

23 IT PROJECT (M&S, 6/98, amended) *36 mins*

The organisation for which you work is about to evaluate a proposal for a major upgrade in its information technology support for office administration staff. Currently the work of these staff is fragmented, lacking integration and cohesion. The proposed upgrade will enable information transfer to be more readily achieved and should improve both the efficiency and effectiveness of the office administration. The suggestion is for each of the fifty staff members to have a high specification personal computer (PC) with associated software (word processing, spreadsheets etc.). All PCs will be linked into a local area network comprising several fileservers to handle shared applications, plus network links into Internet services. At the present time about thirty staff have access to PCs of a variety of types and specifications which are running a number of stand-alone applications. There is limited access on some machines to networked shared services. The capital cost of this proposed upgrade is estimated to be in the region of £250,000.

The Finance Director has asked you to take charge of the proposed project. He wishes the project to focus on two main issues: the cost justification of the expenditure in relation to competing IT project proposals and, if a go-ahead is given, and the achievement of a smooth transition in moving staff and applications to the new office support system. However, he is worried that the review might concentrate exclusively on monetary considerations, such as discounted cash flow, and he feels that this approach would be both simplistic and unsuitable.

Required

(a) The new office support system is believed to be technically feasible but has not yet been cost justified. Explain how you might undertake a non technical evaluation of the proposed investment of £250,000 in office information technology. Your evaluation should cover the treatment of both financial and non-financial criteria. (12 marks)

(b) Outline an approach which you might propose to adopt in planning for and executing an implementation of the new office support system. (8 marks)

(20 marks)

24 WESTPORT UNIVERSITY (M&S, 6/99, amended) *45 mins*

Westport University is a medium-sized educational institution, having achieved university status six years ago. It is located in a large city with a considerable commercial and manufacturing infrastructure. The university has tended to concentrate on vocational courses such as engineering, science and business and management studies. Because of its relative newness it is not a popular university having not yet acquired a strong academic reputation. With a recent growth in university places available, coupled with a small decline in student demand, Westport is currently unable to operate at full capacity. In order to avoid redundancies the university is looking for alternative courses to help them generate both income and students. Bill Loftus is the commercial manager for the business and finance faculty. He recognises that the faculty has a reasonably strong reputation for its degree programmes including an accountancy degree. However this is a full-time programme at undergraduate level. There are currently no postgraduate degrees in accountancy nor any facility for studying professional accountancy qualifications.

Bill realises that accountancy is growing in popularity and that to practice as an accountant and to progress in the profession one has to be a member of one of the professional accountancy bodies. However he also recognises that much of this training is pursued on a part-time basis by students who are already working within a financial environment. Although this area appears to be one with potential, the head of the faculty is unwilling to put resources into offering professional accountancy training until more research has been carried out.

Required

Acting in the position of Bill Loftus:

(a) Present a report to the head of faculty, detailing what research into the professional accountancy training market needs to be carried out, and commenting on the method of research to be used. (10 marks)

(b) Assuming that the university approves the venture to develop professional accountancy training, identify the main marketing strategies that could be used to attract students to the programmes. (10 marks)

(20 marks)

25 PARTNERSHIP (M&S, 6/96, amended) *36 mins*

Siddiqui, Warrington and Company (SW) are a long-established medium sized accountancy practice operating in a large industrial city. The practice had developed a stable and profitable client base over the period between 1970 and the early 1980s, providing advice on taxation and corporate finance, along with the usual steady income stream from audit clients. During this period the practice's main clientele had been owner managed manufacturing and retail businesses within the city and its suburbs. The partners had never actively sought out business and new clients had arrived on the basis of recommendations and personal contacts. In summary, the practice was seen to be the natural supplier of financial and audit services to the small and medium sized business sector of the city. Over the years Siddiqui, Warrington and Company have become conservative in approach and inflexible.

The recessions of the 1980s and 1990s led to a massive shake-out in the manufacturing businesses in the city. Many of these businesses closed, and with restructuring in the manufacturing sector there were numerous mergers and acquisitions. Understandably, as headquarters were relocated and businesses were taken over, the practice began to lose clients to the large international accountancy practices.

In response, Siddiqui, Warrington and Company attempted to attract new business by focusing on the smaller audit and accountancy services sector. This approach brought them into direct conflict with the sole practitioners and other providers of bookkeeping services. The result was not the success which they had hoped for. The very wide range of small clients did not present the opportunities for economy of delivery, and the intense fee competition was producing a large amount of smaller profit margin contracts.

By the end of 1995 the partnership was only just breaking even financially. The long delayed economic recovery was not bringing them the rewards which they had hoped for. Although the older partners recognised the problems, they were undecided as to the way forward. The younger members of the practice were beginning to voice their discontent. One in particular, Dominic Gower, was proposing a more proactive role for the firm. His main concern was that the partnership needed to go out and market itself. It was not enough to be technically proficient. It needed new and profitable business, particularly in the current turbulent and competitive environment. The managing partner agreed that something needed to be done urgently if the firm was to see prosperous times again and decided to encourage Gower to develop his ideas.

Required

(a) In the role of Dominic Gower assess the need to adopt a marketing oriented stance to the management of the partnership and suggest a possible approach to the development of a partnership marketing plan. (10 marks)

(b) Examine the differences that are likely to arise between the marketing of consumer products and the marketing of accountancy services such as auditing and taxation advice. How might these differences influence the way that accountancy services are to be marketed? (10 marks)

(20 marks)

26 KARAOKE *36 mins*

You are an entrepreneur who has decided to launch Opera Karaoke. You have decided to produce the recording of two compact disks. These will be sold together in one box. One CD will contain the orchestral accompaniment to 15 different operatic arias. The other will be singers singing together with orchestral accompaniment, as a tutorial CD.

You have obtained funding from Bumble Records, who will distribute the CDs. You feel that the market will consist of two segments. One is the private individual who enjoys singing in his own home. The other is the professional karaoke machine operator who owns a machine and is hired by pubs and professional party planners.

Requirement

(a) In relation to the above project, describe the elements of the marketing mix to be considered. (12 marks)

(b) Explain the research methods by which the attitudes of prospective private individual purchasers to the product and to the elements of the marking mix you have identified can be measured. Give three examples of the questions that might be asked by the researchers. (8 marks)

(20 marks)

27 PRODUCT LAUNCH (M&S, 6/98, amended) *36 mins*

Klypso Corporation is a medium-sized regional company, producing and distributing fruit flavoured, carbonated drinks. In recent years it has seen a rapid decline in its sales to local stores and supermarkets. There are two main reasons for its poor performance. Firstly the major corporations, selling cola drinks have developed global brands which are now capturing the youth market which is seeking more 'sophisticated' products. Secondly the sales outlets are no longer willing to provide shelf space to products which are not brand leaders, or potential leaders in their product category.

The Managing Director (MD) of Klypso believes that the company needs a drastic turnaround if it is to survive. The soft drinks industry has become too competitive, and the bottling technology too expensive to warrant new investment. However the company feels that its greatest strength is its knowledge and access to distribution channels and therefore its opinion is that it should still stay within the food and drinks industry. Whilst on a fact-finding mission to the United States of America he MD was attracted by a new chocolate confectionery product which claims to provide high energy contact but with low fat. This seemed to be a successful combination of attributes for those consumers, mainly active participants in sporting activities, who were concerned with their diet but who enjoyed an occasional treat. The product has been developed and is owned by a relatively unknown confectionery company in California. The company has agreed to provide Klypso with a licensing contract for manufacture and sales of the product within Klypso's own country.

The MD is convinced that the secret to success will be in the marketing of the product. The company has suffered in its drinks business because it did not develop a distinctive and successful branch. The new product is also unknown in Klypso's own country. In order to get national recognition and acceptance from the major retail outlets the product will need considerable promotional support. As the company has very little experience or expertise in promotional activity it was decided to use a marketing consultancy to provide guidance in developing a promotional plan.

Klypso, being a medium-sized company, has only a limited budget. It will have to focus upon a new and national market instead of its traditional, regional stronghold. It has to develop a new brand in a product area with which it is not familiar. Before committing itself to a national launch Klypso has decided to trial the product launch in a test market.

Required

You have been appointed to act as the business consultant as part of the marketing consultancy team assisting Klypso.

(a) Present a report to the management of Klypso recommending and justifying the types of promotional activity that could be used to support the launch of the new product. (14 marks)

(b) Which factors need to be considered to ensure that the test market produces results which can be reliably used prior to the national launch? (6 marks)

(20 marks)

28 COMPUTER DEPARTMENT

36 mins

ABC plc has a central computer department which works solely for other departments within the company. Its current charge-out rate is £250 per hour. The rate is the same whatever task is being performed. The manager of the computer department has been given a single objective - to recover her department's costs.

Some of the users are dissatisfied with the computer service, and have observed that external agencies often charge as little as £75 an hour. The users are not allowed to use such external agencies.

Required

(a) Recommend what you consider to be a suitable set of objectives for the computer department. (8 marks)

(b) Describe control procedures which could assist in achieving the objectives which you have recommended. (8 marks)

(c) Explain how the computer department could develop a marketing orientation towards its customers. (4 marks)

(20 marks)

29 CASTERBRIDGE OFFICE (M&S, 12/98, amended)

36 mins

Jane Smith has very recently been made a partner in a medium-sized accounting practice with the requirement that she take charge of the practice's Casterbridge office. The office comprises about ten secretarial, technician and part-qualified audit staff. Jane has never worked at the Casterbridge office and, as part of a first attempt to familiarise herself with the office, she has examined the staff files and associated correspondence. She has been surprised to find that staff turnover and sickness are far higher than in the other practice offices and that there appears to have been a succession of quality problems related to poor client care and operational mistakes.

She has also asked the senior partner if he can explain the reasons for the apparent staff related problems to which he replied ' Well we may have had a number of unavoidable changes in partners responsible for Casterbridge over the last few years but remember, Jane, that we do pay staff above market wage rates and provide good working conditions. What we undoubtedly are looking at here is a case of far too slack management control and supervision.'

Required

(a) In the light of relevant theories of motivation and the statement made by the senior partner comment on the apparent staff problems in the Casterbridge office. (12 marks)

(b) Acting in the role of Jane explain how you would proceed in seeking to improve the apparent staff problems in the Casterbridge office. (8 marks)

(20 marks)

30 GRUMIT (M&S, 6/95, amended)

36 mins

David Omega is the finance and administration (F&A) manager of Grumit, a company manufacturing and supplying water filters to the domestic market. Grumit not only manufactures water filters but imports a wide range of filters and associated products from its overseas parent company. All products require installation and after sales service which is carried out by Grumit's trained service engineers.

The numbers employed by Grumit are:

Management and associated administrative and support staff	45
Manufacturing facility	220
Marketing, sales and distribution	75
Installation and after-sales service engineers	65

Trade unions are recognised only in the manufacturing facility - with one for skilled workers, and another for unskilled workers. There is no recognised union in any other part of Grumit, although the majority of field service engineers are thought to be members of an unrecognised union.

For a few years now the manufacturing facility at Grumit has been struggling to break even. Grumit's managing director has just returned from a visit to the parent company and informs David that the manufacturing facility is to be closed as it has not been possible to reach the required levels of quality and productivity. In addition management of the parent company believe that Grumit as a whole is over-staffed in relation to the volume of sales. Management has been given 12 months to produce significant improvements. The manufacturing facility is to be closed as soon as possible and, in future, all products will be imported from the parent company. There will be a need to restructure marketing and also for the re-training of most service engineers to equip them to deal with the new product range.

Grumit's managing director has not told any other employees of the directive from the parent company and is very anxious that the prospective changes are managed so as to minimise loss of morale and keep staff motivated. As F&A also has responsibility for personnel matters, David has been asked to provide advice on three issues: letting people know about the changes, the redundancies arising from the closure of the manufacture plant and the plans for restructuring and re-training.

Required

(a) Recommend and describe a suitable human resource management approach to deal with the situation at Grumit and advise on policy and procedures in relation to the three issues of communication, redundancy and restructuring/retraining. (12 marks)

(b) Examine the lessons which are available to Grumit from other organisations' experience in the successful management of change. (8 marks)

(20 marks)

31 OUTSOURCING *36 mins*

The Directors of AB plc are facing increasing pressure from shareholders to increase earnings per share. The overhead costs of the company have increased as a proportion of total cost over the last three years and the directors are considering outsourcing the financial accounting, payroll, creditor payments and debtors functions in order to reduce the levels of operational gearing. However, the directors are concerned that AB plc will not receive the same level of service from these functions after they have been outsourced.

Required

(a) Explain why an organisation may outsource some of its primary or support activities.

(5 marks)

(b) Summarise how AB plc should proceed to outsource the financial accounting, payroll, creditor payments and debtors functions. Discuss how the directors may be assured of the quality of the service which is subsequently received for these activities. (15 marks)

(20 marks)

32 SPORTS CENTRE *36 mins*

A local administrative authority allowed a supermarket development to go ahead providing that the company concerned built an extension to the authority's sports centre on an adjoining site.

In recent years the sports centre has encountered a growth in competition from local commercial recreation organisations. Simultaneously, the authority had experienced a reduction in its central funding, and has steadily increased its charges for the use of its sports centre facilities.

In reviewing its services at the sports centre, the authority has applied the product life cycle (PLC) model. It has identified the stage within the life cycle at which each of its sports centre services is positioned, as follows.

Introductory stage: Martial arts, with little take up as yet.

Growth stage: Squash playing facilities, which have required capital investment from the authority and on-going maintenance costs of the courts and equipment.

Demand for the facilities is increasing rapidly.

Maturity stage: Gymnasium facilities, which require little maintenance expense and experience steady demand which generates surplus cash.

Swimming, which incurs a continual increase in maintenance and water purification costs.

Decline stage: Badminton, with a continual reduction in demand.

Required

(a) Recommend how the local authority could market its sports centre services. (8 marks)

(b) Comment on the strategic resource allocation implications of each stage of the product life cycle when applied to the sports centre facility.

You are *not* required to describe or draw the product life cycle model. (12 marks)

(20 marks)

33 PREPARATION QUESTION: DIVISIONALISATION

Why are so many very large companies organised into autonomous strategic business units?

34 PREPARATION QUESTION: BURNS AND STALKER

What is meant by bureaucracy? Is there an alternative?

35 PREPARATION QUESTION: CENTRALISATION

What is centralisation? Is it strategically useful?

36 PREPARATION QUESTION: COMPETITIVE ADVANTAGE

What is competitive advantage? How do you know when you have achieved it?

37 PREPARATION QUESTION: LEARNING ORGANISATION

Is organisational learning a route to strategic success?

38 PREPARATION QUESTION: Z SCORE AND BALANCED SCORECARD

Does a Z score do the same thing as a balanced scorecard?

GLOBAL STRATEGY

Questions 39 to 41 cover Global Strategy, the subject of Part D of the BPP Study Text for Paper 3.5.

39 PREPARATION QUESTION: DULCET SPEAKERS LTD

Dulcet Speakers Ltd is a UK company which specialises in the making of high quality loudspeakers for hi-fi systems and public address systems (eg for pop concerts). It is privately owned by Gordon Dulcet, son of the founder Horatio Dulcet. Its craft expertise is widely recognised all over the world. In a recent advertising campaign in the UK, the firm was able to publish statements praising the firm's hi-fi products by ten famous personalities from the worlds of both classical and popular music. Its products are very expensive.

The management of Dulcet Speakers Ltd is obsessive about quality and is continually researching new and better ways of reproducing perfect sound. It pursues a differentiation-focus strategy, by providing a differentiated product to a highly specified segment of the market.

Dulcet Speakers Ltd competes in this segment of the market with three other firms, all based in the UK: Serenity, Keyvalley Sound Systems and Starr. The competition means that prices are slightly lower in the UK market than elsewhere: the other companies have yet to achieve an export presence. Dulcet Speakers Ltd recruits graduates from the local university, where it has established a lectureship in Sound Science, a discipline which covers electronics, acoustics, physics and biology.

Outside the market segment in which Dulcet, Keyvalley, Serenity and Starr are the most important competitors, the hi-fi market is largely dominated by Japanese firms, some of which have factories in Britain and which manufacture for export to continental Europe.

At present, the company's sales are broadly and securely based in Europe and the USA, where it has a powerful position in the segment. However, the managers have decided that to guarantee growth they need to enter the markets of Asia. Their projections reveal growing affluence amongst the general population in the next twenty years.

Their initial analysis reveals the following.

1. Japanese consumers are attracted by 'traditional' British goods like scotch whisky, certain textiles, anything with a craft image. However, they take a basic level of quality for granted in goods like consumer electronics. They wish something distinctive.
2. Japanese houses are fairly small and so there is a cultural bias towards miniaturisation (of products etc).
3. The Japanese market for consumer electronics is ruthlessly competitive with new product innovation one of the keys to success. Recession has hit hard. Companies are reducing the bewildering variety of products on offer and are increasing the time it takes to get products to market. Moreover, companies are now finding it much harder to raise capital for new product innovations. (As an example from a different industry, Honda once imported the Land Rover Discovery, and rebadged it under its own name.)
4. The distribution system in Japan is very complicated and it can take a long time to get products into the distribution chain. Alliances with local retailers and manufacturers can help get over this problem.
5. There is a strong demand in Japan for western classical music.

Required

(a) Analyse the situation faced by Dulcet Speakers Ltd in the light of the ideas of Michael Porter regarding the competitive advantage of a nation's industries. How might Dulcet's competitive strengths in Europe and the USA be relevant to the Japanese market?

(b) Indicate with reasons whether you consider entry to the Japanese market, on the information presented, to be a viable strategy.

(c) On the assumption that management goes ahead with its plan to enter the Japanese market, suggest a mode of entry, giving reasons for your choice. (This part of the question does not depend on your answer to (b). Even if you do not think entry to the Japanese market is desirable, answer this part of the question on the assumption that Dulcet Speakers Ltd has ignored your advice, and you want to protect them from the worst consequences of their folly.)

40 TEMPCO *36 mins*

John Adams is the managing director of Tempco, a medium-sized company, manufacturing and marketing central heating and air-conditioning control systems. The company is a strategic business unit, owned entirely by a major UK conglomerate company. Tempco both manufactures and installs building control systems and has a strong reputation within the European market. About 70% of Tempco's sales are focused on the industrial and business sectors with the remainder going to the household consumer. Exports to continental Europe are about 40% of the total sales.

In the past few years the market within Europe has been very difficult. The recession has curtailed new building programmes and competition is becoming increasingly price dictated. Adams believes that future growth will not be strong in Europe but that the Pacific Rim area offers the most attractive opportunities. Adams favours targeting South East Asia and feels that an investment-led rather than export-led entry mode is most attractive.

Adams has the approval of the headquarters management ream (and the financial support) to develop an entry strategy into one or more of the South East Asian markets. He is however faced with a number of difficult choices including whether to set up Tempco's own 'greenfield site' (literally starting with a green field, that is, with no prior manufacturing facility), whether to acquire a local company operating in the sector or whether to make a strategic alliance with a local producer.

John Adams has asked you, as a member of his staff, to prepare a briefing paper for presentation to the main board of the parent company outlining the merits and demerits of differing entry strategies.

Required

Write a briefing paper for John Adams. The briefing paper should cover the following areas.

(a) The case in support of direct investment as a strategy for entry into the South East Asia market. (5 marks)

(b) The key factors relating to the four options:

(i) A joint venture with local interest
(ii) A wholly owned subsidiary
(iii) A 'greenfield' investment
(iv) The take-over of an indigenous firm. (15 marks)

(20 marks)

41 CLOTHING SUPPLY COMPANY (M&S, 12/97, amended) *36 mins*

The Clothing Supply Company (CSC) is seen as a market leader in the design and manufacture of garments such as knitwear and weatherproof clothing for outdoor sports. The company is over a hundred years old and is based in rural islands of Scotland where it originally used to make and supply hill farmers with outdoor working clothes. CSC prides itself on the use of traditional fabric designs, the craftsmanship of its garment workers and the fact that it buys much of its cloth from local weavers, so supporting the local economy.

In recent years CSC has achieved a degree of dominance over other specialist Scottish clothing manufacturers. The CSC product range now enjoys an international reputation based not only on design and the quality of hand-made tailoring but also on the attractive and well known brand name, which is perceived to be associated with the country lifestyle of wealthy society leaders. CSC garments are distributed to and sold at premium prices through the best department stores in London, New York and Tokyo and are especially popular with overseas tourists visiting the United Kingdom.

CSC had been a family-owned business until 1996 when it was sold to the KZ Corporation, a Pacific rim based multinational conglomerate involved in shipbuilding, construction and consumer electronics. The KZ Corporation is keen to maximise what it sees as the global brand potential of CSC and to justify what some KZ managers see as the excessively high price paid to the owner's family for their controlling shares in CSC.

To address these issues, the vice president of global operations at KZ has commissioned a strategy study to identify ways in which CSC can be integrated into the KZ Corporation.

Required

(a) Using an appropriate framework for analysing national competitive advantage, examine the extent to which international location might determine the competitive position of the Clothing Supply Company. (12 marks)

(b) The initial review of the vice president's strategy study has identified two possibilities in particular. These are not seen as mutually exclusive. Evaluate the risks and opportunities presented by each of the following:

   (i) The strategy study was concerned at the relatively high production cost of CSC clothing products and believed that costs could be substantially reduced by moving production to South East Asia. (4 marks)

   (ii) The study suggested achieving brand synergies by making the CSC brand available world-wide, to be used by other divisions within KZ. (4 marks)

(20 marks)

CASE STUDIES

The 60 mark case study is compulsory. It is likely that it will always include a part-question on mainstream strategy, plus two or three other part-questions that could come from almost any part of the syllabus.

42 CINICENTRE (M&S, 6/96, amended) *108 mins*

The CiniCentre was established in 1960 as a charitable trust to promote and increase public awareness of the cinema as an entertainment and cultural medium. The CiniCentre is managed through a part-time board of governors drawn from representatives of the film industry, from government nominees and from elected nominees of the membership of the CiniCentre Film Institute. The board of governors delegate executive responsibility to a chief executive officer (CEO). CiniCentre has five major activity areas or operational divisions each of which has its own manager. These are as follows.

- The multi-screen Film Theatre (FT) which provides performances for the general public of new releases, classic films and minority interest films.
- The Museum of the Cinema (MoC) which provides a permanent exhibition of the history and development of the film industry.
- The Globe restaurant, bars and cafeteria, which are open to cinema goers and to the general public.
- The Film Archive Unit (FAU), which is concerned with the transfer of old film archive material to video as a means of long-term preservation.
- The CiniCentre Film Institute (CFI), membership of which is open to members of the public by annual subscription. Members receive preferential bookings to events, seat discounts and a free copy of CiniCentre's monthly magazine, 'Film Fan'. The magazine and associated publishing activities also form part of the responsibilities of the film institute.

In addition to the five business units there are also three support units which provide common support services as follows.

- Administration - office services, finance, personnel, computing.
- Buildings - building maintenance, cleaning, security, repairs and renewals.
- Maintenance - technical and technician support for the repair and maintenance of capital equipment.

The three support units come under the control of a Head of Support Services.

The CiniCentre is partly funded by government grant and partly funded from its own commercial activities. However, as a part of government policy to reduce the contribution to the arts, the grant to the CiniCentre will, over the next three years, be reduced by 20%. A financial summary of the current year's operations of the CiniCentre is provided in Table 1.

John Umbasa has recently taken over as chief executive officer of CiniCentre. He has been recruited from a senior position in an international media business. The board of governors at CiniCentre were directed by the government to bring in an external CEO as a result of a series of management problems, which have attracted considerable adverse publicity. These have included the following.

- A failure to stay within government financial guidelines of not operating an annual financial deficit.
- Press criticism about the loss of archive film due to the failure to speed up the transfer to video tape.
- Further press criticism on the recent imposition of an admission charge to the Museum of the Cinema.
- Reports of poor quality service and expensive food in the Globe restaurants.
- Persistent labour relations problems with the public sector staff trade union, which represents almost all the non-managerial museum, film theatre, clerical and catering staff.
- Complaints from the CFI membership that the film season has concentrated too much on popular income earning mainstream films with a subsequent fall in the number of showings of classic and non-English language films.

John Umbasa realises that he faces major challenges in revitalising the CiniCentre organisation and dealing with the proposed sharp reduction in government funding. He believes that what the CiniCentre needs is a vision of its role and priorities plus management control systems which link performance to clear-cut divisional objectives. He has offered you a one year management consultancy contract to assist him.

Table 1 - summary financial data

All figures in £m	*Commercial income*	*Direct costs*	*Apportioned indirect costs*	*Surplus/(deficit)*
Film Theatre	1.20	1.70	0.86	(1.36)
Museum	0.25	2.20	1.11	(3.06)
Globe Catering	1.70	0.90	0.45	0.35
Film Archive	0.00	3.20	1.62	(4.82)
CFI	2.30	1.90	0.96	(0.56)
Total	5.45	9.90	5.00	(9.45)
Government grant				9.00
Surplus/(deficit)				(0.45)

Required

(a) John's background is in profit seeking organisations in which objectives and goals seemed so much more clear-cut than at the CiniCentre. To clarify the 'vision' of the organisation, John has decided to undertake an analysis of all the internal and external stakeholder groups at CiniCentre.

(i) Explain how this analysis can assist John. (16 marks)

(ii) Select and identify four different CiniCentre stakeholder groups, indicating for each, its potential power and influence and its likely expectations of the CiniCentre. (12 marks)

(b) The previous CEO at CiniCentre had not considered strategic management relevant to a non-profit seeking organisation and, although a three year rolling plan was put forward annually to the government as a basis to secure funding, John is unable to find any evidence of formalised processes for strategy development.

Prepare a short management briefing paper, for presentation to the next meeting of the board of governors, justifying the establishment of a more formalised strategic management process. (18 marks)

(c) Management control at the CiniCentre is based on an allocated budget and monthly monitoring to ensure that divisions and support services keep within their budget targets. John believes that, although budgeting is important, what is also needed is a system of non-financial performance assessment.

Explain how performance measurement indicators (PMIs) could assist management at CiniCentre and provide one example of a suitable non-financial PMI for each of the five business divisions (five examples in all). (14 marks)

(60 marks)

43 SPORTAK (M&S, 6/98, amended) *108 mins*

Jerome Gulsand is the owner and chief executive of a chain of twenty sports equipment shops, Sportak. These shops are clustered in the south of the country. The company is privately owned by the family and the freeholds of these shops which the company owns and which are on prime retail sites account for the majority of the assets of Sportak. The company sells a wide range of sports equipment such as golf clubs, tennis, skiing equipment, soccer and other sports equipment. Recently it has expanded its range to include certain types of designer sports clothing.

The company was founded by Jerome's father a quarter of a century earlier when he opened his first small shop. Over the next twenty-five years the company grew steadily. A major reason for this successful development lay with the philosophy of Jerome's father who delegated much of the decision making to the individual shop managers. He believed that this gave the local managers a higher degree of motivation. It also allowed them to respond to local demand conditions as stock ordering was carried out by each shop and was not organised at the head office. The managers were also permitted to develop local marketing activities, using sales promotions and publicity as they felt appropriate. These shop managers were remunerated partly by a basic salary and partly by a sales-related performance bonus which could be up to 40% of their basic salary. These methods of operation were satisfactory whilst the company was operating in a steady growth environment. However by late 1997 there was evidence that Sportak's overall position within the market was weakening. Sales had stabilised, but even more importantly competition was growing from a number of discount traders who were prepared to operate on low profit margins but with larger volumes. It was at this time that Jerome took over the company from his father.

Jerome was impatient with the lack of growth. By nature he was an entrepreneur who sought growth. He was not sure that the steady organic growth was appropriate to these conditions. His father's policy had been to open a store each year, funding this growth out of current earnings. Jerome saw that the market was becoming so competitive that even small and specialist markets were proving to be vulnerable. He believed that only the big, nation-wide retail chains would survive and that the smaller sized groups would be taken over by the larger chains of sports goods retailers who were more profitable and had greater capability to raise finance. He decided that a 'dash for growth' was required if the company was to achieve the critical size to survive in the market place. It had been suggested to him that the franchising of the Sportak brand name would be a reasonable and relative risk-free method of expansion. Growth, using other people's money has its advantages, but it did not appeal to Jerome. He wanted a more 'hands-on' approach.

At about this time another chain of fifteen shops became available for purchase. This group was in a distinctly separate area of the country - about 150 miles from Sportak's current area of operations. As the overall sports equipment and sports wear market was still growing, the price being asked for this acquisition was rather high. However Jerome was convinced that this was too good an opportunity to miss. He believed that Sportak needed this expansion so as to take advantage of the profitable sales still available in this sector. However for an acquisition of this size it was obvious that the growth could not be funded internally. Jerome assumed that he might use the freeholds of the properties Sportak owned as securities for the finance the company needed to borrow. Before approaching the bank Jerome discussed this issue with his accountant and offered the following ideas for his proposed expansion.

In anticipating this proposed expansion and the need to manage an enlarged group Jerome believes that it is time for a strong and centralising leader. Recognising that the current system of product ordering is delegated to individual store managers, he proposes to provide a centralised purchasing function based upon a warehouse owned and controlled by Sportak. Individual shop managers will be permitted to decide upon their stock range but they will have to order from the central warehouse set up by Sportak.

Jerome has also decided to tackle the problem of marketing, and in particular, promotion. The decentralised approach adopted by his father has not brought about the development of a well-known image and therefore the brand of Sportak needs to be strengthened. Under Jerome's plan it is proposed to allocate a substantial budget - 15% of sales - to spend on press advertising and on public relations, and this level of commitment will continue for the foreseeable future. Sports personalities will be paid to appear in all stores which will have to be re-equipped. By a competent use of merchandising it is hoped that these stores will increasingly be recognised as centres for influencing the fashion of both sports equipment and clothing. The shop managers will also be encouraged to stock more expensive lines of products where the margins will be higher and, in addition, they will be expected to hold much more stock. A criticism of the stores when Jerome's father was in charge was that they were often short of stock. Most customers were unwilling to wait for the product to be ordered and they therefore bought from competitors' shops.

Jerome recognised that during this period of change Sportak might lose a number of its key shop managers. These people have enjoyed substantial autonomy, and although they still will have some freedom on the stock range which they offer they might increasingly see their freedom to act as managers being eroded. In appreciating that these shop managers provide much goodwill and their loss would be damaging to the company, Jerome is proposing to increase their sales-related bonuses as an inducement to stay.

Jerome fully understands that the costs incurred in the proposed acquisition involve more than the purchase of the new shops. Store modernisation programmes for all the shops, as well as upgrading stock with a wider and more sophisticated range of products, will also require funding. Forecasts of immediate future sales appear to be attractive. Jerome anticipates that sales per store will rise by about 8% over the next year. He believes that this growth in sales, accompanied by his more aggressive approach to retailing will enable his bold expansion plans for Sportak to be achieved. Above all Jerome wishes to see his company, Sportak, become a national company, no longer having to operate as a regional retailer.

Attached in Table 1 is a summary of the figures that have been prepared by Jerome's accountant for discussion. Part of the data has been obtained from trade association statistics as well as government forecasts.

Table 1

	1997	*1998*	*1999*	*2000*
	Actual	*Budget*	*Forecast*	*Forecast*
	£m	£m	£m	£m
Sales revenue	30.00	29.50	58.80	57.96
Cost of Sales	15.00	14.75	25.28	24.92
Gross Margin	15.00	14.75	33.52	33.04
Expenses	12.00	12.50	29.50	29.75
Operating profit	3.00	2.25	4.02	3.29
Interest paid	0.00	0.00	2.50	2.50
Profit after interest	3.00	2.25	1.52	0.79
Fixed assets	15.00	15.00	34.00	34.00
Current assets	6.00	5.90	9.80	9.66
Current liabilities	3.75	3.69	7.35	7.25
Equity	24.75	24.59	26.15	25.91
Debt	0.00	0.00	25.00	25.00
Gross Margin	50%	50%	57%	57%
Return of Sales	10%	7.63%	6.83%	5.67%
Activity Ratio	1.21	1.20	1.15	1.14
Return on net assets	12.2	9.15	7.85	6.46
ROE	12.2	9.15	5.80	3.04
Industry Sales (1990 = 100)	125	135	140	138

Required

(a) Jerome Gulsand's father was a great believer in the decentralisation of both operations and decision making. To what extent has this process harmed or benefited Sportak? Provide examples to justify your arguments. (12 marks)

(b) Evaluate the key features that you consider to be important and would expect to see in the business plan which Jerome Gulsand would have to present to his bank to support his application for financial assistance. (18 marks)

(c) Acting in the position of Jerome Gulsand's accountant, and using the financial data provided and the intentions developed by Jerome, assess the viability of the strategy that has been proposed by him. (18 marks)

(d) Discuss whether a franchise operation would have been a better option for expansion than an acquisition. (12 marks)

(60 marks)

44 METALCRAFT (M&S, 12/98, amended) *108 mins*

Metalcraft Industries Group plc is a UK company operating mainly in the metal goods manufacturing sector and currently has an annual turnover of £170 million. The company originally concentrated on manufacturing high precision machine tools for use in a wide range of industries, particularly in the transportation sectors – automobiles, lorries and military vehicles. The market for Metalcraft's products is international, with half the total sales destined for markets overseas. During the 1970's the company met increasing competition from more efficient and cheaper suppliers from Europe and the Far East and consequently it decided to operate in a more diversified range of products and markets. It initially bought a company which manufactured electric motors for power transmission and then acquired a range of companies which manufactured a variety of products including wheelchairs for the disabled, wheel rims and nuts and bolts for the motor industry and metal partitioning for the kitchens and toilets used in civil aircraft. In total the company has, within its portfolio, about 20 subsidiary companies, some of them producing an overlapping range of products whilst others manufacture components which could be utilised by other companies within the Group. Many of these subsidiaries have a turnover of less than £5 million and only 5 of the companies have individually sales in excess of £15 million.

Simon Lewis is currently the chairman of Metalcraft Industries and has held that position since 1977. His father had founded the original company in the 1950's and it became a public company, quoted on the Stock Exchange in 1971. Currently the chairman owns 30% of the issued shares, with another 15% being owned by the managers of the subsidiaries. Many of the acquisitions were made during the 1980's. Generally they had been underperforming family-owned companies and had been purchased relatively cheaply. The smaller companies were acquired for cash, without resort to loan finance. However two or three of the larger acquisitions had involved a share exchange.

Having acquired the companies Lewis has then allowed them to operate as if they were still independent companies. When asked why he has not encouraged a greater integration of the companies he replied that his policy has been to delegate authority and control to the local managers as they know the industries and their customers better, and that a strategy of decentralisation improves motivation. Each of the companies promotes itself as if it were independent, using the original company name and not the Metalcraft name. Marketing activities are the responsibility of the individual companies. Each company has its own sales force and its own research and development facility. There are few occasions when a corporate-wide activity is initiated. One company's marketing manager had exhibited at an overseas trade show and had been surprised to see five other of the group's subsidiary companies represented there.

There has been little evidence that the acquisition of these companies has improved their competitiveness. Sales volume in most of the subsidiaries has remained static. This has been primarily because of increased competition despite there being a healthy world-wide market demand for similar products. The group's companies are selling to a wide range of geographic markets, which helps to explain the relatively high ratio of foreign to domestic sales. Unfortunately no individual company has a strong presence in any of these overseas markets, so inhibiting a greater penetration of these areas. It is difficult to state who has developed a strong position within any of the markets it is almost impossible to build up any brand loyalty and consequently most of the sales have been price-led, which inevitably has had an adverse effect on profits.

Because of the lack of co-ordination and co-operation between the subsidiary companies overseas sales often are of an haphazard nature. Overseas agents frequently provide inferior service mainly because the better agents are already under contract to bigger or more focused competitors.

Despite the corporate philosophy of decentralisation the chairman has often contradicted himself by imposing highly centralised constraints on the subsidiary companies. He has insisted that each company should acquire the latest international quality standards approval. He argues that this is sensible for companies operating in the highly competitive manufacturing sectors. He also has required them to seek the Investors in People award (a national award for training), so demonstrating the corporate commitment to manpower development. Whilst these initiatives are encouraged there has been no centralised direction or assistance given to the companies, some of which might have as few as 50 employees. Possibly the most constraining issue of all is that of capital expenditure. The parent company considers itself as the shareholder of the subsidiaries, and as such, requires a given profit from each company. It is very inflexible with regard to its attitude to finance. Any capital investment by a subsidiary has to be approved by the main board. Because of the lack of a strong portfolio of products and the failure to market them in an effective manner, the profits in the group have fallen during the mid and late 1990's. In order to keep shareholders happy with a satisfactory dividend payout the main board has rejected many applications by the subsidiaries for capital investment. This naturally has exacerbated the problem of low profits because product innovation, development and quality have now suffered and have affected sales adversely.

By mid 1998 the poor performance of the group was being reflected in its share value which had gradually deteriorated against a background of a buoyant stock market. External shareholders were becoming hostile. Lewis had considered a share buy-back so as to reduce this pressure but the poor profit performance over recent years prevented him from doing so, despite the current low value of the shares. He has belatedly realised that his strategy has been unsuccessful. He has decided that he must re-structure the holdings of the group. In Lewis' s opinion there appears to be little scope for internal efficiencies and internal development to provide the growth in profits which the shareholders are expecting. The best hope appears to be in selective asset disposals and in new acquisitions. Currently the group is an amalgamation of disparate companies with little or no synergy being evident. The chairman has brought in a new finance director. In addition two new non-executive directors have been appointed to the main Board, one being Ruth McGeorge, a specialist on mergers and acquisitions, to advise the company on its future strategies.

Lewis is conscious of the fact that his previous record of company acquisitions has been rather haphazard and now he is looking for a more logical strategy. Consequently the influence of Ruth McGeorge has grown. She has convinced Lewis that if any acquisitions are to be made in the future they must be more rationally undertaken. Looking at the current portfolio, some of the acquired companies do not fit easily into the group and others are competing against each other. There is a need for some organisational re-structuring. Lewis has asked McGeorge if she will produce a paper for him and the rest of the board identifying the main sources of synergy which can be utilised in a group of companies such as Metalcraft. He is also keen to know if there are any cultural factors within companies which might lead to the successful integration of acquisitions. He believes that with her experience of acquisitions McGeorge must have noticed whether there are any critical success factors or distinctive competences which might be common in successful acquisitions.

A serious problem with Metalcraft is its inability to market its products successfully so as to gain a significant market share. It fails to use a corporate approach to marketing, but its more flexible company-specific approach does not provide it with the market penetration required. The Group needs to be more knowledgeable about its markets and to be more focused in its approach to them.

Details of the financial status of Metalcraft Group plc are given in Table 1 below.

Table 1

handwritten margin note: Don Commonsize Statement to bring them to 100%.

	1995	1996	1997	1998	1999 (forecast)
	£m	£m	£m	£m	£m
SALES	160.0	165.0	170.0	175.0	181.0
Cost of Sales	96.0	100.0	106.0	112.0	120.0
Gross Profit	64.0	65.0	64.0	63.0	61.0
EXPENSES	48.0	50.4	51.5	52.0	54.0
of which					
Marketing	10.0	11.0	12.0	13.0	15.0
R&D	6.0	5.5	5.0	4.5	4.0
OPERATING PROFIT	16.0	14.6	12.5	11.0	7.0
P/E ratio	12	10	9	8	5
Earnings per share (pence)	12	10	8	7.5	6
Dividend per share (pence)	3	4	4	4	4

Required

Acting in the role of Ruth McGeorge:

(a) present a position audit on Metalcraft Industries Group plc, and suggest actions that the management could take to improve the situation other than with asset disposals or acquisitions;   (20 marks)

(b) prepare the briefing paper for the board, requested by Lewis, outlining the main criteria you think would be important in evaluating a company prior to its proposed acquisition;   (15 marks)

handwritten margin note: How do we restructure

(c) comment on the existing management style and suggest how Lewis might provide leadership and direction to the group in order to effect the necessary changes. Support your arguments with appropriate academic theories or models.   (15 marks)

(d) Describe how Metalcraft might effectively segment its industrial market, and discuss the criteria which the company should consider in deciding upon the appropriate segments.   (10 marks)

(60 marks)

45   **ICC (M&S, 12/96, amended)**   *108 mins*

The International Computing Corporation (ICC) is incorporated in the USA and is a major world-wide manufacturer of mainframe processors, associated disk access storage devices, network communications hardware and its own proprietary operating system software. In many countries ICC has traditionally been seen as the first choice provider of computer hardware and software to the data processing departments of large public and private sector organisations. Although generally priced at a premium in the market place, ICC hardware products have long been noted for their high quality and the excellence of their after sales support and service. Historically ICC has been responsible for many of the innovations in large scale computing and traditionally spends about 10% per annum of its sales revenue on research and development (R&D).

There has traditionally been a very strong and distinct corporate culture at ICC based on the belief that the business is the best and employs the best. ICC recruits outstanding university graduates for its management training scheme and expects to pay the highest salaries in the industry. Managers frequently spend their working life with ICC and typically all senior positions are filled internally. ICC has had a no redundancy policy in operation for many years.

ICC manufactures almost all of its own products in its own manufacturing plants and markets these products and associated services direct to its customer base. There are two major customer functions in ICC, the sales and marketing (S&M) function and the sales engineering support (SES) function. Essentially, S&M sells the product and SES installs the product and provides customer technical support and maintenance. SES activity is seen as a key part of ICC's market strategy. SES supports the S&M sales effort by providing a high quality installation service while the longer term SES maintenance contracts provides access to the customer base for exploiting further product sales opportunities. Partly for this reason, ICC has set service contract prices deliberately low so as to deter other maintenance service providers from entering the ICC equipment maintenance market.

The good reputation of ICC among computer professionals has been built in part on the basis of high levels of customer support. It is not untypical for a S&M sales team to spend many weeks with the customer discussing requirements, providing technical specifications and visits to other user sites before a sale is actually made. S&M sales staff are encouraged to develop a close relationship with the data processing managers who make the purchase decision. Sales team/customer relationships are cemented by a variety of *social activities* such as golfing days hosted by S&M and provided free of charge to the customer contact. This substantial level of sales support has been made possible by the very high value of typical sales orders and the high gross margins earned on such sales. Historically, the average gross margin on a typical product sale has been about 55% of the sales value.

In the early part of the 1990s ICC was suddenly and unexpectedly hit by a combination of factors which for the first time in its history resulted in heavy operating losses (see Table 1 for the last four years financial performance). The adverse impact of the losses was far from being purely financial. Employees were shaken by the sudden downturn in business, key customers began to ask questions about the future prospects for ICC, the ICC share price fell dramatically, numerous damaging articles appeared in the business press and there were rumours of possible take-over bids being made by other technological multi-nationals. In general the problems at ICC were seen as arising from factors such as the following.

1 Direct production competition from manufacturers in the Far East who provided comparable equipment to ICC's product range and appeared able to undercut ICC's prices by 10% in many bid situations.

2 A change toward open systems with demands from customers that hardware and software from different vendors be able to operate together in integrated systems.

3 The tendency of many customers to distribute their data processing using networks of small and medium sized computers resulting in a fall in the demand for mainframe systems.

4 The superior price to performance of small and desk based processors as against large system processors.

5 The growth of end-user computing resulting in closer involvement of end-users in the purchase decision for computer hardware and software. The influence of the data processing manager in the technology acquisition decisions was therefore less than in the 1980s.

6 The market entry of many low cost computer maintenance companies able to offer full on-site maintenance for businesses operating hardware supplied by a variety of different vendors.

ICC has two major world-wide customer functions. The sales and marketing (S&M) function which sells the product and the sales engineering support (SES) function which installs the product and provides customer technical support and maintenance. Within each country functional management (S&M, SES and other functions such as Finance) report to the country Vice President (Operations) and also to the functional Vice President located at the Head Office in the USA. For example, the ICC country Finance manager for Germany reports and provides support to the German Vice President (Operations) but also has a line responsibility to the Vice President (Finance) located at head office in the USA.

Within this country however S&M and SES are organised as independent divisions. The S&M division organises its sales teams on the basis of product groups, for example, printers or network hardware. S&M product specialisation is seen as essential if sales staff are to develop the level of product technical expertise deemed necessary to sell advanced technologies to computing professionals. The SES division, on the other hand, organises on the basis of customers not products. The intention is that the customer has only one SES contact for any hardware or software problem and the SES teams are equipped to deal with any aspect of technical support. SES activity is seen as a means of assisting product sales, as potential sales leads are picked up by SES staff and passed on to the S&M sales teams.

Recently there have been a growing number of country based problems in co-ordination between S&M and SES. One result has been a number of instances of sales leads not being passed by SES to S&M. Another has been instances of hardware being sold by S&M which later proved unsuitable in performance terms. This created significant workload problems for SES engineers in reconfiguring to a specification which met the customers performance criteria.

Year	*1991*	*1992*	*1993*	*1994*
Sales revenue				
Hardware/software	3,100	3,300	2,900	2,500
Maintenance	770	775	810	860
	3,870	4,075	3,710	3,360
Cost of sales				
Hardware/software	1,364	1,551	1,392	1,350
Maintenance	462	475	495	530
	1,826	2,026	1,887	1,880
Gross profit	2,044	2,049	1,823	1,480
Operating expenses	1,760	1,800	1,810	1,770
Operating profit	284	249	13	–290
Net assets	1,893	2,040	1,902	1,690

Table 1

Notes

(i) All figures in US$ millions
(ii) 1991 can be taken as typical for the previous ten years

Required

(a) Analyse the strategic position of ICC. Your answer should include:

(i) an analysis of both the past and present strategic and financial position of ICC; and (25 marks)

(ii) an assessment of the apparent failure of ICC management to identify the worsening business situation at an earlier stage. (12 marks)

(b) Driven by the urgent need to reduce costs, ICC management are planning to abandon the 'no redundancy' policy and reduce significantly the number of management levels and the number of managers working within each level. Evaluate the potential *impact* of such a policy decision paying particular attention to the effect on the prevailing *culture*, the role of the *middle manager* and the implications for *management control information*. (13 marks)

(c) Suggest how the adoption of a country based matrix structure combining S&M and SES could assist in resolving the apparent co-ordination problems between the two divisions. (10 marks)

(60 marks)

46 ALG INDUSTRIES (M&S, 12/97, amended) *108 mins*

ALG Industries plc is a multinational conglomerate organisation with its headquarters based in the UK, with an annual turnover in 1996 of £3.3 billion (1 billion = 1,000 million). The company has concentrated mainly in the mature industries and has grown by means of acquisition. The origins of ALG were in the construction industry based within the UK. Successful growth in construction and office building during the 1960s and early 1970s brought significant profits and these were reinvested by acquiring companies within the UK and overseas.

The ALG strategy was to identify asset-rich organisations with negative market value (ie market value compared with balance sheet value). This has tended to occur in mature industries where management had become complacent and where sales were static. Target acquisitions were expected to provide potential synergies when combined with ALG and they were generally acquired with cash rather than an issue of ALG shares. The acquisitions were financed by temporary borrowing which was subsequently repaid by disposing of the surplus and undervalued assets of the acquired company. The intention was to retain a valued core business which in fact had cost the company very little. This strategy proved to be successful for ALG. Between 1971 and 1996 the company's turnover had grown from £120 million to £3.3 billion. Asset values had increased from £95 million to £3.2 billion.

This rapid expansion had coincided with a degree of steady growth prevalent within the geographical markets covered by the company. ALG's businesses now operated throughout the world, but mainly in Northern Europe, the USA and in India. Apart from construction, ALG had integrated backwards into brick manufacturing, and had also moved in forestry development and management so as to guarantee raw materials for the timber-based products required in the construction industry. It also had interests in textile manufacturing based in India and Bangladesh. As the standard of living of the European countries improved, ALG spread its interests into the leisure and entertainment fields. Furthermore, in the early 1990s when share prices were relatively low, ALG bought companies with interests ranging from the manufacture of safety equipment and office furnishings to agricultural equipment distribution. It also acquired three motor vehicle franchises with outlets in the UK, Germany, France and Italy. There was nothing in common between many of the acquisitions except for the following aspects.

- The acquired firms were relatively cheap to purchase
- The assets of the acquired companies were generally undervalued

- Little, if any, capital injection was needed by ALG to stimulate growth and profits
- Asset turnover tended to be rather low

A conventional turnaround strategy involving cost cutting, reduced capital investment, redundancies and tight financial controls ensured that these once tired and neglected companies soon returned to profit. The markets in which they operated were stable, providing steady but unexciting growth. There were very few competitors within these markets who had the resources to fight off aggressive predators such as ALG.

The culture of the company seemed to be clearly portrayed when, in 1995, the late chairman and chief executive officer (CEO) of ALG had an interview with a leading group of fund managers. He was quoted as saying, 'The mission of ALG is to enhance the shareholder value of the company. Whilst we may wish to grow at our current rate of 8% per annum, and whilst we may wish to spread our products and market coverage ever wider, our sole responsibility is to our shareholders. We are not in business for the sake of business but to add value for our owners, whoever they may be. We have been criticised for being an asset stripping company. We strongly disagree with this. We see our role as asset management. Indeed if a competitor company made a bid for us, and if we felt that this was in the interests of our shareholders, then we would welcome the approach.' The views of the chairman were significant, because as the founder of the company he had been dominant in the development of ALG over the years. Even when ALG became a public company with a full Stock Exchange listing in 1969 he still considered it to be his own property and he controlled and directed it in the way he thought best. He was rarely prepared to accept opposition to his ideas.

However, as a result of the untimely death, in early 1996, of the chairman of ALG, the board decided to separate the roles of chairman and CEO. The new chairman had previously been managing director of a leading commercial bank and the CEO had previously been the finance director of ALG.

Within six months of their appointments to the board the new directors planned to make their first move in the acquisitions business. This focused upon a major foreign corporation which was heavily involved in aeronautics and in satellite design and manufacturing technology. The company, Starlink Technologies, had been created as a result of mergers between a number of medium sized Japanese high technology companies. They had amalgamated to create an organisation of sufficient critical size to operate competitively in the new space-oriented industries. The ALG board announced that the acquisition would move the company into a fast moving, high value-added sector of industry. The sales potential was large, with the international scope of the business being enormous. Developing countries are now increasingly able to access high technology telecommunications without having need of the traditional infrastructure existing in the more developed countries, by leapfrogging technology and using satellite systems. Consequently demand for satellite capacity was growing at a rapid rate. Additionally, many customers, such as the telecommunication companies and the defence contractors who needed to use satellites to carry their research instruments, were interested in encouraging another supplier into the market. This enabled them to reduce the supplier power of the existing satellite manufacturers.

The acquisition was regarded by ALG as the first stage of a corporate renewal - the solid, unexciting mature industry liasing with a leading edge technology sector with short term versus long term criteria being part of the mix.

With the proposed acquisition of Starlink Technologies, ALG Industries plc appears to have consciously redefined its strategic purpose. This impetus for change appears mainly to be the result of initiatives from the newly appointed chairman and the recently promoted CEO.

The following figures give financial details of ALG, an example of a typical prior acquisition of ALG and comparable data for Starlink Technologies.

Table 1

	Typical acquisition	*ALG 1997*	*Starlink Technologies*
	£m	£m	£m
Sales	250	3,300	390
Cost of sales	185	2,300	220
Gross profit	65	1,000	170
Sales and administration	35	370	65
Research and development	10	130	80
Operating profit	20	500	25
Net assets	280	3,200	250
Debt	100	800	100
Equity	180	2,400	150
Price earnings ratio	8	11	20
Market value	220	3,600	820

Required

(a) Evaluate the growth strategies which ALG had pursued prior to the new board appointments in 1996. (15 marks)

(b) Acting as a consultant, prepare a briefing paper to present to the board of directors of ALG, evaluating the implications of the proposed acquisition of Starlink Technologies. In support of your analysis use strategic planning tools of your choice, as well as an assessment of the financial consequences of the move. (25 marks)

(c) Identify and evaluate the critical areas which will need to be addressed if the new acquisition is to be successfully integrated within ALG's portfolio of businesses. (10 marks)

(d) Indicate under what circumstances strategy formulation should be initiated either by senior managers or by middle/operational level managers. (10 marks)

(60 marks)

47 SALCHESTER THEATRE (M&S, 12/99, amended) *108 mins*

Bernard Mason has just been appointed as Commercial Manager of the Salchester Theatre. The theatre has just completed a disappointing year with low attendances, culminating in a loss of £57,000. Details of the financial position of Salchester Theatre are given in Table 1. The current Artistic Director had, until now, been responsible for both the commercial and creative activities of the theatre. Mason has been brought in to improve the financial heath of the theatre. His previous experience has been in the financial function within manufacturing industry, and more recently as a finance manager at the town's university. Bernard considers himself to be a man of culture and not just a hard, bottom-line oriented businessman. He has welcomed this challenge to improve the fortunes of Salchester Theatre.

Salchester is situated about 50 miles from London, has a population of about 200,000 people, and is home to one of the newer universities. The main sources of employment are in the commercial sector, including the headquarters of a large insurance company, and in the computing industry. There are also a significant number of commuters who travel daily to work in London. The theatre is reasonably modern, built in the early 1980s, and is located in the centre of town, having a seating capacity of 350. There is also a restaurant/coffee shop which is open throughout the day. However this facility is poorly supported and is only ever busy for pre-theatre meals in the evening. There is also a rehearsal stage which is adjacent to the theatre. The theatre employs 20 full-time actors and actresses and a stage crew of twelve which includes set designers and builders, carpenters, electricians and painters. Ticket sales and administration are handled by two full-time employees. Much of the work done during performances is by the 'Friends of Salchester Theatre' – a small group of active volunteers, many of whom are retired. These people act as bar and restaurant staff. They deal with mailing lists and they also collect tickets, show people to their seats and sell ice cream and confectionery to the audience at the interval. The twenty actors and actresses are usually divided into two groups, each performing a play for three weeks. Whilst one group is performing, the other group is rehearsing for its next three week commitment. Occasionally when a larger cast is required, such as for a performance of Shakespeare, members of one group will supplement the other. In fact, when requirements are for large number of actors, they are helped by volunteers from the drama department of the university. The theatre company operates for 42 weeks in a year. The theatre is closed for one week each year for refurbishment and decoration. The remaining nine weeks are used by touring companies for shows such as opera, ballet and musicals, the Christmas show targeted at young children for the holiday period, and by the local choral society for its concerts.

The funding of the theatre is typical of many regional theatres. The Arts Council (a central government-funded body to support cultural activities throughout the country) provides an annual grant of £180,000, subject to the programme being artistically acceptable. The Arts Council aims to encourage both artistic and cultural development. The town council in Salchester provides another subsidy of £130,000 each year. They believe that the existence of a theatre in Salchester is valuable for a number of reasons. It provides both culture and entertainment for the population of Salchester. Furthermore it enhances the reputation of the town. This is thought to be particularly important in attracting students to the town. The university has currently 8,000 students who provide valuable income to the town, including shopkeepers and providers of student accommodation. With increasing competition for students Salchester does not want to lose a potential attraction. In addition the university has a drama department and the theatre provides both resources and support to this department. Although there is only a nominal charge for this (about £5,000 a year) the theatre does receive help from the graphics and advertising. The rest of the income has to be generated by the theatre itself. Box office receipts have been falling over the past three years and in the financial year just completed amount to only £340,000. Until last year ticket prices had been £8 for weekday performances (Monday – Thursday) and £10 for weekends (Fridays and Saturdays). In order to cut the deficit the prices have been increased to £10 for midweek and £12.50 for weekends. The strategy does not appear to have worked and the receipts have continued to fall.

Mason has decided that there must be a review of the theatre's operations. Attendances are continuing to fall. He has reviewed the productions over the past year and has discovered that on average attendances were less than a third of capacity. There were few shows which could be considered to be financially successful. The twice yearly Shakespeare productions are always popular because the management wisely choose to perform the plays which are being used as the examination texts by the local schools Naturally the local students take the opportunity to see these plays. The Christmas show is successful for about two weeks but unfortunately the performances are scheduled for three weeks, Some of touring groups for opera and ballet are well supported but the cost of attracting these companies is very high and although the attendance is almost at capacity the revenue does not cover the operating costs. However, the main problem appears to be with the resident theatre group. Their costs are escalating but they do not appear to be attracting the public to their productions.

Mason called a meeting with the various groups who have an interest in the theatre's future to look at alternative approaches for improving the situation. The outcome of this meeting has not resulted in an agreed plan of action for the future. The actors and actresses who are looking for challenging modern plays are suggesting that future programmes be more adventurous and modern. One of them said 'We need to educate the audience to accept more creative material. The old favourites are boring and provide no interest for us'. However this view has been totally rejected by the theatre supporters club who do most of the voluntary work. They are looking for an increase in established and popular plays with which the audience are familiar. They want comedies, and easy-to-understand detective plays. This request has met with total opposition from the performers who have said that this type of material is both uninteresting and unacceptable to them. Finally, the members of the local council, who appear to enjoy the privilege of free entry to the theatre as a result of their patronage, seem more concerned with attracting outside companies to the theatre. The presence of nationally known theatre groups and performers apparently enhances the town's reputation.

Bernard Mason is unhappy at this inability to agree a way to resolve the current unacceptable position. There has to be some agreed strategy if the theatre is to survive and yet most of the groups, who have a stake in the theatre, cannot reach an understanding. Unless a viable solution can be found and agreed upon, Salchester Theatre will have to close, just as have many other regional theatres.

It is apparent that the differences in opinions held by actors, the local council and the volunteers will present problems to management and, in particular, to Bernard Mason. He will have to initiate change within the theatre if the required solutions are to be introduced. This will be neither welcome nor easy to implement.

Table 1 Financial details of Salchester theatre (financial year September – August)

	1996/97	*1997/98*	*1998/99*
	£'000	£'000	£'000
Income			
Theatre group	410.00	390.00	340.00
Touring companies	118.00	120.00	140.00
Restaurant	31.00	36.00	32.00
Arts council	180.00	180.00	180.00
Local Authority	130.00	130.00	130.00
University	5.00	5.00	5.00
Hire to local choral groups	3.50	3.50	4.00
Total income	877.50	864.50	831.00
Expenditure			
Wages and salaries	500.00	520.00	550.00
Materials and other costs	100.00	103.00	120.00
Restaurant (food etc)	28.50	30.00	35.00
Fixed costs (rent, lighting, heating)	30.00	33.00	38.00
Costs of touring companies	110.00	115.00	145.00
Total expenditure	768.50	801.00	888.00
Surplus/deficit	109.00	63.50	–57.00

Required

(a) It appears that the stakeholders in the theatre cannot agree on a strategic direction to solve their financial problems. Mason believes that a mission statement for the theatre could draw the conflicting parties closer together. With reference to the problems of Salchester Theatre, identify the major characteristics of a good mission statement, and comment on the problems which Mason may experience in drawing up such a statement (13 marks)

(b) Evaluate the current position at Salchester Theatre and critically review the solutions which the various parties have suggested might improve the financial position of the theatre. (20 marks)

(c) Discuss what actions Mason might take in order to correct the worrying deterioration in the financial position. (17 marks)

(d) Examine why the different parties might resist the introduction of new objectives and new operations. (10 marks)

(60 marks)

48 PLAYWELL (M&S, 6/99, amended) *108 mins*

Alexander Simmonds is the founder and Managing Director of Playwell Ltd, a privately owned UK company specialising in making educational toys for young children and for children with special educational needs. These toys are robust and of simple construction, made from high quality materials, mainly wood, acquired form a local supplier. The main selling lines are building block of different shapes, sizes and colours, and toy trains and carriages (with no mechanical or electrical components). These simple toys are intended to stimulate the imagination of young children and to help them develop their visual and co-ordination skills.

Alexander started the company in the early 1980s. He had initially made toys in his garage for his own children. He soon was persuaded to expand his activities and he had a ready demand for his products from friends and neighbours. In 1983 he was made redundant from his full-time job and he decided to put his redundancy money into setting up his own company. To his surprise the demand for his products grew at a faster rate then he had expected. There was an obvious gap in the market for simple and high quality toys. Young children did not appear to want the complex and high technology products which were expensively promoted on television and in magazines. The early success of the company was helped by being a low-cost operation. At the start, Alexander's sales were made on a direct basis, using no intermediaries. He promoted his products within a fifty mile radius using local newspapers; orders were shipped directly to the customers. Additionally the supplier of the materials provided Playwell with extended and low cost credit until the final payment was made to the company for the completed toys. This arrangement has continued to the present time.

Between 1983 and 1988 sales grew from a figure of £30,000, to almost £700,000. Net profit after tax was about 12% Alexander's policy has been to reinvest these profits into the business. By 1988 he had moved out of his garage and had taken over a small factory in an industrial development area in a nearby town. Skilled labour was relatively easy to acquire. There was high unemployment as a result of recent factory closures. By 1988 Alexander employed nearly 30 people in a range of jobs including design, manufacturing, sales, invoicing and distribution. Labour turnover was, unsurprisingly, very low. The workers were very loyal and Alexander paid them competitive wages and provided them with above-average benefits, particularly attractive in an area where unemployment was still high. The firm continued to grow at a rate of about 20% a year during the late 1980's and early 1990's. Although most of the sales were still marketed directly to the customer, a significant proportion of sales were now made through one retailer who had a group of fifteen shops. This retailer sells products for young children, ranging through clothing, cots and prams as well as toys, and even currently, in 1999, this retailer still relies on Playwell for a significant amount of its toy purchases. About 40% of the UK sales (excluding those to the special educational needs market) are currently made to this retailer. The target market of these shops is professional and middle-class parents who generally value quality above price.

As in any growing organisation Alexander now found himself moving away from hands-on operation and becoming more concerned with future growth and strategy. By the end of 1994 Alexander decided to look at another market to generate increased growth in sales. Although sales were now almost £1.5 million a year and there were nearly 50 employees, the company now had the capacity to double its output. Fixed costs, including labour, accounted for 60% of total costs and any future increase in sales ought to generate improved profit margins. This was important if the company was to prosper and grow and provide security for the workers in an area where employment opportunities were limited. The company was then looking for sales to increase by about 30% per year. However such an increase could not be easily funded out of retained earnings. Playwell's performance and conservative financial record was sufficiently attractive for the company's bank to be more than willing to extend its credit lines so as to provide the necessary working capital.

The new area that Playwell was interested in was the development of toys designed for the 'special educational needs' market. This term is generally used to refer to the education of children who have one or more physical, mental, or emotional disabilities. Toys such as shaped building blocks, sponge balls, pegboards, and three dimensional puzzles can all help children with disabilities to improve their visual perception, spatial awareness, memory and muscle control. In addition there were other products such as balance boards and beams and disks, all made from high quality wood, which can help to co-ordinate mental and muscular activities. However it was likely that the method of marketing and distribution might have to be adapted. The new market segment was much more easily identifiable and accessible. Data bases of parents of children with special education needs were readily available and it was possible to access the parents of these children via the specialist schools which these children attend. These schools were enthusiastic about Playwell's products but they alone could not support the this new range of products. In fact part of Playwell's strategy was to distribute its products to these schools at very low prices in the hope that parents would then purchase these specialist toys for home use. This proved less easy than had been anticipated. Firstly, parents of these children with specialist educational needs incurred many other expenses such as the additional costs of care. Furthermore because of the increased care which these children usually required, one of the parents often had to stay at home or could only take on part-time work. Consequently the parents' discretionary income was significantly less. In addition, whereas the company had hoped that the teachers would recommend its products to the parents, it became apparent that the teachers were no doing so, being worried that the parents would not have the expertise to use some of the equipment properly. As a result the revenues from this market were not as large as had been anticipated, particularly as the products' placement in the schools were seen initially as loss-leaders. Nevertheless sales of Playwell's core products (the non-specialist toys) were still gradually increasing (8% a year), but the momentum of earlier years was now not being maintained. By the beginning of 1997 Alexander decided that any future market expansion should be focused overseas, although he still intended to persevere with the 'special education' venture.

The company had acquired a good reputation within the United Kingdom and was operating in a growing niche market, in which Playwell was a significant participant.

However, the company now decided that exports were to be the favoured means of growth. In an effort to avoid high risks Alexander decided to concentrate his activities in Western Europe. There were a number of advantages to this strategy – the purchasing processes of both parents and children were thought to be similar to that of the domestic market, transportation costs were likely to be lower than sales to America or Asia, and being part of the European Union, there would be no trade barriers. However after an initial period of success, Playwell discovered that sales were not as easily achieved as they had been in the UK. Firstly the major European countries of France, Germany and Italy were at different stages in the business cycle to the UK. Whilst the British economy was growing the continental ones were suffering from recession. Consequently the demand for products such as toys was not buoyant. Furthermore high interest rates within the UK resulted in a high level of the pound sterling against the Euro and other continental currencies. so making any export from the UK an expensive option. It appeared that price was now becoming a serious consideration in the customer's purchasing decision, particularly for a company with no strong overseas reputation. (Table 1 provides financial data for Playwell over the past few years).

Alexander had now made two efforts to expand his business, neither of which could be judged as successful and he was now anxious to determine the future progress of the company.

Table 1

£ Million

	1994	*1995*	*1996*	*1997*	*1998*	*1999 (forecast)*
Sales to General Toy Retailers –UK	1·50	1·62	1·75	1·89	2·04	2·20
Cost of Sales	0·53	0·57	0·62	0·67	0·72	0·78
UK Special Needs Toys Sales		0·30	0·30	0·25	0·25	0·15
Cost of Sales		0·14	0·14	0·11	0·11	0·07
Overseas Sales				0·50	0·55	0·55
Cost of Sales				0·30	0·33	0·33
Total sales	1·50	1·92	2·05	2·64	2·84	2·90
Fixed costs	0·65	0·95	1·00	1·25	1·40	1·40

Required

(a) Alexander Simmonds appear to be the only person who is determining the objectives and strategic direction of Playwell Ltd. Identify any other parties who could have an interest in the success of this company. How might their goals be different from those of Alexander and to what extent would these differences be relevant? (15 marks)

(b) You have been retained as a business consultant by Alexander to provide impartial advice as to the future strategy which the company should adopt. Given its relative failure in its last two ventures, provide a briefing paper recommending a strategy that Playwell should pursue in the next two to three years. You should support your recommendation with appropriate financial analysis and the use of suitable analytical models. (20 marks)

(c) The exporting venture appears to have failed because of inadequate knowledge of the market. Identify the main types of information concerning the company's business environment you would consider to be essential before committing the company to an export strategy, giving reasons to justify your selection. (15 marks)

(d) It has been argued that strategy can emerge rather than be the result of deliberate planning. Explain this statement and consider what factors might influence whether a strategy should be emergent or planned. (10 marks)

(60 marks)

49 LRP

LRP is a division of Stillwell Slim, a large, diversified conglomerate with extensive operations in Europe, North America and the Far East. Originally a UK general engineering business, LRP now operates internationally and specialises in the production of high quality fasteners. Its products range from simple nuts and bolts to complex devices for high stress applications such as submersibles and satellites. The company was sold to Stillwell Slim by its founder, Mr Wingate, when he retired in 1990 and is now managed by Joe Lentaigne, who had joined five years before the sale as Deputy Production Manager.

Stillwell Slim is controlled from a small global headquarters in Lickskillet, Ohio. Its overall strategy may be described as high technology products subject to satisfactory cash flow. Other SBUs include a manufacturer of airliner galleys; an aviation service company whose operations range from engine overhaul to the management of complete airports; a company that builds high capacity trunk telecomms switching nodes; and a design boutique specialising in military standard printed circuits. LRP is a typical Stillwell Slim SBU, having provided a satisfactory return on investment in nine of the past ten years and having funded much of its expansion from its own profits. There is considerable intra-group trade, which is managed by negotiation among the SBUs.

Mr Lentaigne, while essentially a practical engineer, has become accustomed to thinking strategically and globally. LRP has no formal mission statement, but if asked for one, Mr Lentaigne would probably say something along the lines of 'making profit by making very good fasteners'. He feels that the success of the company depends on two main factors: efficiency in production and keeping up with the technology. He has therefore employed Dr Mike Calvert, a recent PhD in metallurgy, to maintain a continuing review of developments in all aspects of the technology. LRP does no research itself, but has developed several new products by applying the research of others, including competitors.

Production efficiency is the responsibility of Jack Masters, the Production Director. His background is in production engineering in the motor components sector. LRP has plants in Ireland, Taiwan and the UK and Mr Masters spends about 180 days a year away from the UK headquarters. He thinks the company has made great progress in both productivity and quality, but does not have the volume of throughput in any of its plants to achieve major purchasing economies. Mr Masters' ambitions for the company include the updating of the machinery in the UK plant, where some machines date back to Mr Wingate's time, and the introduction of computer-based resource scheduling systems to each of the three plants.

Sales and marketing issues are dealt with by Bernard Fergusson, the Sales Director. The market for LRP's more mundane products is very large and competition is tough. Price and delivery are what customers look for, and there is little opportunity to differentiate products. The market is global, but the weight of the products means that airfreight is expensive; on the other hand, intercontinental surface transport inevitably imposes a time penalty on delivery. While the global market is growing at about 4% per annum, historically, the USA has always outstripped the average, and even with the slowdown in the US economy, the lack of a manufacturing facility in North America has always hampered sales.

It has also affected the sale of the more complex, higher value-added products, though not to the same extent, because high and consistent quality is the key to the markets for those products. A more important factor in this market has been the appearance of TIG Products. TIG's production facilities are located in an eastern European country, which combines high technical ability with low costs. Mr Fergusson has recently established that TIG is a joint venture between an established western competitor and a local company, rather than being a wholly owned subsidiary of the competitor. Mr Fergusson made informal contact with the CEO of the eastern European partner company at a recent trade fair and was surprised at a revelation made by him in an unguarded moment late one evening. He stated his belief that the western partner company intends to renege on the joint venture agreement (which was committed to paper but never signed) because it is restructuring its operations. This could lead to major loss for the eastern company. The CEO indicated that he would welcome an approach from LRP to replace the competitor. He went on to explain that such a deal should be very attractive to LRP, since it would enable it to join a price-fixing trade association in a particular regional market that it had never previously been able to penetrate.

Table 1 – Data pertaining to LRP

	1998	1999	2000
Turnover – North America	£7.23m	£7.37m	£7.35m
Turnover – Europe	£27.56m	£28.39m	£29.12m
Turnover – Rest of the world	£14.63m	£15.92m	£17.03m
Profit after capital charges	£4.82m	£6.23m	£6.05m
Market share – basic fasteners	9.76%	9.82%	8.32%
Market share – sophisticated fasteners	4.67%	5.21%	6.83%
Number of employees	147	159	163
Overdraft	£9.78m	£10.24m	£11.02m
WIP*	107%	112%	103%
Finished goods stocks*	98%	115%	121%
Customer returns by value*	57%	87%	124%
Reject rate*	87%	114%	137%
Productivity index*	84%	92%	102%
Average age of machinery	8.6 yrs	9.6 yrs	10.2 yrs

* LRP participates in a confidential benchmarking scheme that includes most major manufacturers of fasteners globally. Industry averages are computed from information provided by member firms; the performance of each member is then assessed against the averages and the results fed back. For example, LRP's productivity index for 2000 means that it achieved 102% of the industry global average productivity.

Required

(a) As a consultant, prepare a report for the CEO of Stillwell Slim assessing the strategic potential of LRP. (You are not required to undertake portfolio analysis of the Stillwell Slim group as a whole.) Mr Fergusson has not revealed his conversation with the eastern European CEO to you. (25 marks)

(b) Discuss the usefulness of the diversified conglomerate business model. (15 marks)

(c) Neither Stillwell Slim nor LRP has any formal policy on business ethics. Discuss the ethical dimension of the TIG partner CEO's proposal. (20 marks)

(60 marks)

50 SCREEN BOOKS

Jack Benfold Limited is a small independent publisher in London. The management of the business is still dominated by the Benfold family, though several professional managers have been recruited in the last fifteen years. At one time the company specialised in medical text books, but it lost substantial ground in this field during the prolonged illness of the then managing director, George Benfold, the founder's son. The present managing director, Thomas Speight, is George's son-in-law. He brought considerable publishing experience when he joined the company as editorial director twelve years ago and he has succeeded in restoring the company's fortunes by moving into the travel and cookery markets. However, the trend in publishing has been towards the creation of ever-larger companies by amalgamations and takeovers, and independent publishers are tending to become niche operators.

Mr Speight has taken a close interest in the development of Internet commerce as a strategic option for smaller businesses. He formed an alliance with John Rogers Books Limited, a small chain of bookshops in the Midlands. The original plan was to sell books over the Internet, with John Rogers Books providing most of the administrative and logistic facilities and Jack Benfold the capital and Internet technology. A joint venture subsidiary called Screen Books Limited was set up in 1996, with a website called Screenbooks.com.

Screen Books expanded quite successfully and more or less in accordance with its business plan. Its advertising and rapid growth attracted the attention of Rupert Coke, who was at school with Thomas Speight and is now a senior merchant banker. Mr Coke's bank was promoting the dotcom business model heavily in the late 1990's and saw Screen Books as a candidate for heavy capital injection. Mr Speight was enthusiastic about this possibility because he had an idea for a technology-based strategy that would require considerable investment to launch.

Mr Speight proposed the development of a small, portable, liquid crystal display (LCD) screen device dedicated to the presentation of text. The device's memory would be capable of holding the equivalent of up to ten 'blockbuster' novels. It would be inherently Internet-capable, though without a proper browser and it would be programmed to connect automatically to Screenbooks.com. Customers would be able to review Screen Books' catalogue, download books and magazines and pay for them by credit card on line.

Mr Speight felt that such a device would appeal to a wide range of potential customers and suggested that such a device was particularly attractive because it exploited the main characteristic of the Internet: the high-speed transfer of information in electronic form. It would be independent of warehouses and carriers and other aspects of physical order fulfilment, with consequent benefits for efficiency and quality.

Such devices had already been produced but not on a large scale: there was a need for considerable technical development, which would be expensive. The success of the venture would also depend on the size of Screen Books' own catalogue and permission from other publishers to offer their titles in electronic form.

Mr Coke was sufficiently impressed with the proposal to arrange an initial injection of loan capital in early 1998. Contracts were let with research agencies and marketing staff were recruited. Such was the interest in the proposed product that a flotation on the London Stock Exchange was undertaken in late 1998 and the initial issue of 10p shares was heavily oversubscribed. More research was undertaken, with in-house staff being hired and a major marketing campaign was planned to launch the new product. To fill the gap until the new device was available, the existing Screenbooks.com website was heavily promoted, with a major advertising campaign and generous discounts. CDs and 'lifestyle' accessories were added to the product range and more marketing, sales and administrative staff were recruited at all levels.

Unfortunately, there are now indications that all is not well. The development of the crucial screen-based device has been held up by fundamental technical limitations. It also seems that the demand for LCD screens has grown to such an extent that prices remain higher than forecast, which will have a major effect on selling price when the device is launched. Expenditure on both research and marketing has been higher than forecast and the marketing director has left the company after only ten months in the job.

There is some doubt about the ultimate demand for the product, as well; research seems to indicate that people are very happy with electronic games consoles, since they offer facilities unobtainable elsewhere, but they do not see the point of the electronic book. A recent article in an influential business newspaper discussed this problem in detail, and some investors are getting cold feet.

Table 1 – Summary data

	1996	1997	1998	1999	2000
Turnover £'000	367	635	1026	2176	4309
Operating loss £'000	42	54	728	1032	1097
Marketing costs £'000	5.5	8.2	198	349	422
Loan capital £'000			500	550	1700
Spending on R&D £'000			204	639	721
Headcount - Marketing	2	4	9	18	42
Headcount – R&D	1	1	17	24	28
Head count - Telesales	4	5	7	16	28
Nominal value of capital at year end £'000	200	200	12498	12498	12498
Share price p high/low	-	-	72/46	85/63	67/17

Required

(a) Assess the strategy adopted by Screen Books to date. (25 marks)

(b) Acting in the role of consultant, consider how Screen Books' operations could be developed in the future. (15 marks)

(c) Screen Books' plans appear to have been heavily dependent on the new screen-based product. How could it have best managed its technological innovation? (20 marks)

(60 marks)

Answers

1 PREPARATION QUESTION: DISTINGUISH

(a) **Intended strategies** are plans. Those intended strategies which actually get implemented are **deliberate strategies.** Deliberate strategies and emergent strategies (patterns of behaviour) together form **realised strategies** (what the organisation actually does).

(b) The **rational model** of strategic management has three elements.

(i) **Strategic analysis** is concerned with understanding the strategic position of the organisation. It deals with the following issues.

(1) **Mission:** the organisation's overall role, its business strategy and value system

(2) **Objectives:** what the organisation hopes to achieve in order to fulfil its mission. These may be set for the individual units in the organisation.

(3) **Environmental analysis, PEST factors** (politics/law, economic issues, social/ cultural factors, technological development), **competitive factors** (eg Porter's five forces) and other factors directly impacting on the organisation (opportunities and threats), such as the expectations of **stakeholder** groups.

(4) **Internal appraisal**: the firm's resource capability, current performance, products, brands and markets (strengths and weaknesses)

(5) These are combined into a SWOT (strengths, weaknesses, opportunities, threats) analysis, ranked in order of importance.

(6) **Gap analysis:** what the organisation wants to achieve may differ from what the organisation will achieve with current projects.

(ii) **Strategic choice** is based on strategic analysis.

(1) **Strategic options generation.** A variety of alternatives are considered.

(2) **Strategic options evaluation**. Each option is then examined on its merits, and assessed for its suitability, feasibility and acceptability.

(3) **Strategy selection** on the basis of (2) above.

(iii) The **implementation of the strategy** has to be planned. This is the conversion of the strategy into **detailed plans** or **targets** for operating units.

The concept of **emergent strategies** holds that a strategy can develop from **patterns of behaviour**, or from decisions taken at operational level. Emergent strategies are not thought out by senior managers before being 'implemented' 'top down'. They can bubble up from below. Strategic management is the process of crafting emergent strategies in the desired direction.

(c) **Strategic decisions** deal with the long term, the organisation's relationship with the environment and the scope of the business and its activities. **Operating** decisions do not.

2 PREPARATION QUESTION: AURORA LIGHTING PLC

(a) **Aurora Lighting plc's strategic planning system**

Aurora plc has a formal strategic planning system, but it is **dormant** and **incomplete.**

(i) Aurora has a **mission statement** - but how relevant is it to the company's **actual** business? Does it conceal rather than enlighten? Does it allow managers to deceive themselves as to what the business is about?

(ii) Aurora has **objectives**, both for profit and for market share, which is a good balance.

(iii) There is **no** evidence, however, of any **environmental monitoring** activities, nor indeed any regular **position audit** or **SWOT analysis**.

(iv) **Age.** Perhaps most damning is that the strategy devised in 1989 is now too old. Helmut still refers to it, yet ignores the changes in the environment. Arguably, there is a **failure of double loop feedback**: the plan itself has to be questioned. In this respect the comments in the Financial News are fair and apt. The company has survived more through luck than judgement.

(b) There are three models of the strategic management process that we can examine to shed some light, as it were, on Aurora Lighting plc's condition.

(i) The **rational model** suggests there are three stages to strategic management: strategic analysis, strategic choice and strategy implementation. Clearly this is **not relevant to Aurora Lighting plc**. Little analysis is carried out, and the various choices made by the business, such as entry to Germany or the developing bespoke product business, are made reactively.

(ii) **Logical incrementalism**. In this case, strategy is made by minor adjustments to existing behaviour, as part of a political negotiation process. This **does not apply** in this case: Aurora Lighting plc is a company, and it appears that the lines of authority are very straight: Helmut and Dawn are both in charge.

(iii) Mintzberg's **crafting strategy** model. An **emergent strategy** develops out of a pattern of behaviour, or out of responses to the particular circumstances in which the business finds itself. Examples in this case would be:

(1) Aurora's **export drive;** and (more importantly)

(2) the continued development and growth of the **bespoke manufacturing business** as opposed to the Borealis range which appears to be absorbing most management attention.

The art of the strategic management of emergent strategies is not simply to let them develop and take over but to **select** those which are most desirable and to **shape them** in the right direction.

The **crafting strategy model** is probably most **appropriate** to Aurora's process of strategic management, but it in no way describes what Aurora **actually** does.

(i) **Manage stability**. Managers should spend more time implementing than planning.

(ii) **Detect discontinuity**. Environments neither change all the time, nor are they all turbulent. In Aurora's case, the company has exploited the opportunities of the environment, but had obviously not considered the collapse of the commercial property market in London.

(iii) **Know the business**. Helmut and Dawn are fairly aware of what goes on. They know the needs of the bespoke business as well as Borealis. However, concentration on Borealis means that not enough attention is being paid to the area of the business that perhaps holds out most hope for the future.

(iv) **Manage patterns**. This means that emerging patterns of business behaviour, such as the bespoke business, must be nurtured and others uprooted.

(v) **Reconcile change and continuity.**

Helmut and Dawn are **failing to craft strategy effectively**. Even the *Financial News* recognises that it is the **bespoke business**, not Borealis, which is crucial to the firm's long term success. Instead they are operating hand-to-mouth, taking advantage of such opportunities as they arise, but not developing them. Perhaps the export business could be expanded. In short, Helmut and Dawn need to ask the basic question: 'What business are we in?'

(c) **Goals and objectives**

(i) The **mission statement** does not describe mission: it is more of an operational goal, which can be turned into objectives, than a mission as such. It is only partly relevant as it deals only with Borealis rather than the bespoke aspect of the business. It **confuses** rather than enlightens.

(ii) There are a number of **formal goals**, not least the goal of achieving market share and the required profit. The profitability goals are those demanded by shareholders. In this case, Aurora is exceeding expectations.

(iii) **System goals**. Survival is obviously one, as is growth. There is nothing wrong with these as such, but there are times when they tend to subvert mission. As the business's stated mission is at variance with reality, these system goals have in fact, paradoxically, acted to the shareholders' benefit. After all, the company has prospered through its export and bespoke production business.

(iv) **Personal goals**

(1) Dawn and Helmut have invested much money and effort in Borealis. Their commitment to the range reflects this past investment rather than an objective assessment of the range's future prospects.

(2) The **production director** of the Borealis range might have been empire building to enhance his importance as the company invests more money in the Borealis range.

3 PREPARATION QUESTION: PLANNING COMPONENTS

(a) The three levels of strategic planning are considered individually below.

Corporate

Strategic analysis

(i) The analysis will deal with **internal factors** (skills available, the organisation's resources and so on) and **external factors** which can be seen in the operating environment (competition, PEST factors).

(ii) Variables of direct relevance to the organisation's plans will be the subject of very **specific** forecasts, frequently of an annual duration. These will include market share, demand and similar factors.

It is on the basis of this analysis that the organisation will make the necessary choices.

(i) The company **mission** is a broad statement of the organisation's purpose, serving to orientate it within its environment and to inform more specific decisions as to its objectives and mode of operation.

(ii) Goals and **objectives** define the targets towards which the organisation will work in the light of the mission.

(iii) **Strategies** give effect to objectives. Taken as a whole, they are the overall means by which the organisation intends to progress towards its strategic goals.

Tactical. This concerns the measures used to follow the strategy and how resources are deployed.

(i) **Policy making** occurs at this level, so that the organisation has a standardised response to particular sets of circumstances. Consistency is thus assured.

(ii) Many control measures such as variances are picked up at this level.

Operational. Planning at this level is very detailed. It includes the setting of **rules**, so that discretion in response is removed in certain circumstances, **procedures** (which are usually a bundle of rules), and **programmes** (which can be viewed as a collection of procedures). **Budgetary planning** allows for feedback, review and therefore control.

Corporate and operational planning are sometimes connected. In a service industry, for example, service quality is achieved at operational level, but must be considered in its minutiae higher up.

Planning can be both top down and bottom up. In practice, both are necessary. Strategists may be unaware of the operational difficulties or pitfalls. At operational level, staff may know more about how the company actually works than the planners.

(b) Mintzberg defines goals as '**the intentions behind decisions or actions**, the states of mind that drive individuals or collectives of individuals called organisations to do what they do.'

(i) **Operational goals** can be expressed as **objectives**. Mintzberg says that an objective is a goal expressed in a form by which its attainment can be measured. Here is an example.

(1) An operational goal: 'Cut costs'
(2) The objective: 'Reduce budget by 5%'

(ii) **Non-operational goals** (or **aims**) on the other hand do not express themselves as objectives. Mintzberg quotes the example of a university, whose goal might be to 'seek truth'. This cannot really be expressed as an **objective**. To 'increase truth by 5% this year' does not make a great deal of sense.

(c) The **environment of a business**

(i) Politico-legal factors include political changes (eg change in government, operation of the executive, openness of political institutions to business influence) and legal developments (eg health and safety legislation, developments in company law).

(ii) Economic factors include overall economic growth levels, interest and exchange rate and the effects of government fiscal and monetary policies.

(iii) Social and cultural factors include the country's demographic profile (eg age structure), the class system, and trends in consumer tastes and wants.

(iv) Technological factors include new product technologies, new materials, and new techniques in production.

4 INTRODUCING STRATEGIC MANAGEMENT

> **Tutor's hint.** Operational management is generally short-term and internally focused when compared with wider strategic considerations. Strategic management can be undertaken in a number of ways. This answer follows the standard rational approach. You could possibly argue that N Ltd has followed, albeit unconsciously, an incrementalist approach, by small scale change when necessary. Strategic management does not only include the rational model - Mintzberg's crafting strategies approach might also be worth a mention, especially in part (b), to reduce the shock of the new approach - but the tone of the question suggests that the rational model was what the examiner is mainly interested in. You need to focus on the specific organisational and cultural issues required by the question.

Strategic management

Strategic management is an integrated management approach drawing together all the elements involved in planning, integrating and controlling a business strategy. The concerns of **corporate strategic decisions** are these.

(i) The **scope** of the organisation's activities, in other words the product and markets the organisation deals with

(ii) The organisation's **fit with the environment** and the relationships it has with stakeholder groups

(iii) Matching its **resource capability** with the environment

(iv) **Resource allocation** between divisions or functions of the business, and direction towards different product-market areas

(v) The organisation's **long term direction**

(vi) **Change**

(vii) **Value systems**

The implementation of a strategic management approach, according to the **rational model,** involves a three-stage process of **strategic analysis** of the organisation's current situation and the environment, **strategic choice** (the generation and evaluation of alternative strategic options) and **implementation** of the chosen strategy. Many strategic decisions are one-off, non-programmable decisions.

Operational management

The concerns of **operational management** are quite different.

(i) Its **scope is restricted** to the particular task in hand

(ii) **Internal.** Operational management is generally more **internally focused** - although day to day relationships with customers are an operational concern.

(iii) **Implementation.** Operations managers have to work with the resource allocation decisions set by the strategy. Their concern is the most **efficient** use of these resources.

(iv) **Time scale.** Operations management is generally **shorter-term** than strategic management

(v) **Routine.** Operational decisions are often more **routine** than strategic decisions and are more likely to be programmed.

There are some cases when short-term decisions are of strategic importance, for example if the survival of the organisation is at stake. Moreover, poor performance at operational level can make or break a strategy.

(b) **Cultural and organisational changes at N Ltd**

There are a variety of different approaches to strategic management. The extent of organisational and cultural change required will depend on the type of strategic management style adopted.

The current strategic management style is incrementalist.

There is little strategic review, and the underlying assumption of managers is that things will continue more or less as they are, any changes being coped with by incremental adjustment at an operational level. The lack of market information is particularly worrying. The company appears to be **reactive rather than proactive**.

Introducing the rational model: organisational changes

(i) **Resources** must be diverted to strategic management.

(1) The strategic management system must be **designed for future use**.

(2) The initial stages of strategic analysis need to be done, and the directors will need some **guidance,** so management consultants may be employed.

(ii) **Intelligence.** Strategic management requires suitable **information systems**. This also requires resources. The scope of the strategic intelligence systems will almost certainly include **marketing research data**.

(iii) **People.** Changes to the **job descriptions** of existing personnel might be needed so that their new responsibilities, especially for information gathering, are outlined.

(iv) **The management accounting system,** if any, must be configured to provide information related **to product profitability**, so the firm can identify life cycle and portfolio issues.

(v) **Objectives and indicators.** Strategic management involves the **setting of objectives**, and so new performance indicators will be needed to ensure that the strategies chosen are implemented successfully.

The **balanced scorecard** approach could probably be adopted - given falling profitability, it is likely that financial indicators assume a great deal of importance. However other operational performance indicators need to be used so that managers do not become too short-termist in their outlook. A technique using some of the insights of management by objectives might be employed.

To summarise, the organisational changes involve new information systems, changes to job descriptions and new performance indicators to encourage a strategic perspective and a more strategic approach to marketing.

Clearly, this involves a **change in the management style** of the company.

(i) **New approach to strategy**. There will have to be a cultural change at board level. Directors will have to consider strategic issues in an active way. This may involve challenging some of their assumptions as to how the business is run.

(ii) **Professional approach, not family management.** The company certainly needs professional management. Hopefully, the decline in profits and turnover provides a sense of urgency, but the family may still find it hard to accept the dilution of its power.

(iii) **A new approach to risk** is needed, especially with regard to products and markets.

(iv) Operational decision-makers who were used to doing more or less what they pleased will be faced with **objectives set by their managers higher up**. This is a resumption of **control**, and operations managers may feel that they are losing power and authority. It may be **demotivating.**

(v) **Innovation** will have to be addressed, both in products and in processes. The existing managers are probably technically aware in their own fields, but the firm needs a **marketing orientation** to ensure its continued success via a proper focus on the needs of its customers.

(vi) A programme of **education** will be needed to convince managers that it is necessary.

Arguably, strategic decisions have **emerged** from patterns of operational behaviour, but this mode of making strategy is obviously insufficient at the moment. Accepting some **bottom-up input** into the strategic decision making process will mean:

- The new system is accepted more **readily**
- The **expertise** of operational decision makers is exploited

5 ELITE FABRICS

Tutor's hint. A few clothing manufacturers have practised forward vertical integration into retailing, such as Laura Ashley and Benetton. Not all these experiments have been happy ones.

Part (a)

Forward integration into dress manufacture and its effect on competitive ability

Forward vertical integration is often justified as it enables the firm to do three things

(a) Earn **more of the profit available** in the value chain

(b) **Control marketing and pricing strategy** (eg Benetton) - the firm can ensure it maintains the image of quality and exclusivity

(c) **Control usage of the product**

EF's main motivation has been to earn more profit. In this, the incorporation of an **in-house clothing design team** has enabled it to increase its profits.

EF has thus extended the value chain. Previously, the process of adding value was simply a matter of designing and producing cloth. Dressmakers then creamed off the value added from turning the cloth into dresses and suits. A consequence is that EF's customer has changed from being the trade customer to being the end consumer. The operations process in the value chain is now more complicated, because **what were previously two value chains in a value system have now become one.**

The firm's success may lead its directors to consider that vertical integration has no drawbacks, hence their suggestion to enter retailing.

The drawbacks of EF's approach

(a) EF has **restricted its market** to the middle aged and middle income market. This is probably a sensible strategy for a clothing design company, but not for a fabric manufacturer. EF has put more eggs into one basket.

(b) EF has **precluded the possibility of other ways of increasing fabric sales**, by exporting for example.

(c) The **dress design company is limited** in its use of fabrics to what EF supplies. Its designers may resent the restrictions and lack of freedom.

(d) EF has to support **two different production operations** - spinning/weaving the fabrics, on the one hand, and dress manufacture on the other. There are thus two sets of machinery and two workforces.

(e) Capacity may not be matched properly. EF will have increased warehousing costs if it needs to manufacture cloth ahead of retail demand.

(f) There are other minor administrative issues such as **transfer pricing**. However, it should not be too difficult to compare cloth prices with competing products on the market.

Forwards vertical integration has made it harder to compete with **other yarn manufacturers**, and EF is now competing for fickle consumers who face many other offers.

Part (b)

Forward vertical integration into retail outlets

EF is proposing copying Laura Ashley and Benetton in having exclusive outlets for its own products. The intention is to earn more of the value in the value system.

Advantages

(a) EF would have **total control over production, pricing and marketing.** It could develop a precise marketing strategy that further differentiates the product, enabling an even more targeted focus on its desired customer base. Moreover, it will have more freedom to develop marketing messages and integrate its marketing strategy.

(b) EF will also be able to ensure that its products are available and visible, and are not competing in the same clothes racks as other competitors - thereby **avoiding price comparisons**. In other words, EF will not depend on retailers' professional buyers to order or display its products.

EF will **become fully informed of its target market.** It may be able to make clothes to order, if customer measurements can be transmitted electronically to the factory: this would be an example of **mass customisation.**

Drawbacks

(a) EF will acquire a range of high street properties, with management problems of their own. **Debt service** will eat into any extra profits that are made on clothing sales.

(b) **Higher risk.** If EF's clothes go out of fashion, the stores will become an expensive liability. Owning a chain of retail outlets involves a much higher proportion of fixed costs than cloth and clothing manufacture. Much depends on the location of the shops.

(c) If EF products are exclusively sold in its own shops, **EF may forgo the sales it would have made at the department stores**. EF might be better advised to bite the bullet and accept that it will have to accept the high customer bargaining power with the stores.

(d) EF will need to produce a wide enough range of products to encourage customers to enter. EF may have to supplement its own wares with others by other suppliers - will it be able to do so cost-effectively?

Competences

(i) As EF is acquiring the chain, it will inherit the many competences needed, providing both that it can keep the staff and that EF's managers integrate the acquisition in a sensitive way.

(ii) Stock management for many small retail stores will be quite complicated. EF may well inherit systems currently employed in the acquired company.

(iii) EF needs to understand high street retailing, display, and merchandising (ensuring a suitable range of clothes is available in the right volumes and at the right time).

competent

(iv) EF needs a more responsive distribution system.

(v) EF is now running three different types of business. To benefit from economies of scale it may need a performance monitoring system for each business.

6 PREPARATION QUESTION: COMPETITIVE FORCES

(a) **Five forces**

(i) **The threat of new entrants.** A new entrant into an industry will bring extra capacity. The new entrant will have to make an investment to break into the market, and will want to obtain a certain market share.

(1) The strength of the **barriers to entry** (eg scale economies, product differentiation, switching costs etc).

(2) The likely **response of existing competitors** to the new entrant.

(ii) **Substitutes.** The products or services that are produced in one industry are likely to have substitutes that are produced by another. 'Substitutes limit the potential returns of an industry by placing a ceiling on the prices firms in the industry can profitably charge. The more attractive the price-performance alternative offered by substitutes, the firmer the lid on industry profits.' (Porter)

(iii) **Bargaining power of customers.** Customers want better quality products and services at a lower price.

(1) Do the customer's purchases represent a substantial **proportion of the producer's total sales**?

(2) Do the customer's purchases from the industry represent a large or a small proportion of the **customer's total purchases**?

(3) Are **switching costs** are high or low?

(4) Are the products supplied by the industry standard items?

(5) A customer who makes low profits will be forced to insist on low prices.

(6) The threat that customers might **take over sources of supply,** if suppliers charge too much.

(7) The **skills** of the customer's purchasing staff, or the price-awareness of consumers.

(8) When **product quality** is important to the customer, the customer is less likely to be price-sensitive, and so the industry might be more profitable as a consequence.

(iv) **Bargaining power of suppliers.** Suppliers influence an industry's profitability by exerting pressure for higher prices.

(1) Whether there are just one or two dominant suppliers to the industry, able to charge monopoly prices.

(2) Are the suppliers threatened by new entrants, or substitute products?

(3) Do suppliers rely on the industry for the majority of their sales?

(4) The importance of the supplier's product to the buyer's business.

(5) Whether the supplier has a differentiated product which buyers need to obtain.

(6) Whether switching costs for buyers would be high.

(v) **Competitive rivalry.** The intensity of competitive rivalry (eg price competition, new products) within an industry will affect the profitability of the industry as a whole.

(1) It can help the industry as **a whole** to expand, by stimulating demand.

(2) It can leave demand unchanged, in which case individual competitors will simply be spending more money, charging lower prices and so making lower profits, without getting any benefits except maintaining or increasing market share.

(b) **The determinants of national competitive advantage**

(i) **Factor conditions** is a term describing a country's endowment of inputs (eg raw materials, land, capital, infrastructure) to production. Different nations have different stocks of factors. Factors can be grouped into these categories.

(1) Human resources
(2) Physical resources
(3) Knowledge (scientific and technical know-how, educational institutions)
(4) Capital (ie amounts available for investment, how it is deployed)
(5) Infrastructure (transport, communications, housing)

An abundance of factors is not enough. It is the efficiency with which they are deployed that matters.

(ii) **Demand conditions.** The **home market demand determines how managers of firms perceive, interpret and respond to buyer needs.** It is not so much the quantity of home demand, although economies of scale are significant, as the information that the home market gives firms and the pressure to innovate, which provide a launch pad for global ambitions.

(iii) **Related and supporting industries.** Competitive success in one industry is linked to success in related industries particularly suppliers. Having a competitive domestic supplier industry is preferable to good foreign suppliers, as 'proximity of managerial and technical personnel, along with cultural similarity, tends to facilitate free and open information' flow at an early stage.

(iv) **Firm strategy, structure and rivalry.** Domestic rivalry is important because:

(1) It is visible.

(2) There can be no special pleading about 'unfair' foreign competition.

(3) With **little** domestic rivalry, firms are happy to rely on the home market.

(4) Tough domestic rivals teach a firm about competitive success.

(5) Firms cannot compete on factor endowments (eg cheap materials) alone.

(6) The industry benefits as each rival can try a different strategic approach.

(7) The stock of knowledge in each firm increases the stock of knowledge of industry as a whole.

7 PREPARATION QUESTION: IMPERIAL TRADERS PLC

(a) (i) **A position audit** is 'Part of the planning process which examines the **current** state of the entity in respect of:

(1) resources of tangible and intangible assets and finance;
(2) products, brands and markets;
(3) operating systems such as production and distribution;
(4) internal organisation;
(5) current results;
(6) returns to stockholders.

The question asked is '**Where are we now?**'. It is the beginning of the long term planning process, on the assumption that in order to reach a desired objective you need to have a good idea as to where you are starting from. This will enable Imperial Traders plc then to assess the extent to which continuing operations can contribute towards the goal, and to develop strategies to fill the gap between the goal and what is currently achievable.

The proposed move to a Pacific Rim location. The position audit will deal with **all** the factors noted for:

(1) **The company as a whole**

(2) **The Head Office entity** in particular.

- The position audit covers the unique functions as a head office in the context of the firm's internal operation, and in its relations with the wider commercial environment and with investors and bankers. (No other strategic change in the company's **operations** is being contemplated. The entity under discussion, therefore, will be Head Office.)

- The gathering of comparative cost information for London and various regional sites

- The current role of Head Office in its existing location

Only after such a position audit is carried out, can management decide:

(1) whether to move at all;
(2) if a move is desirable, where to go to;
(3) how the move will be implemented successfully.

(ii) **Benefits in carrying out a position audit in respect of this decision**

What is the **role of Head Office**?

(1) **Head office might**, like Hanson or BTR, **simply set financial targets** and **let subsidiaries get on with meeting them**, avoiding interference with tactical or day to day decisions. In this case the role of Head Office will be to communicate with the investment community, to be a central location for financial reporting, and as a domicile for the company so that it can take advantage of a favourable tax regime. Thus it might be **better to keep it in the UK** for the benefit of the company's investors. Moreover, the City of London is a centre of world finance, and if the firm's activities require a great deal of financial sophistication, London might be the place to stay.

(2) The **Head Office may take a hands-on approach** to the running of the company. If all its activities are heavily interrelated, Head Office coordination may be essential for the company's successful functioning. A position audit of the company as a whole would identify those **regions**

which are most critical to its long term success. If that region is Japan, for example, this might be a good reason for relocating to that country.

(3) The position audit should identify all the major costs and benefits of such a move, in a formal way, and so should result in a better decision.

(b) **Effects of relocating to a Pacific Rim country**

(i) **Choice of country.** The term **Pacific Rim** is normally held to encompass the west coast of the USA, Indonesia, the Philippines, and the rapidly growing region of southern China as well as the area of Imperial Traders plc's current operations which comprises Japan, Korea, Malaysia, and Australia. The final choice as to which of the latter countries will be the site of the new Head Office will be as significant as the decision to move away at all. Recent financial crises (eg in Korea) do provide opportunities for expansion.

(ii) **Tangible assets**

(1) **Imperial Traders will need to sell its London accommodation.** The price it receives may be a major factor in the economic benefits of the relocation decision.

(2) **Imperial traders will have to buy office space**. The **relative price** of office space in each country will differ significantly. Japan, despite the current slump in land prices, is still extremely expensive. Perhaps an Australian location would be cheaper.

(iii) **Finance**. Imperial Traders will be moving from London, which has one of the world's most developed capital markets. It must ensure that its needs are as well satisfied in one of the Pacific Rim countries? A country with a relatively **open financial system**, such as Australia, might be a better than, say, Korea. The company will already deal with providers of trade finance, so this should not be any great problem.

(iv) **Products, brands, and markets**.

(1) **Products and brands.** We do not know which products are Imperial Traders plc's particular speciality. It might specialise in trading commodity products (like wool from Australia to textile factories elsewhere) or it might specialise in trading manufactured goods. It might not specialise at all.

(2) **Markets.** If Imperial Traders plc is basically a transport and distribution company, active in several areas, then the domicile of its Head Office is unlikely to matter very much in terms of the goods it trades, nor in attracting business. However, moving Head Office closer to its main markets may **enhance head office's market knowledge**. If Head Office plays a coordinating role, it might be able to develop a better strategic vision as to where it wants to be if this function is located in its **main market**.

(v) **Operating systems**. The firm will have to arrange appropriate and secure **telecommunications links**, especially for the transfer of commercial documentation by fax or email. If most of its activities before the move were based in the region, changes should not be too drastic, but the firm will need to develop the right system for the Head Office function.

(vi) The **internal organisation**. This is where the difference will be greatest.

(1) Many of the London based staff may not wish to be relocated, and might leave the company.

(2) The company, moreover, might wish to avoid the expense of relocation, and prefer to **recruit staff locally** or transfer staff from the company's divisions in the regions to the new head office function. There are likely to be redundancy costs in the UK, and the cost of hiring and training staff in the area.

(vii) **Current results**. There will be a number of **costs** entailed in the move, and perhaps some loss of efficiency in the Head Office function. Careful planning should minimise this risk. It is possible that the firm might receive **relocation subsidies** from some countries, or it may be able to negotiate a tax holiday if the country wishes it to locate there.

(viii) **Returns to stockholders**

(1) Initially, there might be an adverse effect, owing to the **costs of the move**.

(2) Later, if the move of Head Office significantly **affects the firm's trading patterns** or financial arrangements, the effect could be large. For example, the firm might have used Sterling more often than necessary as there was a London Head Office. As currency flows are likely to remain within the Pacific Rim region, the **currency risk will be different**. This might significantly affect the reported returns to stockholders, who are based in the UK. Furthermore, if the company can find capital at cheaper rates than in the UK this will reduce its interest charge, and might make certain activities appear more attractive.

(c) **Cultural differences.** Imperial Traders plc's activities are divided between two Commonwealth countries (Australia and Malaysia) and two countries (Japan and Korea) where the UK had no formal colonial presence. Some existing staff may move to the new location, with the consequent disruption to their personal lives.

(i) **Language**. If the Head Office staff relocate to Australia, there will be no problem with language, as English is spoken there. English is used widely in Malaysia. In Korea or Japan, however, while English is taught, staff will find it hard to get by without a good working knowledge of Korean or Japanese.

(ii) **Business culture**. Different cultures have different ways of doing business, arranging deals and so forth. UK staff will have to get used to this in all of the countries mentioned.

(iii) **Different legal systems**. Australia's legal system is probably most like the UK's.

(iv) **Women**. The relative inequality of women in Japanese society is greater than that of the UK. Female executives may find it harder to be accepted by Japanese counterparts. (At the same time, this is an **opportunity** for the firm to recruit talented female employees who might be ignored by more chauvinist local managers.)

(v) **Personal problems**

(1) Newly expatriate staff will need to adjust to different climate, diet and working hours.

(2) Those with **families** will have to find education provision for their children, and perhaps employment for spouses. The firm might have to run a cultural adjustment program to help them cope. People might have initial difficulty in forming friendships if social mores are very different.

8 PREPARATION QUESTION: THREAT OF NEW ENTRANTS

Tutor's hint. This is quite a specialised question dealing with only *one* of the five competitive forces in Porter's model: the threat of new entrants. Although not a scenario-based question you are expected to apply your knowledge of the threat of new entrants to a low-technology industry.

In our answer we have interpreted 'low technology industries' literally, ie such that entry barriers in terms of requiring, for example, the latest computerised production systems, are not present. This may not always be the case - a low technology industry may not necessarily have low barriers to entry and you may have put this into your answer. As always, if your argument is sensible, relevant and supported by evidence it will earn marks.

(a) **Porter's Five Forces model** contends that the long-term profitability of an industry is determined by the interrelationship between five competitive forces: the threat of new entrants; substitute products; customer bargaining power; supplier bargaining power; and the intensity of competition.

A company is concerned with maintaining **competitive advantage** and all of these forces impact on that, especially in the sense that a profitable industry will attract new entrants (purely because it is profitable, if for no other reason). If these newcomers do enter the market, they will increase competition.

The **threat of new entrants** is that risk associated with other firms entering the industry. They will bring in new capacity and compete for the same customers. This may have the effect of driving down prices and profitability. It may also have the effect of driving existing firms out of business. The precise level of the threat posed by new entrants is determined by **barriers to entry** and the likely **response of firms currently in the industry**.

If the barriers to entry are significant and firms currently in the industry are prepared, for example, to cut their prices to protect their market share, new entrants may be deterred. Any new entrant is likely to have to make a significant investment to break into the market and will want to be able to obtain enough market share to provide an **adequate return** on that investment.

Low-technology industries are, however, likely to be characterised by a number of firms, as it is relatively easy to set up in business without significant outlay and with a relatively low cost of failure. There may not be so many barriers to entry (certainly in the technological sense) and so it is likely that competition will reduce industry profitability.

(b) An **assessment of the threat** of new entrants will depend on the following.

(i) The likelihood that new entrants will be **interested** in the industry and its markets, and will be **successful**.

(ii) Their effect on the **future of the industry** as a whole.

(iii) The ability of a firm already in the industry to **repel the threat**. This depends on its **internal capabilities** and the way it adds value for its customers.

By shrewd review of the environment, a firm might have some idea as to potential new entrants. Porter suggests that in carrying out a **competitor analysis** a firm can analyse the following.

(i) The competitor's future **goals**

(ii) The competitor's **assumptions**

(iii) The competitor's current **strategy** - (will it try the same approach to any new industry it enters?)

(iv) The competitor's **capabilities and competences**, which might be relevant to the industry. These include know-how in the area, financial resources, marketing resources and so forth.

All firms currently in the market must therefore use **external information** to assess the environment, as well as looking to their own operations.

The industry ought to be **monitored** for its continuing appeal to new entrants, by assessing what would happen, for example, if prices were decreased or products were altered. This may involve the company 'under threat' in some form of market research to see both how customers, competitors and new entrants would respond.

Customers will always welcome price reductions, which may decrease profitability and thereby deter new entrants. This will depend on the strategy of the new entrant, who may be prepared for initial losses and is taking a **longer term view**. Changing product specifications may be unpopular with customers and therefore an inappropriate strategy to adopt when dissuading new entrants.

This latter point may tie in with an assessment of where in the **product life cycle** the industry's various products lie. If many of them are in the growth stage then the market is attractive to new entrants, with customers increasing in number and companies better able to differentiate their product. An industry with products in a mature phase characterised by little market growth will, as a rule, be less attractive.

A new entrant may be attracted to even a mature market if the anticipated volumes are large enough and the new entrant has **cost advantages**. It is therefore important to ascertain where possible the **cost structure and capabilities** of new entrants. A new entrant may have such access to funds (such as large cash balances, bank loans or debenture stock) that it has plenty of available cash and is looking for places to spend it.

All this information can be collected and analysed in a firm's process of **strategic planning**. As an example, when conducting a corporate appraisal, SWOT analysis can include the likelihood of the threat of new entrants in the market, as identified by some of the above processes.

The firm needs to examine the **future** of its industry as well as the current picture. A number of scenarios can be devised and they can be used for decision-making. Analysing the scenario involves determining the future structure of the industry, developing the implications of the scenario for the attractiveness of the industry and identifying implications for future competitive strategies.

For example, a relatively low-tech industry such as footwear must take into account the likely entry by firms from countries with very low labour costs, such as Brazil and China and react accordingly, by product differentiation or moves to low cost production.

Internal information sources

Porter suggests that competitive advantage rests in **adding value** in a unique way. A model of the process is the value chain, describing the various activities of the firm. Each element of the value chain can be identified to see if there some activities which are weak and/or costly, or which a competitor will exploit.

Reducing weaknesses and **enhancing strengths** should make it that much more difficult for new entrants to compete profitably. The advantage of already being set up in the industry is significant and should be capitalised upon, but lapse of time and perhaps a previous lack of competition may serve to make incumbent firms complacent. Long established players will always be under potential threat from slimmer, younger companies.

(c) Various options are open to a company to counter the threat of new entrants to a low technology industry. The key is to make sure that potential new entrants are aware of them.

As we are trying to deter the threat of new entrants rather than existing competitors, the initial approach is to **discourage them from entry in the first place**, or to drive them off once they have decided to enter.

Raise barriers to entry. Here are some examples.

(i) Fill in any gaps in the product range which a competitor might exploit. Launching a number of **different brands** gives the impression of a market that does not need new entrants. New products from new entrants may be resisted.

(ii) Block access to **distribution** channels (eg by exclusive agreements, volume discounts).

(iii) Even in a low technology industry, effective use of **patents** can raise entry barriers.

(iv) Build or reinforce **customer loyalty** (eg match the entrant's guarantees). Building customer loyalty is not achieved overnight, however, and is expensive.

Raise the new entrant's perception of risk, by making the market appear less attractive and more risky, so that the new entrant goes somewhere else.

(i) The firm should indicate its intention to fight by publicising that it is investing in **new capacity**, brands etc.

(ii) Propose an aggressive **price-cutting strategy** which will make it harder for the new entrant to build market share. Cost savings could be investigated to mitigate the effect of this.

(iii) Challenge the **competitor's assumption** about the future of the industry (eg by reducing stated profit targets).

Counter attack

(i) Disrupt the new entrant's **test markets** (eg by amending the offer).

(ii) Introduce **new products**, processes or variants.

(iii) **Litigation**, if necessary. This could be costly, but it may be considered worthwhile in a cost/benefit analysis. It may buy valuable time while new entrants 'regroup'.

(iv) **Attack the entrant in its home market**, to divert attention and resources from the new entry strategy.

Not all of these tactics can be adopted easily. Much depends on the resources available within the industry. Firms which are weakly profitable will be vulnerable to new entrants, and may not have the resources to spend dealing with the threat or counterattacking.

Long term considerations

(i) **Diversify**. If the new entrant threat results from a long term and permanent change in the structure and profitability of the industry, then the firm might have to reconsider its place in the industry and perhaps diversify.

(ii) **Acquisitions**. The firm might have to accept the new entrant. Rather than attack the new entrant, the firm might seek to take over one of the existing competitors

- or at least its market share - to build up size and strength. The new entrant may have the effect of consolidating the industry.

As a last resort, a firm might decide the threat is so big, or the returns so small, that it is best to give in to the threat and **abandon the market**. For example, if a small pharmacy hears that Boots or Superdrug has got planning permission to open next door, it might decide to withdraw.

Entry barriers might be falling for many reasons, so withdrawal might in any case be **economically sensible** if the structure of the industry is changing.

9 PREPARATION QUESTION: CLASSICS ON THE CHEAP

> **Tutor's hint.** This question basically deals with the ideas of Michael Porter on value chain analysis. The question asks you to conduct an analysis to assess what features in the company's operations, as indicated by its value chain, support its recent success. You should also note the industry structure: the vast majority of publishers subcontract their printing to outside firms.

(a) **Classics for under £1: exploiting cost leadership or possibly a cost-focus strategy**

The strategy depends on **high volume** sales of low priced books, out of copyright, and a willingness to use **novel distribution channels**, such as supermarkets etc, where suitable. The books themselves are competing with other publishers' editions such as Penguin, Everyman and Oxford University Press. Wordsworth offers a different packaging of the same text, but **claims** to be pursuing a **focus** strategy, as its editions are not produced for schools and universities, but for the price-conscious general reader. In practice, the campaign can have two consequences.

(i) **Competitors.** Wordsworth's competitors (Penguin etc) do **not** consider themselves restricted to the school and university market and so Wordsworth's claim not to be competing directly with them looks rather extraordinary.

(ii) The **market for the classics may grow**, so that people who would not consider buying classic literature, for whatever reason, now can do so, as it is so much cheaper than before.

Wordsworth is thus competing in the market for classic titles. **Cost leadership** is the most appropriate description of the strategy: the directors say as much by stating that they cannot be undercut. At the moment no-one can produce books more cheaply.

Wordsworth's **price strategy** used to have another function. It enabled Wordsworth to differentiate its offer to booksellers and other retailers; they were given the freedom to price as they wish; they were not subject to the Net Book Agreement. This flexibility on pricing was probably necessary to attract retailers new to bookselling. The Net Book Agreement has now been abolished.

(b) The **value chain** is a sort of model of how firms create value for their customers. The value chain describes a number of activities carried out in a firm.

Primary activities are directly related to the processes of production and sales.

(i) **Inbound logistics** are those activities involved with receiving, handling and storing inputs to the production system.

(ii) **Operations** convert the resource input into the end product.

(iii) **Outbound logistics** relate to storage and distribution.

(iv) **Marketing and sales** inform customers about the product, and include advertising and promotion.

(v) **After sales service** - this rarely applies to publishing companies.

Support activities obtain purchased inputs, human resources, technology and infrastructure to support the primary activities.

Competitive advantage is obtained by configuring the value chain in certain ways.

Primary activities

(i) There is little in the way of **inbound logistics**. Like most publishers, it subcontracts other firms to do its printing, so it would not need to warehouse stocks of paper. There is little effort required to find books out of copyright.

(ii) **Operations**: editorial work is done in house, but the conversion of paper and ink into books for sale is done by outsiders.

(iii) Outbound logistics and distribution, on the other hand, are very important indeed to reach the right markets at the right time, especially as the firm eschews advertising and promotion.

Of the **support activities**, the size of the firm (ten staff) means that these might be the responsibility of a few people. **Technology development**, for example, would mean reviewing the latest word processing technology, if appropriate; **procurement** is simply a matter of researching back catalogues for old editions. The firm perhaps does not have to bother with market research; the books are so cheap (the price of a Sunday Newspaper) that they are easy to sell.

What Wordsworth does is to **manage the linkages in the value chain,** even though many of the activities in the value chain are contracted to outsiders, **to squeeze out costs**. Wordsworth has combined a number of elements in a normal publisher's value chain and **configured them in its own unique way**. This is why it has been successful.

10 PREPARATION QUESTION: FAMILY DOCTOR

(a) **Key internal and external issues facing the practice**

The appointment of an administrator is a response to the unprecedented change that the practice is undergoing. However it seems that the doctors feel that this is enough and that the problem is mainly administrative.

SWOT analysis brings together an internal appraisal of the organisation's strengths and weaknesses with an analysis of the opportunities and threats seen in the environment. The aim is to neutralise the weaknesses and try and convert threats into opportunities.

Internal issues

Strengths. The practice's strengths include its **reputation** and some of its **clinics**. However, these were developed in the past, and they have to be maintained and nurtured. Furthermore, only two of the partners are concerned about the practice in the **long term**.

Weaknesses. These seem to be in the **internal structure and management** of the practice, not its clinical effectiveness. Although the new administrator sounds very pessimistic, it may be that she has yet to adjust her desire for clear management, as would be expected in the profit-making organisation, with the fact that, in a practice which is a **non-profit making organisation** with a variety of objectives, a **dispersal of power amongst various stakeholders** is inevitable, and, in a service which is publicly funded delivering specialist care, even desirable. However, internal deficiencies can be listed as follows.

(i) **Poor information** regarding the practice's performance. This is serious if doctors are to be paid by results.

(ii) **Poor management of support staff** (an area where distinctly managerial skills are desirable).

(iii) The practice has **no mission**, other than the doctor's professional specialisms.

(iv) Staff are resisting change.

Stakeholders

There is a danger that the administrator is trying to impose a managerial model of the organisation on the practice. The administrator has to negotiate with the various stakeholder groups in the practice.

(i) **The partners, as significant stakeholders, are not united.** Only two want to stay around in the long term. The administrator's relationship is complicated by the fact that each partner is her boss. The practice is a minor example of what Mintzberg calls a **professional bureaucracy**, in which the operating core is supported, rather than controlled, by the managerial infrastructure.

(ii) The administrator also had problems with the **computer expert** who had **expert** and **resources power** over the practice's computer systems.

(iii) **The practice is a public service.** The regional health authority and the patients (who pay for the service out of their taxation) are stakeholders with legitimate interests.

(iv) There has been **no systematic analysis of customer needs** and requirements in the area (eg does it have a higher than average proportion of elderly people?). This would give some guidance as to their performance targets.

External opportunities and threats

The environment provides opportunities and threats. Unlike a business, the practice is controlled by its customers, the public, through a roundabout route, and the only competitive threat is that of losing patients to competing practices. However, the supplier of resources, the government (as customer as well as a supplier) is able to impose changes in management and technique.

Opportunities include **the liaison with the local Health Authority:** the practice, already an innovator, will have advance information about planned developments and will be able to shape developments. The practice might be used as a **testing base** for new ideas in patient care.

Threats include the continued cutting of **resources**, and **competition** from neighbouring practices which are stealing patients, and hence the capitation fees.

Summary

To summarise, the internal issues are those of human resources management, performance information and measurement, and strategic thinking for the practice as an organisation rather than just a place where individuals dispense care. The external factors include potential funding problems and continued change.

(b) **Introducing change**

Sources of change

(i) **Environmental changes** include the new **funding system**, and the more **competitive approach**.

(ii) **Changes in products and services** include **new medicines** and **therapeutic techniques**, and perhaps a new fashion for **alternative treatments**. The practice seems quite innovative in this respect.

(iii) **Changes in technology and working methods:** conceivably this could include the use of expert systems as diagnostic tools.

(iv) **Changes in management and working relationships.** The appointment of an administrator, over the heads of the existing clerical staff, is an example of this.

(v) **Changes in organisation structure.** This has not yet been mooted, but it is difficult to see how this could be achieved, other than by a shuffling of clerical responsibilities.

Preparing the ground for change. The administrator has to consider the initial **climate of change**. She has to create a culture where innovation and change is desirable.

(i) Ensure that everybody understands what innovation is and how it happens.

(ii) Ensure that the partners accept the need for change.

(iii) Encourage people to think creatively.

(iv) The needs of the various stakeholders must be understood and addressed. It is clear that there has been a communications problem in the past: partners have not explained themselves to staff, who have been working to thwart any change.

(v) Recognise and encourage internal change agents: but in a small practice, the administrator herself is a change agent.

Implementing change. The administrator has to sell change (through reasoned persuasion) rather than command it, because of the limits to her power. A useful model is Lewin's unfreeze-change-refreeze model.

(i) The **unfreeze process** can be started by a major event. An example would be the proposed brain-storming session suggested by one of the partners. Senior management are already receptive to change. This could not extend to other members of staff, especially as they will have to be won over eventually. At least there will be the semblance of consultation.

(ii) **Change.** The administrator can suggest that the practice needs a plan, and she can ask for and/or put forward proposals to improve the system of performance measurement employed in the hospital. A well publicised strategic or business plan for the practice, with targets for immunisations etc as well as revenue considerations, can be drawn up. Setting up this system involves disruption and extra effort. If staff, not only the partners, can be told how it benefits them, the change will be easier to implement.

(iii) **Refreeze.** The administrator should ensure the changes are bedded down.

11 SALES TEAM BENCHMARKING

(a) **Objectives and uses of benchmarking**

Benchmarking is 'the establishment, through data gathering, of targets and comparators, through whose use areas of performance (and particularly areas of underperformance) can be identified. By the adoption of identified best practices it is hoped that performance will be improved'.

(i) **Internal benchmarking** compares one operating unit or function with another in the **same firm**.

(ii) **Functional/operational/generic benchmarking** involves the comparison of a business's internal functions with those of the best external practitioners of those functions, regardless of the industry they are in. For example a bank setting up a telephone banking service might benchmark a telephone sales operation, for matters such as speed of answering, courtesy and so forth.

(iii) **Competitor benchmarking.** The firm uses competitors as a benchmark for performance. **Strategic benchmarking** is a type of competitor benchmarking aimed at strategic action and organisational change.

Objectives and value of benchmarking

(i) To keep up with **industry best practice** - perhaps to negate a competitor's operational competitive advantage.

(ii) To enhance the **efficiency and effectiveness** of the function involved in the benchmarking exercise.

(iii) To reduce the need to 'reinvent the wheel' - a firm can climb the learning curve to achieve best practice much quicker if it uses another firm's experience.

(iv) As performance indicators to motivate managers: the **benchmark standards are achievable**, as other firms **have** achieved them.

In all these respects, benchmarking can be used for **planning and control**.

(i) As **planning measures**, they can be used to design systems and to assess the resources required to achieve a certain standard of performance.

(ii) In evaluating operational performance, benchmarks can be used as the 'plan or standard' of a **control system**, and feedback can be used to see whether the plan has been met.

Problems with benchmarking in evaluating operational performance

(i) The benchmark standards do not always take the use of resources into account.

(ii) Managers will be satisfied when they have reached the benchmark standard and will be less motivated to exceed it.

(iii) There may be better ways of enhancing performance (eg by exploiting different linkages in the value chain, outsourcing some value activities etc).

(iv) It is based on copying industry leaders, rather than doing things in a different, more innovative way.

(b) (i) **Using benchmarking to assess the sales team as a whole**

Many organisations have field sales forces organised on an area basis, and so the company is not unique. It can therefore learn from other companies as to the best way of managing and controlling its sales personnel. Benchmarking techniques can be used for two types of information.

(1) The best way to **design and run** a field sales force (eg the optimum balance of salary and commission, the most appropriate way of designing and setting targets).

(2) The **performance** of the sales team, as it is currently managed in the light of other field sales forces (in other words the content of the targets).

Choice of company to benchmark

Competitor benchmarking is probably out of the question, given that any useful and coherent information will be hard to obtain, unless the firm poaches disaffected sales personnel. There is no indication that the firm is considering any major change in strategy, so the approaches which **can** be used are **internal benchmarking** and **functional benchmarking**.

Identifying areas to be benchmarked

The company needs to identify and describe its **current practices** and performance.

(1) **Systems issues** include remuneration systems, territory design and size, and the basis on which targets are set by territory.

(2) **Performance issues** include typical mileage and expenses, the number of sales leads generated and the number of sales leads converted into real orders.

Timescale

The benchmarking exercise needs to carried out over a meaningful timescale, both from the firm's point of view and in terms of the operational realities of the benchmarked firm. **Seasonal factors** need to be taken into account as do any other special circumstances. Whilst the demand for industrial oils is unlikely to be too seasonal, this may not apply for the benchmarked company.

Review

Once the information has been gathered, it can be analysed and converted into a meaningful form by the benchmarking company. The information must be comparable and so a number of adjustments will have to be made. Once this is done, the benchmarking firm can then identify areas of performance or systems where deficiencies are found.

Action

The firm can then take steps to improve its performance and make any necessary changes to the achieve the benchmark.

(ii) **Using benchmarking to assess individuals**

Individual benchmarks are not appropriate.

Whilst the sales team can be reviewed as a whole, and its performance measured on an average basis, individual sales personnel will differ in their performance. Furthermore, it is unlikely that any single individual sales person in the benchmarked company could be used for benchmarking purposes. The benchmarked company may have a different sales territory structure.

Group average

Applying benchmarking to individual sales people will therefore happen at one remove. From the comparison between each company, an overall average measure of performance will be derived. For example, the benchmarked company may show a much better record of converting sales leads into orders.

Suggest and announce changes

This may involve making current targets harder to reach, or introducing new measures, or changing more fundamentally the structure and operations of the sales function. In the company described, changes could include:

- **Redesign of the sales territories**
- The use of **different targets** per individual - in other words setting different targets per territory, depending on the nature of the territory, the ease with which it can be traversed and so forth
- **Amend the payment system** to increase the element of bonus/commission and reducing the level of basic salary

Introduce changes

Clearly, these matters will be better resolved if a **participatory approach** is adopted. Sales staff may offer suggestions to improve performance. An appropriate time might be needed for people to get used to the new system, and so learning curve effects must be allowed for.

New comparisons

Once the new measures are in place, the performance of the sales staff can be compared. To ensure fair comparisons, matters such as the overall level of prosperity and industrial structure of the sales territories can be taken into account to enable more appropriate targets to be set.

12 PREPARATION QUESTION: MISSION, VISION AND STRATEGIC INTENT

Mission

Mission is 'the organisation's basic function in society, in terms of the products and services it produces for its clients' (Mintzberg).

Mission may be seen as having four important elements

Purpose. Why does the company exist?

- To create wealth for shareholders?
- To satisfy the needs of **all stakeholders** (including employees, society at large, for example)?

Strategy and strategic scope . Mission provides the commercial logic for the organisation, and so defines two things

- The **products or services** it offers and therefore its competitive position.
- The **competences** by which it hopes to prosper, and its way of competing.

An organisation's **strategic scope** is defined by the **boundaries** its managers set for it. These boundaries may be set in terms of geography, market, business method, product or any other parameter that **defines the nature of the organisation**.

Policies and standards of behaviour. The mission needs to be converted into everyday performance. For example, a firm whose mission covers excellent customer service must deal with simple matters such as politeness to customers, speed at which phone calls are answered and so forth.

Values and culture. Values are the basic, perhaps unstated, beliefs of the people who work in the organisation.

(a) Principles of business

- Commitment to suppliers and staff
- Social policy eg on non-discrimination or ecology
- Commitments to customers

(b) **Loyalty and commitment**. A sense of mission may inspire employees to sacrifice their own personal interests for the good of the whole. This however has to be reciprocated by company loyalty to its staff (eg long-term staff retention).

(c) **Guidance for behaviour**. A sense of mission helps create a work environment where there is a sense of **common purpose**.

For there to be a strong, motivating sense of mission, the four elements above must be mutually reinforcing.

Vision

A vision gives a general sense of direction to the company, even if there is not too much attention to detail. It is a guiding idea. The strategy draws on the vision. A vision might provide the boundaries (in Simon's description of bounded rationality) for the firm's direction.

A strategic thinker should have a vision for the future. This has three aspects.

- What the business *is* now
- What it *could* be in an ideal world
- What the ideal world would be like

Problems with vision

- It ignores real, practical problems.
- It can degenerate into wishful thinking.

Strategic intent

Hamel and Prahalad suggest that **strategic intent** is similar to vision, but it should to have an emotional core.

- It is a 'dream' that energises a company.
- It implies a 'stretch' beyond current competences.
- Like vision it gives a sense of **direction** and discovery.
- It entails a sense of discovery, as employers learn new things.
- It gives coherence to plans.

Effectively, it aims to enthuse employees with the business strategy. As such, it is possibly less powerful a motivator than mission.

13 PREPARATION QUESTION: COST LEADERSHIP

(a) **Achieving overall cost leadership**

(i) High market share to utilise capacity
(ii) Mass production to achieve economies of scale
(iii) Continual investment in the latest technology
(iv) Focus on **productivity improvements** and **cost reduction**
(v) Regular feedback of cost control information to managers
(vi) A cost cutting culture
(vii) Favourable access to sources supply

(b) **Risks of overall cost leadership**

- (i) Heavy investment required to achieve economies of scale
- (ii) Technological change: cost of keeping up to date
- (iii) Competition from other countries where costs may be even lower
- (iv) Competitors may differentiate the products
- (v) The market may segment

(c) **Two other generic strategies**

- (i) **Differentiation** of the product or value chain.
- (ii) **Focus.** A firm only sells to a particular segment of the market, by adopting a strategy of cost leadership or differentiation for that segment.

14 PREPARATION QUESTION: PHARMIA PLC

Part (a)

A decision tree is provided below. The outcomes are multiplied by the probabilities which are then aggregated. Before the initial investment of £5m is taken into account, the expected value (EV) of each option is as follows.

EV of Tyrix	=	0.03 × £150m = £4.5m
EV of Medvac	=	(£48m × 1/6) + (£27m × 1/3) + (-£10m × 1/2) = £12m
EV of Sonprex	=	£14m

The net payoff, after the investment cost, is as follows.

Tyrix £4.5m – £5m	=	£(0.5m) (ie a loss of £500,000)
Medvac £12m – £5m	=	£7m profit
Sonprex £14m – £5m	=	£9m profit

Part (b)

The appropriateness of expected values and subjective probabilities

Any strategic decision is taken in a state of partial ignorance as to the future: this is why strategies are necessary. You cannot be sure that a quantitative exercise necessarily gives the right result without questioning the **assumptions** on which it is based and the **context** in which it is made. The probabilities in this example are merely **subjective** quantifications of uncertainty. In the cases of the options suggested we can note the following.

(a) **Possible overconfidence about Sonprex.** Can we really be 100% certain about Sonprex's success? The answer has to be **no**, as this would imply that the company's forecasters had an absolute knowledge of the future. However, this does indicate that the project is low risk, but that is all it indicates.

(b) **Sensitivity to the 'risky' Tyrix.** The decision is sensitive to the low (3%) probability of Tyrix's success. Tyrix offers a huge reward. Were the success of Tyrix to have a 5% probability, the EV before investment would be £150m × 5% = £7.5m. A 10% probability of success, still very low, would give it an EV before investment costs of £15m, which would make it, on the basis of EVs alone, an attractive option even though a high risk. The decision is thus sensitive to changes in probability estimates. As these are subjective anyway, they need to be taken with a pinch of salt.

(c) **Bizarre profit/market share figures for Medvac.** How realistic are the market share projections for Medvac?

(i) It is hard to see how an **increase in market share**, even if only 10%, could lead to a loss of £10m, especially after £5m had been invested in advertising, and the loss did not take this advertising into account.

(ii) The difference in payoff between a 10% market share and a 15% market share is extraordinary (£37m). This needs to be looked into. It is unlikely that there would be a sudden jump in market share. When would the outcome be positive? at 11%? or 12%?

To summarise, the decision cannot be taken in isolation from the firm's commercial strategy of innovation, its need to maintain a balanced portfolio of projects in the present, and its need to invest in future successful projects. Furthermore, especially in the case of Medvac, more information is needed.

Part (c)

The relative merits of each drug. This decision should not be taken without considering other products in the portfolio, about which we know little. Nor can we ignore the circumstances of the decision: the £5m is 'unexpected', additional to the existing allocation of resources. The company's policy is to take a **scattergun approach**, investing large sums in R & D in many projects in the hope of producing a sure fire winner.

(a) **Tyrix** is an innovative investment.

(i) **Cheap.** The actual investment (£5m) is small in comparison to the potential reward (£150m) even though the probability of achieving the reward is very low.

(ii) **Safe.** The investment of £5m is hardly critical to the firm's success: otherwise it would not have been conjured out of a hat and made unexpectedly available. The risk is perhaps less important than it would be normally.

(iii) **Strategic conformity.** The firm's overall approach to the market is product **innovation**. Tyrix conforms to this strategy. Sonprex does not.

(b) Medvac

(i) It has already been successfully introduced. The chances of the advertising campaign being successful is about 50%.

(ii) Despite the competition, and the rather bizarre negative payoff resulting from an increase in market share, there are substantial benefits to be had from supporting it. Again, this will depend on the firm's attitude to risk. Risk is spread through a number of different products in the portfolio, and so Medvac may be worth it in the light of the rest of the portfolio.

(c) Sonprex gives the **highest** payoff compared to the other two, but that is the **only** thing in its favour.

(i) Investing in Sonprex will be an investment in a product which would shortly be superseded: a **harvesting strategy**.

(ii) If this means that the firm's portfolio is too heavily weighted towards mature products, the firm's **long term future is in danger.**

(d) **Remaining uncertainties. We do not know much about the timing of the cash flows.**

(i) If Sonprex brings in £14m in the year **after** the investment, this might be used to subsidise investment in the other two. Nor do we know if Medvac's condition will get much worse if the money is not invested.

(ii) If the price of investing in Sonprex is the failure, say, of Medvac, then this must be taken into account when devising expected values. Tyrix is an opportunity: it does not need the investment, whereas Medvac's competitive position may be undermined if it is not supported.

The EVs provide some useful information to make a decision, but because we do not know the state of the **entire product portfolio**; and the firm's attitude to **risk**, a comparison of EVs **cannot** be used as the determining factor in this case.

Expected value of different products

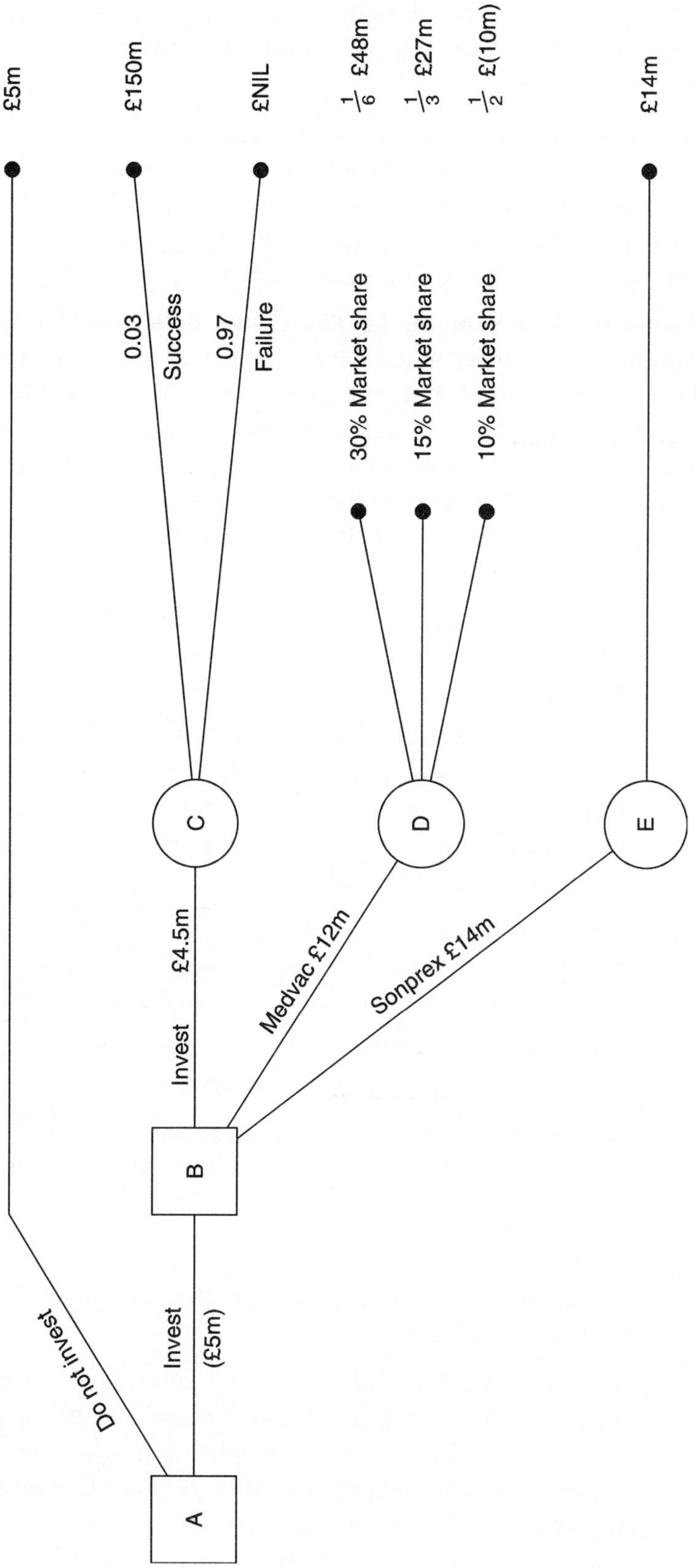

15 PREPARATION QUESTION: CHILDREN'S NOVELTY CONFECTIONERY

> **Tutor's hint**. In part (a) of the question, don't confuse product-market portfolio planning with investment portfolio theory.

(a) **Scope of portfolio analysis.** The compilation of a product-market portfolio will help the marketing function to plan and control the organisation's marketing strategy, by helping to identify the **strengths, weaknesses and gaps** in the organisation's range of products and markets and what **strategy might be needed** to exploit strengths or reduce weaknesses.

BCG. A variety of product-market portfolio techniques have been developed, the most well-known being the **Boston Consulting Group** classifications of products into stars, cash cows, question marks (or problem children) and dogs. Portfolio analysis can include an analysis of a product's expected sales, profitability and cash-generating or cash-consuming features within the context of its expected life cycle.

Use of portfolio planning for novelty confectionery. A company that manufactures **novelty** confectionery might have a number of products with a fairly long life cycle, but it is also likely that other products will have a very short life that ends when the 'novelty' wears off for consumers. A feature of the company's product-market portfolio is therefore likely to be the **continual introduction of new products, and the removal of old products from the market**. In these circumstances, the current and anticipated strengths and weaknesses of the company's entire range of products can usefully be monitored.

(i) **Marketing planning.** Management can try to plan for a portfolio of products that provides a good spread of life cycle 'ages' and a good spread of shorter-life and longer-life products.

(ii) **Profitability planning.** The profitability of products varies at different stages in their life cycle, and according to their market position. Portfolio planning can help management to achieve a satisfactory range of products that are either profitable now or are expected to become profitable in the future. An overall view can be taken of the company's potential for profit and growth.

(iii) **Cash flow planning.** Similarly, portfolio analysis can help management to plan for a mix of products that provides suitable cash flows. 'Cash cows' will generate cash, whereas 'stars' will still use up cash for further investment.

(iv) **Market position.** Management can also use portfolio analysis to plan and control their overall market position with regard to competition.

(v) **Exit.** Portfolio analysis helps management to decide the timing for 'killing off' old products, which is likely to be a frequently-recurring event in ZQ Ltd.

Risk

By helping management to achieve a satisfactory competitive position, a good spread of products, and satisfactory profits and cash flows, portfolio planning is a technique for **controlling or reducing risk**.

(i) **Business risk.** The company should not become exposed to the dangers of an ageing product range, questionable future profits, unsupportable cash outflows because of an excessively large number of new 'star' products in development, or failures to kill off old products when they cease to earn profits or generate cash inflows.

(ii) **Risk and return.** The financial analysis of different product portfolios can also be used to select a portfolio that promises an **attractive return for a tolerable level of risk.**

(b) **Consumer panels.** A consumer panel should consist of a representative cross-section of consumers who agree to give information about their attitudes to a product. A panel might be established for a long-term or a short-term period, and in this situation, it is more likely that the panel will have a long-term duration, for the testing of a series of products that are developed.

Problems with the use of consumer panels

(i) **Affording a representative sample.** Within the budget constraints of the marketing exercise, it will often be difficult to find a 'sample' of consumers who are representative of the market as a whole.

(ii) **Identifying decision makers.** A consumer panel should ideally consist of individuals who make the buying decisions about the product. In some households, children themselves will be the decision-making units, but in other households, parents might take the buying decisions, or might restrict the amount of buying that their children can do.

(iii) **Reliability of children's opinions.** The opinions and judgement of many children might not be sufficiently reliable to provide a basis for marketing planning.

(iv) **Education in techniques.** Panel members tend to become sophisticated in interviewing techniques, and their reactions become 'corrupted' and unreliable.

(v) **No stable membership.** Children grow up quickly, and it will be impossible to maintain a stable personnel for the panel, with stable, consistent views over time.

(c) **Product differentiation** is the creation of actual or perceived differences in a product, that make it seem different from similar rival products in such a way as to appeal to consumers in a particular niche of the overall market.

(i) ZQ Ltd needs to market a range of different products, since novelty is a key feature of their appeal to the market.

(ii) Since the products must be manufactured on the same equipment and within the same factory, the scope for differentiation must be restricted.

The aim of differentiation for a company such as ZQ Ltd should thus be to create maximum novelty at minimum cost; therefore many of the differentiating features between products will be fairly superficial.

(i) **Differences in flavour:** new 'flavours' can be added to an existing range.
(ii) **Differences in packaging.**
(iii) **Moulds.** There will probably be scope for variation in shapes and sizes.
(iv) Differentiation through **advertising**.

16 PREPARATION QUESTION: IMPORT CONCERN

> **Tutor's hint**. Do not suggest that corporate culture automatically leads to decreased profits, and so should be jettisoned at the earliest opportunity. This betrays a confusion as to the meaning of the concept of corporate culture: culture is not the same as ethics, however defined.

(a) **Examining and adapting short-term plans to take account of environmental changes**

Assumption. BM plc's short term plans, before the receipt of this environmental information, were to carry on much as it is at present.

Faced with the trends identified, the management of BM plc might carry out a SWOT (strengths, weaknesses, opportunities, threats) analysis over its entire business.

(i) The only data we are given relates to **threats** from the environment.

(ii) It is not entirely clear what BM plc's strengths and **weaknesses** are. We are not enlightened as to the **market positioning** of the products, whether they are low volume high value items, or whether they are sold in high volumes at low margins. This limits any suggestions for improving the situation. However, we can still assess some of the issues.

Strengths

(i) **Low fixed costs.** BM plc does not carry a high amount of fixed costs. It buys from Asian suppliers, and presumably does not get involved in manufacturing itself.

(ii) **Wide product range**

Weaknesses

(i) **Dependence on reliable Asian suppliers:** presumably these are cheaper than European suppliers but this may not last.

(ii) **Fixed contracts with suppliers** might lock the company into a given level of production.

Opportunities. The obverse of a threat: a competitive market is an opportunity to beat the competition.

Threats

(i) **Long term decline in consumer spending.** (**Tutor's hint**. The phraseology of the question implies a long term decline in absolute terms; more probable is the **decline of the rate in growth** of consumer spending over the five year period.)

(ii) **Import restrictions** threaten the heart of the business

(iii) A very competitive market

(iv) **Political pressure**

Dealing with environmental threats

(i) **Decline in consumer spending**

(1) **Aggressive competitive strategy.** BM plc must make sure that the decline hurts the competition more.

(2) **Enter new markets**, by importing a greater variety of products. BM could consider expanding its operations in Eastern Europe.

(3) **Reduce competition** by acquiring competing firms.

(4) Find **new market segments**. It is unlikely that all segments of the market will be in decline at once. For example, the changing age structure of the population might encourage marketing to the elderly.

(5) **Review distribution channels.** Dell Computers, for example, sells its machines by mail order.

(6) **Identify which products and markets** will be more profitable and should concentrate on those, perhaps keeping a presence in the other markets in

the event of an upturn in the long term. Some of BM plc's product range may be **immune** from the overall decline in consumer spending, if they are necessities rather than luxuries.

(7) **Review costs** and current operations to ensure efficiency.

(ii) **Possible import restrictions**

(1) Many forms of protectionism have been outlawed or are being policed, by the **World Trade Organisation.**

(2) **Import quotas.** By raising overall prices and reducing competition, quotas could enable BM plc to import fewer goods of higher value and quality, thus moving up- market. This would allow BM plc to import higher quality goods and make good profits.

(3) **Higher tariffs**. If this is a real danger, BM plc should consider seriously lobbying to avoid them. The company should bring up the matter with the European Commission first of all, so that it is treated as a competition issue. The company does not want to be on the receiving end of actions for dumping. BM plc might also get some support from the Department of Trade and Industry. Such lobbying might put BM plc's imports in the context of overall trade with the countries it exports to.

(4) **Relocation** in the long term. If importing becomes more expensive, it might be worth BM plc's while to **subcontract its manufacturing elsewhere**, perhaps in an EU country with low wage costs, to keep its cost advantage.

(5) BM plc's short term response should be to investigate alternative sources of supply so that if long term changes are necessary, at least it has some information.

(iii) **Pressure groups:**

(1) Have a direct impact on a company's fortunes
(2) Set the agenda for national policy decisions (eg the environment).

BM plc should not ignore the pressure groups even though they have not targeted the company directly. BM needs to develop a plan for approaching the problem, should the issue become one of public concern. **Public relations** are important here. BM plc needs to investigate the practices of supplier companies. BM plc can set minimum standards of pay and conditions in companies which supply it ('contract compliance').

(b) **Influencing governments' policies.** With no local production facilities, BM plc does not provide employment or investment in the countries where it sells, so it cannot rely on local interest groups to advance its case. Instead its policy will have to be one of persuasion.

(i) Employ **lobbyists** to put the company's case to governments, MPs, MEPs and other decision makers.

(ii) Do **some assembly work** in Europe, or perhaps subcontract some work to European companies. If it sets up the operation in a region that is depressed economically, it might receive government grants, and it certainly will win the support of local political representatives.

(iii) Give **donations to political parties** which support BM plc's cause.

(iv) **Respond to pressure groups**. BM plc could claim that free trade is in the interests of consumers, as it promotes higher quality at lower prices.

(v) **Advertise effectively.** Build up a good reputation for social responsibility (eg sponsorship of the arts, charity, donations to Prince's Trust and so forth, preferably schemes which attract media attention).

(c) **Conflicts between profit and corporate culture.** An **organisation's culture** may be defined as its complex body of shared values and beliefs. Some corporate cultures develop with the growth of the company, and may depend on the attitudes of management. Some companies employ specialists in corporate ethics to help them out of tricky dilemmas.

Short-term profits vs culture. Companies generally exist to pursue profit in the short and long terms. However, they do not to pursue every profitable opportunity even if they could. A company with a culture in which quality was important would not try and deceive customers by using substandard components, as its long-term reputation would suffer. So, where the short-term profit opportunity destroys the whole rationale for the company as expressed in the corporate culture it should be ignored, as in the long term this will be bad for business.

Long-term profits vs culture. What some managers would find more difficult, though, is if the profitable opportunity is of **long-term** benefit to the company as a whole. Managers can:

(i) reject the profitable opportunity;

(ii) 'sell' it to staff or those who influence corporate culture as an a project which does not breach corporate culture after all (ie 'reposition' the project);

(iii) change the corporate culture (eg change of mission statement)- in companies which have bureaucratic role culture, making them more customer-orientated can require organisational changes too;

(iv) ignore the corporate culture, and pursue the profit anyway.

Note that **corporate culture** is a different concept from **corporate ethics**. For example, a policy of customer service and care may be a change in a corporate culture which treated customers and their requests as procedural inconveniences: customer service and care may bring increased profits. Here the customer benefits and profits increase: there is no ethical conflict here.

17 LARGE FINANCIAL SERVICES COMPANY

Tutor's hint. Answers taking a more critical approach – that is, not assuming that a code of conduct is all that is necessary – are likely to score higher marks. It is not clear how many marks were originally allocated to each part of the question, presumably allowing scope for a variety of different approaches to the question. For instance some of the points made in the first part of our answer appear in the second part of the original official solution and *vice versa*.

Our solution is longer than could have been produced in an exam because it aims to cover a variety of different possible answers, and to provide extra material to help with your revision.

In his report the original examiner agreed that 'only exceptional answers would cover all topics in reasonable depth:

- discuss top management responsibility; managerial control
- top management attitudes and communication
- company mission and beliefs system
- existence and enforcement of code of conduct
- organisational culture, and the problems of changing culture
- recruitment and assessment of staff
- the reward system and possible changes
- formal product approval, and separation of this approval from product sales
- trade-offs/balanced conclusions
- the limits of an incremental approach to change, and the risks in rapid change of preventing innovation and losing competitive advantage.

The question does not mention the mis-selling of pensions, but it could be related to this problem which has been discussed extensively in the financial press. It could also be related to the commission-driven approaches of insurance and fund sales staff which have been a problem for many years.'

Discussion of quality control, the enforcement of the code of conduct, corporate governance and corporate image were not relevant.

REPORT

To: Board of Directors
From: A Consultant
Date: XX.XX.XX
Subject: Ethical values

Background

In recent years we have seen the financial services industry come under **increasing scrutiny**, both in terms of formal regulation and in terms of public awareness. This trend is expected to continue. The industry is also **increasingly competitive**, and others appear to have been more successful than this company at responding to the needs of the market.

Corporate **culture** here is based around a **risk-taking strategy** which is **not appropriate** in the current climate. It has therefore been suggested that a **formal code of conduct** be introduced to help **change organisational culture** and **encourage more ethical behaviour** on the part of staff.

Company code of conduct

A corporate code typically contains a series of statements setting out the company's values and explaining how it sees its responsibilities towards stakeholders.

Typical statements in a corporate code	**Comment**
The company conducts all of its business on **ethical principles** and **expects** staff to do likewise.	At present this company conducts its business with a view to maximising **sales and growth**, and encourages staff to promote this aim by giving them maximum freedom to maximise their own sales-related earnings
Employees are seen as the most important component of the company and are expected to work on a basis of trust, respect, honesty, fairness, decency and equality. The company will only employ people who follow its ethical ideals.	Employees are likely to be highly competitive and self-interested. They are attracted to the company because they are offered the chance of earning high rewards.
Customers should be treated courteously and politely at all times, and the company should always respond promptly to customer needs by listening, understanding and then performing to the customer requirements.	The company has been criticised for its treatment of customers. Products do not meet customer requirements in the sense that they appear to be poor value for money.
The company is dedicated to complying with **legal or regulatory standards** of the industry, and employees are expected to do likewise.	There have been no major problems yet, but this may just be a matter of time, since small problems have already forced the withdrawal or modification of products and disciplinary action against staff.

Codes may also contain statements about matters such as above-board dealings with suppliers and competitors, respect for company assets, health and safety, ecological commitments and responsibility to the community. No information is available in the scenario about these aspects.

The impact of a code of conduct on this company

A code of conduct can **set out the company's expectations**, and in principle a code such as that outlined above will **address many of the problems** that the organisation is experiencing.

However, merely **issuing a code is not enough**.

- The **commitment of senior management** to the code needs to be real, and it needs to be very clearly communicated to all staff. The prevailing, sales-maximising culture is clearly very strong, and staff need to be persuaded that expectations really have changed.
- Measures need to be taken to **discourage previous behaviours** that conflict with the code.
- **Staff** need to understand that it is in the organisation's best interests to change behaviour, and become **committed to the same ideals**.

Some employees – including very able ones - may find it very difficult to buy into a code that they perceive may limit their own earnings or restrict their freedom to do their job.

There is a very real danger that the **spirit of innovation** upon which the success of the company is founded **may be harmed**.

Other changes necessary

At senior management level, **new reporting systems** need to be set up, emphasising matters that are now perceived to be important, such as level of customer complaints. It may be necessary to **restrict staff freedom** in developing new products, at least by requiring **more formal authorisation procedures** at senior level. If current products really do offer poor value then they must be changed.

In addition to the general statement of ethical conduct envisaged above, **more detailed statements** (codes of practice) will be needed to set out formal procedures that must now be followed. For instance there should be formal procedures designed to ensure compliance with any new regulation: this should not be left up to individuals.

The increase in regulation is likely to require regular **training** or briefing sessions for all staff whose actions could result in regulations being breached.

Many larger organisations have set up an **ethics office**, to monitor instances of non-compliance with ethical principles. Some have a 'hot-line' that staff might use, for instance if they are being asked to engage in unethical behaviour by their seniors.

Many companies have also set up a range of **other ethical support measures** such as ethical review committees, ethical audits, and ethics counsellors or ombudsmen.

Reward systems in the company need to be thoroughly **overhauled**. Bonuses and commissions (which encourage self-interest) need to be de-emphasised in favour of **rewards based on excellence of customer service**. A similar **change of emphasis** may be necessary in **recruitment** and **personnel policies**: it may be necessary to redefine what is meant by 'very able' staff and find ways other than high rewards to attract and retain staff of the required calibre.

Public perceptions of the company need to be monitored more formally, and it may be possible to enter into closer, more active relationships with consumer bodies.

Finally, it may be possible to conduct **benchmarking exercises** to see if the company is following best industry practice in its operations.

18 ACQUISITION

> **Tutor's hint.** This is a wide ranging question, covering an acquisition and its effect on stakeholders, recalling issues of social responsibility via the question of pollution. In part (a), focus on the word strategic and what this implies about the future for C if it goes ahead. Can it afford the acquisition, and would shareholders support it?

(a) **Strategic factors to be considered before the acquisition**

The disappointing performance of the share price, compared to dividend growth, suggest that investors are not confident that dividends can be maintained in future.

(i) **Competitive environment**. Stern competition is driving down profits. This might be caused by excess capacity in the industry. If there is excess capacity and C buys K, C can benefit in two ways.

(1) C can close down K, reducing the over capacity - every other firm in the industry will be better off because of this, but at C's expense.

(2) C can use K's capacity, either by reaping economies of scale or by investing in K to improve its record and to make it a more fierce competitor. This is a more expensive option.

It appears that the industry needs to be consolidated - the problem is to ensure that C reaps as much benefit as possible from this.

(ii) **Competitive strategy**. We are not told of C's or K's competitive strategy, but cost leadership would appear to be an option. Alternatively, the capacity could be used in a competitive strategy of product differentiation.

(iii) **Business risk**. The possibility of prosecution for effluent discharge makes K far less attractive as a target, at least until a settlement is agreed. C should wait until the case is settled. C would not wish to be lumbered with any liability. Moreover, a large fine might make K cheaper to buy. Either way, the timing is not right.

(iv) **Product-market strategy.** The industry is consolidating, and the purchase of K implies that C intends to pursue a **penetration strategy**, in existing markets. Although supply will be consolidated the firm will have to consider whether existing product-market mix can generate the profits that shareholders want.

(v) **Wait until K goes bankrupt** - the capacity can then be acquired even more cheaply, and K would not be a going concern.

(vi) Acquisition in this case is a way of increasing **market share**. As the competitor is in the same industry, the board of C do not have to grapple with a completely unfamiliar business.

(vii) There are often **management problems** in acquisitions.

(viii) C plc has to set itself **strategic objectives** for the acquisition. For shareholders to support it, it must offer an increase in shareholders' wealth.

(ix) **Cost**. No details are given as to how the acquisition would be financed and how much it would cost. These are obviously related to shareholders' wealth. C will also have to **invest** in K.

(x) **Other prospective purchasers** may drive up the price.

(xi) The underlying **capital structure** might change. C will find it more costly to raise capital, and may have to borrow to fund the acquisition.

(xii) **Contingency plans**. If the bid is unwelcome, then C will have to consider a better means of growth.

(b) (i) **Social and ethical implications**

Employees. Significant redundancies are forecast whichever strategy is adopted. These redundancies would happen anyway if there is over capacity in the industry. If K is failing then redundancies, liquidation or receivership would ensue in the medium term. This is a fact of life. It may be the case that C offers the best hope that at least some of K's employees will have a future with the company.

(1) The **manner in which the redundancies are dealt with** is a matter for ethical concern. **Distributive justice** suggests that people should be rewarded according to the value of their contribution. This can be taken into account in the redundancy settlement. **Ordinary decency** can be satisfied by honest dealings, not raising expectations deceitfully, and adherence to contracts.

(2) In practical terms, the effects of the changes on employees involve other issues for the company, including **morale and insecurity**. These can be bad for business - large scale sackings are known to increase the stress levels suffered by those who remain.

(3) For employees and managers of C, the acquisition may create **career opportunities**. C will certainly want to inject management to 'turn round' K.

Shareholders, not managers', interests. Most shareholders are financial institutions. In the UK at least, financial institutions include pension funds, insurance companies and so forth, who look after people's savings. They have a responsibility to their own investors to **maximise the return** available. The ethical implications are that both K and C must pursue their goals with the benefits of maximising long-term owner wealth in mind.

> **Tutor's hint.** The ethical considerations include the benefit to shareholders, rather than managers. For example, K's shareholders may prefer to sell the business, and so K's managers should seek to get the best deal for its shareholders even though K's managers might want to carry on. It is possible to proceed with further nitpicking here.

(ii) **Environmental issues faced by C**

Although it was suggested in (a) that C wait until the outcome of the litigation, there may be good reasons to proceed before this is dealt with. The following issues should be dealt with.

(1) **Discover the cause of the pollution** at K and deal with the problem.

(2) **Estimate the likely financial penalty**. Offer to settle early, perhaps, to avoid the expense and bad publicity of a court case. Devote management's attention to dealing with the problem.

(3) For C and the newly acquired K, put steps in place to improve its **environmental record** (eg BS 7750, the environmental standard). This will promote best practice, and help the company avoid liability in future.

(4) **Waste reduction** can be pursued in tandem with a quality management programme.

(5) The firm will pre-empt legislation or legal action by bringing its environmental practices **up to date**.

(6) In the short term, **crisis management techniques** will be needed to deal with the public relations problems at K.

(7) C may incur **some short-term costs** up front.

19 PREPARATION QUESTION: PROJECT MANAGEMENT

(a) **Features distinguishing 'project' from 'business as usual' (BAU)**

(i) It is geared to the **introduction of change**, where (BAU) management is geared to controlling operations in a stable environment.

(ii) A **definite start and finish date.**

(iii) A **specific budget**. Since it has a defined duration and purpose, its costs should - and can - be more specifically controlled than BAU.

(iv) A **detailed and defined set of objectives,** including time and performance targets, more precise than ABU.

(v) A hierarchy of detailed plans.

(vi) A **fluctuating work load** and resource requirement: not all team members will be required to work on all stages and areas.

(vii) Team members may be permanently employed by the organisation in functional departments, as well as participating as experts on the project. Each team member therefore has two bosses and dual responsibility.

(b) **Key requirements**

(i) **Clear aims** for what the project is supposed to do, its cost and its deadlines.

(ii) A **sponsor** is a 'champion' of the project in the organisation. The project team is not part of the permanent structure of the organisation. It may also face resistance, as an agent of change.

(iii) A **management structure** will be required within the project team.

A large project may have a **steering committee** defining terms of reference etc, which appoints an overall project director, who is responsible for overall planning and control, co-ordination and resource allocation. There would then be a **project manager**, responsible for the direction of the project team.

(iv) An **owner** of a project is the person or group whose work will be affected by the results of the project. The owner has to continue 'business as usual' management while the project is in progress, while planning for the new post- project level and methods of BAU. Ideally, the owner should have been involved in defining the aims of the project.

(v) A **project team** should be made up of experts in the disciplines required to complete the project. They are therefore likely to be drawn from various functions, and various levels of the hierarchy.

(vi) A **communication system** will be required to link:

(1) The project and its 'owner', who will be affected by developments
(2) The project and other areas which will be less directly affected
(3) The various levels of the project's management structure
(4) The members of the project team
(5) The various sub-projects

(c) **Project planning**

(i) **Specify the objectives** or aims to be achieved.

(ii) **Assess the resources** available and the resources **required**.

(iii) Identify **key results**, those critical points where planned results must be achieved if the objectives are to be met.

(iv) Identify the **key tasks** which will achieve the Key Results.

(v) Define **standards of performance** in the key tasks.

(vi) Define **short-term goals** to motivate and control performance.

(vii) Draw up an **action plan**.

(viii) **Set up a timetable** and method for monitoring progress against short-term goals and standards of performance.

20 PREPARATION QUESTION: RESISTING CHANGE

Key processes in the successful implementation of change

(a) **Planning**. This should begin with a **definition of the objectives** to be achieved by the proposed change. In environments where change takes place at a rapid pace this may be more of an ideal than a target achievable in practice.

(b) **Consultation**. Interested parties can be invited to express their views on the need for the proposed change and more usefully on the methods for implementing it.

(c) **Communication**

(i) Before the change takes place, all employees affected by it should be notified of its aims and its intended effects. Efforts should be made to minimise resistance.

(ii) As the change is introduced, employees should be told what is going on. Any transitional procedures should be clearly explained; for example, if a computerised system is being introduced a form of parallel running may be needed. In that case staff would need to know that for a time they are expected to process data through two systems in parallel.

(iii) After the change has taken place, the results should be reviewed and if the intended benefits have become apparent, they should be pointed out to all concerned.

(d) **Monitoring and review**. Comparison with the original plan will show where implementation of the plan is being carried out successfully and where improvements are needed. Finally, review of the whole process after it is complete will indicate where follow-up action is required to tidy up loose edges. It will also provide benefits when future changes are planned because lessons will have been learnt.

Reasons for difficulties in bringing about change

(a) **Change may be expensive**, particularly if major innovations in working procedures are planned. Any marginal improvement may not be worth the cost.

(b) Managers who are thinking of introducing change may be daunted by the **administrative hurdles** to be overcome.

(c) **Policies and procedures become fixed and inflexible.**

(d) **Employees often resist change.**

(i) Change may alter people's relative pay or status.
(ii) People may resist change which lessens the value of their experience.
(iii) People may resist change which causes disruption to their social life.
(iv) Change may be associated with job insecurity.

21 PREPARATION QUESTION: SEGMENTATION

(a) **Manufacturer of diesel engines**

(i) **End-use markets.** The manufacturer would identify customers who would put his diesels into their products. Thus he might segment into heavy road haulage (large trucks and specialist vehicles) light road users (light commercial vehicles and the rising demand for diesels as car engines) passenger vehicles, (buses, coaches, railcars and locomotives) agricultural equipment and marine usage.

(ii) **Geography.** The diesel engine market could be spread out across the world, ie UK, Western Europe etc. This would be appropriate where single types of diesels are being produced, say just marine diesels or just locomotives.

(iii) **Size of customer.** Clearly certain customers, such as motor manufacturers, would be large buyers of particular products and might therefore warrant special treatment.

If only a few potential major buyers exist for the manufacturer, then he could simply segment his market by using a different marketing approach or service to each individual one.

(b) **Manufacturer of breakfast cereals** (a consumer product)

(i) **Age groupings**, eg young children appeal; older children appeal; adult appeal - with appropriate packaging, cut-out models and so on.

(ii) **Benefits.** Cereals that provide adequate diet fibre, extra vitamins and are helpful to weight watchers and sporty outdoor people, justify this kind of segmentation.

(iii) **Family size**. This will dictate packet size. Small family units may want smaller packets or even variety packets, eight single portions of eight different cereals. Larger families possibly with many children will want giant economy size packages. Similarly hotels and hospitals will want larger packets.

(iv) **Type of outlet**. Cereals are sold through a variety of retail outlets. Consideration must be given to the corner shop, convenience stores, supermarkets and hypermarkets etc. The organisational market must also be considered, ie are they supplied direct or through warehouse outlets?

(v) **Geographical area**. The more sophisticated, vitamin enforced, diet-aiding cereals might appeal best to certain parts of the country and so a cereal manufacturer might produce certain products for a geographical/regional market.

(vi) **Social class.** Tastes in food might vary according to social class, and so a firm manufacturer might target its products accordingly.

22 GRENDALL AND FELIX

> **Tutor's hint**. This is a fairly straightforward question on: quality and choice of suppliers. Close and strategic supplier relationships are now fashionable: quality **assurance** programmes provide the bridge between TQM and supplier relationships. Additional issues you might have mentioned, provided you could tie them in with the general thrust of the answer, include the need for a cultural change in Grendalls to secure quality, and its relevance to competitive strategy. You could also develop the role of quality in the value chain and the value system.

Briefing paper

To: Senior management
From: Head of internal audit
Date: 1 December 20X4
Subject: Quality assurance

(a) **Why Barnhams want us to get BS EN ISO 9000 accreditation**

(i) BS EN ISO 9000 is an internationally recognised standard of quality assurance - Barnhams will be able to rely on accredited suppliers to operate to a specified quality level. This will enhance its own quality control.

(ii) Having accredited suppliers will enable Barnhams to save money on inspection.

(iii) It will be easier for Barnhams to earn BS EN ISO 9000 certification if its suppliers have it, and this will add creditability to Barnhams' own attempts to win business from its own customers.

(vi) Many firms are reducing the number of suppliers they deal with, to develop closer relationships with those remaining.

(b) **Advantages and disadvantages to Grendalls of accreditation**

Advantages

(i) Because BS EN ISO 9000 is internationally recognised, it **communicates** certain facts about the firm's production process to potential customers elsewhere in the world.

(ii) It is a **useful discipline** in that it ensures a rigorous approach to quality and other production issues. The very fact of applying for the standard and the effort necessary might reveal useful improvements in operations. The accreditation will enable us to undertake a systematic and disciplined review of our procedures.

(iii) **Standardised** procedures make it easier to understand what goes wrong.

(iv) The quality manual can act as an aid to **training**.

(v) Hopefully, there will be **less defective production** and so, despite the cost of applying for certification, there will be a positive effect on profit.

(vi) As there are **standard procedures**, there might be less need for direct supervision and unnecessary checking: this might improve motivation.

(vii) **Suppliers** are unlikely to impose their own requirements, if the firm can promise to adhere to a standard.

(viii) It will be **harder for people to cut corners** in their work.

Finally, the internal audit department already requires a high standard of paper work, so we are not totally inexperienced in documenting what we do. We can also contact other suppliers of Barnhams for their advice.

Disadvantages

(i) The cost (in consultancy fees).

(ii) The paperwork and bureaucracy on a long term basis.

(iii) The fact that certification itself does not guarantee high quality product, only that the quality systems are of a certain standard.

(iv) BS EN ISO 9000 is probably better at ensuring conformance quality (ie zero defects etc) than **design quality**, which is as important in meeting customer requirements.

(v) BS EN ISO 9000 is only part of a programme of quality management (see below)

(c) **Quality standards and Total Quality Management**

TQM is 'a **culture** aimed at continually improving performance in meeting the requirements in all functions of a customer'. It is as much a way of doing business as a set of techniques or procedures. That said, TQM relies on meticulous observation and recording of the production and significant analytical rigour to ensure that it is successful. TQM does involve bureaucracy, as it involves scientific analysis of the work process with a view to improving it. TQM involves **continuous improvement,** allied to techniques to ensure a minimum of variation in the production process.

TQM includes such concepts as **zero defects** and **right first time**. It is also a culture in which the production workforce has a crucial part to play, and therefore has serious implications for management.

Successful implementation of TQM does not in itself depend on the adoption of an external standard. A company can adopt BS EN ISO 9000 without being committed to the continuous improvement that is at the heart of TQM.

BS EN ISO 9000 does, however, provide the necessary bureaucratic underpinning for an adoption of TQM, as it is systematic and rigorous.

TQM is an important feature of customer/supplier relationships, with implications for competitive strategy. Quality issues inevitably infect the whole of the **value chain**; the output of one firm's value chain is, in the value system, the input to another. For example Grendall's valves are subcomponents in products which Barnhams supplies to its own end-customers and so the supply chain does not end with Barnhams.

23 IT PROJECT

> **Tutor's hint.** Many candidates will struggle with questions like this, as they do not fit into a neat category. A little lateral thinking is required. If you feel you have to tackle a question like this, remember that relevance to the scenario is *always* important and use key words like *strategy, organisation structure, competitive advantage, value chain, marketing and HRM* to guide your thinking.
>
> Do not be put off by the superfluous word *and* in the third line of the second paragraph of the scenario; minor typos can occur in exam papers; the meaning is clear. Serious errors are rare, but if you have the misfortune to encounter one, report it to the examination staff and ask for guidance.

(a) The project is to be assessed against 'competing IT project proposals'. Such a comparison should **focus on costs and benefits** and would have two main aspects: matters which could be quantified with some precision, such as capital cost, and more **qualitative factors** such as efficiency of working.

Standard investment appraisal techniques such as NPV should be applied to any **quantifiable costs and benefits**. These should include the capital cost of hardware and software, including physical security measures and any structural work such as enhanced fire precautions and installation of ducts and cables; maintenance costs, including an allowance for contingencies; increased insurance cost; the cost of training; extra telephone costs arising from internet access; and any savings which might arise from staff reductions.

These aspects are probably quite simple to determine and assess. However, it is probable that **such an appraisal will produce a negative NPV** for any project, as costs are fairly easy to establish, but **benefits are likely to be largely unquantifiable.** Nevertheless, a successful IT project can offer benefits which are of major significance for an organisation and they must be taken into account.

It would be normal to attempt to deal with this by **ranking competing projects** by scoring them against **objective criteria**. The scoring could be done by a committee or by several individuals separately, with a moderator combining their scores. This would bring a kind of collective judgement to the process, but would be subject to personal bias, which might break out into acrimony in the later stages of selection.

Projects should be assessed against criteria such as those below.

- Expected improvement in quality of **management information** in such matters as speed of provision and completeness
- **Compatibility** with the existing organisation in terms of structure, responsibilities, personalities, culture and skill levels
- Fit with the current **strategic posture** of the organisation, and, if a commercial organisation, contribution to competitive advantage
- **Risk** associated with the technology: is it proven or groundbreaking? How big is the installed base?
- Extent to which **existing equipment** can be reused

When the financial and qualitative assessments are complete, it will be necessary to integrate them. This should only present a problem if they produce radically different solutions; if that is the case, **rational decision rules** such as minimising the maximum possible loss may help.

(b) The broad objectives of project management are as follows.

Quality. The end result should conform to the project specification. In other words, the result should achieve what the project was supposed to do.

Budget. The project should be completed without exceeding authorised expenditure.

Timescale. The installation should be ready for use by the agreed date.

A typical project has a **project life cycle** and is likely to progress through **four stages**:

- **conception and project definition;**
- **planning;**
- **implementation;**
- **completion and evaluation.**

The first stage may be based on the work already done and described in part (a) above. It will be necessary to define the final objectives and agree fundamental and desirable success criteria.

Project planning breaks the project down into manageable units, estimates the resources required for each and establishes the necessary work schedules. Tools such as critical path analysis and Gantt charts may be used where there are time and sequence constraints.

Implementation must be controlled and progress monitored to ensure that, for instance, quality and financial requirements are being achieved. It is often suggested with IT projects that there should be an extended period of parallel running; it must be remembered, however, that this implies a great deal of extra work by the staff involved and may be impractical for all but the most important elements.

When the installation is complete it should be **appraised for success** in meeting user expectations. With internally managed projects, this provides invaluable opportunities to learn from mistakes.

24 WESTPORT UNIVERSITY

Tutor's hint. This is effectively a question about marketing, a subject of which even well prepared candidates may feel they know little. This should not lead you to reject the question out of hand. The examiner does not expect you to be an expert and a glance at the marking scheme will demonstrate that it is possible to score quite well by applying basic knowledge and some common sense.

The question asks you to 'present a report'. Do not waste time on elaborate presentation on layout. Write a business letter, but avoid being too formal.

Part (a)

Head of Faculty
Business and Finance Faculty 1 April 200X

PROFESSIONAL ACCOUNTANCY TRAINING – MARKET RESEARCH

1 We discussed briefly the possibility of the Faculty's using some of its spare capacity to provide professional training in accountancy. I undertook to report on the market research implications of this idea.

2 **Information requirements**

2.1 **Market size.** We need some estimate of the number of students we might reasonably expect to attract to our courses. The total numbers of students registered with each of the main accountancy bodies should be easily ascertained, but we need more than this. The geographical distribution of students will be important, as will their chosen method of study. Our market will probably lie among those who both live close enough to travel to us each day and are able fund their study.

2.2 **Student preferences.** Students' study preferences should be established in detail.

- What size are the markets for full-time and part-time courses respectively?
- How should the cycle of training relate to the professional bodies' exams?
- How would students be funded and at what target cost should we aim?
- Should we provide printed teaching notes or teach from an established text?
- How much tutorial input would students expect and how would it be funded?
- Should we provide generic courses or classes specific to one or more of the professional accountancy bodies.

2.3 **Competition.** It would be important to assess the local competition before committing ourselves to providing training. We need to know the extent to which it is feasible for us to contest the local market.

3 **Methods of research**

3.1 **Desk research.** It will be feasible to obtain much of the information we need from the accountancy bodies. They will almost certainly have well-organised databases that will reveal numbers of students in our area, probably analysed by post code; the stage of their studies; and, possibly, how they study. Potential competitors in both the public and private sector can be assessed on the basis of their prospectuses and other publicity material.

3.2 **Primary research.** Primary research is a highly specialised professional field and is expensive if it is reliable. It is not something that I would recommend we do in house, unless there are members of the academic staff who can claim more than a theoretical acquaintance with the processes involved. It is probably inappropriate for a project of this type. However, if undertaken, it could amplify our knowledge of the potential market generally and of student preferences specifically. A telephone survey would probably be most effective. A postal survey would be cheaper, but this method suffers both from a low response rate and the fact that the respondents self-select.

4 **Conclusion.** A successful entry into the professional accountancy training market will depend on our acquiring greater knowledge about that market than we possess now. Much of the information we need may be obtained by desk research. Greater detail and certainty could be obtained by primary research in the form of a survey, but this is probably too expensive to be practical.

Bill Loftus
Commercial Manager

Part (b)

> **Tutor's hint.** You may wonder, on examining this part of the question, just what marketing strategy is and how it differs from ordinary strategy, especially as marketeers tend to claim that business strategy generally is a component part of their discipline. Well, clearly, for 10 marks you don't have to be too abstruse. Nor does the scenario give you enough information to build up an answer in terms of *Porter's* generic strategies, for instance, or *Ansoff's* product market vector. The examiner's suggested solution simply considers the Faculty's proposed project in terms of the 4 Ps of the basic marketing mix. This solution could have been improved by including the other 3 Ps of the extended marketing mix, as we do, since they are relevant to **services** and that is what the Faculty provides, after all.
>
> Don't forget that the elements of the marketing mix must be consistent with one another.

Marketing strategies

Product. Unfortunately, the examining bodies have different syllabuses and, though there is great similarity in total coverage, there is wide variation between individual examinations. We shall thus have to decide whether or not to provide **courses for more than one set of examinations** to begin with. This will depend in part on the size of the **potential markets** involved.

Our greatest opportunity to add value probably comes from the provision of lectures, since that is what we are best equipped to do. However, we must carefully consider course design, in the light of our market research. Part time courses, including day release and evening classes, may be most appropriate at first. Commercial providers tend to have two types of short course: teaching and revision. We should aim to do the same.

Place. The location of our courses must also be decided. It would be cheapest to use our own premises, but part-time courses may prove more popular if we can take them to the student by establishing local venues.

Price. We probably need to be competitive in our pricing. Many students fund themselves and employers who pay for training are likely to be equally price-conscious. If we are convinced of our excellence we may be able to justify a price premium, but we will be judged by results. At the moment we do not have much experience of the demands of the examinations.

Promotion. This would be a new venture for us and we would need effective promotion to get it off the ground. We must apply the same standards of decorum and academic appropriateness to this project as to any other of our activities. To be effective, our promotion and the media we use must be carefully targeted. Advertisements in the journals aimed at accountancy students will be a good starting point, supplemented by information on the University website and, possibly, direct mail.

People. People are fundamental to marketing services. The members of our target market are older than our undergraduates and likely to be more demanding of lecturers. If they are not satisfied they will vote with their feet.

Process. Similar considerations apply to processes and particularly to administration. Our existing enrolment system, for example, is used to dealing with a bulge of work before the commencement of the academic year. If we are to run short courses, enrolment queries must be dealt with throughout the year.

Physical evidence. Since education is so very intangible, it may be worth considering the provision of physical evidence. An obvious example would be the provision of course notes. A standard textbook written by a member of our staff would be almost too good to be true.

Conclusion. It is important that decisions about these matters are not taken in isolation. If we are to go ahead with this project, I suggest that a marketing committee be formed and charged with responsibility for ensuring that our plans form a coherent whole.

25 PARTNERSHIP

> **Tutor's hint.** Although the marketing mix is normally characterised in terms of the four Ps, in discussing service marketing, three extra Ps are needed. Also remember, that there is a continuum on which any product can be positioned. Many products contain a service element.
>
> The examiner said that answers to part (a) missed the fact that the marketing mix needs to be tailored to the needs of the segment. Answers to (b) concentrated excessively on ethical issues.

(a) **The need for a marketing orientation and a marketing plan.** A marketing orientation involves identifying and satisfying customer needs profitably. The partnership needs a marketing orientation, as their management recipe is no longer a guarantee of success, given competitors and change. Rather than rush in reactively by undercutting competitors on price, this is now the time to reposition the firm.

Identification of customer needs: SW can do some low-level market research on their clients.

(i) SW need to define **who their customers are, and who they might be in future**. The previous customer base has shrunk and there have been difficulties in finding new customers.

(ii) **Dominic Gower's approach does not address this key issue.** A marketing oriented approach identifies a market, perhaps by market research. Gower is suggesting not so much marketing but a greater reliance on advertising and promotion.

(iii) SW can target a particular type of client over a wider geographical area.

Developing a marketing plan, follows a similar process to developing a corporate plan, only it is at the level of marketing rather than the whole firm. Marketing issues - especially in relation to choices of products and markets - are at the heart of corporate planning even though they are conceptually distinct.

Kotler identifies the formulation of **marketing plans** as follows.

(i) **The executive summary**. This is the finalised planning document with a summary of the main goals and recommendations in the plan.

(ii) **Situation analysis**. This consists of the PEST, SWOT analysis, forecasts, an appraisal of customers, competitors etc. The **marketing strengths and weaknesses analysis** will concentrate on current marketing programmes if any. A major weakness of SW is that they have no marketing programmes at all.

(iii) **Objectives and goals. Marketing objectives** needs to be in line with overall corporate objectives (eg profitability, survival cash flow). It is probably not realistic to talk about market share for this business, but objectives and goals of customer retention and new customers can be set.

(iv) **Marketing strategy.** This considers the selection of target markets, the **marketing mix** and marketing expenditure levels. The **marketing strategy** can relate to the Ansoff matrix, in other words market penetration, market development, product development and diversification. SW will need to develop new products/services and also to **find new customers**. The plan will contain quantified, timed objectives of this nature. The design of marketing mix follows directly from the needs of the customers SW chooses to serve.

(v) **Action programme**. This sets out how these various strategies are going to be achieved (eg Dominic Gower should be provided with the necessary resources).

(vi) **Budgets** are developed from the action programme.

(vii) **Controls**. These will be set up to monitor the progress of the plan and the budget. A **plan needs to be controlled** to see if outcomes are successful or if the plan needs changing. SW's business is sufficiently small for control to be exercised informally, but control needs to be exercised nonetheless, given the partnership's previous history of drift. The objectives set earlier in the marketing planning process are convenient bases for control.

(b) **Goods and services**

Kotler defines services as follows.

> '... any activity of benefit that one party can offer to another that is essentially intangible and does not result in the ownership of anything. Its production may or may not be tied to a physical product.' (P Kotler, **Social Marketing)**

Characteristics of services which make them distinctive from the of goods have been proposed.

(i) **Intangibility.** Unlike goods (physical products such as confectionery), there is no substantial material or physical aspects to a service: no taste, feel, visible presence and so on. In practice, intangibility is not an 'either/or' issue, but rather a **continuum**. Most 'offers' to customers **combine** product and service elements. A firm can therefore exploit the service element in a value chain.

(ii) **Inseparability**. Many services are created at the same time as they are consumed. Goods in the vast majority of cases have to be produced, then sold, then consumed, in that order. Services are only a promise at the time they are sold: most services are sold, and **then** they are produced and consumed simultaneously.

(iii) **Variability.** Many services face the problem of maintaining consistency in the standard of output. It may be hard to attain precise standardisation of the service offered.

(iv) **Perishability.** Most services cannot be stored, of course. They are innately **perishable**. The services of a beautician are purchased for a period of time. The service they offer cannot be used 'later'.

(v) **Ownership**. Most services differ from consumer goods: they do **not always result in the transfer of property**. The purchase of a service only confers on the customer access to or a right to use a facility, not ownership. Payment is for the use of, access to or the hire of particular items.

In the context of SW, the issue is not clear cut as their offer to customers has a service element. SW are offering **advice**, and they use their intangible skills to write up books of account, do tax computations and so on. Deploying the service marketing mix is a rather difficult task.

(i) Poor service quality in **one instance** is likely to lead to widespread distrust of everything the organisation does in future.

(ii) If the service is intangible offering a **complicated** future benefit, or is consumed 'on the spot', then attracting customers means promoting an attractive image and ensuring that the service lives up to its reputation consistently.

(iii) Pricing of services is often complicated, especially if large numbers of people are involved in providing the service.

Service marketing involves three additional Ps, people, processes and physical evidence.

(i) **People**. The importance of employees as an element in the marketing mix is particularly evident in service industries. It involves corporate culture, job design, training and motivational issues.

(ii) **Processes.** Processes involve the ways in which the marketer's task is achieved. Efficient processes can become a marketing advantage in their own right. For example SW can employ new software.

(iii) **Physical evidence.** This is very important in some service industries (for example where the ambience of a restaurant is important). This is of some relevance to SW, with the exception of appropriate meeting rooms for meeting clients.

26 KARAOKE

(a) The marketing mix is the set of controllable variables which a marketer may manipulate to influence the returns on a product.

Product

(i) **Selection of arias to be included.** The entrepreneur needs to discover which arias people know of feel able to sing. Popular arias should be included.

(ii) **Design of the packaging**. It may be appropriate to maximise cross-over from pop to Karaoke by choosing a colourful and lively design.

(iii) **Inclusion of lyrics and vocal score.** The inclusion of lyrics will make the product more usable, along with an English translation. The vocal score, too, would be a useful addition for segments of the market wishing to practise seriously at home.

(iv) **Alternative media.** The project is currently to be produced as a compact disc for use with current Karaoke equipment. In addition it could be produced on a cassette tape, perhaps for singing to in the car, or on video for home use complete with pictures of the vocal score and bouncing ball to indicate the words.

(v) **Quality of musicians and recording.** The entrepreneur needs to select an appropriate level of quality. A well known conductor may be a boost to sales.

Price

(i) **Price to general public.** The general pricing level needs to be decided. Opera traditionally is seen as an exclusive preserve and this may enable the charging of a skimming price. Conversely, to maximise sales the firm may prefer a penetration price. The latter policy would also know the advantage of justifying longer production runs which might permit discounts on duplication costs and stocking costs as well as spreading the fixed costs of recording further.

(ii) **Price to distribution channels.** The product will need to be priced to attract the interest of retailers and Karaoke operator. In the call of the former the entrepreneur will need to provide a generous margin to encourage initial take-up of this novel concept. It may be advisable to offer an initially low promotional price to encourage initial stocking. Karaoke operators will act as opinion leaders and it might be worthwhile supplying the disc free at first to encourage a craze to develop.

(iii) **Discounts and credit terms.** In dealing with distributors and retailers the pricing decision should also cover discount policy and credit terms.

Promotion. It seems likely that the entrepreneur will need to promote these discs to both the general public and to distributors.

(i) **Advertisements on television and radio.** If the general public are the target market they may need to be reached by broad media. The costs of this are likely to be prohibitive although the entrepreneur could seek a tie-in advertisement with a major record shop chain.

(ii) **Point of sale posters and displays.** These could be supplied to the retailers for display to help raise customer awareness of the product.

(iii) **Advertisements in magazines.** Display advertisements, perhaps with reply coupon, could be included in classical music magazines, eg Gramophone.

Place

(i) The entrepreneur has already arranged a distribution deal with Bumble Records which will presumably cover record shops. It is not clear whether this is an international arrangement or whether additional distributors should be arranged for overseas markets.

(ii) The entrepreneur could consider using direct selling via mail order. The customer could be attracted by television or press advertisements and call a freephone number to purchase.

(iii) It is not clear whether Bumble has distribution to Karaoke operators. There the entrepreneur may consider arranging parallel distribution through equipment shops.

(b) The suggestions below apply specifically to research into the attitudes of private individuals. Professional Karaoke operators are excluded.

(i) **Assembling potential demand**

It seems unlikely that the general public as a whole will be early purchasers of this product. Instead, like Karaoke in general, it may need to be a craze to gain momentum. In assessing demand it is necessary to examine just those persons already liking opera and/or Karaoke.

The entrepreneur should obtain a client list based upon membership of opera appreciation societies, or canvas persons attending professional and amateur performances. They should be interviewed to assess likely purchase of the product.

(ii) **Researching the product element**

Selection of appropriate arias will be crucial. There are various ways to assess which may be included.

(1) Examine which arias are included on other popular 'introducing opera' CD's.

(2) Present a questionnaire to the target group and ask them to indicate which arias they most enjoy hearing/singing by scaling them on a 1-5 basis with 5 as 'don't know/like'.

(3) Consult the programme of popular opera concerts.

(iii) **Researching the price**

(1) Opera goers could be invited to attend a short research session held in a hired room at the opera house or theatre. Here they could be shown the product and asked to suggest a price for it.

(2) The product could be launched in a restricted range of shops and the prices adjusted through time to ascertain the effects on sales.

27 PRODUCT LAUNCH

Tutor's hint. In part (a) we have given quite a lot of introductory information, before dealing with actual promotion. You must do this if you are asked for a *report*, but, clearly, it should not overwhelm the rest of the answer. Answering part (b) would be made easier by the general awareness which comes from reading the business press.

The Examiner noticed a strong contrast in the quality of the answers submitted to this question. Most candidates produced good answers to part (a), demonstrating a sound knowledge of promotional activities. However, answers to part (b) were disappointing, frequently confusing test marketing with product testing.

(a) REPORT

From: Sharpe & Keene, Marketing Consultants
To: Managing Director, Klypso
Date: 1 January 2000
Subject: Promotion for new confectionery product

Introduction

Klyso has a new low-fat, high-energy confectionery product, licensed from the USA, which it intends to market nationally. The product will be aimed at a niche market: health and exercise conscious consumers. Klyso's core competence is in access to retail distribution channels in its region. To exploit this and expand to national distribution, it will be necessary to establish a national brand. Klyso's promotional budget is small, so expenditure must be carefully planned and controlled. It is intended that national launch should be preceded by test marketing.

Aim

The aim of this report is to recommend and justify appropriate promotional methods for the test launch of the new product.

Promotional objectives

The product must be promoted to two groups; the distributors and the ultimate consumers. The distributors will not be prepared to stock the product unless they believe it will generate turnover. The product is new to this country. The initial objectives therefore will be to raise awareness of the product and its brand name among both consumers and distributors and to persuade the consumers to try it.

Success in these objectives can be measured first by a brand recognition survey and second by interpretation of the value of sales and sales returns.

The target market

The target market has been identified as physically active people who enjoy an occasional treat.

Promotional methods

The name of the new product has not yet been decided, nor has its packaging been designed. These are therefore tentative suggestions which may need modification. The overall theme is the product's contribution to an active life-style.

Advertising

The limited budget means that wide media coverage is inappropriate. Specialist magazines dealing with popular participation games and pastimes will provide the most precise targeting, combined with posters at recreational facilities which have shops and cafes. A life-style approach should be used, emphasising that the product enhances a healthy, active way of life.

Direct sales

There will be a major role for direct selling in the approach to distributors, who will expect help with merchandising and any problems at the time of product launch.

Public relations

This product is tailor made for sponsorship. Possibilities include financing training for a young athlete with national representative potential and promoting a local amateur league in an active game such as squash, soccer or rugby. When the time comes for national launch, endorsement by a well-known sports person may be appropriate. Thought should be given to that now, as such relationships should be undertaken for the long term.

Sales promotion

The distributors must be convinced to stock the product: high initial discounts will be necessary. Consumers must also be persuaded to try the product. The slightly tacky traditional sales promotion measures such as money-off and buy one get one free are inappropriate; a percentage of revenue put into a good cause such as coaching for school children might be more appropriate.

Conclusion

The new product must be promoted to both distributors and consumers. A closely targeted life-style approach will make the best use of the limited budget. Adequate provision must be made for the assessment of the effectiveness of the launch and the promotion in particular.

(b) **Test marketing** is an important part of the **new product development process.** It obtains information about how the test market reacts to the new product and the other marketing mix elements associated with it. The aim is to extrapolate these results to the national market so that the product's prospects can be assessed. Consumer test markets are usually selected geographically, with the area covered by a regional television company used as a basis.

Clearly, it is essential that the test market should be as representative of the national market as possible, so that the correct conclusions may be drawn. The following aspects of the chosen test market should be considered in this context.

- The **structure of the population in demographic terms** such as age and social class distributions; size of ethnic minorities and religious denominations; and number of urban and rural households, should be similar to the national population.
- The **economic characteristics** should be typical; a permanently depressed area such as South Yorkshire would be as inappropriate as one in a permanent boom such as South East England.

- **Distribution channels** should be representative.
- **Promotional media** should be similar to those available nationally.

There are other considerations for test marketing.

- The test must run long enough for reliable results to be obtained. In the case of Klypso's new product, this probably means at least three cycles of ordering by distributors.
- The test market should be reasonably **isolated from the rest of the nation**. This helps to prevent competitors finding out about the new product and gives more representative results.
- Ideally, there will be a **control area**, that is, one which is not subject to the experimental stimulus. This allows the effects of extraneous developments such as economic changes to be assessed.

28 COMPUTER DEPARTMENT

(a) **Objectives of the computer department**

(i) **Recover the costs** spent on central computing services through appropriate charge out rates (given in the question). (The issue of appropriate charge out rates is discussed more in part (c) of this question.)

(ii) **Provide a value for money service**, so that the market rate is used a benchmark or price for a given quality of service. (**Tutor's hint**. The cheap market rate may go with restrictions as to when the external suppliers' services are used, so ABC plc's users might still pay extra for the extra flexibility. Moreover, the market rate may apply only to routine processing and might be considerably more for specialised applications.)

(iii) **Provide information to management** which is timely and relevant to satisfy their existing information needs.

(iv) **Assess, in consultation with user departments, the future information needs** of management and staff, and endeavour to satisfy them.

(v) Ensure that the firm has an **adequate computer capacity**, improved where necessary in line with technical developments, and ensure that it is used at optimum efficiency and effectiveness.

(vi) **Lay down guidelines for computer usage by departments.** Although there is a centralised capacity, it is quite possible that each department will have its own PCs (eg for word processing, and perhaps spreadsheets). Ensure all items of equipment and software purchased meet company standards and are compatible.

(vii) Regularly **review the firm's information technology activities** so that it conforms to the firm's overall business strategy.

(b) **Control procedures to ensure that the objectives are met**

The performance of some of the objectives will be easier to monitor than others. Not all objectives can be quantified.

(i) **Cost recovery**

Identify costs. In order to ensure that the costs of the computer operation are recovered, an accurate and realistic assessment of what those costs are must be arrived at. This will include wages and salary costs, depreciation on equipment as a means of charging the department's capital costs and sundry other overheads.

Relate charge out rate to costs. An issue here must be the charge out rate. Most of the department's cost will be fixed. How much does the current charge out rate reflect the actual cost structure of the services provided? Some jobs may not require the same mix of staff or equipment. The charge out should reflect more exactly the type of service offered.

Set budgets. In order to check that the costs are being recovered, the department will need to set budgets covering both predicted expenditure, and likely usage of its services. This can be identified through consultation with other departments.

Standard costs. For routine tasks, it might also be possible to set standard times and standard costs, so any variances caused by sub-optimal performance, of staff or equipment, can be identified immediately.

(ii) **Providing a value for money service** may be easier said than done. Although the price differential between the market rate and the department's charge out rate is very high, this may be because the department charges all services equally. We do not know whether the market suppliers provide all the services that the department does. For example, the computer department may be much better able to prepare special ad hoc reports, or reports at unusual times at short notice which would not be supplied by outsiders.

In short, an hourly charge out rate, irrespective of the service provided, probably does not reflect the true cost of the service (eg the time of one computer operator is charged at the same rate as that of four programmers) to the department.

The market price is a benchmark, but the department will charge more if it provides a more flexible responsive service.

If the department itself has spare computer capacity, it might try and recover this cost by letting it out to external suppliers. This will spread the fixed costs over a greater number of tasks and jobs.

(iii) **Monitor information's timeliness and relevance.** Timeliness can be measured by the extent to which reports are printed within their deadlines. The department might like to ask management when they want their reports, and structure their activities around that.

As far as relevance goes, this can be monitored with regular meetings with user departments, and a log of proposed modifications which can be compared with what is actually achieved.

(iv) **Assessing management's future needs** requires a strategic approach to information. If sales are to increase, or if the company is to expand into new product or market areas, management will probably require information dealing with these issues. If the computer department knows these requirements in advance, it can prepare to provide the service.

However, the computer department should liaise with user departments on a regular basis, and there should be a system for noting down findings and a record of action taken.

(v) **Ensuring the firm has optimum capacity** and that it is used most effectively. This requires a review of the department's operations in peak or slack times, and the time in which user queries are dealt with by the system.

(vi) **Guidelines and standards** must be drawn up and circulated to the departments concerned. A system of capital expenditure authorisation, which ensured that all IT equipment and software purchases need to be authorised by the computer department, should ensure consistency.

(vii) **Ensuring that the IT strategy conforms with the business strategy** can only be achieved if IT issues are considered to be at the heart of the company's activities.

(c) A marketing orientated department would be one which identifies customer needs, and satisfies them within budgetary and other resource constraints. The marketing orientation is both a cultural issue as well a set of specific practices.

(i) In this case, the computer department should look upon the departments it services as customers (the **'internal customer' concept**) rather than simply people working for the same firm.

(ii) **Competition.** If the computer department sells its services to external customers, the necessary market disciplines should spill over into its relationship with internal customers. At the same time, the true costs and benefits of both policies should be estimated. Outside suppliers might appear cheaper, but there may be long term advantages in a centralised computer department, especially if IT is a critical success factor in the company's overall performance.

However, the real implementation of the marketing concept does not depend on these external factors. Instead the department should research the needs of its internal customers, and devise a service to suit these needs, rather than the other way round. It can then promote those of its services which are little known perhaps, but which users might find attractive. It will thus have to communicate more information about its skills to its internal customers.

29 CASTERBRIDGE OFFICE

(a) The high rates of staff turnover and sickness Jane has identified are **symptomatic of more fundamental problems** of organisational behaviour. They must be tackled at the root, otherwise the poor client care and operational errors are likely to continue and worsen. Jane has encountered a pocket of poor morale and motivation that will be difficult to deal with.

There are a number of theories of motivation. Frederick Herzberg's **two factor theory** is an example of a **content** theory. It may be particularly relevant here as it was based on interviews with well paid professionals. Herzberg asked them what it was about their jobs that gave them satisfaction and what caused dissatisfaction. He found that there were **two distinct categories of factor**. The presence of **motivator** factors can create job satisfaction and are effective in motivating an individual to superior effort and performance. **Hygiene** factors, on the other hand, cannot produce a positive effect, but they will cause dissatisfaction if they are inadequate.

Herzberg's analysis is very useful in the context of the senior partner's remarks to Jane. **Working conditions and salary are classic hygiene factors** and cannot really be expected to motivate. The lack of continuity in management will also have had an undesirable effect. Achievement, recognition and increasing responsibility are important motivators but they are largely dependent on management style and policy; if there have been frequent changes at the apex of the Casterbridge office, it is likely that these factors have been neglected.

The senior partner's remarks are also interesting in that they illustrate Douglas McGregor's **Theory X**. McGregor suggested that managers seemed to subscribe to one of two opposing theories about motivation. Theory X managers believe that subordinates must be driven to perform well; theory Y managers believe that people accept work as natural and respond to challenge and leadership. Probably neither view is completely accurate, but, depending on the circumstances, aspects of both are relevant to the management of people.

Expectancy theories, such as that of Victor Vroom, suggest that individuals' efforts depend on a calculation based on two factors. **Expectancy** is the subjective assessment of the likelihood that behaving in a certain way will result in a particular outcome, while **valence** is the value the individual places on that outcome. This is also relevant to the situation at Casterbridge. If effort has gone unrewarded because managers have come and gone rapidly, this will have undermined individual motivation.

(b) It is important to recognise from the beginning that **poor motivation exists in the Casterbridge office** and it will take time to change this. Morale has been eroded and must be built up again in an atmosphere of mutual trust and respect. This will be difficult, given that there is almost certainly an element of hostility to management at the moment. It will take more managerial input than would be required for an office running normally.

Fortunately, the **basic hygiene factors are in place** in that pay and conditions should be satisfactory. However, company policy and administration are also hygiene factors and it may be difficult to make changes here.

It seems that motivating factors are to some extent missing. The first step to remedying this is a series of **staff interviews** to establish how the poor level of morale arose. This cannot be done in a bald way; staff must be coaxed to talk about themselves, their colleagues and their perceptions of the firm in a way which reveals their feelings and attitudes. This will require open questions and constructive listening.

Such a programme of interviews should reveal both **sources of dissatisfaction** which can be amended and **specific opportunities to introduce improvements**. It is to be anticipated that normal good management practices such as recognising good work, giving guidance where required and providing opportunities for personal growth will gradually improve matters. However, some changes may be required in the local arrangements, such as staff moves.

30 GRUMIT

Tutor's hint. Applying a HRM approach to the scenario it makes it easier to plan the answer around a set of objectives and helps to give the answer some structure. There are only 4-5 marks available for change processes and change models so there would only be time to describe one and mention others where they outline a different approach.

(a) **Human resource management** (HRM) 'is a strategic approach to acquiring, developing, managing and motivating an organisation's key resource - its people' (Armstrong). In order to make an effective contribution it **must complement and advance strategic business objectives.**

(i) **Grumit is changing strategic direction** - it is **leaving manufacturing and is being repositioned as a distribution and service firm,** hopefully expanding its client base. This typical objective will have far-reaching implications for David Omega, acting as HR manager. His approach might begin as follows.

(1) An analysis of the key competences required to fulfil this objective.

(2) A review of the current management capabilities in these areas.

(3) A set of initiatives to close the gap identified between (i) and (ii).

(4) A method of **recruitment** to new posts and promoting existing staff into more senior posts by introducing an assessment-based approach to selection and promotion.

(5) A meaningful and cost-effective programme to deal with staff identified as surplus to requirements.

(ii) Thus **change management** is a key issue: once the initial shock has worn off, the various practicalities of the situation can be smoothed over by a participatory approach.

(1) Local managers, who have had the decision imposed upon them may feel particularly demotivated.

(2) **Union policy.** The union will be consulted in the short term. Grumit may have to change its union relationships in the long term, and might **choose** to follow European directives on implementing a Works Council.

(iii) **Communications: long term.** In its new service role, Grumit will need **better communications** to fit its culture. The policies and practices adopted in the future will affect both the **channel** and the **media**, for example, suggestion box schemes, quality circles, joint consultation committees, company newsletters and notice boards. A **staff association** might be formed to encourage communication and discussion on matters of mutual interest. The management style could be the key to communication flows in the company eg, management by walk about, which facilitates the 'exchanging' of information rather than the 'telling' of it.

(iv) **Service engineers**. Although in the **short term,** the 220 people working in the manufacturing facility are the most affected by the changes imposed on the company, Grumit needs the **continued support of the installation and after-sales service engineers in the long term**. Seeing how their colleagues in the manufacturing facility are treated might influence how they see the company and affect their motivation and morale.

(v) **Communicating and handling the redundancies.** For the immediate redundancy situation, Grumit must decide on the respective **short term roles of top management, line management, the personnel function and the unions**. The unions must be told of the changes that are going to take place as their co-operation may be necessary to avoid disruption. The redundancies must be communicated to everyone concerned in mass meetings, group briefings, or team briefings where questions can be answered. Details of redundancy pay and staff redeployment should be available at the same time.

The manufacturing facility is to close immediately. Therefore the redundancy process is something demanding **immediate management attention** if it is to go smoothly. There are specified **legal requirements** in the UK for days notice of redundancy, notification to recognised trade unions and compensation payments based on age and length of service.

David Omega needs to deal with the unions in a manner which is in line with current agreements and sets the tone for future policy.

(vi) **Training, re-training and staff development.** Grumit needs an active policy for developing the skills of its human resources in the service business.

(1) **Short term**. It may be beneficial to have short secondments to the parent company to improve product knowledge.

(2) In the **long term** Grumit should develop a strategy for human resources in line with its business strategy, so that skills training is part of the wider human resources management process.

- A cost/benefit analysis of training
- Technical training in new equipment
- Learning targets for employees, perhaps linked to management development programmes, career progression, succession planning and appraisal systems

(b) **Managing strategic change**. Some writers have taken a rather mechanistic approach, suggesting that there are a set of 'levers' for change which managers can pull. Others have emphasised the role of the individual as **change agent**, sometimes stressing the charisma and vision of the leader. The process can vary considerably from situation to situation.

Management of the change will obviously be influenced by the **prevailing environment**. For example, the **threat of closure** due to competition in an organisation may enable management to implement radical changes which in normal circumstances employees would find unacceptable. The organisational culture and structure will also affect the management of change. Some companies have a culture which is supportive of change; others find it harder to adapt.

Some people tend to resist **any** sort of change. The reasons for this resistance include:

(i) People's self interest, individual attitudes and personality
(ii) Uncertainty and fear (job loss, security, loss of status)
(iii) Misunderstanding of the situation (poor communication)
(iv) Lack of trust (past history and culture of the organisation)
(v) Different views of the situation
(vi) Low tolerance of change

In Grumit's case, people's self interest is directly affected, especially those who are about to be made redundant. Some hostility should be expected.

Change process models

(i) Once identified, the changes are brought about by **unfreezing** the present level, moving to the new level and then **refreezing** at the new level. Unfreezing will lead to doubts and fear of the unknown, giving managers the opportunity to introduce training and education. Moving to the new level implies the change has been brought about but **refreezing** is necessary to stop people reverting to their previous ways.

(ii) *Conner and Patterson* identified three phases (subdivided into eight stages): **preparation, acceptance** and **commitment.** They argue that commitment to change is necessary for its successful implementation. As with Lewin's model, the change has to be institutionalised so that it becomes the new norm.

31 OUTSOURCING

(a) **Why outsource?**

An organisation will outsource some of its activities to improve **efficiency**, and for **cost control**. The outsourced services are usually those that are **supplementary to the core business activities**, such as IT, facilities management, administration and human resources.

By outsourcing functions such as payroll and creditor payments a company gets the **benefit** of such services (its employees and creditors get paid) without itself having to provide (and therefore **finance**) the resources needed. A **specialist** organisation has the necessary resources and **economies of scale** and should be able to provide the service more efficiently, but it does have to cover its own costs and make a profit.

Main reasons for outsourcing

(i) Better use is made of what **resources** the company has, focusing on the **core business** rather than trying to carry out functions that it does not have the resources to manage, including supervision time

(ii) There is a reduction in **costs** and cash may be realised from selling assets to the outsourcing organisation

(iii) **Capital** resources are freed up

(iv) **Risks** are shared with the outsourcing provider, such as keeping up with changes in **legislation** affecting payment of employees. The recent imposition of the minimum wage would be a good example.

(b) **Outsourcing finance functions**

(i) The directors of AB plc are clear about the **objectives** of their outsourcing strategy. They are under pressure from shareholders to increase EPS, and they have identified **overhead cost control** as one way of achieving this, rather than relying on increased revenue. Overhead costs have been increasing and the expectation is that outsourcing the chosen activities will reverse this.

(ii) **Short termism**

Directors have to be careful that they are not over-emphasising **short term shareholder concerns** at the expense of the overall quality of the company and the **sustainability** of its success in the **long term**. The correct balance of in-house and outsourced service provision must be achieved in order to achieve **competitive advantage**.

(iii) **Avoidable costs**

The directors do need to be sure that the costs of the in-house functions that have been earmarked for outsourcing are the source of the cost control problems. **Cost accounting principles**, such as consideration of the allocation of **fixed overheads**, need to be applied to be sure that the savings that are expected do indeed materialise. For example, certain fixed costs associated with the financial accounting function may not necessarily disappear when that function is outsourced.

Phases in the process of outsourcing

(i) **Sourcing strategy** is the identification of those activities which are to be outsourced. The directors of AB have already done this and have decided that financial accounting, payroll, creditor payments and debtors are non-core activities for the resources of the company.

(ii) **Sourcing preparation** establishes the levels of improvement needed in the soon to be outsourced services. This will involve collecting detailed information on how these functions currently operate, including the costs associated with them.

(iii) **Supply selection** involves identifying the appropriate supplier for each service, with quotes being obtained as the first step. The services may all be provided by one organisation. Some of the large accountancy practices and management consultancies provide comprehensive outsourcing services. Using a large and reputable organisation will help to assure the directors of AB that they will be receiving a quality (and possibly world class) service.

(iv) A **transition period** will be needed for the handover of the functions to the supplier(s). This may include a period of parallel running.

(v) The contract will then need to be **managed** and **monitored** to ensure satisfactory performance by the outsourcing organisation and compliance with the **supply contract**. This is probably one of the most complex areas as it will depend upon the negotiated terms and also upon accurate presentation of the **expected benefits** from the outsourcing programme.

Management of outsourcing

(i) **Involve resources to monitor the contract.** Investment should be made in a **staff team** set up to manage the contract, which will cover roles such as managing the **financial control** of the contract, its **legal** aspects and the **technical** strategy.

For example, AB may want to see an improvement in **debtors collection** periods, and the outsourcing company will be expected to provide regular details such as aged debt reports. **Deadlines** for production of reports from the financial accounting function may be tighter than were imposed on the in-house service.

(ii) **Re-selection.** If the supplier performs well then the **re-selection process** at the end of the contract will be smoother. AB may eventually decide to bring some of the functions back in-house if new resources (more space in a new building, for example) become available.

(iii) **Quality.** The directors have **quality concerns** and it is certainly true that with outsourcing there is a **loss of control** of potentially sensitive areas. External suppliers need to be reliable in terms of product quality and reliability of delivery times, and one way of vetting them is to check that they have certification of the standard of the service they deliver, such as the British certification BS EN ISO 9000.

(iv) **Vulnerability.** There may also be loss of **internal skills** that may be needed in the future if employees are made redundant as a result of the outsourcing programme. Employees who remain in the company may feel threatened and this could have implications for the performance of those functions which are retained in house. There may be increased absenteeism, staff turnover and hence high recruitment and training costs.

32 SPORTS CENTRE

Tutor's hint. The PLC can be applied at any stage of strategic planning process, both to identify the firm's overall product portfolio and in devising marketing strategies for each product or service.

Good marks can be earned by application of an appropriate model, such as the marketing mix. Do not take too restrictive a view and concentrate on promotional activities. Also, in answering part (a) you could have used the PLC for the sports centre as a whole as the starting point for your answer. Part (b), on resource allocation, required each service to be discussed separately: the word 'resources' should be interpreted widely to include human resources not just capital investment and cash, important though these are. You *should* acknowledge the public service nature of the sports centre as for instance in the use of the swimming pool by schools.

(a) **How the local authority can market its sports centre service**

The sports centre as a whole might be positioned at the maturity stage of the product life cycle. It is well established, but other service providers have entered the market. Of course, there does not have to be a decline stage at all, and many marketing strategies can be deployed to maintain and enhance the centre's attractiveness.

Investigate customer needs.

A marketing orientation is built around satisfying the needs of the customers; these have to be discovered first of all. The sports centre has many users, including leisure/sports enthusiasts, schools and so forth. Unlike a business, it is partially funded by public money and so part of its remit might be to promote social objectives (eg keep fit classes for the elderly).

Segment the market

It should be possible to discover groups of potential consumers with common characteristics: these are **market segments**.

Apply the 7 Ps of the service marketing mix.

(i) **Product/service**. The sports centre basically provides facilities for recreational use. It can vary its product offering by offering new facilities (as with martial arts), improving current facilities (eg fitness training) and by amending the circumstances when the service is delivered. The badminton court could be adapted at times for dancing classes, for example. Some additional revenue might be earned by providing a restaurant or bar.

(ii) **Price.** The users of the centre only pay for part of its costs, as user fees. Other funding is provided by the local council. However, prices will have to rise to cope with the cutback in central funding. The council has the discretion to vary prices. It can raise prices for some users, but still keep to its social remit (eg free entry for pensioners) or it can offer a leisure pass (eg £25 pa) which will allow people to get reductions for frequent use. The centre can also price its services by time of day, day of week (eg more at weekends).

(iii) **Promotion** covers all aspects of communications with the consumer. Some promotional techniques (eg personal selling) are of little relevance. Advertising is probably most important, for example, in local newspapers, on local radio, perhaps a leaflet with other local council communications (eg council tax demands). Perhaps the supermarket could be persuaded to assist in this. Promotions need to show the benefits of the centre (eg that it is cheap) as well as basic facts about it (eg opening times). Public relations (eg articles rather than advertising copy) in the local newspaper can also help.

(iv) **Place** is the channel of distribution for the services - this is given, and the service is delivered directly on site.

(v) **People**: the quality of a service depends crucially on the people giving the service. Some staff are involved in administration - basic issues of courtesy and friendliness are important here. Other staff are involved in running the centre and providing training and other services (eg in the gym).

(vi) **Process** denotes the way in which the service is delivered, such as access to the pool, ticketing, booking systems for the squash courts etc. These should be designed for ease of use.

(vii) **Physical evidence** denotes the environment in which the service is delivered. As well essentials such as basic cleanliness and security in the locker room, an attractive environment will encourage people to return.

The elements of the mix have to be **integrated** with each other, in the light of the **marketing objectives** (to increase usage) and available resources. As the centre is not a business, one marketing objective might be to encourage use by people who would not normally visit the centre, or those groups in the community with special needs.

(b) **Strategic resource allocation implications for each life cycle stage**

The sports centre as a whole is well past the introduction stage. Most of its capital costs were incurred by the supermarket development, and so the basic facilities have been quite cheaply provided. The resources needed by any of its individual services are these.

- **Cash** to spend on capital equipment (eg gym machines)
- **People**, properly trained
- A **time** slot
- Special **materials**

Introduction (martial arts)

Martial arts is a service in the introduction phase, with little take-up yet, presumably because too few people know about it and interest has yet to grow.

The main introductory costs for martial arts will be **certain special equipment** (eg judo mats).

(i) The capital equipment is unlikely to be costly.

(ii) Instructors have to be hired or trained: instructors' time is effectively an issue of capacity, which will be built up ahead of demand.

(iii) Promotion will be the principal drain on resources, so that people know that martial arts are available

(iv) Finally, there are the opportunity cost of not offering the space to other activities.

Growth (squash)

Squash courts are in the growth phase. Growth requires investment in new capacity to cope with demand which according to the scenario is growing rapidly.

(i) **Capital investment**. Unlike martial arts, squash does require quite heavy capital investment, in the construction of the squash courts.

(ii) **Capacity rationing**. Some flexibility in pricing is useful here. Higher prices, in the short term, could ration demand, and prices could be lowered later (skimming pricing). There is nothing to stop charging higher prices at peak periods and lower prices at relatively slack periods to use the capacity as much as possible.

(iii) **Revenue costs**. Squash courts require continual maintenance.

Maturity (gymnasium, swimming)

At maturity stage are the **gymnasium** and the **swimming pool**.

The **gym** is obviously a **cash cow**, which generates resources rather than consumes them. This surplus can be applied to the sports centre's other activities. The gymnasium can perhaps be used to generate income (eg aerobics classes).

Swimming pools are fairly expensive to maintain and to run (the need for life guards in permanent attendance). In theory the swimming pool should be generating cash - but the best way to do so is to persuade as many as possible to use it.

(i) The pool is perhaps at the heart of the **public service** ethos. A pool is of value to school sporting provision and family use particularly at weekends.

(ii) **The pool at least should cover its costs,** although in the mature phase of the life cycle in theory it should provide surplus cash for reinvestment elsewhere.

(iii) **Demand in the pool might be developed further.** For example, at weekends, families might enjoy the use of a wave making machine; perhaps a separate area of the pool can be cordoned off for children; some local authorities have women-only swimming sessions; others offer swimming classes to adult non-swimmers.

Decline (Badminton)

The decline stage features lower sales, and falling profits. Although **badminton** is in the decline stage of the life cycle, there are three **contrasting approaches** to dealing with it.

(i) **Reverse the decline.** Conduct market research to find out why the badminton facilities are becoming less popular. Reversing the decline might require a commitment of extra resources.

(ii) **Ignore the decline for the time being.** The badminton facilities can be run down slowly - although, as the sports centre is a public service, it has to cater for a variety of tastes. Few extra resources need be committed. The only problem is whether, in the long term, badminton represents the best use of available space - there might be an opportunity cost consideration here.

(iii) **Dual use of badminton facilities.** The badminton facilities may be shared with other sports. This would require some new equipment.

33   PREPARATION QUESTION: <u>DIVISIONALISATION</u> *The Creation of Multi-Unit Struct--*

Alfred Chandler conducted a detailed historical study of the development of four major US corporations: *Du Pont, General Motors, Standard Oil of New Jersey* and *Sears Roebuck*. He found that all four had evolved a <u>decentralised structure</u> based on operating divisions, though by different routes.

Chandler suggested that during the period 1850 to 1920 (which he describes as the formative years of modern capitalism), the development of high volume production to serve mass markets forced the replacement of entrepreneurial, owner management by innovative professional managers. These <u>managers created the modern, multi-unit corporation</u> as the <u>best response to the administrative problems associated with growth</u>. The <u>divisionalised organisation is thus a response to strategy</u> in its broadest sense.

Chandler discerned two main types of strategy, positive and negative. <u>Positive strategy</u> is aggressive, seeks new markets and leads to **growth by product diversification**. <u>Negative strategy</u> seeks to <u>defend</u> a current position and leads to **growth by vertical integration** based on <u>mergers and acquisitions.</u> In both cases, the initial structural response is likely to be <u>centralised control based</u> on functional departments. Both Du Pont and Sears Roebuck went through this stage.

Unfortunately, this approach has important <u>disadvantages,</u> especially where there is geographic dispersion.

(a) It does not reflect the actual business processes by which **value is created.**

(b) It is hard to establish which <u>products</u> and <u>markets</u> are **profitable** and which are not.

(c) <u>Departmental managers</u> do not have an understanding of how a **whole business** works. This makes it difficult to groom candidates for promotion

(d) There are <u>problems of</u> <u>co-ordinating the work of different specialisations</u> over a range of businesses.

Du Pont therefore created an innovative **decentralised structure** of largely autonomous product-based business units co-ordinated rather than controlled by the corporate headquarters. General Motors copied the idea to overcome a lack of overall control in its loose federation of operating units. Standard Oil of New Jersey followed suit after a series of *ad hoc* responses to crises of control; its particular problem was the need to allocate and co-ordinate resources. Sears Roebuck went through essentially the same process as Du Pont.

The creation of the multi-unit structures thus a logical managerial response to the problems associated with strategies that create very large organisations.

Chandler described four levels of management activity typical of this structure.

(a) The **general office** is the headquarters, responsible for overall performance. It allocates resources to the divisions and controls their performance by setting targets. Divisions are responsible for a product line or sales region.

(b) The **divisional central office** is responsible to the general office. Divisions are organised internally on a functional basis.

(c) Each function, such as production or sales has a **departmental headquarters, which** manages **field units** such as manufacturing plants or a sales team. Only at field unit level do managers carry out day-to-day operational work.

It has been argued that an established and well-functioning structure can influence strategy, as, for instance, when two retail organisations merge because the geographical pattern of their branches is complementary. However, this is really an aspect of organisational strengths and weaknesses analysis. Structure should, if necessary, be adjusted to suit the chosen strategy.

34 PREPARATION QUESTION: BURNS AND STALKER

Bureaucracy is perhaps the term most commonly used to describe a hierarchical rule-bound organisation. When the term was first coined, bureaucracy was regarded as a recipe for efficiency. There are still cases where a bureaucratic approach is well suited to an organisation's objectives. *Weber* specified several general characteristics of bureaucracy, which he described as 'a continuous organisation of official functions bound by rules'. Mintzberg identifies two kinds of bureaucracy.

(a) Machine bureaucracy, similar to Weber's description, based on standardisation of work processes, functional groupings, size.

(b) Professional bureaucracy (eg hospitals) based on standardisation of skills.

Criticisms of bureaucracies

(a) Committees and reports slow down the decision-making process.

(b) Conformity creates ritualism, formalism and 'organisation man'.

(c) Personal growth of individuals is inhibited - although bureaucracies tend to attract, select and retain individuals with a tolerance for such conditions.

(d) Innovation is discouraged.

(e) Control systems are frequently out of date.

(f) Bureaucracies are slow to change.

(g) Over prescriptive rules produce a simplistic approach to problems.

The financial and technical advantages of bureaucratic organisations **usually outweigh** the disadvantages, especially in circumstances of slow change and a large customer/client base, to which bureaucracy is well suited. The dysfunctions, however, still need to be reduced to acceptable proportions.

Bureaucracies and change

Burns and Stalker contrasted the **organic** structure of management (see below), which is more suitable to conditions of change, with a **mechanistic** system of management, which is more suited to stable conditions. A mechanistic structure, which appears very much like a bureaucracy, has the following characteristics.

(a) Authority is delegated through a hierarchical, formal scalar chain, and **position power** is used in decision-making.

(b) Communication is **vertical** (ie up and down the scalar chain) rather than **lateral**.

(c) Individuals regard their own tasks as specialised and not directly related to the goals of the organisation as a whole.

(d) There is a precise definition of duties in each individual job (rules, procedures, job definitions).

Organic organisations: suitability for change

In contrast to mechanistic structures, Burns and Stalker identified an **organic structure** (also called an **organismic structure**). They believed organic structures were better suited to conditions of change than mechanistic structures. The mechanistic structures and the organic structure are contrasted in the table below.

Mechanistic	*Organic*
• Tasks are specialised and broken down into subtasks.	Specialist knowledge and expertise is seen to contribute to the 'common task' of the concern.
• Each individual task is 'abstract', pursued with techniques and purposes more or less distinct from that of the concern. People are concerned with task efficiency, not with how the task can be made to improve organisational effectiveness.	Each task is seen and understood to be set by the total situation of the firm: people are concerned with the task insofar as it contributes to organisational effectiveness.
• Managers are responsible for co-ordinating tasks	Each task is adjusted and redefined through interaction with others. This is rather like co-ordination by mutual adjustment
• There are precise job descriptions and delineations of responsibility.	Job descriptions are less precise: it is harder to 'pass the buck'
• 'Doing the job' takes priority over serving the interests of the organisation.	'The spread of commitment to the concern beyond any technical definition'
• Hierarchic structure of control. An individual's performance assessment derives from a 'contractual relationship with an impersonal organisation.'	Network structure of control. An individual's job performance and conduct derive from a supposed community of interest between the individual and the organisation, and the individual's colleagues. (Loyalty to the 'team' is an important control mechanism.)
• Decisions are taken at the top, where knowledge is supposed to reside.	Relevant technical and commercial knowledge can be located anywhere 'omniscience is no longer imputed to the head of the concern.'

Mechanistic	*Organic*
• Interaction is mainly vertical (up and down the scalar chain), and takes the form of commands and obedience.	Interaction is lateral and communication between people of different rank represents consultation, rather than command.
• Operations and working behaviour are governed by instructions issued by superiors.	Communication consists of information and advice rather than instructions and decisions.
• Insistence on loyalty to the concern and obedience to superiors.	Commitment to the concern's task (eg mission) is more highly valued than loyalty as such.
• Internal knowledge (eg of the organisation's specific activities) is more highly valued that general knowledge.	'Importance and prestige attach to affiliations and expertise valid in the industrial, technical and commercial milieux external to the firm'

The organic organisation

(a) Although organic systems are not hierarchical in the way that bureaucracies are, there are **differences of status**, determined by people's greater expertise, experience and so forth.

(b) The degree of **commitment to the concern** is more extensive in organic than mechanistic system. This is similar to the idea that an organisation's mission should motivate and inspire employees.

(c) The reduced importance of hierarchy is replaced by 'the development of shared beliefs and values'. In other words, corporate culture becomes very powerful. **Control is cultural rather than bureaucratic**.

(d) The two approaches represent **two ends of a spectrum**: there are intermediate stages between bureaucratic and organic organisations. Different departments of a business may be run on different lines. For example, the payroll department of a firm has a **well defined task** (eg paying salaries at the end of the month) with little variation. **Controls** are needed to ensure processing accuracy and to avoid fraud. A **mechanistic** system might be applied here. On the other hand, the '**creative** department' of an advertising agency, with a number of professional experts (copywriters, graphic designers, account executives), may be run on an **organic** basis.

Burns and Stalker recognised **that organic systems would only suit individuals with a high tolerance for ambiguity and the personal stresses involved in being part of such an organisation** - but the freedom of manoeuvre is considered worth this personal cost, for individuals who prize autonomy and flexibility.

35 PREPARATION QUESTION: CENTRALISATION

Centralisation in an organisation means a greater degree of control by the strategic apex over the activities of the departments or divisions. **Decentralisation** means a greater degree of delegated authority.

Advantages of centralisation

Control

Senior management can exercise greater control over the activities of the organisation and co-ordinate their subordinates or sub-units more easily.

Advantage	Comment
Standardisation	Procedures can be standardised throughout the organisation.
Corporate view	Senior managers can make decisions from the point of view of the organisation as a whole, whereas subordinates would tend to make decisions from the point of view of their own department or section.
Balance of power	Centralised control enables an organisation to maintain a balance between different functions or departments.
Experience counts	Senior managers ought to be more experienced and skilful in making decisions.
Lower overheads	When authority is delegated, there is often a duplication of management effort (and a corresponding increase in staff numbers) at lower levels of hierarchy.
Leadership	In times of **crisis**, the organisation may need strong leadership by a central group of senior managers.

Advantages of decentralisation

Advantage	Comment
Workload	It reduces the stress and burdens of senior management.
Job	It provides subordinates with greater job satisfaction by giving them more say in making decisions which affect their work.
Local knowledge	Subordinates may have a better knowledge than senior management of 'local' conditions affecting their area of work.
Flexibility and speed	Delegation should allow greater flexibility and a quicker response to changing conditions. If problems do not have to be referred up a scalar chain of command to senior managers for a decision, decision-making will be quicker.

36 PREPARATION QUESTION: COMPETITIVE ADVANTAGE

Competitive advantage is anything that gives an organisation the ability to perform better than its rivals. *Porter* says that **competitive strategy** means 'taking offensive or defensive actions to create a dependable position in an industry, to cope successfully with . . . competitive forces and thereby yield a superior return on investment for the firm'.

Johnson & Scholes tell us that **core competences** critically underpin the organisation's competitive advantage. They divide competences into two types. An organisation must achieve at least a **threshold** level of competence in everything it does., but its **core competences** are both those where it outperforms competitors and difficult to imitate.

A core competence can be identified in three ways..

(a) **It provides potential access to a wide variety of markets**. GPS of France developed a core competence in 'one-hour' processing, enabling it to process films and build reading glasses in one hour.

(b) **It contributes significantly to the value enjoyed by the customer.** For example, for GPS, the waiting time restriction was very important.

(c) **It should be hard for a competitor to copy.** This will be the case if it is technically complex, involves specialised processes, involves complex interrelationships between different people in the organisation or is hard to define.

In many cases, a company might choose to combine competences.

Competences can be related to **critical success factors** (CSFs), which 'are those factors on which the strategy is fundamentally dependent for its success'. Some CSFs are generic to the whole industry, others to a particular firm. For example, the critical success factor to run a successful **mail order business** is speedy delivery. Underpinning critical success factors are **key tasks.** If **customer care** is a CSF, then a key task, and hence a measure of performance, would include responding to enquires within a given time period. There may be a number of key tasks - but some might be more important than others, or must come first in a sequence.

Competences fulfil the CSF. In the example quoted, competence in organising order processing, picking , packing and despatch supports a CSF of speedy delivery for a mail order business.

37 PREPARATION QUESTION: LEARNING ORGANISATION

There has been considerable theoretical attention paid to the concept of a **learning organisation**, but as yet there is no single coherent model available.

Knowledge as a resource

With the transformation of advanced economies away from manufacturing and towards ever more complex service industries, there has been a growing awareness of the importance of the **knowledge worker**, whose value is based on a high degree of skill and learning, and of the **knowledge-intensive firm**, which employs large numbers of such workers. A firm of accountants is a good example of a knowledge-based firm.

There is an obvious requirement for such firms and workers to maintain, develop and exploit their knowledge, collectively and individually. With this requirement comes recognition of the human resource as a source of competitive advantage.

Nonaka identifies two types of knowledge.

(a) **Tacit** knowledge may be compared to individual skills. It is personal and rooted in a specific context.

(b) **Explicit** knowledge is formal, systematised and easily shared. An example would be the specification for a technical process.

Knowledge creation

The exploitation of knowledge requires that its acquisition or creation is organised in a rational fashion. *Argyris* was one of the early exponents of the need for business learning. He used the term **double loop learning** to describe this process. The term is derived from **control theory**, in which a feedback control system that incorporates the option of changing the target is called a double loop system.

In double loop learning, knowledge is not only acquired, organised, stored and retrieved, but the purposes for which this is done are constantly reviewed. This involves regular examination of the organisation's purpose and objectives in the light of the knowledge already acquired.

The learning organisation

Lynch quotes *Garvin's* definition.

> An organisation skilled at creating, acquiring and transferring knowledge, and at modifying its behaviour to reflect new knowledge and insights.

This clearly reflects Argyris's double loop approach. *Senge* has proposed that strategy development should be seen as a learning process. The essential nature of organisational learning in this sense is **active creativity**. Senge suggests that this is best undertaken by co-operative groups.

Implications for strategy. The learning organisation will generate a flow of fresh ideas and insights. This will promote renewal and prevent stagnation. Increased openness to the environment will enhance the quality of response to events. However, none of this will happen if there is a rigid, prescriptive, **top-down** approach to the strategy-making process. There must be a wide range of inputs and a commitment to **discussion and debate**.

The potential advantages of the learning approach must not be allowed to seduce the organisation into endless, unfocused debate. Senior management must guide the process in order to keep it on track. They must also be prepared to take decisions without consultation when circumstances require them to do so.

38 PREPARATION QUESTION: Z SCORE AND BALANCED SCORECARD

The essential difference between a Z score and a balanced scorecard is that the former is designed for external assessment of a company's success while the latter is part of a system of internal control. *Altman's* original Z score summarised five important ratios, all of which could be obtained from published financial statements. Subsequent versions have followed this approach. A Z score is thus based on publicly available information. It is an aid to potential **investors** and specifically a predictor of **corporate decline**. The essence of the balanced scorecard, however, is that it makes use of information that is generated specifically for the purpose of **top management control** and is unlikely to be widely distributed.

Z scores

Altman analysed 22 accounting and non-accounting variables for a selection of failed and non-failed firms in the USA and from these, five key indicators emerged. These five indicators were then used to derive a **Z score**. Firms with a Z score above a certain level would be predicted to be financially sound, and firms with a Z score below a certain level would be categorised as probable failures. Altman also identified a range of Z scores in between the non-failure and failure categories in which eventual failure or non-failure was uncertain.

Altman's Z score model emerged as:

$$Z = 1.2X_1 + 1.4X_2 + 3.3X_3 + 0.6X_4 + 1.0X_5$$

where

X_1 = working capital/total assets
X_2 = retained earnings/total assets
X_3 = earnings before interest and tax/total assets
X_4 = market value of equity/book value of total debt (a form of gearing ratio)
X_5 = sales/total assets

Other researchers have developed similar models.

The balanced scorecard

The **balanced scorecard** is 'a set of measures that gives top managers a fast but comprehensive view of the business . . . traditional financial accounting measures like return on investment and earnings per share can give misleading signals for continuous improvement and innovation - activities today's competitive environment demands'. (*Robert Kaplan*)

The balanced scorecard allows managers to look at the business from **four important perspectives**

- Customer
- Internal business
- **Financial**
- **Innovation and learning**

Customer perspective

'**How do customers see us?**' Given that many company mission statements identify customer satisfaction as a key corporate goal, the balanced scorecard translates this into specific measures. Customer concerns fall into four categories.

(a) **Time**. Lead time is the time it takes a firm to meet customer needs from receiving an order to delivering the product.

(b) **Quality**. Quality measures not only include defect levels - although these should be minimised by TQM - but accuracy in forecasting.

(c) **Performance** of the product. (How often does the photocopier break down?)

(d) **Service**. How long will it take a problem to be rectified? (If the photocopier breaks down, how long will it take the maintenance engineer to arrive?)

Internal business perspective

The **internal business perspective** identifies the **business processes that have the greatest impact on customer satisfaction**, such as quality and employee skills.

(a) Companies should also attempt to identify and measure their **distinctive competences** and the critical technologies they need to ensure continued leadership. Which processes should they excel at?

(b) To achieve these goals, **performance measures must relate to employee behaviour**, to tie in the strategic direction with employee action.

(c) An information system is necessary to enable executives to measure performance. An **executive information system** enables managers to drill down into lower level information.

Innovation and learning perspective

The question is '**Can we continue to improve and create value?**' Whilst the customer and internal process perspectives identify the *current* parameters for competitive success, the company needs to learn and to innovate to **satisfy future needs**.

- How long does it take to develop new products?
- How quickly does the firm climb the experience curve to make new products?
- What percentage of revenue comes from new products?
- How many suggestions are made by staff and are acted upon?
- What are staff attitudes?
- The company can identify measures for training and long-term investment.

Financial perspective

'**How do we appear to shareholders?**' Financial performance indicators indicate 'whether the company's strategies, implementation, and execution are contributing to bottom line management.'

Financial performance indicators

Measure	For	Against
Profitability	Easy to calculate and understand.	Ignores the size of the investment.
Return on investment (profit/ capital)	Accounting measure: easy to calculate and understand. Takes size of investment into account. Widely used.	• Ignores risk • Easy to manipulate (eg managers may postpone necessary capital investment to improve ratio) • What are 'assets'? (eg do brands count?) • Only really suited to products in the maturity phase of the life cycle, rather than others which are growing fast.
Residual income	Head office levies an interest charge for the use of asset.	Not related to the size of investment except indirectly
Earnings per share	Relates the firm's performance to needs of its shareholders	Shareholders are more concerned about future expectations; ignores capital growth as a measure of shareholders' wealth
DCF measures	Relates performance to investment appraisal used to take the decision; cash flows rather than accounting profits are better predictors of shareholder wealth	• Practical difficulties in predicting future cash flows of a whole company • Difficulty in separating cash flows for products which share resources

Linkages

Disappointing results might result from a **failure to view all the measures as a whole**. For example, increasing productivity means that fewer employees are needed for a given level of output. Excess capacity can be created by quality improvements. However these improvements have to be exploited (eg by increasing sales). The **financial element** of the balanced scorecard 'reminds executives that improved quality, response time, productivity or new products, benefit the company only when they are translated into improved financial results', or if they enable the firm to obtain a sustainable competitive advantage.

39 PREPARATION QUESTION: DULCET SPEAKERS LTD

> **Tutor's hint**. This is a question requiring theoretical knowledge and a willingness to apply it. There is not necessarily a right answer to this question: but any arguments you use should be supported. A point to keep in mind is that demand conditions in the home market - in this case, the UK - are important insofar as they give information about what consumers **might** want in other markets. The acoustic demands of hi-fi enthusiasts in the UK, where Dulcet was born, are likely to be similar to those of hi-fi perfectionists everywhere. But has Dulcet been educated in miniaturisation?

(a) **Existing competitive position**

The **competitive advantage of a nation's industries** is determined by the following variables and the interrelationship between them.

(i) **Factor conditions.** A factor is a resource of inputs to the production process. Factors include human resources, knowledge (eg scientific know-how), capital (eg investment rates, equity versus loan capital, short- or long-termism), and infrastructure (transport, communications).

(ii) **Demand conditions**. The **home market** provides a basis for expansion globally, but also provides the firm with valuable information about what customers actually want.

(iii) **Related and supporting industries**. Success in one industry is linked to success in others.

(iv) **Firm strategy, structure and rivalry.** Porter believes that vigorous competition is the best way to encourage firms to innovate and compete, whether in matters of cost, reliability, delivery or production efficiency. Moreover, the stock of knowledge in each firm increases the stock of knowledge of the industry as a whole.

In the case, we have partial information about two countries, the UK and Japan.

Let us look at Dulcet Speakers Ltd's strengths and those of the industry as a whole in the light of Porter's analysis.

(i) **Factor endowment**. The **workforce is skilled** and obviously trained to a high standard. The firm has secured a source of **technical innovation** by co-operating with the local university. It thus has a strong basis of expertise to build on. We are given no information about the training of the workforce and their productivity. Although it would appear that UK companies dominate this segment of the market, they might suffer from like inadequacies in human resources and production systems, even though the quality of the end product appears not to be a problem.

(ii) **Demand conditions**. Arguably, Dulcet benefits from being in the UK market, where there is a strong presence in recording music, and where classical and popular music are significant leisure activities: the same, however, can be said for western Europe and the USA. **Dulcet's home market** is not precisely defined and **can be viewed as the whole of Europe**. Dulcet has had to export from its earliest days, so already it has been exposed to the demands of specialist global connoisseurs.

(iii) **Related and supporting industries**. A number of Japanese companies manufacture consumer electronics in the UK. It is uncertain, however, how far they interact or how far there is a flow of ideas. It is probable that the research base of these Japanese transnationals is in Japan, so the crossover of technical expertise must be limited, especially if Dulcet and the other companies are worried about any latent competitive threat. It is **hard to see any clusters**, in Porter's sense of the word.

(iv) There are **four competing firms**, all of which are UK based, and all of which appear to serve the same market. This would indicate a **healthy amount of competition** at home: indeed we are told that this has the effect of reducing margins in the UK. It also means that there is a skilled workforce available, and that they have learnt to compete on grounds of product quality.

Japan

(i) **It has its own cluster of competitive industries.** The market in consumer electronics is competitive. Paradoxically, Dulcet Systems Limited, which is surviving competition from Japanese firms in the UK, Europe and the USA by a focus strategy, might be quite well positioned in Japan, providing it can reach its chosen segment. Trading on heritage might be a good idea - Dulcet might position itself as the hi-fi of the connoisseur of western music.

(ii) **Demand conditions are fairly exacting.** Are Dulcet's products small enough for Japanese houses or distinctive enough for Japanese consumers to prefer an unknown foreign brand to a product made by a Japanese company?

(iii) The **structure of the retailing industry** would cause difficulties, as there are a large number of small shops.

(iv) Many Japanese companies are expert in **miniaturisation**. Dulcet might need to develop a competence in this area.

(b) **Is entry to the Japanese market desirable at all?**

(i) **Against.** The firm already has a strong presence in the UK, Europe and the USA, each of which are sophisticated markets in their own right. It might not benefit from the extra hassle, and it might spread its marketing resources too thinly. The Japanese market, as indicated, is hard to enter, especially given recession.

(ii) **For**

(1) The firm needs to grow.

(2) The firm can learn from the competitive disciplines of the Japanese market.

(3) Despite the current slump, Asia, generally, is expected to enjoy rapid economic growth, and the experience of the Japanese market might be useful in marketing to other Asian countries.

(4) Sales might be profitable.

(5) If the firm ignores the Japanese market, a Japanese competitor may make a similar type of product which will then be exported to compete with Dulcet's own products.

On balance, Dulcet is best advised to try and tackle the Japanese market. The choice of entry mode is crucial and is discussed in (c) below.

(c) **Modes of entry**

(i) **Direct export.** Dulcet would ship speakers from the UK to Japan and sell them there.

(ii) **Indirect export.** Dulcet's goods are sold by intermediaries (eg an agent, specialist export management firms etc.)

(iii) **Overseas manufacture** (eg contracting, joint venture, licensing, wholly owned production).

Option (iii) will have to be ruled out for time being, as this would be too daunting a task. It would be prohibitively expensive, and there is no evidence yet of demand.

The choice is between the two types of exporting. The use of intermediaries, option (ii), might be helpful, but it will mean that Dulcet will not have control over the export process. However, to enter the Japanese market, this might be essential if Dulcet's products are to enter the retailing system.

Direct exporting (i) is also possible, but it will be much harder to break down the barriers without the help of the indigenous systems and firms.

40 TEMPCO

> **Tutor's hint**. This question concerned the strategic options for inward investment of an existing product to a new geographic market location. The tricky part of the question was in spotting that there was a trend towards inward investment rather than trading and John Adams was keen to go along this route.
>
> You could have left the introduction till last. Although it fills a presentational role, basically it restates the question.
>
> Your answer may well be different. Direct investment is probably cheaper now, but there are still important issues of local knowledge and so on that you should not ignore.

From: A Consultant
To: Tempco
Date: X/X/200X
Re: Market entry strategies for South East Asia

1 **Introduction**

Issues facing Tempco in its entry into South East Asian markets

(a) The attractiveness of an investment-led rather than an export-led entry mode.

(b) Types of ownership - a joint venture with local interests or a wholly owned subsidiary.

(c) Types of production - a greenfield investment or the take-over of an indigenous firm. All of these considerations are reviewed in the paper.

In an ideal world, a different entry strategy may be appropriate to each market, given differences in culture, environment and infrastructure.

2 **Exporting vs direct investment**

2.1 There are three different ways of entering foreign markets: by overseas manufacture, by exporting directly, and by exporting indirectly via an intermediary at home which then sells to customers overseas.

2.2 **Exporting** is the cheapest, easiest and most common mode of entry. The benefits to Tempco would include:

- The ability to concentrate production in the UK, giving economies of scale and consistent product quality
- Avoiding the cost of investment
- Avoiding the risks of overseas production
- Avoiding political risk

2.3 **Advantages of direct investment**

- A better understanding of the needs of customers in that location
- Decision-making is better informed and probably quicker
- Lower production costs possibly as a result of cheap labour
- Access to local finance
- Overcome tariff and non-tariff barriers to imports and other trade barriers
- Reduced logistics costs
- Reduced risks associated with exchange rate fluctuations
- Win orders in the market, (especially government orders)

2.4 **The most suitable mode of entry varies according to the market.**

(a) There may be too few **suitably qualified distributors** or agents to install, maintain and service the systems, which would preclude exporting.

(b) The South East Asian markets may only allow a **restricted level of imports,** but will welcome direct inward investment by foreign companies who provide jobs and limit the outflow of foreign exchange.

(c) Overseas manufacture gains **market standing** by having direct representation and demonstrating **long-term commitment**.

(d) In some cases, investment-led entry can offer market leadership **if this is desirable** but, especially in developed countries, this is by no means certain.

3 **Joint venture with local interests**

3.1 A **joint venture** would mean that Tempco would join forces with an overseas firm for manufacturing, financial and marketing purposes, each having a share in the equity and the management of the business.

3.2 **Advantages of joint ventures**

(a) Expansion can be achieved quicker and cheaper

(b) The local partner will have better market knowledge

(c) Having host country alliances may improve sales

(d) Some governments discourage foreign firms from setting up independent operations but welcome joint ventures/strategic alliances because they transfer know-how and technology and bring long-term benefits to the industrialisation of the host country.

(e) The risk of government intervention is reduced as a local firm is involved, or at least the firm will not be penalised.

(f) Some governments will be more likely to place orders with local involvement.

3.3 **Disadvantages of joint ventures**

(a) A lack of flexibility in decision-making may cause conflicts of interest.

(b) Disagreements may arise over corporate objectives, management and control, profit shares, amounts invested, marketing strategy and quality issues.

4 **Wholly owned subsidiary**

4.1 With a **wholly owned subsidiary** there are **no conflicts of interest** because in theory there is total control subject to the laws of the host country.

4.2 The firm is **free to make decisions** on the following matters.

(a) Whether to **repatriate or re-invest** profits

(b) **Trading areas.** The firm can integrate its international operations

(c) **Pricing strategies**. Transfer pricing can minimise tax liabilities

(d) **Standards**. The firm can enforce its own manufacturing or quality standards

(e) **Distribution**. The rationalisation of supply routes are easier to manage without the problem of differing objectives, skills, experiences and culture

(f) **Competitive information.** There is no obligation to share commercially sensitive information.

4.3 **Disadvantages**

- The capital investment required

- The difficulty in finding suitable managers
- Repatriating dividends may be a problem

5 **Greenfield site**

5.1 Companies can either set up their overseas subsidiary **from scratch** or merge with or acquire an existing operation. A greenfield site is more often built by companies in the following circumstances.

- Whose products are **technical** in either design or method of manufacture
- Which want **direct** involvement in the development of new markets
- Which are breaking into new ground
- Which can find no suitable partners

5.2 The past reputation of local companies may not be an attraction and it could be the only way to ensure keeping an image intact and serving specific market segments. There may be tax advantages or government funding to develop in certain areas.

For Tempco, the attractions of developing a 'greenfield site' are these.

(a) An **ideal choice of location,** near markets or suppliers to support just-in-time systems.

(b) The chance to build the most **up-to-date production facilities**.

(c) The ability to **hand-pick new staff** with no previous labour relations history.

6 **Local acquisition**

6.1 These benefits must be weighed against those of acquiring an existing operation.

(a) The cost of improving the management and skills level of the acquisition.

(b) Time is of the essence and production can begin more quickly.

(c) The existing firm may have useful distribution networks in the target areas.

(d) An additional firm operating in the market may create a situation of oversupply.

(e) The purchased company may have a good reputation which will benefit Tempco.

(f) The acquirer can pretend to be 'local'.

(g) A local firm has better market knowledge (eg about what design features are suited to local tastes and how the central heating and air conditioning control systems might be marketed successfully).

6.2 The problems associated with acquisitions involve finding the right firm which is agreeable to a deal, negotiating a fair price and integrating activities in the post acquisition phase.

7 **Conclusion**

Overseas investment is more costly in terms of management effort and finance, but may offer major benefits in terms of access and operational flexibility.

41 CLOTHING SUPPLY COMPANY

> **Tutor's hint.** This question was fairly straightforward - but did you read part (a) properly? It asked about national competitive advantage, not just competitive advantage as such. Cite Porter and make sure your answer relates to the diamond. However, markers did look sympathetically at PEST and 'five forces'.

(a) **International competitive position**

Porter identifies four key issues that determine whether an industry based in one country will be successful in global terms. These issues show how national origin can affect competitive advantage. They can be applied to show how the CSC's global success might be influenced by its current position.

(i) **Factor conditions**. Factors are the resources the business uses, such as raw materials, supplies, human resources and so on. CSC benefits from its resources in the Scottish islands, which it has turned into a marketing advantage. If 'Scottishness' is fashionable, then this is a benefit.

However, having an abundant supply of factors can exerts no pressures towards efficiency and innovation. Japan has relatively few resources at home. Russia has an abundance of raw materials.

Advanced factors relate to expertise, not just raw inputs. The CSC benefits from its craft image, an advanced factor.

(ii) **Demand conditions**

Customers in the domestic market educate a firm as to customers' priorities world-wide. If the domestic customer is demanding, then the firm may be attuned to the exacting demands of overseas customers. CSC's original customers who wanted practical outdoor garments, educated CSC about the products needed.

However, CSC's original customers have not **educated CSC as to the demands of the international luxury goods industry**, which, in practice, is where CSC is operating. Clearly, the lifestyles of the tourists buying thc clothes are far removed from CSC's original customers' lifestyles.

CSC is already a successful global business - trading on images of Scotland.

(iii) **Related and supporting industries**

An industry will be successful globally if there is a **cluster of suppliers** nearby, with whom the firm can co-operate. CSC has a network of suppliers, in a relationship of **mutual dependence**. CSC does depend on the quality of its suppliers, to support its brand image.

Other supporting industries, although unrelated

(1) **Tourism**, with London being a centre for tourism. If the UK were not effectively promoted, then CSC clothes would not have any cachet.

(2) **Retailing** is very highly developed in the UK. Retailing success in the UK has doubtlessly helped CSC expand abroad.

(3) **Fashion**. Many British fashion designers have been very successful in global *haute couture*. A supporting 'industry' (or perhaps a factor endowment) is the higher education sector in the UK (eg art colleges).

(4) **Competitive rivalry**. High fashion and luxury goods are always competitive, and there is no shortage of alternatives, whether based in the UK or overseas.

In general, luxury goods are a global commodity, even though segmented towards the affluent. CSC's national origins are important for the *brand image*.

(b) **Strategies**

(i) **Move production to South East Asia**

The opportunities are: **cost savings**, and **low-cost entry into overseas markets**, expanding the reach of the brand.

The **risks are considerable**. CSC will **lose the brand identification within the UK**, and also the **local craft expertise**. These are major reasons why customers chose to buy the products.

Such a move is a **change of competitive strategy from differentiation-focus to cost-focus** for no good reason. The differentiating factor supports the premium price charged.

(ii) **Brand synergies for use by other divisions**

A brand is a differentiating characteristic of a product ('signalling criteria'). Such a move **copies brand strategies adopted by other luxury goods manufacturers**. For example, Calvin Klein originally made clothes but diversified into perfumes. (Even Dunhill, a tobacco brand, is applied to after-shave.)

This move - a brand extension strategy - clearly makes sense, provided it is implemented properly over the appropriate range of goods, perhaps branded luggage, handbags, pens, perfume or after-shave.

The CSC brand is associated with high **quality, traditional fabrics, craft manufacture** and **perhaps Scottishness**. Clearly, these features need to be **maintained in any brand** extension or else the brand as a whole will lose its value. If for example, the brand extension s support low quality products, then the core range will be devalued. Furthermore, customers will become confused.

KZ comes from a different industry background, and neither consumer electronics nor shipbuilding has much in common with premium clothing. However, we do not know the motivation for the purchase. Management of a luxury consumer brand **does not seem to be a core competence**. Merely branding consumer electronic goods with CSC's name would seem pointless - unless the goods support the brand (eg for outdoor use).

42 CINICENTRE

> **Tutor's hint**. Firstly remember that the CiniCentre is a *non-profit organisation*, and so does not follow a *financial objective*. Secondly, note that the *style of strategic management* will change. You might have taken a different approach to part (b) if you felt that formalised strategic planning processes were not appropriate.

(a) (i) **Use of stakeholder analysis in developing vision, mission, goals and objectives**

As John reports to a Board of Governors representing most major stakeholders (except employees), he has no alternative to considering stakeholder interests and the power that they have. It is not simple matter however, because there are potential **conflicts between different stakeholder groups**, and hence multiple objectives to be satisfied.

No dominant stakeholder. Although some stakeholder groups are more powerful than others, no one of them can exercise dominant power. **Central**

government's grant is large. Even though it is being cut by 20% it will still be significant, and indeed has contributed to John's appointment. Yet the government exercises its power at arm's length. Furthermore, as a charitable trust, the Cinicentre is quite unlike a private company or plc where there is a clear line of accountability (eg to shareholders) whose interests must, ultimately, prevail.

Conflict. Potential for conflict can be seen in the example of **admission charges**. Charges displease **visitors and the tourism** industry - but are needed to maintain revenue; other parts of the Cinicentre's work might suffer, for example if the film restoration budget has to be cut. The media and visitors might dispute this, and newspapers will be full of stories of Britain's media heritage slowly decaying away. It is not stated whether the government grant has been given with a purpose: to subsidise restoration or to promote cinema. Like any museum, the Cinicentre is a curious mixture of laboratory, subsidised art form and entertainment park - with the big difference that there is only one British Museum, but a huge number of competing cinemas in the UK which do not have government funding - the Cinicentre has faced complaints from its **members** that it is not **distinctive** enough in its programming.

Value of stakeholder analysis

Analysis of stakeholders' interests and power can inform the Cinicentre's **vision and mission** as well as any necessary **tactical planning**. It forces the planner to look at the **environment** in a systematic way, and poses some necessary questions about **priorities and resources**. The deficit in 1996 was only £45,000. This would be wiped out by a small increase in commercial income to £6m, were it not for the fall in the government grant. [**Tutor's hint**. We are not told of the size of the accumulated deficit.]. On a three year contract, John might be tempted just be to tinker at the margins - but the cut in government funding suggests more radical surgery is needed.

Vision

A **vision** is a desired future state, which the organisation hopes to achieve. John has not been employed as an entrepreneur, nor can he impose his vision on the Cinicentre as a whole. He could decide to **consult stakeholders**. If there are hard choices to be made, these can be asked of the various stakeholders. What sort of Cinicentre do they want in future? Given the preponderance of tactical decision-making he will have to convince the Board of Governors first of all: but this **might only reveal that different stakeholders have widely differing ideas** as to what the centre is all about.

Mission

A **mission** is different in that it describes the reasons why an organisation exists, and can direct both its strategy and its guiding values.

(1) John can review the point of view of different stakeholders. It is clear what the **members** want - but they only represent a small proportion of the filmgoing public. Less clear is what the **government** wants of the Cinicentre.

(2) Agreeing on a mission statement will be **contentious**, but John has no alternatives but to try to get an agreement. A mission taken seriously effectively sets strategic direction, and requires choices as to what priorities are. A good mission statement should address the concerns of major stakeholders.

Goals and objectives

Strangely enough, these might be much **easier to define than mission** and vision, as they can be related to the **existing activities of the directorates**. John might need to identify short-term and long-term goals. Given the Cinicentre's current short-termism, this might also pose a challenge.

(1) **The time-horizons of the different areas of the Cinicentre vary.**

The **Film Archive Unit** is faced with deadlines. If its mission is to preserve the UK's cinema heritage, this means taking action now to avoid more and more films decaying and combusting. This is important for the mission, but is a **short term** issue.

Museum. Communications and operational staff probably plan on a **seasonal basis,** with more visitors to the museum anticipated in school holidays and so forth.

In the **Film Theatre** itself, planning and programming might be planned **months or even years ahead,** for major festivals or seasons by major directors. It would help if this were linked in with production of Film Fan.

(2) Similarly **funding differs between long-term and short-term funding**. The government grant is decided each year, and John knows what it is to be over the next three years. His aim must be to inject some long-term planning into fund-raising to enable him to plan for the long term.

Constraints

Stakeholders exercise constraints over what is achievable. A plan would not ride roughshod over the views of members - it may be the case that some activities which could easily be curbed will not be, because of stakeholder pressure. However, the role of unions has been identified as problematic. John would seek to introduce his changes with their support, rather than endure the bad publicity and loss of revenue that a strike would bring. We are not told of the cause of the persistent labour relations problems - perhaps a new approach to management would help.

(ii) **Main stakeholder groups**

(1) The government (Department of National Heritage)

(2) Members of the society

(3) The public, who visit the museum and the Film Theatre; non-member cinema-goers; film buffs who subscribe to Film Fan

(4) Local government and local residents

(5) Employees and management (John himself has made a major, high-profile career change in taking on the job.)

(6) The media (eg, newspapers, television companies, film-makers)

(7) Schools (museum) and educational institutions running Media studies and related courses in the humanities

(8) English/London tourist authorities keen to promote London as a tourist destination showing people around London

> **Tutor's hint**. We have identified four important stakeholder groups below. However, you might have chosen others. Local government perhaps has similar expectations to central government, but sees the Cinicentre as a major local employer and an attraction for people to visit the borough. Local residents are probably concerned about traffic noise and security.

Stakeholder expectations and interests

(1) **Members of the Centre**. People join such societies for a **variety** of reasons. Some **active members** may want put themselves up for election, providing a suitable number of secondments can be found. Other members may simply be pursuing a **vague interest** in films, and are chiefly interested in the publications and discounts that membership can bring. Members who feel that the Cinicentre is becoming too commercial have protested - however the **deficit** should concern them too.

(2) **Employees and staff.** Their interest is in **continued employment** and the continued interest in the job. Obviously they must love film, particularly in the Film Archive Unit, where specialist expertise is highly valued. Staff in the museum must also enjoy and be skilled at dealing with the public, as expectations of quality rise.

(3) The **government** funds the Cinicentre as it is a public benefit and there would be a major protest, especially in the media, were the Cinicentre to close. It is a tourist attraction to London, it provides jobs, it is prestigious for Britain, and it supports education. Funding the Cinicentre is perhaps similar to funding museums, art galleries, orchestras the National Theatre and so forth. There are many calls on government spending, and the government will be concerned about financial efficiency.

(4) **The media.** Although this might seem surprising to list as a stakeholder, British media firms may see the Cinicentre as a resource for programming ideas. Certainly, the film industry will be keen to promote an interest in the cinema, both as art and as entertainment.

Stakeholder power

Mintzberg suggests that stakeholders can exercise power in three ways: loyalty, exit or voice (ie interfering with what is done so as to change it). The extent to which they can exercise power depends on the sort of relationship they have with the managers.

(1) **Membership**. Members have little power as individuals, unless they are distinguished film-makers, producers, actors etc. Exit is relatively easy for them: they can simply resign or allow their subscriptions to lapse: in the long term this will threaten the existence of the organisation; in the short term, they do of course have the vote, and in theory are able to exercise voice through their representatives on the Board of Governors. This power is probably latent rather than active for the individual. Presumably, at elections, the Governors have to submit a manifesto as to what their main priorities are.

(2) **Employees and management**. In the short term, the staff can disrupt totally the operations of the Cinicentre even if in the long term this would be self-defeating. On the other hand the staff at the FAU have little power in the short term - other than resignation - but they could do long - term damage to the Cinicentre's reputation and mission. As a **manager** John has significant

executive power - but less than he probably had in his previous job. He has no experience of working in a non-profit-orientated organisation.

(3) **Central government's** power is large, as it provides most of the Cinicentre's revenue, covering most of its overheads. Its power of voice is significant.

(4) **Media**. The media have no direct power. They contribute no regular income, other than fees to use films from the archive. But they are powerful nonetheless in that they can mobilise the attention and interest of the public. They have the capacity for setting the agenda in terms of public policy. As the Cinicentre is a multi-stakeholder institution, such power is important.

(b) **Introducing strategic management processes**

Briefing paper

The model of **formal strategic planning and management** I propose to introduce has the following characteristics.

(i) A logical sequence of analysis, choice, evaluation and implementation

(ii) Clear objectives which the strategies must support for the long and short term

(iii) Direction, by and large, by senior management

(iv) Strategies are chosen after an objective evaluation of the facts.

(v) Strategic decisions cover the scope of the organisation's activities, its position in the environment and its general direction.

Although there are other approaches this rational model is perhaps the most suitable at the current time.

Strategic management to date

In the past we adopted the incrementalist approach, which involves small scale adjustments to current activities. **Incrementalism has failed**. There has been no explicit, conscious approach to strategic management, which instead has been **dominated by the budget planning process.** This recognises the realities of the government grant, but has obviously failed to deal with the underlying funding problem, and has not addressed the scope of the Cinicentre's diverse activities.

The crafting strategies approach suggests that management's task is to shape strategies as they emerge from operations. **Crafting strategies is not adequate** to deal with the current situation. We have to respond actively to the wishes of our key stakeholders on the committee. Things cannot carry on as they were in the hope that something will turn up. Of course, the crafting strategies approach may be useful in developing the ideas for implementation, improving our reach with the target audience.

Advantages of formal strategic planning

(i) Other approaches to strategic management do not address our major problems.

(ii) I will be able to use lessons learnt from my experience outside the Cinicentre.

(iii) Cinicentre's problems cover its scope and direction. The model proposed below addresses these uncomfortable questions explicitly - the other models do not always answer these questions.

(iv) The government is more likely to maintain its support if there is a comprehensive strategy in place, especially if this addresses the deficit problem.

The process of strategic management

Strategic analysis

Mission and **objectives** are worked out first of all. In Cinicentre's case, we do not have a mission or vision: these two issues have to be developed after a more fundamental strategic review.

Environmental analysis. This is a key issue given the multiplicity of stakeholders and its ability to secure revenue in future.

(i) **Political factors**. Government and local authority grants are set every year. Governments with other priorities may see the Cinicentre as a waste of money. The Cinicentre needs to cultivate friends in all political parties, and in other departments of government, not just the Department of Culture, Media and Sport. For example, an educational programme will win it friends in government, and also it can exploit the current success of the British Film Industry in 'rebranding Britain'.

(ii) **Economic factors** determine people's prosperity and their willingness and ability to spend on discretionary items such as subscriptions and donations. The Cinicentre is vulnerable to **interest rates** depending on how its borrowings are financed. The exchange rate has a marginal impact, if it affects tourism from overseas. Obviously, in **prosperous times**, leisure spending increases - and as admission charges and catering account for over 50% of revenue, this is important.

(iii) **Social and cultural factors.** Visitors and members have many other calls on their leisure time. An analysis of social and cultural trends can help predict future income from admission or suggest marketing approaches to increasing admissions. It might also suggest means of **segmentation**. The Cinicentre appears at the moment to be alienating its target audience. This is all the more surprising as cinema admissions in the UK have been rising for a number of years, with the development of multiplex cinemas etc and the medium, after years of decline, is flourishing.

(iv) **Technology**. New **management information** systems may be an essential constituent of **strategic control**. Externally, the Cinicentre is bound to be affected by changes in the technology of displaying and distributing the moving image. This has affected film going in the past. The **Cinicentre should not get ossified in one particular technology**. Also, the Cinicentre as a flagship of the arts, should be able to match in quality and comfort what is offered commercially. Technology is relevant to the **FAU's role**. The CFI could consider using the **internet** as a means of drawing people in.

The environmental analysis offers an idea as the long term future of the Cinicentre in a variety of contexts. If the current trend is for a long term fall in the number of visitors, this needs to be addressed on a long term basis. If new technologies change the whole basis and purpose of going to the movies, then again this needs to be addressed. These issues are strategic rather than just financial. **An annual budget review would not pick this up effectively.**

Internal appraisal

An internal appraisal can then assess the state of the Cinicentre.

(i) If the FAU fails to meet appropriate standards, this might lead to a redirection of government funding elsewhere, to meet the same objectives. However, the expertise is thinly spread.

(ii) Review the membership, the Cinicentre's current resources and operations to see if they are employed efficiently and effectively. (Surplus property might be sold off.)

(iii) **Risks**. The Cinicentre is vulnerable to upward pressure in technician salaries and equipment. Moreover, the public expects increasingly high standards of comfort. Maintenance costs are also vulnerable to inflation.

Strategic options generation deals with products/services and markets. We can consider a **competitive strategy** for the Cinicentre. There are other ways of distributing moving images (such as TV) but this is a problem for cinemas generally. Attention must be paid to substitute services (other calls on people's leisure money). (At this stage, the Cinicentre might need to consider fundamental questions about mission, rather than earlier as normal. This is because it is likely to be contentious and all stakeholders will have to be convinced of it.) **Evaluation** covers suitability, feasibility and acceptability.

Control. The strategic plan will have long-term objectives and milestones, as a counter-weight to the short-termism inherent in the budgetary process.

There is some flexibility in the system. The Cinicentre has a mix of long-term income (to a degree, membership subscriptions) and short-term income (government grant).

The **benefits of the strategic management approach** are that it will force the Governors to take a long term view of the Cinicentre, agree what it is for, establish priorities and play to its strengths. Not least, it will present them with a strategy for containing and hopefully reducing the accumulated deficit.

(c) **Strategic control and performance measures**

An approach to strategic control which uses a variety of performance indicators is the **balanced scorecard** (developed by Johnson and Kaplan). The balanced scorecard typically involves identifying performance on the basis of four perspectives.

(i) **Customer perspective** - customers can be defined broadly in this context to include internal customers and stakeholders.

(ii) **Internal business perspective** - this covers the business processes that have greatest impact on customer satisfaction.

(iii) **Innovation and learning perspective**: how far current and future needs are taken into account; employee motivation and learning.

(iv) **Financial perspective**: return on capital, cash flow. This presupposes that the current financial information is of any use. There are major flaws, in particular the way that overheads are treated in Cinicentre's management accounts.

The balanced scorecard does not devalue budgeting etc but shows the **linkages between different areas of a business** for its long term strategic health. In Cinicentre's case the financial perspective has perhaps been inappropriately managed. With the balanced scorecard approach objectives from departments and business units can be **integrated with financial performance**.

The balanced scorecard approach was developed for businesses, but it can be adapted to the particular circumstances of Cinicentre. The **internal business** perspective can be adopted to improve the administration of the centre, for example ticketing if that is a problem, and perhaps procedures in the FAU, which deals with chemically unstable material. The **customer perspective** can be tracked by admissions, repeat admissions, membership subscriptions and participation, as well as market research.

The balanced scorecard also warns against short-termist cost-cutting, as it exposes the hidden costs (eg falling number of admissions) in making savings.

Performance measures

FAU

(i) **Operating measures**: the number films saved; number of films destroyed; alternatively, footage of films saved/destroyed; sponsorship income; the ability to reach government standards; publications.

(ii) **Financial measures:** efficiency (eg buildings costs, administration etc); revenue.

(iii) **Conservation**. This is a long term effort, but some simple measures (eg 'numbers of films saved') are appropriate. However, objectives might be set in terms of **publicity**, and **project planning** and **management**. This ensures that this programme is conducted efficiently and effectively, but clearly the **financial perspective** is not much use other than for overall cost control.

The **other divisions** need perhaps to be restructured on **profit centre lines,** so that the Film Theatre, the museum and catering all come under management structure. This is because they are connected. Visitors to the theatre are likely to eat in the restaurant as are visitors to the museum.

(i) The film theatre should begin to **cover its costs,** at least.

(ii) For the museum and film theatre **numbers of visits** and **repeat visits** are useful indicators of success.

(iii) For the film theatre, **capacity measures** (we were 60% full) are useful. The Cinicentre's mission is not simply to show popular films, but clearly getting higher attendances for its programme will lead to more revenue and greater credibility.

(iv) Growth in membership, reductions in member turnover. Membership offers a fairly stable source of revenue.

(v) Mentions in the press (eg film review sections).

(vi) Success in ensuring publicity.

(vii) Over the long term, **market research can indicate** customer satisfaction.

The **cafeteria** should make a profit and targets should be set to increase profit (eg better food, more seats).

The **marketing activity** performance measures can cover new members, and public awareness and perceptions of the Cinicentre.

43 SPORTAK

Tutor's hint. A good answer to part (a) only requires a careful reading of the scenario. Part (b) is more demanding of knowledge and part (c) of analysis. This is reflected in the mark allocation.

The Examiner commented that many candidates were unfamiliar with the content of a business plan and wrote about the strategy process or aspects of operations. The financial information given was used poorly by some candidates.

(a) Sportak seems to have benefited from decentralisation principally in the degree of motivation of its store managers, as was intended by Jerome's father. These managers' responsibility for their stores' success was emphasised by their sales-related performance bonuses. Decentralised control also allowed the managers to respond rapidly to local demand and manage their own sales promotion activity in a flexible manner. It appears that the policy of decentralisation was successful since the company generated enough funds to support a policy of opening a new store each year.

Decentralisation also has disadvantages and some are now apparent.

(i) **The market has become much more competitive,** with threats from both larger chains of stores and discounted traders. Sportak is poorly placed to meet this competition.

(ii) **Decentralised purchasing means that costs are high** since bulk discounts are not available.

(iii) **Local control of sales promotion** has prevented bulk purchasing in the media, the use of more expensive media such as regional television and development of the Sportak brand.

(iv) The store managers have kept their stocks low, possibly because of a dysfunctional performance measure, thereby losing trade.

(v) Finally, the **hands-off approach** used by Jerome's father has made it difficult for Sportak to standardise on proven good ideas and learn from individual managers' mistakes.

(b) The objective of a formally presented **business plan** is to raise money. It must attract the prospective financier's **attention** and **interest**, emphasise the business's strengths and project the development of the business. It should also demonstrate that the managers of the business know what they are doing and have sound ideas about where it is going. The plan should be reasonably brief, extending to no more than ten or fifteen pages.

The plan proper should be preceded by an **executive summary** to convey the main points of the investment proposal and answer the financier's basic questions such as what does the company do and how much money does the company want to raise and why?

The business plan will then be divided into a number of sections covering the matters indicated below.

(i) **The business.** The background and history of Sportak and what it does should be explained briefly. Aspects of the business that give it a **competitive advantage**, such as the new stock policy, should be highlighted.

(ii) **Markets and marketing.** The principal markets should be described, with details of the **segment targeted**, existing and forecast **market share** and the main **threats** and opportunities. The store modernisation and new emphasis on merchandising should be explained and the main competitors described.

(iii) **Products** and **product development.** The main products should be described, together with details of those planned for the future. Details of any **endorsements** from, for instance, trade journals and surveys should be given.

(iv) **Suppliers.** The introduction of **centralised purchasing** and its anticipated benefits should be emphasised. **Principal suppliers**, their location and financial position should be described and details given of exposure to single sources, delays and inadequate quality.

(v) **Management.** It is most important to demonstrate the **qualities and suitability of management**. Jerome will need to emphasise both the experience and energy of his team. Brief details of the directors and senior managers should be given, including their qualifications and track record.

(vi) **Financial analysis. Summary profit and loss figures** for the last three years and projections for the next three should be given. Key assumptions should be highlighted. There should be clear indication of how management intend to **monitor and control performance.**

It will be necessary to provide detailed financial results and forecasts; these and any other detailed technical information amplifying the material in the plan should appear as appendices.

(c) Jerome has identified weaknesses in Sportak's position and his plan attempts to overcome them.

(i) **Sales growth has stagnated** while competition has increased and Jerome believes the company's survival depends on **rapid expansion** to nation-wide operation. He intends to achieve this by acquiring outlets and by spending heavily on promotional activities.

(ii) His **product strategy** will change slightly by putting more emphasis on **higher margin goods.**

(iii) He will also **centralise purchasing** in order to obtain economies of scale and hold increased levels of stock to enhance customer satisfaction.

(iv) He recognises that a greater degree of central control may **alienate his existing store managers**, thus hampering his plans, but he hopes to overcome this with generous financial rewards.

The forecast information indicates that Jerome's plan may be expected to nearly **double sales and achieve an increase in gross margin** from 50% to 57%. However, the extra costs associated with his new policies mean that expenses increase by about 150%; 1999 operating profit is forecast to be only 34% higher than the 1997 actual figure. This is the high point of the increase, since operating profit for 2000 is expected to decline to a mere 110% of the 1997 result. Furthermore, growth in the industry generally is expected to slow in 1999 and become negative in 2000. **Forecast trading results do not, therefore, justify the planned changes.**

A further concern is the debt burden imposed by the purchase of the new shops. Sportak is currently debt free. After the purchase, debt and equity will be almost equal and the interest burden is forecast to reduce profit after interest to 51% of the 1997 result in 1999 and to 26% in 2000. The extra borrowing incurs significant **financial risk** for the business, which would be increased if the interest rate were variable. The debt capital would not in fact be used profitably as is shown by the **declining return on net assets**. The business would actually be rather precariously poised, a position not improved by a decline in the current ratio from 1.6 to 1.3.

In summary, the expected curtailment of sales growth and the increase in costs lead to significant falls in RONA and ROE. This **erosion of profits** combined with the proposed **debt burden** could be very dangerous for Sportak.

(d) **Franchising is normally seen as a relatively cheap and therefore low risk method of expansion** since franchisees are expected to provide most of the extra capital. The franchiser's input is usually restricted to such matters as brand name, operating expertise and management assistance, though there may be heavy central promotional expenditure. The use of the franchisees' capital also means that expansion can progress rapidly.

Advantages

(i) Franchisees may be expected to be highly committed to the success of their ventures because of their financial stake and at least moderately enterprising. The management problem of motivating and controlling managers at remote sites would therefore be reduced.

(ii) Franchisees might also possess useful local knowledge.

Disadvantages

(i) On the other hand, the expansion of Sportak's profits would not be as fast as its growth in turnover, as profits would have to be **shared with the franchisees.**

(ii) It is possible that disputes might arise which would be costly and inconvenient to resolve.

(iii) The **method of charging for Sportak's input** would have to be carefully thought out to minimise the possibility of **fraud**.

(iv) It may be more difficult to exercise control over essential matters with semi-independent franchisees who are protected by their franchise agreements. For instance, Sportak will want to take a **long term** view of profitability, whereas franchisees may prefer **short term returns.**

(v) Control over **quality of service** may also present problems.

Overall, we may say that franchising is a successful method of expansion, especially in retailing, and has **good potential for Sportak.** It would certainly be preferable to Jerome's plan to expand by acquisition.

44 METALCRAFT

> **Tutor's hint.** This is a typical case study; it takes a strategic approach and includes marketing, organisational, human resources and operational material, all tied together with simple financial statistics. If you can tackle a question like this, you should have nothing to fear from the examination.
>
> In part (b) we have used *Porter's* three tests for diversification as the basis of our answer. The CIMA model answer uses the approach of *Ansoff* and *McDonnell*, which is a valid alternative.

(a) **Metalcraft Group plc**

Position audit

Metalcraft is currently failing to meet its shareholders' expectations. This is largely a result of the policies pursued by group headquarters. Group management have failed to achieve synergy in areas of the business where it is available, while starving the subsidiaries of finance and imposing significant administrative burdens on them.

The **chairman's policy** of allowing the member companies of the group to operate as if they were still independent has failed. The group's efforts **in marketing and R&D** have been **fragmented** and there have been no **economies of scale.** The requirement to achieve high quality accreditation and IIP was probably inappropriate for some companies and has been a distraction for all. Essentially, the **subsidiaries have been unsupported rather than given autonomy**.

The **failure of policy is clearest in marketing**. There has been no attempt to create a single, distinctive **brand. Sales forces are duplicated,** even when operating in connected areas and even in overseas markets there has been **no co-ordination of**

effort. Little is known about the competition overseas, group sales are static, despite healthy demand, and it has not been possible to acquire good agents. Nevertheless, marketing costs have increased by 50% since 1995. All these problems could be addressed much more effectively if export sales were **properly co-ordinated under a single authority.**

R&D has also suffered from **uncoordinated effort**. The group's products, while not at the cutting edge of technology, are reasonably complex and need to be kept up to date. **R&D has been fragmented and constrained by financial policy**. The R&D budget has fallen by one third in four years.

Financially, the group is in decline. As a result of being forced to compete on price because of marketing inadequacies, cost of sales has been growing faster than turnover, leading to declining gross profit. At the same time, expenses have risen and operating profit has more than halved since 1995, despite moderate growth in sales.

It has been policy to maintain dividends despite the decline in profits. **Dividend cover is now dangerously low at 1.5**. Maintaining dividends is a very **short-sighted policy** when it is clear that the group needs extensive investment in new products, marketing and reorganisation.

Improvement in profitability should not be difficult to achieve, without resorting to acquisitions or disposals.

(i) Assuming cash flow does not deteriorate in the immediate future, it should be possible to reap immediate **economies of scale** by a measure of rationalisation in purchasing, R&D and marketing.

(ii) The investment in quality accreditation and IIP should make it possible to build a brand with a good name for quality and service.

(iii) The main area for improvement is marketing. It should be a high priority to identify the most profitable regions, customers and products, the least profitable and those with the greatest potential. This should be done on a group-wide basis. The disparate sales forces could then be drawn together and their efforts focussed.

There may have to be some **structural and personnel changes**, but these should be kept to a minimum in order to contain cost. It is very likely that **extra directors** will have to be appointed at group headquarters to drive the rationalisation, but these can probably be found from within the group.

In the **medium term**, it would probably be advantageous to restructure the group into **product divisions**, with some consolidation of products and facilities. Savings on premises and staff costs may ensue, but this stage would have to be very carefully planned and implemented if **job losses** were not to erode the developing group brand image.

(b) **Metalcraft Group plc**

Board briefing

The evaluation of potential acquisitions

Professor *Michael Porter* suggests that there are **three critical tests** of whether diversification is likely to enhance shareholder value. Acquisition is one of the methods of diversification he considers, so we may use these tests to assess acquisition targets.

a **The attractiveness test.** The industry it is proposed to enter must be **structurally attractive** or capable of being made so. That is to say, it must have good prospects for an **above-average return on investment**. Note that it is prospects for the future that are important: industries which already display high returns are likely to be arenas for intense competition or to have high entry barriers. In the case of an acquisition, the latter would take the form of a high price tag. A company in a currently unattractive industry which is capable of structural change at reasonable cost could be a bargain.

c **The cost of entry test.** Market forces will tend to make the cost of acquisition reflect the potential future cash flows. The more attractive an industry, generally, the more expensive it is to enter. A company which is overvalued will not be a good buy. In this context, methods of company valuation which rely on **past earnings** or asset values are of little use; a much **more commercial, market oriented approach** must be used.

b **The 'better-off' test.** This test asks if the acquisition is likely to bring some significant and continuing **competitive advantage** to the group. Examples would be products that fit well into an existing distribution system, or a distribution system that adds value to existing products. It is important that the advantage is a continuing one. If it accrues once only, as when, for instance, a newly installed management team brings the acquired company up to scratch, there is no reason to hold on to the company in the long term. This test could usefully be applied to our existing subsidiaries to determine which are worth keeping.

In addition to these strategic tests, there are more immediately practical matters to consider in relation to a target, including the convenience or otherwise of its **geographic location**, the acceptability of any continuing **minority shareholding** and whether a reference to the **Competition Commission** might ensue.

R McGeorge

December 1999

(c) At the moment, the group is operating as a collection of independent companies but with the burden of the Chairman's insistence on IIP and quality accreditation and with serious financial constraints. There is no group management worthy of the name, let alone leadership. However, the chairman is aware of the potential motivational effects of autonomy and it should be possible to build on that.

Goold and Campbell categorised organisations into three types according to how strategic decisions were made and performance was controlled.

(i) **Strategic planners** have a small number of core businesses. Head office plays a big part in making the strategic planning decisions for its subsidiaries; the subsidiaries are then required to implement these global plans.

(ii) **Strategic controllers** tend to be diversified. Headquarters is remote and issues general guidelines for strategic planning dealing with general objectives and background assumptions.

(iii) **Financial controllers** allow subsidiaries to take most strategic decisions without head office interference. Head office manages by results in terms of financial performance.

The **strategic planner model** is probably inappropriate for Metalcraft as it has a variety of businesses and products. The **financial controller model** seems close to the present system; it does not provide sufficient support for the group's smaller subsidiaries while at the same time starving them of funds. A system based on the **strategic controller model** is probably required. Such a system would provide the operating companies with **strategic direction without stifling freedom of action**. Its success would depend on the establishment of a rational organisation, possibly along divisional lines. There appears to be considerable room for rationalisation. A measure of consolidation along product group lines and possibly by location could be combined with group direction of marketing and oversight of R&D.

Mintzberg described the **divisional form of organisation** as allowing autonomy to the **middle line**. Each division is monitored by its **objective performance** towards a set of **integrated goals set by the strategic apex**. The divisions are insulated, to some extent from the environment and face less uncertainty than if they were independent. Such an organisation, to be successful, must have certain characteristics:

- There must be appropriate **delegation** of authority by headquarters.
- The divisions must be **large enough** to support the quality of management they need.
- There must be **scope and challenge for the management** of each division and **potential for growth** in its area of operations.

Organisational culture will be an important aspect of any change. Mintzberg speaks of a missionary culture of inspirational leadership; clearly this does not exist and would be difficult to build. The existing culture seems to combine elements of the **role culture**, with the rather bureaucratic approach to performance control and the **power culture**, typified by the chairman's decrees. The group needs a culture of flexibility, co-operation and attainment, similar to the **task culture**. The chairman should promote the team identity of the divisions and the individual creativity of their managers by rewarding talent and achievement.

(d) Certain **standard criteria** for effective market segmentation are widely recognised.

- **Measurability** is the degree to which the size and purchasing power of segments can be determined. This depends upon the availability of relevant data.
- **Accessibility** is the extent to which the business can communicate with and serve the identified segments.
- **Substantiality** is the extent to which the identified segments are large enough to be worth tailoring a marketing program for.

In addition to these criteria, segmentation should be **consistent with the company's strategic stance and capabilities**. There would be no point in segmenting a market on the basis of its need for products that Metalcraft could not produce, or in identifying so many segments that the company's marketing effort could not cope with them. Finally, the basis of segmentation should be sufficiently stable to allow long term predictions to be made.

The simplest approach is **geographic** and Metalcraft will certainly be aware of the major differences between its UK market and any overseas market. Overseas customers can usefully be analysed by **region** as language, market needs and norms of commercial behaviour vary by region.

With its existing variety of products, Metalcraft would find it useful to segment by **industry type**. It currently serves the commercial aviation, motor manufacturing and health care markets, but its machine tools and electric motors could have wider markets than at present identified.

Another useful base of segmentation could be **purchase approach**. Metalcraft is involved in the market for military vehicles. Military specifications and purchase procedures tend to be highly demanding and experience here could be built upon.

Benefit segmentation is a common consumer approach but is also very useful in industrial markets. Metalcraft could, for instance, determine which customers bought on price, which on **service** and which on **quality**.

Finally, **size** is a useful basis of segmentation. This could be judged on the basis of current actual sales or future potential.

A practical approach to segmentation will determine where the company's efforts are best applied. This is likely to involve a combination of approaches to segmentation.

45 ICC

Tutor's hint. This question appears based on IBM's mainframe and service business rather than its personal computer business which also faced vicious competition from clones such as Compaq, Dell and a whole host of other brands. Key strategic developments were the rise of Microsoft and Intel, suppliers initially, who turned into major rivals (eg Microsoft Windows beat IBM's OS2 hands down).

Other approaches. Our answer is based on Porter. You could easily have used the BCG matrix to describe what has happened and suggested that mainframes are a cash cow, although less valuable than before, and that stars should be identified. Even now, the firm has lots to spend on R&D. For a while IBM concentrated on decentralising, even spinning off its printer-manufacturing operations.

The examiner wanted *use* of frameworks, not just a description of them. Furthermore, candidates did not have to calculate all ratios, only the important ones. It was to easy to dwell on the motivational aspects rather than organisation structure.

(a) Strategic and financial position: changes and implications

(i) Past and current strategic and financial position

Financial issues

Some typical ratios are calculated below.

Ratios

Item	*1991*	*1992*	*1993*	*1994*	*Change 1991-1994*
Asset turnover: sales/capital employed	2	1.99	1.95	1.98	
Return on net assets	15%	12.2	0.68%	(17%)	
Maintenance revenue					Up 11%
Hardware/software revenue					Down 20%
Cost of sales: maintenance					Up 14%
Cost of sales: hardware					Down 1%
Gross profit/sales: maintenance	40%	38%	38%	38%	
Gross profit/sales: hardware	56%	53%	52%	46%	
Total gross profit/sales	52%	50%	49%	44%	
Gross margin					Down 28%
Operating expenses					No change

ICC's performance has clearly deteriorated, and the data can enable us to pose some pertinent questions as to why there has been this sudden descent into loss. We do not have information about accounting policies which might elucidate some of the figures.

Sales levels: price and volume falls

It is not clear whether the fall in hardware revenue reflects sales **volume,** sales **price** or both. (With a bit more information a simple variance analysis could be performed.) We must assume both: ICC would have to cut its prices by 10% at least to match its far East competitors. Assuming that prices in 1994 are 10% lower than in 1991, a constant sales volume would have given sales of £2.79bn, as opposed to £2.5bn. Clearly volume sales are falling too.

Asset turnover (sales over capital employed) appears to be fairly stable, indicating that there is some control over investment and asset utilisation. Net assets have been falling – although this is because of the fall in profit. Data about fixed assets would have allowed a more precise investigation.

Cash flow: not a problem

Currently, despite the fall in net assets, the firm still has healthy asset balances. The increasing revenue from maintenance contracts will certainly have a cash element.

Cost of sales and gross margins

Total gross margins are down 28%, largely due to a fall in the margin on the hardware (56% to 46%).This has two causes: the lower selling prices identified above and perhaps a failure of costs to fall in line with sales. As calculated above, sales without price cuts would have been £2.79bn and a gross profit on hardware of (£2.79bn - £1.35bn) £1.44bn, a margin of 51%, still lower than in 1991.

Margins on maintenance have more or less been maintained. In fact, maintenance accounts for 22% of total gross profit as opposed to 15% in 1991.

Operating expenses and net profit

Operating expenses rose from 1991-1993 falling in 1994 near to the level in 1991. These clearly have not kept in line with the business as a whole. Had operating expenses been kept at 45% of sales (1991), in 1994 they would have amounted to £1,512m in 1994, not £1,770m, a difference of £258m, accounting for 88% of the total loss.

The cost profile of the business is not explicit. Almost certainly, a company of ICC's size would have a heavy burden of fixed costs: indeed the R & D budget, historically high, is hard to trim in the short term. Doubtlessly, the firm's staffing policies have contributed to this.

Of course, the staffing policies and R & D have doubtless a strategic value. **Knee-jerk downsizing** has left many firms in a state of **corporate anorexia** without the resources for future growth. However, the financial state of the firm is problematic both for investors and for the firm's wider reputation.

Changes in strategic position

The financial downturn is the results from changes in strategic position and ICC's response to it. ICC might be accused of complacency. After all, many of its virtues – innovation (as suggested by R & D) and closeness to customers – were signs of 'excellence' in the early 1980s.

Competitive forces

Using Porter's five forces analysis, we can assess the changes ICC is experiencing.

(1) **Threat of new entrants. Barriers to entry** have been eroded by technology and globalisation. Costs and so forth have not deterred competitors exploiting low cost manufacturing sites from Asia. Competitors might be able to enter ICC's markets by **configuring the value chain** in quite a different way, by outsourcing components for example. **Outsourcing** gives flexibility as production volumes can be ratcheted up or down depending on

demand. The fact that components for processors are effectively commodities mean that a lower level of R & D is needed to compete. In short, much of what ICC does in-house can be done by outsiders.

(2) **Substitute products** are the products of another industry which serve the same customer needs. In ICC's case this is a matter of definition. Arguably, **distributed processing** using PCs in a network or other server-based systems have become the 'substitute product' to ICC's mainframe systems – of course ICC can try to reposition the mainframe.

(3) **Customer bargaining power**. This has increased as a result of the lowered barriers to entry, and increased rivalry. In fact, by supporting *open systems*, customers are trying to *increase* their bargaining power. In the past, customers had to take what was offered without complaint. They also now have a real choice not only of mainframe, but of service-providers and type of computer configuration. Customers are *using* their power, and the actual user of computer services in the organisation, the end-user is able to specify more precisely what is needed.

(4) **Supplier bargaining power**. ICC has been its own supplier, choosing to manufacture its components itself rather than subcontract. This has enabled it to maintain high quality and control particularly where issues of quality are concerned.

(5) **Competitive rivalry** is hotting up, as is shown by the emergence of lower-cost competitors. The trend to open systems will make it harder to pursue a policy of differentiation on service and proprietary software.

Products and service portfolio. ICC developed in a market place where it was possible to be all things to all people. IT was a costly and specialised activity and there were few competitors. Proprietary operating systems were a high barrier to entry. They provided a valuable **cash cow**. In the past ICC could exploit all **stages of the value chain** to maximise the value created. This, however, has created **operational inflexibility** as production volumes cannot be easily adopted to demand.

Technological changes have transformed this situation more than any other PEST factor. There is no need for all the activities in the value chain to be performed by one companies, and it is clear that ICC's rivals are picking this off one by one.

With hindsight it appears that the **market place is both growing and fragmenting**. In the past, ICC's business model was successful, but compared with the massively expanded industry, ICC appears, to be suffering the dangers of vertical integration. By seeking to retain all the 'value' in the value chain, ICC is effectively **competing in several product-markets**: **hardware** (mainframes and PCs, probably, competing with clones, open systems and an environment), **software** (in competition with specialist software houses such as Microsoft) and **service** (competing with specialist service suppliers who are able to offer a greater variety of expertise, eg in other systems, not just ICC's). **There is no evidence that ICC has reconsidered its portfolio**. Instead of improving its existing services, it could be doing something different with its research budget (eg joint ventures).

Summary

Technology and **globalisation** have lowered barriers to entry and have increased the size of the market. Competitors to specialise in doing particular activities of the value chain, which ICC had kept integrated. Customer bargaining power has increased and end-users want more choice.

(ii) **Management's failure to identify the problem earlier**

Mintzberg identified five different meanings of strategy: plan, ploy, pattern, position and perspective. Position and perspective are useful in this context. Assessing position enables management to address strategy consciously. They can raise their eyes from the nitty-gritty and concentrate on the broad picture.

External factors and strategic position

For many years, ICC's position had been unassailable. It set benchmark standards of quality. It dominated the industry. It had a close relationship with customers throughout the value chain. It recruited the best minds. It was a technological leader. In short, ICC's recipe since its foundation had delivered spectacular success.

Moreover, to support this position, an enormous infrastructure of factories and the sales force had grown up to support it.

This past success and the large internal infrastructure to support the position has two important consequences.

The recipe or paradigm

(1) Senior managers and strategy-makers have a formula by which they interpret the world and the significance of PEST factors and market developments. An example of the recipe would be to promote a proprietary rather than an open system. In the past computers were large, expensive machines made by a small number of mainframe manufacturers. They were sold to specialist personnel for predictable corporate uses. Proprietary software captured a core of compliant customers who could like it or lump it. Similarly, keeping low prices on maintenance contracts was a tried and tested formula for success. Any management team has a recipe.

(2) ICC's recipe had delivered spectacular results over the years. It had succeeded in delivering high profits. The forecasts had been successful, innovations had been introduced. Given its success, the managers who had done so well would be very unwilling to change. Johnson and Scholes suggest that when the recipe begins to fail, managers' immediate reaction is to see it as failure of implementation and control: they assume that more resources are needed, for example, and more control mechanisms are built up. In effect, this is single loop feedback. An example from computing would be to offer ever higher levels of the type of customer service customers wanted before, even though the market signals, correctly interpreted, would suggest that something else was needed entirely.

(3) Only when these control mechanisms do not work is the recipe itself seen to be flawed and in need of change. This double loop feedback is particularly hard to introduce to a large and relatively bureaucratic organisation such as ICC.

Inertia and drift

The recipe is very hard to change in these circumstances. Even applying SWOT and gap analysis is problematic, simply because the recipe is so entrenched. Whole lists of strengths and weaknesses might be trotted out – but, as Mintzberg says, a strength is not a strength until it has been tested in the environment. Arguably, a bloated sales force, once a real strength, might be becoming a liability, draining costs in shrinking market. This inertia leads the firm to aim at survival, drifting rather than moving.

The culture

The culture of ICC is very strong. Its managers and staff have invested a great deal of their lives and relationships in the company as a whole. The culture was perpetuated by ICC's recruitment practices – the 'best brains' were recruited and all promotions are internal. This meant that graduates were recruited at formative stages in their development. ICC – and the 'recipe' – would have been their lifeblood. A strong culture can be an asset to a firm – but it resists change and is another reason for drift.

Power

ICC is a large complex organisation which, for many years, had occupied a fairly stable, if complex, environment. It thus evolved the bureaucratic structure to deal with this. Bureaucracies are riven by internal politics, and it is likely that power-plays and empire building would have interrupted the real work of the organisation.

(b) **Delayering middle managers**

Delayering is the name given to the process whereby firms reduce the number of levels of management between senior managers and the operational workforce.

Advantages

(i) Improving communications, by reducing the number of personnel a message has to pass through.

(ii) Giving senior managers a much better idea as to what is happening on the ground.

(iii) Enabling suitably empowered employees to use their initiative.

(iv) Introduction of flexibility to operations.

(v) Much of **middle management's** role was the provision of information and passing it up and down the corporate hierarchy. This role is no longer necessary. Information technology has removed the need for some middle management jobs.

(vi) The automation of work operations has meant that fewer workers, if more skilled, are needed for a given level of output. Some supervisory jobs are no longer necessary as there are fewer people to supervise.

In theory, both these considerations can apply to ICC. An important link is the connection between **strategy and structure**. In other words, structure should follow strategy. If ICC is going to shrink, then delayering is a natural result. If it is to change its strategy fundamentally, then structural change will follow. Delayering thus might result from:

(i) General changes in technology and communication.

(ii) A change in business strategy.

Disadvantages

Recently, the fashion for delayering has come under attack - like many fads it can be taken too far, and the role of the middle manager can be seen to be quite important.

(i) Middle managers are a **vital co-ordinating link** between the **strategies** of people at the top with the nitty-gritty of operations. It is unrealistic for the empowered workforce always to suggest tactical priorities.

(ii) **Not all decisions can be taken at operational level**. Middle managers can act as a potentially useful filter or else senior managers will be swamped with information, and relatively minor decisions.

(iii) Middle managers are important for motivation and appraisal, but they need to be motivated themselves.

Other changes needed at ICC for delayering to succeed

Delayering can only work if there are other changes to the way a company is run. Too often it is used as a justification for a cost cutting exercise which just leaves the remaining managers over-worked, demoralised, and less effective than before. But as part of a **wider process of corporate renewal,** delayering can be effective.

(i) **Corporate culture**. In a delayered environment, senior management must be more accessible to the workforce, as they will be required to give advice. The existing role culture need not be jettisoned completely, but it will need to be leavened with some feedback. 'Command and control' is no longer appropriate in an environment where people are expected to use their initiative. **A change of corporate culture is needed**. In fact the delayering exercise itself will make a huge difference – the company has practised a **no redundancies** policy for many years, although this is no longer sustainable, and this will indeed be a shock.

(ii) **Structure.** It is pointless delayering for the sake of doing so. The crisis gives the senior management team the opportunity to restructure the firm. It might decide to introduce **strategic business units,** to decentralise operations and authority.

(iii) **The middle manager's job.**

(1) **Management style**. In a delayered firm, the middle manager is expected to be more of a coach than an authoritarian boss. Middle managers are put in a difficult position - whilst they retain responsibility, they have less direct authority. They will have to learn to delegate. Some, used to the old ways, might find this difficult.

(2) **Impact on career development.** Delayering means fewer promotion opportunities. Personnel might have to move *across* the firm rather than up the hierarchy. People that are promoted will face a much greater shift in responsibility, so more resources will have to be thrown at management development.

(3) **Customer contact.** There is a high level of customer contact, possible when margins were high. The budgets for this might have to be redirected, and customers' and end-users' needs anticipated more commercially and cost-effectively.

(iv) **Information and control systems**. As a major computer company, ICC can doubtless afford the most sophisticated information systems available. ICC might need to build systems which can provide it with strategic intelligence. Also, with fewer middle managers, the information systems at corporate level must reflect key indicators and *critical success factors* in performance.

(v) **Performance indicators**. Satisfactory performance indicators for strategic and financial control need to be developed. The balanced scorecard is such an approach. It seeks to align customer, innovation/learning, internal process and financial perspectives. The scorecard does not *design* strategies, and ICC must develop indicators relevant to its strategies so that the indicators are the right ones.

(c) **Changing the structure at country level**

Currently, at **country level, the two divisions act independently,** although each reports, at a senior level to the country vice president, as do other business functions such as finance.

The **problems described are not necessarily caused by poor organisation structure**. Perhaps in their zeal to sell more, **S&M have not been selling entirely appropriate products** – if their performance is based on sales, they would have an incentive sell whatever they could, especially if another division is left picking up the costs and clearing up the mess. Not enough is known about the system of **performance assessment and incentives**.

The S&M function should have correctly ascertained the performance levels required by the clients – this seems like a failure of management and market research not co-ordination as such. However, certain **types** of system configuration might be particularly difficult to maintain.

Possible structural causes of these problems

(i) **Hoarding of information** by different divisions; information is not seen as a corporate resource in a heavily bureaucratic organisation

(ii) **People not knowing** who to direct sales leads to: an excessively vertical chain of command leads to information going up the chain of command rather than horizontally along the gangplanks. There might be reasonable co-ordination at strategic level, but a lack of it at implementation level.

(iii) **Sales leads are not really seen as SES's responsibility**.

Advantages of introducing a matrix structure.

(i) **Better co-ordination** across the value chain – in this case, sales and after-sales service would be better co-ordinated, as far as the customer is concerned.

(ii) **Greater awareness** of the strategic realities facing the different activities. S&M staff would not sell systems which SES find hard to maintain – S&M staff can communicate the necessary performance standards to SES staff.

(iii) Any **potential problems are flagged in advance**, as the maintenance implications of any contract can be described before the final proposal to the client. This will lead to increased customer satisfaction and lower costs in running the maintenance department.

(iv) There should be better management. People are not classified according to the functions they fulfil but their role in promoting the wider success of the organisation.

Drawbacks

(i) Introducing a complex matrix system at country level will almost certainly lead to a **greater level of bureaucracy**, in that decisions will have to be co-ordinated. Decision-making might be slower than before.

(ii) Inevitably this will give **greater power to the country managers** and will weaken the reporting links within S&M and SES globally.

(iii) ICC may have **clients** who themselves are global companies. They may prefer to **deal with the divisions on a product rather than on a country basis.**

46 ALG INDUSTRIES

> **Tutor's hint.** Some parts of the question are a bit ambiguous – precisely *what* sort of growth strategies are required?
>
> The Examiner feels that candidates do not pay enough attention to the financial data in questions such as this. In part (a) focus should be placed on the low-tech nature of the business, so that the dangers of moving into a high-tech sector could be identified. In part (b) candidates made insufficient use of financial analysis, particularly the high p/e ratio and the cost of the acquisition. Candidates should have used portfolio models in their answers. In part (c) candidates could have written more about how operating factors would make the merger difficult.

(a) **Growth strategies pursued until 1996**

ALG has grown by both related and conglomerate diversification. ALG's objective is to maximise shareholder value. There are different ways of doing this, but ALG has chosen to **maximise shareholder value but minimise risk** as far as possible. There is a relationship between risk and return, and so ALG has decided to:

(i) squeeze as much **value out of acquisitions on a one-off basis;**
(ii) **buy new businesses** where other one-off gains can be made;
(iii) **second-guess the stock markets which undervalued** the businesses acquired.

Related diversification is diversification into similar industries by vertical or horizontal integration. **Vertical integration is when a company takes over suppliers or users of its products** to earn more of the profit available in the value chain. ALG has been a construction company, and a brick manufacturer is a source of supply. In practice, though, there is no shortage of bricks in the world, so the expressed **need to 'guarantee' sources of supply seems unconvincing**, although this is a way of earning profits.

Otherwise, ALG has grown by conglomerate diversification, buying businesses and expanding into unrelated sectors, such as textiles.

Clearly, ALG had considered that it could use its management skills to turn round under-performing businesses and to realise some of the value inherent in them, which other investors could not realise. In other words, ALG aimed to apply a **distinctive management competence**. There is **no product-market justification** in this strategy.

The acquired businesses, whilst operating in different product market areas, share certain features, which have enabled ALG to benefit from management synergies.

(i) They operate in relatively **mature industries**. In other words, they are industries which do not expect great change, other than the operating of the business cycle and the state of the economy. The brick industry, for example, is mature, in that demand for bricks is fairly predictable. This maturity gives stability.

(ii) The **products are relatively 'low-tech'** although the **processes** that manufacture them might be high tech. Compared with pharmaceuticals, for example, textiles are a simple product. They can be produced cheaply.

(iii) ALG did not have to **invest** a great deal in the businesses when it took them over. This makes them cheap to run in the short term. In the long term, however, even mature business can be rejuvenated, and such firms are vulnerable to competitors who are more committed to the market.

(iv) **After acquisition**, the **stimulus to growth** and profits was a **one-off injection of new management skills, relying on cost cutting**. To continue to grow requires more than this. For example, Internet selling might supersede the vehicle franchise businesses. **Cutting capital investment might be short-termist.** Although returning the businesses to profit in the short term, **long term expansion might be jeopardised.**

ALG has avoided gearing. By repaying borrowings via asset disposals, it shows a hostile attitude to wards gearing. In practice it may be possible to increase the level of borrowing, enabling further investments and

Finally, ALG's success is riskier than it seems.

(i) It assumes no other fundamental changes in the industries it purchases.

(ii) Low investment might be dangerous – for example new building materials may reduce demand for bricks.

(iii) Little or no competition is assumed.

(iv) It depends on the ability of management to find 'undervalued' investments – however investors may get better at fully understanding the value of the companies.

(v) Mature industries are vulnerable to cheaper overseas competition.

(vi) There will come a point when ALG cannot expand this way any longer.

(b) BRIEFING PAPER

To: Board of Directors, ALG
From: A N Accountant
Date:
Re: Implications of Acquisition of Starlink Technologies

1 **Strategic justification: business portfolio**

1.1 The proposed acquisition of Starlink, whilst **continuing the strategy of conglomerate diversification**, enables the firm to **change its portfolio of businesses**, in order to enhance shareholder value. **In the past**, we have concentrated exclusively on mature industries, **cash cows** in the BCG model, **low risk but low, if predictable, returns.**

1.2 The move enables us to reposition our portfolio of businesses, so that we have some **rising stars.**

1.3 The justification is that we **cannot continue to buy businesses whose products are fixed in the maturity stage of the product life cycle**, important though these products are. We will no longer be able to deliver the increased growth shareholders need, especially as our profits have been driven effectively by company doctoring, not product-market strategy.

1.4 The **satellite business is a new type of business** for us, in which, given the market is expanding, we are positioned at the launch stage of the life cycle. Although satellite technology has been around for many years in the developed world, there is greatly increased market demand, for example in Eastern Europe and the developing world, given the relative cheapness of mobile phone technology. They may be vulnerable to competition are some important differences however.

2 **Product-market and competitive implications**

2.1 Although satellite technology is high-tech, unlike some of our other businesses, it can **provide solid growth, given the worldwide expansion in telecommunications.** Moreover, there are relatively few businesses competing in this market.

2.2 However, there is a high technical content in the product itself, unlike some of the other goods we manufacture. Currently, at ALG we do not have this expertise, although, **if we buy Starlink, we will be buying the expertise as well**.

2.3 The market and **customer bases are totally unfamiliar** to us. We will have to **establish our credibility** with potential clients. Although Starlink's name may be known, ALG will not be known to be in high-tech industries. ALG is a dominant player in some of its businesses, so a newcomer status is new to us. We will be exposed to a new sort of customer.

2.4 The competitive environment is characterised by **intense competitive rivalry**, given that sales are low volume, high value and satellites are expensive, and **high barriers to entry**. However, the substitute products are ocean cables, and the high investment in ground based communications means they may be costlier than satellite transmission. For certain applications, satellites are the only option. The relative bargaining power of customers and suppliers varies. On the one hand, customers are few and far between; on the other hand, there are few suppliers of satellites and customers cannot easily press prices down.

2.5 As far as a choice of **generic strategy** is concerned, **Porter's model fits uneasily** with our situation. Satellites are very expensive, so attention to costs is necessary. Focus is out of the question as it is very hard to see how the market for the hardware could be segmented, other than between satellites for military and domestic use. **Differentiation** is difficult to achieve as there are few 'standard' satellites available to differentiate from. Finally, a lot of the work might be for governments and public corporations and large companies or consortia that may have very precise specifications as to what they want.

3 **Risk implications**

3.1 Although in the long term, growth in the market is assured, there are relatively few units sold in any particular year. The **fixed cost base,** in R & D and manufacture, involves higher risk, and a lot of the firm's assets will be tied up **high cost job production**. The return is more volatile.

3.2 Cash flows are more risky for the business, in that unlike brick say, satellites are one-off purchases, and only a few may be sold in any particular year. Given that all the expenses are incurred up front, **a lot of cash is tied up in working capital**.

3.3 The satellite industry has high barriers to entry, partly because of the investment and technological expertise involved. Purchases of satellites are perhaps vulnerable to the whims of telecommunications companies and governments which

3.4 **ALG's management does not have the competences** needed to understand the complexities of a high tech business. We may apply the recipe that has worked in the high tech business to a totally inappropriate way.

3.5 Starlink is operating in **genuinely global market.** None of the other companies in ALG's portfolio are quite so global. Bricks are rarely exported. Although ALG is exposed worldwide its portfolio of businesses (perhaps with a few exceptions) is multi-domestic.

4 **Financial implications**

Key financial data

	ALG	*Typical acquisition*	*Starlink*
ROCE	15%	7%	10%
Sales and admin costs as a % of sales	11%	14%	16%
Gross profit as % of sales	30%	14%	43%
Operating profit as a % of sales	15%	8%	64%
R&D costs as a % of sales	4%	4%	20%
Debt/equity	33%	55%	40%

4.1 **Cost of acquisition**. Starlink's market value is £820m, over three times as expensive as the traditional purchase. Furthermore, **Starlink's price/earnings ratio is high (20, compared to 8 for a purchase)**. This implies that investors consider that Starlink has a bright future, and so there may not be **hidden assets, which can be sold off**. It shows that investors put a high, not a low, value on Starlink's future.

4.2 The implication of the P/E ratio, especially when compared to the ROCE (around 10%) is that **Starlink is not cheap**. The fact that Starlink is itself the **result of a merger** may mean that some peripheral areas can be sold but this is unlikely in the circumstances. Further evidence for this view is that ALG's typical acquisition has a market value less than the net asset value shown in the accounts (£220m as opposed to £280m). ALG's market value is higher than its book value (£3,600 to £2,400). Starlink's market value (£820m) is higher than its net asset value.

4.3 These figures have to be treated with caution **as we do not know what accounting policies have been applied in the past**, regarding goodwill and asset write-offs.

4.4 **Financing the acquisition**. ALG will not be able to finance the purchase through selling bits of Starlink to other investors. It will either have to borrow, finance it out of cash or issue shares. We do not know how much of ALG's net assets are liquid.

4.5 **Starlink will cost £820m. Borrowing would double ALG's total debt increasing its gearing,** raising the debt equity ratio from 1:3 to 2:3. This will increase interest payments, but is perfectly **feasible**. There seems no reason to issue shares to finance the purchase.

4.6 The Board of Directors could also sell another division to finance the purchase.

4.7 **Performance**. Starlink's return on capital is only 10% - less than ALG's (over 15%), although more than the typical acquisition – therefore the acquisition might reduce ALG's ROCE. Of course, ROCE is an unreliable measure and is susceptible to differences or changes in accounting policy. It may be that ALG will give a lower book value to some of Starlink's assets than Starlink does. This would have the effect of increasing Return on Capital Employed. Furthermore, ALG might **be able to realise some cost savings in administration.**

4.8 **Starlink's cost profile ie very different from ALG's typical acquisition** in certain key respects.

(a) Research and development accounts for 20% of sales as opposed to 4% for the typical acquisition and under 4% for ALG in total. This cannot realistically be reduced.

(b) Sales and administration account for 16% at Starlink, 11% at ALG and 14% at the typical acquisition. Bringing it down to ALG's level would release £20m per year, increasing operating profit to £45m (raising the ROCE to 18%). A reduction of £12.5m in sales and admin costs (to £52.5m) would bring Starlink's ROCE in line with ALG's.

This data underscores the difference in gross profit (43% for Starlink, 14% for the typical acquisition, and 30% for ALG) and operating profit percentages (8% for a typical acquisition, 15% for ALG and 6.4% of Starlink).

5 **Summary**

5.1 Starlink is not necessarily underperforming, and investors are looking kindly on its future. It is an expensive acquisition.

5.2 It is a fundamentally different type of business and ALG's managers are not familiar with it.

5.3 The financial impact is unclear. The only possible savings appear to be in administration.

(c) **Critical areas for the new business**

As indicated above, Starlink is a different type of business, and ALG's directors will have to go through a learning process in order to be able to deal with it.

(i) **Style of strategic management adopted.** In any conglomerate the role of head office varies, as does the use of shared overheads.

A **financial control** style is adopted where head office sets **financial targets only, and it is to the subsidiary/divisional managers to achieve them.** This can provide important discipline, and its effectiveness depends on how well the targets set are appropriate to the business. ALG would not impose the same framework on Starlink as on its other acquisitions, if only because the financial characteristics of the two businesses are so very different. **Some financial targets may be appropriate to encourage efficiency** – ALG's managers would not interfere in product-market decisions they did not understand.

Strategic controller style: **divisional managers set the strategy, under the approval and guidance of head office. As ALG knows little about satellites, it is hard to see what value ALG could add**, unless ALG has a large research department. However, ALG's management may prefer to indicate product-market objectives, and can invest money.

Strategic planner style: in this case, head office determines the strategic plans of the subsidiary companies directly. The subsidiaries execute these plans. This is totally inappropriate.

ALG's management faces a dilemma:

Clearly, they have bought Starlink to benefit from its technological expertise and its promise for development. This is more than just a turnaround strategy and ALG's managers will be tempted to get involved in the new company. They cannot simply leave Starlink's managers to do their own thing - Starlink has to perform.

In summary, ALG's managers' knee-jerk reaction may be to set financial controls, but because of the uncertainty of the new business, ALG's managers, simply to reassure themselves, may equally be tempted to over-intervene.

(ii) **Performance measurement. The Japanese investment culture is different from the UK's** and it is not certain that Japanese firms have been as geared as

UK ones to short-term profit performance. This merely exacerbates the differences between a satellite business and ALG's normal acquisition.

ALG will doubtless set profit and ROCE targets, to ensure that Starlink's performance can be monitored. After all, ALG is supposed to be adding value in some way. **Starlink's managers may have to think much more seriously of shareholder value**.

(iii) **'National' culture**. Starlink is a Japanese firm, and ALG is based in the UK. There are huge cultural differences - they can be overcome, as witnessed by the success of UK subsidiaries of Japanese firms. Here the boot. Culture affects **reward systems**, how **managers communicate**, a preference for **consensus** (Japan) over **authoritarianism** (ALG's cult of the personality to date). In addition, some Japanese firms have a tradition of **lifetime employment**.

(iv) **Corporate culture**. National cultures can affect corporate cultures. We know little of the specifically corporate culture of Starlink, but given the industry it is in and its national origin, this may be another problem.

(v) **Degree of integration.** Here may be some cost savings in integrating some overhead activities, and plugging Starlink into ALG's supplier networks. However, marketing and branding is unlikely to be affected.

In short, the problems of integration suggest that it is hard to identify what value ALG can add to Starlink's business.

(d) **Strategy formulation by senior as opposed to middle managers**

Strategic decisions affect the scope of the business, are long term, can involve change and affect the total allocation of resources within the company.

Head office/divisional managers

ALG currently employs a **divisional form** configuration, and the style of strategic management is that of **financial control**. Head office effectively regards each business unit as an investment. The underlying rationale for the Head Office role is to be a better informed investor than the stock market and to manage the investments to deliver shareholder value.

The Head Office role is that of a portfolio manager. The only strategic decision head office takes is which assets to add to the portfolio of ALG, and the balance between **risk and return**. Head Office's **core competence** is in making assets work and assessing and balancing risk.

Head office **sets objectives for the divisions but does not set strategy**. Therefore, for ALG, the strategy for each operating unit should be set by that unit. The acquisition of Starlink suggests this: head office recognises a good asset when it see one - but they know nothing about the details of the satellite business. **Therefore, Starlink's managers should be able to set their own strategy.**

Senior managers or operational managers

Within each business unit, Mintzberg suggests different ways of dealing with strategy.

Planned or intended strategies are produced by senior managers and are implemented by operational managers. They are top-down and are quite detailed. Operational managers may be involved if their advice is needed, particularly about resource allocation. The senior managers think great thoughts. This process is very analytical.

Where the industry and business cycle are predictable, this approach might make sense in that change is limited and that forecasting is realistic.

The other approach is the **emergent strategies** approach, where strategic developments are not planned but tend to be initiated by lower level managers as small-scale changes. Where the environment is fairly turbulent and uncertain, then an emergent approach may be more effective. Managers' role is to craft emergent strategies as they arise, directing resources to promising areas, or closing off avenues. Clearly, within the ALG group, either style of strategic management may be used.

47 SALCHESTER THEATRE

Tutor's hint. The requirement for this part of the question is rather confusingly worded, making two separate references to 'problems'. You may be tempted to wonder if you are supposed to distinguish between the theatre's problems and Bernard Mason's problems in drawing up a mission statement. Do not be put off by this potential complexity. When in doubt keep it simple and get the easy marks. In this question, they are for discussing the requirements of a mission statement and showing that there is extensive disagreement about what the mission is. The examiner's suggested solution uses the same mission statement framework as the BPP Study Text, as does this answer.

Don't forget that part (b) is also about the theatre's problems, so try to keep your answer to part (a) focussed on the mission statement.

Part (a)

Mission statement for Salchester Theatre

Mintzberg says that **mission** 'describes the organisation's basic function in society'. The concept is one of providing an overall sense of direction for those involved.

It is possible to discern four main components in a good mission statement.

Purpose. Why does the organisation exist? For whose benefit? And to achieve what ends? Bernard Mason is already finding that there is no clear consensus of opinion on this topic. Goals and objectives may be developed from a mission statement to give direction and cohesion to operations, but if the overall mission is in dispute, the danger is that more detailed aims will conflict and hamper one another.

Strategy. Strategy covers such matters as products or services and competences. In broad terms, how does the organisation go about doing its business? There are conflicting opinions about this at the Salchester Theatre, deriving from the various views on what the theatre is for.

Values and culture. Culture is, perhaps, a tricky word to use in this context. Here we mean the prevailing ethos. There is less dissension about this at Salchester Theatre than in other areas, but still no real consensus.

Policies and standards of behaviour. We are given little information in this area, though it is vital at the operational level; the opinions of outsiders, such as theatre-goers, will be heavily influenced by these matters.

It is obvious that there is fundamental disagreement over just what the mission of the Salchester Theatre is. The local politicians see it largely as enhancing the town's image (and perhaps their own). The acting company see it as a vehicle for their own professional and cultural aspirations. The Friends of Salchester Theatre have no time for such matters and look for middle of the road entertainment. Schools and University see it as an adjunct to drama studies. The Arts Council wishes to see artistic and cultural development.

At the moment, Salchester Theatre is poised on the brink of serious decline. It is apparent from the financial information that the continued survival of the theatre depends on achieving a better balance between costs and revenues in two main areas: in-house productions and touring companies. The in-house production problem seems to boil down to a balance between attracting paying customers and art for art's sake. The touring company problem is compounded by the influence of the politicians.

Bernard Mason is not in a position to impose authority on the theatre and must proceed cautiously. Perhaps the best he can do is to ensure that none of the stakeholders is allowed to ignore the financial position.

Part (b)

> **Tutor's hint.** This is where you must combine basic financial analysis with judgement about commercial realities. Make sure you do not include any proposals of your own: they should appear in your answer to part (c)

A review of the current position at Salchester Theatre

Salchester Theatre made a loss of £57,000 in 1998/99. Trading at a loss may eventually threaten the survival of any organisation, and cause a re-examination of its most basic assumptions. These have been discussed above. The suggestions of the various stakeholders are considered below.

Costs and revenues

The Theatre's main activity is its **in-house productions**. Revenue from these has fallen in both of the last two years, with a fall of 13% in 1998/99. Over the same two years, costs have risen: personnel costs by 10% and materials and other costs by 20%. The fall in revenue has occurred despite increases in ticket prices; these increases may, in fact, have accelerated the falling-off of audience numbers.

The second main area of operations is the promotion of performances by **touring companies.** Here also there has been a significant increase in cost unmatched by a corresponding increase in revenue.

Finally, it is clear that there has been a **failure of cost control generally**, with other costs rising by about 25%.

The stakeholders' attitudes

It is tempting to associate the failure of in-house productions to attract audiences to the arrogant attitude of the **acting company**, but there is a question of **responsibility**. Are the actors organised as a soviet, with decisions about the programme emerging from internal debate? If not, the Artistic Director must presumably bear most of the responsibility for the choice of productions and therefore for the failure to attract audiences. There is a clear requirement for the exercise of financial responsibility in the choice of future productions.

The views of the **Friends** should not be given too much weight; they are a self-selecting and unrepresentative minority group. However, they are probably closer to the general public in Salchester than the actors. There is no doubt that in-house productions must generate more revenue and audiences must be attracted if this is to happen. It should not be necessary to produce West End hits exclusively, but greater attention must be paid to **market potential** in the future.

The **touring companies** present a rather different problem because of the political input. In 98/99 there was, for the first time, a trading loss on this activity. We are told that 'some of the touring groups ... are well supported'. The first step of any recovery programme must be to establish which events have the best prospects, with a view to eliminating the others. The politicians must then be confronted.

If they wish to maintain their commitment to the touring groups, it should really be matched by an undertaking to subsidise their performances as a separate item, rather than as part of a global sum. This would force them to confront the realities of their policy.

The objects of the Arts Council may make a move to a more commercial programme difficult for them to support. However, even they cannot expect the Theatre to run at a loss.

Conclusion

None of the courses of action proposed or espoused by the various stakeholders is likely to ensure the survival of the Salchester Theatre. There will have to be compromise. At the same time, closer control by the Theatre management can make a significant contribution to that survival.

Part (c)

> **Tutor's hint.** This is where you make your concrete proposals to lift the Theatre out of its decayed state.

Salchester Theatre has a long-term problem in the failure of its stakeholders to agree on what it should be doing. In the shorter term, Bernard Mason can take a number of positive steps to improve the financial situation.

Revenues

Revenues from **in-house productions** have fallen by 13% in the last year. This represents a sum of £50,000. This development alone would make a significant difference to the theatre's position if it could be reversed. Leaving aside the problem of the type of production, Bernard Mason could address the falling revenues in two ways: sponsorship and promotion.

Sponsorship allows businesses to share in the kudos accruing to cultural activity in return for financial support. High profile financial institutions such as banks are particularly susceptible to offers of this kind. The catering facilities of the theatre could be used for the related activity of **corporate entertainment.**

We are not told what **promotional** activities are undertaken, but it is likely that they could be improved. A programme of visits by actors to schools, for instance, might arouse some interest among younger people.

The touring productions promoted by the Theatre no longer cover their cost. A plan of action to deal with this has been outlined in part (b) above.

The grant from the **Arts Council** has remained unchanged for the last three years. This may be an inevitable result of government policy to the arts generally, but the position could at least be examined in partnership with the Arts Council. The increase in costs (see below) indicates at least some element of unavoidable cost inflation, which may offer some leverage in discussion.

The **university** receives services from the Theatre at a nominal charge. This also has remained unchanged over the last three years. This charge should be reviewed in partnership with the University.

Costs

Costs have **increased in all areas** in both of the last two years, with particularly heavy increases in the last 12 months. Wages and salaries have increased by 10% on the 96/97 figure, materials and other costs by 20%, restaurant casts by 23% and fixed costs by 27%. The increase in fixed costs in particular indicates that there has been some inflation in the currency, since increases in charges for utilities are usually resisted quite aggressively. A programme of cost control and reduction is needed, starting with an examination of headcount and a review of materials and other costs. There may be extravagances to be controlled.

The **catering costs** are particularly interesting since they do not include staff costs. In 98/99 the restaurant did not even generate enough revenue to cover the cost of the food it served. This is a ridiculous state of affairs and immediately raises the possibility of **fraud**. This should be investigated as a matter of urgency.

Part (d)

Resistance to change at Salchester Theatre

It is highly likely that there will be resistance to change from some or all of the individuals and interest groups at Salchester Theatre. The effect of natural conservatism will be compounded by the incompatible proposals and assumptions of the various stakeholder groups.

Change as a threat

The prospect of change is often perceived as threatening to established **benefits and privileges**. The actors will fear losing the challenge of *avant-garde* drama, while the Friends will fear that their role will be diminished. The politicians will fear for their status as patrons of the arts and for their free admission. Staff generally will fear for their jobs, the Arts Council will be wary of any cultural compromise, and the University will be concerned about the continuance of its valuable relationship with the Theatre.

Fear of the unknown

The prospect of change also arouses fear of the unknown. The exact implications of any programme of reform will only become clear bit by bit as time passes. Uncertainty of this type causes **stress** in those who are affected but have no control over the processes involved. This effect is exacerbated if there is an air of **implied criticism** generally, as is often the case when an organisation is in difficulties and a new manager is brought in

Change methodology

The **manner** in which change is introduced can provoke resistance. Time is fairly short at Salchester Theatre and there is little in the way of financial resources to ease changes like redundancies. It will be necessary for Bernard Mason to introduce his proposals in as diplomatic a way as possible, avoiding confrontation and attempting to promote a positive attitude to the need for change. A **problem-solving** approach is more likely to succeed than an approach based on ultimatums.

48 PLAYWELL

> **Tutor's hint**. Many candidates have difficulty with the case study type of question, often being unsure of how to get started. Fortunately, questions of this type are broken down into parts, each with its own specific requirement. This gives you some structure to work to. However, in this question, the 20 mark part (b) is quite open ended and likely to intimidate.
>
> We will show you how to tackle each part in turn.

Part (a)

> **Tutor's hint**. This part of the question is really quite simple: in essence, it asks you to identify stakeholders and discuss their goals. The only problematical element is the requirement to assess the **relevance** of the goals. What does this mean? Relevance to what? This is a good example of how a minute or two spent **understanding** the question can be time well spent. We think that here **relevance** means something like 'potential impact upon the strategy Playwell Limited pursues'.
>
> **Planning** your answer to this part is quite simple: you need a list of stakeholders with their likely goals and an assessment of their impact.

Stakeholders

Alexander Simmonds appears to be the **principal internal stakeholder** in the company and under normal circumstances answerable to no-one. His goals are not clearly stated in the setting, but it would be reasonable to assume that he wishes to see his business survive and grow so that he and his work force may continue to benefit from it. He is described as concerned for the welfare of his work force; also, we may assume that he regards at least some of his business associates, such as the bank and his principal distributor, as important to Playwell Limited's continuing success.

The **members of the work force** are important internal stakeholders. There were 50 of them at the end of 1994 and with the continued expansion of output, it is likely that their number has risen significantly. They live in an area of high unemployment and are paid well. They are likely to be most concerned about **security of employment,** and, perhaps secondarily, about the ability of the firm to **continue** to provide competitive wages and above average benefits. Their influence upon Playwell Limited's future depends upon the extent of A4lexander Simmonds' **sense of responsibility** for them, which seems to be significant, as evidenced by the fact that labour costs are regarded as fixed.

Playwell Limited is likely to count as an import local provider of employment. This is a matter of interest to **local government**. The ability of this stakeholder to influence the company's future actions is probably limited to negative effects, now that government grants to industry are so rare. However, goodwill in such matters as planning permission, building regulation, trading standards and trade with local schools could be quite important to Playwell Limited.

The **bank** has an important financial stake in the firm. This is likely to be **secured,** since banks rarely lend to small businesses without security, but this is far from being the limit of the bank's concern. It needs to **generate income** from interest payments and this depends on Playwell Limited's continuing success. It is likely that the bank manager is in regular contact with Alexander Simmonds and may receive regular management accounts. There is probably some input in the form of advice, therefore. There are also likely to be **loan covenants**, such as required profit percentages and limitations upon total borrowing, which will have direct influence upon the company's courses of action.

Playwell has two major business associates in its extended **value chain**: the materials supplier and the retailer.

The **materials supplier** is dealing in commodities, principally timber. Commodities offer little scope for adding value, and competition on price is usual. It is, therefore, perhaps unsurprising that the supplier has offered attractive credit terms. The supplier's overall aim is likely to be to achieve as much sales volume as possible in order to achieve the maximum **economies of scale**. Were Playwell Limited to expand its requirements significantly, it might expect to obtain even more favourable prices, but this scale of operations is probably a long way off. A more relevant consideration for Playwell Limited is that its business is founded largely on the **quality** of its products; the quality of its raw materials, and particularly its timber, must make an important contribution to that. The supplier thus has little scope for direct influence, but Alexander Simmonds is likely to be cautious about the effect of any new strategy upon this business relationship.

The **retailer** takes 40% of Playwell Limited's non-special needs UK business and is dependent on the company for a significant amount of its supplies of toys. We are not told the overall size of this business: it deals in other goods than toys and with 15 specialist retail outlets, it could be quite large and in a position to exert some influence over Playwell Limited's plans. In any event, it is a significant **business partner** and has interests in common with Playwell Limited. Alexander Simmonds is unlikely to follow any course of action that might hazard this mutually beneficial relationship.

The **special schools** that have been receiving Playwell Limited's toys at advantageous prices clearly have an interest in continuing to do so. However, there seems little advantage for the company in maintaining this relationship. The special schools loss-leader policy is clearly ripe for reconsideration and there is little the schools will be able to do about it. Similar considerations apply to existing overseas customers.

> Notice that when we reach the end of our list of stakeholders we stop. There are no complex arguments to summarise in this section, so there is no point in waffling. Get on to the next bit!

(b)

Tutor's hint. This is the most demanding part of this question since it requires the higher skills of analysis and argument. There is no point in starting to write your answer until you have a good idea of what you are going to recommend and why. Furthermore, before you reach that stage, you must analyse the given information carefully, identifying what is important and how the various considerations link together. A further concern is that the question requirements include 'the use of suitable analytical models'. The examiner's suggested solution is built around a sophisticated version of *Ansoff's* **product-market growth vector** model. The BCG matrix would be an alternative, as would the GE business screen and even a simple SWOT approach.

A good place to start is the table of financial information. Spend a few minutes working out some percentages and ratios on the face of the exam paper: there is no need to provide workings in your answer, just make sure your calculations are correct. In this question, the examiner has even provided some blank cells in the table that you can use for gross profit and GPP for the various parts of the business, and you can enter net profit and net profit percentage at the bottom.

A good area to focus on is trends over time. This can be done by calculating year-on-year percentage changes for salient quantities such as turnover, gross profit and overheads.

It is likely that these calculations will reveal a lot of relevant information and stimulate your thinking. You then have to integrate the relevant pieces of information from the narrative to end up with a coherent picture. A mind map approach may be useful here. Alternatively, you could try using the SWOT analysis structure. You could even combine the two.

When you come to write your report, remember that there will be marks for summarising and analysing the current situation. This forms the basis for your proposals for the future.

We omit the covering letter that would accompany a report in real life: you should do the same.

PLAYWELL LIMITED

BUSINESS STRATEGY REPORT

Playwell Limited's current situation

1 At the moment, Playwell Limited is trading profitably and enjoying moderate growth in its core business. However, it has undertaken entry into two separate new markets in search of significant growth and neither has proved entirely satisfactory.

1.1 **General UK sales** continue to grow at 8% each year and consistently achieve a gross profit percentage (GPP) of 65%. This must be regarded as a successful part of the Company's business.

1.2 Turnover in **special needs products** has been in decline, falling from £300k in 1995 to £150k in 1999. However, a GPP in excess of 50% has been achieved each year. This is less than for general toy sales but still very respectable. It must, however, be seen in the light of the large increase in **fixed costs** associated with the move into this market. 1995 special needs sales were exactly equal to the increase in fixed costs in that year. The part of that increase caused by the continuing expansion of general sales cannot have been very large.

1.3 **European sales** have been steady during the three years of operation in this market, turnover of £550k being achieved last year. GPP in this market is steady, but only 40%, and there was a further increase in fixed costs when this market was entered. However, this increase was not disproportionate: an extra £500k of sales was achieved and fixed costs rose by £250k. Once again, some of that increase was due to the 8% increase in general sales in the year, but even if the whole were charged to European sales, at 50% of the turnover increase, it would not be unreasonable. In the last year before the new ventures commenced, fixed costs were 43% of turnover.

1.4 It is fair to conclude that the new ventures, while far from disastrous, have not achieved the levels of overall growth hoped for.

What went wrong?

2 Both the special needs and European ventures encountered unexpected market conditions that resulted in low growth. We use *Ansoff's* **product/market growth vector** terminology to explain what went wrong.

2.1 Sales of special needs equipment were hampered by the failure of special needs teachers to recommend it to parents and by the limited disposable incomes in the target market. Playwell Limited was in fact not merely **diversifying** by entering a new market with a new product, it was **innovating** by trying to create a new market where none previously existed. This must be recognised as a high risk strategy.

2.2 Expansion into Europe constituted **market development**: the market was new but existing products were to be sold. This is a much lower risk strategy than diversification, but still not risk-free. In the event, Playwell Limited's venture was denied success by macroeconomic factors: recession in the target countries and the strength of sterling on the foreign exchange markets.

2.3 The factors that hampered the expansion strategies were not sudden unexpected developments or concealed underlying trends. **They were all quite predictable.** There appears to have been a **failure of planning** in both cases and in particular a failure to assess the market environment. An application of the **rational model** of strategic planning might have produced different results. Certainly, an appreciation of the conditions in the economic environment would have militated against entry into the European market, while some basic desk research into the special needs market might well have revealed its problems before the company was committed.

A plan for the future

3 The two ventures out of the mainstream business were undertaken in a search for growth, which is not an unreasonable goal, and one that may be assumed for the future. The company's **attitude to risk** is important: it appears to be risk-averse in theory, but not in practice. It is probably time to minimise the company's exposure to risk, and consolidate its position.

3.1 **Special needs equipment.** The company should gradually withdraw from the family special needs market in a measured fashion and with as little fuss as possible. If there is a worthwhile market in the special needs schools alone, this may be targeted, but it must pay its way. The loss leader strategy has failed. The fixed costs associated with this venture must be examined with a view to cost reduction. Where they consist of labour costs, redeployment may be necessary.

3.2 **European sales.** While hindsight enables one to say that the venture into Europe was ill-advised, withdrawal is not necessarily the correct move now. As mentioned above, the venture is inherently less risky than the special needs move and it has been more successful. Turnover in 1999 was £550k and there is huge growth potential in the European market. The misalignment of the business cycle between European countries and the UK could be an important factor for survival during some future UK recession. An appropriate strategy here would be **consolidation,** aiming for modest organic growth with minimal new investment.

3.3 **UK general toy sales.** The company's core business is UK toys: this is what it does best and where it makes its best returns. It should now focus on **market penetration** in this field. It is possible that there has been some distraction caused by the other ventures. The company should now largely return to its 'knitting', in *Peters and Waterman's* terminology, and pursue some of the other aspects they found in successful firms. **Closeness to customers, simplicity** and **productivity through people** would all seem to chime very well with Playwell Limited's historical approach.

3.4 There is probably scope for a close examination of **costs and productivity** after the recent ventures. This will be particularly important if the company is to continue selling into Europe.

Conclusion

4 Playwell Limited is in fairly good overall shape, despite the limited success of its recent strategic moves. It should now consolidate its position and build on its undoubted strengths.

Part (c)

Tutor's hint. It would be possible to produce a good answer this part of the question without mentioning Playwell Limited at all, since the requirement is essentially to describe the environmental analysis and internal audit stages of the rational model of strategic planning. However, you should **always** relate your answer to the setting!

Strategic information

The information necessary for any consideration of future strategy has two principle aspects: **internal** to the organisation and **external** to it. The external analysis may be broken down into **general environmental factors** and the **immediate market environment**.

Internal audit.

It is important to have an objective view of the organisation's **strengths and weaknesses**. In the context of exporting, there are a number of competences which a company must possess if it is to succeed.

- Almost certainly, it must be able to do business in the **language** of the foreign country concerned. This is essential if it wishes to export to France.
- There are **cultural differences** other than language, both nationally and at the level of **business practice**. These must be understood and allowed for since they will colour perceptions and expectations on both sides.
- There are complex legal and administrative **procedures** associated with shipping, credit, contract terms, customs procedures and payment. The documentation associated with exports requires particular expertise.

Environmental analysis.

The general environmental analysis may make use of the PEST acronym.

Political and legal factors include trade protection policy, business law in such areas as contracts and debt collection, permissible business forms and regulations pertaining to advertising.

Playwell Limited has suffered from two aspects of the **economic environment** in its target markets: the strength of sterling and the unsynchronised business cycle. Other economic factors include the levels of interest rates and the availability of credit; trends in economic growth and national income per head; and the outlook for inflation.

Analysis of the **social** aspect of the environment would, for Playwell Limited, focus on attitude to toys and play. In particular, it would be important to assess the overall place in society of toys of the type Playwell Limited specialises in, with their simplicity and high quality construction.

The market environment.

Knowledge of the general environment must be supplemented with details of the immediate market environment. For simple export of goods (as opposed to any kind of local manufacture) this will require consideration of the size and concentration of the market, available distribution channels, the scale and nature of competition, what selling points will be appropriate, how the product is to be promoted and whether there are any unusual commercial practices.

Part (d)

Tutor's hint. To answer this part well you must recognise and respond to the term '**emergent strategy**'. This is a fairly basic piece of textbook knowledge, so if you are unsure about it, go back to the BPP Study Manual!

There are two main parts to a satisfactory answer to this question. First, you must make clear that you know exactly what an emergent strategy is and how it differs from a planned one. A brief mention of other approaches may glean a mark or two. Second, you must consider the factors that might influence the strategic method used.

'**Factors**' are always difficult. Really, you need a mental checklist of things to run your mind over so that you can come up with some appropriate ones. Various bits of theory can be useful here.

- The components of the **value chain** are a useful basis for considering organisational and tactical matters.
- **Culture**, **organisational form**, **management style**, **environment** and **technology** are good keywords to remember for wider-ranging questions like this one.

Emergent strategy.

The **rational model** of planned or deliberate strategy can produce very effective results. It is, however, time consuming and demanding of resources. Its careful, considered processes alone make it questionable for dynamic environments. *Mintzberg* suggests that valid strategies can **emerge** without extensive planning, simply from responding to external stimuli. In this model, action comes first and is followed by thought, which refines, or **crafts**, the emerging strategy. This idea is similar to *Quinn's* description of **logical incrementalism**, in which strategy evolves by experiment, and to the concept of strategy as a **learning** process.

The appropriateness of any form of strategy-making will depend on a range of factors.

Environmental factors

Unstable or **dynamic** environments are less suited to a planned approach, unless the planning is particularly rapid, because a lengthy period of consideration may allow an opportunity to pass. A more **stable** environment, on the other hand, may well reward the strategist who plans with greater care. This is particularly true when the environment is **complex**, as is usually the case when exporting.

Technology is a particularly important example of an environmental variable. It can affect both market offerings and internal methods. Rapidly developing or complex technology is likely to favour emergent strategies, simply because **expertise** is likely to be in limited supply and confined to staff who are fairly junior but close to the market. Nevertheless, where there is a clear need for **transformational change**, this can only be achieved by the strategic apex and implies a deal of careful planning and control.

Internal factors

Size, **culture** and **management style** all have an influence on strategy making. Small businesses often start with a single good idea and exploit it in a flexible fashion. New ideas emerge easily in such an environment. The owners will be close to the daily operations of their business and likely to be willing to try things out. However, the management of a larger business must actively delegate and coach if the same creativity is to exist. If they hold all the threads in their own hands, it will be unlikely that strategy will emerge.

A planned approach may, however, be more appropriate. This will be the case if staff are unwilling or unable to take initiatives or if the costs associated with a change of course are high. In the first case, strategy simply will not emerge from below and must be driven from the top – though it might be incrementally rather than comprehensively planned. In the second case, careful planning is necessary to minimise risk.

49 LRP

Part (a)

> **Tutor's hint.** It is not unusual for case studies to commence by asking you to analyse and comment on the setting. There are marks available here simply for reading, understanding and summarising. A little thought will then bring you a pass mark in that part of the question.

REPORT

LRP FASTENERS

Introduction

The aim of this report is to discuss the strategic value of LRP as an independent entity.

Background

LRP manufactures a wide range of fasteners, ranging from basic nuts and bolts to more sophisticated devices. It became part of the Stillwell Slim group in 1990. Its turnover in 2000 was £53.5m and its profit was £6.05m. It has plants in Ireland, Taiwan and the UK and sells its products globally.

Strengths and weaknesses

Overall, LRP is a sound enterprise and seems properly managed. Its average net profit margin over the last three years has been 11%, while turnover has grown steadily at about 4%. Overdraft has increased in line with the growth in turnover.

The company has a record of sensible product innovation and maintains a review of technical developments.

There is an appropriate emphasis on quality within the company. However, the industry benchmark reports indicate a disturbing upward trend in both internal reject rate and customer returns. These may be linked to recent productivity gains in that output volume may be being achieved at the expense of quality. This is an important point, especially in the market for the more sophisticated fasteners.

There are opportunities for further improvements to productivity. The average age of the plant is rising as time passes and now stands at 10.2 years. While an average gives no detail, it does indicate that if advantage is being taken of recent technical improvements there must be counterbalancing examples of very old machinery. The UK plant is in particular need of investment.

The introduction of computer-based scheduling systems (such as MRP2) is another possible route to improved efficiency. The value of WIP is a little higher than the industry average, indicating scope for improvements in production control.

The level of WIP, while higher than desirable, is fairly constant. However, over the last two years, there has been a significant rise in stocks of finished goods. These are now one fifth higher than the industry average. This rise may be associated with the parallel rise in customer returns, but that possibility is not a proper explanation. Rejected goods should be sold to less demanding customers, reworked or scrapped. They should not accumulate as stock. If they are saleable, with or without rework, their existence should be taken into account in works ordering procedures. This may be further justification for an improved production control system. A review of the saleability of stocks might be an interesting exercise, also.

Opportunities and threats

The global market for fasteners is growing at about 4% annually and LRP should be well placed to at least obtain its share of that growth. However, its market share in basic fasteners has fallen from almost 10% to less than 8½%. The reasons for this are not clear, but two important possibilities are apparent from the data available. The first is the possible falling-off in quality mentioned earlier. The second is the lack of a manufacturing facility in North America, where growth is higher than elsewhere but sales have remained almost constant over the last three years.

It should also be noted that while turnover growth in the European market has been fairly low at 3% and 2.6% in the last two years, the Rest of the World market has grown strongly in the same period, at 8.8% and 6.7%.

It is possible therefore that LRP's manufacturing facilities are significantly mis-matched with its markets, since it has two plants within the EU, none in the NAFTA and only one in the remaining part of the global economy, in Taiwan. Consideration should be given to the possibility of manufacturing in North America. The long term future of the two EU plants should also be reviewed.

Sales of higher-value fasteners have been adversely affected by the increase in competition resulting from the entry of TIG Products into the market. TIG have a cost advantage in that their manufacturing takes place in eastern Europe. Their current success shows that their quality and service must be appropriate. They are in a favourable position to serve the European market, both geographically and in price terms. TIG must be seen as a significant threat to LRP, at least in Europe. However, their ability to compete globally must be constrained by the same factors that hamper LRP, particularly the cost and delay associated with international delivery.

Conclusion

LRP is in reasonably good commercial health, but quality and production planning seem to be areas in which improvements might be possible.

In the longer term, the location of the company's manufacturing facilities should be reviewed in the light of its pattern of trade.

Part (b)

> **Tutor's hint.** This part of the question is particularly useful because this organisational form is typical of most large companies. Many aspects of organisational management are drawn together in a consideration of the divisionalised conglomerate.

Chandler showed that the conglomerate form can provide a very large organisation with a suitable compromise between centralisation and decentralisation. Centralised control through functional organisation becomes unwieldy and inefficient as organisations grow geographically or in terms of products and markets. The other extreme, a loosely linked group of independently managed firms owned by a holding company, fails to achieve any advantage or synergy.

The divisionalised conglomerate is based on combining a high degree of autonomy at the operating division (SBU) level with value-adding input from the strategic apex. High divisional autonomy allows the organisation to operate effectively over a wide range of product-markets. Divisional managers can concentrate on their own operations and markets thus becoming more effective in them. Autonomy also promotes a high degree of motivation.

Mintzberg shows that the strategic apex. has a range of roles that contribute to the success of the organisation.

Management of the strategic portfolio. Portfolio analysis is as applicable to SBUs as it is to products. A conglomerate needs a suitable range of product-market operations. The corporate HQ must decide the overall shape of the organisation, buying and selling divisions to achieve a balanced portfolio.

Control of financial resources. Corporate HQ controls major investment in the SBUs. Its detailed knowledge of their operations and prospects enables it to invest more profitably than the most efficient external market. SBUs often have their liquid assets centralised under a corporate treasurer for more efficient short-term investment. The size and stability of the organisation as a whole enhance its creditworthiness and allow it to raise funds in the capital markets more cheaply than the individual SBUs could.

Performance control. Corporate HQ designs and operates a performance measurement system that supports the roles above. The system also permits assessment of the performance of SBU management. The only real method the HQ can use to deal with unsuccessful management is to replace it. The design of the control system must take account of potential manipulation and must not encourage dysfunctional decision making. Members of the corporate HQ supplement the reporting system by making regular **personal visits** to SBUs.

Support services. Some functions may be organised centrally and provided on a charge-out basis to SBUs. Apart from the services of the HQ itself, these typically include R&D, HR, PR and legal services.

Part (c)

> **Tutor's hint.** Ethical considerations are more prominent in the syllabus for Paper 3.5 than they were in its predecessor. This is emphasised by the fact that the pilot paper included an 8 mark question requirement on this topic.

Ethics is concerned with notions of right and wrong behaviour and is inevitably subject to dispute because of the wide range of cultural, legal, religious and professional influences. The question of price fixing is a common and practical problem for managers.

Johson and Scholes define an organisation's **ethical stance** as the extent to which it will exceed its minimum obligation to stakeholders. To some extent that minimum obligation is defined by law. However, law and ethics are not congruent; they may in fact be opposed to one another, as is often the case in totalitarian states.

The first comment to make on the CEO's proposal is that collusive price fixing is illegal in most western jurisdictions and is therefore something that responsible managers should not countenance. However, it is a fundamental of economic theory that **oligopolies** rarely compete on price. Industry prices are 'sticky' and even when a price war breaks out, it does not usually last long. It is possible, in fact, for a kind of **non-collusive** price fixing to take place, often when there is an accepted **price leader**. This is not illegal. Whether or not it is ethical is anther question.

The CEO's proposal would be more difficult to deal with if such behaviour were legal in the region in question. Global organisations such as LRP and Stillwell Slim are subject to conflicting pressures from stakeholders in different parts of the world. For example, the use of child labour in developing countries can be seen either as a way for those countries to exploit a form of natural economic advantage, thereby contributing to their economic development, or as a shameful neo-colonialist practice. The water is muddied when it becomes apparent that employers of child labour may be ignoring basic health and safety standards while opponents may merely be seeking to protect domestic employment from competition.

To some extent, the problem of differing national legal standards is being eroded by the modern tendency for **extra-territorial legislation**. The USA has been most prolific with this, particularly in its efforts to promote economic sanctions against Cuba. Generally, such legislation has been limited to major wrongdoing, such as war crimes. However, in 1997, the OECD countries and five others adopted a convention to prohibit the bribery of foreign public officials. This is now making its way into UK law.

While corruption might be seen as more serious wrongdoing than price fixing, it is clear that a trend exists. It would be risky for any international company to behave in a way that was illegal in any of the countries where it has a presence.

A further refinement of LRP's ethical problem would arise if the legal position were different from what was generally acceptable to the ethical notions of the local society. For example, the success of Mr Berlusconi in Italian politics, despite his many brushes with the laws relating to corruption, has been attributed to a belief among the Italian electorate that such behaviour is an unavoidable part of the way their society works.

A very simple test for behaviour is the principle known as the **golden rule**, which is often stated as deal with others as you would like them to deal with you. We are told that LRP has never been able to penetrate the regional market in question. If this has been the effect of trade association action that LRP has condemned as improper, it would clearly be cynical and ethically inappropriate to subscribe to the same behaviour when circumstances changed and it offered an advantage.

A final consideration is a practical one: the effect of bad publicity. Another simple ethical test for individuals is whether a particular course of action would be acceptable to their friends. For companies we might substitute 'stakeholders' for 'friends'. It may be that LRP's current and potential investors, customers, employees and business associates would have differing views on any given ethical question, but giving them due consideration would help to indicate a suitable solution to an ethical dilemma.

50 SCREENBOOKS

Part (a)

Screen Books began as a joint venture intended to harness the direct sales potential of the Internet. We are told that it was successful initially in that it grew in accordance with its business plan; its operating losses of £42,000 and £54,000 in 1996 and 1997 would fit this assessment, especially as turnover increased from £367,000 to £635,000 in these two years. We may assume both that the joint venture generated some synergistic effects and that the warehousing and distribution part of the business worked satisfactorily. **Fulfilment** was a common problem area for the Internet business model in the early days.

That being said, such a joint venture is not an obvious strategic choice for a publisher such as Jack Benfold Limited to take. In essence, it is an example of forward vertical integration, requiring skills in distribution and retailing. The alliance with John Rogers Books made the new venture possible. We gather that Mr Speight is prepared to be open minded in his strategic thinking, as indicated when he moved into the travel and cookery markets. From the point of view of John Rogers Books, the Screen Books venture fitted well with their existing business.

The sudden availability of huge amounts of capital in 1998 brought Screen Books into very different territory. There are two important issues here.

(a) **The band waggon effect of the Internet boom of the late 1990s.** There is no doubt that investing in the Internet became extremely fashionable. For many months, normal business considerations such as profitability, cash flow and prudent investment appraisal seemed no longer relevant. The boom rapidly became a classic bubble, with investors so anxious not to be left behind that they would pour money into any Internet-based venture.

Such profligacy on the part of providers of finance is contagious: managers began to think in more and more grandiose terms and less and less of fundamentals (like profitability and so on). In this atmosphere, the least plausible projects could flourish – for a time.

(b) **The screen-based device.** The new device was, in fact, quite a plausible idea and no more outrageous in technical or marketing terms than the Internet-connected refrigerators now in production, that are capable of organising their own re-stocking. However, it was a very risky venture.

It is actually quite difficult to classify the new product in terms of *Ansoff's* product-market growth vector matrix.

Penetration. It could be seen merely as a way of bringing more books to the existing market, though this is likely to be a minority view.

Product development. The strategy certainly contains an element of product development, particularly including the risk. 'Considerable technical development' was required, involving both in-house staff and research agencies. The investment in R&D was enormous, rising to a total that exceeded Screen Books' turnover in 1997. It is not possible to assess the inherent practicability of the idea, but it certainly represented a major step.

Market development. It is arguable that the Screen Books joint venture was merely a new way of reaching an existing market; that is, a new form of distribution rather than an example of market development. However, the LCD device would inevitably attract the attention of the particularly gadget-conscious market segment and sales potential might be well be slanted to this segment. It would certainly be appropriate to ensure that books and magazines dealing with computers and the Internet were well represented on Screen Books publications list.

Diversification. It is even possible to see the new device as an example of diversification, being both a new product and aimed at a new market.

This complexity of possible analyses reflects the complexity of the strategy itself. Such a strategy will inevitably make major demands on the top management of the company.

This brings us to **strategic implementation and control**. We are told that expenditure on both marketing and research has been higher than forecast and, indeed, the table of summary data gives the impression of lack of control over expenditure.

In the case of **marketing,** it is fair to comment that turnover has roughly doubled each year and this must inevitably require an increased marketing budget. Indeed, marketing spending *as a proportion of turnover* has fallen in the last three years. However, it still seems rather high. It would be interesting to establish the proportion of the marketing expenditure that was spent on salaries: the marketing headcount has also doubled each year, which would seem rather excessive.

Research and development expenditure seems to have been under greater control. Indeed, it is partly by comparison with the R&D expense that the growth in marketing expenditure seems so high. Nevertheless, spending on R&D has been very high in absolute terms. It is not possible to comment in detail on the R&D effort, but it is somewhat disturbing to hear of 'fundamental technical limitations' after more than £1.5 million has been spent over three years.

The disturbing feature of the Screen Books strategy is its close correspondence with a classic pattern of business failure: that is, escalating commitment to a single, major high-technology project that ultimately proves unworkable. The profligacy of the Internet bubble, mentioned above, appears to have undermined prudence and financial control to the extent that the continued existence of Screen Books appears to depend on the willingness of lenders to finance it. The ability of the basic Internet sales operation to support the current burden of loan finance must be questioned. Also, if the new product fails to materialise and it becomes necessary to write off much of the past development expenditure, lenders may take the first opportunity to salvage what they can by closing the business down.

In conclusion, we may say that Screen Books' strategy appears to suffer from failings in both intent and execution. It is questionable whether the plan for the new product was ever really feasible and it seems likely that its implementation lacked direction and control.

Part (b)

1 **SWOT Analysis**

Strengths

The **Internet retailing operation** is fundamentally successful and has the crucial fulfilment capacity. While trading at a loss, the company has actually held its losses to not much more than the total of the apparently inflated spending on marketing and R&D. This implies that the basic retailing business is sound.

Extensive experience of both publishing and book retailing is available.

The screen-based device. It is debatable whether this is, in fact, a strength, but if any technical progress has been made it represents a knowledge asset that may have value, if only on disposal.

There would seem to be significant **cash reserves**. The flotation must have raised more than £12 million and cumulative operating losses amount to less than £3 million.

Weaknesses

The **financial position** is dubious. There are a number of elements to this.

- The **share price has collapsed**. This may be due partly to market panic, but also reflects the justified doubt about the viability of the new product. This is bound to bring pressure from shareholders and analysts.
- Ability to generate **positive cashflows** is somewhat suspect. While the basic retailing operation is assessed above as probably healthy, it is doubtful that it could generate enough funds to service the existing debt and make a reasonable profit. If it were to be expanded, this would require further marketing expenditure.
- Contracts have been let with external R&D agencies. These may require continuing payments.

The dot com bubble has burst. It will be very difficult for Screen Books to raise capital or even obtain a sympathetic hearing from existing providers. Internet retailing is no longer a fashion statement and has become little more than an alternative to catalogue shopping.

Opportunities

It is difficult to identify opportunities without further information, other than to say that Internet shopping is now accepted as routine by many customers.

Threats

The *Palm Pilot* type of personal organiser is the subject of continuing development and may make the new product unviable, even supposing it can be brought to market.

The current global economic slowdown would prejudice the launch of the new product.

2 **Comment**

Screen Books is subject to major uncertainty over its new screen-based product. If it is ultimately feasible to bring this to market, the company's strategic position will be very different from the one it would find itself in if it proves impracticable. The first priority therefore, is an authoritative assessment of the project. This should be carried out externally to ensure objectivity.

If the project is judged to be viable, the next thing to be assessed is whether or not it will be necessary to raise more finance. If it is, financial market conditions may mean that it becomes necessary to make an approach to another company in the same field with a view to some form of alliance or even outright sale of the project.

If it is felt that it is possible to bring the product to market with existing resources, it will be necessary to exert stringent control over progress.

Should the new product development be shown to be a dead end, Screen Books must avoid escalating commitment. It must cut its losses as fast as possible, restricting operations to Internet retailing. This will improve its cash flow position, but it is likely to reveal that the company is under-trading to a dangerous extent. It would be necessary to expand profitable turnover significantly in order to service existing debt and satisfy shareholders.

Internet trading may not hold the potential to achieve this. The principals in the joint venture must also consider using their available cash resources to expand their more traditional operations. The acquisition of more high street retail outlets is one possibility. There are legal and taxation implications here, relating to the form of the group and the three businesses, that will require detailed attention.

Any retail expansion will require significant promotional expenditure.

Part (c)

A research and development project such as Screen Books' must be carefully managed if it is to have the best chance of success. Poor or non-existent planning is a recipe for disaster. In particular, **objectives** must be clearly defined and time and cost constraints established. Project management teams often fail to exercise control under changing circumstances. A special problem exists with IT projects: the technical ability of IT staff is no guarantee of management skill.

When an organisation is highly dependent on the success of a single large project, it is particularly important that effective strategic control is exercised. In particular, regular performance reviews against planned targets should be held.

All projects are likely to be subject to difficulties that must be resolved.

(a) **Teambuilding.** The work may carried out by a newly assembled team who must immediately be able to communicate effectively with each other. Arrangements must be made to manage the probable need to cut across functional boundaries within the organisation.

(b) **Unexpected problems** There should be mechanisms within the project to enable these problems to be resolved during the time span of the project without detriment to the objective, the cost or the time span.

(c) **Specialists**. Contributions made by specialists are of differing importance at each stage, but must be carefully managed.

(d) **Unproven technology**. Estimating the project duration can be difficult when it involves new technology or existing technology at its limits. Screen Books' project almost certainly suffered from this.

(e) **Over-optimism.** Costs are often underestimated by optimistic designers, particularly with new technology. Screen Books may well have suffered from this problem.

A development project often arises out of a perceived problem or opportunity. Screen Books' research arose because of the opportunities presented by the Internet and the availability of finance. Under these circumstances it is important that the management *---- process should begin immediately. The problem should be analysed to establish its **precise nature** and to outline possible solutions. When it is determined that technological development is required, the project **objectives** and **success criteria** should be clearly specified and possible routes to achieving them explored.

It should be possible to break the forecast activity down into **stages**. This eases both the assessment of the required resources and the establishment of intermediate objectives. Subsequent control is greatly enhanced if there is clear understanding of what is to be done, by whom and when. A variety of management techniques may then be used to control projects, including Gantt charts and network analysis. Network planning facilitates management by exception by identifying, from the outset, those critical activities that might delay others.

The process of control should include regular **meetings** to review overall progress and undertake financial and quality audit. Review will be undertaken at more than one level of management, with those in immediate control of developments meeting perhaps once a week; a higher level review might take place each month and a strategic review perhaps quarterly.

The final stage of control is **post-audit**, which asks two questions.

- Did the project meet its objectives?
- Was the management of the project successful?

Screen Books has been concerned with a single major project. It is possible to make recommendations for organisations that are concerned with broader aspects of innovation.

R&D should support the organisation's chosen strategy. To take a simple example, if a strategy of differentiation has been adopted, it would be inappropriate to expend effort on researching ways of minimising costs.

Problems of authority relationships and integration arise with the management of R&D. The function will have to liase closely with marketing and with production, as well as with senior management responsible for corporate planning: its role is both strategic and technical.

Pure research or even applied research may not have an obvious pay off in the short term. Evaluation could be based on successful application of new ideas, such as patents obtained and the commercial viability of new products.

Research staff are usually highly qualified and profession-orientated, with consequences for the style of supervision and level of remuneration offered to them.

Encouraging innovation means trial and error, flexibility, tolerance of mistakes in the interests of experimentation, high incentives etc. If this is merely a subculture in an essentially bureaucratic organisation, it will not only be difficult to sustain, but will become a source of immense 'political' conflict. The R&D department may have an 'academic' or university atmosphere, as opposed to a commercial one.

Intrapreneurship is entrepreneurship carried on within the organisation at a level below the strategic apex. The encouragement of intrapreneurship is an important way of promoting innovation. Such encouragement has many aspects.

(a) Encouragement for individuals to achieve results in their own way without the need for constant supervision

(b) A culture of risk-taking and tolerance of mistakes

(c) A flexible approach to organisation that facilitates the formation of project teams

(d) Willingness and ability to devote resources to trying out new ideas

(e) Incentives and rewards policy that support intrapreneurial activity

Strategic Business Planning and Development

BPP Mock Exam 1: December 2001

Question Paper		
Time allowed		**3 hours**
This paper is divided into two sections		
Section A	This question is compulsory and MUST be attempted	
Section B	TWO questions ONLY to be answered	

Disclaimer of liability

Please note that we have based our predictions of the content of the December 2001 exam on our long experience of the ACCA exams. We do not claim to have any endorsement of the predictions from either the examiner or the ACCA and we do not guarantee that either the specific questions, or the general areas, that are forecast will necessarily be included in the exams, in part or in whole.

We do not accept any liability or responsibility to any person who takes, or does not take, any action based (either in whole or in part and either directly or indirectly) upon any statement or omission made in this book. We encourage students to study all topics in the ACCA syllabus and the mock exam in this book is intended as an aid to revision only.

paper 3.5

DO NOT OPEN THIS PAPER UNTIL YOU ARE READY TO START

UNDER EXAMINATION CONDITIONS

Section A – THIS question is compulsory and MUST be attempted

1 Dr John Clarkson is currently Managing Director of BlueSky Analysis Ltd, a research company which obtains date gathered from satellite observations, analyses this data and then sells the information to client organisations. During the 1980s Clarkson had been employed by the United Kingdom's Ministry of Defence, to interpret military data obtained from satellite surveillance. With the end of the Cold War and the change in political regimes in the early 1990s Clarkson believed that the demand for this military intelligence would decline and he accordingly set up BlueSky Analysis Ltd to utilise the technology which he understood and to adapt it for peaceful applications. Together with four other scientists he formed the company in 1992. These five scientists were the only shareholders. Most of the work was then focused on obtaining new customers, and as the technology had, until then, been primarily used for highly confidential military information gathering there were few other potential competitors. It was now possible to buy from both military and civil satellite owners data obtained from a variety of sources. This data could be usefully interpreted and could provide valuable information on a wide range of topics including climate change, crop forecasts, soil conditions and mineral deposits. The potential customers for such information were mainly governmental agencies, operating both nationally and intentionally, including organisations such as the United Nations Food and Agricultural Organisation. Many mining and oil exploration companies also found the information invaluable in helping to select geographical locations for exploration and development.

The initial growth was rapid. The company had to employ more scientists and within two years the company had grown to number about 45 employees including 15 clerical staff. It was an attractive company for the scientists to work for. There was little management structure. Each analyst worked on an individual client's project, specialising on either a geographical area or on a specific industry such as mining, helping to identify the location of mineral deposits. The analysts could concentrate solely on scientific work and were not diverted into administrative activities involving long meetings and planning programmes. Staff turnover was very low. All the scientists required was a project to work on and secretarial support to prepare reports for clients. Otherwise they usually worked alone. Clarkson was the Managing Director, but all five shareholders took in turn to carry out the necessary but, in their opinion, mundane administrative tasks required in any company – personnel, purchasing, finance and marketing activities. They did employ some junior staff or used outside agencies to carry out the routine tasks such as payroll and book-keeping. Even recruitment was contracted out to an agency. These five senior managers were also totally responsible for the critical task of obtaining contracts. However they, like most of the scientists, were at their happiest when they were focusing on the analytical work for clients and not being managers.

Unfortunately, this informal style and structure did not run smoothly. Although the company provided a good social and challenging work environment, it was inevitable that this analyst-led approach should lack direction and that errors in administration would create problems with clients. There was inadequate integration and teamwork within the company, with most of the scientists working independently on their own projects. The five senior scientists began to spend much of their time 'fire-fighting' – correcting mistakes which should never had occurred. Fortunately the company was still a leader in this small specialist field and so did not lose much business to merging competitors.

However by late 1997 it was apparent that this loose management structure was inhibiting the growth of the company. The market for data collection and analysis was becoming more global and competitors wee eroding BlueSky's market position. Its projects were frequently going over budget and many were taking too long to complete. A lack of cohesion and cooperation between the analysts with the company meant that when such delays occurred other staff members could not help to sort out the problems. Furthermore, as the senior managers acted as intermediaries between the client and the scientist responsible for their particular research contract, any negotiations for changes in requirements tended to be lengthy and confusing. The problem was that a move towards greater discipline and structure, necessary for keeping work on target and profitable, was likely to alienate the analysts who enjoyed their independence.

In early 1998 the senior management, now facing declining orders, decided that they could not continue in such an undisciplined manner. They were approached by a much larger company from the USA, United Data Systems (UDS), whose main business was as a software company, providing information systems for major clients throughout the world. These contracts were with both public and private sector clients ranging from automobile manufacturers to governmental tax agencies. UDS was accustomed to dealing with multi-million pound contracts, serviced by specialist teams, and accordingly had the infrastructure and systems to suit such a business. The company employed in excess of 3,000 employees world-wide, with almost half being in support but non-operational roles, compared with a total of 90 employees at BlueSky in 1998. Recognising their lack if interest in administration, Clarkson and his four fellow shareholders agreed to the acquisition by UDS, but still maintained a significant share of the equity. Although technically UDS now owned BlueSky it was not seeking to absorb it. The larger company, seeking to diversify into more innovative areas, saw BlueSky as providing the expertise and access into a rapidly expanding and lucrative market. They did not wish to destroy the research-centred culture of BlueSky because the company's success depended upon the scientists' continued good will and commitment. They agreed to allow the smaller company to continue operating as a subsidiary company in an innovative manner – no large company bureaucracy being imposed upon the scientists. However UDS would now require that all new contracts be investigated by themselves for financial attractiveness. A charge was levied from the centre for this service. This meant that all contracts, regardless of size, were now sent to the headquarters in the USA. This was intended to ensure that BlueSky did not accept contracts where they could not complete on time or which were not profitable.

However this fusion of cultures did generate unforeseen problems. BlueSky had been accustomed to managing smaller contracts with lower margins but now UDS was seeking to impose financial criteria on them which were more suitable for a larger company with a bigger infrastructure to support UDS also had a more formalised system of contract vetting which took time to complete. There was dissatisfaction in both BlueSky and UDS as BlueSky's scientists were seeing contracts being lost and the parent company was not seeing the growth it had expected when it acquired the subsidiary. In addition some of BlueSky's long-standing clients were becoming increasingly worried by the further reduction in quality and service they were receiving. Clarkson was summoned to the USA headquarters to discuss the future of BlueSky. He feared that the proposed solution would be to integrate BlueSky more closely into UDS, by making it an operating division, with both strategy and operations being dependent upon UDS's central control, rather than by allowing it the greater freedom it currently had as a subsidiary company.

Details of the performance and financial position of BlueSky Analysis Ltd can be found in Table 1 below.

Table 1 Financial Data

	1997 (last full year as an independent company)	1999 (first full year as a subsidiary of UDS)
	£	£
Sales Revenue	4,400	4,350
Cost of Sales	3,400	3,250
Expenses	300	480
of which - marketing	100	80
- administration	200	400
Operating profit	700	620
Value of contracts in progress or on order book (31 December)	1,300	750
Employees	85	93
Fixed assets	750	600
Average value of contracts	45	90
Percentage of contracts on cost or time	37	45

Required

(a) **Identify and explain the problems which are now being faced by BlueSky Analysis Ltd, operating as a subsidiary company of UDS.** (15 marks)

(b) **If BlueSky is integrated fully into UDS it is probably that there will be a clash of cultures. Using models of your choice to support your arguments:**

(i) **Comment on the current differences in culture, explaining the main factors which cause these differences;** (10 marks)

(ii) **Explain the ways in which the management at UDS might minimise the conflict which may arise from the cultural differences.** (10 marks)

(c) **Clarkson, fearing an imposed solution by UDS which would be unwelcome to both employees and clients of the BlueSky subsidiary, has decided to put forward his own solutions.**

Provide a brief report for Clarkson which he will present to the senior management of UDS, suggesting how the current situation might be improved. (15 marks)

(d) **With reference to BlueSky identify and explain the main factors that can cause a project to fail to meet its original objectives.** (10 marks)

(60 marks)

2 Matthew Sanders is the Operations Director of Chestlands Insurance Ltd. Chestlands is a medium-sized company, operating in a specific niche within the financial services sector. It has found a reasonably profitable segment focusing on the lower income end of the personal insurance market. Its customers are generally unskilled workers, single parent families or older people with poor pensions. The

common factor is that they all have little discretionary income. Most other financial companies see this segment as being unattractive and unlikely to yield high profits and as a result Chestlands have had few competitors. By concentrating on this one segment it can obtain economies of scale, particularly in collection and administration. Furthermore it does not need to provide a wide portfolio of products as most other financial companies are obliged to.

Most of the business is for cheap insurance policies to cover future contingencies – the cost of essential household repairs, furniture and even funerals. These clients generally have insufficient money to pay for these types of bill out of current income and therefore they need to save for them. Unfortunately some of them do not have bank accounts and so savings have to be collected in a more direct manner. Others, with bank accounts, rarely use them for saving, and it is not unknown for these accounts to be mismanaged. The company uses agents who make weekly calls at the clients' homes to collect their payment. These agents also are responsible for seeking new business by following up enquiries from potential customers who have heard of Chestlands through advertising in the local newspapers or from word-of-mouth recommendations from other customers. Because the company inevitably works on low margins the payment to these agents is low and a significant proportion of its is commission based. Consequently this 'salesforce' is mainly unskilled and turnover is high.

Recently Sanders has received an increasing number of complaints from his customers and new business has been declining. Existing customer have not renewed policies and there have been fewer new customers. The complaints have centered around the sales staff, involving incomplete and unfinished documentation, missed appointments, financial irregularities and an aggressive attitude towards selling new policies. Sanders is aware that his company is only profitable because it has volume sales in a focused market. Any loss of business will damage his company's reputation and profits. He has come to the conclusion that quality is the key to recovery and so he has decided to implement a system of checking the paper work so as to ensure a more acceptable level of delivery. He feels confident that this will solve the problem.

Required

(a) **Discuss whether Sanders' proposed solution will correct the problems currently being experienced by Chestlands.** (10 marks)

(b) **It has been suggested to Sanders that a system of Total Quality Management should be introduced into Chestlands.**

Describe the actions which must be undertaken within the organisation to ensure that this quality initiative is successfully implemented. (10 marks)

(20 marks)

3 Simon Darby is the Managing Director of a small company which specialises in producing high quality prints of original paintings. When framed these prints are most attractive and have become very popular as decoration in fashionable hotels and modern business premises. The company pays royalties to the owners of the original paintings, usually to a consortium of the museums and the owners of country houses where the original paintings are kept. The company has enjoyed five successful years since Darby started the company. He advertised originally in art magazines and by direct mail, but his reputation soon spread and with his products

becoming very fashionable he now relies almost entirely on customers contacting him. This demand has enabled him to charge premium prices as he has no distribution network to maintain. He employs 10 workers, equally split between printing, packaging and dispatch. His annual turnover is approximately £575,000. The largest single expense is the payment of royalties - £125,000. This is linked directly to the volume of sales achieved.

He has now been offered the opportunity to pay an annual lump sum royalty payment for rights to make prints of the paintings, regardless of the numbers produced. Given his current market size this would be relatively expensive. However he has substantial printing capacity and could easily double his output without any further investment or additional labour. Unfortunately, his current market, although expending, could not absorb that increase in supply. He has decided to look at marketing overseas and he has identified three key markets – Germany, Japan and the United States – which he intends to export to.

Required

(a) **Identify and explain the problems which Darby might face in exporting to the three proposed markets.** (10 marks)

(b) **It is unlikely that Darby's company will be able to use a standardised marketing approach.**

Discuss the changes that may need to be made to the marketing mix if the proposed overseas marketing approach is to be successful. (10 marks)

(20 marks)

4

The JayBee organisation provides services in relation to corporate communications technology and has been growing very rapidly in the last two years owing to both an increased market for such services and an increasing share of the market.

The increase in new customers and the volume of business through existing customers has placed severe strains on the sales accounting operations within JayBee. The use of temporary contract accounting staff and excessive overtime worked by current staff, have been used as ways of coping, but a more permanent solution based on the recruitment of additional staff has been agreed by senior management. Management are now anxious that the recruitment is carried out as soon as possible.

John Lee is the recently appointed assistant financial controller at JayBee and his job includes responsibility for the sales accounting department. The department is currently managed by a sales administrator with the assistance of three senior and four junior clerical assistants. It is expected that at least four new appointments will need to be made if overtime and contract staff are to be eliminated.

John Lee has been given the task of organising the recruitment and selection of the new staff. John has examined the company's staff file but has failed to find any job descriptions for the existing department staff, or in fact for many positions within JayBee. John believes that this is probably due to the time pressure resulting from the rapid expansion of all JayBee's operations. John's immediate line manager, the JayBee financial controller does not see this as a problem and argues that 'if we recruit four good people we can sort out exactly who does what when they are in post - the essence is speed. Contract staff and overtime are proving far too expensive and we are still not getting the levels of quality work that we would with an expanded team.'

Required

(a) **In the context of the comments of the financial controller, examine the purpose and role of a job analysis and job description exercise on the sales accounting department prior to recruitment and selection.** (10 marks)

(b) **Draw up a checklist for John Lee of the key stages which must be successfully carried out to ensure an effective recruitment and selection process for the four new posts.** (10 marks)

(20 marks)

ANSWERS TO MOCK EXAM 1

DO NOT TURN THIS PAGE UNTIL YOU HAVE COMPLETED THE TEST PAPER

WARNING! APPLYING THE MARKING SCHEME

If you decide to mark your paper using the marking scheme, you should bear in mind the following points.

1 The BPP solutions are not definitive: you will see that we have applied the marking scheme to our solutions to how good answers should gain marks, but there may be more than one way to answer the question. You must try to judge fairly whether different points made in your answers are correct and relevant and therefore worth marks according to the ACCA marking scheme.

2 If you have a friend or colleague who is studying or has studied this paper, you might ask him or her to mark your paper for you, thus gaining a more objective assessment. Remember you and your friend are not trained or objective markers, so try to avoid complacency or pessimism if you appear to have done very well or very badly.

3 You should be aware that BPP's answers are longer than you would be expected to write. Sometimes, therefore, you would gain the same number of marks for making the basic point as we have shown as being available for a slightly more detailed or extensive solution.

It is most important that you analyse your solutions in detail and that you attempt to be as objective as possible.

Professional Examination - Paper 3.5 **Marking Scheme**

Strategic Business Planning and Development

This marking scheme is used only as a guide to markers in the context of the suggested answer. Scope is given to markers to award marks for alternative approaches to a question, including relevant comment, and where well-reasoned conclusions are provided. This is particularly so in case scenario questions where there may be more than one acceptable solution.

Unless otherwise stated, it is expected that candidates will set their answers within the context set by the question case scenario.

A PLAN OF ATTACK

It is a good idea to think about the nature of any examination before the day you sit it. You must be sure you know what the Examiner wants from you in terms of number of answers and which questions are compulsory and so on. Paper 3.5 is quite simple in this respect. You **must do** question 1 and you must answer two questions from Section B.

Note that Section A is crucial. You are highly unlikely to pass on the strength of your answer to Question 1 alone, but you are highly likely to fail if you do not make a creditable attempt at it.

You must have clear view of your overall preference about the order in which you will attempt questions before you enter the exam room. This is something you must do for yourself. Many people will advise that because Question 1 is so important you should definitely answer it first. Other people find that answering a shorter question first builds their confidence, especially if it is on a topic they are confident about. Only you can decide.

However, we would advise you that it would be very risky to leave question 1 to the end. This is a recipe for running out of time. While there are certain to be two or, more probably three, separate requirements, you cannot deal with them in isolation from each other; you must make sure you do not end up repeating yourself by using the same ideas too early, for example. So you must allow sufficient time to complete **all** the requirements. If you leave question 1 to the end, you may not manage to do this.

You do not have a lot of choice in this examination. The overall requirements and the likely nature of the questions mean that you will be examined on much of a very wide syllabus. Do not despair if you find you are probing the boundaries of your knowledge. Most of your contemporaries will be in the same boat. Make sure you cover the essentials, use common sense and experience as much as possible, relate your answers to the settings and **do not** ramble or dump theory.

The aim is not to cover pages with ink. Write concisely. This will release time for planning and checking. You **must** allow time to think.

A very important thing to remember in this exam is that there is bound to be more than one way of answering most of the questions: uniquely correct answers do not exist in a subject like this. If you can analyse data sensibly, apply theory appropriately and reach reasonable conclusions **you will pass.**

1

Part (a)

> **Tutor's hint**. This part of the question places a premium on your ability to analyse the given data - there is little scope for the introduction of theory. Questions like this are easier to tackle if you have experience of the way businesses are run. Unfortunately, few students have much experience of that type. It is important that you both cultivate an awareness of what is happening in your own organisation and supplement that awareness by reading the business pages of your newspaper and other, more specialised publications, such as *The Economist*.

BlueSky and UDS are two very different companies. The only things they have in common are project based activity and high technology and even here there are important differences: UDS deals in IT exclusively while BlueSky provide a wide range of environmental information from satellite imagery; BlueSky's projects are much smaller than those of UDS. Add to these differences the more obvious factors of company size, nationality and managerial approach and it becomes clear that the two companies are extremely ill-matched.

This poor match is evident in the very different way the two companies have been accustomed to do their business. To some extent the difference is cultural, but it also appears in basic management practice, particularly where marketing is concerned. The five senior scientists have been essentially dilettante in their approach to their market and to administration. Their business succeeded initially because they were exploiting a new product. The emergence of better-run competitors revealed the company's management inadequacies

BlueSky finds itself in a managerial straitjacket that has done little about its fundamental problems. All that was needed was an injection of senior management competence in order to address two main problem areas:

- Poor project control resulting in missed deadlines and cost overruns
- Lack of prompt attention to changes in client requirements

Both problems could have been tackled by the appointment of scientifically competent but market oriented project managers. In fact, an extra layer of management has been imposed with the result that a much higher percentage of contracts now overrun on cost or time.

The new procedure of contract vetting by UDS appears to have reduced the informal flexibility that was one of BlueSky's strengths. The average value of contracts has doubled, as has administrative expense, perhaps indicating an emphasis on larger customers with more formal procedures. This would be the influence of UDS at work, accustomed as they are to thinking in terms of multi-million pound IT contracts. It is probably an inappropriate approach for BlueSky.

Turnover has fallen slightly and appears likely to fall further, judging from the state of the work-in-progress and order book. This may be partly the result of a market perception of falling ability to give a satisfactory service. There has also been a reduction in marketing expenditure, which has perhaps contributed to the falling order book.

BlueSky is now in an unenviable position. Its order book is shrinking; competition is mounting; its reputation is in decline; and its new business model is at odds with its culture.

Part (b)

(i) As outlined above, BlueSky and UDS are very different organisations. BlueSky is a pleasant place for scientists to work, offering great independence and a minimal burden of administration. In terms of *Harrison's* classification of organisations it is closest to the **existential** type, which exists for the benefit of its members rather than its members serving the ends of the organisation. Such an organisation depends on the talent of the principal members; management is largely dependent on their continuing consent to being managed. Staff whose roles are purely managerial or administrative are likely to have lower status than those whose work forms the core of the organisation's activities. The culture in this type of organisation is likely to support professionalism, individualism and a very light hand on the managerial reins.

BlueSky is also identifiable in *Mintzberg's* typology as a **professional bureaucracy.** It has an operating core of highly trained professionals who require no real supervision: indeed they would be highly likely to reject attempts to control their work. Power is based on expertise and the work processes are too complex for supervision by any form of technostructure.

There is a great contrast with UDS, which is a large organisation run in a rational and systematic fashion. We are not told very much about UDS, but we may deduce that it displays at least some of the characteristics of Mintzberg's **machine bureaucracy**, with importance attached to formal control systems, documentation and standardisation. No doubt there is also a degree of the flexibility required to manage large projects, so we may see UDS as exhibiting a combination of the characteristics of the machine bureaucracy and the **adhocracy**, or in Harrison's terms, of the **role culture** and the **task culture**.

Thus, there is no head on clash between the cultures of the two companies, but we may expect there to be frequent instances of mismatch. UDS is more likely top call for routine reports, for instance, and to have set administrative procedures.

These cultural differences arise largely from the **scale of operations**. It will have been possible for co-ordination of effort in BlueSky to have existed largely on a basis of **mutual adjustment**. UDS, however, is far too large for such a system, and even though the company is used to team-working methods, overall financial control and the need to deliver on time and to specification will have made some degree of central control inevitable. This will have knock-on effects. Some proportion of the technical staff working in each company would be unhappy with the prevailing ethos in the other: there will be BlueSky scientists who resent any control at all, just as there will be UDS managers who are disappointed in BlueSky's rather chaotic arrangements. Management style will be rather different, being more formal and probably rather better in UDS, more tentative, informal and amateurish in BlueSky.

The other main influence on culture is likely to be **nationality**. We are not specifically told that BlueSky is a UK company, but it appears clear that it is. UDS, on the other hand, is stated to be a US company. Without descending into stereotypes, we may anticipate some differences of approach and attitude as a result.

(ii) The integration of BlueSky into UDS implies a significant change management problem. Minimising the clash of cultures will be part of this process. There are a number of models that might be applied, at least in part, to such a process of change.

The **Gemini 4Rs** framework for planned strategic change aims to cover all the important components of the organisation's identity. Each of the four dimensions of the process has three components.

Reframing involves fundamental questions about what the organisation is and what it is for. This is very relevant to BlueSky's situation.

- **Achieve mobilisation**: create the will and desire to change.
- **Create the vision** of where the organisation is going.

- **Build a measurement system** that will set targets and measure progress.

Restructuring is about the organisation's structure, but is also likely to involve cultural changes.

Revitalising is the process of securing a good fit with the environment and so is less relevant to the cultural aspect of BlueSky's problem

Renewal ensures that the people in the organisation support the change process and acquire the necessary skills to contribute to it. The components here may be of value to BlueSky.

- **Create a reward system** in order to motivate.
- **Build individual learning.**
- **Develop the organisation** and its adaptive capability.

The change process

Lewin/Schein's three stage approach to changing human behaviour is relevant hare. It may be depicted thus.

UNFREEZE existing behaviour	⟶	Attitudinal/ behavioural change	⟶	REFREEZE new behaviour

Unfreeze is the most difficult stage of the process, concerned mainly with 'selling' the change, with giving individuals or groups a **motive** for changing their attitudes, values, behaviour, systems or structures.

If the need for change is immediate, clear and necessary for the survival of the individual or group, the unfreeze stage will be greatly accelerated. It is likely that the scientific staff at BlueSky will be unsympathetic to the notion of change, however.

Unfreezing processes need four things.

(a) **A trigger.** A crisis is an effective trigger, so BlueSky is part-way there.

(b) Someone to **challenge** the existing behaviour pattern. This could be the present MD.

(c) The involvement of **outsiders.** UDS can act here.

(d) Alterations to the **power structure**. To some extent this has started, in the form of the UDS control of contracts.

Change is mainly concerned with identifying what the new, desirable behaviour should be, communicating it and encouraging individuals and groups to adopt it. The new ideas must be shown to work.

Refreeze is the final stage, implying consolidation or reinforcement of the new behaviour. Positive reinforcement (praise, reward) or negative reinforcement (sanctions applied to those who deviate from the new behaviour) may be used.

Peter Honey suggests that each of the sources of resistance to change identified below can be dealt with in a different way.

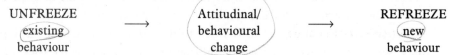

Cause	How to deal with it
Parochial self-interest	**Negotiation** (eg offer incentives to those resisting on grounds of self-interest).
Misunderstanding	This is best dealt with by **educating and reassuring** people. Trust has to be earned.

Cause	How to deal with it
Different viewpoints of the situation	Change can be promoted through participation and by **involving potential resisters.**
Low tolerance of change	Force the change through and then **support** the new behaviours it requires. People may have to be coerced (by carrot and stick methods) to adopt the new methods.

When dealing with resistance to change, managers should consider three aspects of the change.

- Pace
- Manner
- Scope

Pace of change

The more gradual the change, the **more time** is available for questions to be asked, reassurances to be given and retraining (where necessary) embarked upon.

Presenting the individual concerned with a ***fait accompli*** may short-circuit resistance at the planning and immediate implementation stages. However, it may cause problems later.

The manner of change

The **manner** in which the changes at BlueSky are introduced will be important for their success. Talking through areas of conflict may lead to useful insights and the adapting of the programme of change to advantage. The change will have to be sold, particularly to the scientific staff. **Information** should be sensible, clear, consistent and realistic.

Scope of change

The **scope of change** should also be carefully reviewed. Total transformation would be more difficult than moderate innovation. It may be possible to minimise the impact of the change of BlueSky's status.

Part (c)

To: UDS Vice-President for Operations
From: J Clarkson, Managing Director, BlueSky Analysis Limited
Date: 6 June 200X

Subject: **BlueSky Analysis Limited**

Introduction

Since becoming a subsidiary of UDS, BlueSky Analysis Limited (BSL) has not developed as well as we hoped it would. While turnover has remained more or less constant, operating profit has fallen significantly, largely because of the doubling of administrative expense. The rate of generation of new business has fallen markedly, with a significant deterioration in the value of our order book.

Diagnosis

The intention when BSL and UDS became linked was that BSL should retain its innovative and flexible technical approach while having grafted on to it some of UDS's expertise in the acceptance and management of contracts. Unfortunately, the necessary balance has not been struck. UDS contract vetting has proved administratively expensive and tended to reject small but potentially profitable contracts. At the same time, the individualistic approach of BSL's staff has hampered the proper management of the larger projects we have undertaken.

Future improvements

A different approach is needed to the management of BSL, an approach that will combine flexibility with discipline across the company. At the moment, discipline seems confined to the contract vetting function and flexibility to the technical staff.

It would seem appropriate that those responsible for the strategic control of BSL should deploy more flexibility of approach, while a greater degree of co-ordination should be applied to the work of the technical staff.

The contract vetting criteria applied by the central staff at UDS should probably be modified to allow more projects to be accepted. At the same time, the technical staff must work in a more controlled way, especially where the larger contacts are concerned.

Recommendation

BSL needs an injection of on-site senior management skill. This could be achieved by seconding managers from UDS to BSL. These managers would have responsibility for contract approval and overall project management. They should be people who understand both the financial imperatives of wider strategy and the motivation of the scientific staff. They should be skilled in financial management but sufficiently intelligent and open-minded to be credible in the eyes of the scientific staff at BSL. There is probably a need for a chief executive and two project managers.

At the same time, the scientific staff will have to undergo a process of education, above all to lead them to accept that the way we do things has to change. This should, perhaps, be the first task for the new executives. The requirement for an improved system of project management and budgetary control should be explained to them and there should be an introduction to the necessity of controlled and effective team working, especially with regard to quality and delivery. The overall aim of this process of development would be to inculcate a proper degree of commercial awareness but without constraining the creativity and scientific credentials of the specialists.

John Clarkson

Managing Director

Part (d)

> **Tutor's hint**. The Examiner's marking scheme for this question appeared to be a condensed version of the relevant section of the BPP Study Manual, to the extent of including some identical wording.

Project management is a distinct branch of management expertise with its own problems and techniques. Many projects go wrong: this is usually manifested as a failure to complete on time, but this outcome can arise for a variety of reasons.

Unproven technology

Then use of new technological developments is likely to be a feature of any project. The range of such developments extends from fairly routine and non-critical improvements, through major innovations capable of transforming working practices, costs and time scales, to revolutionary techniques that make feasible projects that were previously quite impracticable. As the practical potential of a technical change moves from minor to major, so too moves its potential to cause disruption if something goes wrong with it. A classic example is Rolls Royce's attempt to use carbon fibre in the design of the RB211 engine in the early 1970s. Not only did the project fail to meet its objectives, its failure led to the company's financial failure, which necessitated its rescue by government.

Changing client specifications

It is not unusual for clients' notions of what they want to evolve during the lifetime of the project. However, if the work is to come in on time and on budget, they must be aware of what is technically feasible, reasonable in their aspirations, prompt with their decisions and, ultimately, prepared to freeze the specification so that it can be delivered. The failure of the TSR2 aircraft project forty years ago was in large part caused by major, unrealistic changes to specification.

Note that the term 'client' includes *internal* specifiers.

Politics

This problem area includes politics of all kinds, from those internal to an organisation managing its own projects, to the effect of national (and even international) politics on major undertakings. Identification of a senior figure with a project; public interest and press hysteria; hidden agendas; national prestige; and political dogma can all have deleterious effects on project management. **Lack of senior management support** is an important political problem.

Poor project management

This comes in several guises

- **Over optimism**. This can be particularly troublesome with new technology. Unrealistic deadlines may be accepted, for instance, or impossible levels of performance promised.
- **Over-promotion of technical staff**. It is common for people with a high level of technical skill to be promoted. Only then is it made clear that they lack management and leadership ability. This is a particular problem with IT projects.
- **Poor planning**. Realistic timescales must be established, use of shared resources must be planned and, most fundamental of all, jobs must be done in a sensible sequence.
- **Poor control**. Progress must be under continuous review and control action must be taken early if there are problems. The framework of control must provide for review at all levels of management and prompt reporting of problems.

Marking scheme

			Marks
1	(a)	Problems associated with culture differences	to 4
		Problems with structure and contract vetting	to 4
		Worsening delays and over-run on costs	to 3
		Quality/service deterioration	to 2
		Sales fall, marketing spend fall, admin increase	to 3
		Lower order book and contract size	to 3
			(max 15 marks)
	(b)	(i) Comparison between a centralised culture and a decentralised one – use of *Mintzberg or* Handy	to 5
		Type of employee	1 - 2
		Size of company	1 - 2
		Attitude towards risk	1 - 2
		Structure of firm	1 - 2
		Formality within hierarchy	1 - 2
		Management style	1 - 2
		Time frame	1 - 2
			(max 10 marks)

(ii) Criteria for change management	
Participation	1 - 2
Education/communication	1 - 2
Power/coercion, manipulation	1 - 2
Negotiation	1 - 2
Use of *Mitzberg* missionary model (if used)	to 4
Peters and Waterman	1 for each point made
	(max 10 marks)
(c) Summary of problems to be solves	to 3
Development of task orientated culture	to 4
Introduction of project managers	to 4
Training in budgets	to 2
Training in time management	to 2
Danger of formal integration	to 2
	(max 15 marks)
(d) Unproven technology	2 - 3
Change of client specification	2 - 3
Poor resourcing	2 - 3
Lack of senior management support	2 – 3
Poor project management	4 – 6
	(max 10 marks

2

Part (a)

A system of checking is an obvious measure to deal with errors, especially those of procedure, and is routinely used in tasks such as aircraft operations where performance must be highly standardised. A system of checking the paperwork will address some of the unsatisfactory occurrences that Chestlands Insurance has suffered. Incomplete documentation will be detected at an early stage; financial irregularities and mis-selling may also be affected for the better.

Nevertheless, simple checking is probably not the best way to address the current quality problems. The process of checking would not add value to correctly completed documentation but it *would* increase costs and the complexity of operations. Checking is something to be avoided if possible.

A more modern approach to quality would be to take steps to eliminate the creation of errors. This is the quality assurance approach, rather than the quality control approach, which depends on inspection or quality checking. Quality assurance requires that members of staff accept responsibility for the quality of all aspects of their work. Such an approach would address all of the problems now apparent in Chestlands Insurance's operations.

However, taking the quality control approach would require significant changes to the company's management of its human resources, since success would be dependent upon the motivation and skill of the individual employee.

(a) It would be necessary to review the recruitment policy so that only people with suitable personal qualities started work.

(b) Identifiable poor performers would have to go, preferably by natural wastage, but by dismissal if necessary.

(c) Effective training would be required, both for new recruits and for existing staff who were not working satisfactorily.

(d) The remuneration policy should be reviewed. There should be incentives that promote the behaviour the company needs. At the moment, the large element of commission will tend to encourage dubious selling practices and poor attention to documentation. An adjusted system, with a higher level of basic pay, would encourage sales people to take a longer-term view of their customers. A performance related bonus could include an element of penalty for inadequate documentation.

It will be difficult to strike the right balance between the need for more effective staff and the need to hold down costs, but a quality assurance approach is the best way to approach the problem.

Part (b)

Total Quality Management (TQM) is an extension of the quality assurance approach to every activity in the organisation, with the aim of ensuring complete customer satisfaction both externally and *internally*. Quality lies in the eye of the consumer and this applies as much to those products that are consumed *within* the organisation as to those that are marketed externally. Total Quality Management thus views the organisation as an integrated whole and quality as an organisation-wide concern.

TQM is more of a philosophy of business than a collection of techniques. A high degree of commitment is necessary if it is to be implemented. Senior management, in particular, must support its introduction and promote the necessary changes. This can be a particularly difficult thing to achieve, since it demands changes of practice, not just lip service. A TQM initiative can also be expensive, especially if there is much training to undertake. It is necessary to take a long view and maintain the momentum of the programme over the longer term.

Staff at lower levels must be prepared to accept responsibility for their performance and to undergo appropriate training. A problem Mr Sanders will have to solve is the likelihood that staff will expect greater remuneration in return for improved performance and for accepting greater responsibility. In the longer term, improved productivity and quality should pay for these extra costs.

The development of a TQM programme inevitably requires the participation of the workforce. They have the greatest knowledge of the details of the work and they will see the effects of changes first. Quality circles are a possible technique for promoting their continued input. Participation in development is also likely to encourage internalisation of the principles of the new approach.

It will not be enough to rely on the positive motivational effects of participation to ensure compliance with the aims of the new approach. Work procedure should be reviewed with a view to simplification and standardisation, both of which will improve performance. Also, the philosophy must be supported by improvements in control and discipline to ensure that poor performance is checked.

Marking scheme			Marks
2	(a)	Show that proposed solution addresses symptoms	1 - 2
		Distinguish between quality control, assurance and TQM	4 - 5
		Need to correct recruitment, training and wage structures	3 - 4
			(max 10 marks)
	(b)	Employee participation	1 - 2
		Commitment of management	1 - 2
		Training	1 - 2
		Long time frame	1 - 2
		Work standardisation	1 - 2
		Company-wide involvement	1 - 2
			(max 10 marks)
			Total 25 marks

3

Part (a)

Strategic considerations – marketing

A move into exporting would be a major development in Mr Darby's business and would require significantly more marketing effort than is expended at present. It is possible that Mr Darby's original marketing approach of magazine advertising and direct mail would be as successful overseas as it has been at home. However, it would be necessary to tailor his promotional material to the needs of the markets concerned. This would include the use of a foreign language in two cases, and even in the USA, copy suitable for use in the domestic market might be ineffective.

It is also likely that greater marketing effort would be required, particularly in research, since each of the three target markets has its own culture and customs. Fashionable hotels and modern business premises make up Mr Darby's existing market. There is no guarantee he will achieve the same success with this type of customer in any other country. On the other hand, there may be other market segments that could be successfully targeted. It will also be necessary to consider the state of competition in each market. Mr Darby seems to enjoy rather favourable conditions in his home market, but it is unlikely that he will be so lucky in a foreign market. At the moment, Mr Darby has too little knowledge of his three target markets for him to be able to enter them successfully.

Simultaneous ventures into all three markets would be very difficult, both from the marketing point of view and because of the practical matters dealt with below. It would be cheaper and less risky to try one market at a time.

Strategic considerations – finance

Mr Darby is tempted to seek expansion to realise a substantial economy of scale. A doubling of turnover is mentioned, but we are not told the size of the increased royalty payment. Mr Darby should consider that a doubling of turnover is likely to take time to achieve – possibly several years – but the increased payment must be found immediately. There would be other significant expenses, both for the extra marketing effort mentioned above and for the practical matters discussed below.

Practical considerations

Exporting will bring extra work and cost.

- Export documentation is complex and demanding.
- Insurance costs will inevitably rise.

- Physical distribution will presumably be by carrier; it will be necessary to find one with international capabilities.
- There may be barriers to trade to take into account, including tariffs and customs procedures.
- Exporting will expose Mr Darby to exchange rate risk, unless he can prevail upon customers to accept invoices denominated in sterling.

Part (b)

It is highly likely that cultural and practical differences will prevent Mr Darby from using the same marketing approach in all three of his target markets.

Product

It will be necessary to give careful consideration to the **product**, since what is successful in the domestic market may not be so successful overseas. Works by previously unfeatured artists might be required, possibly including those native to each target country. Mr Darby will have to give careful consideration to the terms of his royalty agreement. He will be poorly placed if he finds that he needs to offer works that it does not cover.

It is important to present a full product range. At the moment, Mr Darby seems to be able to restrict his range to unframed prints. He may find it necessary to enhance his product offering, perhaps by framing or by providing picture lighting accessories. He may even find that potential customers expect to be shown a full range of art works, including sculptures and ceramics, for instance.

Price

It is common in exporting to adjust price downwards in order to achieve high volumes and hence significant economies of scale. This is probably inappropriate for Mr Darby: while the anticipated doubling of his output will reduce his unit costs significantly, he will have significant extra expenses, as discussed above. A premium price policy may be possible, so long as the rest of the marketing effort promotes a quality image. A knowledge of the going rate and what the market will bear would be invaluable – but difficult to obtain. Mr Darby will probably have to proceed by trial and error, taking care to cover his costs.

Promotion

The competitive environments of the target markets are likely to be significantly different from that of Mr Darby's home market and from each other. It is a commonplace of marketing that promotion has to be carefully tailored to each market and the folklore abounds with examples of promotion howlers. There may also be regulatory constraints on what can be done. Finally, if it becomes necessary to target different segments in different countries, as may be the case, promotion will have to be adjusted accordingly. It may be, for instance, that private individuals form an important market segment in one of the countries concerned.

Place

Mr Darby is likely to find that distribution of his products presents significant problems. We presumed earlier that he currently uses the services of carriers. Several large companies offer international delivery, but the administration involved is much more complex and inevitably subject to delay. Documentation is a particular problem. Mr Darby should consider the use of local agents to ease his logistics problems. The confidence of foreign customers will be enhanced if they have a local point of contact and Mr Darby should find the complexity easier to manage if he has someone with local knowledge to deal with problems.

Suitable local agents would also be able to assist with the other aspects of the marketing effort.

Marking scheme

			Marks
3	**(a)**	Over-stretched resources	1 - 2
		Lack of expertise	1 - 2
		Need for financial funding	1 - 2
		Lack of marketing knowledge	1 - 2
		Currency volatility	1 - 2
		Trade barriers	1 - 2
		Freight cost and insurance	1 - 2
		Competition	1 - 2
			(max 10 marks)
	(b)	Recognition for need for changes up to 5 marks	
		SLEPT	
		Competition	
		Position in product life cycle	
		Reason for change in: product	2 - 3
		price	2 - 3
		promotion	2 - 3
		place	2 - 3
			(max 10 marks)
			Total 25 marks

4

Tutor's hint. This question should pose few challenges, despite the specific description of the business. Job analyses and descriptions are suited to bureaucracies where it is possible to define roles easily. JayBee, experiencing rapid growth, is not a machine bureaucracy.

Other ways of approaching the answer. Many management issues are a matter of opinion. Our answer broadly agrees with the financial controller's view. You may well have thought otherwise and considered that a formal job analysis was necessary.

Examiner's comment. Part (b) was a gift for many students - surprisingly some forgot to mention the need to make the job offer, contracts etc.

(a) **Role of job analysis and job description**

The purpose of **job analysis and description** exercise is to ensure that the **needs of the firm are identified,** that these needs are translated into a role and that the right people are recruited for the role.

A **job analysis** collects data about a job or the tasks needed. Some **aspects of the 'job' may be superseded** by technology (business process re-engineering). Tasks may be allocated to different job holders. In many cases, the analysis will indicate the need for the job and tasks are collected into one job.

With the task in hand, the **financial controller is quite right to rush ahead**. He knows that his current needs are not being met adequately, in that contract staff are employed. There is no need for a job analysis exercise - the jobs are there, but they are filled by temporary staff.

A **job description** outlines the tasks and duties of the job, to guide the job holder as to his or her responsibilities and identifies the skills and experience needed. A **person specification** should be developed in the light of the job analysis and description so that the recruitment process can target the right people.

The financial director is clearly concerned not to got too worried about bureaucratic detail. Too **rigid a person specification will not help the department to grow and develop**, and might restrict people's initiative.

Moreover, a **job description presupposes a coherent and stable reporting structure**. Clearly, the financial controller has not yet decided on an appropriate structure for the department. The best way of seeing who should be in charge of what is to let people to show their metal.

Instead, he might be more concerned with the role profile, that is, the overall mission of the job in the organisation as a whole. Given that JayBee is experiencing rapid growth, he is right to let people grow into the role. Getting new people on board now will enable any backlog to be dealt with. The **needs of the department may indeed have changed in** six months time, when a structure can be sorted out.

The financial controller wants 'good people', a vague person specification. By 'good' he probably means people who have:

(i) Experience of sales accounting
(ii) Initiative to cope with the unexpected
(iii) Willingness to work hard, independently

He needs to be pressed further on this. Skills, qualifications and experience can be easily defined. Personal qualities can only be assessed on meeting the candidate.

(b) **Checklist**

(i) The **need for new staff** has been identified and recruitment has been authorised.

(ii) The financial controller has a reasonable idea what he wants - but in other circumstances a detailed **job analysis exercise** might have been carried out.

(iii) Develop a **role profile** of what the job is supposed to achieve, even if the tasks are not specified in detail - other firms may have developed detailed job descriptions.

(iv) Develop **a person specification** (more than 'good people') describing what candidates should be able to do, what experience and qualification they have and so on.

(v) Brief a **recruitment agency**, if this is used, to find permanent staff. Alternatively identify suitable media (eg newspapers) and draft an advertisement, describing the job and indicating where candidates should send their responses.

(vi) **Review CVs** and **select candidates for interview**. CVs can be scored and analysed for suitability.

(vii) **Interview favoured candidates.** The interview may be **supplemented by testing procedures** to assess the candidate's competence. The interview should also be used to let the candidates know about the job. In many firms, interviews are conducted by a panel. The company might draw up a short list.

(viii) **Second interviews** might be conducted.

(ix) Once the firm has reached a decision, the favoured candidates are made **a formal offer in writing**. During this period, the firm will **follow up any references**, to check the basic accuracy of the candidate's CV and any clouds over the candidate's departure.

(x) The offer is made **unconditional once references have been received.**

(xi) An induction program is drawn up.

The firm needs to arrange start dates, accommodation and so on. Throughout the firm needs to follow equal opportunities legislation.

Marking scheme

			Marks
4	**(a)**	Place in recruitment process	2 - 4
		Typical content	2 - 4
		Relevance to JayBee	2 - 4
		Relevance to financial controller's approach	2 - 4
			(max 10 marks)
	(b)	Job analysis/description	1 - 2
		Person specification	1 - 2
		Advertising/use of agencies	2 - 3
		Shortlisting – CVs, application forms	1 - 2
		Interviews	1 - 2
		Offer subject to references	1 – 2
		Induction	1 - 2

Strategic Business Planning and Development

BPP Mock Exam 2: Pilot Paper

Question Paper	
Time allowed	**3 hours**
This paper is divided into two sections	
Section A	This question is compulsory and MUST be attempted
Section B	TWO questions ONLY to be answered

paper 3.5

DO NOT OPEN THIS PAPER UNTIL YOU ARE READY TO START UNDER EXAMINATION CONDITIONS

PART A

1 Angus Cairncross has recently been appointed as Head of Strategic Operations to the main board of Global Industries plc. This company is a UK-based conglomerate organisation, which had achieved significant expansion during the 1960s and 1970s when focusing on core businesses was not the fashion. The company has managed to maintain a leading position with the UK but is increasingly meeting competition from foreign competitors, both at home and abroad. Angus, prior to this recent appointment, had been Managing Director of one of Global Industries' subsidiary companies, Control Systems Ltd. This subsidiary company had focused on building control systems, including central heating, air conditioning and security equipment. The market had been mainly in the industrial sector as distinct from the general housing market. This subsidiary had traditionally not been a significant profit earner for Global Industries but Angus had been able to radically improve the position by his ability to control costs and, with judicious capital investment, improve the output per employee. He had also identified new markets overseas, particularly in China, and the rapidly developing countries of South East Asia. The recent economic problems faced by these countries had only marginally affected Control Systems' business and now sales are again following an upward trend.

The Chairman and Managing Director of Global Industries are both impressed with Angus and are hoping that his proven abilities in managing a focused company can be transferred to managing a conglomerate. Recently Global Industries has experienced a downturn in profits. The variety of businesses incorporated in the Company is large. The presence in industrial markets is considerable, ranging from design and construction within the nuclear power industry, railtrack construction, components for the motor vehicle assembly industry and the building control systems. As can be imagined the demand for these products is volatile and depends upon the state of economic activity within a country. So as to avoid over-dependence on one market Global Industries has set up sales and manufacturing facilities in overseas markets. This has enabled Global Industries to break into new foreign markets. Without a manufacturing presence the company would find it difficult to overcome trade barriers, and transport costs. It is also benefiting from access to cheaper labour and from local government grants so as to attract foreign investment.

Apart from the industrial sector Global Industries is also heavily involved in the defence industry, particularly in weapon systems and avionics. This is also an uncertain environment with demand being mainly determined by government policy which is highly dependent on the state of public finances. Finally Global Industries has a significant position within the consumer durable industry. It manufactures electric cookers and refrigerators within its kitchen appliance subsidiary, and also has recently purchased a number of franchises in the automobile distribution sector.

The problem which Global Industries is facing is that it appears to be exposed in too many markets and product areas. Its strategy of diversification has enabled it to be less dependent upon one market or one industrial sector. However it has created a difficult control system for management. Most of the technologies in which it operates are complex and the markets are dynamic, responding to increasing social, technological and political change. It has proved impossible to manage these industries from the centre, because no central organisation could possibly cope with the complexities of such a widespread business. Consequently the business is organised on divisional lines with each subsidiary reporting to the centre on a financial basis only. Each subsidiary is given financial targets by the centre (after consultation with the subsidiary) and then strategy formulation, implementation and control are delegated to the subsidiary companies. Because there appears to be little synergy between the companies their corporate and brand names are not even related to each other. At the end of a financial year most of the profits are returned to the Global Industries Headquarters, with a proportion being available for re-investment. The company acts in a shareholder role. It takes no active part in management but if profits from a subsidiary are considered to be inadequate then the likelihood of funds for investment in innovation or on new capital equipment will be low. In the final resort the subsidiary may be sold off. Angus has sympathy with this management philosophy. Its attitude towards delegation and the freedom to develop strategies had benefited him at Control Systems. However he also is concerned with a lack of support from the centre. Each subsidiary, by acting as an independent company has to provide its own support infrastructure - R&D, marketing and sales, finance and human resources. He believes that there must be some benefit in developing an organisational structure which can provide some direction and help, other than the Global Industries' Headquarters controlling the subsidiaries only through financial discipline.

However Angus appears to have a more urgent task to attend to as The Board has become very concerned about the performance of its kitchen appliance subsidiary. Over the past few years the performance of this company has deteriorated. This subsidiary originally produced and marketed these appliances within the UK market. However over time it acquired five foreign companies with their own product brands - two in Europe, two in the Far East and one in South America. The management at that time decided that it would be worthwhile continuing to promote these products under their original brand names. It also believed that by maintaining separate production facilities the kitchen appliance subsidiary could still appear to be a local company, so customising products for distinctive markets. Initially this had seemed to be a sensible strategy. Sales actually increased for a short time. However over the past three years sales have fallen significantly. Competition is mainly from one major global company who has grown rapidly over the past few years by pursuing a focus strategy. Its strategy has been to concentrate on a restricted number of models, both of cookers and refrigerators, promoted under a single corporate brand name. It has also decided to source its products from just two manufacturing sites. Its marketing strategy has also been centralised, with apparently little reference to local demand conditions. Initially the Global Industries' kitchen appliance subsidiary attempted to correct its position by increasing its promotion. However the inability of the company to halt the slide in sales, and the resultant loss in profits now means that Global Industries is now unwilling to finance any increased expenditure. Whereas Angus still believes there is profit potential within the kitchen appliance industry the majority of the members of the Board of the Global Industries plc do not believe that the subsidiary can be turned around and are considering disposing of the company. Unless the Board can see an improvement in sales or at least be presented with a strategic plan which will identify opportunities to turn around the situation then it will look for a buyer or starve the subsidiary of cash, milk the current operations and then withdraw from that sector.

Angus has analysed the company accounts and has been able to draw up the following table. The figures for the competitor's internal costs are estimates based on media expenditure statistics and assessment on costs for new product development. Whilst these figures cannot be guaranteed they should give a sound guide to the current situation and the relative competitive positions. Table 1 shows selected data and is not intended as a comprehensive set of accounts.

Table 1 **£ million**

	1998	1999	2000	2001 (forecast)
Sales of Global Industries' kitchen appliances				
domestic	14.2	13.5	12.8	11.4
overseas	8.5	7.5	7.2	7.0
total	22.7	21.0	20.0	18.4
Cost of Sales of Domestic Industries				
domestic	8.8	8.2	7.8	7.5
overseas	4.8	4.9	5.0	5.2
total	13.6	13.1	12.8	12.7
Gross profit (domestic and overseas)	9.1	7.9	7.2	5.7
Expenses	6.4	6.9	7.4	8.0
of which				
marketing	2.0	2.2	2.5	2.7
R&D	3.0	3.1	3.2	3.4
administration	1.4	1.6	1.7	1.9
Operating Profit (Loss)	2.7	1.0	-0.2	-2.3
Number of employees	1,300	1,350	1,250	1,250
Work in progress	3.5	3.7	4.0	4.2
Stock	2.4	2.9	3.2	4.1
Competitor:				
Sales revenue	18.0	19.5	22.5	25.0
Cost of sales	10.4	11.1	12.6	13.8
Gross profit	7.6	8.4	9.9	11.2
Expenses	4.6	4.9	5.4	6.3
of which				
marketing	1.4	1.5	1.7	2.0
R&D	2.2	2.2	2.4	2.8
administration	1.0	1.2	1.3	1.5
Operating profit	3.0	3.5	4.5	4.9
Number of employees	800	850	950	1,000
Work in progress	2.7	2.4	2.2	1.9
Stock	1.9	1.8	2.0	2.1

Required

(a) As Angus Cairncross prepare a report identifying the main problems which the kitchen appliance subsidiary has, particularly when compared with its major competitor. (20 marks)

(b) Discuss the benefits and problems which Global Industries plc is likely to experience, operating as a decentralised group of companies, using mainly financial controls as the major management control system. Suggest how the company can provide more help from the Headquarters, without becoming over-involved in day-to-day operations. (25 marks)

(c) Examine the factors which should be considered before a company decides to dispose of a subsidiary. Consider how each of these factors might relate to the disposal of the kitchen appliance subsidiary by Global Industries plc. (15 marks)

(60 marks)

Section B – TWO questions ONLY be to attempted

2 Karen Lee has been a qualified accountant for several years and currently works for a large partnership with international links. Although successful in her career she feels that there is still more she could achieve. Being part of a large organisation can be limiting. There is a tendency for large partnerships to become increasingly specialised. This is understandable because such a move can lead to efficiencies. However the disadvantage with this is that the employees tend to find their work becoming repetitive and occasionally boring. Also, because the client base consists of very large firms, Karen tends to concentrate her activities on only two or three firms. Her line manager has told her that although the work she does is specialised the benefit to her and the organisation is that she can now focus on the issues in greater depth. However Karen is looking for a breadth of experience rather than increased depth in specialist areas. She is not alone in feeling this way and knows a number of colleagues and friends who are also seeking a greater challenge.

Despite the tendency towards 'big being beautiful' Karen is also aware that a number of clients prefer to deal with smaller accountancy firms. Rather than dealing with several accountants employed by one large firm, each dependent upon the type of service required, these clients would like to develop a business relationship with smaller accountancy firms who could provide a more integrated and friendly service. Karen has decided that the opportunities are available to set up more local partnerships, which will meet both the requirements of clients and the aspirations of some of the accountancy staff. She and five other friends and colleagues have decided to set up their own partnership. She realises that initially she will have to market the partnership vigorously if the venture is to prove successful. This is an area where she has little experience. She approaches a colleague who works in marketing and seeks their advice.

Required

(a) As the colleague, explain in report format, the major issues which the proposed partnership must address if it is to be successfully launched. (12 marks)

Karen is proposing to base her partnership's pricing strategy on costs, because she feels that she and her colleagues lack knowledge of the market and therefore cannot make any other informed judgement.

(b) Evaluate cost-based pricing as a suitable pricing strategy for Karen's proposed partnership. (8 marks)

(20 marks)

3 John Staples is the Finance Director of Nadir Products plc, a UK-based company which manufactures and sells bathroom products – baths, sinks and toilets – to the UK market. These products are sold through a selection of specialist shops and through larger 'do-it-yourself' stores. Customers include professional plumbers and also ordinary householders who are renovating their houses themselves. The company operates at the lower end of the market and does not have a strong reputation for service. Sales have been slowly declining whereas those of competitors have been improving. In order to encourage increased sales the Board of Directors have decided to pay senior staff a bonus if certain targets are achieved. The two main targets are based on profit levels and annual sales. Two months before the end of the financial year the Finance Director asks one of his staff to check through the orders and accounts to assess the current situation. He is informed that without a sudden improvement in sales before the year end the important sales targets will not be met and so bonuses will be adversely affected.

The Finance Director has proposed to other senior staff that this shortfall in sales can be corrected by taking one of the following decisions.

1. A significant discount can be offered to any retail outlet which takes delivery of additional products prior to the end of the financial year.
2. Scheduled orders due to be delivered at the beginning of the next financial year can be brought forward and billed before the end of this year.
3. Distributors can be told that there is a risk of price increases in the future and that it will be advisable to order early so as to circumvent this possibility.

The Board is not sure of the implications associated with such decisions.

Required

(a) **As a consultant, prepare a report for the Board of Nadir Products examining the commercial and ethical implications associated with each of the proposed options mentioned above.** (8 marks)

(b) **Identify the main weaknesses of using profits and sales as the sole indicators of performance and suggest other indicators which may be more appropriate.** (12 marks)

(20 marks)

4 Coxford Doors is a family owned wood products company, specialising in producing doors and windows to be sold directly to house builders. There are currently no sales directly to homeowners who may wish to purchase doors and windows to replace their existing ones. In recent years the industry has become much more competitive. Most of the customers are now large nationwide builders, the industry having gone through a period of consolidation. These customers generally require standardised products in large volume, and they buy on the basis of low prices and guarantees of regular delivery. This has put great pressure on companies such as Coxford Doors. This company is still operating as if it were dealing with the fragmented market of twenty years ago. The family, in seeking uninterrupted growth, has permitted the workforce to have a substantial degree of self-management. This has avoided industrial unrest but there have been disadvantages to this approach. This delegated decision-making has led to delays in manufacturing and problems with quality. There has appeared to be a lack of focus. Consequently the company has lost important contracts and is gradually seeing its sales volume and profits decline.

The family has employed Andrew Smith as the new Managing Director, giving him the responsibility for turning the company around. He has decided that power and control must now return to the centre. The passive style of management pursued in the earlier years is now giving way to a more centralised and autocratic approach. However it is obvious that such a change in management style could create even further problems for the company.

Required

(a) **Discuss the benefits and problems which this more direct style of management might bring to Coxford Doors.** (10 marks)

(b) It is apparent that such a change in management style could bring opposition from the workforce. How might this change be implemented with minimal disruption? (10 marks)

(20 marks)

ANSWERS TO MOCK EXAM 2

DO NOT TURN THIS PAGE UNTIL YOU HAVE COMPLETED THE TEST PAPER

WARNING! APPLYING THE MARKING SCHEME

If you decide to mark your paper using the marking scheme, you should bear in mind the following points.

1 The BPP solutions are not definitive: you will see that we have applied the marking scheme to our solutions to how good answers should gain marks, but there may be more than one way to answer the question. You must try to judge fairly whether different points made in your answers are correct and relevant and therefore worth marks according to the ACCA marking scheme.

2 If you have a friend or colleague who is studying or has studied this paper, you might ask him or her to mark your paper for you, thus gaining a more objective assessment. Remember you and your friend are not trained or objective markers, so try to avoid complacency or pessimism if you appear to have done very well or very badly.

3 You should be aware that BPP's answers are longer than you would be expected to write. Sometimes, therefore, you would gain the same number of marks for making the basic point as we have shown as being available for a slightly more detailed or extensive solution.

It is most important that you analyse your solutions in detail and that you attempt to be as objective as possible.

Professional Examination - Paper 3.5 **Marking Scheme**

Strategic Business Planning and Development

This marking scheme is used only as a guide to markers in the context of the suggested answer. Scope is given to markers to award marks for alternative approaches to a question, including relevant comment, and where well-reasoned conclusions are provided. This is particularly so in case scenario questions where there may be more than one acceptable solution.

Unless otherwise stated, it is expected that candidates will set their answers within the context set by the question case scenario.

A PLAN OF ATTACK

It is a good idea to think about the nature of any examination before the day you sit it. You must be sure you know what the Examiner wants from you in terms of number of answers and which questions are compulsory and so on. Paper 3.5 is quite simple in this respect. You **must do** question 1 and you must answer two questions from Section B.

Note that Section A is crucial. You are highly unlikely to pass on the strength of your answer to Question 1 alone, but you are highly likely to fail if you do not make a creditable attempt at it.

You must have clear view of your overall preference about the order in which you will attempt questions before you enter the exam room. This is something you must do for yourself. Many people will advise that because Question 1 is so important you should definitely answer it first. Other people find that answering a shorter question first builds their confidence, especially if it is on a topic they are confident about. Only you can decide.

However, we would advise you that it would be very risky to leave question 1 to the end. This is a recipe for running out of time. While there are certain to be two or, more probably three, separate requirements, you cannot deal with them in isolation from each other; you must make sure you do not end up repeating yourself by using the same ideas too early, for example. So you must allow sufficient time to complete **all** the requirements. If you leave question 1 to the end, you may not manage to do this.

You do not have a lot of choice in this examination. The overall requirements and the likely nature of the questions mean that you will be examined on much of a very wide syllabus. Do not despair if you find you are probing the boundaries of your knowledge. Most of your contemporaries will be in the same boat. Make sure you cover the essentials, use common sense and experience as much as possible, relate your answers to the settings and **do not** ramble or dump theory.

The aim is not to cover pages with ink. Write concisely. This will release time for planning and checking. You **must** allow time to think.

A very important thing to remember in this exam is that there is bound to be more than one way of answering most of the questions: uniquely correct answers do not exist in a subject like this. If you can analyse data sensibly, apply theory appropriately and reach reasonable conclusions **you will pass.**

1

Part (a)

> **Tutor's hint.** The question asks for an answer in the form of a personalised report. Do not get carried away with the format of your answer. At this level there are very few marks for it.

To: Board Members, Global Industries plc
From: Head of Strategic Operations
Date: 1 December 2001

Kitchen Appliance Subsidiary

Scope of the report: Analysis of the problems faced by the kitchen appliance subsidiary

Introduction

1.1 The kitchen appliance subsidiary (KAS) has suffered falling sales and profits in its global operations for the last three years and the downward trend is forecast to continue next year. This is despite increases in promotional expenditure of about 10% each year. KAS lost £200K in 2000 and a loss of £2.3M is forecast for 2001.

Analysis

1.2 There appear to have been failures of management at both the strategic and operational levels at KAS. The strategy of market customisation has not led to increased turnover. At the same time, there has been a lack of control over manufacturing and costs.

Strategy

1.3 Global turnover has fallen by 12% over three years, at the same time as the major competitor (MC) has increased turnover by 25%. Their strategy is in marked contrast to ours. We have retained separate brand names and manufacturing plants in each of our markets as part of our polycentric strategy. MC have consolidated manufacturing on two sites and market a standardised range under a single brand name. On the face of it, it would seem that theirs is the more appropriate strategy. I do not have any data on selling prices; however, it is safe to assume that MC have reaped economies of scale from their policies, both in manufacturing and in promotion, and are probably the cost leader. I anticipate, therefore, that we will find that their competitive advantage lies at least partly in lower prices.

1.4 There are two possibilities to consider here.

1.4.1 The market for differentiated products exists in each of our markets, but is smaller and more demanding than we had anticipated. If this is the case, we may only be able to pursue our present policy by reducing the scale of our operations still further and moving upmarket.

1.4.2 Kitchen appliances have become commodities, with no significant market for differentiation at all. If this is the case, we may choose to compete on price and promotion or to withdraw completely.

Operations

1.5 There appears to be poor cost control at KAS. While I accept that there was a conscious decision to increase spending on promotion, I am concerned about the increases in R&D and administrative costs. I accept that R&D, if focused and controlled, is as important in lean times as in good, but I feel an actual increase in R&D spending is inappropriate.

1.6 Stock rose from 39 days in 1998 to 50 days in 1999 and then to 58 days in 2000. Again, I accept that if turnover slumps, some increase in stock is to be expected. However, it should not be allowed to go on accumulating for two years. There has clearly been insufficient attempt to control output. This is borne out by the 14% increase in WIP since 1998 and the fall in turnover per person from £17462 in 1998 to £16000 in 2000. I am alarmed to observe that stock is actually forecast to *increase* to 81 days in 2001, more than double the level in 1998.

Comparison with MC

1.7 At the same time as KAS has been faltering, MC has increased turnover by 39% and operating profit by 163%, WIP has fallen in absolute terms while stock has fallen from 39 days to 31, and turnover per person has increased from £22500 to £25000.

Conclusion

1.8 Our product market strategy for KAS has been proven unsatisfactory. While improvements in operational management may enable us to contain our short-term losses, for the longer term we must reassess our strategy of differentiation. It may be that we must either accept a market niche or compete on price.

Angus Cairncross

Part (b)

> **Tutor's hint.** In the main part of our answer we cover much the same ground as the Examiner's own suggested solution. However, we do not reach the same conclusion as he does about the best role for the Global Products plc headquarters. He suggested that the HQ could act as a provider of optional corporate services. You should understand that **there is unlikely to be a single correct answer** to any question in this paper and that a large part of what you must be able to do is to argue sensibly from theory and the scenario in order to reach a **reasonable conclusion**. Note that the introduction to the marking scheme for the Pilot Paper says:
>
> 'Scope is given to markers to award marks for alternative approaches to a question, including relevant comment, and where well reasoned conclusions are provided. This is particularly so in case scenario questions where there may be more than one acceptable solution.'

Global Industries plc is highly diversified and its subsidiaries are spread over the world. It is involved in a variety of complex technologies and dynamic markets. It is almost inevitable, therefore, that its approach to strategic management should be that identified by *Goold and Campbell* as '**financial controller**'. This allows the individual businesses to develop their own longer-term plans, requiring only that they produce a proper return on their assets.

This approach has its advantages.

Each operating company can exploit its knowledge of the market fully and rapidly, without the need for regular reference to the global headquarters. Market developments and opportunities can be exploited and tactics tailor-made for local conditions.

The senior managers of each SBU should be **motivated** by their independence and freedom of action, which may have a positive effect on their commitment and efforts.

Devolution of power and responsibility will **provide experience in general and strategic management for the senior managers**. This will provide an element of practical training and also act as a proving-ground, creating a pool of candidates for appointment to more demanding roles. These include the most senior posts in the global organisation and 'trouble-shooting' or 'turn-round' posts in under-performing subsidiaries.

The financial control approach means that the global headquarters can be a **small and therefore inexpensive** organisation, perhaps concentrating on overall group performance and structure through acquisitions and disposals.

Assessment against financial targets is the simplest way of making **performance comparisons** between diverse subsidiaries. Indeed it may be the only practical way of doing so. There may be similar elements that can be compared directly, such as the operation of a road transport fleet, but the core operations of businesses as diverse as the manufacture of refrigerators and the construction of railways cannot really be compared except in terms of financial outcomes.

However, this approach is not perfect. In particular, it makes little attempt to co-ordinate across companies in order to **exploit synergies and value chain** linkages.

One obvious area where performance could be improved is the achievement of **economies of scale**. It is likely that large savings could be made in the purchasing of supplies and raw materials, for instance. This does not mean that all purchasing would have to be done centrally, imposing delays and reducing flexibility. Rather, a small centralised staff could negotiate appropriate discounts with favoured suppliers, on a global or country basis, that individual companies could then exploit. A more sophisticated approach would be the creation of a global computer database of suppliers and terms that could then be rationalised and exploited.

Economies of scale could also be achieved in other functional areas such as marketing, by the rationalisation of brands and in R&D by means of a global review of what was being done and the most efficient means of doing it. There may well be elements of duplication that could be avoided also.

An important disadvantage of financial controls is that they tend to encourage a short-term approach, with possible dysfunctional effects. The tension between the short-term and the long-term is easily seen in the area of **maintenance**, where a cost cutting approach brings an immediate improvement to short-term financial performance, but at the risk of degraded performance or even major failure in the future.

A similar dysfunctional outcome can be seen in investment decisions where ROI is used as the main performance measure, as is common. ROI varies according to two quantities: profit and the value of the investment base. A fall in profit will reduce ROI, but so will a rise in the value of the assets in use. The use of ROI therefore discourages investment, since capital expenditure increases the value of the asset base.

Global Industries plc can overcome these problems by instituting a more comprehensive system of reporting and performance assessment, with regular meetings between SBU and HQ staff.

Where SBUs operate autonomously, a dysfunctional lack of cohesion may arise between them. This is apparent in Global Industries plc's kitchen appliance subsidiary, where the national operating companies have been allowed to go their own way without any overall guidance.

If Global Industries plc is to continue as a multi-national conglomerate, it should almost certainly continue its policy of operational independence for subsidiaries. However, the global HQ must **lay down the rules** by which they operate, providing a strategic framework for them to work within. This means using its privileged access to detailed information to take an overview of the SBUs themselves and the relationships between them.

In the case of the kitchen appliance subsidiary, for instance, this is as much a problem of **structure** as of anything else. There is a clear need for rationalisation of both production and marketing effort, with realignment of brands, standardisation of design and concentration of manufacturing. This would be a major strategic change, but once it has been done, devolved management may recommence.

Other areas in which the corporate HQ should be involved include long term investment plans, corporate ethics and treasury operations. These all form part of the strategic framework for operations. More detailed operational input should be kept to a minimum and should concentrate on detecting and exploiting potential synergistic effects such as economies of scale and value chain linkages.

It is probably inappropriate for the HQ to undertake the provision of services such as marketing on an optional, consultancy basis. Such things can be bought in by the operating companies as they find they need them. This approach eliminates all the problems of overhead absorption and charge-out rates.

Part (c)

> **Tutor's hint.** The most important thing about answering this question is to do what it tells you and **relate your discussion to Global Industries' kitchen appliance subsidiary**.
>
> The Examiner's suggested solution to this question was a largely unstructured sequence of short discussion paragraphs. We conclude that he will regard such an approach as satisfactory in answering a question like this. We think it is possible to add value by answering in terms of the appropriate part of the rational model: strategy evaluation and selection.

Disposal of a subsidiary is an important strategy option and should be subject to the same assessment for suitability, feasibility and acceptability applied to other possible courses of action.

Suitability

A strategy is suitable if it supports the organisation's mission and overall strategic stance. Global Industries plc is a highly diversified conglomerate operating internationally in a wide range of markets. We are not told how it has defined its mission, if at all, but it seems that it would be difficult to identify a type of business that was unsuitable for Global Industries plc to undertake. Probably, the only real criterion for suitability in this sense is that the component parts of the organisation should achieve an acceptable return on investment over the long term.

It would be appropriate therefore to carry out a full financial analysis of the disposal in terms of the present value of the **relevant costs and benefits** involved.

Another aspect of suitability is the extent to which the strategy supports other strategic activities. A strategy's suitability is enhanced if it enhances the balance of the organisation's portfolio of activities, for instance by selling into the same markets or complementing existing products. In the case of this disposal, Global Industries plc should be sure that it will not be left with a rump of associated activities that will wither without the presence of the kitchen appliance subsidiary. This seems unlikely from the information we are given, however.

Feasibility

Feasibility is usually assessed in financial terms, so the analysis mentioned above would cover this.

Acceptability

Johnson and Scholes say that acceptability may be assessed in terms of **risk, return** and **stakeholder reactions**. Return will be dealt with by financial analysis. Risk may be considered to be minimal given that the strategy involves withdrawal. Stakeholder reactions, however, are a very important consideration. There are two main groups of stakeholders to consider: employees and governments.

Employees will inevitably see the disposal as a threat to their employment. This will probably lead at least to a bad press and possibly to strikes and more violent unrest. There will be an interaction with the response of governments, who will be equally concerned about the possible economic impact of the disposal. As Global Industries plc operates in the nuclear power, railway and defence industries, its relations with governments are particularly important since they are either the major customers in those markets or have major influence over them.

Marking scheme

			Marks
1	**(a)**	Duplication of activities – costs associated with polycentricity	
		As opposed to geocentricity: standardisation versus customisation	
		With reference to marketing, production and R&D	12
		Poor control of costs	
		- R&D	3
		- employee numbers	3
		- stocks	3
		- work-in-progress	3
			(max 20 marks)
	(b)	Benefits	(up to 3 each)
		- motivation	
		- training	
		- speed in response	
		- control/comparison	
		- 'bottom line' dominance has political impact	
			(max 10 marks)
		HQ provides core services with examples 'arm's length' pricing considered	(max 6 marks)
			(max 25 marks)
	(c)	Reasons for not shutting down company, with specific Reference to Global Industries	(up to 4 each)
		- integration of products/facilities	
		- existence of dominant customer	
		- value of assets/goodwill	
		- importance of the company to the host country	(max 15 marks)
			Total maximum 60 marks

2

Part (a)

Tutor's hint. The implication of the last three sentences of the setting is that this part of the question is about major issues of *marketing*. Similarly, taking the requirement at face value, one could answer the question in terms of *launch* considerations, such as publicity, premises and internal administration. However, it is clear from the mark scheme and the Examiner's own suggested solution that he was actually thinking of wider strategic considerations. In fact, 50% of his suggested solution consists of a mini-strategic analysis.

Do not be discouraged by this: refer to our comments on question 1(b).

To: Karen Lee
From: A Marketeer
Date: December 2001

REPORT – PROPOSED PARTNERSHIP

You asked me to advise on your new partnership project. As you know, my main area of expertise is marketing, so I have concentrated on marketing aspects of the project, though this inevitably includes some consideration of wider strategic matters.

Strategy

As an accountant working in practice you are no doubt familiar with the requirements of a business plan. You seem to have a firm idea of the satisfactions you intend to offer your target market, in the form of a variety of professional accountancy services. You also seem to have identified a gap in the market for such services provided by a small but integrated practice. No doubt your financial planning has been careful and you are assured of sufficient capital and liquidity to enable you to build up your business.

It would probably be appropriate at this stage to carry out an analysis of your group's strengths and weaknesses and the opportunities and threats present in the market. For instance, while I have no doubt that you have an appropriate mix of professional skills available, are you happy that the mundane administration of the practice will be carried on well enough to support rather than hinder your professional efforts? To what extent will your cash flow depend on the prosperity of any single client or industry?

Your aim should be to exploit the strengths and opportunities you identify, while avoiding the threats and converting the weaknesses into strengths.

Marketing

We have already considered the **product** aspect of the marketing mix, and, to some extent, **price. Place**, or distribution, is not really an issue for the type of services you are proposing to supply. I would merely suggest that you give proper consideration to the almost subliminal messages your premises will send to your clients, and ensure that they are in keeping with the overall image you wish to promote.

Promotion, as you realise will be an important input to the success of your venture. You are subject to professional rules governing promotion, but I would urge you to budget considerable resources, not least your own time, to the promotion of your practice.

You will be engaged in the supply of services and there are therefore three further marketing elements to consider: **people, processes** and **physical evidence**.

Your colleagues will no doubt be aware of the importance of the impression made by the staff of any service business. They must give a lead in matters such as appearance, friendly attitude and reliability so that your support staff form the correct impression of what is required. We both know how easy it is to regard the clients as an annoying distraction from the real work of the practice!

Your working processes and administrative procedures must also be designed to provide the maximum satisfaction to your clients. You will know better than I what is involved here.

Finally, because services are so intangible, you must give serious consideration to the physical evidence you actually put into your clients' hands. This is likely to consist largely of communications of one sort and another. Remember that you will be judged by such things as the correctness of your grammar and spelling and the quality of your notepaper. I suggest that you consult a trained designer before having your letterheads and so on printed.

Part (b)

> **Tutor's hint**. This part of the question allows you to make use of material from other parts of your ACCA studies, since you will have covered pricing as an aspect of financial management. Also, if you have experience of how accountancy practices work, you can use that knowledge as background input into your answer.

We are told that Karen is a qualified accountant and we may assume that she and her colleagues intend to trade as members of their professional body, or bodies. If this is the case, it is important to point out that their conduct in relation to their fees, as with so much else, will be subject to the appropriate rules of professional conduct. These are such that most practices do in fact base their fees largely on cost, charging on the basis of time spent and degree of skill deployed.

That said, there is wide discretion available to the practitioner as to the size of any fee note issued, so other considerations other than cost may be introduced into the fee by adjusting the mark-up.

There are many factors that may be considered in setting a price. Fortunately, many of them, such as market skimming and penetrating are not really relevant to professional services. For Karen and her colleagues, the main considerations are economic: supply and demand will determine what price the market will bear.

There is likely to be competition from both qualified and unqualified accountants. While Karen's practice will have an advantage over the latter in professional credibility and the capacity to provide audit opinions, it is likely that they will be in competition with them for at least some of their business. Similarly, though they hope to serve a niche market, there is no guarantee that larger competitors will not try to attract the same clients. All this will tend to drive their fees down.

The level of demand in the market will also affect the prices they can charge. This may well differ between the various professional specialities Karen and her colleagues offer. For instance, there is currently a gradual erosion of demand for audit services because of changes to the law relating to audit of smaller limited companies. On the other hand, there is an expanding market for taxation services resulting from the introduction of self-assessment and an increase in the number of people falling into the higher tax bracket.

Marking scheme

			Marks
2	(a)	Major issues to be addressed	
		- internal resources, finance and skills	up to 4 marks
		- having suitable external market	up to 4 marks
		- ability to be able to formulate appropriate marketing mix	up to 4 marks
			(max 12 marks)
	(b)	Relationship between costs and volume	up to 3 marks
		Recognition of competition	up to 3 marks
		Recognition of demand	up to 3 marks
			(max 8 marks)
			Total maximum 20 marks

3

Part (a)

> **Tutor's hint**. While this question clearly has an important ethical slant, it is important to deal with the commercial impact of the proposed courses of action. If you feel your experience has not prepared you to do this, think in terms of stakeholder theory and ask yourself what connected stakeholders like customers are reasonably entitled to expect and how *you* would react to these ploys.
>
> Do not spend more than a minute on dealing with the report form requirement: a suitable heading and, perhaps, numbered paragraphs are all that are required. A short introductory paragraph giving the reason for the report is a good way to get started.

REPORT

To: Board Members, Nadir Products plc
From: A Consultant
Date: December 2001
Subject: Proposed adjustments to turnover reporting

You asked me to comment on the commercial and ethical implications of suggestions that had been made about the value of this year's turnover. There was concern that a current decline in sales will adversely affect the level of bonuses paid to senior staff.

My first comment is that the assumption behind the suggestions appears wrong. The aim of the bonus scheme was surely to provide an incentive for senior staff to take appropriate action to improve performance. If performance has not improved, it would be perverse to adjust the numbers so that they receive the bonuses anyway. There is an element of **moral hazard** here: if the bonuses are in effect guaranteed and not dependent on improved performance, the incentive effect disappears and the scheme might as well be abandoned.

I understand that there is concern that staff will be adversely affected by the downturn in sales value. However, I must point out the questionable nature of the suggestions from an ethical point of view. It is likely that the detailed proposals will create a **conflict of interests** since each has the potential to disadvantage shareholders. It would be ethically inappropriate to pursue any course of action that reduced shareholder value in order to enrich senior staff.

I will now examine the individual proposals.

Discount for additional sales. A discount is an unexceptional sales promotional device that may be used, for instance, to increase or defend market share or to shift excess stock. It has a cost, in the form of reduced margin, and it is a matter of commercial judgement to decide whether the benefit is greater than the cost. It may also have the effect of merely bringing sales forward in time, so that later trading periods suffer.

Of the three suggestions, this is the most defensible. However, it is quite *indefensible* if it is undertaken solely in order to boost bonuses, because of the conflict of interest discussed above.

Bringing forward scheduled orders is a form of **window dressing**. Your auditors will deploy checks on such activities as a matter of course, and may succeed in detecting this. The accounts would then have to be adjusted, since there is no commercial justification for the practice. It can be seen as detrimental to shareholders since the reported profit would be overstated and, while this may have a positive effect on share value in the short term, were it ever discovered, it would bring into question the company's **corporate governance**. Such a scheme is also likely to irritate customers who may respond by delaying payment and even seeking a new supplier. This would clearly disadvantage the company.

This suggestion is unacceptable on both ethical and practical grounds.

Warning of possible price rises. I take it as read that there are no actual plans to raise prices? If this is the case, to say that such plans exist is untruthful and therefore inappropriate for a company that wishes to maintain high ethical standards. Further, to hide behind a form of words such as 'there *may* be price rises' would be equally dishonest, since the intention would be to create a specific, incorrect impression in customers' minds. When the warning is eventually shown to be spurious, customers' estimation of the company will fall, with an eventual knock-on effect on turnover.

This ploy is comparable to the previous one in its potential effect on shareholders and customers but is even more unethical

Conclusion. None of the suggestions is acceptable ethically or commercially as a solution to the senior staff bonus problem.

Part (b)

> **Tutor's hint**. You may suppose that performance measurement is a mainstream management accounting topic and be surprised to see it in a strategy paper. First, don't forget that the professionally qualified accountant should be able to bring significant breadth of knowledge to bear. Real life problems do not fall neatly into separate, syllabus relevant categories. Second, remember that **control** is an important aspect of strategic management and control implies measurement. The **balanced scorecard** is an obvious solution to the second part of the question requirement but if you are able to discuss some other suitable scheme, perhaps from experience, do not hesitate to do so. Markers are always ready to give credit for practical solutions from real life.

There are two main categories of problem connected with restricting performance measurement to consideration of turnover and profit.

- Concentration on these two measures can actually be counter-productive and encourage **dysfunctional decision making**.
- There are many **other aspects of business activity** that are critical to the continued health and success of the organisation and that should be monitored.

While both turnover and profit are clearly important aspects of performance measurement, senior managers must be aware that both are subject to manipulation. A **trade-off** between the two can often be achieved, as when margin is sacrificed by discounting to increase volume or promotion budgets are cut to boost profitability. The latter example is also an instance of the way short-term profitability can be increased by cost cutting that actually prejudices longer-term results. Similar **tensions between short-term and long-term results** may be observed when considering the costs of R&D, training, market research and equipment upgrades.

Turnover and profit are respectively the top and bottom lines of the profit statement. The lines in between are not merely costs: they represent the varied activities that any business must undertake, and each activity has two aspects: it represents a **cost** and it **adds value** to output. Each activity must be managed so that the value it adds is greater than its cost: this means that a wide range of measures of performance is required. Some of these will be of departmental importance only, but some will be strategic in nature.

Kaplan and Norton suggested that attempting to run a business by reference to a single performance measure such as profit was like trying to fly an aircraft by reference to a single instrument. They proposed the adoption of a **balanced scorecard** that provided information on four strategically vital perspectives.

- Customer concerns

- Financial performance
- Internal processes
- Innovation and learning

Effective performance from the **customer perspective** may be assessed by measures such as failure rates for products, delivery times, reliability of service and changes in market share.

Internal processes should all create value, though some, such as legal compliance requirements are more concerned with avoiding the long-term *destruction* of value through infringements. Other internal processes may have significant impact on customer satisfaction. These include order handling, service staff training and quality procedures. Performance measures must relate to staff behaviour and proficiency; they may be particularly difficult to establish.

The internal process perspective may also include consideration of **core competences** where these are process based.

The **innovation and learning perspective** considers the organisation's potential to achieve **future success**. This is another area in which performance measures are difficult to design. Possible indicators include the percentage of revenue generated by products introduced during the last three years and the average time taken to bring a new product to market.

The **financial perspective** shows how the business appears to shareholders. Performance measures are well-established here and include ROE, EPS, dividend cover and capital growth as measured by market valuation. This perspective is the acid test of performance. Successful innovation and learning and efficient internal processes are only useful if they are translated into customer satisfaction; similarly, success with customers is only worthwhile if it leads to satisfactory financial performance.

Marking scheme

			Marks
3	**(a)**	Review of the three suggestions considering both Ethical and commercial implications	up to 3 marks for each
	(b)	Problem of manipulation with numbers	up to 5 marks
		Balanced scorecard or other better performance indicators	up to 2 marks for each appropriate suggestion
			(max 7 marks)
			(max 12 marks)
			Total maximum 20 marks

4

Part (a)

This company seems to have operated more like a soviet than a business. No doubt there has been much job-satisfaction, but the company's ability to compete and add value has deteriorated.

A participatory style of management has been shown in many studies to enhance personal **motivation** and **commitment** to the organisation's mission. This occurs via the process of **internalisation**, whereby the members of the workforce adopt the corporate goal as their personal goal. This can lead to better industrial relations, higher quality and better service. However, there is no conclusive evidence that such an approach necessarily leads to improved overall performance. This is borne out by the situation at Coxford Doors.

Andrew Smith's style of management is likely to bring the focus that has been missing in the past. He will no doubt speed up the decision making process (probably by making most decisions himself) plan effectively and issue clear instructions. Confusion and delay should be reduced and control enhanced. This will improve the business's responsiveness and ability to satisfy customers.

However, Andrew Smith is likely to encounter resistance from a work force used to proceeding according to its own ideas of what is appropriate. Morale and loyalty are both likely to suffer from the loss of autonomy. There is likely to be a lack of co-operation and, possibly, active resistance to the new order. The commercial position might deteriorate further as a result.

Even if there is acceptance that the trading position demands change it is unlikely to be wholehearted. A strong undercurrent of resentment may be created, resurfacing at some time in the future, perhaps when the commercial situation has improved.

Part (b)

> **Tutor's hint**. We use the Lewin/White model of the change process in our answer to this part of the question. Be aware that the **systems intervention strategy** would be just as appropriate.

Any significant change in the workplace is likely to provoke a mixture of reactions including resigned acceptance, hostility and outright opposition. Many people are simply naturally averse to change of any kind, being happiest with what they know and understand. With a change of the kind proposed here, many workpeople will lose a degree of independence in their working practices and are likely to object. The danger is that Andrew Smith's gathering up of the reins will provoke serious disruption perhaps extending to a strike.

The theoretical models proposed for the management of change offer no magical solutions to the problems of human behaviour. They simply provide a rational framework within which reason, diplomacy, tact and communication skills may be deployed to the best advantage. The general idea is to obtain agreement about the **need** for change and to manage it in as harmonious a manner as possible.

Lewin and White's model divides the change process into three stages: **unfreeze, change, refreeze.**

Unfreeze is the most difficult stage of the process. The aim is to **sell** both the need for change and the proposed changes themselves. Individuals and groups must be provided with **motives** for changing their attitudes, systems and behaviour. If the need for change is immediate, clear and perceived to be associated with the survival of the individual or group (for example change in reaction to an organisation crisis), the unfreezing process will be eased. Andrew Smith should use the decline in financial performance to illustrate the necessity for change at Coxford Doors, since it seems likely that without change, the organisation is doomed to ultimate failure. This may involve takeover or winding-up but is certain to be more inimical to the interests of the workforce than any possible change to working practices.

Routine changes are harder to sell than **transformational** ones if they are perceived to be unimportant and not survival-based.

Culture change is perhaps hardest of all, especially if it involves basic assumptions. This is certainly the case at Coxford Doors. However, the necessary precondition for change are in place. Andrew Smith is himself an **outsider**, prepared to challenge and expose, in a visible way, the existing behaviour pattern; his appointment will act as a **trigger**; and **alterations to the power structure** will be an inherent part of his actions.

The unfreeze stage is likely to include extensive **communication** and **consultation processes**, but the objective must be kept in sight; concern for proper treatment of employees must not be allowed to subvert the overall aim.

Change is the second stage of the process and is mainly concerned with introducing the new, desirable behaviours and approaches. This will involve retraining and practice to build up familiarity and experience. Individuals must be encouraged to take ownership of the new ways of doing things. For this to happen they must be shown to work.

Refreeze is the final stage, involving consolidation and reinforcement of the new behaviour. Positive or negative reinforcement may be used, with praise, reward and sanctions applied as necessary.

It will be important for Andrew Smith to retain **control of the process** at all times, since the company's history of participative management will tend to undermine his move towards a firmer style. He must make it clear from the outset that change must take place, while remaining flexible on the detail and the style of its introduction. It would be advisable to aim for an intermediate style of management, in which the workforce retain a voice. Operational control must be improved, but it should not be necessary to move to a completely autocratic way of doing things.

Marking scheme

			Marks
4	**(a)**	Benefits - reduced confusion in decision-making - ability to integrate activities - swiftness in actions Problems - less commitment - less motivation - less co-operation	up to 2 marks for each point (max 10 marks)
	(b)	Lewin's model – 'freeze, unfreese – refreeze' or Systems Intervention Model (diagnosis, design and implementation) .	(up to 10 marks for either depending upon depth and relevance) **Total max 20 marks**

REVIEW FORM & FREE PRIZE DRAW

All original review forms from the entire BPP range, completed with genuine comments, will be entered into one of two draws 31 January 2002 and 31 July 2002. The names on the first four forms picked out on each occasion will be sent a cheque for £50.

Name: ______________________ **Address:** ______________________

____

____

How have you used this Kit?
(Tick one box only)

☐ Self study (book only)

☐ On a course: college (please state)__________

____

☐ With 'correspondence' package

☐ Other __________________

Why did you decide to purchase this Kit? *(Tick one box only)*

☐ Have used the complementary Study Text

☐ Have used other BPP products in the past

☐ Recommendation by friend/colleague

☐ Recommendation by a lecturer at college

☐ Saw advertising in journals

☐ Saw website

☐ Other __________________

During the past six months do you recall seeing/receiving any of the following?
(Tick as many boxes as are relevant)

☐ Our advertisement in *Student Accountant*

☐ Our advertisement in *Pass*

☐ Our brochure with a letter through the post

☐ Our website

Which (if any) aspects of our advertising do you find useful?
(Tick as many boxes as are relevant)

☐ Prices and publication dates of new editions

☐ Information on product content

☐ Facility to order books off-the-page

☐ None of the above

When did you sit the exam? ______________________

Which of the following BPP products have you used for this paper?

☐ Study Text ☐ MCQ Cards ☑ Kit ☐ Passcards ☐ Success Tape ☐ Breakthrough Video

Your ratings, comments and suggestions would be appreciated on the following areas of this Kit.

	Very useful	*Useful*	*Not useful*
'*Question search tools*'	☐	☐	☐
'*The exam*'	☐	☐	☐
'*Background*'	☐	☐	☐
Preparation questions	☐	☐	☐
Exam standard questions	☐	☐	☐
'*Tutor's hints*' *section in answers*	☐	☐	☐
Content and structure of answers	☐	☐	☐
Mock exams	☐	☐	☐
'*Plan of attack*'	☐	☐	☐
Mock exam answers	☐	☐	☐

	Excellent	*Good*	*Adequate*	*Poor*
Overall opinion of this Kit	☐	☐	☐	☐

Do you intend to continue using BPP products? ☐ Yes ☐ No

Please note any further comments and suggestions/errors on the reverse of this page. The BPP author of this edition can be e-mailed at: glennhaldane@bpp.com

Please return this form to: Katy Hibbert, ACCA range manager, BPP Publishing Ltd, FREEPOST, London, W12 8BR

REVIEW FORM & FREE PRIZE DRAW (continued)

Please note any further comments and suggestions/errors below.

FREE PRIZE DRAW RULES

1 Closing date for 31 July 2002 draw is 30 June 2002. Closing date for 31 January 2002 draw is 31 December 2001.

2 Restricted to entries with UK and Eire addresses only. BPP employees, their families and business associates are excluded.

3 No purchase necessary. Entry forms are available upon request from BPP Publishing. No more than one entry per title, per person. Draw restricted to persons aged 16 and over.

4 Winners will be notified by post and receive their cheques not later than 6 weeks after the relevant draw date.

5 The decision of the promoter in all matters is final and binding. No correspondence will be entered into.

See overleaf for information on other
BPP products and how to order

ACCA Order - New Syllabus

To BPP Publishing Ltd, Aldine Place, London W12 8AA
Tel: 020 8740 2211. Fax: 020 8740 1184
email: publishing@bpp.com
online: www.bpp.com

Mr/Mrs/Ms (Full name) ______
Daytime delivery address ______
Postcode ______
Daytime Tel ______ Date of exam (month/year) ______

	2/01 Texts	8/01 Kits	9/01 Passcards	MCQ cards	Tapes	Videos
PART 1						
1.1 Preparing Financial Statements	£19.95 ☐	£10.95 ☐	£5.95 ☐	£5.95 ☐	£12.95 ☐	£25.00 ☐
1.2 Financial Information for Management	£19.95 ☐	£10.95 ☐	£5.95 ☐	£5.95 ☐	£12.95 ☐	£25.00 ☐
1.3 Managing People	£19.95 ☐	£10.95 ☐	£5.95 ☐		£12.95 ☐	£25.00 ☐
PART 2						
2.1 Information Systems	£19.95 ☐	£10.95 ☐	£5.95 ☐		£12.95 ☐	£25.00 ☐
2.2 Corporate and Business Law (6/01)	£19.95 ☐	£10.95 ☐	£5.95 ☐		£12.95 ☐	£25.00 ☐
2.3 Business Taxation FA 2000 (for 12/01 exam)	£19.95 ☐	£10.95 ☐ (4/01)	£5.95 ☐ (4/01)		£12.95 ☐	£25.00 ☐
2.4 Financial Management and Control	£19.95 ☐	£10.95 ☐	£5.95 ☐		£12.95 ☐	£25.00 ☐
2.5 Financial Reporting (6/01)	£19.95 ☐	£10.95 ☐	£5.95 ☐		£12.95 ☐	£25.00 ☐
2.6 Audit and Internal Review (6/01)	£19.95 ☐	£10.95 ☐	£5.95 ☐		£12.95 ☐	£25.00 ☐
PART 3						
3.1 Audit and Assurance Services (6/01)	£20.95 ☐	£10.95 ☐	£5.95 ☐		£12.95 ☐	£25.00 ☐
3.2 Advanced Taxation FA 2000 (for 12/01 exam)	£20.95 ☐	£10.95 ☐ (4/01)	£5.95 ☐ (4/01)		£12.95 ☐	£25.00 ☐
3.3 Performance Management	£20.95 ☐	£10.95 ☐	£5.95 ☐		£12.95 ☐	£25.00 ☐
3.4 Business Information Management	£20.95 ☐	£10.95 ☐	£5.95 ☐		£12.95 ☐	£25.00 ☐
3.5 Strategic Business Planning and Development	£20.95 ☐	£10.95 ☐	£5.95 ☐		£12.95 ☐	£25.00 ☐
3.6 Advanced Corporate Reporting (6/01)	£20.95 ☐	£10.95 ☐	£5.95 ☐		£12.95 ☐	£25.00 ☐
3.7 Strategic Financial Management	£20.95 ☐	£10.95 ☐	£5.95 ☐		£12.95 ☐	£25.00 ☐
INTERNATIONAL STREAM						
1.1 Preparing Financial Statements	£19.95 ☐	£10.95 ☐	£5.95 ☐	£5.95 ☐		
2.5 Financial Reporting (6/01)	£19.95 ☐	£10.95 ☐	£5.95 ☐			
2.6 Audit and Internal Review (6/01)	£19.95 ☐	£10.95 ☐	£5.95 ☐			
3.1 Audit and Assurance services (6/01)	£20.95 ☐	£10.95 ☐	£5.95 ☐			
3.6 Advanced Corporate Reporting (6/01)	£20.95 ☐	£10.95 ☐	£5.95 ☐			
SUCCESS IN YOUR RESEARCH AND ANALYSIS PROJECT						
Tutorial Text (9/00) (new edition 9/01)	£19.95 ☐					

SUBTOTAL £ ______

POSTAGE & PACKING

Study Texts

	First	Each extra	
UK	£3.00	£2.00	£
Europe*	£5.00	£4.00	£
Rest of world	£20.00	£10.00	£

Kits/Passcards/Success Tapes/MCQ cards

	First	Each extra	
UK	£2.00	£1.00	£
Europe*	£2.50	£1.00	£
Rest of world	£15.00	£8.00	£

Breakthrough Videos

	First	Each extra	
UK	£2.00	£2.00	£
Europe*	£2.00	£2.00	£
Rest of world	£20.00	£10.00	£

Grand Total (Cheques to *BPP Publishing*) I enclose a cheque for (incl. Postage) **£** ______

Or charge to Access/Visa/Switch

Card Number ______

Expiry date ______ Start Date ______

Issue Number (Switch Only) ______

Signature ______

We aim to deliver to all UK addresses inside 5 working days; a signature will be required. Orders to all EU addresses should be delivered within 6 working days. All other orders to overseas addresses should be delivered within 8 working days. * Europe includes the Republic of Ireland and the Channel Islands.

EXORCISM, ILLNESS AND DEMONS

Sidestone Press

EXORCISM, ILLNESS AND DEMONS

IN AN ANCIENT NEAR EASTERN CONTEXT

The Egyptian magical Papyrus Leiden I 343 + 345

Susanne Beck

PALMA 18

PAPERS ON ARCHAEOLOGY OF THE LEIDEN MUSEUM OF ANTIQUITIES

PALMA: Papers on Archaeology of the Leiden Museum of Antiquities (volume 18)

Volume editor: Maarten J. Raven

Published by Sidestone Press, Leiden
www.sidestone.com

Lay-out & cover design: Sidestone Press

Photograph cover:
The Egyptian magical Papyrus Leiden I 343 + 345,
photo: Karsten Wentink

Photographs book: Robbert-Jan Looman (National Museum of Antiquities)

Printed and bound in Great Britain by
Marston Book Services Ltd, Oxfordshire

ISBN 978-90-8890-539-1 (softcover)
ISBN 978-90-8890-540-7 (hardcover)
ISBN 978-90-8890-541-4 (PDF e-book)

ISSN 2034-550X

Contents

Preface

I first had the pleasure of dealing with the extraordinary papyrus Leiden I 343 + 345 during my PhD thesis *Sāmānu. Ein vorderasiatischer Dämon in Ägypten* (Ludwig-Maximilians-Universität, Munich, 2014/2015) under the supervision of Friedhelm Hoffmann, Hans-Werner Fischer-Elfert, Walter Sallaberger and Manfred Krebernik. This manuscript was a major source for the object of my study, the ancient Egyptian disease demon Sāmānu. During the analysis of this remarkable demonic being, it soon became clear that a new edition of papyrus Leiden I 343 + 345 could not be feasibly worked into my dissertation, which focused on an analysis of the Mesopotamian and Egyptian forms of Sāmānu from a modern perspective and the transfer of knowledge from the Ancient Near East to Egypt.[1] Maarten J. Raven and I therefore agreed to give the re-edition the space and time it deserves.[2] I would like to extend my sincerest gratitude to him for giving me the opportunity to prepare a re-edition of papyrus Leiden I 343 + 345 for the Papers on Archaeology of the Leiden Museum of Antiquities (PALMA) series.

I would also like to thank Katherine E. Davis and Ramadan B. Hussein for their input on Egyptological terminology in English. Last but not least I would like to thank Michael Jumic for proofreading the manuscript.

1 Beck 2015b.

2 For an overview of all previous publications and mentions of the papyrus in the literature, see Chapter I.

PART I

Introduction

Introduction

1. Origin and date

The Leiden magical papyrus I 343 + 345 is kept in the Rijksmuseum van Oudheden, Leiden. The two unequal parts of the manuscript – I 343 and I 345 – were purchased separately. Originally, papyrus Leiden I 343 was part of Giovanni Anastasi's[3] collection, and upon its arrival in Leiden it received inventory number AMS 28. It was purchased by the Dutch government in 1828.[4] The Rijksmuseum van Oudheden's original sale's list states that the manuscript originated in Memphis.[5] The second segment – papyrus Leiden I 345 – comes from the collection of Maria Cimba,[6] and it was given inventory number CI 11b. It was acquired in Leghorn (Italy) in 1827.[7] The origin of papyrus Leiden I 345 is not listed but it is very likely that it comes from Memphis too, as both manuscripts are part of the same papyrus.[8] François Chabas seems to be the one who established a connection between both objects.[9] In the *Description raisonnée*, Conrad Leemans wrote that papyrus Leiden I 345 resembles the aforementioned manuscripts, namely papyri Leiden I 343 and 344, both of which hail from Memphis.[10]

The handwriting, spelling, language, and content of the manuscript indicate that the papyrus dates to the Ramesside period (19th–20th Dynasty).[11]

3 For G. Anastasi, see Bierbrier 2012, 19–20, with further references. See Dawson 1949, 158–160.

4 See Bierbrier 2012, 19; Massart 1954, 1.

5 Correspondence with M. Raven (email 08.08.2012). See also Leemans 1840, 112.

6 For M. Cimba, see Bierbrier 2012, 122–123, with further references.

7 Correspondence with M. Raven (email 08.08.2012). According to Leemans 1846–1862, Text II, 63, the manuscript was acquired in 1826.

8 See Massart 1954, 1; Müller 2008, 275. The latter assumes that both papyri – like most of the other papyri in the RMO – come from an archive in Saqqara (Müller 2008, *ibid.*). See also Raven's statement: Raven 2012, 78–83.

9 At least, Chabas mentions that both manuscripts are written in the same hand and contain similar texts: Chabas 1862, 70; Chabas 1902, 142.

10 Leemans 1840, 111–113.

11 It is impossible to narrow down the dating to a single dynasty, because there has been no recent reappraisal for handwritings of the New Kingdom. The attempt to reduce the dating to one of the dynasties with the aid of the *Paläographie der nicht-literarischen Ostraka der 19.–20. Dynastie* (Wimmer 1995, I–II) did not result in a definitive statement.

2. Bibliography

The papyrus is first mentioned in Leemans's *Description raisonnée* (1840), but the manuscript is only briefly described.[12] In the catalogue *Monumens égyptiens du musée d'antiquités des Pays-Bas à Leide*, the manuscript is described and a facsimile is given.[13] In the same book, Chabas gives a short summary of the papyrus's content.[14] His article was republished several times.[15] According to Massart, A. Massy transcribed and translated papyrus I 345 in 1887, which may be erroneous.[16] In 1925, František Lexa translated parts of papyrus I 345.[17] Alan H. Gardiner and Warren R. Dawson included short translations and references to this text in their publications.[18]

The first publication dealing with the entire papyrus and containing a transcription, translation and commentary as well as photographs was produced by Adhémar Massart in 1954.[19] The manuscript's recipes are integrated in H. Von Deines and H. Grapow's *Grundriss der Medizin*, Th. Bardinet's *Les papyrus médicaux de l'Égypte pharaonique*, and W. Westendorf's *Handbuch der altägyptischen Medizin*; these works also include short descriptions of the papyrus.[20] In more recent times, the incantations and conjurations in the text were translated by M. Müller and partially translated by J.F. Borghouts and H.-W. Fischer-Elfert.[21] The present author's book *Sāmānu. Ein vorderasiatischer Dämon in Ägypten* deals with the incantation against Sāmānu/Akhu.[22]

12 Leemans 1840, 111–113.

13 Leemans 1846–1862, Text II, 63; Leemans 1855, II.16, Pls. XCVIII–CIV, CXXVI–CXXXVIII.

14 Chabas 1862, 62–64, 66–67.

15 Chabas 1901, 5–13, 16–19; Chabas 1902, 135–139, 142–145.

16 This publication cannot be found but is mentioned as: Massy, A., 1887: *Études égyptiennes III, Le papyrus de Leyde I 345*, Ghent.

17 Lexa 1925, 55–56.

18 *E.g.* Gardiner 1915, 262–269; Dawson 1927, 97–107; Dawson 1934b, 185–188. In the commentaries on specific incantations, spells, etc., references to these articles will be given.

19 Massart 1954.

20 GdM IV.1, 77, 79, 83, 258, 265, 316; IV.2, 76–78, 80–81, 201, 197, 237; V, 132–133, 135, 441, 453–454 (with transcription, translation, and commentary); Bardinet 1995, 231, 475–477 (with translation and commentary); Westendorf 1999, 65–68 (with translation and commentary).

21 Müller 2008, 275–293 (including information on the papyrus, translation, and commentary); Borghouts 1978, 18–21, 102; Fischer-Elfert 2005, 43–44, 135; both with translations and commentary.

22 Beck 2015b, 98–161 (including information on the object, transcription, transliteration, translation, and commentary).

3. Description of the manuscript

The manuscript can be reconstructed to a length of 510 + x cm. The beginning of the papyrus is broken off (papyrus Leiden I 343) and only one third of what is now the first column has been preserved. The manuscript's first lines contain the end of an incantation, so there must have been at least one other column at the beginning. Additionally, the size of the missing parts between the fragments of columns R:XXIII, V:XXI, and V:XXII cannot be ascertained. The manuscript has an average height of 18–20 cm, which is common for the book style in the New Kingdom.[23] The upper and lower edges are torn. Müller claims the manuscript was rolled together with papyrus Leiden I 344, and notes that the state of preservation confirms this.[24] The state of preservation in fact does not corroborate this view, as the beginning and end of the papyrus are intact (except for the missing part at the beginning noted above), but the middle is mostly fragmentary.[25]

The fibres on the recto side run horizontally and those on the verso side run vertically. The recto consists of 28 columns and the verso of 25 columns.[26] On the recto, the pages have 12 lines on average, while those on the verso have 11. The average width of the columns is 16.7 cm, but the narrowest column is only 6.5 cm (V:VIII) and the widest column is 34.2 cm (R:XXI).[27] A slight tendency for wider columns on the verso can be observed. The papyrus has darkened and the ink has partially rubbed off, especially at the beginning of papyrus Leiden I 343. The surface of the papyrus has a slight sheen, probably due to older conservation treatment.[28] The manuscript has been written in beautiful, even handwriting.[29] 'Verse points' only appear on the recto, with the exception of

23 Möller 1927, 5; Černý 1952, 8, 16–17.

24 Müller 2008, 275.116; cf. Enmarch 2005, 3–5.

25 For the state of preservation, see Borghouts 1971, 2. Due to its condition, it is impossible to detect the length of the manuscript's pages or to say something about the gluing.

26 The column count follows Massart's edition. For the former names of the columns, see Massart 1954, 3–6.

27 The widest column can also be part of the original inscription, because the phrasing and content do not resemble the other texts.

28 For the state of preservation, see also the table in Appendix II.

29 Chabas remarks that a change in handwriting can be observed in V:VI, but concedes that the content remains similar. The ductus of the rush is indeed thinner, but the scribe's hand is still the same; Leemans 1846–1862, Text II, 68.

Incantation	Recto	Verso	Remarks
1	I1–4	II4–10	*s-m-n*/*ꜥḫ.w* are not mentioned, the preceding incantation is against *ꜥḫ.w* (No. 11); similar, but no duplicates
2	I4–III2	III1–IV8	*s-m-n* (rt.) and *ꜥḫ.w* (vs.)
3	III2–IV9	V8–VII5	*s-m-n* (rt./vs.) and *ꜥḫ.w* (rt./vs.)
4	IV9–VI2	VII5–VIII12	*ꜥḫ.w* (rt. ?) and *s-m-n* (vs. ?)
5	VI2–VIII9	XI, XII, XIII	*s-m-n* (rt.) and *ꜥḫ.w* (vs.?); partially duplicated by oLeipzig ÄMUL 1906 (R:VI2–VII4) and oStrasbourg H. 115 (R:VII6–VIII8)
6	VIII10–X9	XIV, XV	*ꜥḫ.w* (rt./vs.)
7	X9–XI1	XVI	*s-m-n*/*ꜥḫ.w* are not mentioned, but the epithet 'you that are submerged' and the Deities-Hathors-Formula are used
8	XI2–14	XVII	*ꜥḫ.w* (rt.) and *s-m-n* (vs. ?)
9	XXII1+ x+1–2	–	*s-m-n*; originally also part of the verso (?)
10	–	I1–8	*ꜥḫ.w*; originally also part of the recto (?)
11	–	I8–II3	*s-m-n*/*ꜥḫ.w* are not mentioned, initial *k.t* suggests an incantation against that demon; originally also part of the recto (?)
12	–	IV9–V8	*ꜥḫ.w*; not duplicated, part of the original inscription
13	–	IX1–X2	*ꜥḫ.w*; not duplicated, part of the original inscription
14	–	XXII1–3	*ꜥḫ.w*; originally also part of the recto (?)

Table 1. *Duplicates of the incantations against Sāmānu/Akhu.*

incantation 13 (V:IX1–X2), which shows verse points on the verso as well. The different incantations, spells and remedies are divided by means of rubra. Usually, the beginning and the cure's ingredients or the quanta are written in red. The text of the papyrus is positioned upside down on the verso in relation to the recto and is a palimpsest. Incantations 12 (V:IV9–V:V8) and 13 (V:IX1–X2) are written in the same hand and could be part of the original text, since they do not show any signs of palimpsest.[30] The ends of the papyrus (on both sides) are left blank,[31] so that the verso page ends with *k.t* 'another'.

4. Reconstruction of the papyrus in its original form

For a reconstruction of the manuscript and its original form, see Adhémar Massart's detailed description[32] and the table in Appendix II.

5. Content

The Leiden magical papyrus I 343 + 345 mainly contains a collection of incantations against the ancient Near Eastern disease-demon Sāmānu (*s-m-n*) and his Egyptian equivalent Akhu (*ꜥḫ.w*). Usually, Sāmānu is addressed on the recto, while Akhu is dealt with in the duplicated incantations on the verso (see Table 1).

The manuscript contains a total of 14 spells against the demon, eight of which are duplicates. Incantations 12 (V:IV9–V8) and 13 (V:IX1–X2) are unique in the papyrus.[33]

30 See Massart 1954, 6–7.
31 There are approx. 6 cm on the recto and 29 cm on the verso.
32 Massart 1954, 2–6.
33 See Section I.3 above.

Pages (*recto*)	Directed against:	Pages (*verso*)	Directed against:
I1–4 (incantation 1)	*s-m-n* (?)	I1–8 (incantation 10)	*ʿḫ.w*
I4–III2 (incantation 2)	*s-m-n*	I8–II3 (incantation 11)	*ʿḫ.w* (?)
III2–IV9 (incantation 3)	*s-m-n*	II4–10 (incantation 1)	*ʿḫ.w* (?)
IV9–VI2 (incantation 4)	*ʿḫ.w* (?)	III1–IV8 (incantation 2)	*ʿḫ.w*
VI2–VIII9 (incantation 5)	*s-m-n*	IV9–V8 (incantation 12)	*ʿḫ.w*
VIII10–X9 (incantation 6)	*ʿḫ.w*	V8–VII5 (incantation 3)	*ʿḫ.w*
X9–XI1 (incantation 7)	*s-m-n* (?)	VII5–VIII12 (incantation 4)	*ʿḫ.w* (?)
XI2–14 (incantation 8)	*ʿḫ.w*	IX1–X2 (incantation 13)	*ʿḫ.w* and *ʿ* (blow ?)
XII–XXI (fragmentary)	?	XI–XIII (fragmentary, incantation 5)	*ʿḫ.w* (?)
XXII1+x+ 1–2 (incantation 9)	*s-m-n*	XIV–XV (fragmentary, incantation 6)	*ʿḫ.w*
XXIII–XXV1+x+2 (fragmentary)	?	XVI (fragmentary, incantation 7)	*ʿḫ.w* (?)
XXV1+x+2–XXVI2 (conjuration (?) 1)	*s.t-ʿ* of god, the dead, opponents	XVII (fragmentary, incantation 8)	*s-m-n* (?)
XXVI7–9 (remedy 1)	a swelling of the feet or any limb	XVIII–XXI (fragmentary)	*ʿḫ.w* (?)
XXVI9–10 (remedy 2)	ditto	XXII1–3 (incantation 14)	*ʿḫ.w*
XXVI11 (remedy 3)	ditto	XXII3–4 (conjuration (?) 4)	*mn.t nb.t* 'any pain'
XXVI11–12 (remedy 4)	ditto	XXIII1–7+x+1 (conjuration 5)	sore feet/*wḫd.w*
XXVI12–XXVII6 (conjuration 2)	inflammation of the leg (?; *sḏꜣ*)	XXIII7+x+1–XXIV	ditto or same conjuration?
XXVII6–XXVIII5 (conjuration 3)	ditto	XXV1–2 (spell 1)	for 'falling water'
		XXV2–4 (spells 2+3)	ditto

Table 2. *Distribution of incantations, spells, and remedies in the papyrus.*

Spells 9 (R:XXII1+x+1–2), 10 (V:I1–8), 11 (V:I8–II3), and 14 (V:XXII1–3) may originally have been part of the recto or verso (spell 9), but have not been preserved as such. Because the beginning of the papyrus is missing, no name is known for this composite manuscript. The various spells usually start with *k.t šn.t* 'another incantation' on the recto and *k.t* 'another' on the verso. Only R:X9 (incantation 7) is without a superscription, and R:XI2 (incantation 8) begins with just *k.t*. A typical epithet of the demon is 'you that are submerged', and the incantations often end with the 'Deities–Hathors–Formula' (hereinafter DHF) and remedies. The incantations usually consist of themes which are not common to Egyptian literature. Allusions to Canaanite myths abound.[34] Incantation 14 seems to use only genuine Egyptian topics.

34 See the specific commentaries on the Sāmānu/Akhu incantations below; Beck 2015b, 242–244.

Somewhere between fragmentary columns R:XXII–XXV and V:XXII, the content of the papyrus changes. The remaining conjurations are mainly against inflammations of the legs (2–3), sore feet (5), any kind of pain (4), and the effects of gods, the deceased, opponents, etc. Remedies 1–4 describe a therapy for swelling of the feet or any other limb caused by *wḫd.w*, and spells 1–2 shall cause the 'falling of water' (see Table 2).

6. Language and grammar

The papyrus is mainly written in classical Middle Egyptian – some texts are even pure Middle Egyptian – but the influence of Late Egyptian is obvious in the spellings, the use of words not found in Middle Egyptian, and/or in the grammar. Words that are generally written in Late Egyptian spelling include *wꜥr* (R:II6, V:IV2; WB I, 286), *jꜣ.t* (R:IV6; WB I, 26), *bšꜣ* (R:I12, V:II5, V:III7; WB I, 478), *pḥ.ty* (R:IV12, R:X5, V:VII7; WB I, 539), *nrw* (V:XXI1; WB II, 277), *swhj* (R:VII2; WB IV, 71), *fꜣj* (R:VII3, R:IX9, V:V3; WB I, 572), *ḥwj* (R:III4, 5, IV3, 4, V1, VII4, IX5, 10–11, XI13; V:II5, 7, V10, VI1, VIII1, 9, XIV2, XVIII1, XX2; WB III, 46–48), *ꜥmꜥꜣ.t* (R:IX8; WB I, 186), *šnw* (R:XXIx+2; WB IV, 495), *šrj* (V:V5; WB IV, 523), and *tnr.w* (R:IX13–14, V:III2; WB V, 382–383). The *t*-ending is usually omitted in infinitives and participles. To a certain extent, typical Late Egyptian words are used, such as the negations *bn* (V:XV1) and *bw* (V:IV10) and the adverbs *r-bnr* (R:II7, V12; V:IV2.3, VII2, XV1, XVIII1) and *dy* (V:VII1.2). Examples of Late Egyptian grammar include the use of the suffix *=w* for the third person plural (R:VII6.7, V:VII1, V:XII1), the Late Egyptian participle *j:ḏd* (V:V7) and the aforementioned negations *bw* and *bn*. In general, the definite article (*pꜣ, tꜣ, nꜣ*) is frequently used and the construction *pꜣ n.ty* etc. appears often. The construction *jw=f ḥr sḏm* is widely used, and seems to have replaced the older *sḏm=f* and *sḏm.n=f*. It is not always possible to tell whether it is used as a Middle Egyptian adverbial clause, a 'narrative' clause or – depending on the context – a virtual relative clause. In a few cases, one finds a Late Egyptian first person present clause (R:V11, V:IV2). The periphrastic construction with the verb *jrj* is common in the papyrus. On the whole, a somewhat greater preference for Late Egyptian words and grammar can be noted on the verso.

7. Importance of the text

The disease demon Sāmānu (*s-m-n*) and his Egyptian equivalent Akhu (*ꜥḫ.w*) are only known from a handful of other incantations and remedies, most of which date to the New Kingdom. The oldest attestation of Sāmānu/Akhu in Egypt is preserved in papyrus BM EA 10059. This manuscript dates to the 18th Dynasty and contains two different spells: one against Sāmānu (R:VII6–7) in a foreign language and one against Akhu (V:XIV1–7) in Egyptian – which, surprisingly, are written on different sides of the papyrus. Thus it is not clear whether Sāmānu really corresponds to Akhu, as in papyrus Leiden I 343 + 345.[35] Only one spell in papyrus Leiden I 343 + 345 (incantation 5) is repeated in other Egyptian texts: ostracon Leipzig ÄMUL 1906[36] and ostracon Strasbourg H.115.[37] The former replicates the incantations at the beginning (R:VI2–VII4) and the latter repeats the end of the spell (R:VII6–VIII8). Another spell against Akhu is preserved in papyrus Leiden I 348, which dates to the 19th Dynasty (R:XII7–11).[38] The themes used in this incantation are genuinely Egyptian. Papyrus Chester Beatty VI recto (papyrus BM EA 10686) contains two remedies against Akhu (R:VI8–11): 'manual of all remedies of medicine: remedy to repel Akhu on the anterior trunk, to treat his sides.'[39] Akhu is mentioned as a potential cause of death in papyrus Turin 1996 (V:II9, 20th Dynasty).[40] In the oracular amuletic decree papyrus Turin 1983, both Sāmānu and Akhu are mentioned (V:29–31). They form

35 See *e.g.* Leitz 1999, 63, 80, Pls. 32, 39; Beck 2015b, 93–98, 247–248 with further references.

36 See Černý/Gardiner 1957, I, 5, 30, Pls. CXIV3, XIV5, XIVa5; Beck 2015, 126–140.

37 See Koenig 1997, 10, Pls. 50–52, 117; Mathieu 2000, 248–249; Müller 2000, 280–281; Beck 2015b, 127–140.

38 See *e.g.* Borghouts 1971, 26, 125–129, Pls. 12–12A, 29; Beck 2015b, 162–164 with further references.

39 See *e.g.* Gardiner 1935, I 53–54, II Pls. 31–31A; Beck 2015b, 164–165 with further references.

40 See *e.g.* Roccatti 2011, 30–33, 171–172; Beck 2015b, 166–167 with further references.

a group with other skin diseases, but they appear in different sentences, so it is not clear whether Sāmānu still equals Akhu in this manuscript.[41] The most recent attestation dates to the early Ptolemaic Period. Amazingly, in this amulet Akhu is said to afflict the bones (papyrus Cologne 3545).[42]

As the syllabic writing of his name clearly shows, Sāmānu is foreign to Egypt. This demon is well known from numerous texts from Mesopotamia, including incantations in Sumerian and Akkadian and bilinguals, remedies, lexical lists, and astronomical diaries. In Mesopotamia, the demon could afflict gods, men, animals (sheep, cattle, asses), and plants (rust/fungus and pests), as well as rivers.[43] In Egypt, as the texts show, he is only attested as a human disease. Sāmānu is clearly a kind of skin alteration or skin disease in Mesopotamia – and probably in Egypt too.[44]

It is remarkable that the incantations against Sāmānu/Akhu in papyrus Leiden I 343 + 345 contain numerous allusions to Canaanite myths and legends, *e.g.* the Baal Cycle and the Legend of Keret. Often it is not clear whether the texts refer to Baal or Seth, so the term 'weather god' is used in the translation, in line with a suggestion from M. Müller.[45] Alongside the weather god, who appears as the main opponent of Sāmānu/Akhu, and of course the Egyptian deities, Canaanite deities play a major part in the incantations: Reshep (R:XI13–14, R:V6), Anat (R:III12, R:VI11), Astarte (R:VIIIx+1), Ishkhara (V:II2), and the moon god ('the god above') (R:II11/V:IV6, R:V56/V:VIII2). Some deities are only attested in papyrus Leiden I 343 + 345: Nikkal (R:V6/V:VIII3, R:IX12), Shala (V:XVII1), and Adamma (R:V7/V:VIII5). Certain beings and themes cannot be identified, but are clearly not genuinely Egyptian, *e.g.* the demonic Ḏhr and Nḳpḥn/Pḳsn (*Ḏꜣ-hꜣ-r' ḥnꜥ Nḳp-ḥꜣw-nꜣ/Pw-ḳ-sꜣw-njꜣ*, R:II8/V:IV4), Mrj (*Mꜥw-r'-jꜣ*, R:VI7), Mšr (*mꜥ-šr*, R:III3/V:V9), Ṯmkn (*ṯꜣ-mꜥ-nꜣ-kꜣ*, R:III4/V:V10), and Jbsn (*jb*(*w*)-*sw-nꜣ*, R:III5/V:V10–11). The same can be said of subjects like 'the dry land/desert will drink you (= Sāmānu/Akhu). The dry land/desert has drunken you', 'the poisons of deity X are against you', and the DHF. Even if the demon, the gods (though not all of them), and the themes used in the incantations are not typically Egyptian, the structure, language, and methods are characteristic of Egyptian spells, hence the use of historiolae, rhetorical questions, and analogies (Horus as patient, magician as god X, magician's assignment of his spell to a god/goddess, deification of the body/'*Gliedervergottung*').[46]

It is remarkable that 'foreign deities and subjects are only used in the incantations against Sāmānu/Akhu. The other conjurations, remedies, and spells are *really* Egyptian. Furthermore, the rear part of the papyrus focuses on swelling and inflammation of the legs or feet, which leads one to wonder if there was a reason for collecting these spells in one composite manuscript.

41 See Edwards 1960, I 57–61, II Pls. XXa–XX, XXIa–XXI; Beck 2015b, 167–168.

42 See Kurth 1980, 9–53, Pls. I–III; Fischer-Elfert 2015, 174–208; Beck 2015b, 168–169 with further references.

43 See Beck 2015b, 171–208.

44 The disease could probably be identified with cutaneous leishmaniasis, impetigo contagiosa, furuncle and erysipelas with some limitations; see Beck 2015b, 182–193; Beck 2016c, 33–46. Whether the demon covers the same potential ailments in Egypt as in Mesopotamia is not clear.

45 Müller 2008, 276–277.

46 See Beck 2015b, 246; Beck 2015a, 94–100, which compares the Mesopotamian and Egyptian incantations against Sāmānu.

PART II

Text with transliteration, translation and commentary

Text with transliteration, translation and commentary

1. Incantation 1 (R:I1–I4/V:II4–II10)

In the first incantation neither Sāmānu nor Akhu is mentioned. On the verso, however, the incantation follows an incantation against Akhu (incantation 10; V:I1–8), so one may assume that this spell was directed against the demon as well. Due to the fragmentary state of the papyrus, the content is difficult to interpret. On the recto, only the last three lines have been preserved. It should be noted that the incantations resemble each other but are not true duplicates.[47]

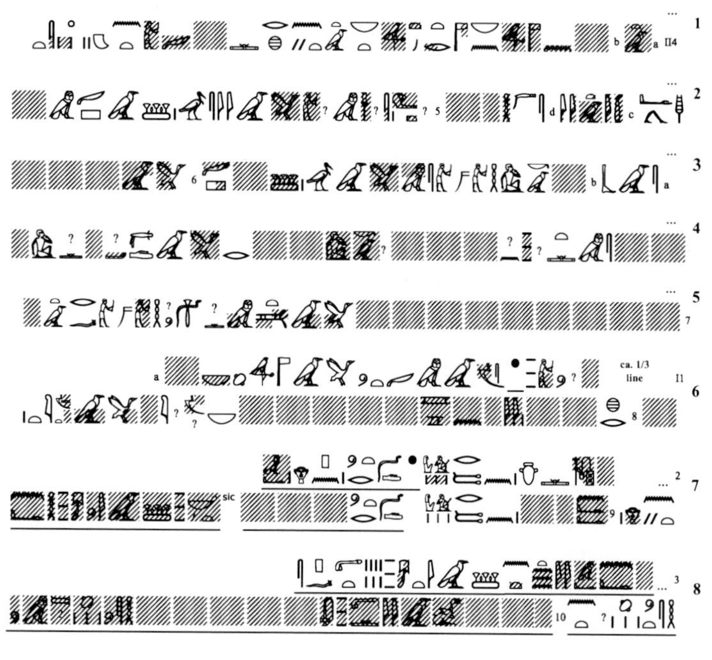

R:I approx. 1/3 of the line is missing; 1a traces could fit mꜣꜥ.t; V:II4a–b not visible any more; 4c–d according to Gardiner, a 'mere guess', traces match his suggestion; 5a–b group difficult to read due to sticky tape.

47 See Massart 1954, 49.

Transliteration

	Recto		Verso	
1		*not preserved*	II4	*tꜣ* [...] *n nṯr nb n ntr.t nb.t tꜣ n.ty rḫ* [...] *n.t ḥmt st*
2		-//-	II4–5	*ꜥḥꜥ*[*.tj tꜣ*]*y=s mḥ*[*.t m*] *ḥꜣ.t=s* [*sḫ*]*m* [*p*]*ꜣy=s b*(*ꜣ*)*šꜣ m* [...]
3		-//-	II5–6	*sꜣb* [...] *kꜣ ḥwj=s* [*m p*]*ꜣ b*(*ꜣ*)[*šꜣ*] *pꜣ* [...]
4		-//-	II6	[...]*sm.wt n* [...] *kꜣ* [...] *r* [*p*]*ꜣ šd* [...]
5		-//-	II7	[...] *pꜣ tm w*(*ꜣ*)*ḏ ḥwj r=f tꜣ* [...]
6	I1	[...] ° *smꜣ*(*m*) *tw pꜣ nṯr nb* [*mꜣꜥ.t*?]	II7–8	*ḫr* [...] *y*[*m*]*n* [...] *nb mꜣ*[*ꜥ.t*] *pꜣ mꜣꜥ.t*(*j*)
7	I2	[... *s:nꜥꜥ*] *jb n*(*.j*) *r*(*m*)*ṯ* ° *dd.tw r' pn hr m*[*y.t* ...]	II8–9	*n.ty ḥr* <*s:*>[*nꜥꜥ jb*] *n*(*.j*) *r*(*m*)*ṯ dd.tw r*[*' pn* ... *k.wt šꜣj.w ḥnꜥ*]
8	I3	[*ḥnꜥ my*]*.t n.t šꜣj.w*(*t*) *7 ṯꜣ.y pfs*[*.w*]	II9–10	*ḥs*(*w*){*.t*} *n.t*? [... *šꜣj.w*] *ṯꜣ.y.w pfs*(*.w*) [... *ḥs*(*w*) *t* ... *mw*]
9	I4	[...]	II10	[*dd.w* ...]

Translation

1 The [...] for every god (and) for every goddess, she who knows [...] of copper. She
2 has stood up, her fea[ther (?) in] front of her. Her axe exerts power over [...]
3 She shall strike [with th]e ax[e ...]
4 the (?) [...] May [...] the reciter (?) [...]
5 [...] the unfruitful one who strikes against him the [...]
6 (rt.) [...] the god, lord of truth (shall) kill you [...]
6 (vs.) fall (?) [...] Se[a ...] lord of tru[th ...] the righteous one,
7 who pleases the heart of men. This spell is to be said over uri[ne] of pigs and
8 urine/dung of seven boars, to be cooked [...] dung [...]
9 [...] to be placed [on it/him].

Commentary

1 V:II4: Massart 1954, 104.1 and Müller 2008, 289, suggest that *k.t* 'another' was written at the end of line 3. Theoretically there is enough space at the end of that line, but the papyrus seems to be blank. Perhaps the manuscript was intensively rubbed off there. A new incantation begins in line 4 because a recipe ends in the previous line. — V:II4 *tꜣ* [...]: It is not clear what term comes next. Massart 1954, 104.3, proposes *ḥn.wt* 'mistress' as a restoration, similarly Müller 2008, 289. The feminine article implies that a word in the feminine follows, as does the adverbial clause with the pronoun *st* and the feminine ending of the stative, which seems to refer to *tꜣ*.

1–2 V:II4 *st ꜥḥꜥ*[*.tj*]: This is a rare appearance of the Late Egyptian first present clause in the manuscript. For the pronoun, see Černý/Groll 1984, 32–33 and Junge 2008, 118.

2 V:II4 *mḥ*[*.t*]: Perhaps *mḥ* can be restored to *mḥ.t* 'feather' as in R:IV5/V:VII12 and V:XXII1. See the translation in WB II, 123.6. Massart 1954, 104.5, suggests the restoration

mḥn.yt 'encircler (the Uraeus)' (WB II, 129.3–6). Müller 1954, 289.199, cautions against certainty regarding the specific lemma because only *mḥ* has been preserved. The preposition *m* can be assumed to have stood at the end of the line so that *m-ḥ3.t* could be constructed with the next line. — V:II5 *bš3* 'axe, chisel': See Hoch 1994, 110–111, for the term. According to Gardiner 1947, I, 69*.169, this tool is used for chipping rather than cutting. He points to papyrus Turin 138.4 (Pleyte/Rossi 1869, II, Pl. 138), where a head injury is inflicted by a *bš3*. — [*sḫ*]*m* ... *m*: For usage with cutting instruments, see WB IV, 248.2. The *sḫm*-scepter looks a bit odd in hieratic, but the other signs are clear, see Massart 1954, 104.7.

3 Massart 1954, 105.10, suggests restoring [*r*] at the end of the line. The verb *ḥwj* can also be constructed with a direct object, see WB III, 46. — V:II6 *p3* [...]: Massart 1954, 105.10, proposes restoring *ʿḫ.w* after the definite article. The traces on the papyrus do not accurately match Sāmānu or Akhu.

4 V:II6 *šd*: This could also be translated as 'saviour' (WB IV, 463.10–11).

6 V:II8 [...] *y*[*m*]*n*: See incantation 4 (below § 4) line 5 for this unusual spelling of the word 'sea'. — V:II8 *nb m3*[*ʿ.t*]: Massart 1954, 105.14, suggests restoring [*p3 nfr nṯr*] 'the good god' as the preceding phrase.

7–8 R:I2–3/V:II8–10: Urine is used on the recto, while excrement is specified on the verso. In Egypt, urine was used in bandages, ophthalmic agents, incense materials, ointments and enemas (GdM VI, 235–237; Nunn 1996, 149). The use of animal urine is rare; see GdM VI, 236–237, which refers only to the urine of a dun ass and does not mention the urine of sows and boars. Urine contains, among other things, urea, enzymes, hormones, water, and metabolic and surplus products from the body (Krebs 1942, 19–20; Höting 1997a, 64–68; Thomas 1999, 110–111; Pschyrembel 2011, 825, table (*Harn*)). The curative effect of urine is mainly due to urea and hormones. Urea smoothes the skin and supplies it with moisture; it is antimicrobial and antipruritic (Krebs 1942, 33, 85; Höting 1997a, 67–68; Höting 1997b, 18–19; Thomas 1999, 183; Győry 2002, 54; Pschyrembel 2011, 828 (*Harnsäure*)). Some of the hormones found in urine, for example corticosteroids, are anti-inflammatory and inhibit allergies (Krebs 1942, 19, 26; Höting 1997a, 64–68; Höting 1997b, 20–23). Urine is traditionally used in cold and warm compresses for treating skin alterations, wounds, sunburns, ulcerations and mycosis in general (Krebs 1942, 96; Höting 1997a, 90–92, 166–171; Thomas 1999, 67, 108–110). The specific composition of the urine depends on various factors, i.e. nutrition, health, and environment. No information is available for animal urine; see Höting 1997b, 109–111; Thomas 1999, 27–29. The statements here are based on human urine. Faeces were used for topical as well as internal therapies in Egypt, but the focus was definitely on topical treatments such as bandages and ointments (GdM VI, 353–362; Nunn 1996, 149, 220). The *Dreckapotheke* has played a part in medicine since time immemorial. It is commonly used in analogical treatments (Goede 2006, 8–14; Kolta/Schwarzmann-Schafhauser 2000, 143–145; Sipos *et al.* 2004, 211). Faeces contain approximately 75% water and 25% solid matter, of which 30% is mixed with bacteria, 15% is inorganic matter, and 5% is fats. Glucocorticoids, hormones, enzymes, and various vitamins can also be detected. Of course, faeces contain waste products, which are toxic. The enzymes in faeces are supposed to enhance the curative effects of ointments. Parts of the bacteria, specifically their metabolic products, enable faeces to function as an antibiotic and possibly also as an antimycotic. Excrement burns well due to high levels of fats and raw fibres, and is therefore often used in incense. At the same time, the smoke has narcotic effects due to sulphuric substances. See Westendorf 1992, 259; Sipos *et al.* 2004, 212; Pschyrembel 2011, 1115 (*Kot*). The statements here are based on human faeces.

8 V:II9 [*š3j.w*] *ṯ3y.w*: lit. 'masculine pigs'. For general information on swine, see Hopfner 1913, 61–62; Dawson 1928, 597–608; el-Huseny 2006; Volokhine 2014, 233–238, especially 234–235. For special properties of the number seven, see Sethe 1916, 33–37; Dawson 1927, 97–107; Goyon 1985, 185–188; Kees 1987, 158–159; Rochholz 2002, 200–201.

2. Incantation 2 (R:I4–III2/V:III1–IV8)

The incantation's beginning is severely damaged. The spell is directed against Sāmānu on the recto and against Akhu on the verso. At the beginning, the magician asks for strong words to utter. The weather god then fights the demon, smashing his dwelling and eventually dispersing his companions. Then Sāmānu/Akhu is blinded, and a strange episode with two otherwise unknown deities (*Nkpḥn*/*Pḳsn* and *Ḏhr*) follows; they deflower the maidens and emasculate the gods. The incantation ends with a recipe for a bandage. In several parts of the spell there are tangible allusions to Canaanite myths.

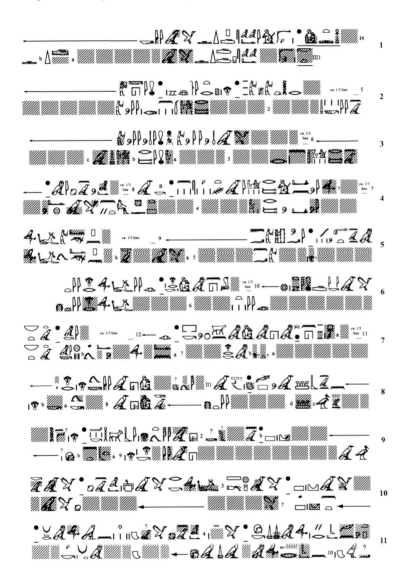

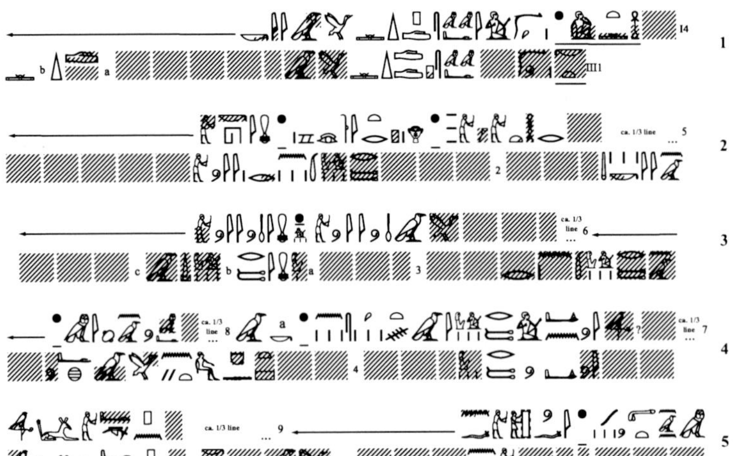

R:I7a traces are visible above and , remains of the palimpsest; 10a under the line; 11a Gardiner reads ; R:II1a traces; 1b verse point and no longer visible; V:III1a–b traces of palimpsest above the line; 3a or ; 3b–c barely legible; 5a–b barely legible; 6a–b no longer legible; 7a no longer legible; 7b no longer legible; 7c–d no longer legible; 8a–b barely visible; 9a–b no longer legible.

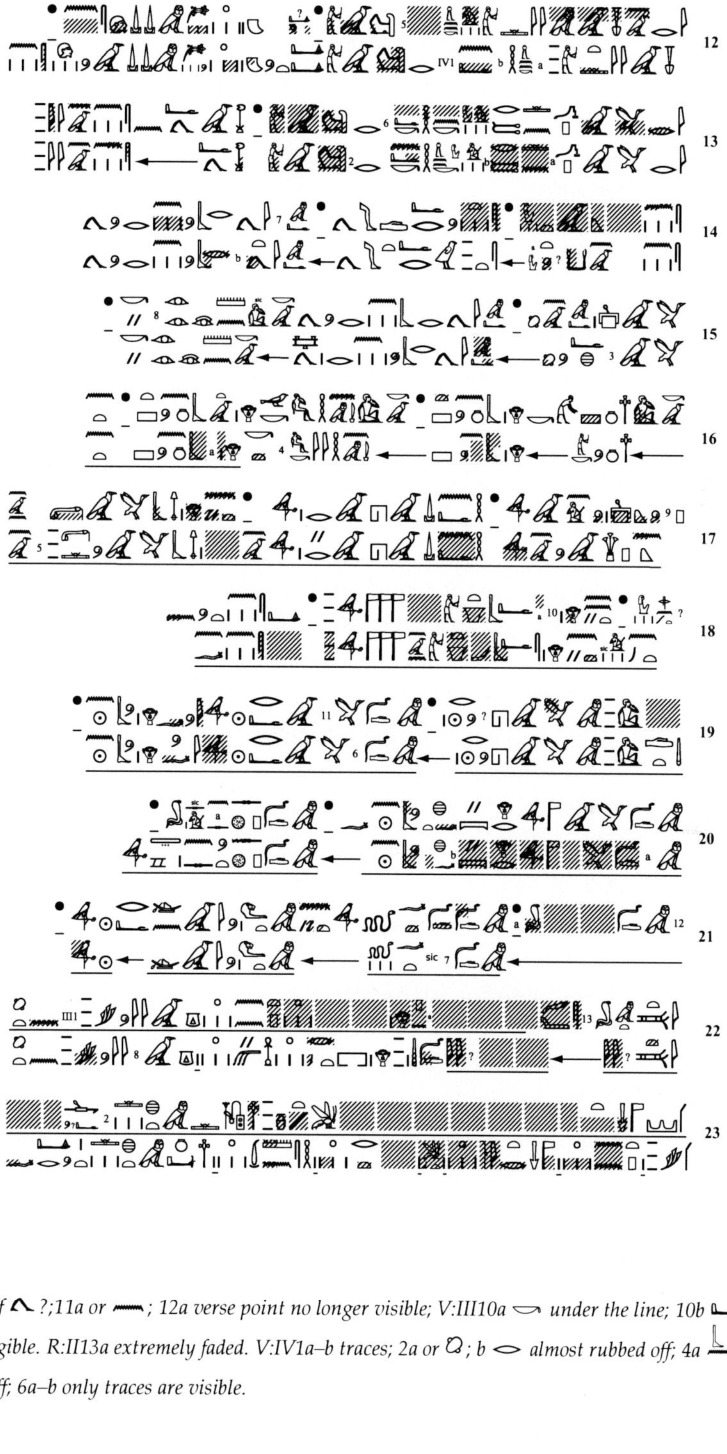

R:II10a if ?;11a or ; 12a verse point no longer visible; V:III10a under the line; 10b no longer legible. R:II13a extremely faded. V:IV1a–b traces; 2a or ; b almost rubbed off; 4a almost rubbed off; 6a–b only traces are visible.

Transliteration

	Recto		Verso	
1	I4	[k.t] šn.t° ns=j jmm spd pꜣy=k	III1	k.t ns[=j j]mm spd{d} pꜣ[y=k … jmm] [sp]d[{d}]
2	I5	[…] r(?) [ḥ]w.t_° ḥr p{t}rj_° mj kh	III1–2	nꜣy=k md[w.wt …] r(m)ṯ.w tnr(y).w […]
3	I6	[…]{p} <n> ꜣ ḫrw.y.w_° mj ḫrwy.w	III2–3	nꜣ r(m)ṯ tnr[y.w …] mj r(m)ṯ ḏꜣ[…]
4	I7–8	[…] jw ḏj n=j r(m)ṯ jꜣ.wt=sn_° kꜣ […] [sꜣ]-mʿw-nꜣ jm_°	III3–4	[…] jw ḏj(w) <n=j> r(m)ṯ [… s].t-ḥmz n.ty pꜣ ʿḫ.w [jm](?)
5	I8–9	m nꜣ n(.w) mt.w_° jw=f ḳd n=f […] [kꜣ] pnʿ Stẖ(?)	III4–5	[… ḥr ḳd] n=f […] pꜣ […] kꜣ pnʿ Stẖ(?)
6	I9–10	pꜣy=k d[mj.t …] nhm(.w) ḥr=k_° jr.y Stẖ(?) ḥr.yt	III5–6	[pꜣy=k dmj …] jr.ywt [… jr] Stẖ(?) ḥr.y[t]
7	I11–12	[mꜣ]j.w nh{_°}mhm(.w) m-ẖnw=k_° jr […] jm=k_° tꜣ nb.t	III6–7	[…] tw m-ḥr=k […] ʿn[…] ʿ[w] zp-sn jm=k tꜣ nb.t
8	I12–II1	n(.t) nꜣ n(.j) bšꜣ(w)_° šmꜣ(?) […] j[… kꜣ] hꜣ.y=k ḥr ḥr=[k]?	III7–8	[n(.t) n]ꜣ n(.j) b(ꜣ)šꜣ [… ḥr.]yt kꜣ hꜣ[.y]=k [ḥr]=k ḥr
9	II1–2	[ḥr tbn.t n.t] ḏw_° [n]ꜣ [… D56(?) <jr>=k] hꜣy.t ḥr jbḥ.w=k_° ḥr nḏḥ[.t=k ḥr(?)]	III8–9	bꜣ […] h[ꜣ.y] ḥr=k ḥr [tbn.t]
10	II2–3	[…] pꜣ ḏw_° pꜣ ḫpš Stẖ(?) r=k pꜣ sꜣ-mʿ-nꜣ_° pꜣ k(ꜣ)	III9	n.t ḏw pꜣ […] pꜣ
11	II3–4	tp(w) n(.j) Bʿyr' m ḏꜣḏꜣ=k_° p[ꜣ sꜣ]-mʿ-nꜣ pꜣ ḥmt n(.j) ḥr.w m wp.t=k_°	III9–10	[…]fw n(.j) Bʿ[y]r m [ḏ]ꜣḏꜣ[=k …] ḥmt […] m wp.t=k
12	II4–5	jr nꜣ zmꜣ{m}.yw jn.n=k [ḥnʿ=k r] ʿḥꜣ_° ḏj[.t]w ḥmt ʿšꜣ(.w) m ḏꜣḏꜣ=sn_°	III10–IV1	[jr nꜣ n.w] zmꜣ.yt jn.n=k ḥn[ʿ] <=k> r ʿḥꜣ dd.tw ḥmt ʿšꜣ(.w) m ḏꜣḏꜣ.w=sn
13	II5–6	jr pꜣ stp(.w) n(.j) r(m)ṯ [jn].n=k ḥ[n]ʿ=k r ʿḥ[ꜣ]_° ḫꜣʿ.n=sn nꜣy(w)	IV1–2	jr pꜣ stp(.w) [n.j r(m)ṯ] jn.n=k ḥnʿ=k r [ʿḥ]ꜣ ḫꜣʿ=sn nꜣy(w)
14	II6–7	=sn [nꜣ]ḳꜣ.wt_° st wʿr(d)(.w)_° mj r-bnr	IV2	=sn nꜣkꜣ.wt st wʿr(t)(.w) mj(.t) r-bnr
15	II7–8	pꜣ sꜣ-mʿ-nꜣ_° mj r-bnr kꜣ <kꜣ>mn jr.tj=ky_°	IV2–3	pꜣ ʿḫ.w m[j](.t) r-bnr kꜣmn jr.tj=ky
16	II8	kꜣ nḏ=k ḥr bnw.t_° kꜣ nmḥ=k ḥr tꜣ bnw.t_° n.t	IV3–4	nḏ(w)=k ḥr bnw<.t> nmḥ(y)=k {k.t} ḥr bnw<.t> n.t
17	II8–9	Pw-ḳ-sꜣw-njꜣ_° ḥnʿ Ḏꜣ-hꜣ-r'_° n.ty ḥr wbꜣ nꜣ n(.j)	IV4–5	Nkp-ḫꜣw-nꜣ ḥnʿ Ḏꜣ-hꜣy-r' nꜣ [n.ty] wbꜣ(w){.w} nꜣ
18	II9–10	rwn.wt_° n<ꜣ> n.ty ḥr [s]ʿb.t [nꜣ n.j] nṯr.w_° ḏj=sn tw n	IV5	<rn>n.wt n.ty ḥr sʿb.t nꜣ n(.j) nṯr.w [ḏj]=sn n={f}<=k>
19	II10–11	[mdw.]wt m pꜣ hrw_° m-ḏd pꜣ Rʿ(w) jw=f ḥr wbn_°	IV5–6	md(w).wt m pꜣ hrw m-ḏd pꜣ Rʿ(w) jw=f ḥr wbn
20	II11	m-ḏd pꜣ nṯr ḥr.y ḫft wbn=f_° m ḏd Zp-nz-{z}<tꜣ>	IV6	m-ḏd p[ꜣ] nṯr ḥr.y ḫf[t] wbn<-f> m-ḏd Zp.tw-n=z-tꜣ
21	II12	m ḏd […]_° m-ḏd ḏdf.t n.ty m-ḥꜣ.t wjꜣ n(.j) Rʿ(w)_°	IV6–7	m-ḏd <ḏd>f.{w}t m-ḥꜣ.t wjꜣ Rʿ(w)
22	II12–III1	Jtm.t s[ḳ] [dd.tw r' pn hr …] tpnn gꜣy.w n(.j) wḥꜣ.t	IV7–8	Jtm[.t …]y […]y [ḏd] md(w).w ḥr pr.t-šn(y) 1 gꜣy.w n(.j) wḥꜣ.t
23	III1–2	sntr […] bj.t nḏ(.w) s:nʿʿ m (j)ḫ.wt wʿ(.t) [ḏj.w r=f]	IV8	1 tp[nn] 1 snṯr 1 bj.t 1 [ḏꜣ]r.t 1 ḥsmn 1 nḏ(.w) m (j)ḫ.wt wʿ.t ḏj.w r=f

Translation

1 [Another] incantation/Another: O my tongue, let your [utterance ...] be sharp, let your speech

2 be sharp [...] to [stri]ke upon the battlefield so as raging [...] strong people

3 [...] {the (*sing.*)}<the (*pl.*)> enemies/strong people, so as enemies/people [...]

4 [...] The people flee from me. [...] the [...] the dwelling place in which Sāmānu/Akhu is,

5 within the vessels. He builds himself [a town (?) ...]. The weather god shall

6 destroy your town! [...] made [...] rejoices at you. The weather god shall spread terror.

7 [Li]ons which roar inside you. It (?) makes [...] in you twice. The mistress

8 of axes is wandering (?) around. [...] You shall fall upon your face.

9 [...] You shall [fall (?)] upon your teeth, upon [your] tu[sks ... upon (?)] the top

10 of the mountain! Seth's *khopesh* is against you, o Sāmāna/[o Akhu]. The

11 *ketep* of Baal is in your head, o Sāmānu/[o Akhu]. Horus' copper is in your vertex!

12 As to the band whom you have brought with you to fight: in their heads, much copper shall be given.

13 As to the choicest of people whom you have brought with you to fight: they abandoned

14 their trulls (?). They have fled. Come out,

15 o Sāmānu/o Akhu! Come out! Both of your eyes shall be blinded!

16 You shall grind on a millstone. You shall slave on the millstone of

17 Pḳsn/Nḳpsn and Ḏhr who deflower the

18 maidens (and) who emasculate the deities. They give you

19 words during the day (so as) Re says (when) he is shining,

20 (so as) the god above says while he is shining, (so as) Zepnesta says

21 (so as) [*a goddess*] says, (as) the serpent says which is in front of Re's barque,

22 Itemet who strikes (?) [...] Words to be said over [...] cumin/pine nuts (?), 1 nutgrass (?) of the oasis (1)

23 incense/cumin, 1, [...]/incense, 1, honey, 1, [...], (1), natron, (1), to be ground (finely) to a mass, to be applied to him/it.

Commentary

1 (R:I4/V:III1): According to Müller 2008, 278–279.138, the gap after *pꜣ[y=k ...]* is too big for the simple sequence of two consecutive requests on the verso that Massart 1954, 52, has suggested. One has to consider that the word in the gap has not been preserved and that it could have been extended by an attribute. Furthermore, it is conceivable that the phrase 'my tongue' was picked up again, which would definitely fit with the other word in the gap. There is no space for another request on the recto; see also Massart 1954, 53.4.

2 R:I5 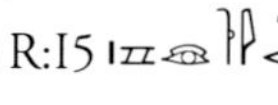: The word mixes the spelling of the verb 'to see' (WB I, 564.1–19) and the substantive 'battlefield' (WB I, 532.1); see also Massart 1954, 53.7.

4 R:I7 *jw dj n=j r(m)ṯ jꜣ.wt=sn*: lit. 'The people give me their backs.' On the verso (V:III3), <*n=j*> is omitted. A similar phrase, *dj n=f sꜣ*, is used in Sinuhe (B57/R81: Blackman 1932, 19.13–14; Koch 1990, 34.5–7; Gardiner 1916b, 34–35.57 with further attestations). *Jꜣ.t* is used for *sꜣ* here; see also Massart 1954, 54.10.

4–5 R:I8 [*sꜣ*]*-mꜥw-nꜣ jm*° *m nꜣ n*(*.w*) *mt.w*°: The phrasing *m nꜣ n*(*.w*) *mt.w* seems to specify the adverb *jm*, which is somewhat uncommon. Several phrases are specified in other incantations on the papyrus, for example in R:VIII1 (incantation 5); see also Massart 1954, 54.12. For information on the word *mt.w* 'vessels', see Breasted 1930, 109–113; Jonckheere 1947, 17.9; GdM I, 20–21, 43, 72–74; Walker 1996, 158, 236, 270; Nunn 1996, 44; Westendorf 1999, I, 127.

5–6 R:I9/V:III5 *kꜣ pnꜥ Stẖ*(?) *pꜣy=k dmj.t*: For this episode, compare a passage of the Baal Cycle in which Baal introduces himself before the fight with Yamm (CAT 1.2 IV 4–5) *ṯm.ḫrbm.its.anšq [b]htm* 'There, (with) a sword I will destroy! I will burn the houses!' See Parker 1997, 102. CAT suggests the restoration [*p*]*itm* 'temple'.

6 R:I10 *nhm*(*.w*) *ḥr=k*: The word *nhm* can be neither a stative nor a participle, because one would expect a feminine ending in reference to the goddess (whose identity has not been preserved). Note however that this goddess could be part of a mixed group of deities. See also Müller 2008, 279, who translates *nhm* as 'to triumph'.

7 R:I11 [*mꜣ*]*j.w nh*{°}*mhm*(*.w*) *m-ẖnw=k*: This passage is missing on the verso. The clause possibly refers to Baal, who is known as 'lion of heaven' and whose roaring is a synonym for thunder: Dhorme/Dessaud 1949, 100–101; see also V:VII7–8 (incantation 4): 'The lion is roaring inside you'. — V:III7 *ꜥn*[…]: Perhaps this can be restored to the goddess *ꜥntj* 'Anat'. For this deity, see Grdseloff 1942, 20–36; Stadelmann 1967, 88–96; Helck 1971, 460–463; Gray 1979, 320–324; Cornelius 1994, 75–76; Day, Anat ענת, in: Van der Toorn/Becking/Van der Horst 1995, 62–71; Cornelius 2004, 4 (previous literature); Tazawa 2009, 7, 72–82, 163–165.

8 R:I12–II1/V:III7 *šmꜣy*(*.t*): The reading of the sign cannot be verified in *šmꜣ* 'to wander' (WB IV, 470); the ending is odd but the determinative fits. The traces on the verso should instead be read as *ḥr.yt* 'terror' (WB III, 147–148).

8–10 R:II1–2/V:III7–9 'You shall fall upon your face. [...] You shall [fall (?)] upon your teeth, upon [your] tu[sks ... upon (?)] the top of the mountain!': For this passage, compare king Keret's reply when Yassib, his son, asked if he could assume the throne (Legend of Keret, CAT 1.16 VI 57–58): *tqln.bgbl šntk.bḫpnk.wtꜥn* 'You shall fall upon the tip of your teeth and you shall be humiliated by your greed/with your fist.' See Parker 1997, 42. *Šntk* is usually translated as 'your years', though *šnt* can also be 'teeth'; see DUL 832.

9 R:II2 *jbḥ* and *nḏḥ.t*: Both words have the meaning 'tooth' (WB I, 64, II, 304). A distinction between the meaning of the two words cannot be established at present. See GdM I, 41; Nunn 1996, 50, Fig. 3.4; Walker 1996, 266, 271; Westendorf 1999 I, 165–166.

10–11 R:II3/V:III9 *pꜣ ktp*: The word *ktp* is used here as a parallel for *ḫpš* 'sickle sword' and describes a similar kind of sword; see O'Callaghan 1952, 37–42; Hoch 1994, 337–338; also Bordreuil/Pardee 1993, 68; Vita/Watson 2002, 147; AHw I, 465. On the verso, the remains do not match *ktp* unless one opts for the reading *ktf*, which would be highly unexpected.

11 RII3/V:III10 *Bꜥyr'*: Usually the text only reads so it is not obvious if it refers to Seth or Baal. The spelling is therefore translated as 'weather god', in line with a proposal by Matthias Müller (Müller 2008, 276–277). Baal is only spelt in full five times (R:II3, V1; V:III10, VII5, 8). For this deity, see Dhorme/Dessaud 1949, 96–102, 362–363; Stadelmann 1967, 16, 27–47; Helck 1971, 447–450; Cornelius 1994, 8–10, 134–233; Wyatt 1999, 544–545. See Schwemer 2001 for weather deities in the ancient Near East. For Baal, see *ibid.* 510–542; Tazawa 2009, 5–6, 13–37, 114–116, 126–130, 154–158. For Seth, see Te Velde 1967.

10–11 R:II2–4/V:III9–10 'Seth's *khopesh* is against you, o Sāmānu/[o Akhu]. The *ketep* of Baal is in your head, o Sāmānu/[o Akhu]. Horus' copper is in your vertex!': Compare a similar passage in the Legend of Keret, where Keret answers his son Yassib when the latter asks if he can ascend to the throne (CAT 1.16 VI 54–57): *yṯbr ḥrn.ybn. yṯbr.ḥrn rišk.ꜥṯtrt.šm.bꜥl qdqd{r}*<*k*> 'May Ḥoron crack, o son, may Ḥoron crack your skull, Astarte name-of-Baal, <your> head!'. See Parker 1997, 42; similarly in CAT 1.2 II 7–8. Perhaps Horus appears here because his name is similar to that of Ḥoron. This does not mean that the two deities are identical.

12 R:II5/V:IV1 *dj*[*.tw*]*/dd.tw*: The verbs show different forms. The form seems to be a subjunctive ('may be given') on the recto and a substantival present *sḏm=f* ('that is (usually) given') on the verso. The substantival *sḏm=f* in the latter case is the subject of an adverbial clause (emphatic construction; 'That much copper is [usually] given, is in their heads.' → 'In their heads, much copper is [usually] given.'). — R:II5/V:IV1 : Besides the meaning 'numerous, rich', the word also describes a quality, i.e. 'common' or 'third-rate' (WB I, 228.21; Hayes 1942, 32; Arnold 1990, 118.N 42), so the translation could also be 'In their heads, common/third-rate copper is given.' This common/third-rate copper would be in contrast to Horus' copper in the previous line (suggestion by H.-W. Fischer-Elfert).

12–13 R:II4–6/V:III10–IV2 'As to the band whom you have brought with you to fight: in their heads, much copper shall be given. As to the choicest of people whom you have brought with you to fight (...)': This passage could be compared with incantation RIH 78/20 8–10 *aphm kšpm.dbbm.ygrš.ḥrn ḥbrm.wġlm.dʿtm* 'immediately afterwards, Ḥoron cast out the companions (with) sorcery (and) incantations (?) and the boy the fellows.' (Bordreuil/Caquot 1980, 346). The term *ġlm* 'boy' is an epithet of Ḥoron; see Rahmouni 2008, 266–268.

13 R:II5/V:IV1 *stp*(*.w*) *n*(*.j*) *r*(*m*)*ṯ*: See WB IV, 399.1–2 for this phrase. — R:II6/V:IV2 *ḫ3ʿ*(*.n*)*=sn*: The different verb forms – *sḏm.n=f* and *sḏm=f* – should be noted.

14 R:II6/V:IV2 : Müller 2008, 249.171, suggests associating this word with the Hebrew נאק or the Akkadian *nâqu* 'to cry, to groan' (HAL II, 622; AHw II, 744 CAD N.1, 341) and notes that the syllabic spelling is not quite what one would expect in Egyptian. The Egyptian verb *ḫ3ʿ* cannot be used with the meaning 'to moan/wail' or 'to express/utter a lament'; see WB III, 227.3–228.25, which opposes Müller's interpretation. Perhaps the Akkadian root *niāku* 'to have illicit sexual intercourse, to fornicate (repeatedly)' (CAD N.1, 197–198; AHw II, 784) can be presumed, in this case as an active participle (*nā'iku, nā'iktu*). — R:II6/V:IV2 *st wʿr*(*d*)(*.w*): This sentence is a rare instance of the first present clause in the manuscript. Massart 1954, 56.37, suggests *ḥr* + infinitive and not a stative. For the writing *wʿr*(*d*), which is very common for the Ramesside Period, see Gardiner 1937, 3.7–3a.7c, 140. See also Massart 1954, 65.37.

15 R:II7 : This spelling is the result of confusion over the particle *k3*, which is used exclusively in the phrases that follow on the recto. — R:II7–8/V:III3 'Both of your eyes shall be blinded!': Compare this passage with a section of the Epic of Aqhat. Danil, Aqhat's father, directs his accusations against the city of Abiluma, where his son died (CAT 1.19 IV 5): *ʿwrt.yštk.bʿl.lht* 'May Baal strike you blind!' See Parker 1997, 75.

16 R:II8/V:IV3 (*k3*) *nḏ*(*w*)*=k*: Fischer-Elfert 2005a, 44, translates this passage in the passive voice. On the recto, the particle *k3* implies a subjunctive, which is normally constructed with a *tw*-passive; see Schenkel 2005a, 211; Erman 1933, 135–136, 137/§288–289, §291; see also the remarks in Müller 2008, 279.149. Fischer-Elfert 2005a, 135, refers to CAT 1.6 II30–35, where Anat fights against Mōt: *tiḫd bn.ilm.mt.bḥrb tbqʿnn.bḥṯr.tdry nn.bišt. tšrpnn brḥm.tṯḥnn.bšd tdrʿ.nn* 'She seizes the divine Mōt. With a sword, she splits him. With a sieve, she winnows him. With fire, she burns him. With two mill stones, she crushes him. In a field, she sows him.' (CAT 1.6 II30–35; Parker 1997, 156). By contrast, Sāmāmu/Akhu is forced to work at the mill stone and is not crushed on it. — V:IV4 {*k.t*}: The verso unexpectedly shows *k.t* 'another', and the lines that follow are written in red, including the names of deities, which are usually written in black, e.g. V:XXII2 and 3. See Posener 1949, 77–81. — V:IV4 : The feminine ending is omitted on the verso. The nisbe *n.t* that follows is constructed correctly.

17 R:II8–9/V:IV4 *Pw-ḳ-s3w-nj3/Nḳp-ḥ3w-n3 ḥnʿ Ḏ3-ḥ3-r'*: The name of the first god is written differently on the verso and recto. Müller 2008, 279.143, tends towards the reading *P-ḳ-ḥ-n* on the recto, so there would be a metathesis and only the initial *n* would be missing. The signs on the papyrus clearly do not support such an interpretation. Müller 2008, *ibid.*, suggests connecting

the name *Nkpḥn* with the root *nqp* 'to subdue, to pull over, to skin' (HAL III, 681–682) or with *nqb* 'to perforate, to pierce' (DUL 639; HAL III, 678–679), and the second part with *ḥn* 'grace, beauty, favour' (DNWSI 386–387; HAL I, 318–319), so that both parts together would mean something like 'the one who subdues/pierces the beauty', which would match the description that follows on the papyrus. It is currently not possible to identify these two deities from other sources. The paired order reminds one of Ugaritic twin gods such as *Kṯr w Ḫss, Šḥr w Šlm, Ṯkmn w Šnm, Gpn w Ugr*, etc. — R:II9/V:IV4 *(n3) n.ty ḥr wb3*: The definite article is omitted on the recto. For *wb3* as 'to deflower', see Papyrus Chester Beatty VII R:IV2–3 *Zp-nz-t3 ẖ.t tp.t n p3* (3) *Rꜥ ḏd=s rn=s n Ḥr(.w) ḥr rnp.t 3 jw znf.w jmn* [...] *m mn.ty=s ḏr wb3 s(y) Ḥr(.w)* 'Zepnesta, the first body for Re. She tells her name to Horus in three years during which the hidden blood is [...] on her thighs since Horus opened/deflowered her' (Gardiner 1935, I, 58.8, II, Pl. 34). See also WB I, 29.13; Massart 1954, 56.43.

18 R:II9/V:IV5 / *rwn.wt*/<*rn*>*n.wt*: As Massart 1954, 56.44, has correctly pointed out, the scribe omitted <*rn*> in *rnn.wt* on the verso. The sign on the recto seems to be a combination of the signs *s* and *r* with the phonetic value *rw*. The word *rwn.t* has the meaning '(young) girl, virgin' (Meeks 1980, I, 213/77.2345) and seems to be identical to the Coptic **ⲣⲟⲟⲩⲛⲉ**. The word is probably a derivation of *rwny.t* 'heifer' (WB II, 409.1); see Clère 1952, 629–642; see also the remarks in Müller 2008, 279.145. — R:II9 : For *n-n.ty* as *n3 n.ty*, see Gardiner 1937, 90.3–90a.3a, 140a; Massart 1954, 56.45. — R:II10 *sꜥb*: The traces do not actually fit on the papyrus, but the signs are indisputable on the verso.

18–19 R:II10/V:IV5 'They give you words during the day': This passage is not the same on the recto and verso. The meaning is uncertain.

20 R:II11/V:IV6 : The 'god above' should be identified as the moon god, a counterpart to the sun god Re. In R:V6/V:VIII2, he is mentioned together with his wife Nikkal; similarly Massart 1954, 67–68.16; Müller 2008, 280.147. — R:II11/V:IV6 / : Zepnezezi/Zeptunesta is known as one of the wives of Horus. Her full name reads *spr.tw-n/r=s-spr.n=s-t3*; see Borghouts 1971, 149–150; Gardiner 1935, I, 56.6; and the listing of all the name's spellings in Massart 1954, 57.51.

21 R:II12: Before the phrase '(as) the serpent says', another goddess is mentioned; her name has not been preserved. Perhaps this is a mistake and the word is a dittography for Zepnezezi, because nothing of the kind occurs on the verso; see also Massart 1954, 57.52. — V:IV6–7: One sign group for *ḏd* is omitted as a haplography; see also Massart 1954, 57–58.53, who cites further literature for *ḏdf.t* and snakes' names generally.

22 R:II12/V:IV7 *Jtm.t*: In this context, it seems to be the snake's name. Itemet designates a female form of Atum and is usually manifested as a kind of snake. She can have a protective function; see Myśliwiec 1978, 104–113; Myśliwiec 1983, 297–304; Refai 2001, 89–94. See also Massart 1954, 58.54; Müller 2008, 280.149. — R:II12 : The word seems to be a shortened variant of the verb *sḳr* 'to strike' (WB IV, 306.10–307.11). It is probably used as an attributive of Itemet. — R:II13/V:IV7: The two recipes start differently. On the recto, the traces might be restored to [*ḏd.tw r' pn ḥr*] 'this spell is said over', whereas the verso reads [*ḏd*] *mdw.w ḥr* 'words to be said over'; see Massart 1954, 58.55.

22–23 R:II12–III2/V:IV7–8: The lists of ingredients differ on the two sides, and quantities are only given on the verso. In Egypt, cumin is archeologically attested from the New Kingdom onwards. Usually *tpnn* is equated with cumin (*Cuminum cyminum* L.; Germer 1979, 101–102; Germer 2002, 43) and not black cumin (*Nigella sativa* L.), because the former is native to the Mediterranean area (Hiller/Melzig 2010, 173) and the latter comes from Western Asia (Frohne 2002, 381). Both species are archeologically attested and the word *tpnn* probably specifies both seeds (Pommerening 2006, 110.45; cf. Keimer 1924, I, 41–42). Cumin is used in internal and topical therapies (GdM VI, 556–557; Draby/Ghalioungui/Grivetti 1977, 799–800; Germer 1979, 102–105; Manniche 1989, 96–98; Germer 2002, 44–45; Germer 2008, 153–154). The active ingredient of both species is the essential oil found in the seeds. Although the active ingredient is not identical in cumin and black cumin, both are spasmolytic and carminative. Cumin also has analgetic, antibacterial, and antimycotical properties (Hoppe 1958, 296; Manniche 1989, 96–98; Nunn 1996, 154, 215; Kolta 2001, 45; Frohne 2002, 134; Germer 2002, 44; Pommerening 2006, 110–111; Hiller/Melzig 2010, 173). In folk medicine, it is used in compresses to treat skin ailments (Alpin 1980, 181–182; Flora III, 679). The term *pr.t-šn* has been identified as pine nuts (Ebbell 1937, 132; Charpentier 1981, 296–297; Nunn 1996, 154; Germer 1985, 9), the fruits of conifers in general (Keimer 1984, II, 23), and blossom of the sweet acacia (Loret 1975, 85–86). Currently a definite identification is not possible. The ingredient was used internally and topically in Egypt; no specific application can be detected and no pharmaceutical effect is known (Hoppe 1958, 696; Schneider 1974, V.3, 78; Germer 2008, 69–71). The term *gj.w n.j wḫꜣ.t* is identified as the species cyperus, particularly nutgrass (*Cyperus rotundus* L.), although some features of the description and usage do not support this identification (Germer 1979, 207–209; Germer 1985, 247; Germer 2008, 147–148). The plant was used in internal and topical treatments in Egypt (Germer 1979, 203–206; Germer 2008, 146–147). The term *snṯr* is usually identified with frankincense (*Boswellia* spp.). An identification with the resin of the turpentine tree (*Pistacia terebinthus* L.), at least for the period of the New Kingdom, is also possible (Loret 1949, 61; GdM IV.1, 265; Manjo 1975, 124; Nunn 1996, 225; Nicholson/Shaw 2000, 442, 458–459; Serpico/White 1998, 1038; Germer 1979, 69–70, 81–82; Germer 2008, 121, 212; Charpentier 1981, 596–601; Steuer 1937, 3). In Egypt, *snṯr* was used in both internal and topical remedies, but mostly in topical treatments for skin alterations (GdM VI, 449–451, 452–454; Germer 1979, 76–80). Both substances – frankincense as resinous gum and turpentine as resin – are anti-inflammatory (Hoppe 1958, 145, 708; Germer 1979, 80–81; Germer 1985, 108; Westendorf 1992, 259; Vieillescazes-Rambier 1992, 11–12; Baum 1994, 22, 25–26; Kolta 2001, 50; Frohne 2002, 109–110; Germer 2002, 99–100; Germer 2008, 211, 320; Hiller/Melzig 2010, 95, 458). Honey (*bj.t*) is one of the most frequently used ingredients in Egyptian medicine (Mininberg 2008, 61) and was used extensively in internal and topical therapy (GdM VI, 156–167; Germer 2002, 155). Honey has antibacterial, antiseptic, and antimicrobial properties. It reduces the swelling of wounds (Hoppe 1958, 971; Manjo 1975, 117–118; Nunn 1996, 148; Westendorf 1999, I, 517; Sipos *et al.* 2004, 213; Mininberg 2008, 62; Veiga 2009, 61; Hiller/Melzig 2010, 302). Natron (*ḥsmn*) was used internally and topically in Egypt; it is hygroscopic and therefore reduces swelling. These salts are antiseptic and antibacterial like honey, and drain pus from infected wounds (Schneider 1975, VI, 153; Nunn 1996, 145–146; Westendorf 1999, I, 517; Guiter 2001, 231). — V:IV8 : The remains of the word can be restored to *ḏꜣr.t*, *ḥmꜣr.t* or *shr.t*, whereby only *ḏꜣr.t* and *shr.t* would match the gap in the papyrus. *Ḏꜣr.t* has been identified as carob or colocynth. The respective medicinal usage of the two substances favours the former. Colocynth is a rather strong purge, while carob is only a mild laxative and therefore corresponds better to the usage of *ḏꜣr.t* in medical texts; see Manniche 1989, 85–87; Germer 1979, 359–360; Germer 1985, 127; Germer 2008, 166–168, 223; Győry 2002, 52–53. According to Guiter 2001, 229–230, it can be carob and colocynth; see also Westendorf 1999, I, 511, who refers to Aufrère 1983, 28–31. Charpentier 1981, 860–861 says it is carob. Draby/Ghalioungui/Grivetti 1977, 699–701 give both possibilities; cf. Keimer 1984, II, 17, 19.29, 52; Dawson 1934a, 41–44, who identifies the term with colocynth; also GdM, 1959, VI, 586–592. For medicinal usage, see especially Hoppe 1958, 199–200; Schneider 1974, V.1, 267; Alpin 1980, 16–17; Boulos 1983, 119–123; Moursi 1992, 99; Frohne 2002, 149–150; Hiller/Melzig 2010, 129; see also Nunn 1996, 154, 215; Veiga 2009, 67. For the plant, see e.g. Löw 1967, II, 393–407; Flora III, 24–25. *Shr.t* is a mineral used in internal and topical therapies (GdM VI, 458–459). According to Dawson (see Barns 1956, 19.24), it is chalcedony, while Caminos 1954, 89, claims it is an unidentified stone. Aufrère 1983, 1–17, suggests *shr.t* could be a resin.

3. Incantation 3 (R:III2–IV9/V:V8–VII5)

The third incantation of the papyrus is directed against Sāmānu/Akhu, who is addressed by both names on the recto and the verso. A number of otherwise unknown demons are also mentioned (e.g. *Ṯmkn, Jbsn, Mšr*). It presents an episode where Re slays asses in the desert. He cuts himself and Anat has to help him. Eventually, Sāmānu/Akhu and his companions are defeated. The incantation ends with a recipe.

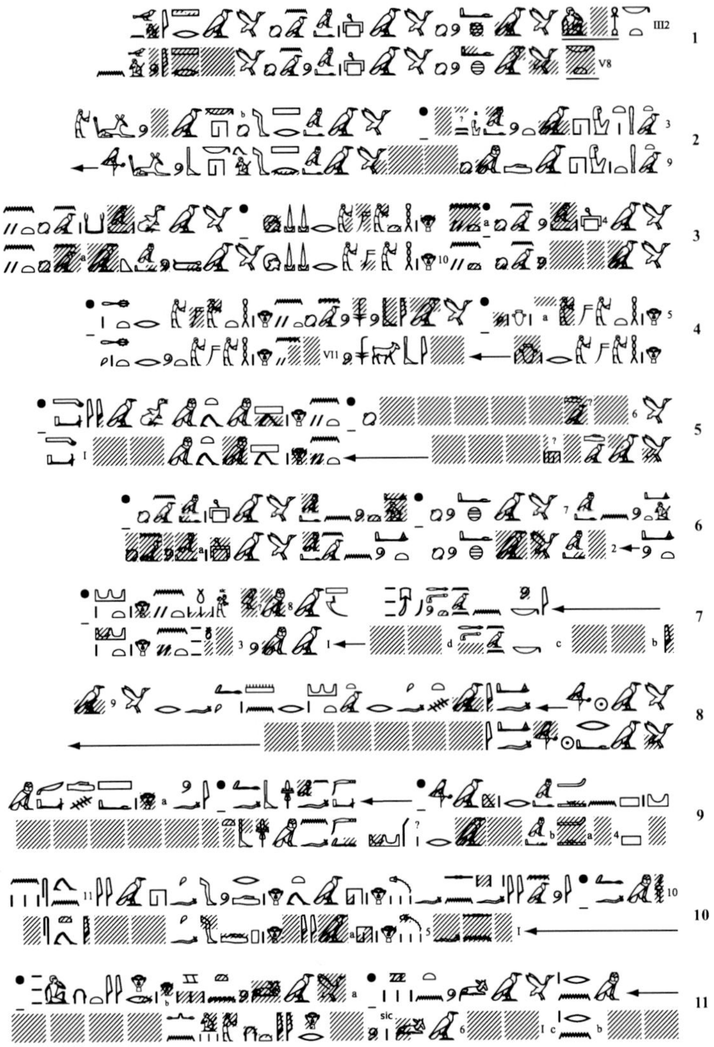

R:III3a *not* *; 3b alternatively* *according to Gardiner clearly* *; 4a strongly faded; 5a perhaps read* *?; 9a no longer legible; 11a & b no longer legible; V:V10a no longer legible; V:VI from I onwards papyrus I 345, before that a gap; 2a–b traces, 2c–d traces; 4a–b no longer legible; 5a no longer legible, 5b–c barely legible.*

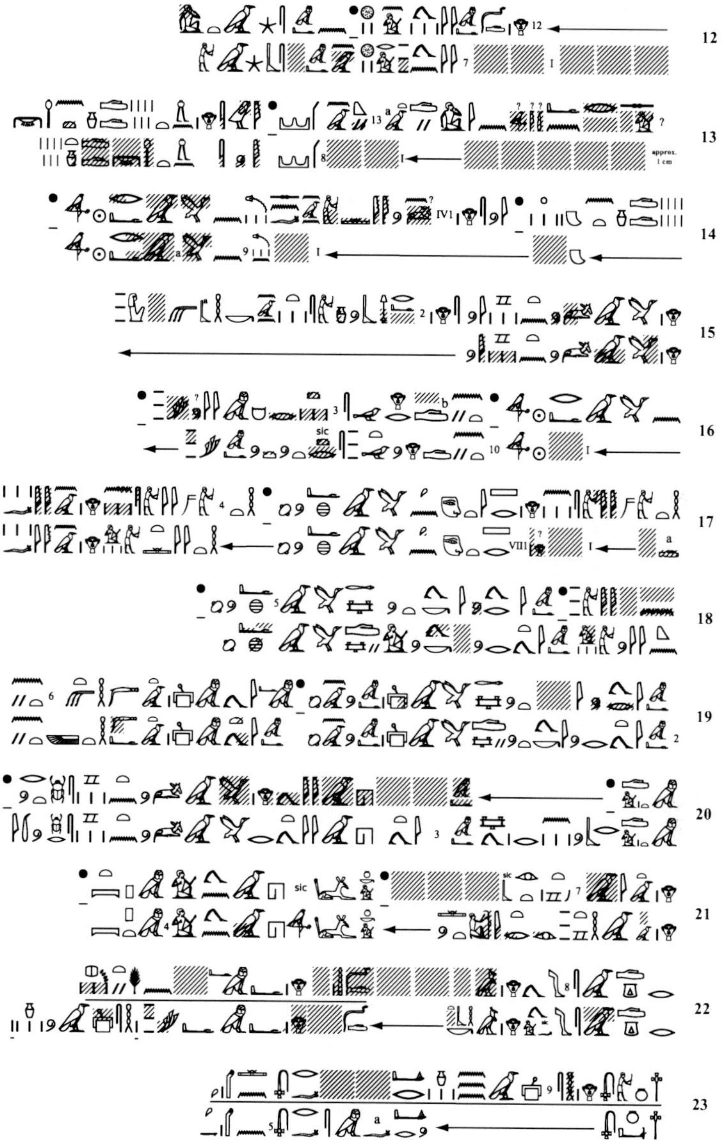

R:III12a or ; *R:IV2a or* ; *2b traces above* , *perhaps palimpsest; V:VI I from I onwards papyrus I 345, before that a gap; 9a no longer legible; 10a or* ; *V:VII4a traces or a stain above* .

Transliteration

	Recto line	Recto	Verso line	Verso
1	III2	k.t šn[.t] pꜣ ʿḫ.w pꜣ sꜣ-mʿ-nꜣ pꜣ šrj n(.j)	V8	k.t pꜣ ʿḫ.w pꜣ sꜣ-mʿw-nꜣ p[ꜣ] šrj(w) n(.j)
2	III3	tꜣ ḥm.t Hꜣ-tw-mʿ […]nn[?]° pꜣ Mʿ-šr khꜣ[b].w	V9	tꜣ ḥm.t Hꜣ-d-m […] pꜣ Mʿ-šr khb.w
3	III3–4	pꜣ sꜣ-[mʿ]w-nꜣ° [n.ty] ḥr ḥ(w).t r ḏꜣḏꜣ° pꜣ Ṯꜣ-[mʿ]-kꜣ-nꜣ n.ty	V9–10	pꜣ [sꜣ-mʿ]w-nꜣ n.ty ḥr ḥ(w)<.t> r ḏꜣḏꜣ pꜣ Ṯw-mʿ-ḳ[ꜣ-nꜣ] n.ty
4	III5	ḥr ḥ(w).t [r'-]jb° pꜣ Jbw-sw-nꜣ n.ty ḥr ḥ(w).t r ẖ.t°	10–VI1	ḥr ḥ(w)<.t> r'-jb [pꜣ] Jb-sw-[nꜣ] n.[t]y ḥr ḥ(w)<.t>{tw} r ẖ.t
5	III5–6	pꜣ […] D[?]ꜣ […]° n.ty ḥr šm.t m ṯꜣy°	VI1	pꜣ Dꜣ[…] n.ty ḥr šm.t m [ṯꜣy]
6	III6–7	ḏj=j tw njm pꜣ ʿḫ.w° ḏj=j tw njm pꜣ sꜣ-mʿ-nꜣ°	VI1–2	ḏj<=j> tw [n]jm pꜣ ʿḫ.w ḏj<=j> tw nj{nꜣ}m pꜣ sꜣ-mʿw-nꜣ
7	III7–8	jw=k n nꜣ n(.j) ʿꜣ.w(t) šmꜣ(m).w n.ty ḥr ḫꜣs.t°	VI2–3	j[w …]=k <n> nꜣ n(.j) ʿꜣ[.w šm]ꜣ(m).w n.ty ḥr ḫꜣs.t
8	III8–9	pꜣ Rʿ(w) ḏj=f jꜣ.t=f r tꜣ ḫꜣs.t rmn=f r pꜣ	VI3	pꜣ Rʿ(w) ḏj=f j[ꜣ.t …]
9	III9	ḏw n(.j) Ḥw-mʿ-r'-ḳꜣ° mḥ.n=f m (j)ꜣb(.j)=f° jw=f ḥr šʿd m	VI3–4	[ḏ]w [n.j] Ḥw-mʿ-[ḳ]ꜣ-r' mḥ.n=f m (j)ꜣb[.j=f …]
10	III10–11	wmn(.j)=f° jw nꜣy=f znf.w ḥr hꜣ.t ḥr rd(w)=f hꜣy.n=sn	VI4–5	[wnm.j=f jw nꜣy=f znf].w ḥr hꜣy[.t] ḥr p(ꜣ)d=f [hꜣy{.t}]=s[n]
11	III11	m r' n(.j) pꜣ jwtn° [p]ꜣ jwtn [ḥr] ḥr.yt°	VI5–6	[m] r' n(.j) [pꜣ jwtn p]ꜣ jw[tn ḥr] ḥry.t nn […]
12	III12	ḥr ḏd my n=j zp-sn° njm sbꜣ{t}	VI6–7	[… m]j-n r=j zp-sn n{ꜣ}(j)m sbꜣ
13	III12–13	z [r … ʿntj[?]] n<.t> J-dy-tꜣ-ḳy-nꜣ° jw=s ḥr jn.t 7 dd n.t ḥḏ	VI7–8	[z …] jw=s jn.t [ḥḏ dd.(w)]t 7
14	III13–IV1	8 dd n.t ḥmt° jw=s ḥr {n}jw(y) nꜣ n(.j) znf.w n(.j) pꜣ Rʿ(w)°	VI8–9	ḥmt [dd.wt 8 jw=s ḥr jwj nꜣ n.j zn]f.w n(.j) p[ꜣ] Rʿ(w)
15	IV1–2	ḥr pꜣ jwtn jw=s ḥr rḏ [.t] wbꜣ st nꜣ n(.j) Kḥb.w	VI9	ḥr pꜣ jwtn jw[=s …]
16	VI2–3	n pꜣ Rʿ(w)° n.ty dḥr st r ḥmy.w°	VI9–10	[… R]ʿ(w) n.ty dḥr{.wt} [st r] tw-tw-mʿ
17	IV3–4	ḥ(w){t}.y=sn ḥr šrj.t n<.t> pꜣ ʿḫ.w° ḥ(w){t}.y=sn ḥr nꜣy=f	VI10–VII1	d[…] [ḥw=sn] ḥr šr.t n<.t> pꜣ ʿḫ.w ḥ(w){t}.y=w ḥr nꜣy=f
18	IV4–5	[ḳ]n(y).w° mj rwj=k tw ʿꜣ pꜣ ʿḫ.w°	VII1	ḳn(y).w mj{.t} rw[j]=k {wj}<tw> dy pꜣ ʿḫ.w
19	IV5–6	mj rwj[=k] tw ʿꜣ pꜣ sꜣ-mʿw-nꜣ° mj m-sꜣ tꜣ mḥ.t n.ty	VII2	mj{.t} rwj=k tw dy pꜣ sꜣ-mʿw-nꜣ mj{.t} m-sꜣ tꜣ mḥ.t n.ty
20	IV6	m ḏr.t=j° mj hꜣy ḥr pꜣ jwtn s:ḫpr tw°	VII2–3	m ḏr.t=j r-bnr mj{.t} hꜣy{.t} r pꜣ jwtn s:ḫpr(w) tj
21	IV6–7	ḥr tꜣ jꜣ.t jr.t b[…]° jnk Stḫ(?) hꜣ.n=j m p.t°	VII3–4	ḥr [t]ꜣ ꜣḥ.t jr<.t> trj tw<=k>jnk Stḫ(?) hꜣ.n=j m p.t
22	IV7–8	r dg(ꜣ)s ḥr nḥ[b.t=k] dd mdw hr ʿmʿ[ʿ…] n(.j) b(d).ty	VII4	r dg(ꜣ)s{=f}{=j} ḥr nḥb.t=k [ḏd mdw] ḥr ʿmʿ 1 ḥsꜣ(w) 1
23	IV8–9	nd(.w) ps(.w) ḥr hsꜣ dj(.w) r[=f m s]rf n(.j) dbʿ	VII4–5	nḏ(.w) ps(.w) ḏj(.w) r=f m srf n(.j) ḏbʿ {n}

Translation

1 Another incantation/another: O Akhu, o Sāmānu, o son of
2 the slave woman (of ?) Hatum who [...], o *Mšr* who rages,
3 o Sā[mā]nu who strikes at the head, o *Ṯ[m]kn* who
4 strikes at the sto[ma]ch, o *Jbsn* who strikes at the body,
5 o *D[...]* who walks (around) secretly.
6 To whom (shall) I hand you, o Akhu? To whom (shall) I hand you, o Sāmānu?
7 You belong to the wandering asses which are in the desert.
8 Re, he turns (lit.: gives) his back to the desert, his shoulder to
9 the mountain *Ḥmrḳ/Ḥmḳr*. After he has seized them (= the asses) with his left, he slits
10 (their throats) with his right hand. His blood fell on his lower leg/knee. It dropped (down)
11 into the maw (lit. opening) of the ground. The ground is frightened
12 (and) says: 'Help me! Help me (lit.: Come to me! Come to me!)! Who is it who teaches
13 a man?' [to (?) ... Anat] of *Jdtḳn*, she brings seven silver dishes
14 (and) eight copper dishes. She separates the blood of Re
15 from the ground. She causes the *Kḫb.w*
16 of Re (?) to serve that (= the blood) which is more bitter than fenugreek (?)/asant.
17 As it was darted upon the nose of Akhu, it was darted upon
18 his companions! Come, you shall go away from here, o Akhu.
19 Come, you shall go away from here, o Sāmānu. Follow (lit. come behind) the feather which
20 is in my hand (out)! Come, fall upon the ground which created you,
21 upon the field/mound which respected you! I am the weather god. To tread
22 on your neck, I descended from the sky. Word(s) to be said over grain of emmer wheat/grain (1), mucilage (1),
23 to be ground, to be boiled with mucilage/to be boiled, to be applied lukewarm (lit.: warmth of finger).

Commentary

1–2 R:III2–3/V:V8–9 *šrj n(.j) ḥm.t*: Fischer-Elfert 2011, 193.18, thinks this passage has a rather pejorative meaning and compares it with the expression 'son of a bitch'. He also considers the possibility that this phrase could be a translation of the Ugaritic *bn 'amt*, for which see Loretz 2003, 346–365.

2 R:III3/V:V9 *tꜣ ḥm.t*: Grapow 1939, 22, erroneously translated this as 'majesty', see Massart 1954, 60.2. — : The appellation of the demon's 'mother' is difficult to interpret. Müller 2008, 280.152, thinks it could be connected with the root *hdm* 'ravaging/destroying, ravager/destroyer etc.' and that it could be further evidence for Hoch's attestations (Hoch 1994, 220–221.303). With some reservations, he suggests that Rešep is related. The term could possibly also be interpreted as the slave woman's origin, even if the determinatives do not support this assumption.

In papyrus 1116A of the Hermitage (St. Petersburg), which dates to the 18th Dynasty, a country/district called Hatum is mentioned twice; it is similar to the mother's appellation: *pꜣ nḏs n(.j) hꜣ-tw-mꜥ* 'the commoner of Hatum' and *hꜣ-tj-tw-mꜥ ḥ(n)k.t n.w* 10 *ḥkꜣ.t* 7 'Hatitumian people, 10 (jars) of beer (made) of 7 bushel (grain)'; see Golenischeff 1913, 2–5, Pls. XVII line 78, XXII line 183. This country or district cannot currently be identified; see Gauthier 1927, IV, 3; Aḥituv 1984, 107. — / : Müller 2008, 280.153, suggests the root *mšl*$_1$ 'to rule' (DNWSI II, 702–703; 'the ruling one/the ruler') as a potential derivation. Fischer-Elfert 2011, 192.16, favours the Ugaritic verb *mšr* 'to drag, to set a vehicle in motion, to go for a drive, to drive it (?)' (Tropper 1990, 39–42; DUL 593; see CAD M.1, 359–360: 'the one setting out (on a journey)'). Another Ugaritic term that appears here, *mšr* 'justice', is also attested as the name of a god (DUL 593–594; see also Watson, Misharu מישור, in: Van der Toorn/Becking/Van der Horst 1995, 1081–1083), but one wonders whether this deity would make sense in this particular context.

3 R:III4/V:V10 / : Müller 2008, 280.154, proposes the Northwestern Semitic word *smk*$_2$ 'support' (DNWSI II, 792) with nunation. Fischer-Elfert 2005a, 135, refers to the Babylonian lord of wild beasts, about which see Rahmouni 2008, 220–222. But why would this god fight alongside with Sāmānu/Akhu? Caquot 1960, 88, derives the root from the Arabic verb *damaqa* 'to beat' or the Ethiopian verb *damaqa* 'to smite, to trample', which would make sense in this context ('the beating one/the smiting one').

4 R:III5 ⌊*r'*-⌋*jb*: The recto probably has to be restored to *r'-jb*, as on the verso. There are still traces of the ideogram. — R:III5/V:V10–VI1 / : Massart 1954, 60.3, refers with some reservations to the divine king Ibbi-Sîn, a ruler in the Ur-III-Period, but also considers the Ugaritic composite deity Ib-Nikkal, which could be written in a shortened writing as Ib. Ibbi-Sîn was the last ruler of the Ur-III-Period. The dynasty perished under his rule, so he has a certain negative connotation (Sallaberger/Westholz 1999, 172–178). It is doubtful that this word conceals king Ibbi-Sîn: while his reputation was far from spotless, he was probably not demonised in an almost literal sense. Perhaps the word can be derived from the Ugaritic *ib* 'enemy' (DUL 4) with the attributive extension *ṯn* 'second, other' (DUL 921), 'a second/another enemy'. The Ugaritic term *ṯn* also has the meaning 'crimson' (DUL 921–922), but this is only attested in reference to fabrics. — *ḥ(w).t r ḫ.t*: Fischer-Elfert 2011, 191.14, refers to Stadler 2004, 115, 173–175, who is able to show that – at least for Demotic – the term *ḥwy-ḫ(e.t)* has the meaning 'to go into labour' or 'to miscarry'. Here, the patient, and *not the slave woman*, is struck on the belly. In either case, the miscarriage or the slave woman's labour would be far too late because the demon has already been born.

5 R:III6/V:VI1 / : The demon's name has not been preserved on either side. — *n.ty ḥr šm.t ṯꜣy*: For the construction *ḥr šm.t* instead of *m šm.t*, see Erman 1933, 231 §476.4; Wente 1959, 43–44, 84, 96–98, 168; Frandsen 1974, 14 §11.1a, 76 §42.2; Junge 2008, note 85.

6 R:III6/V:VI1 *ḏj=j tw njm pꜣ ꜥḫ.w ḏj=j tw njm pꜣ sꜣ-mꜥ-nꜣ*: As Fischer-Elfert 2011, 193–194.19–20, has pointed out, these rhetorical questions are a rather atypical introduction to a magical text; see Morschauser 1991; Nordh 1996, 3–8.

7 V:VI2: An additional sentence appears on the verso. — R:III7–8/V:VI2–3 'You belong to the wandering asses which are in the desert': Fischer-Elfert 2011, 193, refers to a curse formula used on Kudurrū (boundary stones) which appears to be similar: *kīma serrēmu ina kamât šubtišu lirtappud* 'may he always roam as an onager in the desert of his dwelling place'; see Watanabe 1984, 100–104, especially 104, as well as 106–109. For a more detailed discussion, see Fischer-Elfert 2011, *ibid.* On the verso, <*n*> has to be added. For 'wandering asses', Massart 1954, 61.11, also refers to *Zaubersprüche für Mutter und Kind* (MuK: V:VI4; Erman 1901, 51; Yamazaki 2003, 52–53, Pl. 16), Papyrus Harris (VI2; Lange 1927; Chabas 1860, Pl. VI) and the festival calendar of Edfu (Chabas 1930, 399); all these sources mention asses. For general information on asses in magic, see Hopfner 1913, 102–104.

8–9 R:III8–9/V:VI3 'Re, he turns (lit.: gives) his back to the desert, his shoulder to the mountain *Ḥmrk/Ḥmkr*': The sun god seems to be positioning himself for combat. Massart 1954, 61.14, refers to the Magical Papyrus Harris (papyrus BM 10042), which at R:V3–4 reads: *rmn=k°̲ <ḥr> ḏw(.w) pn n.ty m Jgr.t°̲* 'you rest <on> this mountain which is in *Jgr.t*' (Lange 1927, 39, 42, 46.17'; Chabas 1860, Pl. V; Leitz 1999, Pl. 16); the word *rmn* is determined with the flesh sign (F51), so the shoulder has to be assumed in this passage.

9 R:III9/V:VI4 : A god's determinative is used on the recto, while on the verso a determinative for foreign countries is used. Perhaps this term is used again in R:XXIIIx+3 [...]. Much has been said on the meaning of this word. Görg 1987, 14–15, suggests connecting the term with *amlq*, which designates both an area and a divine mountain. Becking, Amalek עמלק in: Van der Toorn/Becking/Van der Horst 1995, 44–45, took it up with some reservations; more recently, it was addressed by Ayali-Darshan 2015, 87–89. Fischer-Elfert 2011, 193, 194.25, cautiously mentions ᵈ*Ammarigu*, which is part of the divine mountains; see Haas 1981, 251–257. See also the indications by Müller 2008, 281.156. In this context, it is obvious that a mountain is meant because of the phrase *ḏw n(.j) Ḥmrk/Ḥm[k]r*. In either case, the transformation of ꜥ into *ḥ* in Egyptian is not without problems.

10 R:III10/V:VI5 : On the recto, the word *rd* 'foot' (WB II, 461–462.1–15; Walker 1996, 85–86; GdM I 91–92) is used, while *p(ꜣ)d* 'knee(cap)' (WB I, 500.7–12; Walker 1996, 269; GdM I, 93) is written on the verso.

10–13 'His blood fell on his lower leg/knee. It dropped (down) into the maw (lit. opening) of the ground. The ground is frightened (and) says: 'Help me! Help me (lit.: Come to me! Come to me!)! Who is it who teaches a man?'': Massart 1954, 62.19, refers to Gen 4, 11, the episode with Cain and Abel. Here the ground has opened its mouth to receive Abel's blood. See also Fischer-Elfert 2011, 194–195.

12 V:VI7 : In R:III12, the word *njm* 'who?' is written. Massart 1954, 62.22, suggests *njm-ḥr* as an emendation, but the gap on the papyrus would be too small for *ḥr*. The sign would fit; see WB II, 263, for this spelling. For the combination of *jn* and the interrogative pronoun, see Gardiner 1988, 176 §227; Erman 1933, 375–376 §743; Junge 2008, 189 note. — R:III12/V:VI7 : The *t*-ending has to be emended on the verso. Even the determinative is unexpected. The sense remains obscure; see also Massart 1954, 62.23; Fischer-Elfert 2005a, 43.

13 R:III12–13/V:VI7–8 : For the goddess Anat, see the commentary to incantation 2, line 7 V:VIII7. The toponym *Jdtkn* cannot be located. Aḥituv 1984, 52, suggests an identification with 'Adidagān. See also Burchardt 1910, II, 11; Gauthier 1925, I, 125; Müller 2008, 281.157; Fischer-Elfert 2011, 195.

13–14 R:III13/V:VI8 '(...) she brings seven silver dishes (and) eight copper dishes': The sequence of the numbers seven and eight is not uncommon in Ugaritic myths; see Quack 1994, 207–208, and Fischer-Elfert 2011, 195.28, with further citations. The different constructions for the materials should be noted. On the recto, the typical construction for Late Egyptian – an indirect genitive extension – is used; see Černý/Groll 1984, 85–86; Erman 1933, 94 §210. An apposition – the material followed by the object – is used on the verso, which is a very common construction in Middle Egyptian; see Gardiner 1988, 68 §90. The feminine *t*-ending is omitted on the recto. The nisbe, however, is correctly constructed. For the *dd.t*-dish, see Urk. IV, 631 No. 17; Janssen 1975, 423–425; Vercoutter 1956, 342–343, Pl. LIII; DUL 265–266; Tropper 2008, 28. See also Fischer-Elfert's statements (Fischer-Elfert 2011, 195.30).

14 R:IV1 : Massart 1954, 62.28, assumes the verb *jwy* 'to irrigate' (WB I, 49.1–2), but concedes that it would not make sense in this context. On the papyrus, the sign is clearly written above the sign , so the word has to be read *njw*. In CT I, 288b (spell 67), there is talk of four *nms.t*-jars which are *nj.t*: *wꜥb=k m fd.t jpwt nms.t nj.t* 'You shall be purified with these four [...] *nms.t*-jars.' According to Meeks 1981, II, 184 (78.1974), *nj* is a verb form – 'to fill with water' – which does not make sense in the context either. The {*n*} probably has to be deleted and the verb *jw* 'to separate, to

cut' (WB I, 48.1–2) should be assumed. However, this verb seems to be attested only in connection with limbs (the neck) and is usually constructed with the preposition . Fischer-Elfert 2005a, 43, translated it as 'fing auf (?)', and six years later wrote 'collected/took away (?)' (Fischer-Elfert 2011, 192). Drioton 1955, 164, suggests *jwy* could be an archaizing variant of *ꜥwꜣy* 'to rob'.

15 R:IV2 : *kḥb.w* or *kḥw.w*. This word is a *hapax legomenon*. The meaning of the word cannot be ascertained from the context.

15–16 R:IV2 *jw=s ḥr rd[.t] wbꜣ st nꜣ n(.j) Kḥb.w n pꜣ Rꜥ(w)*°: This sentence could be translated either as 'She causes the *Kḥb.w* of Re (?) to serve that (= the blood) (...)' or 'She causes the *Kḥb.w* to serve that (= the blood) to Re (...)'. Massart 1954, 62–63.29, assumes that *st* is the direct object and *Kḥb.w* the subject of the verb *wbꜣ*, which would give the translation 'She causes the *Kḥb.w* to serve it (= the blood)', whereby the could be understood either as a preposition ('to Re') or a nisbe ('of Re'). In either case, Massart 1954, 59, uses it twice in his translation ('she causeth the *kḥb* of Prēʿ (...) to present (?) it to Prē''). If the *n* is in fact used as a preposition, that is, to introduce the indirect object, the sense would be rather odd: why would these *Kḥb.w* offer Re his own blood? *Wbꜣ st* could perhaps be a construction for the semantic object of the infinitive with *Kḥb.w*; it would be an indirect object, with the introducing *n* omitted as a haplography – it would have to be restored (<*n*>) – so the translation would be 'She causes that it (= the blood) is served <to> the *Kḥb.w* of Re.' The meaning would still be obscure.

16 R:IV3/V:VI10 : *Ḥmy.w* is written on the recto. The word can be partially identified with *ḥmꜣ.w* 'fenugreek' (Charpentier 1981, 468–469, 470–471, refers to *ḥmꜣ.w*; Lesko II, 113, provides it with a question mark; Gardiner 1947, I, 21, refers to Loret; Loret 1935, 866–868, especially 868), 'bitter shrub/tree' (*Bitterstrauch/-baum*) (Westendorf 1999, I, 502) or 'bitter almond' (Germer 1979, 223–224). According to Janssen 1975, 375, it is a kind of grain. GdM IV, 349, states that it is an unknown plant. Cf. Edel 1970, 24, who argues against the identification with fenugreek. On the verso, the word *ttm* is used as an alternative; Fischer-Elfert 2005a, 43–44, translates it as 'bitter almond/mandragora (?)'. Müller 2008, 281.159, refers to Drioton 1955, 165, who connects this term with the Hebrew דודי 'mandragora'; so also Helck 1971, 461, as well as Germer, *ibid.* The Egyptian word for 'mandragora' is probably *rrm.t* (WB II, 439.14–16). The Ugaritic term *tyt* (plural: *tytm*) designates a plant or vegetable substance (buttercup, ranunculus, *Asa foetida*; DUL 884). Tropper 2008, 130, connects this word specifically with *Asa foetida* = *Ferula assa-foetida* L. 'asant' which is known for its bitter and acrid flavour.

17–18 R:IV3–4/V:VI10–VII1 'As it was darted upon the nose of Akhu, it was darted upon his companions!': Here – as one can clearly see – Akhu/Sāmānu has an entire band collaborating with him; see Beck 2015a, 98, 100. The spelling of the verb form as is unusual. A *w*-passive is probably being used. The {*t*} could be written for graphical reasons, so *ḥw{t}.y* should be read. As a substantival form of the verb *ḥwj*, the *w*-passive voice could be used with a pronominal subject; see Gardiner 1988, 337–338 §420, 339–340 §422.1; Schenkel 2005a, 216–217; Schenkel 2005b, 40–49.

18 V:VII1 . Massart 1954, 63.34, remarks that the enclitic pronoun *wj* was erroneously written and that the *tw* in the following line is correct. Furthermore, he says that a seldom used form of the second person singular masculine suffix pronoun *=kwj* (WB V, 83.2–3; Erman 1933, 29–30 §65) existed in Late Egyptian and was used here, so the text still makes sense. It must however be noted that the second person masculine suffix *=k* is used exclusively in papyrus Leiden I 343 + 345. — R:IV4/V:VII1 : On the verso, the Late Egyptian *dy* (WB V, 420.4–8) is used for the Middle Egyptian *ꜥꜣ* (WB I, 164.7–9) that appears on the recto, as already noted by Massart 1954, 63.35; see also R:IV5/V:VII2.

20 R:IV6/V:VII3 : For *tj* as a by-form of *tw*, see Erman 1933, 40 §88.

21 R:IV7/V:VII3 : The mound's function has not been preserved on the recto. The statement was probably similar to the one on the verso. Perhaps it could be restored to *jr.t b[wꜣ=k]* 'who is highly esteemed (by the mound)' (WB I, 454.11). The periphrastic construction takes the suffix *=k* as an object and not an enclitic pronoun. If one assumes an object

pronoun, something has definitely been omitted. The correct form would be *tw=k*, so the form has to be emended to *tw*<=*k*>.

22–23 R:IV8–9/V:VII4–5: Quanta are only mentioned on the verso. The word *ꜥmꜥꜥ* can be used alone or together with various species of grain. It can probably be identified with *triticum diccocum* 'emmer' when used alone or in combination with *bd.t* (WB I, 186.3–4; Massart 1954, 64.41; GdM VI, 91–94; Draby/Ghalioungui/Grivetti 1977, 489–490; Germer 1979, 149, 152–153; Charpentier 1981, 154–155; Westendorf 1999, I, 496, II, 835). In Egypt, *ꜥmꜥꜥ* was used topically for swelling and wounds (Jéquier 1922, 111–112; Germer 1979, 255–257). The term *ḥsꜣ* 'mucilage' (WB III, 160.6–16) appears in Egyptian recipes for various internal and topical remedies. It is made of grain that is soaked in water and fermented (GdM VI, 364–369). — R:IV9/V:VII4–5  / : This term is also used in Papyrus Ebers 4:10, 8:2, 9:14 and 10:6 (Wreszinski 1913, 6, 8, 9, 10) and in papyrus Berlin 3038 XII11 (Wreszinski 1909, 28). The exact meaning is not known; see also Massart 1954, 64.44; GdM VII.2, 779–781.

4. Incantation 4 (R:IV9–VI2/V:VII5–VIII12)

This incantation starts with an allusion to Baal's Cycle (Baal's combat against Yamm, the Sea), which is followed by an episode where the demon is blamed. Afterwards, different Egyptian and Canaanite deities use their 'poisons' to defeat Sāmānu/Akhu. Eventually, he is extinguished. The spell ends with the DHF and a recipe.

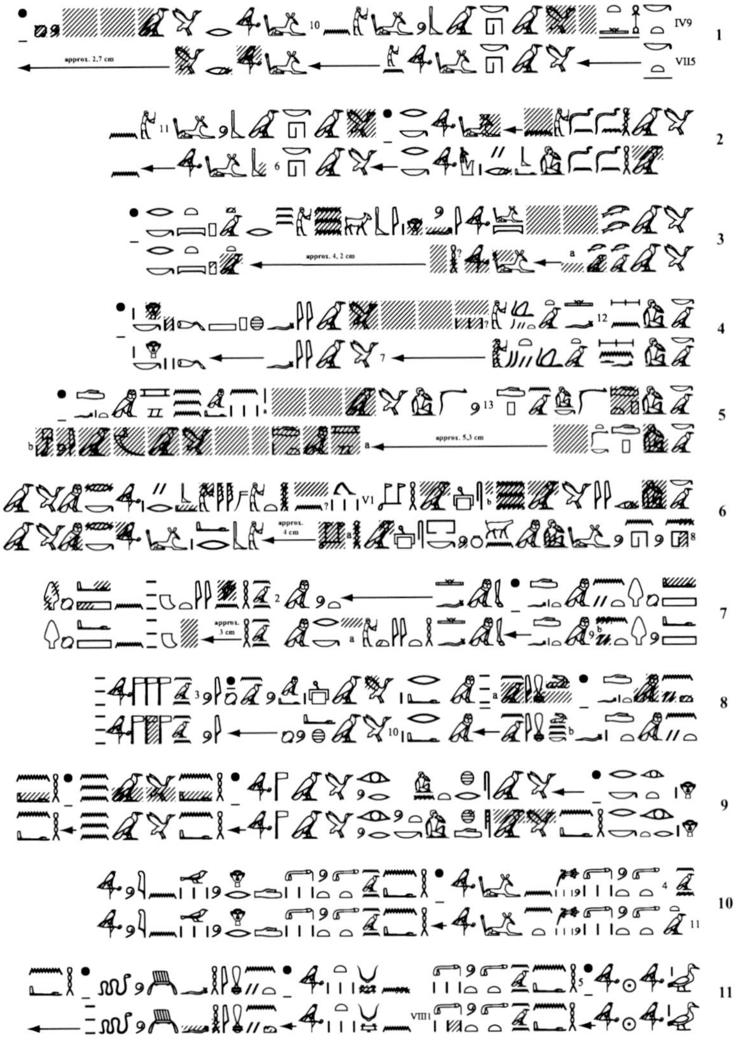

R:IV13a if ?; b traces after ; R:V2a added later in red; V:VII 6a the upper fibres are missing; 7a–b rip in the line; 8a half missing; 8b broken off at the end; 9a upper fibres are broken off; 9b under the line.

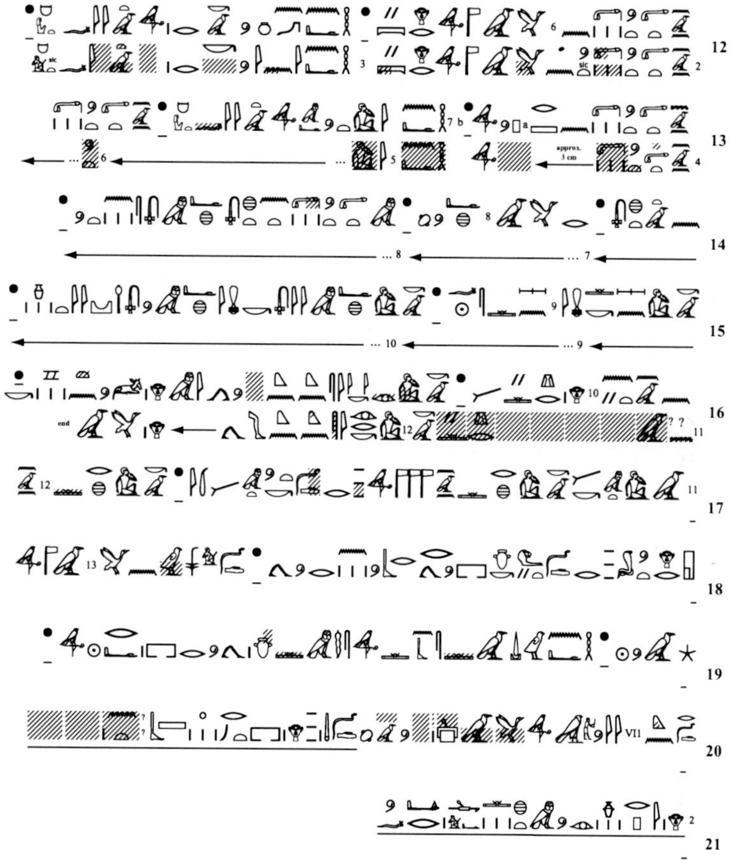

R:V6a–b written between the columns V and VI.

Transliteration

	Recto		Verso	
1	IV9–10	k.t šn.t pꜣ kh(ꜣ)b(w) n(.j) Stẖ(?) r pꜣ [ꜥḫ].w°_	VII5	k.t pꜣ kh(ꜣ) n(.j) Stẖ r p[ꜣ s-m-n]
2	IV10–11	pꜣ ḥḏnḏn n(.j) Stẖ(?) r=k°_ pꜣ kh(ꜣ)b(w) n(.j)	VII5–6	[p]ꜣ ḥḏnḏn Bꜥyr' r=k pꜣ khb n(.j)
3	IV11	pꜣ ẖꜣ[ẖꜣ.tj] jw=f ḥr jb ḥ(w)<.t> r tꜣ p.t r=k°_	VII6	pꜣ ẖꜣẖꜣ[.tj {ḥ?} jw=f ḥr jb ḥw.t r] tꜣ p.t r=k
4	IV11–12	kꜣ ꜥḏn=f tꜣ pḥ.ty [...] pꜣy=f ḫpš 2 ḥr=k°_	VII6–7	kꜣ ꜥḏn=f tꜣ pḥ.ty pꜣy=f ḫpš 2 ḥr=k
5	IV12–13	kꜣ dp{.t}=k nꜣ dp(w) pꜣ [...]n-mꜥ m ḏr.t=f°_	VII7	kꜣ dp{.t}=k [nꜣ dp pꜣ ...nm] m ḏr.t[=f jr.y?] pꜣ mꜣj
6	IV13–V1	kꜣ jr.y pꜣ mw sꜣḥ={n}<k> [ḥ]{t}(w)y Bꜥyr' r=k m pꜣ	VII8	nh(w)nh(w) m-ẖnw=k sꜣḥ [tw pꜣ mw ḥw]j Bꜥr' r=k m pꜣ
7	V1–2	ꜥš n.ty m ḏr.t=f°_ wḥm=f tw m nꜣ n(.j) ḥny.wt n(.wt) ꜥš	VII8–9	ꜥš(w) n.t[y] m ḏr.t=f wḥm=f ḥ{t}(w)y.t r=k m nꜣ n(.j) ḥ[ny.wt] n(.wt) ꜥš
8	V2–3	n.ty m ḏr.t=f°_ wn[n=k] mj nꜣ.w m-r'-ꜥ pꜣ sꜣ-mꜥw-nꜣ°_ jw nꜣ n(.j) nṯr.w	VII9–10	n.ty m ḏr.t=f wnn=k mj nꜣ m-r'-ꜥ pꜣ ꜥḫ.w jw nꜣ n(.j) nṯr.w
9	V3	ḥr jr.t r=k°_ pꜣ s:ḫr.t n(.j) jrr{w} pꜣ nṯr°_ ḥnꜥ pꜣ mw°_ ḥnꜥ	VII10	ḥr jr.t r=k ḥnꜥ pꜣ sḫd.tw=k jrr.w pꜣ nṯr ḥnꜥ pꜣ mw ḥnꜥ
10	V3–4	nꜣ n(j) mtw.wt ꜥšꜣ.w<t> n<.wt> Stẖ(?)°_ ḥnꜥ nꜣ n(.j) mtw.wt dḥr.w<t> n<.wt> Šw	VII11	tꜣ mtw.t ꜥšꜣ(w)<.t> n.(w)t Stẖ(?) ḥnꜥ nꜣ n(.j) mtw.wt dḥr.w<t> n<.wt> Šw
11	V4–5	zꜣ Rꜥ(w)°_ ḥnꜥ nꜣ n(.j) mtw.wt n<.wt>Wp-wꜣ.wt°_ n.ty mj ḥfꜣw°_ ḥnꜥ	VII11–VIII1	zꜣ Rꜥ(w) ḥnꜥ nꜣ n(.j) mtw.wt n<.wt> Wp-wꜣ.wt n.ty mj ḥfꜣw.w
12	V5–6	nꜣ n(.j) mtw.wt n<.wt> pꜣ nṯr-ḥr.y° ḥnꜥ Nw-kꜣ-r' tꜣy=f ḥm.t°_	VIII2–3	nꜣ n(.j) mtw.wt{wt} n<.wt> pꜣ nṯr-ḥr.y ḥnꜥ Jn-jw-k[ꜣ]-r' tꜣ[j]j=f ḥm.t
13	V6–7	nꜣ n(.j) mtw.wt n<.wt> Ršpw ḥnꜥ J-tw-mꜥ tꜣy=f ḥm.t°_ nꜣ n(.j) mtw.wt	VIII4–6	nꜣ n(.j) mtw.wt [n.wt Ršpw] ḥnꜥ J[tm tꜣy=f ḥm.t nꜣ n.j mt].wt [...]
14	V7–8	n<.wt> tꜣ ḫ.t°_ r<=k> pꜣ ꜥḫ.w°_ m mtw.wt n.(w)t ḫ.t ꜥḫm=sn tw°_	VIII7–8	[...]
15	V8–9	kꜣ ꜥḏn=k mj ꜥḏn sf°_ kꜣ ꜥḫm(y)=k mj ꜥḫm(w) ḥḏw.yt°_	VIII9–10	[...]
16	V9–10	n nꜣ n.ty ḥr ẖr.y-mwt°_ kꜣ jr.y=k jsḳnḳn(w) jm ḥr <pꜣ> jwtn°_	VIII11–12	n [n]ꜣ [n.ty ḥr] ẖr.y-<mwt> kꜣ jr=k jsḳnḳn ḥr pꜣ (end)
17	V11–12	kꜣ mwt=k kꜣ rḫ nꜣ n(.j) nṯr.w r-ḏd tw=k mwt.tj°_ kꜣ rḫ nꜣ n(.j)		missing on the verso
18	V12–13	Ḥw.t-ḥr.w.w r-ḏd ḥꜣ.ty=k pr.w r-bnr°_ ḏd=j sw n pꜣ nṯr-		-//-
19	V13	dwꜣ.w°_ ḥnꜥ wḏꜣ snb s:nḏm jb jw(.w) r pr Rꜥ(w)°_		-//-
20	V13–VI1	r-ḏd ḳn(yw) Ḥr(.w) pꜣ sꜣ-[mꜥ]w-[n]ꜣ dd mdw.w ḥr pr.t šb[n.t ...]		-//-
21	VI2	ḫr jrp jr.w m (j)ḫ.wt wꜥ<.t> {z} dj.w r=f		-//-

Translation

1 Another incantation/another: The rage of Seth is against [Ak]hu/[Sāmānu].

2 The uproar of Baal is against you. The rage of

3 the storm while it is thirsting for rain from the sky is against you.

4 It shall exhaust its (bodily) strength [...] (lit. to put an end to), his two arms above you.

5(rt.) You shall taste that which the [S]ea has tasted by his hand!

5(vs.) You shall taste that which the [S]ea has tasted by his hand! The lion

6(rt.) The water shall approach you! Baal shall strike against you

6(vs.) is roaming inside you. [The water] shall approach [you]! Baal shall strike against you

7 with <spears> of coniferous wood which are in his hand. He repeatedly strikes against you with spears of coniferous wood

8 which are in his hand. You shall be alike like that, o Sāmānu/Akhu! The gods

9 act against you (and) the accusing/your blame which the god makes and the water and the

10 numerous poisons of the weather god and the bitter poisons of Shu

11 the son of Re, and the poisons of Wepwawet which are like those of a snake/snakes,

12 (and) the poisons of the god above and Nikkal his wife,

13 the poisons of Rešep and Adamma, his wife, the poisons

14 of the flame are against <you>, o Akhu. The poisons of the flame are those which will extinguish you!

15 You shall expire as yesterday expired. You shall be extinguished as the light (lit. lamp) is extinguished

16 for those who are moribund. You shall retreat (?) (there), upon <the> ground.

17 You shall die! The gods shall learn that you are dead. The Hathors

18 shall learn that your heart has come forth. I shall tell it to the morning

19 god and welfare (and) health which delight the heart are coming to the house of Re

20 with the words (that) Horus has conquered Sāmānu. Words to be said over seed of me[lon (?) ...]

21 with wine, to be made into a mass, to be applied to it/him.

Commentary

1 R:IV9/V:VII5  : *Kh(ꜣ)b* (WB V, 137.2–15) and *kh(ꜣ)* (WB V, 136.10–15) are synonyms. The word *kh* is only used here; elsewhere in the text, *khb* is always written; see also Massart 1954, 65.1. — R:IV9/V:VII5 [Ak]hu/[Sāmānu]: The recto's gap seems large enough to allow the restoration 'Akhu'. The hole on the verso would fit the word Sāmānu.

2 V:VII5 : Because of the appearance of Baal in the second part of the *parallelismus membrorum* on the verso, Seth is used as a translation for the weather

god graph in the first part. For the weather god, see the commentary to incantation 2 (above § 2), line 11 R:II3/V:III10.

3 R:IV11/V:VII6 / : *Ḫꜣḫꜣ.tj* 'storm'. The writing after the two pikes (K4) on the recto cannot be determined with any degree of certainty. It was probably , or something similar and ; see the spellings in WB III, 363.8–9; Faulkner 1962, 102. Since the storm is always written with the god's determinative, it seems to be another variant of the weather god. This is further indicated by the suffix *=f*, which refers to all three. See Massart 1954, 67.3; Borghouts 1978, 102.60.

5 R:IV12–13/V:VII7 / : The recto and verso both read *kꜣ dp{.t}=k* instead of the expected *kꜣ dp=k*; see also Massart 1954, 66.6; Borghouts 1978, 19, 102.61. — R:IV13 : The graph for 'sea' is odd. On the verso, only the determinatives have been preserved. In Turin A V:III10, the spelling is used for 'sea' (Gardiner 1937, 124–124a.7). See also V:II8 (incantation 1); Meeks 1997, 37.52; Hoch 1994, 52–53.52.

1–5 R:IV9–13/V:VII5–7 'The rage of Seth is against [Ak]hu/[Sāmānu]. The uproar of Baal is against you. The rage of the storm while it is thirsting for the rain from the sky is against you. It shall exhaust its (bodily) strength [...] (lit. to put an end to), his two arms above you. You shall taste that which the [S]ea has tasted by his hand!': Here an allusion to the Baal Cycle is used, specifically to the episode where Baal fights against Yamm, the sea (CAT 1.2 IV7–33; Smith 1994, 318–361; Parker 1997, 103–105), as already noted by Müller 2008, 282.162.

5–6 V:VII7–8 *pꜣ mꜣj nhnh m-ḫnw=k*: This sentence is only attested on the verso. The weather god is known as 'lion of heaven' and his roaring is a symbol of storms and thunder; see Dhorme/Dessaud 1949, 100–101. — : *nh(w)nh(w)* probably for *nhmhm* (WB II, 286.3–4, 7).

6 R:IV13–V1/V:VII8: On the recto, *kꜣ jr.y pꜣ mw sꜣḫ={n}<k>* is written. Massart 1954, 66.8, suggests restoring for the gap on the verso, but the gap is large enough for the restoration *sꜣḫ [tw pꜣ mw ḥ(w).y] Bꜥr'*.

7 R:V1, 2/V:VII8, 9 : At present, it is not certain which coniferous species is meant by the term *ꜥš*. For the word, see e.g. WB I, 228.1–6; GdM VI, 110; Gardiner 1947, 8–9.1; Lefebvre 1949, 147.34; Lucas/Harris 1962, 429–439; Germer 1979, 12; Charpentier 1981, 176–179; Germer 1985, 7–8, 92; Manniche 1989, 64; Moorey 1994, 349–350; Nibbi 1994, 35–52; Nibbi 1996, 37–59; Nunn 1996, 154; Serpico/White 1998, 1037–1048; Westendorf 1999, I, 497, 504; Nicholson/Shaw 2000, 431–443; Germer 2002, 64–65; Nibbi 2003, 69–83; Germer 2008, 49, 233. In any case, the species of timber has to be one which can be used to make spears. See also Schwemer 2001, 227.1575; Müller 2008, 282.164.

6–8 R:V1–2/V:VII8–9 'Baal shall strike against you with <spears> of coniferous wood which are in his hand. He repeatedly strikes against you with spears of coniferous wood which are in his hand': For this passage, see CAT 1.4 VII40–41: *ꜥn.bꜥl.qdm ydh ktǵḏ.arz.bymnh* 'Baal sees the orient. His hand flips, the cedar in his right hand.' (CAT 1.4 VII40–41; Parker 1997, 137).

9 R:V3/V:VII10 / : Both phrases have basically the same meaning. On the recto, *s:ḫr* is used for *s:rḫ*; see WB IV, 199.1. The infinitive has a *t*-ending and is combined with the substantival present *sḏm=f* in an indirect genitive construction, so the literal translation would be 'the accusing of 'that the god makes'.' On the verso, *sḫd* 'to blame' is used (WB IV, 267.1) for *s:rḫ.t*. Here, the infinitive has a *tw*-ending – because of the final sound *d* – in the *status pronominalis*; see Junge 2008, 80 note, 84 note. The word *jrr.w* is an imperfective relative form with a nominal subject. For *sḫd* in general, see Jacquet-Gordon 1960, 16–17; Jansen-Winkeln 1997, 174 note n.

10–14: The theme 'the poisons of deity X are against you' is not typically Egyptian, nor can it currently be found in ancient Near Eastern sources.

12 R:V6/V:VIII2–3 and / : Here, in this context, the term *nṯr ḥr.y*

designates the moon god because his wife, Nikkal, is mentioned too. In contrast to claims in Gardiner 1906, 97; Helck 1971, 469; and LGG IV, 251, the goddess referred to is probably not the Sumerian goddess Ningal, but rather her Canaanite/Akkadian counterpart Nikkal, because the incantations of this papyrus were transferred via the Canaanite area to Egypt; see Beck 2015b, 237–249. At present, Nikkal is only attested in the present manuscript; see also the spelling in R:IX12.

13 R:V6–7/V:VIII4–5 and : Rešep is the god of epidemic plagues and death; his aspects are expanded with war and fertility in Egypt. See for example Boreux 1939, 673–687; Grdseloff 1942; Stadelmann 1967, 47–76; Helck 1971, 450–454; Fulco 1976; Cornelius 1994, 4–8, 25–133; Lipiński 2009, especially 161–221; Tazawa 2009, 6, 38–59, 116–118, 158–160; Münnich 2013, especially 80–119. The graph *J-tw-mꜥ* was identified – partially, and with some reservations – with Edom (Chabas 1842, 125 67; Cook 1930, 112; Grdseloff 1942, 25; Stadelmann 1967, 125; Knauf, Edom אדם in: Van der Toorn/Becking/Van der Horst 1995, 520–522). As Morenz 1999, 373–375, has shown, the term *J-tw-mꜥ* can only name Adamma, Rešep's wife. For this goddess, see also Lipiński 2009, 51–75; LGG I, 611. See the remarks made by Massart 1954, 68.19, who refers to Burchardt 1910, II, 10.177, and Posener 1940, 64.E1, as well as Müller 2008, 282.166. Like Nikkal, Adamma is only attested in the present papyrus.

14 RV8 *m mt.wt n(.w) ḥ.t ꜥḥm=sn tw°*: Here a Late Egyptian *jn*-construction is used; see Massart 1954, 68.21; Gunn 1924, 56–58.

15 R:V9 : *Ḥdw.yt* is translated as 'lamp, light (or the like)' in WB III, 213.23, whereas Massart 1954, 68.22, remarks that most of the attestations could also be translated as 'oil' or 'wick', e.g. the stelae of Taharqa (No. III, line 8, Macadam 1949, I, 6, II, Pls. 5–6; No. VI, line 4, Macadam *ibid.* I, 34, II, Pls. 13–14). Borghouts 1978, 102.62, suggests that it could be understood as 'the lamp of life which is extinguished'.

16 R:V10/V:VIII11 *ḫr.j-mwt/ ḫr.j-<mwt>*: Literally 'being under death'; this term is otherwise only attested in Papyrus Chester Beatty VIII R:IV7 (Gardiner 1935, I 68, II, Pl. 60) and in Papyrus Pushkin 127 R:I9–10 (Caminos 1977, 11, 17, Pls. 3–4). In both cases, the word *mwt* is written out and is used as a substantive. Here it seems to be used in a pseudo-verbal construction (*ḥr* + infinitive). — R:V10/V:VIII12 : As Massart 1954, 69.24, has suggested, the determinatives of the word *ḳnḳn* 'to beat, to pound up (med.)' (WB V, 55.4–56.9) indicate another meaning, something like 'to stagger'. Meeks II, 50/78.0489, proposes a translation 'to beat fighting a retreat' (*jsḳnḳn*) and refers to Borghouts 1978, 19, as well as Hannig 1995, 861, who refers to the word *ḳnḳn*, 'to thrash, to beat'. — V:VIII12: The verso ends after V:VIII12. This incantation is not carried on.

15–17 'You shall expire as yesterday expired. You shall be extinguished as the light (lit. lamp) is extinguished for those who are moribund. You shall retreat (?) (there), upon <the> ground. You shall die!': Perhaps a typical sequence of phrases with four units is used here. Such sequences are very common in Akkadian and Ugaritic incantations, e.g. in RIH 78/20: *wtṣ'u lpn ql ṯꜥy kqṭr 'urbtm kbṯn ꜥmdm kyꜥlm ẓrh klb'im skh* 'and you flee before the voice of the priest like smoke through an opening, like a snake at a foundation wall, like mountain goats towards the summit, like a lion in (its) den' (Fleming 1991, 146). See also the sequence of phrases in *Maqlû* III edited by Abusch/Schwemer 2008, 152–153 (lines 154–179); Meier 1937, 27–28 (lines 158–183).

17–20 R:V11–VI1 'The gods shall learn that you are dead. The Hathors shall learn that your heart has come forth. I shall tell it to the morning god and welfare (and) health which delight the heart are coming to the house of Re with the words (that) Horus has conquered Sāmānu': The 'Deities-Hathors-Formula' (DHF) is only attested in this manuscript and in the ostracon Strasbourg H.115, which partly duplicates incantation 5 (below § 5). This formula is used several times in the papyrus:

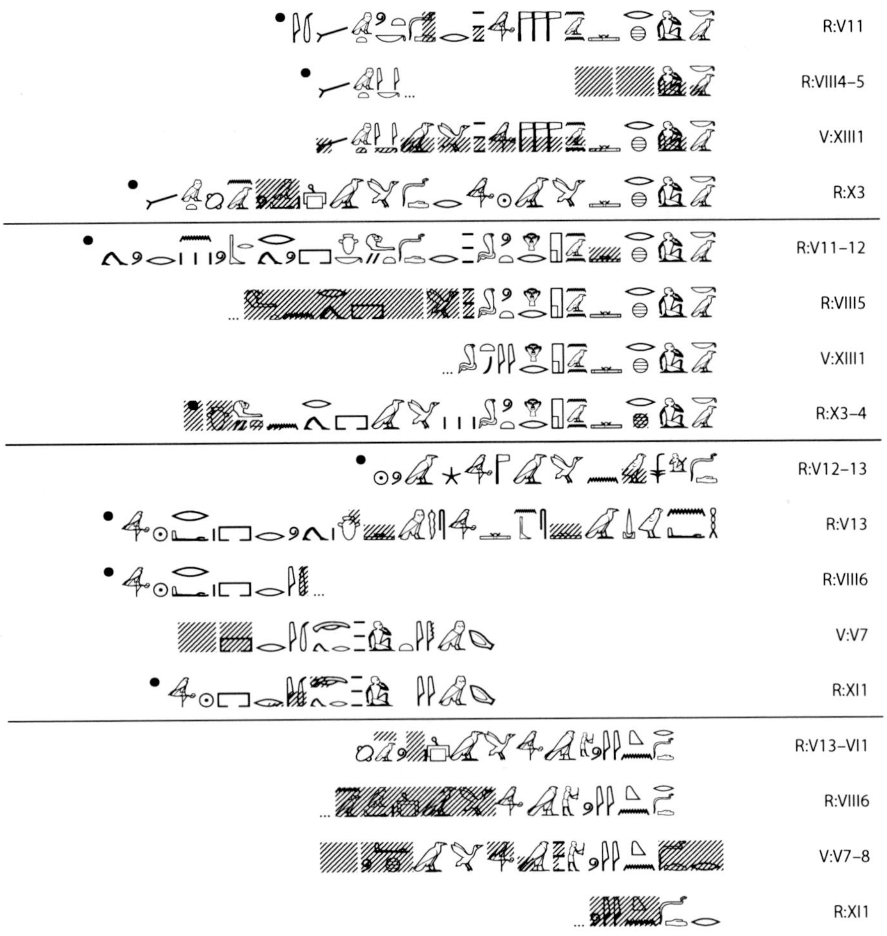
R:V11
R:VIII4–5
V:XIII1
R:X3
R:V11–12
R:VIII5
V:XIII1
R:X3–4
R:V12–13
R:V13
R:VIII6
V:V7
R:XI1
R:V13–VI1
R:VIII6
V:V7–8
R:XI1

17 R:V12 : The Hathors are a group of goddesses who determine one's fate. For the different spellings, see Černý, 1932, 52.20, and Massart 1954, 69–70.30, both with further citations. For general information about the Hathors, see Bissing/Blok 1926, 83–93; Helck 1977, 1033; Hubai 1992, 280–282; Pinch 1994, 37; Rochholz 2002, 45–49, 64–92; Raue 2005, 247–261. These goddesses cannot be connected with the Koṯarāt, because the latter are evoked in blessings at weddings and conceptions and do not determine one's fate; see Pardee, Kosharoth כשרות, in: Van der Toorn/Becking/Van der Horst 1995, 915–917; Spronk 1999, 285–286; Del Olmo Lete 2008, 47, 93, 94–95.

18–19 R:V13 : *Nṯr-dwꜣ* designates the morning god or morning star (LGG IV, 445–446); see Krauss 1997, 216–234.

20 R:V13–VI1 *ḳn(yw) Ḥr(.w) pꜣ sꜣ-[m⌝]w-[n]ꜣ*: It is remarkable that the deity Horus conquers Sāmānu/Akhu. Horus does not figure prominently in battles against the demon. It is the weather god (Seth/Baal) who usually defeats him. One possibility could be that Horus is mentioned in his quality of a patient recovering from a disease (suggested by F. Hoffmann). Another would be that Horus was chosen to conquer Sāmānu/Akhu because his name is similar to that of the Canaanite god Ḥoron, who is often invoked in

incantations or threat formulae (suggested by M. Krebernik; see Rüterswörden, Horon חרן, in: Van der Toorn/Becking/Van der Horst 1995, 806–807; Stadelmann 1967, 78–79; Del Olmo Lete 2014, 31, 205–207). This however does not mean that Ḥoron is identical to Horus here; see Beck 2015b, 234.

20–21 R:VI1–2: The recipe is very fragmentary. The term *pr.t-šn* is translated as seeds of melon or cucumber. An exact identification is not possible. This drug is rarely used; it is applied in bandages and ointments (GdM VI, 485–486; Germer 1979, 126–127; Germer 2008, 130). Two melons were common in Egypt: *Cucumis melo* L. and *Citrullus lanatus* (Thumb.) Mats. & Nakai (Germer 2002, 41). No therapeutic effects are known (Hoppe 1958, 293, 294, 295; Frohne 2002, 209–210; Frohn 2007, 332; Hiller/Melzig 2010, 147, 172). In ancient times and in folk medicine, melon seeds were used, among other things, for bladder problems and kidney diseases and also as a vermifuge (Schneider 1974, V, 394–398; Alpin 1980, 163; Boulos 1983, 75; Moursi 1992, 111–112 133; Hiller/Melzig 2010,172). Wine (*jrp*) was used for internal and topical treatments in Egypt – usually as a solvent or for soaking. Used internally, wine can reduce body temperature (GdM VI, 48–49; Germer 1979, 86–89; Germer 1985, 117; Manniche 1989, 155-156; Kolta 2000, 767; Nicholson/Shaw 2000, 581; Germer 2002, 152; Germer 2008, 363; Schneider 1968, II, 19–20; Schneider 1975, VI, 204–205; Frohne 2002, 577; Hiller/Melzig 2010, 628–629). The alcohol concentration of wine is between 10–11% and does not exceed 16%, so it cannot be used as a disinfectant: only liquids with an alcohol concentration of between 16% and 70% have disinfecting properties (Germer 1979, 87–89; Nicholson/Shaw 2000, 590). Wine seems to have a positive effect on angiogenesis (the growth of new blood vessels from pre-existing vessels; Sipos *et al.* 2004, 213). Its intoxicating effect does not seem to have been used in Egypt (Germer 1979, 87–89; Germer 2002, 152; different GdM VI, 48–49). Lastly, one must consider the psychological component of using wine in recipes, because it was a luxury good in Egypt (Germer 1979, 89; Nicholson/Shaw 2000, 581; Germer 2008, 32).

21 R:VI2 : One would expect *wʿ.t*. — 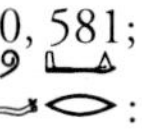: Note the odd order of the signs.

5. Incantation 5 (R:VI2–VIII9/V:XI, XII, XIII)

At the beginning, the magician explains that he has overcome the demon who was submerged in the patient's body, and that he belongs to the family of *Jrtḳn* who are able to speak with snakes. Then the weather god and Anat are mentioned and the magician increases his power by suckling at Anat's teat and drinking out of the weather god's cup. After a fragmentary passage, the dry land and desert drink up Sāmānu/Akhu. A long list follows, describing where the demon afflicted the patient's limbs. The incantation ends with the DHF and a rather fragmentary recipe.

This incantation is the only one in papyrus Leiden I 343 + 345 for which there exist parallels. It appears on two other objects: ostracon Leipzig ÄMUL 1906 and ostracon Strasbourg H.115. The former contains the beginning (R:VI2–VII4) and the latter the end (R:VII6–VIII8). Amazingly, ostracon Leipzig starts with the ending of a different incantation and ends with the beginning of another spell against Sāmānu.[48]

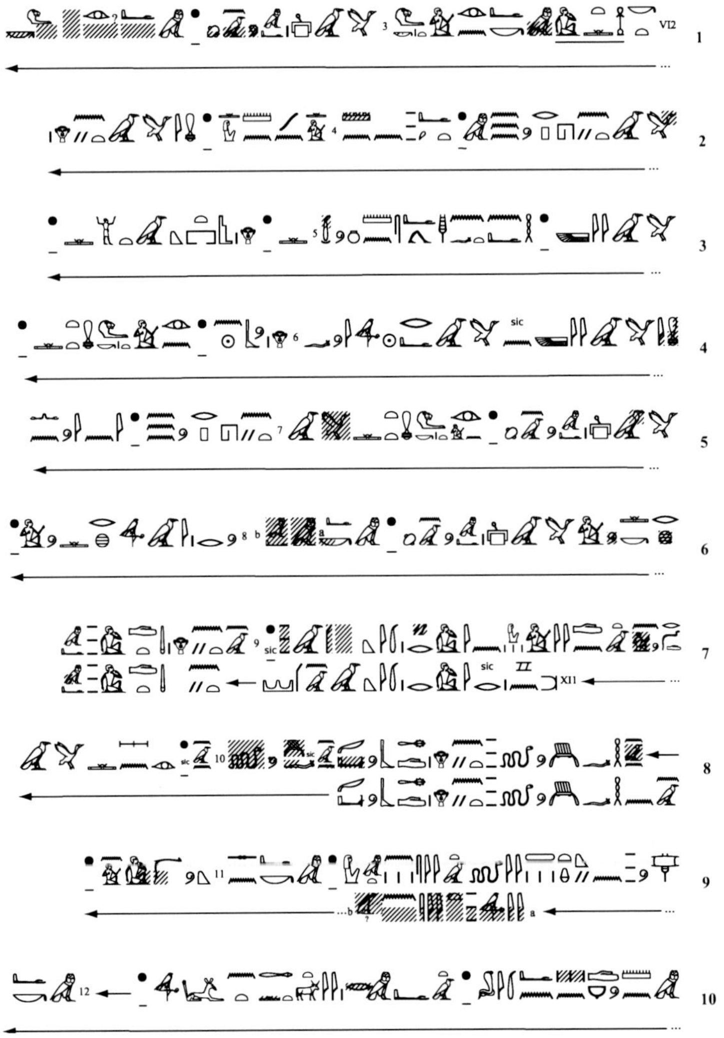

R:VI7a–b no longer legible; 9 <ḫ>f3w, see ḫf3w in the same line; V:XI2a–b lower part of the line is broken off, only traces partially visible.

48 For the ostraca, see Beck 2015b, 126–140, with further citations. Below, the publication will not be cited.

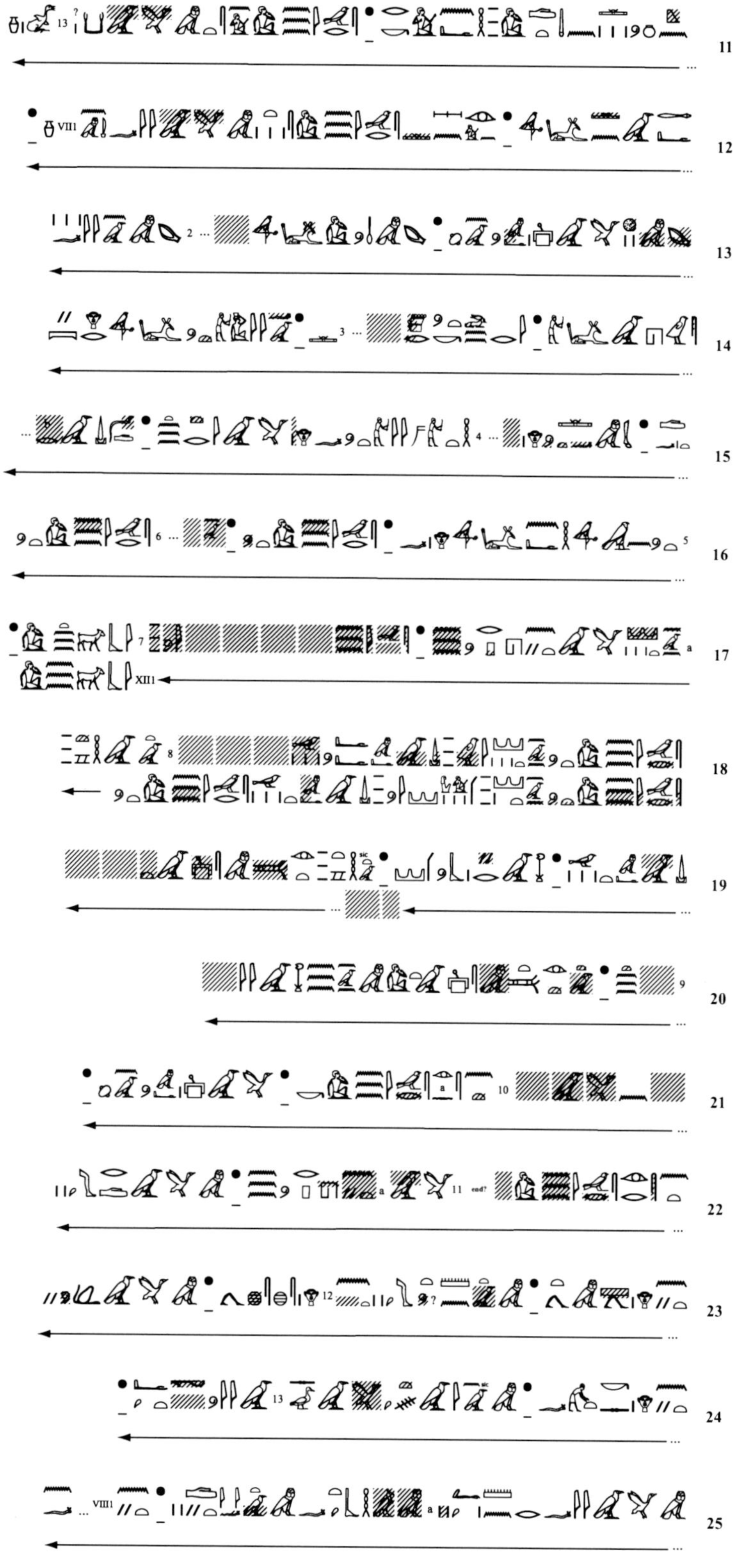

R:VII6a the ⸺ *above is no longer legible; 10a Gardiner writes* ⊂⊃ *and suggests* ⸺*, clearly* ⸺*; 11a no longer legible; 13a no longer legible.*

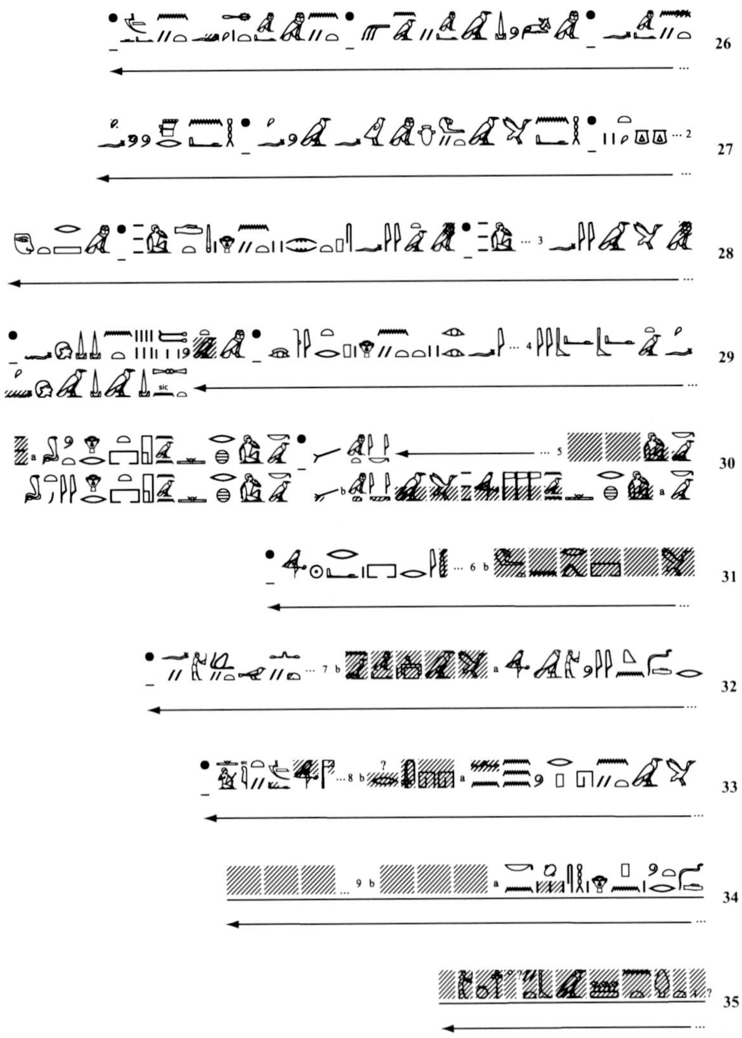

R:VIII5a–b almost illegible 6a–b only partially legible; 7a–b only partially legible; 8a–b traces of rubrum; V:XIII1a–b lower part of the line is broken off.

Transliteration

		Recto		Verso
1	VI2–3	*k.t <u>šn.t</u> m=k jr.n=j ḥꜣ.t=k pꜣ sꜣ-mꜥw-nꜣ*° *m[=k] jr[.n=j] ḥꜣ[.t]=k*		[...]
2	VI3–4	*pꜣ n.ty hrp.w m*° *ꜥ.wt n(.wt) mn ms.n mn<.t>*° *mj pꜣ n.ty ḥr*		[...]
3	VI4–5	*pꜣ(y)*° *ḥnꜥ ntf ꜥḥꜥ s:mn.w*° *ḥr s.t ḳꜣ.t*°		[...]
4	VI5–6	*mj pꜣ(y){.n} pꜣ Rꜥ(w) jw=f ḥr wbn*° *jr.n=j ḥꜣ.t=k mj.t(j)t*°		[...]
5	VI6–7	*pꜣ sꜣ-mꜥw-nꜣ*° *jr.n=j ḥꜣ.t=k mj.t(j)t pꜣ n.ty hrp.w*° *jn-jw nn*		[...]
6	VI7–8	*rḫ=k wj pꜣ sꜣ-mꜥw-nꜣ*° *m=k m Mꜥw-r'-jꜣ rḫ wj*°		[...]
7	VI8–9	*r-ḏd n(.j) wj tꜣ dny<.t> n<.t> J-y-r'-tj-ḳ[...]ꜣ.w nꜣ n.ty ḥr md(w).t m-ꜥ*	XI1	*[dnj.t] n<.t>{r} j-r'-tj-ḳꜣ-nꜣ n.ty (ḥr) md(w).t m-ꜥ*
8	VI9–10	*nꜣ n(.j) h̤fꜣw.w n.ty ḥr ẖdb(w) nꜣ n(.j) <ḥ>f[ꜣw.w] nꜣ n*° *jr ꜥḏn pꜣ*	XI1	*nꜣ n(.j) h̤fꜣw.w n.ty ḥr ẖdb(w)*
9	VI10–11	*ṯꜣw(.w) n(.w) Ḳy-t'-y tꜣy=sn mw.t*° *m=k znḳ(w).n=j*°	XI2	*[... Ḳt]y.w t[ꜣ]y=sn mw.t [...]*
10	VI11–12	*m mnd.w n(.w) ꜥntj tꜣ ꜥ-m-r'-y.t ꜥꜣ.t n.t Stẖ*(?)° *m=k*		[...]
11	VI12–13	*ḳn.w n(.w) md(w).wt ḥnꜥ=j r=k*° *swr(j).n=j st m pꜣ kṯ*		[...]
12	VI13–VII1	*ꜥꜣ n(.j) Stẖ*(?)° *jr.n=j ꜥḏn swr(j) st m pꜣy=f nm*°		[...]
13	VII1–2	*sḏm zp-sn pꜣ sꜣ-mꜥw-nꜣ*° *sḏm ḫrw Stẖ*(?) *[...] sḏm nꜣy=f*		[...]
14	VII2–3	*swh(ꜣ)*° *jr wnn{.tw}=k ḏr [...]*° *fꜣ(y) tw Stẖ*(?) *<ḥr> ḥr.y*		[...]
15	VII3–4	*<m> ḏr.t=f*° *wḥm=f tw ḥr [...] ḥ(w){t} y{tw}=f <tw> ḥr pꜣ jtr(.t)*° *ḏd Ḏꜣr[...]*		[...]
16	VII5–6	*tw n Ḥr.w ḥnꜥ Stẖ*(?) *ḥr=f*° *swr(j) tw*° *nꜣ [...] swr(j) tw*		[...]
17	VII6–7	*nꜣ n(.j) ḫꜣs.wt pꜣ n.ty hrp.w*° *s[wr](j) [tw ... jw=w] jb.t*°	XII1	*[...] jb*
18	VII7–8	*swr(j) tw nꜣ n(.j) ḫꜣs.wt jw=w ḏmꜥ{ꜥ}.w<t> [swr(j) tw ...] tꜣ ꜣḥ.(w)t*	XII1	*swr(j) tw nꜣ n(.j) ḫꜣst.jw jw=w ḏmꜥ.wt swrj tw*
19	VII8	*ḏmꜥ.(w)t*° *ḫꜣ-y-r'-bw*° *tꜣ <ꜣ>ḥ.(w)t jr.t tm sꜣ.t [...]*		[...]
20	VII9	*[...]t*° *tꜣ jr(r).t tm sꜣ.t m nꜣ n(.j) mw ḫꜣy [...]*		[...]
21	VII9–10	*[...] n(.j) pꜣ [...] nts jr=z swr(j)=k*° *pꜣ sꜣ-mꜥw-nꜣ*		[...]
22	VII10–11	*nts jr swr(j) [tw] pꜣ [n.ty] hrp.w*° *m pꜣ rd 2*		[...]
23	VII11–12	*n.ty ḥr šm.t*° *m tꜣ mn.t(w) 2 n.t[y] ḥr sḫsḫ*° *m pꜣ pḥ.wj*		[...]

		Recto		Verso
24	VII12–13	*n.ty ḥr kz.t=f° m {nꜣ}<tꜣ> jꜣ.t pꜣ zꜣy(w) <n.j> ꜥ.t°*		[…]
25	VII13–VIII1	*m pꜣy=f rmn 2 m nḥb.t=f m t[ꜣ]y=f ḏr.ty 2° n.ty […] n=f*		[…]
26	VIII1	*n.ty m-ꜥ=f° m jw-ḏꜣ-mꜥy-nꜣ° n.ty m mẖt(.w)=f n.ty mꜣꜥ(.w)°*		[…]
27	VIII2	*[m] gg.t 2° ḥnꜥ pꜣ ḥꜣ.ty m wfꜣ(w)=f° ḥnꜥ ḏrw.w=f*		[…]
28	VIII2–3	*m pꜣy=f […]° m tꜣy=f sp.t 2 n.ty ḥr md(w){w}.t° m {rš}<šr>.t*		[…]
29	VIII3–4	*=f tꜣ ꜥbꜥb(y.t) [m tꜣj]j=f jr.tj 2.t n.ty ḥr ptr(j)° m tꜣ ṯ(ꜣ)z.(w)<t> 7 n.t ḏꜣḏꜣ=f°*	XIII1	*ṯ(ꜣ)z.t n<.t> ḏꜣḏꜣ=f*
30	VIII4–5	*kꜣ […]° [pꜣ]y=k mwt° kꜣ rẖ nꜣ n(.j) Ḥw.t-ḥr.w*	XIII1	*kꜣ rẖ nꜣ n(.j) nṯr.w pꜣy=k mwt kꜣ rẖ nꜣ n(.j) Ḥw.t-ḥr.yt*
31	VIII5–6	*p[ꜣ] pr<.t> n(.j) ḥꜣ.ty[=k]° […]tj r pr Rꜥ(w)°*		[…]
32	VIII6–7	*r-ḏd ḳn(yw) Ḥr(.w) pꜣ sꜣ-mꜥ-[nꜣ] […] jw.ty pḥ.ty=fy°*		[…]
33	VIII7–8	*pꜣ n.ty hrp.w nn [hh r …] nṯr mꜣꜥ.ty°*		[…]
34	VIII8–9	*dd.tw r' pn ḥr ḥs kn […]*		[…]
35	VIII9	*[… .t n.t šꜣb.yt(?) nḏ(.w) …]*		[…]

Translation

1 Another incantation: Behold, I have overcome you, o Sāmānu. Be[hold, I] have over[come] you,

2 [the] one who is submerged in the limbs of NN whom NN has born, like the one who

3 is flying up and established permanently at the high place,

4 like Re flies up during his rising. In like manner, I have overcome you,

5 o Sāmānu. In like manner, I have overcome you, the one who is submerged. Will you

6 not recognize me, o Sāmānu? Behold, Mauri is the one who knows me

7 with the words: I belong to the family of *Jrtḳn*, those who speak with (?)

8 the snakes, who kill the snakes, those (who) put an end to

9 the breath of Qety, their mother. Behold, I suckled

10 at the breasts of Anat, the great cow (?) of the weather god. Behold,

11 numerous words are with me against you. I have drunk them out of the great

12 chalice of the weather god. Out of his chalice, I have drunk them.

13 Listen, listen, o Sāmānu. Listen to the voice of the weather god. […] Listen to his

14 roaring! If you will be […] The weather god shall lift you

15 up <with> his hand. He shall lift you up once again on […] He shall strike you at the river (during) *Ḏꜣr*[…] says […]

16 you for this reason to Horus and the weather god. The [...] shall drink you. The deserts

17 shall drink the one who is submerged. [The ...] shall dr[ink you] which thirst.

18 The deserts shall drink you while they are dry. The dry

19 field, the desert, the <fi>eld, which is not satiated [...]

20 [...] which is not satiated by [...] water

21 [...] It is it (= the dry field) which will drink you, o Sāmānu.

22 It is it (= the dry field) which drunk [you], the one who is submerged in the two lower legs

23 that walk, in the two thighs that run, in the back

24 that bows, in the spine, the beam of the body,

25 in his two shoulders, in his neck, in both his hands that [...] for him,

26 which is with him in the *Jḏmn* (?) which is in his entrails which are in good condition,

27 [in] the two kidneys (?) and in the heart, in his lung and his sides,

28 in his [two ears that hear (?)], in his two lips that speak, in his

29 nose, the bubbling one (?), [in his] both eyes that see, in the seven orifices of his head.

30 The gods shall learn of your death. The Hathors shall learn

31 of [the coming forth of your] heart. [The goss]ip [reached] the house of Re

32 with the words (that) Horus has conquered [Sāmānu]. [...] without his strength,

33 the one who is submerged. There is no [blast (of fire) against (?) ...] the god, the righteous one.

34 This utterance is to be said over faeces of [...]

35 [...] of the *šꜣb.t*-plant, to be ground [...].

Commentary

1 R:VI2 : Literally 'I made your beginning'. It is translated as 'to get in front of, overcome' in WB III, 21.11–12 with reference to the present manuscript (WB III, 21.12). This phrase is used several times in the papyrus, so also V:IV10: *m=k jr.n=j ḥꜣ.t=k bw jr=k ḥꜣ.t=j* 'Behold, I have overcome you. You did not overcome me!' See also Gardiner 1928, 87.7; Massart 1954, 72.2.

2 R:VI3 : The phrase 'the one who is submerged' is a typical epithet of Sāmānu/Akhu in papyrus Leiden I 343 + 345. This epithet is also used in R:VI7, VII6, 11, VIII7, 11, X10, V:IV9. Massart 1954, 72.3, thinks that the metaphor of something evil being submerged was readily understandable to the Egyptians because they were used to crocodiles submerged in the Nile. For *n.ty hrp.w*, see e.g. papyrus BM EA 10042 (Magical Papyrus Harris) R:III7, R:VIII7 (Leitz 1999, Pl. 14, 19).

2–3 *ḥr pꜣy*: The infinitive of the verb *pꜣj* 'to fly (up)' can be constructed with or without a *t*-ending; for details, see the references in WB I, 494.1–12.

3 R:VI4 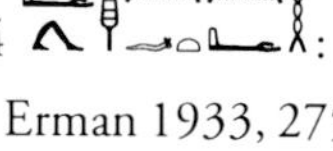: For this construction, see Gardiner 1988, 130 §171.3, 226 §300 Obs.; Erman 1933, 275–276 §575; Gardiner 1928, 87.8; and Černý 1949, 25–30, to whom Massart 1954, 73.5, refers.

4 : Massart 1954, 73.6, assumes that {*n*} has to be emended. In this context the present *sḏm=f* makes more sense because the sun's rising is an action which should take place over and over again. The translation *mj pꜣ(y).n pꜣ Rꜥ(w)* 'like Re flew up' is also possible. [*J*]*mn-Rꜥ(w)* is written instead of *Rꜥ(w)* in the parallel of ostracon Leipzig ÄMUL 1906 R:5.

6 R:VI7–8 : Müller 2008, 283.170, remarks that *w* is uncommon after *mꜥ* and suggests the reading *ḥꜣw*, which cannot be confirmed. The graph *mꜥw* is very unusual for syllabic writings, but Sāmānu is written with *mꜥw* several times in the text. The name of this creature is otherwise unknown. Müller, *ibid.*, tentatively suggests that the creature's name can be connected with Meriri (van der Toorn: Meriri מרירי, in: Van der Toorn/Becking/Van der Horst 1995, 1064–1065). See also statements by Burchardt 1910, II, 24–25; LGG III, 333.

7–9 'I belong to the family of *Jrtḳn*, those who speak with (?) the snakes, who kill the snakes, those (who) put an end to the breath of Qety, their mother': For a recent view on this passage, see Matić 2015, 57–60, who assumes this refers to two different kinds of snakes. It is also possible that there is only one group of snakes to whom the people of *Jrtḳn* first speak and which they then kill.

7 R:VI8–9/V:XI1 sic / : On the recto the determinatives are omitted, probably due to the haplography with *nꜣ n.ty* that follows. The determinatives on the verso clearly mark the word as a toponym. *Jrtḳn* has been identified with Elteqon (אֶלְתְּקֹן; Burchardt 1910, II, 7–8; Gauthier 1925, I, 99). Aḥituv 1984, 92–93, rejects this because of the minor significance of that city. Matić 2015, 60–61, suggests connecting *Jrtḳn* with one of the names of the foreign country of the northern people listed in Karnak on the northern wall of the seventh pylon during the reign of Thutmose III: (Urk. IV, 788.139; Mariette 1875, 53.3, Pl. 21.139). The transformation *k* to *ḳ* and *ṯ* to *t* poses difficulties for this interpretation; see Hoch 1994, 409, 411. Hoch, *ibid.*, remarks that *t* is interchangeable with *ṯ* in monumental inscriptions. Apart from that, one has to consider that time passed between the two texts and that sometimes the spelling of foreign country names changes over time. Furthermore, there was a city with the name *yarqānu* (^uru^*i-ia-ar-qa-ni*, ^uru^*ia-ar-qa-ni*), which at present cannot be located. Perhaps the toponym can be identified with this city provided the *t* is omitted; see van Soldt 2005, 26. See also statements by Massart 1954, 73.10; Müller 2008, 283.171.

8 R:VI9/V:XI1: The feminine article refers to *dnj.t* 'family'. — *nꜣ n(.j) <ḥ>fꜣ.w(.w)*: The parallel on ostracon Leipzig 1906 R:8 alternatively writes *nꜣ n(.j) fy(.w)* 'the vipers'. For snakes in general, see Gardiner 1947, II, 69*.1; for *fy*, see Newberry 1948, 118; Leitz 1997, 64–135.

9 R:VI10/V:XI12 [...]: The mother snake is called *Ḳty* (rt.) in the text. On the verso only the last signs have been preserved. The parallel on ostracon Leipzig ÄMUL 1906 R:8–9 gives a different name and omits the determinatives: *Kjpw* . This name is otherwise unattested.

8–9 R:VI10–11 'Behold, I suckled at the breasts of Anat, the great cow (?) of the weather god': In ostracon Leipzig ÄMUL 1906 R:9–V:1, the subject of the sentences is different: 'Behold, she suckled at the breasts of Anat, the great cow (?) of the weather god.' Here, the mother snake (see above) or alternatively the family of *Jrtḳn* suckles milk at Anat's teat, and not the magician as in papyrus Leiden I 343 + 345. Anat is known as a wet-nurse from the Ugaritic myths, e.g. the Legend of Keret: *ynq.ḥlb.ꜥ[ṯ]trt mṣṣ.ṯd.btlt.[ꜥnt] mšnq[t.ilm]* 'He suckled the milk of Astarte, he sucked at the virgin [Anat's] breast, the wet-nurses [of gods]' (CAT 1.15 II26–28; see Parker 1997, 25).

9 R:VI11 : Massart 1954, 73.15, suggests connecting the word with the Sumerian amar 'calf' and refers to CAT 1.10, where, according to the scholarly consensus at that time, Baal copulates with Anat as a cow. This derivation from the Sumerian amar is to be rejected. CAT 1.10 tells the story of Baal; he is on a hunting trip at a pasture with many cattle, and Anat is following him. According to the rather fragmentary context, Baal, in the form of a bull, copulates with a cow and begets a bull and a heifer, which he presents to Anat, so Anat cannot conceivably be that cow; see Parker 1997, 181–186; Day 1995, 64. Hoch 1994, 67–68, proposes connecting the word *ꜥmry.t* with the Semitic root *ḥlb* 'milk' on the one hand, and with *ꜥwl* 'suckle' on the other.

Vittmann 1997, 281, rejects this with a sound explanation. For the phrase 'cow of Seth' in the inscriptions of Ramses II, see Couroyon 1964, 453–456, who ultimately claims that this epithet should be read 'bull of Seth' instead of 'cow of Seth', because it is generally used as an epithet of Ramses II. The word (ostracon Leipzig ÄMUL 1906 V:1) cannot be simply derived from any of these words, even if the determinative clearly implies that it has to be a kind of cow.

11–12 R:VI12–VII1 'I have drunk them out of the great chalice of the weather god. Out of his chalice, I have drunk them': Here, the conjurer imbibes himself with words from Baal's chalice – an action which will obviously empower him. The next phrase confirms this; see also Borghouts 1978, 102.64. In ostracon Leipzig ÄMUL 1906 V:2–3, the demon Akhu is forced to drink these words, which in this case probably have a harmful effect. The chalice seems to be an expression of royal dignity. In the Baal Cycle, a goblet is placed in Baal's hands and other deities pay tribute to him: *ytn.ks.bdh krp[[m]]nm.bkl'at. ydh bkrb.ʿẓm* 'Put a cup in his hand, a chalice in both of his hands, a mighty goblet' (CAT 1.3 I10–12; Parker 1997, 106; Smith/Pitard 2009, 94–96); see the statements by Müller 2008, 284.174. — For , see WB V, 148.9–10; Massart 1954, 74.18; Hoch 1994, 338–339.502. — Massart 1954, 73.17, thinks that the pronoun refers to suckling at Anat's teat. The reference clearly seems to be to .

13–14 R:VII1–2 'Listen, listen, o Sāmānu. Listen to the voice of the weather god. [...] Listen to his roaring!': Note the climax used in the sentences.

14 R:VII2 : Massart 1954, 74.23, refers to Gardiner 1909, 28–29, and Gardiner 1930, 226, who prefers to translate the word as 'to be in confusion'. In the context – as Massart, *ibid.*, has stressed – the translation 'roaring' fits better. The spelling is common for the 19th Dynasty (WB V, 71). For this term, see also Vandier 1950, 217–218.g. — R:VII2 : {*tw*} has to be emended. For the construction *jr wnn*, see Schenkel 2005a, 328–333; Černý/Groll 1984, 561.

14–15 R:VII3 *fꜣ(y) tw Sth*[(?)] <*ḥr*> *ḥr.y* <*m*> *ḏr.t=f:* The same phrase is used in R:IX10, in accordance with which <*ḥr*> was restored here. Gardiner's transcriptions (Massart 1954, 19) show *jr.t*, with the remark one has to read *ḏr.t*; so does Massart 1954, 74.25. The manuscript clearly shows *ḏr.t*.

15 R:VII4 : For the rearrangement of *tw* + suffix into suffix + *tw*, see Gardiner 1937, 141a, who lists various examples; see also Massart 1954, 74.27. — [...] : This creature is otherwise unknown. — Ostracon Leipzig ÄMUL 1906 V:6–8 ends with 'Strike [...] the hard stone of *Sḏr* [...] on it. <You> will not stand up. There is no ima<ge> of you in [his] limbs.' Papyrus Leiden I 343 + 345 is too fragmentary for restoring this passage and providing a translation. Borghouts 1978, 20, 102.66, thinks that the version in the parallel is more correct than the one on the papyrus, because of papyrus Leiden I 349 R:15 *ḥw.tw=f ḥr pꜣ jnr wʿb* 'he is thrown on the pure stone' (De Buck/Stricker 1940, 57 + Pl.).

16: A new subject in the incantation starts here. The demon is removed by the dry deserts, which drink him up. This is also where the second parallel, ostracon Strasbourg H. 115, begins. The beginning is not exactly the same. — R:VII5: In the lacuna after *swr(j) tw nꜣ* [...] a word qualifying a kind of dry land must have been written. See Massart 1954, 74.28, who refers to Papyrus Chester Beatty II V:V7–8 *šn(t).n=j* (8) *pzg.n=j swr(j).n=j tn* 'I invoked (you). I spat you out. I drank you!' (Gardiner 1935, II, Pl. 37) and papyrus Vatican Mag. II3 *swr(j)=j tw* 'I drink you' (Suys 1934, 70–71), where an ailment is also consumed.

17–22: The 'deserts shall drink you' theme is not genuinely Egyptian.

18 V:XII1 : For this spelling as 'foreign land, hill country' and not 'foreigner, desert dweller', see WB III, 235.14. — R:VII7/V:XII1 / : The word *ḏmʿ(ʿ)* 'parched' is only attested in papyrus Leiden I 343 + 345 and the parallel on ostracon Strasbourg H. 115 R:2 (); see WB V, 574.10–11; Hoch 1994, 386; Müller 2002, 42.581. In contrast to papyrus Leiden I 343 + 354, on the ostracon the word qualifies the desert as an attributive and is not used as an adverbial clause. The word is used again in line 19 (R:VII8).

19 R:VII8 : Massart 1954, 71, 74.33, translates it as 'the dry land of Kharabu' and notes

that the term is not used in the sense of 'Aleppo' but as a paraphrase for Hebrew חרב 'be dry, dried up'; see Burchardt 1910, II, 39.736, Gauthier 1927, IV, 151–152. The translation given by Massart, *ibid.*, is not possible because an indirect genitive would be used in such a construction. The verse points also argue against this translation. Hoch 1994, 249, translates *ḫrb* as 'desert', which fits the context quite well. See older interpretations by Leemans 1842, 67; Chabas 1902, 138.

20 R:VII9 : The word qualifying the water is not clear. Perhaps it has to be connected with *ḥy* 'flood (the high one)' (WB III, 238.8), but this word is not attested before the Greek Period. The parallel (R:3) reads [...] *mw n.w ḥj<j>[.t]* 'rainwater'.

21 R:VII9 : The parallel (R:4) reads: *(verb of motion?).n*(?) *pꜣ Rꜥ(w)* but the context is too fragmentary for a translation. R:VII9 should probably also be restored as *pꜣ [Rꜥw]*.

21–22 R:VII10–11 'It is it (= the dry field) which will drink you, o Sāmānu. It is it (= the dry field) which drank [you], the one who is submerged (...)': The sentences are constructed with a Middle Egyptian *jn*-construction, the former in the future tense, the latter in the perfect tense. Massart 1954, 71, and Borghouts 1978, 20, translate them in the present tense. Müller 2008, 284, uses the future tense in his translation. The parallel on ostracon Strasbourg H. 115 R:4–5 constructs the sentence in the plural (*ntsn jr=sn swr* [...] *n.ty hrp.w*).

22–29: In the following lines, several body parts which Sāmānu/Akhu has afflicted are listed. The body parts are specified by a possessive pronoun or the possessive article in the third person masculine. The parallel on ostracon Strasbourg H. 115 at first uses the second person masculine possessive pronoun (*=k*) and the second person masculine possessive article (*pꜣy=k*; R:5–7), but later follows papyrus Leiden I 343 + 345.

23 R:VII11 : For this construction, see the commentary to line 5 of incantation 3 (above § 3).

24 R:VII13 : One would expect a plural or another word denoting the whole body, like *ḥꜥ.w*.

25 R:VII13 '(...) in his neck, in both his hands that [...] for him': The parallel differs slightly: 'in his neck which is intact [...]' (ostracon Strasbourg H. 115 R:7). Müller 2000, 284.181, reads *ḏꜣ.t* (WB V, 516.5–7), the old lexeme for 'hand', as does Mathieu 2000, 248. The ostracon clearly has *wḏꜣ.t* modifying the neck as an adjunct. The function of the hands has not been preserved in papyrus Leiden I 343 + 345.

26 R:VIII1 : The term seems to designate something in the entrails – an organ or part of an organ. The parallel reads and omits the determinative (ostracon Strasbourg H. 115 R:8). Hoch 1994, 48.44, suggests connecting the term with the Hebrew אזמימאות 'knots, fringes' or the Akkadian *azaʾīlu* 'sack with netlike reinforcement' (CAD A.2, AHw. I, 92a–b), both of which are supported by the determinative for hair. According to Müller 2008, 284–285.182, the parallel is to be restored as *jw-<ḏꜣ>-mꜥ-r'*, whereby the final *r* represents *l*. See also the Ugaritic *azml/izml* 'sack, garment' (DUL 137, Hoch 1994, 48). Perhaps the term *jw-mꜥ-r'* is to be connected with *ʾbr*$_2$ 'limb' (DNWSI I, 7).

28 R:VIII2–3: The ears with their features have to be written in this lacuna because the other of the seven orifices of the head – the mouth, nose, and eyes – are mentioned. The remaining determinatives suggest a verb of perception like 'to hear'. The lexeme used for 'ear' cannot be determined with certainty due to the gap. See also Müller 2008, 285.183.

28–29 R:VIII3 : Here, the term *šr.t* 'nose' is written with the metathesis *rš.t*. For this spelling, see WB IV, 523.

29 R:VIII3 [...] : The term *tꜣ ꜥbꜥb.y[t]* is not attested anywhere else. Perhaps it is a metathesis of *bꜥbꜥ* 'to bubble' (WB I, 447.1–4; Allen 1984, 577; Ward 1977, 274–278), which would give something like 'the bubbling one'. The sense is still odd; see also Massart 1954, 75.49; Müller 2008, 285.184. The remains in the parallel on ostracon Strasbourg H. 115 R:10 fit *sn* 'to smell' (WB IV, 153.8–154.7) – if the reading is correct. — R:VIII4/V:XIII1 '(seven) orifices of his head': Usually the word *bꜣbꜣ.w* 'holes' (WB I, 419.1) is used for *ṯ(ꜣ)z.t* 'knot'. According to Wendrich 2006, 252, the seven *ṯ(ꜣ)z.t* of the head can also be referring to the seven vertebrae of the neck. This has to be

rejected because the seven holes of the head are mentioned earlier in the papyrus and the enumeration of these seven holes ends with *ṯ(ꜣ)t.t 7 n.t ḏꜣḏꜣ=f*.

30–33: The DHF follows, see the commentary to lines 17–20 of incantation 4 (above § 4).

32: The parallel differs from papyrus Leiden I 343 + 345: 'the killed one for you (?)'. Due to its fragmentary state, the meaning is obscure. Ostracon Strasbourg H. 115 ends here.

34–35: A rather fragmentary recipe follows. It mentions faeces and the *šꜣb.t* plant, which is qualified by something lost in the gap. The parallel on ostracon Leipzig 1906 mentions grain and water as ingredients. For faeces, see the commentary to lines 7–8 of incantation 1 (above § 1). The *šꜣb.t* plant is sometimes connected with *šb.t* (incantation 4 (above § 4), commentary to lines 21–22). It is used externally in bandages and ointments. An exact identification is not possible (GdM VI, 476; Germer 1979, 318; Charpentier 1981, 646–647; Germer 2008, 125. See also the discussion in Westendorf 1999, I, 506).

33 R:VIII8 : Dawson 1934b, 187, suggests the reading *js kk*, but admits that it is improbable that words were spoken over the 'brain of a weevil'; see also Massart 1954, 76.56.

6. Incantation 6 (R:VIII10–X9/V:XIV, XV)

In this spell, Sāmānu/Akhu is accused by several deities before the demon is ripped out. After a rather fragmentary passage, the creature is struck at the moon god's jar and falls to the ground. At the end, the vessels containing the demon open up to spit out their contents (= the demon). The incantation ends with the DHF and a very fragmentary recipe. It is remarkable that the scribe alternates between Sāmānu and Akhu. This clearly shows that the two names were interchangable for the Egyptians.

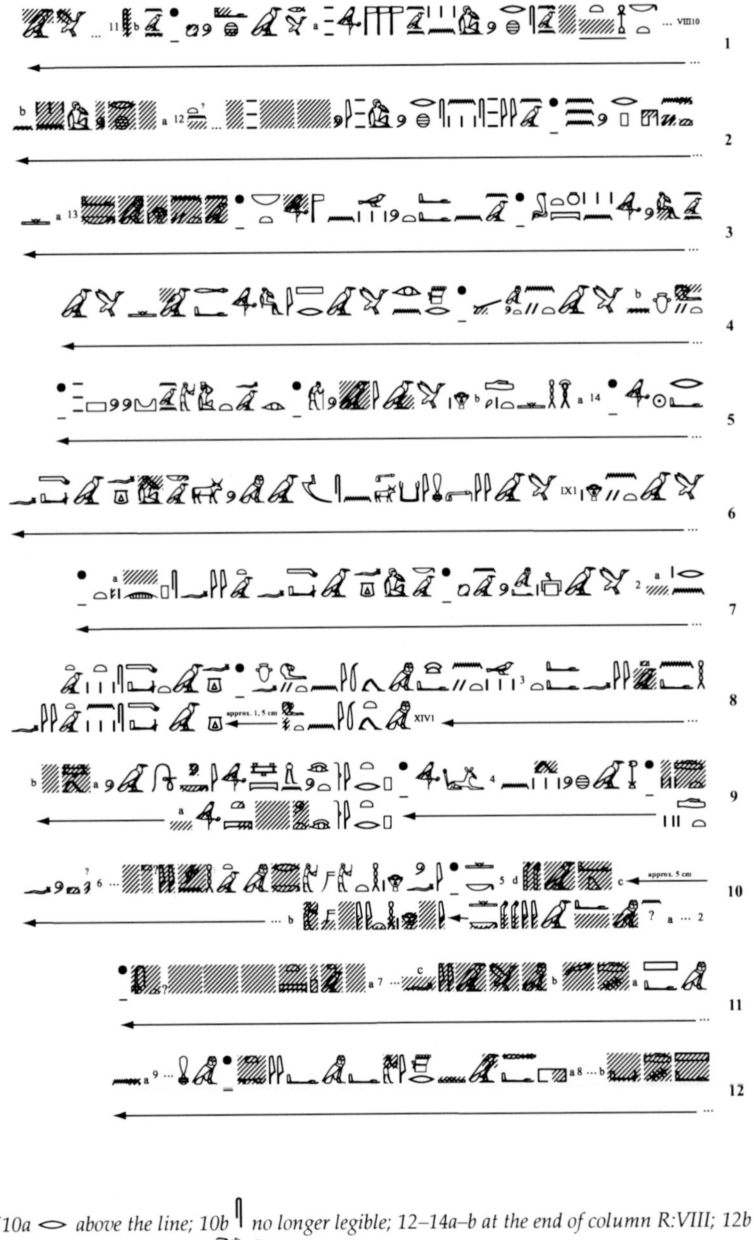

R:VIII10a above the line; 10b no longer legible; 12–14a–b at the end of column R:VIII; 12b no longer legible; IX1a traces of ; 2a on the edge of the rip; 4a–b almost faded; 4c–d partially legible; 6a–b almost faded; 6c almost faded; 7a–b difficult to read due to a rip in the papyrus, signs are faded; 8a & 9a perhaps nothing is missing; V:XIV1a traces; 2a–b lower part of the line is broken off.

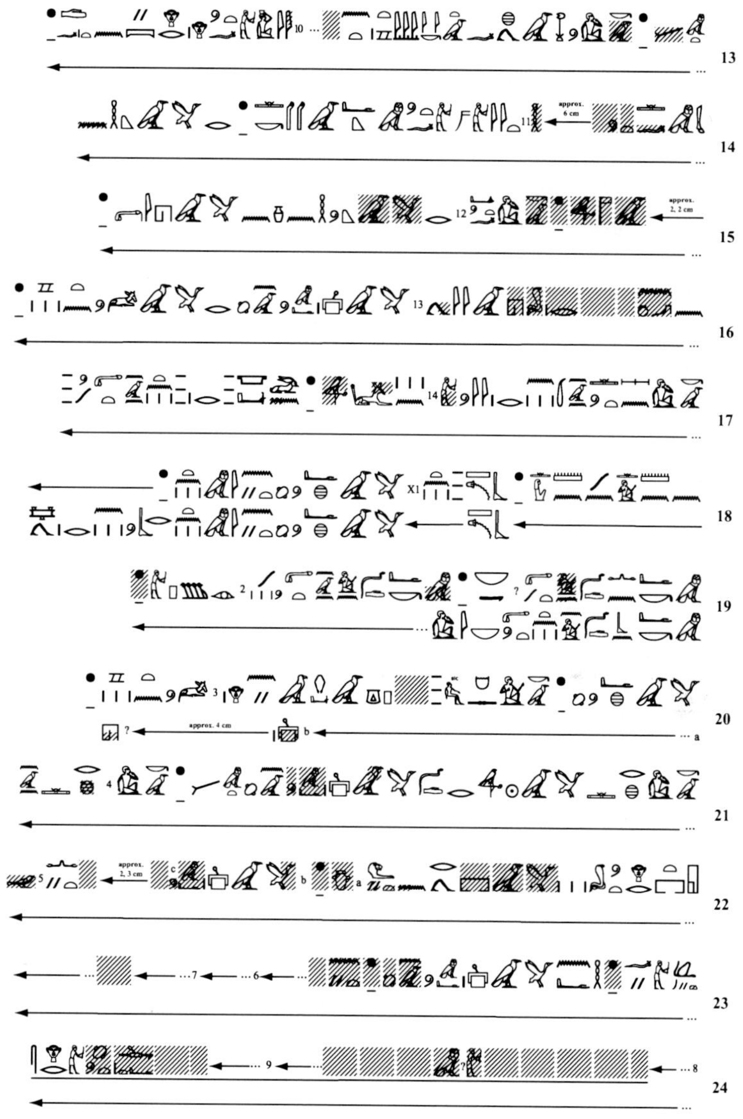

R:X4a–b almost faded, line is half broken off; 4c no longer legible; V:XV2a–b; traces.

Transliteration

	Recto		Verso	
1	VIII10–11	k.t š̲n̲[.t̲] nꜣ n(.j) srẖ.w n(.w) nꜣ n(.j) nṯr.w r pꜣ ꜥ[ẖ].w°̲ nꜣ [n(.j) srẖ.w n(.w) r] pꜣ		[…]
2	VIII11–12	n[.ty] hrp.w°̲ nꜣy=sn srẖ.w j[w …] tn[… srẖ.w n(.w){n}]		[…]
3	VII12–13	nꜣ n(.j) ẖrd.w n(.w) Nw.t°̲ nꜣ n(.j) ꜥꜥ.(w)t n<.t> nṯr nb{.t} <r=k>°̲ [nꜣ n.ty ḥr mk]		[…]
4	VIII13	[ḥ]ꜣ.ty [n(.j)] pꜣ n.ty mwt°̲ ḏr jr.n pꜣ šrj ꜥꜣ <n.j> [p]ꜣ		[…]
5	VIII13–14	Rꜥ(w)°̲ wꜣḥ ḏr.t ḥr p[ꜣ] j[ꜣ]w°̲ jr fꜣ.t nꜣ n(.j) ḏw.w°̲		[…]
6	VIII14–IX1	pꜣ n.ty ḥr pꜣy mj kꜣ n smꜣ(m).w [k]ꜣ fgꜣ=f		[…]
7	IX1–2	r’ n(.j) pꜣ sꜣ-mꜥw-nꜣ°̲ kꜣ fgꜣ=f tꜣy=f sp[.t] 2.t°̲		[…]
8	IX2–3	ḥnꜥ [tꜣ]y=f ꜥꜥ.(w)t n.ty ẖꜥm.tj n ḥꜣ.ty=f°̲ fgꜣ{.t} st tꜣ<y=f>	XIV1	[ẖꜥ]m{t}.tj n [ḥꜣ].t[y=f f]gꜣ sn tꜣy=f
9	IX3–4	[ḏr.t 2]°̲ ẖꜣẖ{.w}.n Stẖ(?)°̲ ptr(j) tw Jn-ḥr.t jw=k wꜣ.w	XIV1	ḏr.t 2 ptr(j) {wt} <tw> [Jn-ḥr].t
10	IX4–6	[… m-ꜥḳꜣ]=k°̲ jw=f ḥr ḥ(w).t [r=k] m tꜣ ḥ[ny.t … t]w=f	XIV2	[…]{n} m-ꜥ[ḳ]ꜣ(y)=k j[w=f ḥ]r ḥ(w).t […]
11	IX6–7	m šꜥ[d m pꜣy=f … tꜣ p.t … t]°̲		[…]
12	IX7–9	[šꜥd …] ꜥꜣ ḏrj ꜥmꜥy[.t]°̲ m-mj[.tjt …] n		[…]
13	IX9–10	mwt°̲ k[ꜣ] wẖꜣẖ=f tꜣy=k sẖ.t n.t [… fꜣ]y.{tw}=f <tw> ḥr ḥr.y n ḏr.t=f°̲		[…]
14	IX10–11	wḥm[=f tw … ḥ](wy).t{tw}=f <tw> m-ꜥḳꜣ=k°̲ r pꜣ ḳḥ[n]		[…]
15	IX11–12	[n.j pꜣ nṯr°̲ kꜣ] ḏj{tw}=f <tw> r [pꜣ] ḳ(w)ḥn n(.j) pꜣ hj°̲		[…]
16	IX12–13	n(.j) [Nw-kꜣ-r’ h]ꜣy pꜣ sꜣ-mꜥw-nꜣ r pꜣ jwtn°̲		[…]
17	IX13–14	kꜣ ꜥḏn tw nꜣ n(.j) tnr(y).w n(.w) [S]tẖ(?)°̲ wn.w r’.w=tn nꜣ n(.j) mt.w		[…]
18	IX14–X1	n(.j) mn ms.n mn<.t>°̲ bš.w tn pꜣ ꜥẖ.w n.ty jm=tn°̲	XV1	bš(.w) pꜣ ꜥẖ.w n.ty jm=tn r-bnr
19	X1–2	m=k nn ḏd=[j n] mt nb°̲ m=k ḏd=j n nꜣ n(.j) mt.w jr šzp[°̲]	XV1	m=k bn ḏd{n}=j <n> {tn} mt(w) nb j
20	X2–3	pꜣ ꜥẖ.w°̲ kꜣ ḥmz(w)=[tn] pgꜣ.tjwny ḥr <pꜣ> jwtn°̲	XV2	[… sꜣ …] h
21	X3–4	kꜣ rẖ pꜣ Rꜥ(w) r-ḏd pꜣ sꜣ-[mꜥw]-nꜣ mwt(.w)°̲ kꜣ r[ẖ] nꜣ n(.j)		[…]
22	X4–5	Ḥw.t -ḥr.w [pꜣ p]r<.t> n(.j) ḥꜣ[.ty=k°̲ p]ꜣ sꜣ-[mꜥw-nꜣ …] jw.ty		[…]
23	X5–7	pḥ.[t]y=fy [°̲] ḥnꜥ pꜣ sꜣ-mꜥw-[nꜣ°̲ n.ty …]		[…]
24	X8–9	[… m … jr.w m jẖ.t wꜥ.t wt.w] ḥr=s		[…]

Translation

1 Another in[cantation]: The accusations of the gods are against Akhu. The [accusations of the gods (?) are against] the one

2 who is submerged. Their accusations [... The ac]cusations

3 of the children of Nut, the accusal of every god [who protects (the)]

4 heart [of] whom is dead, <are against you>, since the elder/eldest son of

5 Re has laid down the hand upon the ol[d on]e who carries the mountains,

6 the one who copulates like a bull (copulates) with wild cattle. He [sh]all tear

7 out the maw of Sāmānu. He shall tear out his two lips

8 and [hi]s accusal which approaches harmfully his heart. His two hands

9 shall tear them out. As the weather god has hastened: Onuris sees you whilst you are (still) remote.

10 [...] towards you. He strikes [at you] with the s[pear ...] He is

11 a cutt[ing one with his ... the sky ... fire (?)]

12 [cut ...] great [...] Solid is a throwing [stick] like[wise (?) ...] of

13 death (?). He sh[all] seek your field of [...] He shall lift <you> [up] with his hand.

14 [He] shall [lift you up (?)] once again [...] He strikes <you> – facing you – at the cauld[ron (?) ...]

15 [of the god]. He [shall] give <you> to [the] cauldron (?) of the husband

16 of [Nikkal]. Sāmānu shall [fa]ll to the ground.

17 The might of the [wea]ther god shall finish you. Open your mouths, o vessels

18 of NN whom NN has born. Spit (you) out Akhu which is within you.

19 Behold! I do not speak to any vessel. Behold, I do speak to the vessels which have received

20 Akhu. [You] shall sit after you have opened to <the> ground.

21 Re shall learn that Sā[mā]nu is dead. The Hathors

22 shall lea[rn of the coming for<th> [of your] he[art], o Sā[mānu. ...] without

23 his strength and Sāmā[nu who ...]

24 [... to be made into one mass, to be bandaged] with it.

Commentary

2 R:VIII11 *nȝy=sn srḫ.w jw* [...] *tn*: The auxilary *jw* seems to initiate a dependent clause which specifies the *srḫ.w*. The *tn* at the end is odd. One would expect the article  because of the *srḫ.w* that follows; see also Massart 1954, 78.3–4.

3 R:VIII12 : The word is only attested in the present manuscript (WB I, 169.3), see also R:IX2–3. —<*r=k*> : <*r=k*> is omitted in the last sentence of the list of accusations. Since Akhu is mentioned before this, the accusations that follow are probably also directed against him. Müller 2008, 285, translates it as '[<Mögen sich> d]ie Vorwürfe der Kinder der Himmelsgöttin <gegen> die Anschuldigungen eines jeden Gottes <richten>', which does not make sense. Müller, *ibid.*, follows Massart 1954, 78.6, who restores <*r*> after . — : The children of Nut are Osiris, Seth, Isis, and Nephthys.

4 R:VIII13 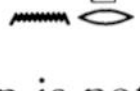: Massart 1954, 78.10, suggests emending {*n*} in *jr.n* because this construction is not possible in Middle Egyptian. The preposition *ḏr* is followed by the perfect *sḏm=f* or *sḏm.t=f*, whereas a *sḏm.n=f* is generally used after *ḏr.n*; see Gardiner 1988, 394 §483. In Late Egyptian *sḏm.n=f* could be used in temporal clauses or with conjunctions, in other words after *ḏr/m-ḏr* (Erman 1933, 149–150 §314), so the text would not have to be emended. — 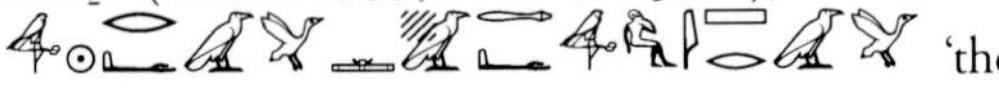 'the elder/eldest son of Re': Both Horus (e.g. CT VII, 430c *Ḥr.w wr.w Rꜥ.w*, 432c *Ḥr.w wr.w Rꜥ.w*, 514h *Ḥr.w wr.w Rꜥ.w*) and Ihi (CT IV, 179c *jnk* (= *Jḥy*) *mtw.wt jptw tp.(w)t n.(w)t Rꜥw*, 180a *jnk* (= *Jḥy*) *zꜣ tp pn n(.j) Rꜥw*) are known as the eldest sons of Re.

5 R:VIII14 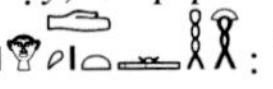: The gesture of laying one's hand upon someone is a sign of support. The phrase is used with this meaning in line 7 of the Metternich stela (Golenischeff 1877, Pl. IV.58) and in papyrus Leiden I 348 V:XII5–6 (Borghouts 1971, Pl. 14–14a, 31); so too is it used here; see also Massart 1954, 78.12. — 'the ol[d one] who carries the mountains': It is uncertain which deity is being meant with *pꜣ jꜣw*. The sun god Re can have this epithet, for example in papyrus Turin 84.1, where it is written as *sḫn nwn jn jꜣw ḏz=f* 'Nun is embraced by the old one himself' (Pleyte/Rossi 1869, II, Pl. 84). Similarly, in papyrus Turin 132.2 Re is called *jꜣw(t) nṯr.y* 'the divine old one' (Pleyte/Rossi 1869, II, Pl. 132). Compare also a passage in the tomb of Seti I (Hornung 1982, 26, 46). Fischer-Elfert 2011, 196.34, suggests this passage refers to the supreme god of the Ugaritic pantheon, El. El is considered to be a king and sacred. He appears as an aged deity. El is also known as a bull, in reference to his dignity and strength; see Hermann: El אל , in: Van der Toorn/Becking/Van der Horst 1995, 523–524; Becking, Ancient of days, in: *Ibid.*, 78–79. In CAT 1.4 VIII1–6, there is a similar passage. Two messengers of Baal are sent out to two mountains: *idk.al.ttn.pnm ꜥm.ǵr.trǵzz ꜥm.ǵr.ṯrmg ꜥm.tlm.ǵṣr.arṣ ša.ǵr.ꜥl.ydm ḫlb.lẓr.rḥtm* 'Then you shall decamp to the mountain Trǵzz and the mountain Ṯrmg, the two mountains at the edge of the Earth. Lift the mountain with both your hands, the mountain above the back of your palms.' (CAT 1.4 VIII1–6; Parker 1997, 138).

6 R:VIII14–IX1  '(...) the one who copulates like a bull (copulates) with wild cattle': Alternatively, the translation 'the one who copulates like a bull of the wild cattle' is also possible. Compare Papyrus Chester Beatty VII, V:16 *jw=f pꜣy mj pꜣy rhn(t) jw=f ḥr ꜥmḳ=st mj ꜥmḳ* [...] 'He copulates like a ram copulates. He mounts her like [...] mounts' (Gardiner 1935, II, Pl. 36). — V:IX1 : This word is only attested with this particular spelling in the present papyrus (WB I, 580.5). Massart 1954, 78.15, remarks that it probably belongs together with the words *fḳꜣ* and *fḳ(w)* (WB I, 579.11–12.14), Coptic: **ϥⲱϭⲉ**, **ϥⲱϫ**. See also Gardiner 1911b, 39*.14; Crum 1939, 626–627.

9 R:IX3 : Used here for *ḫꜥm* (WB III, 364.14). — R:IX3–4 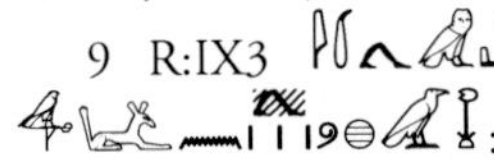: 'As the weather god has hastened' or alternatively 'for the weather god they were hastening'. The term *ḫꜣḫ.w* 'the hastening/fast ones' is only known in reference to the messengers of Re, who are sent to retrieve ochre from Elephantine in order to dye beer to get Sekhmet drunk (Hornung 1982, 6, 34–35, 39; see also Hornung 1975/6 I, 173, II, 83). They do not seem to be associated in any way to the weather

god/Seth, so the text is probably to be emended to *ḫꜣḫ{.w}.n*. — R:IX4 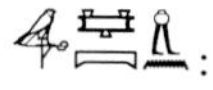: For Onouris, see Junker 1917; Vandier 1957, 269; Schenkel 1982, 573–574.

10–11 R:IX6 *tw=f m šꜥd m pꜣy=f* […] 'He is a cutt[ing one with his ...]': The *tw=f* at the beginning can also be the remains of a *tw*-passive voice. The word *šꜥd* should then be translated as 'sword' (WB IV, 423). The double use of the preposition *m* seems odd, but a similar sequence is used in *The Instructions of Dua-Kheti*: *wrš=f m šꜥd m jz.w* 'he spends the day cutting in reed' (Papyrus Anastasi VII = papyrus BM EA 10222 x+3, 3; tablet Louvre N693 V:31; ostracon BM EA 29550 + ostracon DeM 1546 R:10). Due to the rather fragmentary state of the papyrus, it is not possible to state exactly what is happening.

11 R:IX7 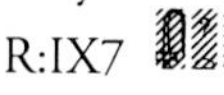: Other restorations besides *ḫ.t* 'fire' are possible: *ḏnḏn.t*, *dšr.t*, *tkꜣy.t*, *tꜣ.yt*, *kꜣp.t*, *sḏ.t*, *sḫm.t*, etc. The fragmentary state of the manuscript prevents a definite conclusion.

12 R:IX8 : 'Solid is a throwing [stick] like[wise (?) ...]' or 'pierces a throwing [stick] through like[wise]'. As a verb the word *ḏr* has the meaning 'to hinder, to put an end to', or, in the context of spears, 'to pierce'. Note that it would be difficult to pierce someone with a throwing stick. The adjective verb *ḏrj* 'to be hard/solid' (WB V, 599; Faulkner 1962, 232; Osing 1976, 609, remark 604) is possible and more likely.

13 R:IX10 : The phrase 'to the top/upwards' is usually written with the prepositions *n-ḥr.w* (WB III, 143.8) or *r-ḥr.w* (WB III, 143.2–6). On a stela of Thutmose III, arms are raised (*ḥr ḥr.w*) to ward off evil (WB III, 143.7). — *n*: Here used for *m*.

13–15 R:IX10–11: For the rearrangement of *tw* + suffix into suffix + *tw*, see the commentary to line 15 R:VII4 of incantation 5 (above § 5).

14 R:IX11 *kḫn*: The gap that follows is far too big (approx. 2.2 cm) to contain only the beginning of the article [*p*]*ꜣ*. The cauldron probably had an adjunct.

15 R:IX11 : Perhaps [*p*]*ꜣ nṯr* is to be amended with <*ḥr.y*> to *pꜣ nṯr ḥr.y* 'the god above', because his wife Nikkal is mentioned next.

16 R:IX12: Nikkal is the moon god's wife. See the commentary to line 12 R:V6/V:VIII2–3 of incantation 4 (above § 4).

17 R:IX13–14  'the might of the [wea]ther god': Literally 'the mighty deeds of the weather god' (Lesko IV, 91).

19 R:X1–2/V:XV1 'Behold! I do not speak to any vessel. Behold, I do speak to the vessels which have received Akhu': Massart 1954, 79–80.34, refers to papyrus Turin 131.10–11, where vessels are addressed in a similar manner: *mt.w n.w ḥꜥ.w(t)=j* [*n*]*n wn r'=tn šzp=tn rḏw* […] 'o vessels of my body, your mouth(s) shall not open so that you can(not) receive the discharge [...]' (Pleyte/Rossi 1869, II, Pl. 131); similarly papyrus Leiden I 348 R:VII 3–6: *mt.w=k nn wn=tn r'=tn šzp rḏw.t n ḏw.t* […] *bš šzp.n=tn m (j)ḫ.t nb ḏw.t* […] 'o my vessels, you shall not open your mouth(s) so that you can(not) receive the discharge of the evil [...] spit out, after you had received any evil [...]' (Borghouts 1971, Pl. 7–7a, 24). The negation  is used on the recto and  is used on the verso. For the term *mt* 'vessel, cord, etc.', see Breasted 1930, 109–113; Jonckheere 1947, 17.9; GdM I 1954, 20–21, 43, 72–74; Lesko I, 251; Nunn 1996, 44; Walker 1996, 236, 270; Westendorf 1999, I, 127.

20 R:X2 : Massart 1954, 80.37, refers to WB I, 562.8–9, where the term is translated as 'eine Art zu sitzen oder zu stehen'. Perhaps the word can be connected with *pgꜣ* 'to unfold, to open up' (WB I, 562; Lesko I, 184; Meeks II, 144/78.1533), which makes sense because the vessels are being asked to spit out the demon.

21–23 R:X3–7: The DHF follows with slight changes: the sun god Re is mentioned instead of the deities (*nṯr.w*). The incantation in R:X6–7 cannot be restored. For a detailed discussion of the DHF, see the commentary to lines 17–20 of incantation 4 (above § 4).

24 R:X8–9: The incantation ends with a rather fragmentary recipe which was to be applied topically.

7. Incantation 7 (R:X9–XI1/V:XVI1–2)

This rather short incantation without a title starts with a sequence of rhetorical questions. The sorcerer identifies himself as the servant of Horus and the weather god strikes the demon with his sword. In the end the evil being dies. Neither Akhu nor Sāmānu are mentioned in this spell but because of the epithet 'the one who is submerged' and the short version of the DHF, it is obvious that the incantation is directed against the demon Sāmānu/Akhu.

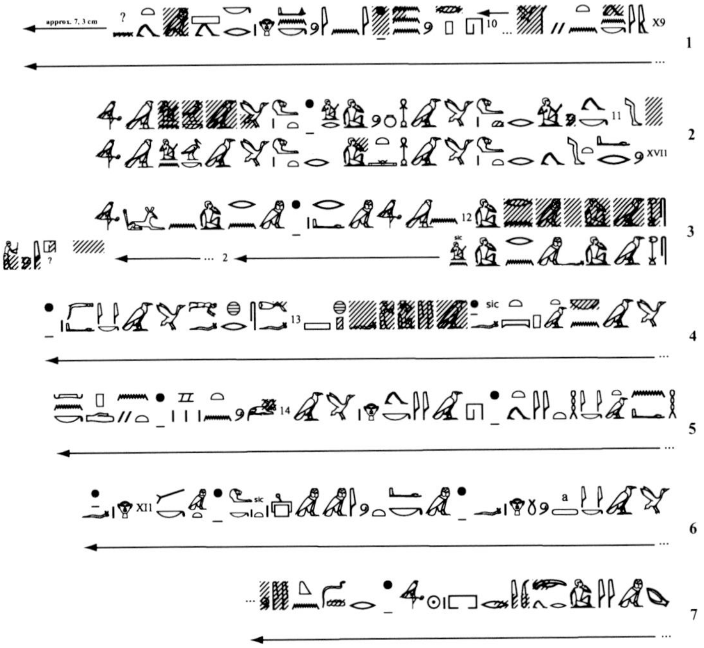

R:X14a at first glance the sign looks like ⊂⊃ but it is actually ⊂⊃ (S130A).

Transliteration

	Recto	Recto	Verso	Verso
1	X9–10	*jy.n=k ṯny [... pꜣ n.ty] h[r]p.w° jn-jw dj.n=k ḥr=k r š[m].t [n]*		[...]
2	X10–11	*[... wꜥr]=k {wj} r-ḥꜣ.[t] pꜣ šn.w r-° ḥꜣ.t p[ꜣ bꜣk n(.j)] Ḥr(.w)*	XVI1	*wꜥr(t)<=k> r-ḥꜣ.t pꜣ šn.t r-ḥꜣ.t pꜣ bꜣk n(.j) Ḥr(.w)*
3	X11–12	*s[ẖꜣ=f m rn] n(.j) Ḥr(.w) m-r'-ꜥ° m rn n(.j) Sth(?)*	XVI1–2	*sẖꜣ=f m rn{=j} n(.j) [...] hjw [...]*
4	X12–13	*pꜣ [nb] n(.j) tꜣ p.t° [fꜣy=f] ḫ[p]š=f s:ḫr=f pꜣy=k mḥ°*		[...]
5	X13–14	*ḥnꜥ tꜣy=k ḥt.yt° hꜣy=k ḥr pꜣ [j]wtn° n.ty pd.n=k*		[...]
6	X14–XI1	*pꜣy=k dꜣj.w ḥr=f° m=k tw jm m-sꜣ {ḥꜣ.t}<ḥꜣ.tj>=k° mwt=k ḥr=f°*		[...]
7	XI1	*sḏm.y(t) sp[r.t]j r pr Rꜥ(w)° r-ḏ[d] kn[y(w) Ḥr.w pꜣ s-m-n]*		[...]

Translation

1 Where have you come from [...]? [... the one who] is sub[mer]ged? Did you turn your face to go?
2 Do you [fle]e from the conjurer, the servant of Horus
3 while he calls to mind the name of Horus (and) likewise the name of the weather god,
4 the [lord] of heaven? [He shall lift] his *kh[op]esh*. He shall cast down your arm
5 and your throat (?). You shall fall upon the [gro]und on which you have spread out
6 your cloth. Behold, you are there according to your heart('s wish). You shall die there!
7 The gossip re[ach]ed the house of Re (that) [Horus has] conque[red Sāmānu].

Commentary

1 R:X9: The incantation starts abruptly. Perhaps this text was used as a template for amulets (suggestion by F. Hoffmann). — R:X9–10: Massart 1954, 81.1, suggests restoring [*pꜣ s-m-n pꜣ n.ty*] at the end of the line. Müller 2008, 286.187, points out with good reason that the gap on the papyrus is far too big for this restoration. He proposes restoring another question in the gap, but the lacuna seems too small for one. In one of the incantations of the *Zaubersprüche für Mutter und Kind* (MuK) a question is similarly constructed: *jn-jw jy.n=t zn ḥrd pn* 'Did you come to kiss this child?' (MuK R:II1; Yamazaki 2003, 14, Pl. 31; Erman 1901, 12). Compare BD chapter 29 *jn-jw jy.n=k r jṯj ḥꜣ.ty=j pn n(.j) ꜥnḫ.w* 'Did you come to take this, my heart of the living?' (Budge 1910, 126); so too Massart, *ibid.*

2 R:X10–11/V:XVI1 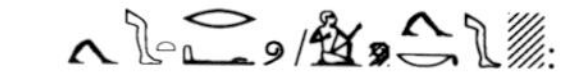: Both spells seem to be corrupt at this point; {*wj*} is to be emended on the recto and the suffix <*=k*> has to be added on the verso. It is not possible to say whether the sentence was framed as a question. — R:X11/V:XVI1 : The spellings are different but in both cases the word seems to designate the conjurer. For the different spellings, see WB I IV, 496.7. — R:X11/V:XVI1 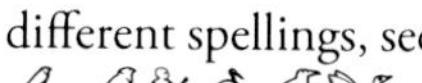: The 'servant of Horus' is also mentioned in papyrus Turin 134.1: *j[nk] bꜣkj Ḥr.w* 'I am the servant of Horus' (Pleyte/Rossi 1869, II, Pl. 134); see also Massart 1954, 81.5.

3 R:X11/V:XVI1 : Massart 1954, 81–82.7, suggests translating this verb form in the passive voice since – according to him – *sẖꜣ* cannot

be constructed with the preposition *m*. In Late Egyptian, it would be possible to construct the direct object of *sḫꜣ* with *m* (WB IV, 232.13). Here it seems to be used with the meaning 'to call someone's name to mind' (WB IV, 233.13). — R:X12 : For the construction with *m-r'-ꜥ*, see Erman 1933, 341; Černý/Groll 1984, 129.

4 R:X12–13 : The word *ḫpš* with this determinative can have the meaning '(fore)arm' or 'scimitar' (WB III, 268–270). The verb *s:ḫr* can be used with or without weapons (WB IV, 257–258), so it is not possible to determine the exact meaning. — R:X13 : The word *mḥ* is translated as '(fore)arm' and is often used together with *ꜥ* 'arm, hand' (WB I, 156–157); see WB II, 120.1. This term is not used in medicinal contexts (GdM I, 51.1). See also Walker 1996, 269.

5 R:X13 : Massart 1954, 82.11, suggests emending this word to *ḥty.t* 'throat' (WB III, 181.4–16), which Müller 2008, 286, follows. The word is only attested here with this particular spelling. Walker 1996, 273, proposes defining the word specifically as the wind-pipe/trachea, as does GdM I, 47, which specifies that the upper part is probably meant. In WB III, 182.7, the word is translated as 'Schritt o.ä.'. Because the demon later dies, the slitting of the throat is very likely.

5–6 R:X14 'on which you have spread out your cloth': When and why did the demon spread his cloth out on the ground? This part is odd.

6 R:X14 : The hieratic shows . The sign resembling is actually sign S130a. The reading *dꜣj.w* was suggested by Massart 1954, 82.12. For the hieratic spelling, see Devaud 1911, 106–116 and the statements in Janssen 2008, 52. The word *dꜣj.w* designates a kind of kilt or skirt which was worn by male and female workers (Janssen 1975, 265–267; Janssen 2008, 52–55); see also Staehelin 1970, 125–133. — R:X14–XI1 : The referent of *ḥr=f* is not clear. It can be translated as 'thereupon' – in the sense of dying upon the cloth ('You shall die thereupon.') – or as 'because of that' – in the sense of a wish ('You shall die because of that').

7 R:XI1: The incantation ends with an abridged version of the DHF; see the commentary to lines 17–20 of incantation 4 (above § 4).

8. Incantation 8 (R:XI2–14/V:XVII)

This short, fragmentary spell evokes Akhu. At the beginning, the demon is told to wake up. Then the weather god is mentioned. The vegetation goddess Shala – she is known as the wife of Baal – is named as bringer of the inundation, probably together with her husband, the weather god. The weather god strikes again and Akhu is directed to those whom Rešep kills and those who are in front of the distant one (?) of Onuris. Large parts of the middle and the end of the incantation are lost.

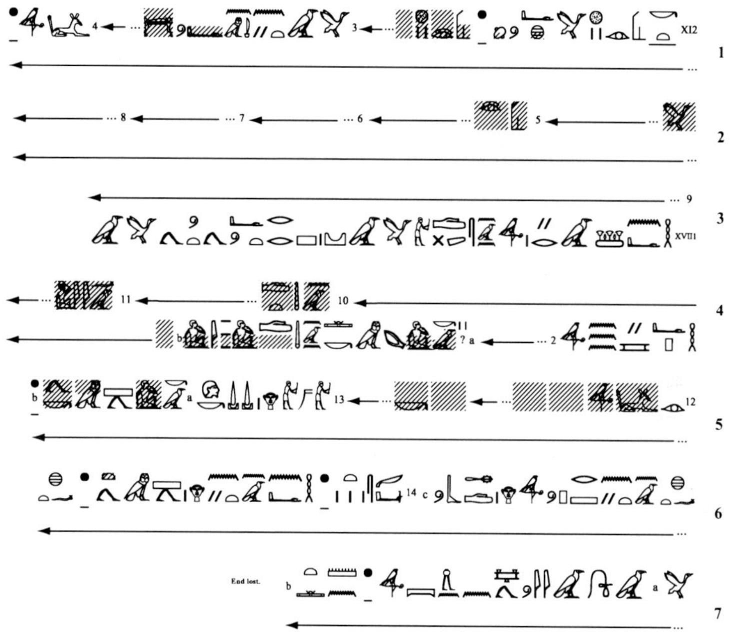

R:XI13a Gardiner places a verse point; 13b now broken; 13b–c & 14a–b on Pl. 2 fragment 5 papyrus Leiden I 345; V:XVII2a–b lower part of the line is partially broken off.

Transliteration

		Recto
1	XI2–4	<u>k.t</u> *srs zp-sn pꜣ ꜥḫ.w*° *s[rs zp-sn pꜣ n.ty hrp.w ...] pꜣ n.ty nm[ꜥ.w ...] Stẖ*(?)°
2	XI4–8	*[pꜣ ...] srs [zp-sn ...]*
3	XI9	[...]
4	XI10–11	*[nꜣ <n.j> md(w).t ... fꜣy ...]*
5	XI12–13	*jr [Stẖ*(?) *... k ... ḥw.t] ḥr ḏꜣḏꜣ=k*° *kꜣ š[m=k]*°
6	XI13–14	*ḫft nꜣ n.ty Ršpw ḥr ḫdb(w) st*° *ḥnꜥ nꜣ n.ty ḥr šm[.t]*° *ḫft*
7	XI14	*pꜣ wꜣ.yw n(.j) Jn-ḥr.t*° *mn.t* (end lost)

	Verso
	[...]
	[...]
XVIII1	*ḥnꜥ Šꜣ-y-rꜥ nꜣ n(.j) sd pꜣ ḏw r rḏ.t(w) jw.t pꜣ*
1–2	*Ḥꜥpy [...] k[ꜣ] sḏm=k nꜣ n(.j) md[(w).w j ...]*
	[...]
	[...]
	[...]

Translation

1 <u>Another</u>: Wake up, wake up, o Akhu! Wa[ke up, wake up, the one who is submerged! ...] the one who sle[eps ...] the weather god,

2 [the ... Wake up, wake up (?) ...]

3 and Shala, those who break open the mountain to allow the coming of

4 the inundation [...] You sh[all] listen to the wo[rd]s [... to lift ...]

5 [The weather god] makes [... strikes (?)] at your head. [You] sha[ll go]

6 in front of those whom Rešep kills, and those who go in front of

7 the distant one (?) of Onuris likewise.

Commentary

1 R:XI2 *k.t*: Here the incantation begins with *k.t* and not with the usual *k.t šn.t*. — *[pꜣ n.ty hrp.w]*: Massart 1954, 83.1, suggests restoring this phrase, which would fit the lacuna. Müller 2008, 287, argues in favour of the restoration *[pꜣ s-m-n]*. The original text in the lacuna on the papyrus cannot be restored.

2 R:XI4 : Perhaps the epithet *pꜣ nb n.j tꜣ p.t* is to be restored as in R:X12 (incantation 7, above § 7). — R:XI5 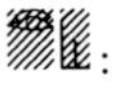: Massart 1954,83.4, suggests restoring *[tw r=k]*, which would be unparalleled in this incantation. The restoration *[zp-sn]* is more likely.

3 V:VXIII1 : Shala is a vegetation goddess who has the epithet 'goddess of mountains'. She is Baal's wife; see Dhorme/Dessaud 1949, 101; Massart 1954, 83–84.6; Helck 1971, 468–469; Haas 1994, 166–167, 442, 446; Müller 2008, 287.189. Fischer-Elfert 2011, 197–198, suggests with some reservations that this passage could be connected with the Ugaritic double deity *Mt-w-Šr* and refers to CAT 1.23 8–11: *mt.wšr.yṯb. bdh.ḫṭ.ṯkl.bdh ḫṭ.ulmn* 'Mōt and Šarru sit down, in his hand a scepter of barrenness, in his (other) hand a scepter of widowhood' (CAT 1.23 8–11; Parker 1997, 208). As CAT discusses death, sterility and widowhood, it is fairly unlikely that the passage under consideration here refers to *Mt-w-Šr*. This spell deals with the fertile aspects of the inundation rather than the destructive ones. See also the remarks on this deity by Hallo/Younger 1997, 276–277.13.

4 V:XVIII1 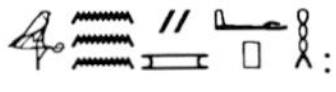: The word can refer to the Nile (WB III, 42.11–16), the inundation (WB III, 42.17–43.4), or the god Ḥapi (WB III, 43.5–12); see De Buck 1948, 1–22; cf. Drioton 1955, 165–166; see also Massart 1954, 84.7; Koenig 1992, 241; Müller 2008, 287.190.

5 R:XI13 : Massart 1954, 84.10, suggests that this could be the complex preposition *ḥr-ḏꜣḏꜣ* (WB V,531.8). The WB states that the verb *ḥwj* is only used with the prepositions *r* and *ḥr* (WB III, 46.1–48.15); see also Erman 1933, 327 §611, Černý/Groll 1984, 121.

5 R:XI13 and 6 R:XI14 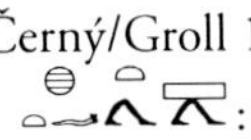: According to WB IV 464.17, the combination *šm.t ḫft* means 'to step

forward (vor jemanden hintreten)'. The connection to the demon in this passage is obscure. It is also unclear who Rešep's victims are and who steps forward to the distant one (?) of Onuris.

6 R:XI13: For Rešep, see the commentary to incantation 4 (above § 4), line 13.

7 R:XI14 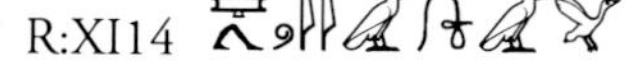 'the distant one': The meaning of the word is uncertain. See also the passage in R:XI14 (incantation 6, above § 6, line 9) and Massart 1954, 84.14. For a general commentary on the word, see Quack 1993, 62. For Onuris, see the commentary to line 9 of incantation 6 (above § 6).

9. Fragments recto (R: XII–XXII1)

The part of the papyrus that follows is very fragmentary. Each column only contains one to three lines from the lower part of the manuscript. It is often very difficult to determine the meaning of these pieces. They could also be directed against the demon Sāmānu/Akhu,[49] but there is no way to be certain.

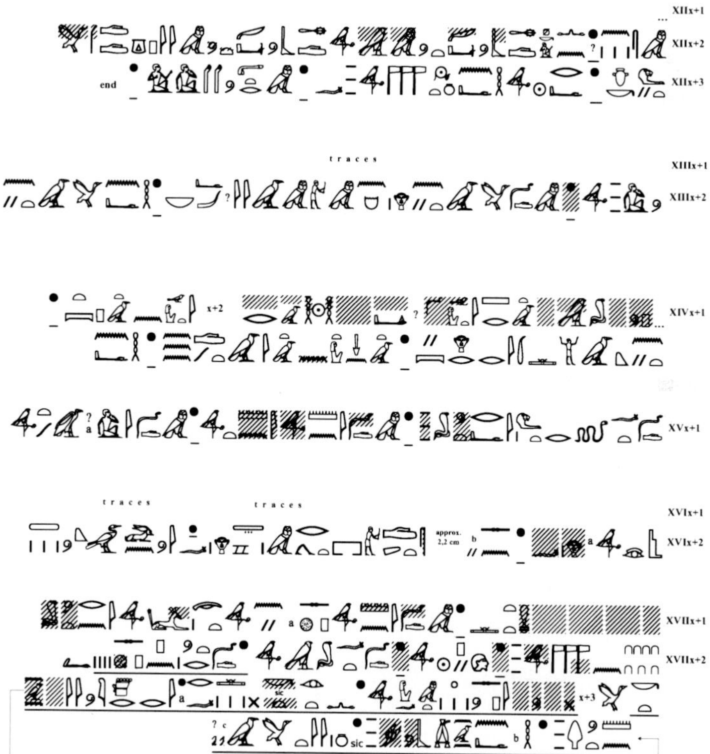

R:XII–XXI: Lower part of the column; R:XVx+1a or  *; R:XVIx+1a or*  *; x+1b either* 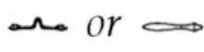 *; R:XVIIx+1a probably*  *; x+3a perhaps only dots of ink; x+3b–c below R:XVIIIx+2.*

49 The only fragment which mentions the demon (R:XXII1+x+1–2) is found here, in incantation 9 (see below, § 10).

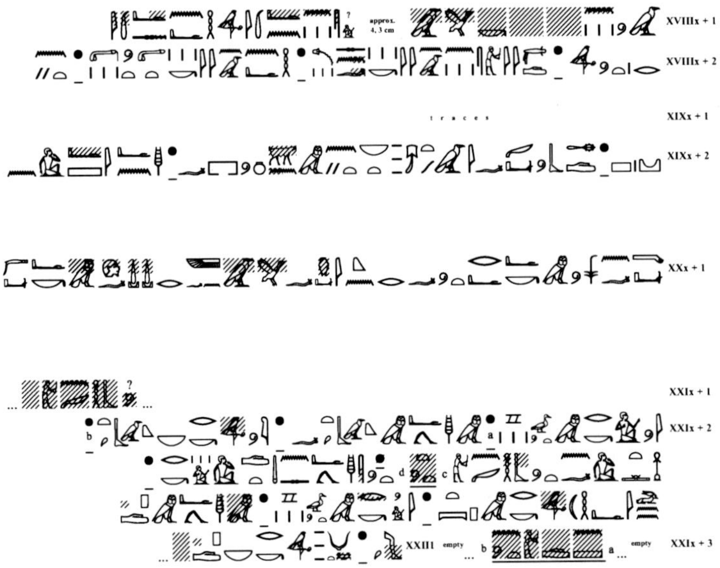

R:XXIx+2a verse point no longer legible; x+2b -//-; x+2c–d much faded, Gardiner writes ?; x+3a–b much faded.

Transliteration

		Recto
1	XIIx+1	[...]
2	XIIx+2	*m=sn°_(?) nn [j]nk ḫd[b].w tw [m Ḥ]r(.w) ḫdb.w [tw] m Ypgdd [...]*
3	XIIx+3	*ḥ3.ty=k°_ Rʿ(w) ḥnʿ psḏ.t=f°_ m mtr.w<.w>*
1	XIIIx+1	[...]
2	XIIIx+2	*[...]°_ m-ḏd p3 n.ty ḥr nḥm m 3yʿ nb°_ ḥnʿ p3 n.ty*
1	XIVx+1–2	*[...] pw [... Ḥ]r.w t3 šrj.t [... ḏ ... ḏj(?) ...] [n]ḥḥ [...] r [t3 š]rj.t n<.t> t3 p.t°_*
2	XIVx+2	*n.ty ḳ3.tj r-ḥr.y°_ t3 sn.t [n]<.t> j3d.t°_ ḥnʿ*
1	XVx+1	*ḏdf.t r-ḥ3.t {jrʿ[.wt]} <jʿr[.wt]>°_ m-[ḏ]d Jmn [Jmn].t m-ḏd J-mt-t*
1	XVIx+1	[...]
2	XVIx+2	*Wsjr ḥr=f°_ zny [...]* (gap) *sd.t pr.t m t3 ḥr=f°_ jw wn ʿḳ.w*
1	XVIIx+1	*[... m]-mj.t(j)t°_ m-[ḏ]d J[m]n Zpny Sp.t-[S]tẖ Jrn[.wt]*
2	XVIIx+2	*70 [n(.j) nṯr.w°_] tp.y-Rʿ(w)[°_] ḏdf.t Ḥr.w°_ <u>dd.tw r' pn zp 4</u> grḥ*
3	XVIIx+2–3	*<u>k.t</u> p[3 ... <u>w ...] j zp.w mw.t=f° n jr.t(w) <n>[kt] r=f</u> °(?) <u>jr-dr šw.y[...] n3 n(.j)</u>*
4	XVIIx+3	*<u>mn.wt ḥnʿ n3 n(.j) ḏb3[.w] °nw-yt-p3[...]</u>*
1	XVIIIx+1	*3wn [...]=k(?) p3 [...]=s[n ʿ]ntj ḥnʿ [ʿ]z[t(j)]*

2	XVIIIx+2	*r.t° šd(y)=sn nꜣy=k zn[f].w° ḥnꜥ nꜣy=k mtw.wt° n.ty*
1	XIXx+1	*(traces)*
2	XIXx+2	*ḏw° ẖdb(w)=f jꜣw.t nb.t n.ty m-ẖnw=f° ꜥḥꜥ.n (j)ꜥš.n*

1	XXx+1	[...]*.n=f sw m=k rḏ.tw=f r ḳnj=f* [*pꜣ*]*.n=f r* [*ḏ*]*ꜣ*[*ḏ*]*ꜣ=f* [*m*]*=k mḥ*

1	XXIx+1	*(traces)* [...] *bḥn* [...]
2	XXIx+2	*jw=j r=k m zꜣt.w° m ꜥḥꜥ(.w) m ḳꜣb.t=f° Šw r=k nb ḳꜣb.t°*
3	XXIx+2	*šnt(j).n=f tw bḥn{t}=tw tw° s:ꜥḥꜥ.n=z md(w).wt=j r=k°*
4	XXIx+2	*wnn Jꜥḥ r=k m p.t° jw=j* [*r*]*=k m zꜣt.w°* [*m*] *ꜥḥꜥ(.w) m p(ꜣ)d°*
5	XXIx+3–XXII1	*(empty)* [...] *nšd.n.tw* [...] *(empty) Wp-wꜣ.wt r=k nb p(ꜣ)d*

Translation

1[R:XII] [...]

2 with them (?). It is not I who killed you, (but) it is [Hor]us who killed [you] with Ypgdd (?) [...]

3 your heart. Re and his Ennead are witnesse<s>. *(end)*

1[R:XIII] [...] *(traces)*

2 [...] as says the one who rescues for every 'valour' and the one who [...]

1[R:XIV] [... Hor]us, the daughter [...] gives (?) [...] eternity [... the daug]hter of the sky

2 who is high above, the daughter of dew and [...]

1[R:XV] [(as) the] snake [says] in front of the Uraei, (as) Amun (and) Amaunet [sa]y, (as) Imetet says [...]

1[R:XVI] [...] *(traces)*

2 Osiris is above it (?). [...] who breaks, who comes forth out of the earth because of it, while there is bread [...]

1[R:XVII] [... the same] (as) A[mu]n says, Zepeny, the-lip-of-[Se]th, Irn[ut],

2 [the 70 gods], the first one of Re (and) the snake of Horus. This utterance is to be said four times. ending.

3 Another: th[e ...] the remedies of his mother. <No>thing was made against him. As soon as [the] roots

4 and the lea[ves] are dried [...]

1[R:XVIII] [...] your [...] their [... A]nat and [A]sta-

2 rte, they take away your bloo[d] and your poisons which [...]

1 R:XIX [...] (*traces*)

2 [...] mountain (?). He shall kill every animal which is wi[th]in him (?). Then called [...]

1 R:XX [...] he [...] him. Behold, he was given into his bosom after he had [flown] up to his [h]ea[d]. [Be]hold, fill [...]

1 R:XXI [... cut off (?) ...]

2 [...] (as) I am against you on earth! Do not stand in his breast! Shu is against you, the lord of the breast.

3 After he had exorcised you, you <u>were</u> cut off. She has set up my words against you.

4 (As) Jah is against you in the sky, (as) I am [against] you on earth! Do [not] stand in [his] kne[e]!

5 (*empty*)[... <u>was torn to pieces (?)</u> ...] (*empty*) Wepwawet is against you, the lord of the kn[ee].

Commentary

R:XII–XXV: Due to the rather fragmentary state of the papyrus and the missing context, it is almost impossible to provide an adequate translation for the lines which have been preserved. Massart 1954, 84–90, cites these lines as §9 and § 10 recto.

1 R:XIIx+1 : Two readings are possible: 'with them' or 'in them'; it is impossible to say which is more suitable. —  and 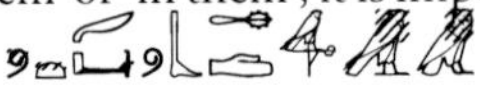: Both sentences are cleft sentences; the latter demonstrates a typical Late Egyptian construction. The form of the former is somewhere in between: half Middle Egyptian, half Late Egyptian. In Middle Egyptian, one would expect  as the negation, whereas in Late Egyptian, the subject would be negated with . Negation with 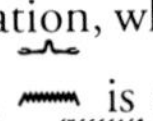 is a transitional form; see Erman 1933, 380 §751; see also Massart 1954, 85–86.1. — : The meaning of the word is not certain. It could be a kind of weapon which Horus uses to kill. Alternatively, it could be a toponym for the place where the killing happens. The term looks like a loan word, but in this case one would expect a syllabic writing. See also Massart 1954, 86.2.

2 R:XIIx+2 *ḥꜣ.ty=k*: It is not certain how this phrase is connected to the previous line.

2 R:XIIIx+2 : These could be the remains of a god's name, see Massart 1954, 86.4. — : The word is otherwise unattested. Massart 1954, 86.5, refers, on the one hand, to *ꜣꜥj* 'Kraft o.ä.' (WB I, 2.12) and, on the other, to Gardiner 1948, 16–18, who discusses words with this spelling. Whatever it is, it does not seem pleasant.

1 R:XIVx+1 : Perhaps the name of the goddess *Jpwy.t* is to be restored (see LGG I, 221; Gardiner 1947, II, 75*), or *Rpw.t* (see LGG IV, 662–663). It is not clear how the goddess relates to Horus in this context.

1–2 R:XIVx+1–2 *tꜣ šrj.t* [... *ḏ* ... *dj*(?) ... *n*]*ḥḥ* [...] *r* [*tꜣ š*]*rj.t n<.t> tꜣ p.t*° *n.ty kꜣ.tj r-ḥr.y*° *tꜣ sn.t* [*n*]*<.t> jꜣd.t*° 'the daughter [...] gives (?) [...] eternity [... the daug]hter of the sky who is high above, the daughter of dew': Fischer-Elfert 2011, 197, suggests that this passage is an allusion to one of the daughters of Baal. Baal's daughters are Ṭallay, Pidray and Arṣay. All of them classify different forms of dew; see Loretz 1990, 161–164; Healy 1995, 473–475. The adjunct 'who is high above' seems to emphasise this, because Ṭally has the epithet *ṭl šmm* 'dew of the sky' (DUL 889; Tropper 2008, 130).

1 R:XVx+1 : [*m-ḏd*] should probably be restored in front of *ḏdf.t*, as it is written in the phrases that follow; so too Massart 1954, 86.10. — : For the different spellings of the word Uraei, see Erman 1909, 102–103; see also Massart 1954, 86–87.12. — : The reading of the bird sign is not certain. It could also be read , or . None of these readings helps to identify this goddess.

1 R:XVIx+2 : or . It is not clear what the suffix *=f* refers to. — and : Both participles have a *t*-ending, so the antecedent has to be feminine.

1 R:XVIIx+1 : This god is otherwise unattested. Drioton 1955, 163, suggests that it could be a goddess of trees; see also Massart 1954, 87.17; LGG VI, 268. It is possible that this god's name is another shortened version of the goddess *Spr.tw-n=s-spj-n=s-tꜣ* (a wife of Horus), because it comes before the name of the goddess *Sp.t-Stẖ*, who is probably a wife of Horus too. For the wives of Horus, see Borghouts 1971, 149–151.358; Massart 1954, 57.51. — : The 'lip-of-[Se]th' is also attested in Papyrus Chester Beatty VII V:VI3 (Gardiner 1935, II, Pl. 37; LGG VI, 268). She could also be a wife of Horus; see Borghouts 1971, 150.358. — : Massart 1954, 87.19, suggests connecting this goddess with Renenutet. LGG IV, 686–689, lists this passage as an attestation for this deity.

2 R:XVIIx+2 : For the 70 deities, see LGG IV, 555; Chassinat 1892, 192–195, 197–199, Pl. XXIVb; Chassinat 1930, 17; Chassinat 1934, 5–11, Pl. LXXXVIII; Drioton 1938, 109–110, 110.1–3; Massart 1954, 87.19a. For this number of gods in Ugaritic myths, see Smith/Pitard 2009, 48, 628–630. — : The 'first one of Re' could be Shu; see LGG VII, 390; see also Massart 1954, 87.20; Massart 1957, 174. Compare also the commentary to line 4 of incantation 6 (above § 6).

2–3 R:XVIIx+2–3 *k.t pꜣ*: After the instruction to utter the spell four times, another incantation begins (*k.t*) with a definite article (?). A rubrum starts abruptly in the next line. As Massart 1954, 87.21, has already suggested, this rubrum could be part of the previous text on the papyrus. The structure of this recipe differs from that of the other recipes in the papyrus, but the handwriting seems to be the same. The line is also essentially longer than the other lines (approx. 22,6 cm; on average); see the introduction (I.3). The whole remedy is rather strange.

3 R:XVIIx+3 : This should perhaps be read <*n*>*kt*. — : Massart 1954, 87.25, suggests connecting the word with 'to be empty, to be devoid of' (WB IV, 427.14). The meaning 'to dry, to be dry' (WB IV, 429; GdM VII.2, 841) seems to fit better in this context.

3–4 R:XVIIx+3 *nꜣ n(.j) mn.wt° ḥnꜥ nꜣ n(.j) dbꜣ[.w]*: The plant whose roots and leaves are to be used is not specified.

4 R:XVIIx+4 : The meaning of the last word is not clear. It could be a kind of drug (?).

1 R:XVIIIx+1 : The beginning of the line cannot be reconstructed. The sign should probably be interpreted as a suffix pronoun for the second person masculine. It is followed by *pꜣ*. — : The verb has not been preserved.

1–2 [ꜥ]*ntj ḥnꜥ* [ꜥ]*z*[*t*]*r.t*: For Anat, see the commentary to line 7 of incantation 2 (above § 2). For Astarte, see Mercer 1949, 218–220; Stadelmann 1967, 96–110; Helck 1971, 456–458; Cornelius 1994, 73–75; Cornelius 2004, 4, 21–22; Tazawa 2009, 7–8, 83–95, 120–121, 128–129, 133–135, 163–165.

2 R:XVIIIx+2 'your bloo[d] and your poisons': The referent of the second person masculine singular is not clear. Massart 1954, 88.30, thinks that this passage refers to the disease's blood and poisons, which are under attack. This is highly likely. The blood is constructed in the plural, which is not uncommon in medicinal texts; see WB III, 459.2–3.

1 R:XIXx+1 'which is wi[th]in him': The resumptive pronoun is odd. One would expect it to refer to the animals, but they are in the plural and

therefore would need the suffix pronoun *=sn* or *=w*. Perhaps it refers to the person who will kill the animals. The passage is strange.

1 R:XXx+1 : Massart 1954, 88.32, suggests restoring the verb *ṯ3j* 'to take' (WB V, 364.1–347.20), but the determinatives which have been preserved provide opportunities for other reconstructions. It is difficult to determine the correct solution without the context.

1–5 R:XXx+1–XXII1: The fragments which follow contain parts of a deification of body parts (*Gliedervergottung*) where different limbs are identified with various gods based on similarities in sound, depiction, function etc.; see Massart 1959, 227–246.

2 R:XXIx+2 : This sentence is more understandable in connection with the previous part, which reappears later in the line. Massart 1954, 90.2, refers to papyrus Turin 124.13: *mtw=tw ḏj.t jꜥḥ r=k m t3 p.t° jw Stḫ r=k m*$^{(?)}$ *z3t.w* 'One shall cause that Jaḥ is against you in the sky while Seth is against you on earth!' (Pleyte/Rossi 1869, I, 160, II, Pl. 124). For *Jꜥḥ*, see Helck 1982, 192–196; Derchain 1962, 17–67. — : Here a prohibitive is used. Very similar forms for the apotropaic deification of body parts (*Gliedervergottung*) can be found in Papyrus Chester Beatty VII, V:II5–V10 (*nn ꜥḥꜥ=ṯ m* (…); Gardiner 1935, II, Pls. 36–37), papyrus Vatican II–IV (*nn ꜥḥꜥ=ṯ m* (…); Suys 1934, 63–87) and papyrus Geneva MAH 15274 II (*nn ꜥḥꜥ=ṯ m* (…); Massart 1957, 172–185), but in these manuscripts a negated future is used. Both forms are followed by the same formula 'the god X is against you, the lord/lady of limb Y'. For *Gliedervergottung* in general, see Ranke 1924, 558–564; Dawson 1931, 23–28; Altenmüller 1977, 624–627; Walker 1993, 83–101; DuQuesne 2002, 237–271; see also Massart 1954, 90.3.

5 R:XXIx+3 : The manuscript is blank before and after this phrase. These probably are the remains of the previous text. — R:XXII1 : A small sign or group of signs appears next to ▯, as in R:XXIx+2.

10. Incantation 9 (R:XXII1+ x+1–2)

Only two lines of this rather fragmentary incantation have been preserved. The demon wanders down the body, starting at the head.

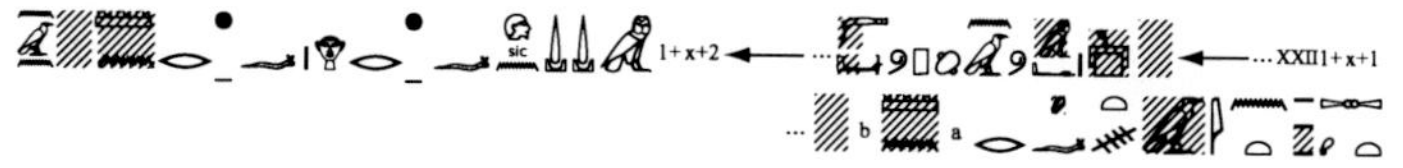

R:XXII1+x+ 2a–b reading uncertain.

Transliteration

		Recto
1	XXII1+x+1–2	*[… pꜣ sꜣ-m]ʿw-nꜣ pw m[ḥ …] m ḏꜣḏꜣ{n}=f° r ḥr=f ° r-[mn-m] nꜣ n(.j)*
2	XXII1+x+2	*ṯ(ꜣ)z.[w]t n.(w)t j[ꜣ].t=f r-[mn-m …]*

Translation

1 [… it is Sām]ānu who seiz[es …] from his head, over his face [to] the

2 vertebrae of his ba[ckbo]ne, t[o …]

Commentary

1–2 R:XXII1+x+1–2: The incantation is extensively destroyed. Massart 1954, 91, cites this spell as §11 recto.

2 R:XXII1+x+2: There is enough space to restore *r-mn-[m]* (WB II, 64.3–5). The complex preposition *r-mn-r'-ʿ* may also have been used as an alternative (WB II, 394.8) in the second line.

11. Fragments recto (R: XXIIIx+1–XXV1+x+2)

The part of the papyrus that follows is very fragmentary. Each column only contains one to three lines from the lower part of the manuscript. It is often very difficult to determine the meaning of these pieces. They could be directed against the demon Sāmānu/Akhu,[50] but in their present state there is no way to be certain.

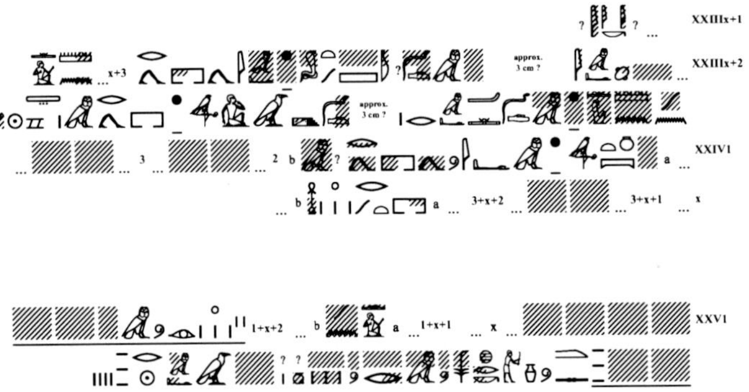

R:XXIV1a–b much darkened and faded; 3+x+2a–b much darkened; R:XXV1+x+1a-b much darkened.

Transliteration

		Recto
1	XXIIIx+1	[...]*y=k* [*j*...]
2	XXIIIx+2–3	[...] *mj* [...] *m*-[*ḏ*]*d Ḳ*[*d*]*š.t*° *mj pr* [*m*]*n*
3	XXIIIx+3	[*ms*].*n* [*mn*<.*t*> *m*]-*ḏd Ḥw-m*ᶜ- *r'*-[*ḳ* ... *m-ḏ*]*d sjꜣ*° *pr m tꜣ R*ᶜ(*w*)
4	XXIV1–3	[... *m-ḏd*] *Nw.t*° *mj p*[*r m*(?) ...]
5	XXIV3+x+1–2	[...] *pr.t šn*[*j* ...]
1	XXV1–1+x+2	(traces) [... *mn ms.n mn.t* ...] <u>*jr.w m* [*jḫ.t w*ᶜ.*t*(?)</u>]
2	XXV1+x+2	[...] *gs*(*w*).*ẖr=k* [*s*]*w* [*m* ... *r* ...*w.w* ...] *ꜣ*[*m*]ᶜ *r hrw 4*

Translation

1 R:XXIII [... your (?) ...]
2 [...] Come, [come forth ...] (as) Qedshet (?) [sa]ys. [Co]me, come forth [of] NN,
3 [whom NN has born, (as)] Ḥmr[ḳ] (?) says. [... Come, come forth (as)] Sia [sa]ys, who came forth out of the land of Re [...]
4 [(as)] Nut [says]. Come, co[me forth of ...]
5 [...] pine nuts (?) [...]

1 R:XXV [... NN whom NN has born ...] <u>is to be made into [one mass (?) ...]</u>
2 [...] then [you ano]int [h]im with [...] on four days.

50 The only fragment which names the demon (R:XXII1+x+1–2) is found here, in incantation 9 (see above, § 10).

Commentary

1–3 R:XXIIIx+1–3: According to Gardiner (Massart 1954, 27), there is a space of about 3 centimeters between the two fragments. That the gap is in fact roughly 3 cm in length cannot be stated with certainty, because the sequence of phrases used in this incantation has not been completely preserved. The two fragments have a total length of 15.2 cm, which with 3 additional centimeters would give a total length of roughly 18 centimeters. The average length of the columns in the papyrus is 16 cm.

1 R:XXIIIx+1 : These are perhaps the remains of a second person masculine singular possessive article; so too Massart 1954, 91.3.

2 R:XXIIIx+2 : The reading of this word is not entirely certain. For Qedšet, see Stadelmann 1967, 110–123; Helck 1971, 463–466; Tazawa 2009, 8, 96–101, 121–123, 129, 135–136, 163–165.

3 R:XXIIIx+3 [...] : This word should perhaps be amended to *ḥmr*[*k*], as in R:III9/V:VI4. There it is definitely used to specify a mountain. Here it seems to be a deity. For the word, see the commentary to line 9 of incantation 3 (above, § 3). Müller 2008, 287, suggests deriving the word from the Semitic 'ass' (*ḥmr*), but has some reservations. — : For this god, see Gardiner 1916a, 43–54, 83–95.

5 R:XXIV3+ x+2 : It is not possible to state whether the pine nuts (?) belonged to the recipe of the incantation or something else. The drug *pr.t-šn* is identified with different substances, among them pine nuts (Ebbell 1937, 132; so too Charpentier 1981, 296–297; Germer 1985, 9; Nunn 1996, 154; Müller 2008, 280.151), the small fruits of conifers in general (Keimer 1984, II, 23), or the blossoms of the needle bush (*Vachellia farnesiana*; Loret 1975, 85–86). Loret *ibid.* admits, however, that the latter is native to America. According to Müller 2008, 280.151, *pr.t-šn* could also be a misspelling for *šnj-tꜣ* 'seeds of fenugreek'. A definite identification is not possible. Pine nuts (?) were used internally and topically in chewing remedies, suppositories, enemas, ointments, and bandages for gastro-intestinal problems, to treat skin diseases, as a hair restorer and, probably due to their pleasant scent, in incense materials. There is no specific focus for their application (GdM VI, 200–202; Germer 1979, 268–271; Germer 2008, 69–71). Pine kernels are not known to have any pharmaceutical effects (Hoppe 1958, 696; Schneider 1974, V.3, 78; Germer 2008, 69–71).

1 R:XXV1+x+2 [...] : The remains of the word can be connected to a variety of substances: *mnj* 'unidentified substance (med.)' (WB II, 76.13), *ḫꜣnn* 'part of the fruit of the doum palm' (WB III, 231.18), *ḫntj* 'ochre/pigment' (WB III, 301), *sk.j* 'flour' (WB IV, 314.15–16), *ḳsn.tj* 'a mineral (med.)' (WB V 71.5), *gmnn* 'an edible plant (legume?)' (WB V 170.7), *gnn* 'legume (bean)' (WB V, 176.6–7), *ṯḥtj* 'copper, bronze (?)' (WB V, 396.11), *dḥ.wj* '(officinal use)' (WB V, 480.10) or *ḏḥtj* 'lead' (WB V, 606.4–6). — : This is probably to be restored to ⌊*jh.t wꜥ.t*⌋.

2 R:XXV1+x+2 : The substance with which the patient was to be anointed cannot be reconstructed. Whatever it was, it was constructed with an indirect genitive. Massart 1954, 92–93.6, suggests restoring *šꜣmꜥ* as a *nomen rectum* and refers to Papyrus Hearst III10: *ḫꜥꜥ n.w šꜣmꜥy* 'Abfälle (?) von dem Getränk *šmy*' (Wreszinski 1912, 9, 74–75). The traces before *ꜣ* do not match *šꜣ*.

12. Conjuration (?) 1 and remedies 1–4 (R:XXV1+x+2–XXVI12)

The conjuration (?) is directed against the *s.t-ꜥ* of any god, deceased person, or opponent and the remedies are directed against swelling of the feet or any other limb. The papyrus is fragmentary in the middle of column R:XXVI, so it is not certain what came after the conjuration – perhaps another one. All the motifs used in this part of the papyrus are genuinely Egyptian.

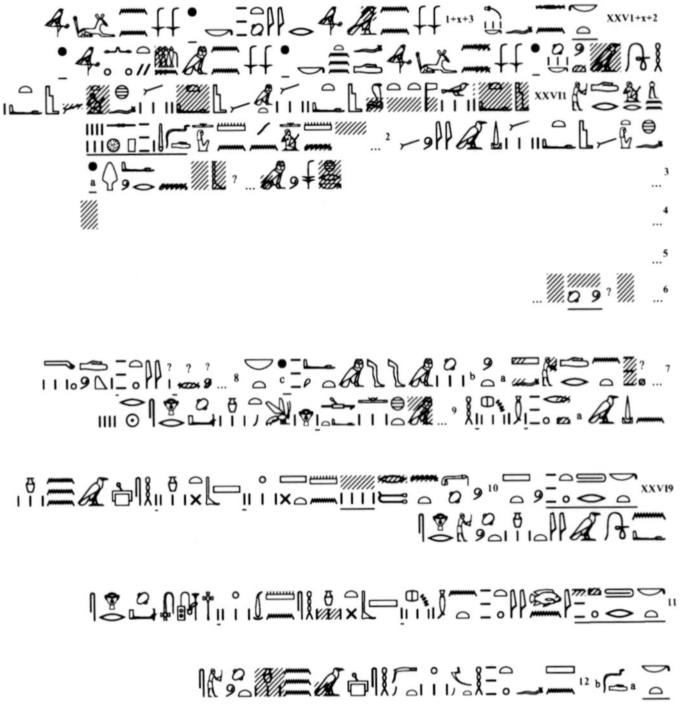

R:XXVI3a verse point no longer legible; 7a–b this part of the papyrus does not exist anymore, the beginning and the ending of the previous and the following groups are missing too; 7c verse point almost illegible; 11a–b deleted.

Transliteration

		Recto
1	XXV1+x+2–3	*k.t [z]nf.w=k nn [Ḥ]r(.w) ry.t=k° nn Stẖ*
2	XXV1+x+3	*ḥw[ꜣ](ꜣ).[t]=k° n[n] Stẖ fd.t=k° nn M[ḫn]t.y-jr.tj°*
3	XXV1+x+3–XXVI1	*jn.n=j r dr [s.t-ꜥ] nṯ[r].t s.t-ꜥ mwt s.[t-ꜥ] ḫf[t].(j) s.t-ꜥ*
4	XXVI1–2	*ḫft.(j) <t> s.t-ꜥ ḏꜣ.yw [...] m[n] ms.n mn<.t> dd md(w).w zp 7*
5	XXVI3	*[... .ḫr=k] sw m [... b(?)... n(.j)] ꜥr.w°*
6	XXVI4	[...]
7	XXVI5	*(gap)*
8	XXVI6	[...] *w[t.w(?)* ...]

1	XXVI7–8	*[... pẖr.t] n.t dr [šf.wt] m rd.wj m ꜥ.wt° nb.(w)t [... wr]y.t 1 dḳ.w*
2	XXVI8–9	*n(.j) ḏꜣr.t 1 bnr 1 ḥ[smn(?) ... jr.w m] (j)ẖ.wt wꜥ.t 1 ḥr bj.t wt(.w) ḥr=s r hrw 4*
1	XXVI9–10	*k.t phr.t w<z>š.t(w) [n.]t [r](m)ṯ 1 mnš.t 1 šb.t 1 ḥsꜣ*
2	XXVI10	*n(.j) ꜥwꜣ.yt wt(.w) ḥr=s*
1	XXVI11	*k.t phr.t jny.t n.t bnr 1 šb.t <1> ḥsmn 1 nḏ(.w) s:nꜥꜥ ps(.w) wt(.w) ḥr=s*
1	XXVI11–12	*k.t {ḏd} šnf.t ḥmꜣ.t mḥ.t ḥsꜣ wt(.w)=s*

Translation

1[XXVI] Another: This is your [bl]ood, [H]orus! This is your pus, Seth!

2 This is your put[refac]tion, Seth! Th[is] is your sweat, Me[khen]ti-irti,

3[XXVI] which I have brought so as to remove the [effect] of a god[dess], the effect of a dead person, the ef[fect] of a male enemy, the effect

4 of a female enemy, the effect of an opponent [...] N[N] whom NN has born. Words to be said seven times.

5 [... then you ...] him with [...] of the ꜥrw-tree.

6 [...]

7 (*gap*)

8 [... to be band[aged with it (?) ...]

1[XXVI] [... Remedy (?)] to remove a [swe]lling on both the feet (and) any other limb [...] 1, flour

2 of ca[ro]b 1, dates 1, na[tron (?) ... to be made in]to a mass with honey, to be bandaged with it for four days.

1[XXVI] Another remedy: exc<re>ment [o]f [hu]man beings 1, (red) ochre (?) 1, mash 1, mucus

2 of fermented substance (?), to be bandaged with it.

1 Another remedy: seed of dates 1, mash <1>, natron 1, to be finely ground, to be heated, to be bandaged with it.

1 Another: {to say} a plant product, northern salt, mucus, to be bandaged with it.

Commentary

1–8 R:XXV1+x+2–XXVI2: The conjuration only starts with *k.t*, so it is not clear what it is directed against. The verse points seem to be randomly placed and do not reflect the structure of the spell. Massart 1954, 92–94, cites this part of the manuscript as §12 recto.

1 R:XXV1+x+2 : The blood is in the plural, which is not uncommon in medicinal texts; see GdM VII.2, 762–765. — R:XXV1+x+3 : For *ry.t*, see WB II, 399.13–14; GdM VII.1, 521; Nunn 1996, 224.

1–2 R:XXV1+x+3 : Amazingly, the god is named twice in succession. It is quite certain that neither of these mentions designates Baal due to the typical Egyptian themes and structure of the text.

2 R:XXV1+x+3 : For *ḥw3(3).t*, see WB III, 51.2; GdM VII.2, 589. — : For Mekhenti-irti, see Junker 1942; Griffith 1958, 192–193; Brunner-Traut 1965, 155–156; Chassinat 1966, 315–333; Brunner-Traut 1975, 926–930; Müller 2008, 291.208.

3–4 R:XXVI1–2: The sequence which follows seems to be abridged. The only pair is *ḫft.j* and *ḫft.j*<*t*>, otherwise one of the forms is missing; see also remarks by Massart 1954, 93.12–13; Müller 2008, 291. For this sequence, see GdM VII.2, 701–703. For more generally, see WB I, 157.4–5; Gardiner 1912, 261.14; Polotsky 1929, 39–40; Ritner 1993, 56–57.

5 R:XXVI3: The broken instruction in the recipe could also be part of a remedy. — ?[...]: The part of the tree which is to be used has not been preserved. Massart 1954, 93–94.17, suggests restoring *g3b.t* 'leaf', but the nisbe which follows is masculine and not feminine, as one would expect in that case. The *ʿr.w* tree is a holy drug. It has yet to be identified. The tree – particularly its leaves and sawdust – was used internally and topically. It was used almost exclusively to treat ailments caused by magic; see Jéquier 1922, 212–213; Keimer 1924, I, 69; GdM VI, 105–107; Germer 1979, 259–260; Charpentier 1981, 170–171; Germer 2008, 45–46.

8 R:XXVI6 : This has probably to be amended to *w[t.w]* 'to be band[aged]', but it can also be *w[t]* 'bandage' (WB I, 379.6).

1 R:XXVI7: Massart 1954, 94–95, cites these remedies as §13. — ?[...]: The signs which have been preserved and the feminine nisbe that follows make the restoration *[pḫr.t]* very likely, as does the fact that the remedies which follow start with *k.t pḫr.t*. — ?[...]: Massart 1954, 94.2, refers to papyrus Berlin 3038 R:XI1–5 (*pḫr.t n.t dr šf.w(t)t m rd.wj*; Wreszinski 1909, 24–25, 79–80 Nos. 125–135; GdM IV.1, 76–77, IV.2, 76, V, 131–132), which contains a series of 11 recipes for swelling of the feet; and Papyrus Hearst IX6–8 (*k.t pḫr.t n.t dr šf.wt m ʿ.wt nb.(w)t*; Wreszinski 1912, 30, 99 Nos. 127–128; GdM IV.1, 230, IV.2, 181, V, 399) and XV15–XVI1 (*k.t pḫr.t n.t dr šf.wt m ʿ.wt nb.(w)t n.(w) z*; Wreszinki 1912, 55, 128–129 Nos. 235–236; GdM IV.1, 230, IV.2, 181, V, 400–401). The ingredients used are the same to a certain extent, but none of the remedies are identical. — *[pḫr.t] n.t dr* 'remedy (?)] to remove': The literal translation would be 'remedy of removal'. — ? ? ?: The remains of some drug. Massart 1954, 95.4, does not provide any suggestions for a restoration. GdM IV.1, 77, reservedly suggests restoring *rj.t* 'dye' or, more generally, the remains of some drug (GdM IV.2, 76). Westendorf 1999, I, 67.89, also prefers restoring *rj.t*. The signs which have been preserved are nearly illegible and not clear. Besides *ry.t* 'dye, ink' (WB II, 399.9–12), potential identifications could be *jwr.yt* 'beans' (WB I, 56.14–15), *mrr.yt* 'lumps (of incense)' (WB II, 100.14), or *nṯr.yt* '[a substance related to natron (med.)]' (WB II, 366.14). If the reading of the traces of the signs is correct, then only the restoration *jwr.yt* 'beans' is possible.

1–2 R:XXVI7–8 'flour of ca[ro]b': For this drug, see the commentary to lines 22–23 of incantation 2 (above § 2).

2 R:XXVI8 *bnr* 'date': Dates and their ingredients are mostly used in remedies that are taken orally, but they occasionally appear in ointments. Dates in therapeutical treatments have no specific common indication and were probably used as a carrier substance or base for other drugs (GdM VI, 172–173, 177–178; Germer 1979, 154, 162; Manniche 1989, 133–134; Germer 2002, 84–85; Germer 2008, 59–60, 64). Dates consist of 60–80% of carbohydrates, and the fruit of the date tree (*Phoenix daytylifera* L.) contains proteins and coumarin (Täckholm/Drar 1950, II, 186; Hoppe 1958, 663; Draby/Ghalioungui/Grivetti 1977, 724, 729–730; Germer 1979, 163–164; Germer 1985, 232–233; Germer 2002, 85; Germer 2008, 314–315; Hiller/Melzig 2010, 443–444). It also contains tannins, which are adstringent (Kolta 2001, 46). Due to the high level of sugar, dates are hygroscopic and their effect

on wounds should be similar to that of honey (Guiter 2001, 226, who mentions the hygroscopic effect only in reference to contraceptives). In ancient times, dates were used to cleanse wounds, among other things (Schneider 1974, V.3, 53; Alpin 1980, 42–43; Boulos 1983, 140; Moursi 1992, 241). — R:XXVI8–9 [...]: This sign is perhaps to be restored to *ḥ*[*zmn*] 'natron'. Massart 1954, 95.6, alternatively suggests amending *ḥsꜣ* 'mucus', *ḥsꜣ n(.j) ꜥwꜣ.yt* 'mucus of fermented substance' or *ḥmꜣ.t mḥ.t* 'northern salt'. Northern salt is also suggested by GdM IV.2, 76. For natron, see the commentary to lines 22–23 of incantation 2 (above § 2); for the other drugs, see the remedies below. — R:XXVI9 : This phrase is probably to be amended to [*jr.w m*] *(j)ḫ.wt wꜥ.t* '[to be made] into one mass'. GdM IV.1, 77, IV.2, 76, comments that the stroke after *wꜥ.t* is red; it was probably added later. The group does not seem to be dense, so the scribe perhaps confused it with the quantities. — *bj.t* 'honey': For honey, see the commentary to lines 22–23 of incantation 2 (above § 2).

1 R:XXVI9–10 *w<z>š.t(w)* [*n*].*t* [*r*](*m*)*ṯ* *1*: The word *wzš.t* generally has the meaning 'excrement' and can be used to designate faeces or urine. The manuscript generally uses *mwy.t n.t r(m)ṯ* for urine; see GdM IV.1, 77, VI, 142–143; Nunn 1996, 226; Westendorf 1999, I, 76, 201, II, 837. For excrement in general, see the commentary to lines 7–8 of incantation 1 (above § 1). — R:XXVI10 : The word *mnš.t* perhaps designates ochre, but it is not clear whether red or yellow ochre is meant. In any event, the substance would not be toxic because it is also used internally. This drug is topically used for skin alterations and wounds; see Dawson 1934b, 188; GdM IV.1, 77, VI, 246–248; Harris 1961, 146–147; Schneider 1968, III, 42; Schneider 1975, VI, 102; Bardinet 1995, 476; Nunn 1996, 146; Westendorf 1999, I, 67. — : *Šb.t* is 'mash'; see Charpentier 1981, 664–665; GdM VI, 486–489.

1–2 R:XXVI10 'mucus of fermented substance (?)': This is sometimes translated as 'fermented dough'; see Jéquier 1922, 151–152; Gardiner 1947, II, 236*; GdM VI, 488–489; WB III, 160.12; Faulkner 1962, 177.

1 R:XXVI11 : For 'seeds of dates', see Schneider 1974, V.3, 53; GdM VI, 174–175, 178; Germer 2008, 61. For general information on dates, see the commentary to line 2 R:XXVI8 of remedy 1 (above § 12). — : This phrase is probably to be amended to *šb.t* <1> *ḥsmn* 1; see GdM IV.1, 77, IV.2, 76; Bardinet 1995, 476; Westendorf 1999, I, 67.91. For *ḥsmn* 'natron', see the commentary to lines 22–23 of incantation 2 (above § 2).

1 R:XXVI12: Unlike the others, this remedy does not give any quantities. — : Massart 1954, 94, 95.17, reads *mnf.t* and suggests emending *šnf.t* to *mnš.t* 'ochre'. GdM IV.2, 77, refers to Massart *ibid.* and suggests it could also be a misspelling of *šnf.t*, which Westendorf 1999, I, 68.93, follows. The signs on the papyrus are clear; they read *šnf.t*. This drug is probably a kind of plant product which was used in bandages and ointments; see GdM VI, 498–499; Germer 1979, 329–330; Westendorf 1999, I, 517; Germer 2008, 134–135. See also Charpentier 1981, 684–685, who thinks it is a fruit in a non-perishable form or the juice of this fruit. — 'northern salt': This drug was identified with sodium chloride and was used internally and topically, with a focus on topical therapies (bandages and ointments). It is osmotic like natron, but larger doses have to be used (GdM VI, 340–341, 343; Schneider 1975, VI, 154–155; Nunn 1996, 147, 220; Guiter 2001, 231). — : The substance that needs to be chewed to make the mucus is not specified.

13. Conjurations 2 and 3 (R:XXVI12–XXVIII5)

These two incantations are directed against inflammations of the leg (?). The term used for leg (*sḏꜣ*) is only attested in the present manuscript. The topics used in the spells are genuinely Egyptian and include typically magical elements, such as threatening the gods (*Götterbedrohung*) and various analogies. Both incantations end with a recitation, and the latter adds instructions for making an amulet.

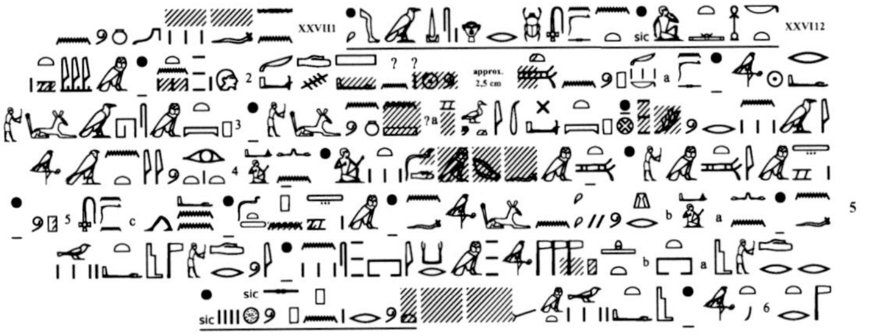

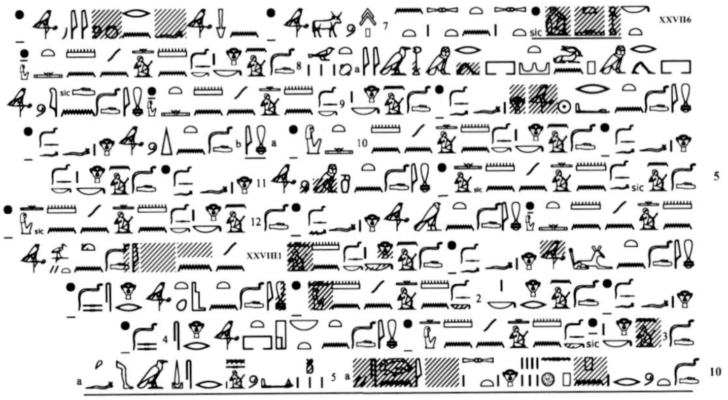

R:XXVII1a under the line; 2a no verse point; 3a no verse point; 4a–b later added above the line; 4c read ; 5a–b read ; 7a perhaps ; 10a–b added later above the line; R:XXVIII4a approx. 6 cm from the end of the line to the end of the papyrus; 5a approx. 11 cm from the end of the line to the end of the papyrus; the last part of the papyrus is blank.

Transliteration

		Recto
1	XXVI12–XXVII1	*k.t šn.t° n.t nz ḫpr ḥr sḏꜣ° znf.w<=k> nw n(.j)*
2	XXVII1–2	*Rꜥ(w)° nz<p>.w=k pw n(.j) T[m … m hr]w š[ꜥ]d(.w) tp.w=t[n]° m sḫ.t*
3	XXVII2–3	*jꜣ(n)r[.w]° p.t ktkt.tj zꜣ[t]° [nš]n.w° p.t m shꜣ°*
4	XXVII3–4	*tꜣ m jtm(.w)° tm[=f sḏm(.w)] [ḏ]d.wt=j° nn ḏj=j jr.t twy n.t Ḥr(.w)*
5	XXVII4–5	*n=f° nn ḏj=j ḫr.wy n(.j) Stẖ n=f° m tꜣ p[n] ḏ.t° ꜥnn ns{n}w pw°*
6	XXVII5	*r dr {s.t}<s.t-ꜥ>° ḥt[p] nṯr.w m kꜣr(j).w=sn° jw dr(.w) s.t-ꜥ*
7	XXVII5–6	*nṯr ntr.t s.t-ꜥ mwt [mwt.t ḥmw.t-r’] [dd.t]w r’ pn zp(w) 4°*
1	XXVII6–7	*k.t [šn.t]° ṯz.t tn ṯz.t n.t Ḥp(w)° n sn[=f] R[nw]y°*
2	XXVII7–8	*pr m Pwn.t pr m ẖꜣ.(y)t° ḏd.n=j ḥr=k ḏz=k mn ms.n mn.t°*
3	XXVII8–9	*mj ḏd.t.n Rꜥ(w) [ḥr]=f ḏz=f° ḏd.n=j ḥr=k ḏz=k mn ms.n mn.t° mj ḏd.{d}<t>.n Šw*
4	XXVII9–10	*ḥr=f ḏz=f° ḏd.n=j ḥr=k ḏz=k mn ms.n mn.t° mj ḏd.t.n Spd.w ḥr=f ḏz=f°*
5	XXVII10–11	*ḏd.n=j <ḥr=k> ḏz{=f}<=k> mn ms.n mn<.t>° mj ḏd.t.n Ḫn[m.w] ḥr=f ḏz=f° ḏd.n=j ḥr=k ḏz=k*
6	XXVII11–12	*mn ms.n mn.t° mj ḏd.t.n Ḥr(.w) ḥr=f ḏz[=f]° ḏd.n=j ḥr=k ḏz=k mn ms.n mn<.t>°*
7	XXVII12–XXVIII1	*mj ḏd.t.n Stẖ ḥr=f ḏz=f° ḏd.n=j [ḥ]r[=k] ḏz=k mn ms.n [m]n[.t] [m]j [ḏ]d[.t].n Ḏḥw.tj*
8	XXVIII1–2	*ḥr=f ḏz=f° ḏd.n=j ḥr=k ḏz[=k] mn ms.n mn<.t>° [m]j ḏd.t.n ꜣs.t ḥr=s ḏz=z°*
9	XXVIII2–4	*ḏd[.n=j] ḥr=k° ḏz=k mn ms.n mn<.t>° mj ḏd.t.n Nb.t-ḥw.t ḥr=s ḏz=z°*
10	XXVIII4–5	*dd.tw r’ [pn] zp 7 ḥr ṯz.t […] j[ns.y] dj.w n z r sḏꜣ=f*

Translation

1[XXVI/II] Another incantation of an inflammation occurring on his leg (?): This <your> [blo]od belongs to

2[XXVII] Re. These, your woun<d>s belong to At[um on the da]y of c[ut]ting off yo[ur] heads in the fiel[d]

3 of r[eeds]. The sky is quivering (and) the [earth is rag]ing. The sky is in confusion (and)

4 the earth in breathlessness! [Does he] not [listen to that which I am [say]ing, (neither) will I give (back) to him this eye

5 of Horus (nor) will I give (back) to him these testicles of Seth in th[is] land eternally! It is a warding off of the inflammation

6 to remove the {place} <effect>. May the gods res[t] in their shrines while the effects of

7 a god (and) a goddess, the effects of a dead man (and) [dead woman (?)] are removed. This spell is to be [said] four times.

1[XXVII] Another [incantation]: This knot is the knot of Apis for [his] brother Ren[uy],
2 who came forth from Punt, who came (healthy) [forth] from the [il]lness! I have spoken for your benefit, NN whom NN has born,
3 as that which Re has spoken for his (own) benefit. I have spoken for your benefit, NN whom NN has born, as that which Shu has spoken
4 for his (own) benefit. I have spoken for your benefit, NN whom NN has born, as that which Sopdu has spoken for his (own) benefit.
5 I have spoken <for> his[!] benefit, NN whom NN has born, as that which Khn[um] has spoken for his (own) benefit. I have spoken for your benefit,
6 NN whom NN has born, as that which Horus has spoken for hi[s] (own) benefit. I have spoken for your benefit, NN whom NN has born,
7[XXVIII] as that which Seth has spoken for his (own) benefit. I have spoken for [your] benefit, NN [whom NN] has born, [as that which] Thoth [has sp]oken
8 for his (own) benefit. I have spoken for your bene[fit], NN whom NN has born, [as] that which Isis has spoken for her (own) benefit.
9 [I have] spoken for your bene[fit], NN whom NN has born, as that which Nephthys has spoken for her (own) benefit.
10 [This] spell is to be said seven [ti]mes over the knot [of *jnsy*-cloth] to be given to the man to his leg (?).

Commentary

1–7: This incantation is cited by Massart 1954, 95–97, as §14.

1 R:XXVI12  : The introduction of this incantation has to be a scribal error because a sequence of remedies (*pẖr.t*) is listed with no other spells; so too Massart 1954, 96.1. — 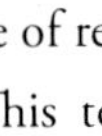: This term is mentioned twice in the text; it appears again in R:XXVI14 as . Usually the word *nzr* 'fire, flame' (WB II, 335.13–18) would be used. The abbreviated variant *nz* existed since the Old Kingdom. For *nzr/nz* as inflammation, see Breasted 1930, 385–386, 387, 388; Cannuyer 1990, 109; Nunn 1996, 223. — : This term is only attested in the present manuscript. Massart 1954, 97.2, remarks that WB IV, 379.16 brings up the possibility that this word could be connected with *sḏ(ꜣ)ẖ* 'lower leg, shin' (WB IV, 394.1–4). Müller 2008, 292, also seems to assume *sḏẖ*. The word *sḏꜣ* literally means 'the walking one (*der Geher*)' (GdM VII.2, 830; Westendorf 1999, I, 223).

2 R:XXVII1 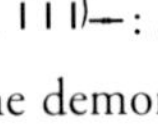: *nz* 'injury' (WB II, 321.4). The scribe has probably omitted the *p* sign due to the demonstrative pronoun *pw* which follows, or to confusion with *nz*[*r*] above (?), so the term is to be amended to *nz*<*p*>*.w* 'wounds' (WB II, 319.9; Kees 1925, 9; Faulkner 1962, 139; Van der Molen 2000, 247). — 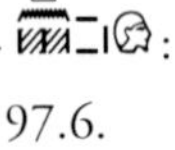: The context does not make clear whose heads are cut off; so too Massart 1954, 97.6.

2–3 R:XXVII2 : For the field of reeds, see Weill 1936; Bayoumi 1940, 1–12, 14–16, 35–45, 70–93; Leclant 1975, 1156–1160. This spelling of the word is common in the New Kingdom (WB I, 32).

3 R:XXVII2 : This abbreviated writing is not easy to interpret. Massart 1954, 97.9, suggests reading *sḏ.tj* 'is damaged' (WB IV, 373.8–375.7) or *ḥḏ.tj* 'is broken' (WB III, 212–213). He admits that neither of the words exists in this abbreviated variant. Alternatively, *zꜣw* (WB III, 427.1–4; Lesko III, 8; Černý/Gardiner 1957, I, LXXXVIII5) or *zwꜣ* (WB III, 419.12; Lesko II, 17) can be read. Abbreviated variants of both terms are attested, but they are generally not used in connection with the sky and earth. The verb *ktkt* 'to quiver' (WB V, 146.2) can be used in this way, but at present it is not attested in an abbreviated writing.

4 R:XXVII3 : Contrary to the view of Massart 1954, 97.12, the construction is not 'certainly abnormal'. It is a negated subjunctive; see Schenkel 2005a, 229.

5 R:XXVII4–5 : For this typical construction, see GdM VIII, 214 §289bb, and Massart 1954, 97.15, who lists several examples, including Papyrus Ebers VIII9–10: *rḏ.t w<z>š pw z* 'It is the causing of urinating of a man' (Wreszinski 1913, 9) and papyrus Leiden I 348 R:VIII6: *šnꜥ ḫft.jw pw* 'It is the detaining of the enemies' (Borghouts 1971, Pl. 8–8a, 25).

1–10: This incantation is cited by Massart 1954, 98–100, as §15.

1 R:XXVII7 : For Apis, see Otto 1938, 11–34; Vandier 1949, 233–236. — : According to the text, Renui is the brother of Apis; he came from Punt. He seems to be attested only in the present manuscript; see WB II, 429.10; LGG V, 678.

2–9 R:XXVII8–R:XXVIII4 *ḏd.n=j ḥr=k ḏz=k mn ms.n mn.t mj ḏd.t.n* GN *ḥr=f/s ḏz=f/s*: The spell has a consistently identical structure in the lines that follow. The construction is emphatic and focuses on the speech of the god. The translation would literally be 'That which I have said over you yourself, NN whom NN has born, is like that which GN has said over him/her him-/herself.'

10 R:XXVIII4 : The gap after *ṯ(ꜣ)z.t* is almost too large to contain nothing but the preposition . In any case, the lacuna has to contain a word introducing the material of the amulet. For general information on knots and amulets made of knots, see Wiedemann 1910, 21–23; Murray 1922, 14–19; Pinch 1994, 83–84, 126; Eschweiler 1997, 197–219; Raven 1997, 275–281; Wendrich 2006, 243–269. The number of knots (one!) is due to the number of knots in the introduction of this spell; see also Massart 1954, 99.10. — : Müller 2008, 293, writes four times instead of seven times. — R:XXVIII4–5 : The term *jns.y* describes a kind of red cloth commonly used in amulets. For this word, see Gardiner 1947, I, 65–66; Massart 1954, 100.12. For general information on the colour red, see Kees 1943, 446–464. GdM IV.1, 83, IV.2, 80, mentions that the red colour could refer to the colour of the inflammation. — R:XXVIII5 : This phrase is very common after instructions for making an amulet of knots; it gives instructions on where the amulet is to be placed on the patient's body. For similar phrases, see the compilation by Massart 1954, 100.13.

14. Incantation 10 (V:I1–8)

In this spell, several deities vilify the demon Akhu. The relation between the different parts of the incantation is often unclear due to the rather fragmentary condition of the papyrus. In contrast to the other incantations against Sāmānu/Akhu, which conclude with a topical treatment, this one ends with a knot amulet being made for the patient. This text has no duplicate.

V:I4a–b traces, no longer legible.

Transliteration

		Verso
1	I1	[k.t(?) p3 ʿḫ.w] š[m(.t) … s:ḥwr]
2	I1–2	tw [nṯr] nb s:[ḥ]wr [tw] n[t]r.t <nb.t> s:ḥwr [t]w t[3] p.t […]
3	I2–3	[…] jm=k [s]:ḥ[wr tw p]3 […]8 nṯr ṯ3.j[j] s:ḥwr
4	I3–4	[tw t3 … n]ṯ[r].t ḥm.t s:[ḥ]wr t[w] psḏ.t [ʿ3.t s:ḥwr tw psḏ.t]
5	I4	nḏz.w<t> s:ḥ[wr tw p3 jwt]n ḥ[nʿ] n.[t]y-nb kt[k]t [ḥ]r=[f]
6	I5	[… jw ḫr ḥr=k ḥnʿ ḏbʿ.wj n(.wj) ʿ.wj(?) šn.wt(?) … ptr(j)]
7	I5–6	[jr.t n<.t> p3 Rʿ(w) s:ḥwr tw šr]j.w s:ḥwr [tw p]3 Rʿ(w) [s:ḥwr]
8	I6–7	[tw p3] šn.w n(.j) J[t]n [s:ḥwr tw …] ḥḏ [t3]
9	I7–8	ḥnʿ w[ḏ3.t … dd.tw r' pn ḥr … jr.w m]
10	I8	ṯ(3)z[.t] 7 dj.w r=f

Translation

1 [Another (?)]: o Akhu who goes […] Every [god]
2 shall [vilify] you, <every> god[d]ess shall vilify [y]ou, t[h]e sky shall vilify [you …]
3 […] in you (?). [T]he […]8 male gods shall vi[lify you. The …] female godd[esses]
4 shall vili[fy you]. The [great] Ennead shall vi[li]fy [you. The] little [En]nead
5 shall [vilify you. The grou]nd shall vili[fy you and] everyone mo[vi]ng u[po]n it.
6 [… Your face and both your fingers of both your hands (?) fall … while the eye of]

7 [Re looks. The little o]nes [shall vilify you]. Re shall vilify you. [The] circuit of

8 the sun disk [shall vilify you. [... shall vilify you which] enlightens

9 [the land] and [the *wedjat*-eye ... This utterance is to be said over ... to be made to]

10 seven kno[ts], to be applied to it/him.

Commentary

1–10: The consistent structure of the incantation makes it possible to restore the spell in most cases (*s:ḥwr tw*). Massart 1954, 101–102, cites this incantation as §1 verso.

1 V:I1 [*k.t*$^{(?)}$]: Massart 1954, 101.1, suggests restoring [*šn.t n.t dr*] in front of . It should have been partially written down in the previous column. The incantation could also simply have started with . — V:I1 ? ? : The readings *m* and *t* are uncertain.

3 V:I3 :Massart 1954, 102.7, states that the graph for the numeral 70 would fit the space. The traces on the papyrus do not support this. The traces could perhaps be restored to the numeral 50.

3 & 4 V:I3 and : The male and female deities remind one of the male and female deities named in several Hittite texts, e.g. in Hittite state treaties (see i.a. Wilhem 2005, 120, lines 50–51) or prayers like Muwatalli's prayer to the assembly of gods (Singer 1996, 37, lines 53, 172–173). *Nṯr.w ṯ3y.w* (WB II, 360.14) and *nṯr.wt ḥm.wt* (WB II, 362.14) are usually named together; see also Massart 1954, 102.8.

4–5 V:I3–4 and : It is also possible to restore [*wr.t*] instead of [*ꜥ3.t*], but *ꜥ3.t* is more common for the 'great Ennead'. For general information on the Ennead, see Barta 1973.

6 V:I5: At the beginning of the line, a cobra is legible. It could perhaps be the determinative for a goddess's name. — '[... Your face and both your fingers of both your hands (?) fall ...]': The meaning of this passage is uncertain due to the fragmentary condition of the papyrus.

6–7 V:I5 'the eye of Re looks': It is unclear how this sentence is to be syntactically integrated in the incantation.

7 V:I6 : It is not clear who are referred to as 'the little ones'; see also Massart 1954, 102.18, and the entries in LGG VII, 108, 109.

8 V:I7 : An appearance of the sun could also have been written in front of *ḥḏ t3* (WB III, 207.27), as already noted by Massart 1954, 102.20; the lexeme 'dawn, morning' (WB III, 208.7–9) is also possible. The space on the papyrus is not large enough to restore *s:ḥwr tw ḥḏ-t3* 'The morning shall vilify you.'

9 V:I7 : For the *wedjat*-eye, see Junker 1917, 143, 144, 154–156, 158–159; LGG II, 646.

9–10 V:I7–8: The recipe that follows is almost completely destroyed. According to what is left, a kind of knot amulet was made. This is unexpected. Usually the demon Sāmānu/Akhu is treated with various mixtures of drugs.

15. Incantation 11 (V:I8–II3)

This incantation is highly fragmentary throughout, so it is difficult to understand. Sāmānu/Akhu is not mentioned, but *k.t* at the beginning indicates that this spell was also directed against the demon. At the beginning, some kind of flame is mentioned together with a mother. Various kinds of waters are then evoked, and the magician seems to purify his words with them. The flame is called by name and connected to Nut and Ishkhara. The incantation ends with a fragmentary recipe.

V:I8a–b traces fit 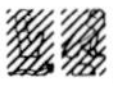 *; II1a traces of ink of the papyrus.*

Transliteration

		Verso
1	I8–9	*k.t tꜣ ẖ[.t] šd [... mw.t=f] š[d].yt <tꜣ> ẖ[.t ḥnꜥ nꜣ n(.j) ...]yw*
2	I9–10	*rꜥw.t pꜣ šnꜥ n(.j) tꜣ [p].t [ḥnꜥ nꜣ n(.j) ...] n [p]ꜣ [tꜣ ...]*
3	I10–11	*[... w] nꜣ n(.j) sbꜣ.w n.ty m tꜣ p[.t ... r ...]*
4	I11	*[... sp.tj]=j [r s:]wꜥb nꜣ n(.j) md(w).wt n.ty [ḥ ... pr.t(?) ...]=f [j]r [...]*
5	I11–II1	*[...] rn [n(.j) ẖ.t(?) ... ḥr] dm.w [r]n n(.j) ẖ.t [...]*
6	II1–2	*[...] rn=s rn n(.j) Nw.t [{t} ... J]-ḳ[ꜣ]-ḏꜣ-*
7	II2	*[j]j[.t] hꜣ(j) [...] J-š[ꜣ-ẖꜣ]-rw [dd.tw r' pn ...]*
8	II3	*[... hrw tp.y n mdw.t ... jr.w m (j)ẖ.wt wꜥ.t dj.w r=f]*

Translation

1 Another: O fla[me] which saves [... his mother] who sav[es] <the> fla[me and the ... wa]ter,

2 the discharge (?), the storm (cloud) of the [s]ky [and the ...] of the [earth ...]

3 [wa]ter (?), the stars which are in the sk[y ... water (?) ... to the sea (?) ...]

4 [...] both my [lips] in order to purify the words which [... come forth (?) ...] his [...] As to [the pronun-]

5 [citation] of the name of [the flame (?): [...] with pronunciation of the [na]me of the flame [...]

6 [...]. Her name is the name of Nu[t ...]ḳḏ-]

7 [yt ...] Ishkhar[a. This utterance is to be said ...]

8 [... first day of words (?) ... to be made into one mass, to be applied to it/him.]

Commentary

1–8: Large parts of the incantation are translatable, but its purpose is difficult to discern. It is obvious that different kinds of water play an important role and contrast with the flame, which also figures prominently in the spell. A pivotal moment occurs in line 4, when the aforementioned waters are used to purify the words of the magician (?). Massart 1954, 102–104, cites this incantation as §2 verso.

1 V:VI8 : Since only the first part of the word has been preserved, different lexemes can be restored. Massart 1954, 103.2, suggests *šdj* 'to take (away)' (WB IV, 560.8–562.19) followed by the restoration ⌊*pꜣ ꜥḫ.w*⌋, which would fit the gap. He admits that this restoration is difficult to connect with 'his mother'. *Šdj* can also be translated as 'to save, to rescue' (WB IV 563.2–9), 'to dig, to carve' (WB IV, 563.1), 'to recite, to read' (WB IV, 563–564.16) or 'to suckle, to educate' (WB IV, 564.17–565.15). Keeping 'his mother' in mind, the translation 'to save' or 'to recite' seems most suitable. Müller 2008, 289, translates this passage as 'to save'. — : It is not quite clear who is saving whom. 'His mother' could save the flame or be saved by the flame. There is no way of knowing whether the meaning 'to suckle' would be suitable. Müller 2008, 289,197, suggests that the ending of the particle *-yt* could perhaps mark a generic passive voice (one has to assume a *w*-passive voice): '... *seine Mutter. Das Feuer wurde fortgenommen* ...'. Due to the fragmentary context, it is unclear if the flame is used in a positive or a negative sense. The interpretation with the *w*-passive voice should be rejected, because when this form appears in the papyrus it is always written with a -ending, as in the numerous recipes in this papyrus. — V:I9 : Perhaps this is one of several rather unusual spellings for 'the sea' used in the manuscript; see incantation 4 (above §4) line 5.

2 V:VI9 : This word is otherwise unattested. According to the determinative, it has to be something unpleasant or bad. Müller 2008, 289, seems to connect it with *ry.t* (WB II, 399, 13–15). — '[and the ...] of the [earth ...]': Massart 1954, 103.7, suggests restoring ⌊*jtr.w n.w*⌋, which does not fit the traces on the manuscript.

2–3 V:I9–10 : The determinative indicates that it has to be a kind of water; in V:I10 this determinative is used twice, and one of these writings is with signs depicting a canal (N36 and N23).

4 V:I11 : It is not clear what word followed *n.ty*. Some of the signs are quite difficult to interpret. — V:I11 *jr*: The word ⌊*dm*⌋ 'to pronounce, to mention' (WB V, 499.8–450.6) should probably be restored, as in line 5 V:II1; Massart 1954, 103.11, already noted this.

5 : It is difficult to say who is speaking here.

5–6 V:II1: Perhaps the restoration ⌊*jr dm rn*⌋ 'As to the pronunciation of the name' is possible after *ḫ.t* 'flame'.

6 V:II1 : The suffix pronoun *=s* probably refers to the flame, as already noted by Massart 1954, 103.13.

6–7 V:II1 : The syllabic spelling shows that the word is a loanword. It is probably a toponym; see also Massart 1954, 103.14; Müller 2008, 289.198.

7 V:II2 : Ishkhara designates a Mesopotamian goddess; see Drioton 1955, 163; Helck 1971, 470; Prechel 1996; see also Massart 1954, 103.16. Her purpose in this spell is not clear.

7–8 V:II2–3: The incantation ends with a rather fragmentary recipe. Judging by the remains it was probably a mixture for a topical treatment.

8 V:II3 *hrw tp.j n mdw.wt*: The phrase could also be translated as 'first day for words' instead of 'first day of words'.

16. Incantation 12 (V:IV9–V8)

In this incantation, the conjurer overcomes the demon by controlling his and his mother's procreation. A fairly obscure passage follows, the content of which is far from clear. Akhu is then forced to leave the patient's body, particularly the vessels of his arm, and Anat strikes him with her chisel. The spell ends with the DHF. This incantation only appears on the verso. It should be noted that the Mesopotamian topic 'Sāmānu as dog' is used here.

V:IV10a under the line; 10b no longer legible; 10c under the line; 10c–d traces of palimpsest under the line; V:V3a–b no longer legible; 4a traces of ; 8a–b traces.

Transliteration

		Verso
1	IV9	*k.t pꜣ ꜥẖ.w pꜣ [n.ty ḥr …]w jw=f hrp.w [p]ꜣ*
2	IV9–10	*jwjw wšꜥ [{.t}] ḳs.w m=k jr.n=j ḥꜣ.t=k bw jr=k [ḥꜣ.t=j pꜣ ꜥẖ.w …]*
3	IV10–V1	*[… n šꜣꜥ.n=j jr.t ḥꜣ.t=k m-mj.t(j)t pꜣ ꜥẖ.w] nḏr<.tj> jr.n=j tꜣy=k*
4	V1–2	*mw.t{t} jwr<.t> jm=k ms{t}[=s m]j-jẖ jw=s(t) ḥr šn.t ḥr rmy.t n*
5	V2	*pꜣ ḫfꜣw pw pꜣ rḏ.n n=k pꜣ nṯr [j]w ḏj=z {ḏj} šp(y)[=s(?) jw=s ḥr]*
6	V2–3	*s[ḏr] ḳdjw ḳdw=s n[ꜣ]y=f ẖrd.w mj […] ḳdw=s p[ꜣ]*
7	V3–4	*[… fꜣy]=k rd.wj=ky r sẖs[=k] pꜣ ꜥẖ.w r ẖt[m].w r' n(.j)*
8	V4–5	*p[ꜣ … gꜣ]b.t 2 n(.t) šrj=f <n.ty> ḥr ss[n] n=f ṯꜣw {m}*
9	V5–6	*tꜣy=f jr.t 2 n.ty {m}<ḥr> p[tr(j) … tꜣ 7] ṯz.t n<.t> ḏꜣḏꜣ[=f] {m} mt nb n(.j)*
10	V6–7	*[gꜣb].t=f ḏj.tw tꜣ mḏꜣ.t n<.t> ꜥntj m mꜣꜥ[=k …=k] nꜣ n(.j) md(w).wt*
11	V7	*j:[ḏd](w) pꜣ p[zg](ꜣ) sḏm.y(w) t spr.tj r [pr Rꜥ(w) r-ḏd]*
12	V7–8	*ḳn(yw) Ḥr(.w) [pꜣ ꜥẖ.w]*

Translation

1 [An]other: O Akhu, the one who [...] while he is submerged, [o]

2 dog who chews bones. Behold, I have overcome you. You did not [overcome me o Akhu! ...]

3 [... likewise, I began to overcome you, o Akhu], while <you> are seized. At the time when I created your

4 mother who was pregnant with you: [H]ow can [she] give birth while she is suffering (and) crying? Because of

5 the snake, it is – the one the god has given to you. She causes [it (?)] to become blind, [while she]

6 [spends] the night sleeping. She surrounds its (?) children like [cows (?)]. She surrounds t[he]

7 [...] You shall [lift up] both of your feet until [you] hasten, o Akhu, until the mouth of

8 [the patient (?)] is sealed, the two [ho]les of his nose <which> breathe air for him,

9 his two eyes which se[e ... the seven] orifices of [his] head, every vessel of

10 his [arm]. The chisel of Anat shall be given into [your] temple. [...] The words

11 which the spitting one said. The gossip reached the [house of Re that]

12 Horus has conquered [Akhu].

Commentary

1–12: Massart 1954, 105–107, cites this incantation as §5 verso.

1 V:IV9 : Massart 1954, 106.1, suggests amending [*wnm*] 'to eat', and is followed by Müller 2008, 289. The traces of do not support his opinion. — : Here *jw=f hrp.w* is used instead of the more common *n.ty hrp.w*.

1–2 V:IV9 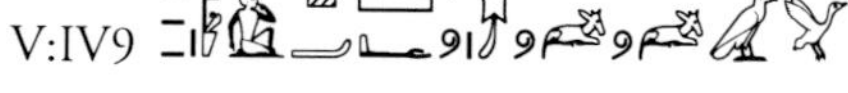 : For the 'Sāmānu as dog' theme, see Beck 2015b, 176–179.

2 V:IV10 *jr.n=j ḥ3.t=k*: For this phrase, see the commentary to line 1 R:VI2 of incantation 5 (above § 5).

4 V:V1 : This spelling for mother is also used in Papyrus d'Orbiney (Möller 1927, II, sign 194). — : As *jwr* refers to 'the mother', <*t*> has to be amended. Massart 1954, 106.7, amends <*tj*> with some reservations.

4–5 V:VI1–2

Massart 1954, 105, translates 'she readeth an incantation weeping' and comments that the mother's way of giving birth is mysterious (Massart 1954, 106.9). Müller 2008, 289–290, translates this passage as 'Wie soll sie gebären, indem sie leidet? Es ist die Träne der Schlange, die der Gott dir gab.' Müller *ibid.* emends *šnj* 'to conjure' (WB IV, 496.2–6) into *šnj* 'to suffer' (WB IV, 494.15–18), which the present commentary follows. After this he reads {*ḥr*} *rmy.t n<.t> p3 ḥf3w pw p3 rḏ.n n=k p3 nṯr* (Müller 2008, 290.202). Alternatively he suggests: '*ḥr-<m> rmy.t* '... indem sie weswegen weint?' The sentence that follows is taken to be a pseudo cleft sentence in which *pw* and *p3* have the same grammatical meaning. The translation is not without difficulties because 'the tear of the snake' is feminine and thus cannot be connected to the phrase 'the god has given to you', which refers to a masculine antecedent. One would expect *tꜣ* rather than *pꜣ*. That is why is understood as the conjunction 'because of', which in this case is followed by a bipartite *pw*-sentence and extended with the phrase *pꜣ rḏ.n n=k pꜣ nṯr*. The last part refers to the snake. The meaning is still obscure.

5 V:V2 : Massart 1954, 106.12, restores [*=f jw=s ḥr*] after *špy*, which is very likely. The question is who blinds whom. The suffix *=s* can only refer to 'the mother'. It is impossible to decide with any certainty whether to restore [*=f*] or [*=s*] as the object after *špy*. The second {*dj*} has to be emended.

6 V:V2–3 : The word *sḏr* seems to be an infinitive. The word *ḳd.w* which follows is probably a stative with the invariable *w*-ending, if the ending is not merely a phonetic complement, in which case it would be another infinitive. — V:V3 : As the possessive article is masculine, it can only refer to the snake – or possibly to the god. The meaning is not certain. — : The sign or signs before the cow determinative are no longer legible.

7–8 V:V4 *r' n(j) p*[*ꜣ* …]: A phrase for 'patient' is to be expected after the article *pꜣ*, as in Massart 1954, 106.16.

8 V:V4–5 'two [ho]les of his nose': This combination is only attested in the present manuscript (WB V, 154.6). Usually, the term *gꜣb.t* is used as 'arm' (WB V, 154.1–5).

9 V:V5 *m ptr(j)*: The phrase is to be emended to {*m*}<*ḥr*> *ptr(j)*, see also Massart 1954, 106.20. — V:V5–6 : Note that the mouth and the ears are omitted in the list of the seven orifices of the head. See also the commentary to line 29 R:VIII4/V:XIII1 of incantation 5 (above §5).

10 V:V6 : The term *gꜣb.t* is used here in its common meaning; see also line 8. — *ꜥntj*: For the goddess Anat, see the commentary to line 7 V:VIII7 of incantation 2 (above §2).

11 V:V7 : The only late Egyptian relative form in the entire manuscript is used here. — : The 'spitting one' is otherwise unattested. For spitting and salvia and their use in magical texts, see Ritner 1993, 74–92.

11–12 V:V7–8: The incantation ends with an abridged version of the DHF; see the commentary to lines 17–20 of incantation 4 (above §4). In contrast to other attestations of the DHF, here *pꜣ ꜥḥ.w* is named instead of *pꜣ s-m-n*.

17. Incantation 13 (V:IX1–X2)

The demon has taken possession of the patient's arm. As long as he remains there, the cosmic order is disturbed and Re will not rise on his daily journey. The spell ends with a recipe. This incantation starts in the middle of a sentence and large parts of the central section are missing. In contrast to all the other texts on the verso, this one uses verse points. That, as well as the broken beginning, indicate that the incantation could be part of the original inscription on the papyrus. The spell has no duplicate.

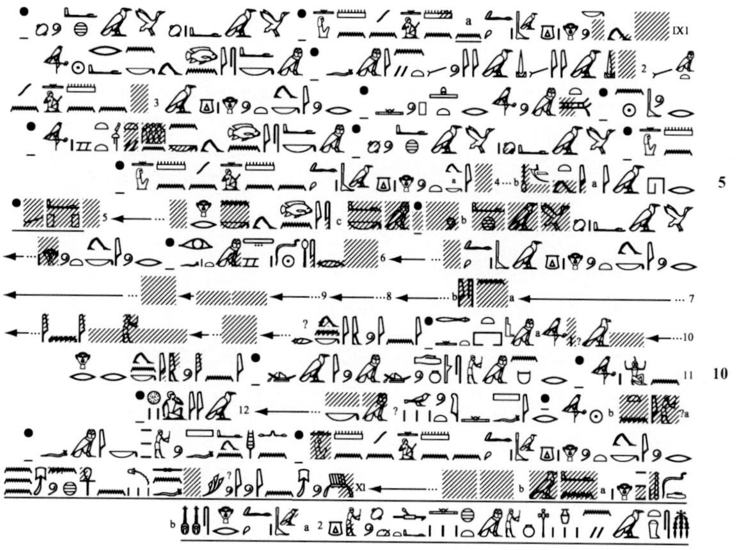

V:IX1a added above the line; 3a–b line broken below; 4a strange; 4b–c line broken below; 7a–b reading uncertain; 10a the curve of goes far under the line; 11a–b line broken above; 12a–b hardly visible; V:X2a–b much darkened.

Transliteration

		Verso
1	IX1	*[rwj]=k [t]w ḥr g3b n(.j) mn ms.n mn<.t>°̲ p3 ꜥ p3 ꜥẖ.w°̲*
2	IX1–2	*mwt <mwt .t(?)> [ḏ]3.y(w) ḏ3.yw(t) n .ty jm=f°̲ m=k s:jn n=k Rꜥ(w)*
3	IX2–3	*r wbn°̲ (J)t[m].w r ḥtp(w)°̲ rwj=k tw ḥr g3[b] n(.j) mn ms.n*
4	IX3	*mn<.t>°̲ p3 ꜥ p3 ꜥẖ.w°̲ m=k s:jn n[=k Ḫnt.y]-jmn.t(t)*
5	IX3–4	*r h3y.t m3[ꜥ-ḫrw rw]j=k tw ḥr g3b n(.j) mn ms.n mn<.t>°̲*
6	IX4–5	*p3 ꜥ [p3 ꜥẖ.w]°̲ [m=k] s:jn [n=k] Ḥr[... ꜥpp°]*
7	IX5–6	*rwj=k tw ḥr g3b [n.j mn ms.n mn.t p3 ꜥ p3 ꜥẖ.w m=k s:jn n=k ... r] s:ḥḏ t3 m jr.t=f°̲ rwj=k tw [ḥr g3b n.j mn ms.n mn.t p3 ꜥ p3 ꜥẖ.w ...]*
8	IX7–9	*[...] n sj [...]*
9	IX10	*[...]tjw m s.t ꜥ3.t°̲ jn-jw jy[.n]=k r [wj3 ... jn-jw ... r wj3]*
10	IX11	*n(.j) Ḥḥ°̲ r nḥm s:ḳd m wj3°̲ jn-[j]w [j]y.n=k r ḥr(.t)*
11	IX11–12	*[Jtn]°̲ r jšf šw.t [m=k ... h]3y zp-sn°̲*
12	IX12	*rwj=k tw ḥr g3b n(.j) mn ms.n m[n<.t>]°̲ nn ꜥḥꜥ nšf(w)=k jm=f°̲*
13	IX12–X1	*dd [mdw].w ḥr [ꜥnt.(j)w ... nr3].w njwj znf.w n(.w) [ꜥn]ḫ(w) mw*
14	X1–2	*mst3ny nḏ(.w) m (j)ḫ.(w)t wꜥ.t wt(.w) g[3]b ḥr=s nfr nfr*

Translation

1 You shall [remo]ve yourself from the arm of NN whom NN has born, o stroke, o Akhu,

2 dead man, <dead woman (?)>, male [op]ponent, female opponent who are within him! Behold, Re is waiting for you

3 to rise, Atu[m] to set. You shall remove yourself from the ar[m] of NN whom NN has

4 born, o stroke, o Akhu! Behold, [Khenti]amentiu is waiting for [you],

5 to descend trium[phant]! You shall [rem]ove yourself from the arm of NN whom NN has born,

6 o stroke, [o Akhu. Behold,] Ḥr[...] is waiting [for you ... Apophis].

7 You shall remove yourself from the arm [of NN whom NN has born, o stroke, o Akhu. Behold, ... is waiting for you, to] illuminate the earth with his eye. You shall remove yourself [from the arm of NN whom NN has born, o stroke, o Akhu! ...]

8 [... is waiting for yo(?) ...]

9 [...] in the great place. Did you come to [the barque ...Did you come ... to the barque]

10 of the Millions to prevent travel in the barque? [Did] you come to keep away

11 [the sun disk], to enlarge (?) the emptiness? [Behold, ...He,] he!

12 You shall remove yourself from the arm of NN whom NN has born. Your poisons (?) shall not remain (lit.: stay) in it!

13 [Words] to be said over [myrrh (?) ...] of the [i]bex, mint (?), blood of a [g]oat, water

14 of mestani, to be ground, to be made into a mass, to be bandaged with it. Very good!

Commentary

1–14: It is possible to restore many parts of the incantation because of the consistent pattern of the spell, even though large parts are fragmentary. It is not clear how much is missing at the beginning. This incantation is noteworthy because it uses only genuine Egyptian themes. Massart 1954, 107–110, cites this spell as §8 verso.

1 V:IX1 : The term is only attested in this text (WB I 159.12). As Massart 1954, 108.4, has correctly stated, the word is an epithet of Akhu, because the pronouns used for him are always in the second person singular masculine. Müller 2008, 290, following Massart 1954, 107, translates the term as 'bad influence (?)/ (schlechter) Zustand'. Perhaps one should assume the simplex *ꜥ* for the compound word *s.t-ꜥ* 'stroke'; see Ritner 1993, 56–57 (suggestion by H.-W. Fischer-Elfert).

2 V:IX2: Massart 1954, 108.5, suggests restoring [*mwt.t*] 'dead woman' after , which Müller 2008, 290, follows. There is a tiny bad spot at the beginning of the line, but the space does not allow the restoration [*mwt.t*]. The scribe probably omitted the word and it is to be amended as <*mwt.t*>. — : The feminine ending is omitted in *dꜣ.ywt*, as is often the case in this manuscript. — : The verb can mean 'to wait' (WB IV, 38.4–8) and 'to hurry, to run' (WB IV, 38.9–39.9). For the meaning 'to wait', see Gardiner 1911a, 100–102; compare Massart 1954, 108.6; for information on the verb in general, see Westendorf 1981, 27–31. In the present context, the meaning 'to wait' seems more adequate, because the deities can only fulfill their typical duties once the demon has removed himself from the patient's arm.

4 V:IX3 : For Khentiamentiu, see Grieshammer 1975, 964–965; LGG V, 783–786 with further citations.

5 V:IX3 : The term *mꜣꜥ-ḫrw* 'to be justified, to be triumphant' (WB II, 15.1–21) qualifies the verb form as a stative.

6 V:IX4 : Massart 1954, 108.10, suggests restoring *Ḥr.j-rw.t-sš* (older spelling: *Ḥr-Ḥr.yt-sš.w*), who binds Apophis in the Book of the Dead, spell 39: *ḳꜣs(w).n sw Ḥr.j-rw.t-sš* 'the one above the ink bound him (= Apophis)' (Naville 1886, I, Pl. LIII9). According to Erik Hornung, this name is an epithet of Thoth (Hornung 1990, 108.28, 440). This god is attested with the spellings *Ḥr.j-rw.t-sš* and *Ḥr.j-rw.t* (WB II, 400.2; LGG V, 370–371, 371); see also the statement in Müller 2008, 290.205. — : The name of the opponent of the sun god is typically written in red; see Posener 1949, 77–81, especially 77. For the reading Apopis instead of Apophis, see Gardiner 1935, I, 30.4; see also Massart 1954, 109.11.

7 V:IX6 : An appearance of the sun god needs to be amended in front of this phrase; see also Massart 1954, 109.12–13.

8 V:IX7–9: These lines are almost completely broken.

9 V:IX10 : The meaning of this line is not clear. After this, a new theme starts with interrogative clauses. Perhaps the beginning of V:IX10 also belongs to this list. The bird sign in the name of the deity could also be read as *nh*; see Müller 2008, 290.

9–10 V:IX10–11 : Read [*wjꜣ*] *n(.j) Ḥḥ* 'barque of the Millions'. This barque designates the boat in which the sun god crosses the sky. It has a devastating effect on the world if it comes to a standstill; see Müller 2006, 452–543; Massart 1954, 109.16.

11 V:IX11 : In line with the structure of the previous sentence, this word should be an infinitive and should be followed by an object. No verb form is attested with this spelling – unless one considers deriving it from the word 'saliva' (WB I, 135.1), which does not make any sense in this context. Perhaps it could be connected with *šfw* 'to swell' (WB IV, 455.8–11), in which case the determinative would be odd. Müller 2008, 291.207, reservedly suggests connecting this word with the Semitic loanword *jšf* 'to burn' (Caminos 1954, 93; Fischer-Elfert 1983, 147; Sivan/Cochavi-Rainey 1992, 19, 78; Hoch, 1994, 41), here not in syllabic writing.

12 V:IX12 : The meaning of this word is not entirely clear. In WB II, 339.11, it is defined as a part of a snake or a poison fang (?). GdM IV.1, 84, VII.1, 484, writes 'Gift', referring to the present manuscript, as does Westendorf 1999, I, 67. According to Reintges 1996, 140, *nšf.w* are 'drops of poison'. Massart 1954, 109.21, reads *šf.w*, so *n* has to be part of the verb form *ꜥḥꜥ*. In

Middle Egyptian, the negation *nn* is not used with *sḏm.n=f* (Gardiner 1988, 80, §105.2); in Late Egyptian, it is used with this verb form very rarely (Erman 1933, 383 §754).

13–14 V:IX12–V:X2: A partial, fragmentary recipe for a bandage follows.

13 V:IX12 *ꜥnt.(j)w*: The term *ꜥnt.jw* is usually identified with myrrh, but it can also be frankincense, or both, or a designation for resin in general (GdM VI, 101–103; Westendorf 1999, I, 67, 497; Manjo 1975, 124; Germer 2002, 98, 118; Goyon 2003, 55; Nunn 1996, 158, 217, Chemettre/Goyon 1996, 58.30; Nicholson/Shaw 2000, 434–436, 438–439, 439–442; Steuer 1933, 31–48; Steuer 1937,102; Bardinet 1995, 477; Daumas 1975, 107; Charpentier 1981, 160–165). It is used internally and topically in recipes, mostly to treat wounds and snake bites (GdM VI, 99, 101–103; Germer 1979, 68–69; Germer 2008, 43–44). See also the discussion on *ꜥnt.jw* and *snṯr* in Beck 2015b, 217–218. — 13 V:X1 : Massart 1954, 109.22, suggests restoring [*nrꜣ*].*w* 'ibex' (WB II, 280.3). It is not clear what part of the ibex should be used. See also GdM, IV.1, 84; Bardinet 1995, 477; Westendorf 1999, I, 67; Müller 2008, 291. — *njwjw*: Probably a variant of *njꜣjꜣ*. The drug is occasionally identified with 'mint' (Guiter 2001, 228; Westendorf 1999, I, 501; Germer 2008, 298; Long 1984, 145–159; cf. Loret 1984, 145–159I; GdM VI, 293–295; Germer 1979, 280–283; Charpentier 1981, 374–375; Germer 2002, 61). In Egypt, *njwjw/njꜣjꜣ* is used internally and topically in oral remedies, bandages, ointments, fumigations, and suppositories. The focus is on afflictions in women. The plant is only used in medicinal texts (GdM VI, 293–295; Germer 1979, 280–283; Germer 2008, 81–82). Different species of mint (*Mentha* spp.) are common in Egypt (Long 1984, 156–157; Germer 2008, 297). The active ingredient of mint is its essential oil. The composition depends on the particular species (Hoppe 1958, 574, 569; Hiller/Melzig 2010, 383–284). The essential oil is antibacterial and helps to relieve itching. The plant is carminative, analgetic, and spasmolytic (Hoppe 1958, 574; Schneider 1974, V.2, 312; Boulos 1983, 104; Long 1984, 154–155, 157; Guiter 2001, 228; Frohne 2002, 366; Frohn 2007, 421, 423–424; Germer 2008, 297; Hiller/Melzig 2010, 383–384). — *znf.w n(.w) ꜥnẖ(w)*: The 'blood of a goat' is only mentioned twice in Egyptian recipes – for a bandage (here) and for an oral remedy (GdM VI, 444). The blood of other animals (for instance asses, fish, swallows, cattle, vultures, pigs, dogs, bats, etc.) is a common ingredient in topical remedies for hair, lashes, and eyes. It is seldom used in internal treatments (GdM VI, 444–448; Nunn 1996, 149).

13–14 V:X1 *mw mstꜣnj*: The drug *mstꜣnj* is mentioned several times in Egyptian medicinal texts. It is used topically in ointments and bandages and in enemas and suppositories. This drug probably has a viscous consistency, with *mw mstꜣnj* being a more fluid variant. The substance cannot currently be identified (GdM VI, 286–287; Massart 1954, 109.24).

18. Fragments verso (V:XVIII1–XXI3)

These fragments seem to be part of the incantations too. It is usually not clear against what or whom they were directed. It cannot be excluded that they were against Sāmānu/Akhu.

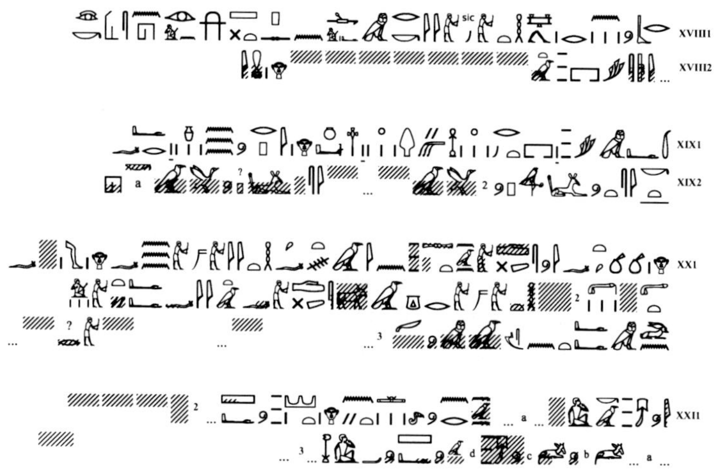

V:XVIII–XXI: Upper part of a column; V:XIX2a or ▬ *V:XXI1a space between the fragments not certain; 2a space not certain; 2a–b no longer exists; 2c–d lower part of the line almost completely broken off.*

Transliteration

		Verso
1	XVIII1	*r-bnr ḥ{t}(w).y r=k m wꜥ n(.j) pzš.t jr<.t>.n=j nhs=k*
2	XVIII2	[...] *js.w tꜣ* [...] *ḥr mj*
1	XIX1	*tjꜥm 1̱ pr.t šn(y) 1̱ nḏ(.w) ḥr jrpw 1̱ ḏj(.w) r=f*
2	XIX1–2	*k.t jst(w) Stẖ pw [pꜣ ...] js[t(w) Stẖ pw pꜣ] k$^{(?)}$h[...]*
1	XX1	*ḥr gg.t=f jw s[d](.w) nꜣ n(.j) [ṯ(ꜣ)z].wt n(.wt) jꜣ.t=f ḥ{t}y=f ḥr rd=f*
2	XX1–2	*mt[w.wt ... ḥ(w).t] r g[ꜣ] sd[=f] tꜣy[=f] ꜥꜥ.t[y]w*
3	XX2–3	*wn(n) m ꜥꜥ.t n sm[ꜣ(mw) ... r$^{(?)}$...]*
1	XXI1–2	*[m(ꜣ)$^{(?)}$]j.w kꜣ [...] nꜣ n(.j) nr.w n.ty ḥr ẖꜣs.wt wšꜥ [...]*
2	XXI2	[... *jwjw.w*] *nꜣ* [*n.j w*]*šꜥ(w) ẖꜣ*[...]

Translation

1 V:XVIII [...] out. That it was struck against you, was with a reed stem/cane which I have made in order that you awaken.

2 [...] reed the [...] upon (?) [...]

1 V:XIX *tjꜥm* plant, 1, pine nuts, 1, to be ground with wine, 1, to be applied to it/him.

2 Another: Now, it is Seth [who ...]. No[w, it is Seth who rages furiously (?) ...]

1 V:XX [...] upon his kidneys (?). The ve[rtebr]ae of his spine were br[ok]en. He sheds upon his le[g]

2 poi[so]ns [...] to strike against the [*gw*-bull (?). He] shall eliminate hi[s] acc[us]ers (?),

3 who exist with the accusation of slay[ing ...]

1 V:XXI [... lio]ns (?) then (?) [... the] fears which are upon the foreign countries while chewing [...]

2 [... dogs] th[e ch]ewing ones of [...]

Commentary

1–2 V:XVIII1–2: The meaning of the texts is obscure due to their fragmentary state.

1 V:XVIII1 (sic): This verb form is a *w*-passive used in an emphatic construction; see Gardiner 1988, 337–338 §420, 339–340 §422.1; Schenkel 2005a, 216–217; Schenkel 2005b, 40–49. — : WB I, 555.1, translates the word as 'Matte o. ä.'. TLA writes 'Rohrstängel, Matte/carpet, matting' (18.02.2016). — : The relative form has to be amended to *jr.<t>.n=j* because the antecedent is feminine (*pzš.t*).

2 V:XVIII2 : It is impossible to tell whether *js.w* is used here with the meaning 'workshop, chamber' (WB I, 127.2–6; perhaps a kind of word play) or 'reed' (WB I, 127.21–22); a reed is mentioned in the previous line, making that reading more likely, although here the determinative would be strange; so too Massart 1954, 111.4. — : The translation can also be '[...] face like [...]'.

1 V:XIX1 : The *tjꜥm* plant is an as yet unidentified plant which is only mentioned in medicinal texts. The drug is used in oral remedies, laxatives, ointments, bandages, and inhalations against cough, gastro-intestinal diseases, bladder problems, and skin ailments; see WB I, 241.12–13; GdM VI, 548–549; Germer 1979, 342–343; Charpentier 1981, 788–789; Westendorf 1999, I, 517; Germer 2008, 150. — : For pine nuts (?), see the commentary to lines 22–23 of incantation 2 (above §2). — : For wine, see the commentary to lines 20–21 of incantation 4 (above §4).

2 V:XIX2 : Something new starts here. Seth seems to play a major part. — : Here the word is used without a god's determinative (G7). — : The word is perhaps to be amended to *khꜣ* 'to storm' (WB V, 136.10–12) or *khb* 'to roar' (WB V, 127.2–15). See also the opening lines of incantation 4 (above §4).

1 V:XX1 : Massart 1954, 111.14, states that the sign is a scribal error and suggests reading *ḥwj* 'to strike', as in the line that follows (V:XX2). The water sign is very tightly written, but the writing is a bit sloppy in this part of the manuscript. Being liquids, poisons can be poured or shed (WB III, 48.16–22). It is not clear who is shedding the poisons upon whose legs.

2 V:XX2 : The word is perhaps to be connected with *gw* 'bull' (WB V, 159.5).

2–3 V:XX2 & : The word is only attested in this papyrus (WB I, 169.3). The determinatives suggest that the term designates a kind of person; and on the other hand, it is in the plural, which creates an incongruence with the possessive article *tꜣy=f* later in the same line, but without any determinatives. See also the commentary to line 3 (R:VIII12, IX2–3) of incantation 6 (above §6).

1 V:XXI1 [...]: The remains of the word can be amended to *mjw.w* 'cats' (WB II, 42.13) or *mꜣj.w* 'lions' (WB II, 11.14–19); so too Massart 1954, 111.19.

2 V:XXI2 [...]: The first part of the word is now missing. For this phrase, see also V:IV9, where Akhu is described as 'dog who chews bones' (lines 1–2 of incantation 12, above §16).

19. Incantation 14 (V:XXII1–3)

The beginning and the end of this incantation are missing and the middle part is broken off. The magician evokes Akhu and uses different tools to try to banish the demon. The incantation probably ends with the mention of an amulet.

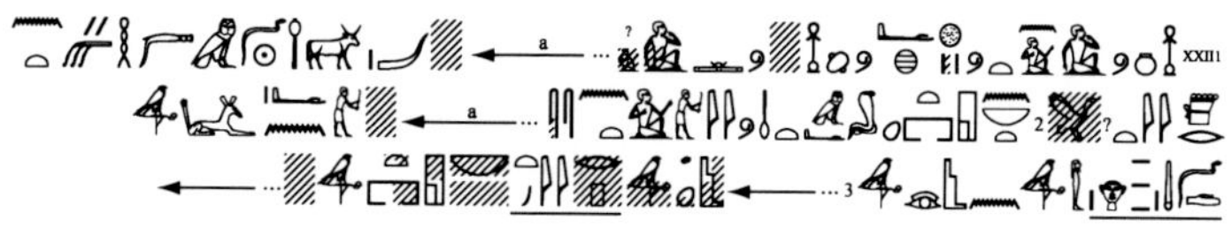

V:XXII1a, 2a: the distance between the fragments is uncertain.

Transliteration

		Verso
1	XXII1	*šn(w).n=j tw zp-sn <p3> ꜥḫ.w šn(w).[n]=j [tw zp-sn ... m] ꜥb n(.j) k3 ḥḏ m mḥ.y(t) n.t*
2	XXII1–2	*ḏry.t n(.t) Nb.t-ḥw.t m-dj.t ḫrw.y nts s[...] ꜥ n(.j) Stḫ(?)*
3	XXII2–3	*<u>ḏd mdw.w ḥr</u> twt n(.j) Wsjr [... 3s.t <u>rp]y.t</u> [Nb.t-ḥ]w.t [...]*

Translation

1 I conjured you, I conjured you, <o> Akhu! I conjured [you, I conjured you ... with] a horn of a white bull, with a feather of

2 a kite of Nephthys because of the disturber (?). It is she [...] the arm of the weather god (?).

3 <u>Words to be said over</u> an image of Osiris [... Isis, an <u>im]age</u> of [Nepht]hys [...].

Commentary

1–3 V:XXII1–3: It is not clear how much is missing at the beginning. Massart 1954, 112–113, cites this incantation as §14 verso.

1–2 V:XXII1–2 : Isis and Nephthys are known as kites. The Book of the Dead states: *jr šw.tj=fy m tp=f šm.t pw jr.n 3s.t ḥnꜥ Nb.t-ḥw.t rḏ.n=sn st r tp=f m wn=zn ḏr.ty* 'As to both the feathers of his head: Isis and Nephthys came and gave them to his head as they were kites' (BD Spell 17, 16–17; Naville 1886, I, XXIII); so too Massart 1954, 112.4.

2 V:XXII2 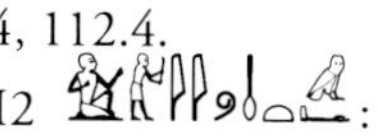: This passage is difficult to understand. For the meaning 'because of' for the preposition, see Lesko I, 201. It could also be translated as a prohibitive: 'Do not bluster!'– in this case the last determinative (sign A1) would have to be emended. — : The verb after the lacuna cannot be restored. It is not clear which particular meaning ꜥ has here. Ultimately one has to consider whether the weather god is acting here or Seth. The latter is more likely.

2–3 V:XXII2–3: The incantation ends with fragmentary instructions for making an amulet. The term *rpy.t* is usually used for female figures (Lesko II, 60), while the word *twt* is often used for images of male beings (WB V, 255.10). See also Massart 1954, 112–113.7, who compiled various instructions for amulets.

20. Conjuration 4 (V:XXII3–4)

This rather fragmentary piece gives the initial two lines of a conjuration (?) against any type of pain. Almost the entire spell is lost.

V: XXII3b–c: partially only traces.

Transliteration

		Verso
1	XXII3–4	*[...] hr m[n.w] nb{.t} mj.t n=j zp-sn Mw.t [... Wsjr ...]*

Translation

1 [V:XXII] [Incantation (?)] against any pain: Come to me, come to me, Mut [... Osiris ...]

Commentary

1 V:XXII3: At the beginning of the line, a term for incantation, spell or the like has to be amended. Obviously, it is at this point in the papyrus that the spells not directed against Sāmānu/Akhu begin. Massart 1954, 112–113, cites this spell as §14 verso. — *Mw.t*: For general information on Mut, see LGG III, 251–252, with further references. — *Wsjr*: For information on Osiris, see LGG II, 528–534, with further references.

21. Conjurations 5 and 6 (?) (V:XXIII1–XXIV6)

This incantation is (or: these incantations are) directed against afflictions of the feet which are not otherwise described, except for the fact that they hurt. The term *wḫd.w* is mentioned several times, and perhaps this is the cause of the ailment. It is not clear whether there are one or two spells, because the middle part is missing and only traces of a rubrum are visible (though wholly illegible).

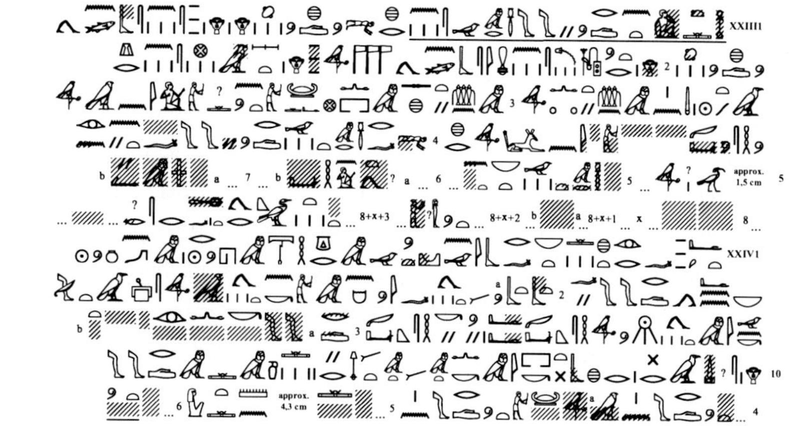

V:XXIII6a–b: partially only traces; 7a–b: partially only traces; 8+x+1a–b: traces in red; V:XXIV2a: 9 above the line; 3a–b lower part of the line is broken off; 4a is no longer legible.

Transliteration

		Verso
1	XXIII1	*[šn.t] n.t rd.wy mr=sn ḥr wḫd.w ḥr ḥr.w=sn s[b]n*
2	XXIII1–2	*wḫd.w [ḥr] t(w)r(.w)=sn mj sbn nṯr.[w] ḥr {spꜣ.tj.w} <spꜣ.wt> =sn ẖr*
3	XXIII2–3	*ꜣ.t mdw n(.j) Mḫnt.y-jr.tj m-ḫnt.y zẖm wḥꜥ.n.tw=j jn Ḥr(.w)*
4	XXIII3–4	*wḥs[(w).n(?).tw(?) ...] jn Stẖ ḥr r=f mr.(w)t rd.w[y]=f n.ty jr[.n]*
5	XXIII4–7	*[...] ꜣḫ [... mr].(w)t nb.(w)t n.t[t ...]t n=j ḥ[... wnm.y(?) ...]*
6	XXIII8–8+x+3	*[...] tw[t ...]t.wt ꜥḳ r [ẖ].t=f r sr [...]*
7	XXIV1	*ꜥ.wt=f jr(.w) (j)ḫ.wt nb.(w)t r=f bjn ḏw.(w)[t] m grḥ m hrw m nw*
8	XXIV1–2	*nb ꜥnn rd.wy=fy [t]btb.w nmt.t=f jw nḥm.n=k nmt.t [Ḥr(.w)] s:(j)ꜣt.*
9	XXIV2–3	*n=k {jm} nmt.t Jꜣḫ.w ḥsḳ(.w) [ꜥ].wy=ky ḥsḳ(.w) [r]d[.wy]=k[y] n [...] jr [...]t*
10	XXIV3	*ḥr s[ḏ]ꜣ {r' r} <r r'> ẖ[b].t=k jm=k mwt mwt.t ḥmw.t-r' ẖnm m rd.wy[=fy]*
11	XXIV4–6	*[... wḥꜥ.t]w rd [n(.j)] Ḥ[r(.w)] wḥ[ꜥ].tw rd n(.j) [Jꜣḫ.w ... mn ms.n] mn.t [...] tw [...]*

Translation

1 V:XXIII [Incantation] of both feet which are ill: 'pain' befalls their face. 'Pain'

2 sl[id]es [over] their red one (= blood) like the gods slide over the nomes under

3 the strength of the staff of Mekhenti-irti, the one in front of Letopolis. By Horus, I was released,

4 by Seth, [... was cut] off. Fall down, illness of bo[th] of his feet which d[o ...]

5 [...] every [ill]ness which [...] for me (?) [... right hand (?) ...]

6 [...] image [...] which enters his [tr]unk to [...]

7 V:XXIV his limbs. Everything was made against him, evilness (and) vicious[ness] by night (and) by day, at any

8 time. Both of his feet shall turn back while his stride staggers (?). You checked the stride of [Horus] (and) you twisted

9 the stride of Jakhu. (Just as) both of your [ar]ms were cut off, (so) both of your fe[et] were cut off. [...] not do [...]

10 bringing to the opening of your place of ex[ecu]tion. You shall not – dead man, dead woman etc. – unite with both of [his (?)] feet.

11 [...] The foot [of] Horus is [released]! The foot of [Jakhu] is released! [... NN whom] NN [has born ...]

Commentary

1–11: Massart 1954, 113–116, cites the incantation(s) as §15 verso.

1 V:XXIII1 : The term *wḫd.w* has been widely discussed, and scholars are still looking for a standardised meaning. See Wreszinksi 1913, 34–35; Ebbell 1938, 16–18; Steuer 1948; Jonckheere 1949, 267–270; Saunders 1963, 22–27, who adapts Steuer 1948; GdM VII.1, 207–215; Ghalioungui 1968, 44–45; Manjo 1975, 129; Westendorf 1992, 126–128; Bardinet 1995, 115, 120, 128–137; Nunn 1996, 61–62; Westendorf 1999, I, 329, 340–343; Kolta/Tessenow 2000, 38–52. See also Stephan 2001, 127–130, who only criticises these publications without offering any new approaches. The most convincing assumption is that *wḫd.w* designates a kind of aetiological principle, as suggested by Steuer 1948, 21, and Kolta/Tessenow 2000, 50–52. See also Massart 1954, 114.2.

2 V:XXIII2 : The literal translation is the 'red one', which designates blood. See WB V, 386.13; Blackman/Fairman 1943, 7.h; Harris 1961, 154–155; Wilson 1997, 1169. — : The meaning of the phrase is not entirely certain because of the word . If the word is indeed to be read *spꜣ.tj.w*, then the translation would be '... like the gods slide over the dwellers of the nome'. But if that is the case, an appropriate determinative, such as or the like, is missing. That is why the emendation of {*spꜣ.tj.w*} to <*spꜣ.wt*> is suggested. The sign (Aa8) is erroneously used for (N24). The former reading, *ḏꜣ.t* (to which Massart 1954, 114.4, refers besides *spꜣ.t*) had fallen out of use; see Berlev 1972, 234–238; Hannig 1995, 1101; Allen 2002, 32.

3 V:XXIII2 : Massart 1954, 114.5, suggests translating *ꜣ.t* as 'strength' (WB I, 2.3–4) rather than 'moment, instant, time' (WB I, 1.12–2.2) and refers to Gardiner 1948, 13–15, who says that the two interpretations go together and only express different shades of the term's meaning. In PT 325 (532a), the phrase is attested as 'under the strength/might before' (Sethe 1908, 271). — : For Mekhenti-irti, see the commentary to line 2 of conjuration 1 (above §12). See also Massart 1954, 114.7. — R:XXIII3 : Massart 1954, 114.8, suggests emending *m-ḫnt.j* to {*m*}-*ḫnt.j*, claiming the *m* is due to a dittography, but the reading *m-ḫnt.j* as a nominalised nisbe is also possible. — : As Massart 1954, 114.9, suggested, the determinatives are incorrectly written after .

4–6 V:XXIII4–8+x+3: The lines which follow are fragmentary or nearly broken off.

4 V:XXIII4 : The meaning of the word is not quite certain. It is perhaps to be amended to *ꜣḫ-bꜣ.w*; see LGG I, 24.

5 V:XXIII6 : Due to the fragmentary context, the signs *n=j* can designate the indirect object of the sentence or the ending of a *sḏm.n=f* form.

6 V:XXIII8+x+1: The remains of this line show traces of red ink, but they are illegible. They can be part of a rubrum, in which case this conjuration (5) ends here and a conjuration (6 ?) with identical content follows. It is also possible that the traces of red ink are merely remains of the name of a hostile creature such as Apophis, and that the spell simply continues. See also Massart 1954, 115.12. — V:XXIII8+x+3 ▨: This group is covered with tape.

8 V:XXIV2 〔hieroglyphs〕: The term is not attested with these determinatives. The determinative ⌐ suggests a negative action. It is perhaps to be connected with *dbdb* 'to cut up' (WB V, 442.6–12) or *ḏbḏb* 'to crush (by treading)' (Lesko IV, 158; Černý 1976, 318; Dawson/Peet 1933, Pl. XXIX line 7; Hannig 1995, 1005). In reference 2 of WB II, 297, it is translated as 'schwanken (?) (to stagger)'. The translation 'to stagger' or 'to crush' would fit the context.

8–9 V:XXIV2 〔hieroglyphs〕: For the meaning of the word *s(j)ꜣt* as 'to distort/twist', see Vogelsang 1913, 94.99–100b, 98.105, 178.250; WB IV, 27.3–4; see also Massart 1954, 115.15.

9 V:XXIV2 〔hieroglyphs〕: Jakhu designates (sun)shine or radiance, particularly that of Re. If the stride of Jakhu is halted, the sun stagnates. Massart 1954, 115.16, refers to PT 456 (852d–e): *wn n=k ṯpḥ.wt pt(r).w snfḫfḫ n=k nmt.wt Jꜣḫ.w* 'For you, the caverns of 'seers' are opened, for you, the stride of Jakhu is loosened' (Sethe 1908, 475); PT 503 (1078a–d): *wn p.t wn tꜣ wn.y ṯpḥ.wt ptr.w wn.y nmt.wt Nn.w sfḫḫ nmt.wt jꜣḫ.w (...)* 'The sky opens (and) the earth opens. The caverns of 'seers' are opened (and) the stride of Nun is opened, the stride of Jakhu is loosened (...)' (Sethe 1910, 93); and PT 604 (1680b–c): *wn n=k ṯpḥ.t pt(r) jsḥ n<=k> n<m>j.t{=k} jꜣḫ.w* 'For you, the cavern of the 'seer' is opened, for <you>, the str<id>e of Jakhu is loosened (?)' (Sethe 1910, 388). A similar statement is found in BD 67: *wn ṯḥp.wt jm.j.w Nn.w znfḫfḫ nmt.wt jm.j.w Jꜣḫ.w* 'The caverns are opened for those who are in Nun, the stride is loosened for those who are in Jakhu' (Naville 1886, I, LXXXIX). For general information on Jakhu, see Englung 1994, 173–175; Jansen-Winkeln 1996, 206–208.

10 V:XXIV3 〔hieroglyphs〕: One expects the determinative ⌒, not ✕. See WB IV, 378.13, 378.18; so too Massart 1954, 115.18.

10–11 V:XXIV3–4 〔hieroglyphs〕: Massart 1954, 115.20, suggests restoring *rd.wj=[ky]*. *Rd.wj=[fy]* would be more appropriate in this context because the ailment is addressed in the second person masculine singular and the feet have to belong to a patient.

11 V:XXIV4–5 '[...] The foot [of] Horus is [released]! The foot of [Jakhu] is released! [... NN whom] NN [has born ...]': The last part of the conjuration implies that the patient's feet have been released the same way the feet of Horus and Jakhu were released, in other words the feet of the patient have been healed; see also Massart 1954, 115.21.

22. Spells 1–3 (V:XXV)

These very short spells are for the 'falling of water'. The last one consists only of *k.t* 'another' and approx. 29 cm of blank space, so one gets the impression that the scribe's intention was to finish the papyrus later.

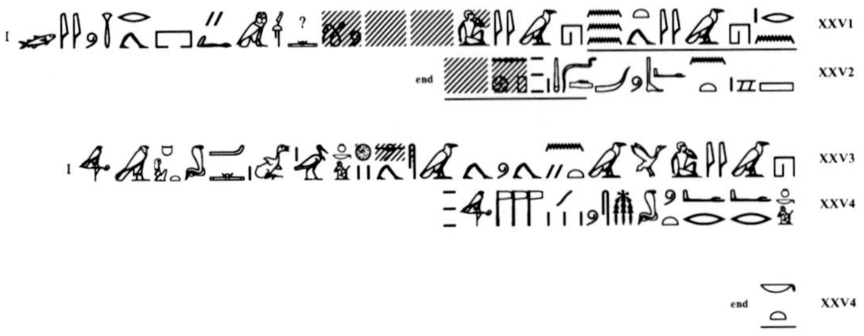

V:XXVI From the end of this column to the end of the papyrus approx. 29 cm are blank.

Transliteration

		Verso
1	XXV1	*r' n(.j) hꜣy.t mw hꜣy [...] rwḏ(?) wnm.y pr <m> wꜣḏy(.t)*
2	XXV2	*n.t ꜥb(w) ḏd mdw.w zp [...]*
1	XXV3	*hꜣy pꜣ n.ty jw ꜣs zp-sn jnk Bꜣ-ṯꜣ-ḥw ḥm.t Ḥr(.w)*
2	XXV4	*jnk ꜥrꜥr(w).t ms{.w} nṯr.w*
1	XXV4	*k.t*

Translation

1 V:XXV Spell of falling of water: O, [...] the right hand which comes forth from Wadji-
2 of-the-horn. Words to be said [...] times.
1 V:XXV Jubilation to the one who comes in great haste. I am Baṯaḥ, the wife of Horus.
2 I am the serpent, the child of the gods!
1 V:XXV Another.

Commentary

1–2, 1–2, 1 V:XXV1–4: Massart 1954, 116, cites these spells as §16 verso.

1 V:XXV1  'Spell of falling of water': The meaning of the spell is not certain. It does not seem to be an utterance for rain magic, because Egyptian has several words for 'rain', for example *mw n.j p.t* (WB II, 51.2) and *ḥw.t* (WB III, 49.1–3). Massart 1954, 116, discusses the meaning as 'utterance for the falling <into> water', but admits that someone who was drowning would not have time to recite a spell and the content of the text 'lack[s] the note of danger or anxiety which certainly would be present if such was the meaning' (Massart 1954, 116). Another possibility

would be that the meaning refers to urinating in a rather euphemistic way. But if this were the case, the expression would be otherwise unattested and, again, the content does not imply something like this. — : The remains of the word allow no certain restoration. One possible restoration is *rwḏ* 'firmness, strength' (WB II, 412. 10–12), which can be used in connection with the arms but is only attested with the lexeme ꜥ. The translation would then be 'o, firmness of the right hand (...)' – a genitive construction – or 'o, firm-of-right-hand (...)' – the accusative of respect.

1–2 V:XXV1–2 : Massart 1954, 46, suggests reading or . The sign seems to be *wꜣḏ* (M13), even if the upper 'stroke' is missing. See for example *wꜣḏ* in V:II7. The nisbe implies that the word originally was feminine. The toponym (?) is otherwise unattested. The determinative of *wꜣd.y(t)* suggests it was a kind of lake or pool. There exists a species of fish with the name *wḏj* (WB I, 399.7–8), which the 'lake' was probably named after. Alternatively, it could be connected with the word *wḏ* 'Bezeichnung für ein Gewässer ?' (WB I, 399.11).

2 V:XXV2 : The number of times the spell was to be recited has not been preserved.

3 V:XXV3: This spell (?) starts without any other introduction. The scribe probably omitted the *k.t* at the beginning. Massart 1954, 116, writes '[<u>*Another*</u> (?)]' at the end of the previous line. It is very unlikely that *k.t* was written there because the end of the line is blank. — : This wife of Horus is only attested here. For general information on the wives of Horus, see Borghouts 1971, 149–151 and the commentary to line 1 R:XVIIx+1 of the recto fragments (above §9).

2 V:XXV4 : This is an alternative writing of *jꜥr.t* '(divine) serpent, Uraeus' (WB I, 42.1–4). — : The term is difficult to integrate in the context. Massart 1954, 116, translates it as 'the offspring of the gods', whereby the plural has to be emended (*ms*{.*w*}). Alternatively, it is possible that the feminine *t*-ending was omitted, in which case *ms*{.*w*}<.*t*>would have to be amended, so the translation would be 'I am the serpent who has given birth to the gods' (participle) or 'I am the serpent whom the gods bring forth' (relative form). The (divine) serpent or uraeus is brought forth by Re or can designate different kinds of goddesses, including a primeval goddess (LGG I, 140–141). The meaning is still odd.

1 V:XXV : The introduction of another spell follows. Obviously the scribe never came back to finish his work.

Abbreviations

ACES	Australian Centre for Egyptology Studies
AE	Ancient Egypt and the East
ÄA	Ägyptologische Abhandlungen
ÄAT	Ägypten und Altes Testament
ÄOP	Ägyptische und orientalische Papyri und Handschriften des Ägyptischen Museums und Papyrussammlung Berlin
AfO	Archiv für Orientforschung
AH	Aegyptiaca Helvetica
AHw	Akkadisches Handwörterbuch, see Soden, W. von, 1965–1981
ALASP(M)	Abhandlungen zur Literatur Alt-Syrien-Palästinas (und Mesopotamiens)
AO	Der Alte Orient
AOAT	Alter Orient und Altes Testament
AoF	Altorientalische Forschungen
AOS	American Oriental Series
ArOr	Archiv Orientální: Quarterly Journal of African and Asian Studies
ASAE	Annales du service des antiquités de l'Égypte
ASJ	Acta Sumerologica Japonica
AW	Antike Welt
BACE	Bulletin of the Australian Centre for Egyptology
BAe	Bibliotheca Aegyptiaca
BD	Book of the Dead
BIFAO	Bulletin de l'Institut français d'Archéologie Orientale
BiOr	Bibliotheca Orientalis
BN	Biblische Notizen
CAD	The Assyrian Dictionary of the University of Chicago, see Gelb, I.J., *et al.* (eds.), 1956–2010
CAT	The Cuneiform Alphabetic Texts from Ugarit, see Dietrich, M./Loretz, O./Sanmartín, J., 1995
CdÉ	Chronique d'Égypte
CT	Coffin Texts, see Buck, A. de, 1935–1961
DE	Discussions in Egyptology
DFIFAO	Documents de fouilles de l'institut français d'archéologie orientale du Caire
DHF	Deities-Hathors-Formula
DNWSI	Dictionary of the North-west Semitic Inscriptions, see Hoftijzer, J./Jongeling, K., 1995
DUL	Dictionary of the Ugaritic Language, see Olmo Lete, G. del/Sanmartín, J., 2003

ET	Études et travaux, Travaux du centre d'archéologie méditerranéenne de l'académie polonaise des sciences
Flora	Flora of Iraq, see Guest, E./ar-Rawi, A., *et al.* (eds.), 1966–1985
FS	Festschrift
GdM	Grundriss der Medizin der Alten Ägypter, see Grapow, H./Deines, H. von/Westendorf, W., 1954–1962
GM	Göttinger Miszellen
GOF	Göttinger Orientforschungen, IV. Reihe, Ägypten
HÄB	Hildesheimer Ägyptologische Beiträge
HAL	Hebräisches und Aramäisches Lexikon, see Koehler, L./Baumgartner, W., 1967–1995
HdO	Handbuch der Orientalistik, I. Abteilung
JEA	Journal of Egyptian Archaeology
JMC	Le Journal des médecines cunéiformes
JNES	Journal of Near Eastern Studies
JRAS	Journal of the Royal Asiatic Society of Great Britain and Ireland
LÄ	Lexikon der Ägyptologie
LGG	Lexikon der Götter und Götterbezeichnungen, see Leitz, C. (ed.), 2002–2003
LingAeg	Lingua Aegyptia, Journal of Egyptian Language Studies
MÄS	Münchner Ägyptologische Studien
MARI	MARI, Annales de Recherches Interdisciplinaires
MDAIK	Mitteilungen des Deutschen Archäologischen Instituts, Abteilung Kairo
Meeks	Année lexicographique, see Meeks, D., 1980–1982
MIFAO	Mémoires publiés par les membres de l'institut français d'archéologie orientale
MMAF	Mémoires publiés par les membres de la mission archéologique française au Caire
MPER	Mitteilungen aus der Papyrussammlung der Österreichischen Nationalbibliothek Erzherzog Rainer
NISABA	Religious Texts Translation Series, NISABA
OBO	Orbis Biblicus et Orientalis
OLA	Orientalia Lovaniensia Analecta
OLZ	Orientalistische Literaturzeitung
OMRO	Oudheidkundige Mededelingen uit het Rijksmuseum van Oudheden
Or	Orientalia
OrAnt	Oriens Antiquus
PdÄ	Probleme der Ägyptologie
PIFAO	Publications de l'institut français d'archéologie orientale du Caire
PMMA	Publications of the Metropolitan Museum of Art (Egyptian Expedition)
PSBA	Proceedings of the Society of Biblical Archaeology
PT	Pyramid Texts
RdÉ	Revue d'Égyptologie

SAK	Studien zur Altägyptischen Kultur
SANER	Studies in Ancient Near Eastern Records
SAOC	Studies in Ancient Oriental Civilisation
SBL	Society of Biblical Literature
SDAIK	Sonderschrift des Deutschen Archäologischen Instituts, Abteilung Kairo
SourcesOr	Sources orientales
Syria	Syria, Revue d'art oriental et d'archéologie
TUAT N.F.	Texte aus der Umwelt des Alten Testaments, Neue Folge
UF	Ugarit-Forschungen, Internationales Jahrbuch für die Altertumskunde Syrien-Palästinas
UGAÄ	Untersuchungen zur Geschichte und Altertumskunde Ägyptens
Urk. IV	Urkunden der 18. Dynastie, Historisch-biographische Urkunden IV, see Sethe, K., 1956
VIO	Veröffentlichungen des Instituts für Orientforschung, Deutsche Akademie der Wissenschaften zu Berlin
WB	Wörterbuch der aegyptischen Sprache, see Erman, A./Grapow, H. (eds.), 1926–1950
WZKM	Wiener Zeitschrift für die Kunde des Morgenlandes
ZÄS	Zeitschrift für ägyptische Sprache und Altertumskunde

Bibliography

Abusch, T./Schwemer, D., 2008: Texte aus Mesopotamien, 3: Das Abwehrzauber-Ritual *Maqlu* („Verbrennung"), in: Abusch, T. (ed.), Omina, Orakel, Rituale und Beschwörungen, TUAT N.F. 4, Gütersloh, 128–186.

Aḥituv, S., 1984: Canaanite toponyms in Ancient Egyptian documents, Jerusalem.

Allen, J.P., 1984: The inflections of the verb in the Pyramid Texts, Bibliotheca Aegyptia 2, Malibu.

Allen, J.P., 2002: The Heqanakht papyri, PMMA 27, New York.

Alpin, P., 1980: Plantes d'Égypte, 1581–1584, traduit du latin, présenté et annoté par R. de Fenoyl, Voyageurs occidentaux en Égypte, Cairo.

Altenmüller, H., 1977: Gliedervergottung, in: LÄ II, Wiesbaden, 624–627.

Arnold, F., 1990: The control notes and team marks, the south cemeteries of Lisht, II, PMMA 23, New York.

Aufrère, S., 1983: Études de lexicologie et d'histoire naturelle I–III, BIFAO 83, 1–31.

Ayali-Darshan, N., 2015: The identification of *ḥmrḳ* in Leiden Magical Papyrus I 343 + I 345 in light of the Eblaite texts, JNES 74, 87–89.

Bardinet, T., 1995: Les papyrus médicaux de l'Égypte pharaonique, traduction intégrale et commentaire, Penser la médicine, Paris.

Barns, J.W.B. (ed.), 1956: Five Ramesseum papyri, Oxford.

Barta, W., 1973: Untersuchungen zum Götterkreis der Neunheit, MÄS 28, Berlin.

Baum, N., 1988: Arbes et arbustes de l'Égypte ancienne, la liste de la tombe thébaine d'Ineni (n° 81), OLA 31, Leuven.

Baum, N., 1994: *sntr*: une revision, RdÉ 45, 17–39.

Bayoumi, A., 1940: Autour du champ des souchets et du champ des offrandes, Cairo.

Beck, S., 2015a: Sāmānu: Konzepte der Dämonendarstellung, in: Neunert, G./Simon, H./Verbovsek, A./Gabler, K. (eds.), Text: Wissen – Wirkung – Wahrnehmung, Beiträge des vierten Münchner Arbeitskreises Junge Aegyptologie (MAJA 4), 29.11. bis 1.12.2013, GOF IV/59, Wiesbaden, 89–103.

Beck, S., 2015b: Sāmānu, ein vorderasiatischer Dämon in Ägypten, ÄAT 83, Münster.

Beck, S., 2015c: Sāmānu as a human disease, JMC 26, 33–46.

Berlev, O.D., 1972: Trudovoye naseleniye Egipta v epokhu srednego tsarstva, Moscow.

Bierbrier, M.L., 2012: Who was who in Egyptology, London.

Bissing, F.W. von/Blok, H.P., 1926: Eine Weihung an die sieben Hathoren, ZÄS 61, 83–93.

Blackman, A.M., 1932: Middle-Egyptian stories, I, BAe 2, Brussels.

Blackman, A.M./Fairman, H.W., 1943: The myth of Horus at Edfu, II, JEA 29, 2–36.

Bordreuil, P./Caquot, A., 1980: Les textes en cunéiformes alphabétiques découverts en 1978 à Ibn Hani, Syria 57, 343–367.

Bordreuil, P./Pardee, D., 1993: Le combat de Baʿlu avec Yammu d'après les textes ougaritiques, MARI 7, 63–70.

Boreux, C., 1939: La stèle C.86 du musée du Louvre et les stèles similaires, in: Extrait des mélanges syriens offerts à M.R. Dussaud, II, 673–687.

Borghouts, J.F., 1971: The magical texts of Papyrus Leiden I 348, Leiden.

Borghouts, J.F., 1978: Ancient Egyptian magical texts, NISABA 9, Leiden.

Boulos, L., 1983: Medicinal plants of North Africa, Algonac.

Breasted, J.H., 1930: The Edwin Smith Surgical Papyrus, I, Chicago.

Brunner-Traut, E., 1965: Spitzmaus und Ichneumon als Tiere des Sonnengottes, in: Schott, S. (ed.), Göttinger Vorträge vom Ägyptologischen Kolloquium der Akademie am 25. und 26. August 1964, Göttingen, 123–163.

Brunner-Traut, E., 1975: Chenti-irti, in: LÄ I, Wiesbaden, 926–930.

Buck, A. de, 1935–1961: The Egyptian coffin texts, I–VII, Chicago.

Buck, A. de, 1948: On the meaning of the name *ḥ'pj*, Orientalia Neerlandica, Leiden, 1–22.

Buck, A. de/Stricker, B.H., 1940: Teksten tegen schorpioenen naar pap. I 349, OMRO 21, 53–62.

Budge, E.A.W., 1910: The chapters of coming forth by day or the Theban recension of the Book of the Dead, the Egyptian hieroglyphic text edited from numerous papyri, I, London.

Burchardt, M., 1910: Die altkanaanäischen Fremdworte und Eigennamen im Aegyptischen, Listen der syllabisch geschriebenen Worte sowie die altkanaanäischen Fremdworte und Eigennamen, II, Leipzig.

Caminos, R.A., 1954: Late-Egyptian miscellanies, London.

Caminos, R.A., 1977: A tale of woe, from a hieratic papyrus in the A.S. Pushkin Museum of Fine Arts in Moscow, Oxford.

Cannuyer, C., 1990: Recherches sur l'onomasiologie du feu en ancien Égyptien, ZÄS 117, 103–111.

Caquot, A., 1960: Les rephaim ougaritiques, Syria 37, 75–93.

Černý, J., 1932: The abnormal-hieratic tablet Leiden I 431, in: Mond, R. (ed.), Studies presented to F.Ll. Griffith on his seventieth birthday, London, 46–56.

Černý, J., 1949: On the origin of the Egyptian conjunctive, JEA 35, 25–30.

Černý, J., 1952: Paper & books in Ancient Egypt, London.

Černý, J., 1976: Coptic etymological dictionary, Cambridge/London *et al.*

Černý, J./Gardiner, A.H., 1957: Hieratic ostraca, I–II, Oxford.

Černý, J./Israelit-Groll, S., 1984: A late Egyptian grammar, Rome.

Chabas, F., 1860: Le papyrus magique Harris, Chalon-sur-Saône.

Chabas, F., 1862: Notice sommaire des papyrus hiératiques égyptiens I.343–371 du Musée d'Antiquités des Pays-Bas à Leide, in: Leemans, C. (ed.), Monumens égyptiens du Musée d'Antiquités des Pays-Bas à Leide, Monumens de la religion et du culte public et privé, II.21, Leiden, 62–79.

Chabas, F.J., 1901: Notices sommaires des papyrus hiératiques égyptiens I. 343–371 du Musée d'Antiquités des Pays-Bas à Leyde, Paris.

Chabas, F., 1902: Œuvres diverses II, Bibliothèque Égyptologique 10, Paris, 131–171.

Charpentier, G., 1981: Recueil de matériaux épigraphiques relatifs à la botanique de l'Égypte antique, Paris.

Chassinat, É., 1892: Le temple d'Edfou, I, MMAF 10, Paris.

Chassinat, É., 1930: Le temple d'Edfou, V, MMAF 22, Paris.

Chassinat, É., 1934: Le temple de Dendera, II, Cairo.

Chassinat, É., 1966: Le mystère d'Osiris au mois de Khoiak, 1, PIFAO, Cairo.

Chemettre, M./Goyon, J.-C., 1996: Le catalogue raisonné des producteurs de styrax et d'oliban d'Edfou et d'Athribis de Haute Égypte, SAK 23, 47–82.

Clère, J.J., 1952: La lecture de la fraction "deux tiers" en Égyptien, ArOr 20, 629–641.

Cook, S.A., 1930: The religion of ancient Palestine in the light of archaeology, Schweich lectures of the British Academy 1925, London, 112.

Cornelius, I., 1994: The iconography of the Canaanite gods Reshef and Ba'al, Late Bronze and Iron Age I periods (c 1500–1000 BCE), OBO 140, Freiburg (Switzerland).

Cornelius, I., 2004: The many faces of the goddess, the iconography of the Syro-Palestinian goddesses Anat, Astarte, Qedeshet, and Ashera *c.* 1500–1000 BCE, OBO 204, Freiburg (Switzerland).

Couroyon, B., 1964: Trois épithètes de Ramsès II, Or 33, 443–462.

Crum, W.E., 1939: A Coptic dictionary, Oxford.

Daumas, F., 1975: L'offrande simultanée de l'encens et de l'or dans les temples de l'époque tardive, RdÉ 27, 102–109.

Dawson, W.R., 1927: The number 'seven' in Egyptian texts, Aegyptus 8, 97–107.

Dawson, W.R., 1928: The pig in Ancient Egypt, a commentary on two passages of Herodotus, JRAS 28, 597–608.

Dawson, W.R., 1931: Notes on Egyptian magic, Aegyptus 11/1, 23–28.
Dawson, W.R., 1934a: Studies in the Egyptian medical texts – III, JEA 20, 41–46.
Dawson, W.R., 1934b: Studies in the Egyptian medical texts – IV, JEA 20, 185–188.
Dawson, W.R., 1949: Anastasi, Sallier, and Harris and their papyri, JEA 39, 158–166.
Dawson, W.R./Peet, T.E., 1933: The so-called poem on the King's chariot, JEA 19, 167–174.
Derchain, P., 1962: Mythes et dieux lunaires en Égypte, SourcesOr V, 17–67.
Dévaud, E., 1911: A propos d'un groupe hiératique, ZÄS 49, 106–116.
Dhorme, É./Dessaud, R., 1949: Les religions de Babylonie et d'Assyrie, Les religions des Hittites et des Hourrites, des Phéniciens et des Syriens, I–II, Paris.
Dietrich, M./Loretz, O./Sanmartín, J., 1995: The cuneiform alphabetic texts from Ugarit, Ras Ibn Hani and other places (KTU: second, enlarged edition), ALASPM 8, Münster.
Draby, W.J./Ghalioungui, P./Grivetti, L., 1977: Food, the gift of Osiris, I–II, London/New York/San Francisco.
Drioton, É., 1938: Note sur un cryptogramme récemment découvert à Athribis, ASAE 38, 109–116.
Drioton, É., 1955: Boekbesprekingen – Egyptologie: A. Massart, The Leiden Magical Papyrus I 343 + 345, Leyde 1954, BiOr 12, 163–166.
DuQuesne, T., 2002: La déification des parties du corps, correspondances magiques et identification avec les dieux dans l'Égypte ancienne, in: Koenig, Y. (ed.), La magie en Égypte: à la recherche d'une définition, Actes du colloque organisé par le musée du Louvre les 29 et 30 septembre 2000, Paris, 237–271.
Ebbell, B., 1937: The Papyrus Ebers, the greatest Egyptian medical document, London/Copenhagen.
Ebbell, B., 1938: Alt-ägyptische Bezeichnungen für Krankheiten und Symptome, Skrifter utgitt av det Norske Videnskaps-Akademi i Oslo, II. Hist.-Filos. Klasse, 3, Oslo.
Edel, E., 1970: Die Felsengräber des Qubbet el Hawa bei Assuan, II: Die althieratischen Topfaufschriften, I: Die Topfaufschriften aus den Grabungsjahren 1960, 1961, 1962, 1963 und 1965, 2. Teil, Text (Fortsetzung), Wiesbaden.
Edwards, I.E.S., 1960: Oracular amuletic decrees of the Late New Kingdom, I–II, Hieratic Papyri in the British Museum, Fourth Series, London.
Englund, G., 1994: La lumière et la répartition des textes dans la pyramide, BdÉ 106 I (= FS J. Leclant I), 169–180.
Enmarch, R., 2005: A world upturned, commentary on and analysis of the dialogue of Ipuwer and the Lord of All, Oxford.
Erman, A., 1901: Zaubersprüche für Mutter und Kind aus dem Papyrus 3027 des Berliner Museums, Berlin.
Erman, A., 1909: Assimilation des ʿAjin an andre schwache Konsonanten, ZÄS 46, 96–104.
Erman, A., 1933: Neuaegyptische Grammatik, Leipzig.
Erman, A./Grapow, H. (eds.), 1926–1950: Wörterbuch der aegyptischen Sprache, I–VI, Berlin/Leipzig.
Eschweiler, P., 1994: Bildzauber im Alten Ägypten, OBO 137, Freiburg (Switzerland).
Faulkner, R.O., 1962: A concise dictionary of Middle Egyptian, Oxford.
Fischer-Elfert, H.-W., 1983: Textkritische und lexikographische Notizen zu den Late Egyptian Miscellanies, SAK 10, 141–149.
Fischer-Elfert, H.-W., 2005a: Altägyptische Zaubersprüche, Stuttgart.
Fischer-Elfert, H.-W., 2005b: Abseits von Maʿat, Fallstudien zu Außenseitern im Alten Ägypten, Würzburg.
Fischer-Elfert, H.-W., 2011: Sāmānu on the Nile: the transfer of a Near Eastern demon and magico-medical concepts into the New Kingdom, in: Collier, M./Snape, S. (eds.), Ramesside studies in honour of K.A. Kitchen, Bolton, 189–198.
Fischer-Elfert, H.-W., 2015: Magika Hieratika in Berlin, Hannover, Heidelberg und München, mit einem Beitrag von M. Krutzsch, ÄOP 1, Berlin/Munich *et al.*
Fleming, D., 1991: The voice of the Ugaritic incantation priest (RIH 78/20), UF 23, 141–154.
Frandsen, P.J., 1974: An outline of the Late Egyptian verbal system, Copenhagen.
Frohn, B., 2007: Lexikon der Heilpflanzen und ihrer Wirkstoffe, Augsburg.

Frohne, D., 2002: Heilpflanzenlexikon, ein Leitfaden auf wissenschaftlicher Grundlage, Stuttgart.

Fulco, W.J., 1976: The Canaanite god Rešep, AOS/Essay 8, New Haven.

Gardiner, A.H., 1906: Miszellen: the goddess Ningal in an Egyptian text, ZÄS 43, 97.

Gardiner, A.H., 1909: The admonitions of an Egyptian sage from a hieratic papyrus in Leiden (Pap. Leiden 344 recto), Leipzig.

Gardiner, A.H., 1911a: "To wait for" in Egyptian, ZÄS 49, 100–102.

Gardiner, A.H., 1911b: Egyptian hieratic texts, I, Papyrus Anastasi I and the Papyrus Koller, Leipzig.

Gardiner, A.H., 1912: Review, PSBA 34, 257–265.

Gardiner, A.H., 1915: Magic (Egyptian), in: Hastings, J. (ed.), Encyclopedia of Religion & Ethica, 8, Edinburgh/New York, 262–269.

Gardiner, A.H., 1916a: Some personifications II, Ḥu "Authoritative Utteranc", Sia "Understanding", PSBA 38, 43–54, 83–95.

Gardiner, A.H., 1916b: Notes on the story of Sinuhe, Paris.

Gardiner, A.H., 1928: An Egyptian split infinitive and the origin of the Coptic conjunctive tense, JEA 14, 86–96.

Gardiner, A.H., 1930: A new letter to the dead, JEA 16, 19–22.

Gardiner, A.H., 1935: Hieratic papyri in the British Museum, Third Series, I–II, London.

Gardiner, A.H., 1937: Late-Egyptian miscellanies, BAe 7, Brussels.

Gardiner, A.H., 1947: Ancient Egyptian onomastica, I–II, Oxford.

Gardiner, A.H., 1948: The first pages of the Wörterbuch, JEA 34, 12–18.

Gardiner, A.H., 1988: Egyptian grammar, Oxford.

Gauthier, H., 1925–1931: Dictionnaire des noms géographiques contenues dans les textes hiéroglyphiques, I–VII, Cairo.

Gelb, I.J., *et al.* (eds.), 1956–2010: The Assyrian dictionary of the Oriental Institute of the University of Chicago, 1–21, Chicago/Glückstadt.

Germer, R., 1979: Untersuchung über Arzneimittelpflanzen im Alten Ägypten, Hamburg.

Germer, R., 1985: Flora des pharaonischen Ägyptens, SDAIK 14, Wiesbaden.

Germer, R., 2002: Die Heilpflanzen der Ägypter, Dusseldorf/Zurich.

Germer, R., 2008: Handbuch der altägyptischen Heilpflanzen, Philippika: Marburger altertumskundliche Abhandlungen 21, Wiesbaden.

Ghalioungui, P., 1968: La notion de maladie dans les textes égyptiens et ses rapports avec la théorie humorale, BIFAO 66, 37–48.

Goede, B., 2006: Die „Dreckapotheke" der Ägypter, das Erwachen der Heilkunst im Alten Ägypten, AW 37/6, 8–14.

Görg, M., 1987: Ein Gott Amalek?, BN 40, 14–15.

Golenischeff, W.S., 1877: Die Metternichstele in der Originalgröße zum ersten Mal herausgegeben, Leipzig.

Golenischeff, W.S., 1913: Les papyrus hiératiques No 1115, 1116A et 1116B de l'Ermitage impérial à St.-Pétersbourg, St. Petersburg.

Goyon, J.-C., 1985: Les dieux-gardiens et la genèse des temples (d'après les textes de l'époque gréco-romaine), les soixante d'Edfou et les soixante-dix-sept dieux de Pharbaethos, BdÉ 93, Cairo.

Goyon, J.-C., 2003: Sources d'étude de la parfumerie sacrée de l'antique Égypte. Résines, gommes-résines, et oléo-résines. Essai de bilan et problèmes à résoudre, in: LeBlanc, C., *et al.* (eds.), Parfums, onguents et cosmétiques dans l'Egypte ancienne: actes des rencontres pluridisciplinaires tenues au Conseil national de la culture, Le Caire, 27–29 avril 2002, Memnonia, Suppl. 1, Cairo, 51–65.

Grapow, H., 1939: Wie die Alten Aegypter sich anredeten, wie sie sich grüssten und wie sie miteinander sprachen, I: Zum Formalen und Syntaktischen der Anreden, Anrufe, Ausrufe, Wünsche und Grüße, Abhandlungen der Preußischen Akademie der Wissenschaften, Philosophisch-historische Klasse, 11, Berlin.

Grapow, H./Deines, H. von/Westendorf, W., 1954–1962: Grundriss der Medizin der Alten Ägypter, I–VIII, Berlin.

Gray, I., 1979: The blood bath of the goddess Anat in the Ras Shamra texts, UF 11, 315–324.

Grdseloff, B., 1942: Les débuts du culte de Rechef en Égypte, Cairo.

Grieshammer, R., 1975: Chontamenti, in: LÄ I, Wiesbaden, 964–965.

Griffiths, J.G., 1958: A postscript on Khenty-ierty, CdÉ 33, 192–193.

Guest, E./ar-Rawi, A., *et al.* (eds.), 1966–1985: Flora of Iraq, I–IV, VIII–IX, Glasgow/Baghdad.

Guiter, J., 2001: Contraception en Égypte ancienne, BIFAO 101, 221–236.

Gunn, B., 1924: Studies in Egyptian syntax, Paris.

Győry, H., 2002: „Öffnen des Sehens", Gedanken über das Rezept Ebers 344, GM 189, 47–57.

Haas, V., 1981: Zwei Gottheiten aus Ebla in hethitischer Überlieferung, OrAnt 20, 251–257.

Haas, V., 1994: Geschichte der hethitischen Religion, HdO I, 15, Leiden/New York *et al.*

Hallo, W.W./Younger, K.L. Jr. (eds.), 1997: The context of scripture, canonical compositions from the biblical world, Leiden/New York *et al.*

Hannig, R., 1995: Großes Handwörterbuch Ägyptisch-Deutsch (2800–950 v. Chr.), Kulturgeschichte der Antiken Welt 64, Mainz.

Harris, J.R., 1961: Lexicographical studies in Ancient Egyptian minerals, VIO 54, Berlin.

Hayes, W.C., 1942: Ostraca and name stones from the tomb of Sen-Mūt (No. 71) at Thebes, PMMA 15, New York.

Helck, W., 1971: Die Beziehungen Ägyptens zu Vorderasien im 3. und 2. Jahrtausend v. Chr., ÄA 5, Wiesbaden.

Helck, W., 1977: Hathoren, sieben, in: LÄ II, Wiesbaden, 1033.

Helck, W., 1982: Mond, in: LÄ IV, Wiesbaden, 192–196.

Hiller, K./Melzig, M.F., 2010: Lexikon der Arzneipflanzen und Drogen, Heidelberg.

Hoch, J.E., 1994: Semitic words in Egyptian texts of the New Kingdom and the Third Intermediate Period, Princeton.

Höting, H., 1997a: Lebenssaft Urin, die heilende Kraft, Augsburg.

Höting, H., 1997b: Heilkraft des Urins, Diagnose – Anwendung – Wirkung, Munich.

Hoftijzer, J./Jongeling, K., 1995: Dictionary of the north-west Semitic inscriptions, I–II, HdO I, 21.1–2, Leiden.

Hopfner, T., 1913: Der Tierkult der Alten Ägypter nach den griechisch-römischen Berichten und den wichtigeren Denkmälern, Denkschrift der Kaiserlichen Akademie der Wissenschaften in Wien, Vienna, 60–63.

Hoppe, H.A., 1958: Drogenkunde, Handbuch der pflanzlichen und tierischen Rohstoffe, Hamburg.

Hornung, E., 1975–1976: Das Buch von der Anbetung des Re im Westen (Sonnenlitanei), nach den Versionen des Neuen Reiches, I–II, AH 2–3, Basel/Geneva.

Hornung, E., 1982: Der Ägyptische Mythos von der Himmelskuh, eine Ätiologie des Unvollkommenen, OBO 46, Freiburg (Switzerland).

Hornung, E., 1990: Das Totenbuch der Ägypter, Zurich/Munich.

Hubai, P., 1992: Eine literarische Quelle der Ägyptischen Religionsphilosophie? Das Märchen vom Prinzen, der drei Gefahren zu überstehen hatte, in: Luft, U. (ed.), The intellectual heritage of Egypt, studies presented to László Kákosy by friends and colleagues on the occasion of his 60th birthday, StudAeg 14, Budapest, 277–300.

el-Huseny, A.M., 2006: Die inkonsequente Tabuisierung von Sus scrofa Linnaeus, 1758 im Alten Ägypten, seine ökonomische und religiöse Bedeutung, Berlin.

Jacquet-Gordon, H.J., 1960: The inscription on the Philadelphia-Cairo statue of Osorkon II, JEA 46, 12–23.

Jansen-Winkeln, K., 1996: „Horizont" und „Verklärtheit": Zur Bedeutung der Wurzel *ꜣḫ*, SAK 23, 201–215.

Jansen-Winkeln, K., 1997: Eine Grabübernahme in der 30. Dynastie, JEA 83, 169–178.

Janssen, J.J., 1975: Commodity prices from the Ramessid Period, an economic study of the village of necropolis workmen at Thebes, Leiden.

Janssen, J.J., 2008: Daily dress at Deir el-Medîna, words for clothing, Egyptology 8.

Jéquier, G., 1922: Matériaux pour servir à l'établissement d'un dictionnaire d'archéologie égyptienne, BIFAO 19.

Jonckheere, F., 1947: Le papyrus médical Chester Beatty, la médicine égyptienne 2, Brussels.

Jonckheere, F., 1949: Rezension: Livres: Steuer, R. O., '*Wḫdw*' aetiological principle of pyaemia in Ancient

Egyptian Medicine, Baltimore 1948, CdÉ 48, 267–270.

Junge, F., 2008: Einführung in die Grammatik des Neuägyptischen, Wiesbaden.

Junker, H., 1917: Die Onurislegende, Kaiserliche Akademie der Wissenschaften in Wien, Philosophisch-historische Klasse, Denkschriften 59, 1 & 2, Abhandlungen, Vienna.

Junker, H., 1942: Der sehende und der blinde Gott (*Mḫntj-jrtj* und *Mḫntj-n-jrtj*), Sitzungsberichte der Bayerischen Akademie der Wissenschaften, Philosophisch-historische Klasse, 7, Munich.

Kees, H., 1925: Zu den ägyptischen Mondsagen, ZÄS 60, 1–15.

Kees, H., 1943: Farbensymbolik in ägyptischen religiösen Texten, Nachrichten von der Akademie der Wissenschaften in Göttingen, Philologisch-historische Klasse, 11, Göttingen, 413–479.

Kees, H., 1987: Der Götterglaube im alten Ägypten, Berlin.

Keimer, L., 1924: Die Gartenpflanzen im Alten Ägypten, I, Ägyptologische Studien, Hamburg/Berlin.

Keimer, L. (Germer, R., ed.), 1984: Die Gartenpflanzen im alten Ägypten, II, SDAIK 13, Mainz.

Koch, R., 1990: Die Erzählung des Sinuhe, BAe 17, Brussels.

Koehler, L./Baumgartner, W., 1967–1995: Hebräisches und Aramäisches Lexikon zum Alten Testament, I–V, Leiden/Cologne/New York.

Koenig, Y., 1992: L'eau et la magie, BdÉ 110, Cairo, 239–248.

Koenig, Y., 1997: Les ostraca hiératiques inédits de la Bibliothèque nationale et universitaire de Strasbourg, DFIFAO 33, Cairo.

Kolta, K.S., 2000: Wein als Opfergabe und Medizin in altägyptischer und koptischer Zeit, Naturheilpraxis mit Naturmedizin 5/2000, 761–771.

Kolta, K.S., 2001: Altägyptische Heilpflanzen – einst und heute, Naturheilpraxis mit Naturmedizin 1/2001, 42–51.

Kolta, K.S./Schwarzmann-Schafhauser, D., 2000: Die Heilkunde im Alten Ägypten, Sudhoffs Archiv, Zeitschrift für Wissenschaftsgeschichte, Beihefte 42.

Kolta, K.S./Tessenow, H., 2000: „Schmerzen", „Schmerzstoffe" oder „Fäulnisprinzip"? Zur Bedeutung von *wḫdw*, einem zentralen Terminus der altägyptischen Medizin, ZÄS 127, 38–52.

Krauss, R., 1997: Astronomische Konzepte und Jenseitsvorstellungen in den Pyramidentexten, ÄA 59, Wiesbaden.

Krebs, M., 1942: Der menschliche Harn als Heilmittel, Geschichte/Grundlagen/Entwicklung/Praxis, Stuttgart.

Kurth, D., 1980: I. Hieratischer Text, 1. Magischer Papyrus gegen Krankheiten, in: Kurth, D./Thissen, H.-J./Weber, M. (eds.), Kölner Ägyptische Papyri (P. Köln ägypt.), Abhandlung der Rheinisch-Westfälischen Akademie der Wissenschaften, Papyrologica Coloniensia IX, Paderborn/Munich *et al.*

Lange, H.O., 1927: Der magische Papyrus Harris, Copenhagen.

Leclant, J., 1975: Earu-Gefilde, in: LÄ I, Wiesbaden, 1156–1160.

Leemans, C., *et al.*, 1839–1905: Monumens égyptiens du Musée d'Antiquités des Pays-Bas à Leide, Leiden.

Leemans, C., 1840: Description raisonnée des monumens égyptiens du Musée d'Antiquités des Pays-Bas à Leide, Leiden.

Lefebvre, G., 1949: Romans et contes égyptiens de l'époque pharaonique, Traduction avec introduction, notices et commentaires, Paris.

Leitz, C., 1997: Die Schlangennamen in den ägyptischen und griechischen Giftbüchern, Akademie der Wissenschaften und Literatur, Abhandlung der Geistes- und Sozialwissenschaftlichen Klasse 1997/6, Stuttgart.

Leitz, C., 1999: Magical and medical papyri of the New Kingdom, Hieratic Papyri in the British Museum, VII, Cambridge.

Leitz, C. (ed.), 2002–2003: Lexikon der Götter und Götterbezeichnungen, I–VIII, OLA 110–116, 129, Leuven.

Lesko, L.H. (ed.), 1982–1990: A dictionary of Late Egyptian, I–V, Berkeley.

Lexa, F., 1925: La magie dans l'Égypte antique, de l'ancien empire jusqu'à l'époque copte, II, Paris.

Lipiński, E., 2009: Resheph, a Syro-Canaanite Deity, OLA 181, Leuven.

Löw, I., 1967: Die Flora der Juden, I–IV, Hildesheim.

Long, B., 1984: À propos de l'usage de menthes dans l'Égypte ancienne, in: Mélanges Adolphe Gutbub, Montpellier, 145–159.

Loret, V., 1935–1938: Pour transformer un vieillard en jeune homme (Pap. Smith, XXI,9–XXII,10), in: Mélanges Maspero I: Orient ancien 2, MIFAO 66.2, Cairo, 853–877.

Loret, V., 1949: La résine de térébinthe (sonter) chez les Anciens Égyptiens, Recherches d'archéologie, de philologie et d'histoire 19, Cairo.

Loret, V., 1975: La flore pharaonique d'après les documents hiéroglyphiques et les spécimens découverts dans les tombes, Hildesheim/New York.

Loretz, O., 1990: Ugarit und Bibel, Kanaanäische Götter und die Religion im Alten Testament, Darmstadt.

Loretz, O., 2003: Ugaritisch *abd* „Sklave, Diener, Vasall", eine Studie zu ug.-he. *abd alm*|| *bn 'amt* (KTU 1.14 III 22–32a et par.) in der juridischen Terminologie altorientalischer Verträge, UF 35, 333–389.

Lucas, A./Harris, J.R., 1962: Ancient Egyptian materials and industries, London.

Macadam, M.F.L., 1949: The temples of Kawa, I–II, London.

Manjo, G., 1975: The healing hand, man and wound in the Ancient World, Cambridge (MA), 69–140.

Manniche, L., 1989: An Ancient Egyptian herbal, London.

Mariette, A., 1875: Karnak, étude topographique et archéologique avec un appendice comprenant les principaux textes découverts ou recueillis pendant les fouilles exécutées à Karnak, Leipzig.

Massart, A., 1954: The Leiden magical papyrus I 343 + I 345, OMRO 34 Suppl., Leiden.

Massart, A., 1957: The Egyptian Geneva Papyrus MAH 15274, MDAIK 15, 172–185.

Massart, A., 1959: À propos des 'listes' dans les textes égyptiens funéraires et magiques, Studia Biblica et Orientalia 3/Analecta Biblica 12, 227–246.

Mathieu, B., 2000: Rezension: Hieratische Ostraca, OLZ 95, 245–256.

Matić, U., 2015: Eine Anmerkung zu *ḳ-t-y* und pLeiden I 343 + I 345 (Recto VI: 7–10), GM 244, 57–66.

Meeks, D., 1980–1982: Année lexicographique, Égypte ancienne, I–III, Paris.

Meeks, D., 1997: Les emprunts égyptiens aux langues sémitiques durant le Nouvel Empire et la Troisième Période Intermédiaire, les aléas du comparatisme, BiOr 54, 32–61.

Meier, G., 1937: Die assyrische Beschwörungssammlung Maqlu, AfO Beih. 2, Vienna.

Mercer, S.A.B., 1949: The religion of Ancient Egypt, London.

Mininberg, D.T., 2008: Honey in Ancient Egyptian medicine, mechanisms of efficacy, GM 217, 61–63.

Möller, G., 1927: Hieratische Paläographie, die Aegyptische Buchschrift in ihrer Entwicklung von der fünften Dynastie bis zur römischen Kaiserzeit, II: Von der Zeit Thutmosis' III. bis zum Ende der einundzwanzigsten Dynastie, Leipzig.

Molen, R. van der, 2000: A hieroglyphic dictionary of Egyptian Coffin Texts, PdÄ 15, Leiden/Boston *et al.*

Moorey, P.R.S., 1994: Ancient Mesopotamian materials and industries, the archaeological evidence, Oxford.

Morenz, L.D., 1999: Rescheph und „*jtwm* (= Ada(m)ma), seine Frau", ein altsyrisches Götterpaar in einem ägyptischen medico-magischen Text und zur *Göttin Edom, UF 31, 373–375.

Morschauser, S., 1991: Threat-formulae in Ancient Egypt, a study of the history, structure and use of threats and curses in Ancient Egypt, Baltimore (MD).

Moursi, H., 1992: Die Heilpflanzen im Land der Pharaonen, Ägyptisch-Nubische Volksmedizin, Cairo.

Müller, M., 2000: Rezension: Y. Koenig, Les ostraca hiératiques inédits de la Bibliothèque nationale et universitaire de Strasbourg, DFIFAO 33, 1997, LingAeg 7, 271–288.

Müller, M., 2002: Rezension: Hoch, J.E., Semitic words in Egyptian texts of the New Kingdom and Third Intermediate Period, Princeton 1994, OLZ 97, 30–43.

Müller, M., 2006: Magie in der Schule? Die magischen Sprüche der Schülerhandschrift pBM 10.085 + 10.105, in: Moers, G./Behlmer, H./Demuß, K./ Widmaier, K. (eds.), *jn.t ḏr.w*, Festschrift für Friedrich Junge, I–II, Göttingen, 449–465.

Müller, M., 2008: Levantinische Beschwörungen in ägyptischer Übersetzung; in: Abusch, T. (ed.), Omina, Orakel, Rituale und Beschwörungen, TUAT N.F. 4, Gütersloh, 275–293.

Münnich, M.M., 2013: The god Resheph in the Ancient Near East, Orientalische Religionen in der Antike 11, Tübingen.

Murray, M.A., 1922: Knots, AE 22, 14–19.

Myśliwiec, K., 1978: Studien zum Gott Atum, I, HÄB 5, Hildesheim.

Myśliwiec, K., 1983: La mère, la femme, la fille et la variante du dieu Atoum, ET 13, 297–304.

Naville, E., 1886: Das Aegyptische Todtenbuch der XVIII. bis XX. Dynastie aus verschiedenen Urkunden zusammengestellt, I–II, Berlin.

Newberry, P.E., 1948: *Fy* 'Cerastes', JEA 34, 118.

Nibbi, A., 1994: Some remarks on the cedar of Libanon, DE 28, 35–52.

Nibbi, A., 1996: Cedar again, DE 34, 37–59.

Nibbi, A., 2003: Cedar yet again, DE 56, 69–83.

Nicholson, P.T./Shaw, I., 2000: Ancient Egyptian materials and technology, Cambridge.

Nordh, K., 1996: Aspects of Ancient Egyptian curses and blessings, conceptual background and transmission, Uppsala.

Nunn, J.F., 1996: Ancient Egyptian medicine, London.

O'Callaghan, R.T., 1952: The word *Ktp* in Ugaritic and Egypto-Canaanite mythology, Or 21, 37–46.

Olmo Lete, G. del, 2008: Mythologie et religion de la Syrie au IIe millenaire AV.J.C. (1500–1200), in: Olmo Lete, G. del (ed.), Mythologie et religion des sémites occidentaux, OLA 162.2, Leuven, 25–162.

Olmo Lete, G. del, 2014: Incantations and anti-witchcraft texts from Ugarit, with a contribution by Rowe, M., SANER 4, Boston/Berlin.

Olmo Lete, G. del/Sanmartín, J., 2003: A dictionary of the Ugaritic language in the alphabetic tradition, I–II, HdO I 67.1–2, Leiden.

Osing, J., 1976: Die Nominalbildung des Ägyptischen, SDAIK 3, I–II, Wiesbaden.

Otto, E., 1938: Beiträge zur Geschichte der Stierkulte in Aegypten, UGAÄ 13, Berlin.

Parker, S.B. (ed.), 1997: Ugaritic narrative poetry, SBL Writing from the Ancient World 9, Atlanta.

Pinch, G., 1994: Magic in Ancient Egypt, London.

Pleyte, W./Rossi, F., 1869–1876: Papyrus de Turin, I–II, Leiden.

Polotsky, H.J., 1929: Zu den Inschriften der 11. Dynastie, UGAÄ 11, Leipzig.

Pommerening, T., 2006: Überlegungen zur Beurteilung der Wirksamkeit altägyptischer Arzneimittel aus heutiger Sicht, in: Zibelius-Chen, K./Fischer-Elfert, H.-W. (eds.), „Von reichlich ägyptischem Verstande", Festschrift für Waltraud Guglielmi zum 65. Geburtstag, Philippika: Marburger altertumskundliche Abhandlungen 11, Wiesbaden, 103–112.

Posener, G., 1940: Princes et pays d'Asie et de Nubie, textes hiératiques sur des figurines d'envoûtement du Moyen Empire, Brussels.

Posener, G., 1949: Les signes noires dans les rubriques, JEA 35, 77–81.

Prechel, D., 1996: Die Göttin Išḫara, ein Beitrag zur altorientalischen Religionsgeschichte, ALASPM 11, Münster.

Pschyrembel, W. (ed.), 2011: Pschyrembel, Klinisches Wörterbuch, Berlin/NewYork.

Quack, J.F., 1993: Ein altägyptisches Sprachtabu, LingAeg 3, 59–79.

Quack, J.F., 1994: Die Lehre des Ani, ein neuägyptischer Weisheitstext in seinem kulturellen Umfeld, OBO 141, Freiburg (Switzerland).

Rahmouni, A., 2008: Divine epithets in the Ugaritic alphabetic texts, HdO I 93, Leiden.

Ranke, H., 1924: Die Vergottung der Glieder des menschlichen Körpers bei den Ägyptern, OLZ 27, 558–564.

Raue, D., 2005: Die sieben Hathoren von *Prt*, ASAE Suppl. 34.2, 247–261.

Raven, M.J., 1997: Charms for protection during the epagomenal days, in: Dijk, J. van (ed.), Essays on Ancient Egypt in honour of Herman te Velde, Egyptological Memoirs 1, Groningen, 275–291.

Refai, H., 2001: Nebet-Hetepet, Iusas und Temet, die weiblichen Komplemente des Atum, GM 181, 89–94.

Reintges, C., 1996: Pyr. 426a revisited, ZÄS 123, 138–157.

Ritner, R.K., 1993: The mechanics of Ancient Egyptian magical practice, SAOC 54, Chicago.

Roccati, A., 2011: Magica Taurinensia, il grande papiro magico di Torino e i suoi duplicati, AnOr 56, Rome.

Rochholz, M., 2002: Schöpfung, Feindvernichtung, Regeneration, Untersuchungen zum Symbolgehalt der machtgeladenen Zahl 7 im alten Ägypten, ÄAT 56, Wiesbaden.

Sallaberger, W./Westenholz, A., 1999: Mesopotamien, Akkade-Zeit und Ur III Zeit, OBO 160.3, Freiburg (Switzerland).

Saunders, J.B. de C.M., 1963: The transitions from Ancient Egyptian to Greek medicine, Logan Clendening Lectures on the History and Philosophy of Medicine 10, Lawrence.

Schenkel, W., 1982: Onuris, in: LÄ IV, Wiesbaden, 573–457.

Schenkel, W., 2005a: Tübinger Einführung in die klassisch-ägyptische Sprache und Schrift, Tübingen.

Schenkel, W., 2005b: Das *śḏm(.w)=f*-Passiv, Perfekt vs. Futur, nach dem Zeugnis der Sargtexte, ZÄS 132, 40–54.

Schneider, W., 1968–1975: Lexikon zur Arzneimittelgeschichte, Sachwörterbuch zur Geschichte der pharmazeutischen Botanik, Chemie, Mineralogie, Pharmakologie, Zoologie, I–VII, Frankfurt.

Schwemer, D., 2001: Die Wettergottgestalten Mesopotamiens und Nordsyriens im Zeitalter der Keilschriftkulturen, Materialien und Studien nach den schriftlichen Quellen, Wiesbaden.

Serpico, M./White, R., 1998: Chemical analysis of coniferous resins from Ancient Egypt using gas chromatography/mass spectrometry (GC/MS), in: Eyre, C. (ed.), Proceedings of the Seventh International Congress of Egyptologists, Cambridge, 3–9 September 1995, OLA 82, Leuven, 1037–1048.

Sethe, K., 1908–1910: Die Altägyptischen Pyramidentexte, nach Papierabdrücken und Photographien des Berliner Museums, I–II, Leipzig.

Sethe, K., 1916: Von den Zahlen und Zahlworten bei den alten Ägyptern und was für andere Völker und Sprachen daraus zu lernen ist, Strasbourg.

Sethe, K., 1956: Urkunden der 18. Dynastie, Historisch-biographische Urkunden IV, 1–4, Berlin.

Singer, I., 1996: Muwatalli's prayer to the assembly of gods through the storm-god of lightning (CTH 381), Atlanta.

Sipos, P./Győry, H./Hagymási, K./Ondrejka, P./Blázovics, A., 2004: Surgical history, special wound healing methods used in Ancient Egypt and the mythological background, World Journal of Surgery 28, 211–216.

Sivan, D./Cochavi-Rainey, Z., 1992: West Semitic vocabulary in Egyptian script of the 14th to the 10th centuries BCE, Beer-Sheva: Studies by the Department of the Bible and Ancient Near East 4, Be'er-Sheva.

Smith, M.S., 1994: The Ugaritic Baal Cycle, introduction with text, translation and commentary of KTU 1.1–1.2, I, Supplements to Vetus Testamentum 55, Leiden/New York *et al.*

Smith, M.S./Pitard, W.T., 2009: The Ugaritic Baal Cycle, introduction with text, translation and commentary of KTU/CAT 1.3–1.4, II, Supplements to Vetus Testamentum 114, Leiden.

Soden, W. von, 1965–1981: Akkadisches Handwörterbuch (AHw), I–III, Wiesbaden.

Soldt, W.H. van, 2005: The topography of the city-state of Ugarit, AOAT 324, Münster.

Spronk, K., 1999: The incantations, in: Watson, W.G.E./Wyatt, N. (eds.), Handbook of Ugaritic studies, Leiden/Boston *et al.*, 270–286.

Stadelmann, R., 1967: Syrisch-Palästinensische Gottheiten in Ägypten, PdÄ 5, Leiden.

Stadler, M.A., 2004: Isis, das göttliche Kind und die Weltordnung, neue religiöse Texte aus dem Fayum nach dem Papyrus Wien D. 12006 Recto, MPER 28, Vienna.

Staehelin, E., 1970: Bindung und Entbindung, Erwägungen zu Papyrus Westcar 10,2, ZÄS 96, 125–139.

Stephan, J., 2001: Ordnungssysteme in der Altägyptischen Medizin und ihre Überlieferung in den europäischen Kulturkreis, Hamburg.

Steuer, R.O., 1933: Myrrhe und Stakte, Schriften der Arbeitsgemeinschaft der Ägyptologen und Afrikanisten in Wien, Vienna.

Steuer, R.O., 1937: Über das wohlriechende Natron bei den Alten Ägyptern, Interpretation, Darstellung und Kultur des *sntr*, Leiden.

Steuer, R.O., 1948: *Wḫdw*, aetiological principle of pyaemia in Ancient Egyptian medicine, Bulletin of the History of Medicine 10 Suppl., Baltimore.

Suys, P.E., 1934: Le papyrus magique du Vatican, Or 3, 63–87.

Täckholm, V./Drar, M., 1941–1969: Flora of Egypt, I–IV, Bulletin of the Faculty of Science, 28, 30, 36.

Tazawa, K., 2009: Syro-Palestinian deities in New Kingdom Egypt, the hermeneutics of their existence, BAR International Series 1965, Oxford.

Thomas, C., 1999: Ein ganz besonderer Saft – Urin, Munich.

Toorn, K. van der/Becking, B./Horst, P.W. van der (eds.), 1995: Dictionary of deities and demons in the Bible, Leiden/New York *et al.*

Tropper, J., 1990: Der ugaritische Kausativstamm und die Kausativbildungen des Semitischen, eine morphologische Untersuchung zum Š-Stamm und zu den umstrittenen nichtsibilantischen Kausativstämmen des Ugaritischen, ALASP 2, Münster.

Tropper, J., 2008: Kleines Wörterbuch des Ugaritischen, ELO 4, Wiesbaden.

Vandier, J., 1949: La religion égyptienne, Paris.

Vandier, J., 1950: Moʿalla, la tombe d'Ankhtifi et la tombe de Sébekhotep, BdÉ 18, Cairo.

Vandier, J., 1957: Le dieu Shou dans le Papyrus Jumilhac, MDAIK 15, 268–274.

Veiga, P.A. da Silva, 2009: Health and medicine in Ancient Egypt, magic and science, BAR International Series 1967, Oxford.

Velde, H. te, 1967: Seth, god of confusion, PdÄ 6, Leiden.

Vercoutter, J., 1956: L'Égypte et le monde égéen préhellénique, étude critique des sources égyptiennes (du début de la XVIIIe à la fin de la XIXe dynastie), BdÉ 22, Cairo.

Vieillescazes-Rambier, C., 1992: Contribution à la connaissance des materiaux résineux utilisés en Égypte ancienne, caracterisation par C.L.H.P. et spectroscopie, Avignon.

Vita, J.-P./Watson, W.G.E., 2002: Are the Akk. terms *Katappu* (Ug. *ktp*) and *Katinnu* Hurrian in origin?, AoF 29, 146–149.

Vittmann, G., 1997: Rezension: Hoch, J.E., Semitic words in Egyptian texts of the New Kingdom and Third Intermediate Period, Princeton 1994, WZKM 87, 277–288.

Vogelsang, F., 1913: Kommentar zu den Klagen des Bauern, UGÄA 6, Berlin.

Volokhine, Y., 2014: Le porc en Égypte ancienne, Liège.

Walker, J.H., 1993: Egyptian medicine and the gods, BACE 4, 83–101.

Walker, J.H., 1996: Studies in Ancient Egyptian anatomical terminology, ACES 4, Warminster.

Ward, W.A., 1977: Lexicographical miscellanies, SAK 5, 265–292.

Watanabe, K., 1984: Die literarische Überlieferung eines babylonisch-assyrischen Fluchthemas mit Anrufung des Mondgottes Sîn, ASJ 6, 99–119.

Weill, R., 1936: Le champ des roseaux et le champ des offrandes dans la religion funéraire et la religion génerale, Études d'Égyptologie 3, Paris.

Wendrich, W., 2006: Entangled, connected or protected, the power of knots and knotting in Ancient Egypt, in: Szpakowska, K.M. (ed.), Through a glass darkly, magic, dreams and prophecy in Ancient Egypt, Swansea, 243–269.

Wente, E.F., 1959: The syntax of verbs of motion in Egyptian, Chicago.

Westendorf, W., 1981: Eilen und Warten, GM 46, 27–31.

Westendorf, W., 1992: Erwachen der Heilkunst, die Medizin im Alten Ägypten, Zurich.

Westendorf, W., 1999: Handbuch der altägyptischen Medizin, I–II, HdO I 36.1–2, Leiden.

Wiedemann, A., 1910: Die Amulette der alten Aegypter, AO 12.1.

Wilhelm, G., 2005: Der Vertrag Šuppiluliumas I. und Ḫukkanna von Ḫajaša, in: Breyer, F./Lichtenstein, M. (eds.), Staatsverträge, Herrscherinschriften und andere Dokumente zur politischen Geschichte, TUAT N.F. 2, Gütersloh, 107–121.

Wilson, P., 1997: A Ptolemaic lexicon, a lexicographical study of the texts in the temple of Edfu, OLA 78, Leuven.

Wimmer, S., 1995: Hieratische Paläographie der nichtliterarischen Ostraka der 19. und 20. Dynastie, I–II, ÄAT 28, Münster.

Wreszinski, W., 1909: Der grosse medizinische Papyrus des Berliner Museums (Pap. Berl. 3038), Leipzig.

Wreszinski, W., 1912: Der Londoner medizinische Papyrus (Brit. Museum Nr. 10059) und der Papyrus Hearst, Leipzig.

Wreszinski, W., 1913: Der Papyrus Ebers, Umschrift, Übersetzung und Kommentar, I, Leipzig.

Wyatt, N., 1999: The religion of Ugarit, an overview, in: Watson, W.G.E./Wyatt, N. (eds.), Handbook of Ugaritic studies, Leiden/Boston *et al.*, 529–585.

Yamazaki, N., 2003: Zaubersprüche für Mutter und Kind, Papyrus Berlin 3027, Achet, Schriften zur Ägyptologie B2, Berlin.

Internet:

- http://aaew.bbaw.de/tla/index.html

Appendix I: Glossary

1. General

ꜣ.t 'strength, time'
V:XXIII2

ꜣyʿ 'valour (?)'
R:XIIIx + 2

ꜣḥ.t 'field'
R:VII8, V:VII3

ꜣs 'to hasten, to rush'
V:XXV3

jꜣ.t 'spine, back'
R:I7, III8, VII12, XXII1 + x + 2, V:VI3, XX1

jꜣ.t 'place, mound'
R:IV6–7

jꜣw.t (*ʿw.t*) 'animals, herds'
R:XIXx + 2

jꜣw 'old man'
R:VIII14

jꜣb.t 'left hand'
R:III9, V:VI4

jrʿ.t 'uraeus'
R:XVx + 1

jꜣd.t 'dew'
R:XIVx + 2

jy, jwj 'to come'
R:V13, X9, V:IX10, 11, XVII1, XXV3

jwjw 'dog'
V:IV9, XXI2

jwr 'to conceive, to become pregnant'
V:V1

jw.tj 'who/which not (*negative relative adjective*)'
R:VIII7, X4–5

jwtn 'ground, earth'
R:III11, IV1, IV6, V10, IX13, X3, 14, V:I4, VI6, 9, VII3

jb 'heart'
R:I2, V13

jbj 'to be thirsty'
R:IV11, VII7, V:XII1

jbḥ 'tooth'
R:II2

ypgdd 'kind of weapon (?)'
R:XIIx + 1

jmj 'not be (*negative verb*)'
V:XXIV3

jm 'there'
R:I8, V10, X14

ym 'sea'
R:IV13, V:I9, 10, II8, VII7

jmn 'right hand'
R:III10, V:XXV1

jn 'by (*of agent*)'
V:XXIII3

jnj 'to bring'
R:II4, III13, XXV1 + x + 3, V:III10, IV1, VI8

jny.t 'seed'
R:XXVI11

jns.y 'red(-dyed) linen or bandage'
R:XXVIII4–5

jnk 'I (*indep. pron. 1st pers. sing.*)'
R:IV7, XIIx + 2, V:VII3, XXV3, 4

jr 'concerning, according to, as to'
R:II4, VII2, XVIIx + 3, V:I11, IV1

jr.t 'eye'
R:II7, VIII4, XXVII4, V:I5, IV3, V5, IX6

jrj 'to do, to make, to create'
R:I10, 11, IV7, 13, V3, 10, VI2, 3, 6, 10, 13, VII8, 9, 10, X2, XI12, XVIIx + 3, XXV1 + x + 2, V:III5, IV10, V1, VII3, 10, VIII12, XVIII1, XXIII4, XXIV1, 3

jrp 'wine'
R:VI2, V:XIX1

(j)ḫ.t 'thing, mass'
R:III1, VI2, XXVI9, V:II3, IV8, X1, XXIV1

jz 'reed (?)'
V:XVIII2

jsḳnḳn 'to retreat (?)'
R:V10, V:VIII12

jsṯ 'now (*particle*)'
V:XIX1, 2

jšf 'to enlarge (?)'
V:IX11

jtm.w 'breathlessness'
R:XXVII3

jtn 'sun disk'
V:I6, IX11

jw-ḏꜣ-mꜥ-nꜣ 'something in the entrails (?)'
R:VIII1

ꜥ 'arm'
V:XXII2, XXIV2

ꜥ 'stroke (?)'
V:IX1, 3, 4

ꜥ.t 'limb, member'
R:VI3, VII13, XXVI7, V:XXIV1

ꜥꜣ 'great, senior'
R:VI11,13, VIII13, IX8, V:IX10

ꜥꜣ 'here, there'
R:IV4, 5

ꜥꜣ 'ass'
R:III7, V:VI2

ꜥꜥ.t 'accusation'
R:VIII12, IX2–3, V:XX2

ꜥꜥ.ty 'accuser (?)'
V:XX2

ꜥwꜣ.yt 'fermented substance (*med.*)'
R:XXVI10

ꜥb 'horn'
V:XXII1

ꜥbꜥy.t 'the bubbling one (?)'
R:VIII3

ꜥmꜥ 'kernel, grain'
R:IV8, V:VII4

ꜥmꜥy.t (*ꜥmꜥꜣ.t*) 'throwing stick'
R:IX8

ꜥmry.t 'cow (?)'
R:VI11

ꜥnn 'to return, to turn back'
R:XXVII4, V:XXIV1

ꜥnẖ 'goat'
V:X1

ꜥnt.jw 'myrrh (?)'
V:IX12

ꜥrw 'ꜥrw-tree'
R:XXVI3

ꜥrꜥr.t 'serpent'
V:XXV4

ꜥḥꜣ 'to fight'
R:II5, 6, V:IV1, 2

ꜥḥꜥ 'to stand (up), to get ready to do'
R:VI4, XXIx + 2, V:II4, IX12

ꜥẖm 'to extinguish'
R:V8, 9

(j)ꜥš 'to call, to summon'
R:XIXx + 2

ꜥš 'coniferous wood'
R:V1, 2, V:VII8, 9

ꜥšꜣ 'numerous, common'
R:II5, V4, V:IV1, VII11

ꜥḳ 'to enter'
V:XXIII8 + x + 3

ꜥḳ.w 'loaves (of bread)'
R:XVIx + 2

m-ꜥḳꜣ 'at'
R:IX4–5, IX11, V:XIV2

ꜥḏn 'to complete, to finish'
R:IV11–12, V8, 9, VI10, 13, IX13, V:VII6

wꜣj 'to be far (away from)'
R:IX4

wꜣḥ 'to lay (down)'
R:VIII14

wꜣḏ 'to flourish'
V:II7

wjꜣ 'ship, processional barque'
R:II12, V:IV7, IX10, 11

→ *wjꜣ n.j ḥḥ* 'barque of the Millions'
V:IX10–11

wꜥr 'to flee'
R:II6, X10–11, V:IV2, XVI1

wbꜣ 'to open, to deflower'
R:II9, V:IV4

wbꜣ 'to present'
R:IV2

wbn 'to shine, to rise (sun, moon)'
R:II11, VI6, V:IV6, IX2

wp.t 'top (of the head), vertex'
R:II4, V:III10

wfꜣ 'lung(s)'
R:VIII2

wn 'to exist, to become'
R:V2, VII2, XVIx + 2, XXIx + 2, V:VII9, XX2

wn 'to open'
R:IX14

wnm.j 'right hand'
V:XXIII7

wḥꜣ.t 'oasis'
R:III1, V:IV8

wḥꜥ 'to release'
V:XXIII3, XXIV4

wḥm 'to repeat'
R:V1, VII3, IX10, V:VII9

wḥs 'to cut (off)'
V:XXIII3

wḫꜣ 'to seek'
R:IX9

wḫd.w 'pain (?)'
V:XXIII1

w<z>š.t 'excrement'
R:XXVI9–10

wšꜥ 'to chew'
V:IV9, XXI1, 2

wt 'to bandage'
R:X9, XXVI6, 9, 10, 12, V:X1

wḏꜣ 'well-being, welfare'
R:V13

wḏꜣ.t '*wedjat*-eye'
V:I7

bꜣk 'servant'
R:X11, V:XVI1

bj.t 'honey'
R:III1, XXVI9, V:IV8

bjn 'bad things'
V:XXIV1

bw '(*negation*)'
V:IV10

bn '(*negation*)'
V:XV1

bnw.t 'millstone'
R:II8, V:IV3, 4

bnr 'date'
R:XXVI8, 11

r-bnr 'out'
R:II7, V12, V:IV2, 3, VII2, XV1, XVIII1

bḥnj 'to cut (off, up)'
R:XXIx + 1, x + 2

bš 'to spit, to vomit'
R:IX14, V:XV1

bšꜣ 'axe, chisel'
R:I12, V:II5, III7

bd.t 'emmer'
R:IV8

p.t 'sky, heaven'
R:IV7, 11, IX7, X12, XIVx + 2, XXIx + 2, XXVII2, 3, V:I2, 9, 10, VII4, 6

pꜣj 'to fly'
R:VI4, 5, XXx + 1

pꜣy 'to copulate with, to fertilise'
R:IX1

p(ꜣ)d 'knee, kneecap'
R:XXIx + 2, XXII1, V:VI5

pw '(*copula*)'
R:XXII1 + x + 1, V:V2

pnꜥ 'to turn upside down'
R:I9, V:III5

pr 'house'
R:V13, VIII6, XI1, V:V7

prj 'to go forth, to come forth'
R:V12, XVIx + 2, XXIIIx + 2, x + 3, XXIV1, XXVII7, V:I11, XXV1

pr.w 'motion'
R:VIII5, X4

pr.t 'seeds, kernels'
R:VI1

pr.t-šn.t 'pine nuts (?)'
R:XXIV3 + x + 2, V:IV7, XIX1

prj 'battlefield'
R:I5

pḥ.wj 'end, back'
R:VII12

pḥ.tj 'physical strength'
R:IV12, VIII7, X5, V:VII6

pẖr.t 'remedy'
R:XXVI9, 11

pzš.t 'reed stem/cane, carpet'
V:XVIII1

psj 'to cook, to heat'
R:I3, IV8, XXVI11, V:II10, VII4

psḏ.t '(divine) ennead'
R:XIIx + 2, V:I3, 4

pgꜣ 'to open up'
R:X2

ptr 'to see, to behold'
R:VIII4, IX4, V:I5, V5, XIV1

pḏ 'to spread'
R:X14

fꜣj 'to lift, to carry'
R:VII3, VIII14, IX9–10, X12, XI11, V:V3–4

fgꜣ 'to tear out'
R:IX1, 2, 3, V:XIV1

fd.t 'sweat'
R:XXV1 + x + 3

m 'in, with, of, etc.'
R:I12, II3, II5, 10, III9, 11, IV6, 7, 13, V1, 2, 8, VI3, 7, 11, 12, 13, VII11, 12, 13, VIII1, 2, 3, IX6, X1, 11, 12, XIIx + 1, XIIx + 2, XXII1+ x + 2, XVIx + 2, XXIx + 2, XXIx + 2, XXIIIx + 3, XXIV1, XXV1 + x + 2, XXVI3, XXVI7, XXVI9, XXVII2, 3, 4, 5, 7, V:I2, IV1, I8, 10, II3, III7, III10, IV1, 5, 8, V1, 5, 6, VI4, VII2, 4, 7, 9, IX2, 10, 11, 12, XV1, XVI1, XVIII1, XX2, XXIV1, 3

m-ꜥ 'in the hand of, together with'
R:VI9, IX2, X5, V:I4, 7, 8, XI1

m-dj 'with, from, in possession of'
V:XXII2

m '(*imperative of the negative verb*)'
R:XXIx + 2

mꜣj 'lion'
V:VII7, XXI1(?)

mꜣꜥ 'to be just, to be true'
R:VIII1, V:IX3

mꜣꜥ.t 'truth'
R:I1(?), V:II8

mꜣꜥ.tj 'the righteous one'
R:VIII8

mꜣꜥ 'temple (of the head)'
V:V6

mj 'come (*imperative*)'
R:II6–7, 7, III12, IV4, 5, 6, XXIIIx + 2, XXIV1, V:IV2, 3, VI6–7, VII1, 2, 2–3, XXII3

mj 'like, according as'
R:I5, 6, V2, 5, 9, VI4, 5, IX1, XXVII8, 9, 10, 11, 12, XXVIII1, 2, 3, V:III3, V3, VII9, VIII1, XXIII2

mj.t(j)t 'the like, the same'
R:VI6

m-mj.t(j)t 'likewise, similarly'
R:XVIIx + 1, V:IV10

mj.t 'urine'
R:I3

mw 'water'
R:IV11, 13, V3, VII9, V:VII10, X1, XXV1

mw.t 'mother'
R:VI10, XVIIx + 3, V:I8, V1, XI2

mwt 'to die, to be dead'
R:V11, VIII13, X3, X14

mwt 'death'
R:VIII5, IX9, V:XIII1

mwt 'dead man'
R:XXVI1, XXVII6, V:IX1, XXIV3

mwt.t 'dead woman'
V:XXIV3

r-mn-[*m*] 'as far as, to'
R:XXII1 + x + 2

mn 'NN'
R:VI3–4, IX14, XXIIIx + 3, XXV1 + x + 1, XXVI2, XXVII8, 9, 10, 11, 12, XXVIII2, 3, V:IX1, 3, 4, 12

mn.t 'NN (*fem.*)'
R:VI4, IX14, XXIIIx + 3, XXVI2, XXVII8, 9, 10, 11, 12, XXVIII2, 3, V:IX1, 3, 4, 12, XXIV5

mn.t 'the like'
R:XI14

mn.w 'suffering, pain'
V:XXII3

mn.t 'thigh'
R:VII11

mnw.t 'root (*med.*)'
R:XVIIx + 3

mnš.t '(red) ochre (?)'
R:XXVI10

mnḏ 'chest, breast'
R:VI11

mr 'to be ill, to suffer'
V:XXIII1

mr.t 'illness, evil'
V:XXIII4, 5

mḥ 'to fill, to be full'
R:XXx + 1

mḥ 'to seize'
R:III9, XXII1 + x + 1, V:VI4

mḥ 'arm'
R:X13

mḥ.j 'northern'
R:XXVI12

, , *mḥ.t* 'feather'
R:IV5, V:VII2, XXII1

mḫt(w) 'intestines, entrails'
R:VIII1

msj 'to give birth'
R:VI4, IX14, XXIIIx + 3, XXV1 + x + 1, XXVI2, XXVII8, 9, 10, 11, 12, XXVIII1, 2, 3, V:V1, IX1, 3, 4, 12

ms.w 'children, offspring'
V:XXV4

mstꜣnj 'a kind of liquid (*med.*)'
V:X1

, *m=k, m=tn* 'behold! (*particle*)'
R:VI2, 7, 10, 12, X1, 14, XXx + 1, V:IV10, IX2, 3, 4, XV1

mkj 'to protect'
R:VIII12–13

, *mt* 'vessel, cord, etc.'
R:I8, IX14, X1, V:V6, XV1

mtw.t 'poison'
R:V4, 5, 6, 7, 8, XVIIIx + 2, V:VII11, VIII2, 4, 6, XX1

mtr.w 'witness'
R:XIIx + 3

mdw 'staff, sacred staff'
V:XXIII2

mdwj 'to speak'
R:VI9, VIII3, V:XI1

, *mdw.t* 'word, speak, matter'
R:II10, IV8, VI1, 12, XI10, XXIx + 2, XXVI2, V:I11, III1, IV5, 7, V7, IX12, XVII2, XXII2, XXV2

mḏꜣ.t 'chisel'
V:V6

n '(*negation*)'
R:XVIIx + 3, V:XXIV3

n 'to, for, from, etc.'
R:III12, XXVIII5, V:V2

n 'belonging to'
R:III7, VI8, V:VI2

njwjw '[a medical plant], mint (?)'
V:X1

njm 'who?'
R:III6, 7, 12, V:VI2, 7

nw 'time, moment'
V:XXIV1

nb 'lord'
R:I1, X12, XXIx + 2, XXII1, V:II8

nb.t 'mistress, lady'
R:I12, V:III7

, *nb, nb.t* 'every, all'
R:I1, VIII12, X1, XIIIx + 2, XIXx + 2, XXVI7, V:I1, II4, V5, XV1, XXII3, XXIII5, XXIV1

nfr 'good, beautiful, perfect'
V:X2

nm '[a large vessel]'
R:VI13–VII1

nmꜥ 'to (go to) sleep'
R:XI3

, *nmḥ* 'to slave'
R:II8, V:IV3

nmt.t 'stride'
V:XXIV2

nn '(*negation*)'
R:VI7, VIII7, X1, XIIx + 1, XXVII3, 4, V:VI6, IX12

nn 'these (*demonstrative pronoun pl.*)'
R:XXV1 + x + 3

nr.w 'fear, terror'
V:XXI1

[*nrꜣ*].*w* 'ibex'
V:X1

nhm 'to rejoice'
R:I10

nhmhm 'to roar'
R:I11

nhnh 'to roar'
V:VII8

nhsj 'to awaken'
V:XVIII1

nḥb.t 'neck, nape of the neck'
R:IV8, VII13, V:VII4

nḥm 'to take away, to rescue'
R:XIIIx + 2, V:IX11, XXIV2

nḥḥ 'eternity'
R:XIVx + 1

nk/ḳ.t 'trull (?)'
R:II6, V:IV1

nz 'inflammation'
R:XXVI12, XXVII4

nz<p>.w 'wounds'
R:XXVII1

ns 'tongue'
R:I4, V:III1

nšnj 'to storm, to rage'
R:XXVII2

nšd 'to reduce to small pieces'
R:XXIx + 3

<n>kt 'matter, thing'
R:XVIIx + 3

n.ty 'the one who/which (*relative pronoun*)'
R:III4, 5, 6, IV2, 6, V1, 2, 9, VI3, 4, 9, VII6, VIII1, 12, 13, VIII1, 3, 4, 7,11, 12, 13,14, IX3, X1, 5, 14, XI13, 14, XIIIx + 2, XIVx + 2, XVIIIx + 2, V:I10, 11, II4, 8, III4, 4, IV9, V5, 9, 10, VI1, 10, VII2, 8, 9, XI1, IX2, XV1, XXI1, XXIII4, 5(?), XXV3

n.ty-nb 'everyone (who)'
V:I4

ntf 'he (*indep. pron. 3rd pers. masc. sing.*)'
R:VI4

nts 'she (*indep. pron. 3rd pers. fem. sing.*)'
R:VII10

nṯr 'god'
R:I1, II10, V3, 11, VIII8, 10, 12, IX11, XVIIx + 2, XXVII5, V:I1, 3, II4, IV5, V2, VII10, XIII1, XXIII2, XXV4

nṯr.t 'goddess'
R:XXVI1, XXVII5–6, V:I2, 3, II4

nḏ 'to grind, to crush'
R:II8, III1, IV1, 8, VIII9, XXVI11, V:IV3, 8, VII4, X1, XIX1

nḏr 'to seize, to hold fast'
V:V1

nḏḥ.t 'tooth, fang'
R:II2

nḏs 'small, little, weak'
V:I4

r 'to, against, in order to, etc.'
R:I5, II3, III4, 5, 8, IV3, 7, 9, 10, 11, V1, 3, VI2, 12, VIII6, 7, 10, IX13, XI1, XXII1+ x + 2, XVIIx + 3, XXx + 1, XXIx + 2, XXII1, XXV1 + x + 3, XXVI9, XXVII5, XXVIII5, V:I8, II7, IV1, 8, V4, 10, VI1, 7, 10, VII3, 4, 5, 6, 8, 9, 10, IX2, 3, 10, 11, XVII1, XVIII1, XIX1, XX2, XXIII4, 8 + x + 3, XXIV3

r' 'mouth, opening, utterance, speech'
R:I2, III11, VIII8, IX1, 14, XVIIx + 2, XXVII6, XXVIII4, V:II2, 9, V4, VI5, XXIV3, XXV1

r'-jb 'stomach'
R:III5, V:V10

m- r'-ʿ 'also, likewise'
R:V2, X12, V:VII9

ry.t 'pus (*med.*)'
R:XXV1 + x + 3

rʿw.t 'discharge (?)'
V:I9

rwj 'to go away, to expel, to drive off'
R:IV4, 5, V:VII1, 2, IX1, 2, 4, 5, 6, 12

rwn.t 'young girl'
R:III9

rpy.t 'statue'
V:XXI3

rmj 'to weep'
V:V1–2

rmn 'shoulder'
R:III8, VII13

r(m)ṯ 'human being, man, people'
R:I2, 7, II5, XXVI10, V:II9, III2, 3, IV1

rn 'name'
R:X11, 12, V:I11, II1, XVI1

<rn>n.t 'maiden'
V:IV5

rḫ 'to know, to learn'
R:V11, VI7, 8, VIII5, X3, 4, V:II4, XIII1

rs 'to wake'
R:XI2, 5

rd 'foot'
R:III10, VII11, XXVI7, V:V4, XX1, XXIII1, 4, XXIV1, 3, 4

rḏj, ḏj, jm(m) 'to give, to cause'
R:I4, 7, II5, 6, 7, III8, IV2, 9, VI2, IX11, X10, XIVx + 1, XXx + 1, XXVII3, 4, V:I8, II10, III1, 3, 10, IV1, 8, V2, 6, VI1, 2, 3, VII4, XVII1, XIX1

hꜣ(y) '(*interjection*)'
V:IV11–12, XXV1, 3

hꜣj 'to descend, to fall'
R:II1, 2, III10, IV6, 7, IX12, X13, V:III7–8, 8, VI5, VII3, IX3, XXV1

hj 'husband'
R:IX12

hrw 'day'
R:II10, XXV1 + x + 2, XXVI9, V:II3, IV5, XXIV1

hrp 'to submerge, to sink'
R:VI3, 7, VII6, 11, VIII7, 11, X10, V:IV9

hh 'blast (of fire)'
R:VIII7

ḥꜣ.t 'forepart, beginning, front'
R:VI2, 3, 6, V:IV10

m-ḥꜣ.t 'in the front of, before'
R:II12, V:II5, IV7

r-ḥꜣ.t 'first, before'
R:X11, XVx + 1, V:XVI1

ḥꜣ.tj 'heart'
R:V12, VIII2, 5, 13, IX3, X4, 14(!), XIIx + 2

ḥwꜣꜣ.t 'putrefaction'
R:XXV1 + x + 3

ḥwj 'to strike, to flow, to flood'
R:I5, III4, 5, IV3, 3–4, V1, VII4, IX5, 10–11, XI13, V:II5, 7, V10, VI1, VII1, 9, XIV2, XVIII1, XX1, 2

ḥm.t 'woman, wife'
R:V6, 7, V:I3, VIII3, XXV3

ḥmꜣ.t 'salt'
R:XXVI12

ḥmy.w 'fenugreek (?)'
R:IV3

ḥmw.t-rꜣ 'etc.'
V:XXIV3

ḥmsj 'to sit (down), to dwell'
R:X2, V:III4

ḥmt 'copper, copper ore'
R:II4, 5, III13, V:II4, III10, IV1, VI8

ḥny.t 'spear'
R:V2, IX5, V:VII9

ḥnꜥ 'with, and, together with'
R:I3, II5, 9, V3, 4, 5, 6, 7, 13, VI4, 12, VII5, VIII2, X5, 13, XI14, XIIx + 3, XIIIx + 2, XIVx + 2, XVIIx + 3, XVIIIx + 1, x + 2, V:I4, 5, 7, 8, 9, II9, III10, IV1, 4, VII10, 11, VIII3, 4, XVII1

ḥr 'to, on, from, up, etc.'
R:I2, 5, II1, 2, 8, 9, 11, 13, III4, 5, 6, 8, 9, 10, 11, 13, IV1, 3, 4, 6, 8, 11, 12, V3, 10, VI1, 2, 5, 6, 9, VII3, 4, 5, 11, 12, VIII3, 4, 8, 12, 14, IX5, 10, X2, 9, 13, 14, XI1, 13, XIIIx + 1, XIVx + 2, XVIx + 2, XXVI9, 10, 11, 12, XXVII8, 9, 10, 11, 12, XXVIII1, 2, 3, 4, V:I4, 5, 7, II1, 8, III4, 8, IV3, 4, 5, 6, 7, 9, V1, 5, 10, VI1, 3, 5, 6, 9, 10, VII1, 3, 4, 7, 10, IX2, 4, 5, 6, 12, X2, XI1, XIV2, XVIII2, XX1, XXI1, XXII2, 3, XXIII1, 2, XXIV3

ḥr 'face, sight'
R:II1, X10, XXII1 + x + 2, V:I5, III8, XXIII1

ḥr.j 'being upon, being above'
R:VII3, IX10

r-ḥr.j 'up, upwards'
R:XIVx + 2

ḥrj 'to be far, to remove (oneself)'
V:IX11

ḥr.yt 'fear, dread'
R:I10, III11, V:III6, VI6

ḥs 'faeces'
R:VIII8, V:II9, 10

ḥsꜣ 'mucus, mucilage'
R:IV8–9, XXVI10, 12, V:VII4

ḥsmn 'natron'
R:XXVI8–9(?), 11, V:IV8

ḥsḳ 'to cut off'
V:XXIV2

ḥty.t 'throat (?)'
R:X13

ḥtp 'to set, to rest'
R:XXVII5, V:IX2

ḥḏ 'to be white, to be bright'
V:I7, XXII1

ḥḏ 'silver'
R:III13, V:VI8

ḥḏw.yt 'lamp (?)'
R:V9

ḥḏnḏn 'uproar, raging'
R:IV10, V:VII5

ẖ.t 'flame'
R:V7, 8, V:I8, II1

ḫꜣ.(y)t 'disease, illness'
R:XXVII7

ḫꜣꜥ 'to throw, to abandon'
R:II6, IV2

ḫꜣḫ 'to come in haste, to be fast'
R:IX3

ḫꜣs.t 'hill-country, foreign land, desert'
R:II8, VII6, 7, V:VI3, XII1, XXI1

ḫꜥm (*ẖꜥm*) 'to approach, to reach'
R:IX3, V:XIV1

ḫb.t 'place of execution'
V:XXIV3

ḫpr 'to come into being, to become'
R:XXVI12

ḫpš 'arm, foreleg'
R:IV12, V:VII7

ḫpš 'scimitar'
R:II2, X12–13

ḫft 'in front of, while, against'
R:III11, XI13, 14, V:IV6

ḫft.j 'male enemy'
R:XXVI1

ḫft.j(t) 'female enemy'
R:XXVI1

m-ḫnt.j 'in front of, in the face of'
V:XXIII3

ḫr 'by'
V:II8

ḫr 'to fall, to fell, to befall'
V:I5, XXIII1, 3–4

ḫrw 'voice, sound'
R:VII1, V:IX3

ḫrw.y 'enemy, disturber (?)'
R:I6, V:XXII2

ḫꜣ-y-r'-bw 'desert'
R:VII8

ḫtm 'to seal, to close'
V:V4

ẖ.t 'body, belly'
R:III5, V:VI1, XXIII8 + x + 3

ẖꜣẖꜣ.tj 'storm'
R:IV11, V:VII6

m-ẖnw 'within, in the interior of'
R:I11, XIXx + 2, V:VII8

ẖnm 'to unite'
V:XXIV3

ẖr 'under'
V:XXIII2

ẖr.wj 'testicles'
R:XXVII4

ẖr.j-mwt 'being under the dead (?)'
R:V10, V:VIII11

ẖrd 'child'
R:VIII12, V:V3

ẖdb 'to kill'
R:VI9, XI13–14, XIIx + 2, XIXx + 2, V:XI1

z(j) 'man'
R:III12, XXVIII5

zꜣ 'son'
R:V5, V:VII11

zꜣ(y)w 'beam'
R:VII12–13

zꜣt.w 'earth, ground'
R:XXIx + 2, XXVII2

zp 'time, occasion'
R:XVIIx + 2, XXVI2, XXVII6, XXVIII4,V: XXV2

zp-sn 'twice (*reciting note*)'
R:VII1, V:IX12, XXII1, 3, XXV3

zp 'remedy'
R:XVIIx + 3

zmꜣ.yt 'band, troop'
R:II4, V:III10

znf 'blood'
R:III10, IV1, XVIIIx + 2, XXV1 + x + 2, XXVII1, V:VI4–5, 8, X1

s.t 'place'
R:VI5, V:IX10

s.t-ꜥ 'effect'
R:XXVI1, XXVII5, 6

m-sȝ 'following after, after'
R:IV5, X14, V:VII2

sȝj 'to be satiated, to be sated'
R:VII8, 9

sȝḥ 'to approach'
R:IV13–V1, V:VII8

s:(j)ȝt 'to twist, to cheat'
V:XXIV2

s:jn 'to wait'
V:IX2, 3, 4

sꜥb 'to castrate, to emasculate'
R:II10, V:IV5

sw 'he, him (*depen. pron. 3rd pers. masc. sing.*)'
R:V12, XXx + 1, XXV1 + x + 2, XXVI3

s:ꜥḥꜥ 'to set up'
R:XXIx + 2

s:wꜥb 'to cleanse, to purify'
V:I11

swr 'to drink'
R:VI12, 13, VII5, 6, 7, 10, V:XII1

swhj 'roaring'
R:VII2

sbȝ 'star'
V:I10

sbȝ 'to teach, to punish'
R:III12, V:VI7

sbn 'to slide (away)'
V:XXIII1, 2

sp.t 'lip'
R:VIII3, IX2, V:I11

spȝ.wt 'nomes, districts'
V:XXIII2

spr 'to arrive at, to reach'
R:XI1,V:V7

spd 'to be sharp, to make sharp'
R:I4, V:III1

sf 'yesterday'
R:V9

smȝ 'to slay, to slaughter'
R:I1, V:XX2

smȝ 'wild bull'
R:IX1

s:mn 'to establish, to make endure'
R:VI4

sn 'brother'
R:XXVII7

sn.t 'sister'
R:XIVx + 2

s:nꜥꜥ 'to grind something fine'
R:XXVI11

s:nꜥꜥ jb 'to please the heart'
R:I2, V:II9

snb 'health'
R:V13

snḳ 'to suckle'
R:VI10–11

snṯr 'incense (?)'
R:III1, V:IV8

s:nḏm 'to make pleasant, to delight (*jb*)'
R:V13

srf 'to warm, to be warm'
R:IV9, V:VII4

srḫ(!) 'to accuse'
R:V3

srḫ 'accusation'
R:VIII10, 11, 12

shȝ 'confusion'
R:XXVII3

sḥwr 'to vilify'
V:I1, 1–2, 2, 2–3, 4, 6

s:ḥḏ 'to make bright, to shine, to illuminate'
V:IX6

sḫ.t 'field, marshland'
R:IX9, XXVII2

s:ḫȝ 'to call to mind, remember'
R:X11, V:XVI1

s:ḫpr 'to create, to bring into being'
R:IV6, V:VII3

sḫm '(divine) power'
V:II5

sḫs(ḫ) 'to run, to hasten'
R:VII12, V:V4

s:ḫr 'to overthrow, to cast down'
R:X13

sḫḏ 'to blame'
V:VII10

ssn 'to smell, to breathe'
V:V5

sḳ(r) 'to strike'
R:II13

sḳdj 'to travel'
V:IX11

, *st* 'she, her, it (*depen. pron. 3rd pers. fem. sing.*)'
R:IV2, 2–3, VI12, 13, IX3, XI14, V:II4

st 'they (*indep. pron. 3rd pers. plur. com.*)'
R:II6

stp 'choice, select'
R:III5, V:IV1

sd 'to break'
R:XVIx + 2, V:XVII1, XX1, 2

sḏꜣ 'leg (?)'
R:XXVI12, XXVIII5

sḏꜣ 'to bring'
V:XXIV3

sḏm 'to hear'
R:VII1, 2, XXVII3, V:XVII2

, *sḏm.yt* 'gossip'
R:XI1, V:V7

sḏr 'to lie, to sleep, to spend the night'
V:V2–3

šꜣj 'pig'
R:I3, V:II9

šꜣʿ 'to begin, to be the first (to do something)'
V:IV10

šʿd 'to cut (off)'
R:III9, IX6, 7, XXVII1

šwj 'to dry, to be dry'
R:XVIIx + 3

šw.t 'emptiness'
V:IX11

šb.t 'mash'
R:XXVI10, 11

, *šb(n).t, š(ꜣ)b.t* 'cucumber(?)'
R:VI1, VIII9

šp 'to be blind, to blind'
V:V2

šf.wt 'swelling'
R:XXVI7

šmj 'to go'
R:III6, VII11, X10, XI13, 14, V:I1, VI1

, *šmꜣ* 'to wander, to be wild'
R:I12–II1, III7–8, V:VI2–3

šn.w 'circuit'
V:I6

šnj 'to suffer'
V:V1

šnj 'to conjure, to exorcise, to curse' R:XXIx + 2, V:XXII1

, *šn.w* 'conjurer, magician'
R:.X11, V:XVI1

šn.t 'incantation, conjuration'
R:I4, III2, IV9, VI2, VIII10, XXVI12, XXVII6, V:XXIII1

šnʿ 'storm cloud'
V:I9

šnf.t '[a plant or plant product]'
R:XXVI12

, , *šr.t* 'nose'
R:IV3, VIII3, V:V5, VII1

, , *šrj* 'child, son, little one'
R:III2, VIII13, V:I6, V8

šrj.t 'daughter'
R:XIVx + 1, XIVx + 2

šzp 'to receive'
R:X2

šdj 'to take (away), to rescue'
R:XVIIIx + 2, V:I8

šd.y 'reciter (?)'
V:II6

ḳꜣj 'to be high'
R:VI5, XIVx + 2

ḳꜣb.t 'chest, breast'
R:XXIx + 2

ḳnj 'embrace, bosom'
R:XXx + 1

ḳnj 'to conquer'
R:V13–VI1, VIII6, XI1, V:V7–8

ḳn.y 'companion'
R:IV4, V:VII1

ḳn.w 'many, numerous'
R:VI12

, *ḳḫn*'cauldron (?)'
R:IX11, 12

ḳs 'bone'
V:IV9

ḳd 'to build'
R:I8, V:III4

ḳdj 'to go around, to return'
V:V3

ḳd 'to sleep'
V:V3

kꜣ '(*particle*)'
R:I7, II1(?), 8, IV11, 12, 13, V8, 9, 10, 11, VIII4, 5, IX1, 2, 9, 11, 13, X2, 3, XI13, V:II5, 6, III5, 7, VII6, 7, VIII11–12, XIII1, XVII2, XXI1

kꜣ 'bull'
R:IX1, V:XXII1

sic *kꜣmn* 'to be blind, to blind'
R:III7–8, V:IV3

kꜣr 'chapel, shrine'
R:XXVII5

ky, k.t 'another'
R:III2, IV9, VI2, VIII10, XI2, XVIIx + 2, XXV1 + x + 2, XXVI9, 11, 12, XXVII6, V:I8, III1, IV4, 9, V8, VII5, XIX1, XXV4

kh 'to rage (furiously), to raise (the voice)'
R:I5, R:III3, V:VII5, XIX2(?)

khb 'to roar'
R:IV9, 10–11, V:V9, VII5–6

kḥb 'Keḥeb (?)'
R:IV2

kzj 'to bow'
R:VII12

ktp 'sickle sword'
R:II3

ktkt 'to quiver'
R:XXVII2(?), V:I4

kṯ 'chalice (?), [a metal drinking vessel]'
R:VI12–13

gꜣ (*gw*) '[a bull]'
V:XX2

gꜣb 'arm'
V:IX1, 2, 4, 5, 12, X1–2

gꜣb.t 'arm'
V:V6

gꜣb.t 'hole (?)'
V:V4–5

gꜣy.w 'nutgrass (?)'
R:III13, V:IV7–8

grḥ '(*ending*)'
R:XVIIx + 2

grḥ 'night'
V:XXIV1

gs 'to anoint'
R:XXV1 + x + 2

gg.t 'kidney (?)'
R:VIII2, V:XX1

tꜣ 'land, earth, ground'
R:XVIx + 2, XXIIIx + 3, XXVII3, 4, V:I7, 9, IX6

tjꜥm '[a plant (*med.*)]'
V:XIX1

twt 'statue, image'
V:XXII2, XXIII8 + x + 2

tw-tw-mꜥ 'asant (?)'
V:IV10

tbn.t(!) 'top'
V:III9

tbtb 'to stagger (?)'
V:XXIV2

tp 'head'
R:XXVII2

tpnn 'cumin'
R:II13, V:IV8

tm '(*negation*)'
R:VII8, 9, XXVII3

tm 'to cease, to perish'
V:II7

trj 'to respect'
V:VII3

ṯꜣ.y 'male'
R:I3, V:I3, II10

m-ṯꜣy 'secretly, in secret'
R:III6, V:VI1

ṯꜣw 'air, wind, breath'
R:VI10, V:V5

ṯꜣz.t 'knot, orifice'
R:VIII4, XXVII6, XXVIII4, V:I8, V6, XIII1

ṯꜣz.t 'vertebrae'
R:XXII1 + x + 2, V:XX1

ṯnj 'where?, whence?'
R:X10

ṯnr 'strong, effective, energetic'
V:III2

ṯnr 'mighty one'
R:IX13

t(w)r.(w) 'blood, gore'
V:XXIII2

dꜣj.w 'loin cloth'
R:X14

dy 'here, there'
V:VII1, 2

dpj 'to taste'
R:IV12, V:VII7

dp.t 'taste'
R:IV12

dm 'to pronounce, to mention'
V:II1

dmj.t 'town'
R:I9

dnj.t 'family'
R:VI8, V:IX1(?)

dr 'to drive away, to repel, to remove'
R:XXV1 + x + 3, XXVI7, XXVII5

dḥr 'bitter'
R:IV2, V4, V:VI10, VII11

dḳ.w 'flour, powder'
R:XXVI8

dd.t 'dish'
R:III13, V:VI8

ḏ.t 'eternity'
R:XXVII4

ḏꜣ.yw 'male opponent'
R:XXVI1, V:IX2

ḏꜣy.t 'female opponent'
V:IX2

ḏꜣr.t 'carob (?)'
R:XXVI8

ḏꜣḏꜣ 'head'
R:II3, 5, III4, VIII4, XI13, XXx + 1, XXII1 + x + 2, V:III10, IV1, V6, 10, XIII1

ḏw 'mountain'
R:II1, 2, III9, VIII14, XIXx + 2, V:III9, VI3, XVII1

ḏw.t 'evil, viciousness'
V:XXIV1

ḏbꜣ.w 'leaves, foliage'
R:XVIIx + 3

ḏbʿ 'finger'
R:IV9, V:I5, VII5

ḏmʿ(ʿ) '(to be) parched'
R:VII7, V:XII1

ḏr.t 'hand'
R:IV6, 13, V1, 2, VII3, 13, VIII14, IX3, 10, V:VII2, 7, 9, 13, XIV1

ḏr 'since'
R:VIII13, XVIIx + 3

ḏr.(y)t 'kite, falcon'
V:XXII1

ḏrj 'to be hard, to be solid'
R:IX8

ḏrw.w 'side'
R:VIII2

ḏz 'self, person'
R:XXVII8, 9, 10, 11, 12, XXVIII1, 2, 3, 4

ḏd 'to say'
R:I2, IV8, V12, VI1, VII4, VIII8, X1, XVIIx + 2, XXVI2, XXVII3, 7, 8, 9, 10, 11, 12, XXVIII1, 2, 3, 4, V:I7, II2, 9, IV7, V7, VII4, IX12, XV1, XXII2, XXV2

m-ḏd 'as follows'
R:III11, 12, XIIIx + 2, XVx + 1, XVIIx + 1, XXIIIx + 2, x + 3, V:IV5, 6

r-ḏd 'that, with the word'
R:V11, 12, 13, VI8, VIII6, X3, XI1, V:V7

ḏdf.t 'snake'
R:II12, XVx + 1, XVIIx + 2, V:IV6–7

2. Numerals

, *wʿ* 'one'
R:III2, VI2, X9, XXVI8, 9, V:II3, IV8, X1, XVIII1

jfd.w 'four'
R:XVIIx + 2, XXV1 + x + 2, XXVI9, XXVII6

sfḫ 'seven'
R:I3, III13, VIII4, XXVI2, XXVIII4, V:I8, V5, VI8

ḫmn 'eight'
R:III13

'seventy'
R:XVIIx + 2

ḥḥ 'million'
V:IX10

tp.j 'first'
R:XVIIx + 2, V:II3

3. Deities and demonic beings

ꜣs.t 'Isis'
R:XXVIII2, V:XXII3

Jꜣḫ.w 'Jakhu'
V:XXIV2

Jꜥḥ 'Jah, moon'
R:XXIx + 2

Jbsn '[a demon]'
R:III5, V:V10–VI1

Jmw.t(?) '[goddess] (?)'
R:XVx + 1

Jmn 'Amun'
R:XVx + 1, XVIIx + 1

Jmn.t 'Amaunet'
R:XVx + 1

Jn-Ḥr.t 'Onuris'
R:IX4, XI14, V:XIV1

Jrn.wt 'Renenutet (?)'
R:XVIIx + 1

Jšḫr 'Ishkhara'
V:II2

(J)tm 'Atum'
R:XXVII1, V:IX2

Jtm.t 'Itemet'
R:II12, V:IV7

Jtm 'Adamma'
R:V7, V:VIII5

ꜥpp 'Apophis'
V:IX5

ꜥntj 'Anat'
R:III12, VI11, XVIIIx + 1, V:III7(?), V6

ꜥḫ.w 'Akhu'
R:III2, 7, IV3, 5, V8, VIII10, X1, 2, XI2, V:I1, III4, IV3, 9, 10, V4, 8, VI2, VII1, 10, IX1, 3, 4, XV1, XXII1

ꜥzt(j)r.t 'Astarte'
R:XVIIIx + 1–2

Wꜣy.w 'the distant one (?)'
R:XI14

Wp-wꜣ.wt 'Wepwawet'
R:V5, XXII1, V:VIII1

Wsjr 'Osiris'
R:XVIx + 2, V:XXII2, 4

Bꜥl 'Baal'
R:II3, V1, V:III10, VII5, 8

Bṯḥ 'Bathah (wife of Horus)'
V:XXV3

Pḳsn '[god] (?)'
R:III8–9

Mw.t 'Mut'
V:XXII3

Mrj '[god] (?)'
R:VI7–8

Mḫnt.j-jr-tj 'Mekhenti-irti'
R:XXV1 + x + 3, V:XXIII2

Mšr '[a demon]'
R:III3, V:V9

Nw.t 'Nut'
R:VIII12, XXIX1, V:II1

Nb.t-Ḥw.t 'Nephthys'
R:XXVIII3, V:XXII2, 3

Nkl 'Nikkal'
R:V6, IX12, V:VIII3

Nḳpḥn '[god] (?)'
V:IV4

Nṯr-ḥr.j 'the god above (the moon god)'
R:II11, V6, V:IV6, VIII2

Nṯr-dwꜣ 'the morning god, morning star'
R:V13

Rꜥ(w) 'Re, the sun'
R:II11, 12, III8, IV1, 2, V4, 13, VI5, VIII6, 13, X3, XI1, XIIx + 3, XVIIx + 2, XXIIIx + 3, XXVII1, 8, V:I5, 6, IV6, 7, VI3, 9, VII11, IX2

Rnwy 'Renuy (brother of Apis)'
R:XXVII7

Ršp 'Reshep'
R:V6, XI13, V:VIII4

Ḥꜥpj 'Hapi, flood'
V:XVII1

Ḥw.t-ḥr.wt 'Hathors'
R:V12, VIII5, X4, V:XIII1

Ḥp.w 'Apis'
R:XXVII7

Ḥr.w 'Horus'
R:II4, VI1, VII5, VIII6, X11, XIIx + 2, XIVx + 1, XVIIx + 2, XXV1 + x + 3, XXVII4, 11, V:V8, XVI1, XXIII3, XXIV2, 4, XXV3

Ḫnt.j-jmntj.w 'Khentiamentiu'
V:IX3

H̱nm.w 'Khnum'
R:XXVII10

Zp-ny '[goddess]'
R:XVIIx + 1

Zp-ns-tꜣ 'Zepnesta'
R:II11, V:IV6

Sp.t-Stẖ 'the-lip-of-Seth'
R:XVIIx + 2

sꜣ-mꜥ(w)-nꜣ 'Sāmānu'
R:I8, II3, 3–4, 7, III2, 4, 7, IV5, V2, VI1, 3, 6, 7, VII1, 10, VIII6, IX2, 13, X3, 4, 5, XXII1 + x + 1, V:V8, 9, VI2, VII2

Sjꜣ 'Sia'
R:XXIIIx + 3

Spd.w 'Sopdu'
R:XXVII10

Stẖ(?) 'weather god, Seth'
R:I9, 10, II3, IV7, 10, V4, VI11, 13, VII1, 3, 5, IX4, 14, X12, XI4, 12, XXV1 + x + 3, XXVII4, 12, V:III5, 6, VII3, 5, 11, XIX1, 2, XXII2, XXIII3

Šw 'Shu'
R:V4, XXIx + 2, XXVII9, V:VII11

Šl 'Shala'
V:XVII1

Ḳty '[a mother snake]'
R:VI10, V:XI2

Ḳdš.t 'Qedshet'
R:XXIIIx + 2

Ṯmk/ḳn '[demon]'
R:III4, V:V10

Ḏr[...] '[god] (?)'
R:VII4

Ḏhr '[god] (?)'
R:III9, V:IV4

Ḏḥw.tj 'Thoth'
R:XXVIII1

4. Toponyms

Jrtḳn '[toponym] (?)'
R:VI8, V:XI1

Jḳḏy.t '[toponym] (?)'
V:II2

Jdḳn '[toponym] (?)'
R:III12–13, V:VI7(?)–8

wꜣḏy(.t) n.t ꜥb(w) 'Wadji-of-the-horn (a lake?)'
V:XXV1–2

Pwn.t 'Punt'
R:XXVII7

Ḥt/dm '[toponym] (?)'
R:III3, V:V9

Ḥmḳr '[toponym] (?)'
R:III9, XXIIIx + 3, V:VI4

Zḫm 'Letopolis'
V:XXIII3

sḫ.t jꜣ(n)r.w 'field of rushes'
R:XXVII2

Appendix II: Present appearance of the papyrus

Sheet	Column (lines, remarks)	Condition
343 Sheet 1 recto	R:I (12) R:II (13) R:III (13)	Papyrus quite dark due to older conservation treatment; mostly legible; bottom edge frayed
343 Sheet 1 verso	V:I (11) V:II (10) V:III (10, beginning)	Papyrus quite dark; ink severely rubbed off, making it difficult to read; top edge frayed
343 Sheet 2 recto	R:IV (13) R:V (13) (R:IV)	Papyrus quite light; ink in good condition, slightly rubbed off
343 Sheet 2 verso	V:III (10, end) V:IV (10) V:V (10, beginning)	Papyrus quite light; ink often in good condition, severely rubbed off at the beginning (V:III)
343 Sheet 3 recto	R:VII (13) R:VIII (14, beginning at line 12)	Papyrus slightly darker than 343 Sheet 2; ink often legible; broken off at top (R:VII, VIII)
343 Sheet 3 verso	V:V (10, end) (V:VI) V:VI (10, beginning)	Papyrus slightly darker than 343 Sheet 2; ink often legible; broken off at bottom
345 Sheet 1 recto	R:VIII (14, end) R:IX (14) R:X (14) R:XI (14, beginning)	Papyrus relatively dark; ink clearly legible; large hole at the beginning (R:VIII, IX); middle completely broken off towards the latter part (R:X, XI); *passim* tears fixed with tape
345 Sheet 1 verso	V:VI (10, end) V:VII (11) V:VIII (12) V:IX (12)	Papyrus darker around the holes; ink clearly legible; large hole at the beginning (V:VII); middle completely broken off towards the latter part (V:VIII, IX)
345 Sheet 2 recto (5 fragments, top-down)	R:XI (14, fragment 5) R:XII (fragment 5) R:XIII (fragment 5) R:XIV (fragment 4) R:XV (fragment 4) R:XVI (fragments 4 & 3) R:XVII (fragments 3 & 2) R:XVIII (fragments 3 & 2) R:XIX (fragment 2) R:XX (fragments 2 & 1) R:XXI fragment 1, beginning)	Papyrus slightly darker at the edges; only one to three lines preserved from the lower part; ink often clearly legible, rubra rubbed off in places; *passim* tears

Sheet	Column (lines, remarks)	Condition
345 Sheet 2 verso (5 fragments, bottom-up)	V:X (fragment 5) V:XI (fragment 5) V:XII (fragment. 4) V:XIII (fragment 4) V:XIV (fragment 3) V:XV (fragment 3) V:XVI (fragment 2) V:XVII (fragment 2) V:XVIII (fragment 1) V:XIX (fragment 1)	Papyrus slightly darker at the edges; only one to three lines preserved from the upper part; ink often clearly legible, rubra rubbed off in places; *passim* tears
345 Sheet 3 recto (4 fragments)	R:XXI (fragment 3, end) R:XXII (fragments 1 & 3) R:XXIII (fragments 4a & 4b) R:XXV (fragment 2, end) R:XXVI (12, fragment 2 beginning)	Papyrus considerably darker at the edges; ink often clearly legible; *passim* tears
345 Sheet 3 verso (4 fragments)	V:XX (fragment 3) V:XXI (fragments 3 & 4a) V:XXII (fragment 4b, beginning) V:XXIV (fragment 2) V:XXV (fragment 2, beginning)	Papyrus darker at the edges; ink often clearly legible; *passim* tears
345 Sheet 4 recto (3 fragments)	R:XXIV (fragments 1 & 3) R:XXV (fragment 3, beginning)	Papyrus darker at the edges; ink often clearly legible; *passim* tears; fragment 2 traces of ink (palimpsest?), cannot be joined
345 Sheet 4 verso (3 fragments)	V:XXII (fragment 3, end) V:XXIII (fragments 1 & 3)	Papyrus considerably darker at the edges; ink often clearly legible; *passim* tears; fragment 2 traces of ink (palimpsest?), cannot be joined
345 Sheet 5 recto	R:XXVI (12, end) R:XXVII (12) R:XXVIII (5)	Papyrus partially shows dark spots; edges frayed; ink often clearly legible, rubra partially rubbed off (R:XXVIII); last part of the page blank (6–10 cm)
345 Sheet 5 verso	V:XXV (4, end)	Papyrus partially shows dark spots; edges frayed; ink often clearly legible; last part of the page blank (29 cm)

Indices

1. General

2. Deities & demonic beings

- eye of 86–87
- first one of 71, 73
Renenutet 71, 73
Renui 85
Reput 72
Reshep 16, 43, 45, 67, 68, 69
'the righteous one' 22, 53
Sāmānu 15–16, *passim*
Seth 16, 27, 28, 43, 44, 46, 55, 61, 63, 74, 79, 84, 98, 99, 102
- testicles of 83
Shala 16, 67, 68
Shu 43, 72, 73, 84
Sia 76
Sopdu 84
sun god 30, 37, 62, 64, 95
Ṭallay 73
Thot 84, 95
Tjemk/qen 16, 35, 36
Uraeus 23, 105
weather god 16, 24, 27, 28, 35, 43, 44, 46, 48, 52, 53, 54, 55, 61, 62, 63, 64, 65, 67, 68, 99
Wepwawet 43, 72
Yamm 28, 40, 44
Yassib 28
Zepnesta 27, 30
Zepni 71, 73

3. Drugs

acacia, sweet
- blossom of 31
almond, bitter 38
asant 35, 38
bitter shrub/tree 38
blood
- of animals 96
- of goat 94, 96
carob 31
- flour of 79, 80
colocynth 31
conifer
- fruits of 31, 77
cucumber
- seeds of 47
cumin 30–31
cyperus 31
date 80–81
- seeds of 81
Dreckapotheke 23
emmer 39
faeces 23, 57, 81
- of pig 23
fenugreek (?) 38, 77
frankincense 31, 96
grain 38, 39
gum 31
honey 31, 81
ibex 96
leaf 80
mandragora 38
melon 47
- seeds of 47
mineral 31, 77
mint (?) 96
mucilage 39
mucus 81
myrrh 96
natron 31, 80, 81
nutgrass 31
ochre 62, 77, 81
pine nut 31, 77, 98
salt
- northern 81
resin 31, 96
root 73
turpentine 31
urea 23
urine 23, 81
- pigs 23
water 39, 57, 96
wine 47, 98
Asa foetida 38
Boswellia spp. 31
Citrullus lanatus (Thumb.) Mats. & Nakai 47
Cucumis melo L. 47
Cuminum cyminum L. 30
Cyperus rotundus L. 31
Ferula assa-foetida L. 38
Mentha spp. 96
Nigella sativa L. 30
Pistacia terebinthus L. 31
Triticum diccocum 39
jwr.yt 80
jns.y 85
jrp 47
ʿmʿʿ 39
ʿr.w 80
wzš.t 81
bj.t 31
bd.t 39
pr.t-šn 31, 47, 77
mnš.t 81
mstȝnj
- *mw* 96
rj.t 80
rrm.t 38
ḥmȝ.w 38
ḥmy.w 38
ḥmȝ.t
- *mḥ.t* 81
ḥmȝr.t 31
ḥsȝ 39, 81
- *n(.j) ʿwȝ.yt* 81
ḥsmn 31, 81
snṯr 31, 96
shr.t 31
š(ȝ)b.t 57, 81
šnf.t 81
gȝb.t 80
gj.w n.j wḥȝ.t 31
tjʿm 98
tpnn 30–31
ttm 38
ḏȝr.t 31

4. Grammatical/lexical remarks

5. Persons

6. Toponyms

7. Quoted texts, Egyptian

8. Quoted texts, Near Eastern

Sketch of the papyrus

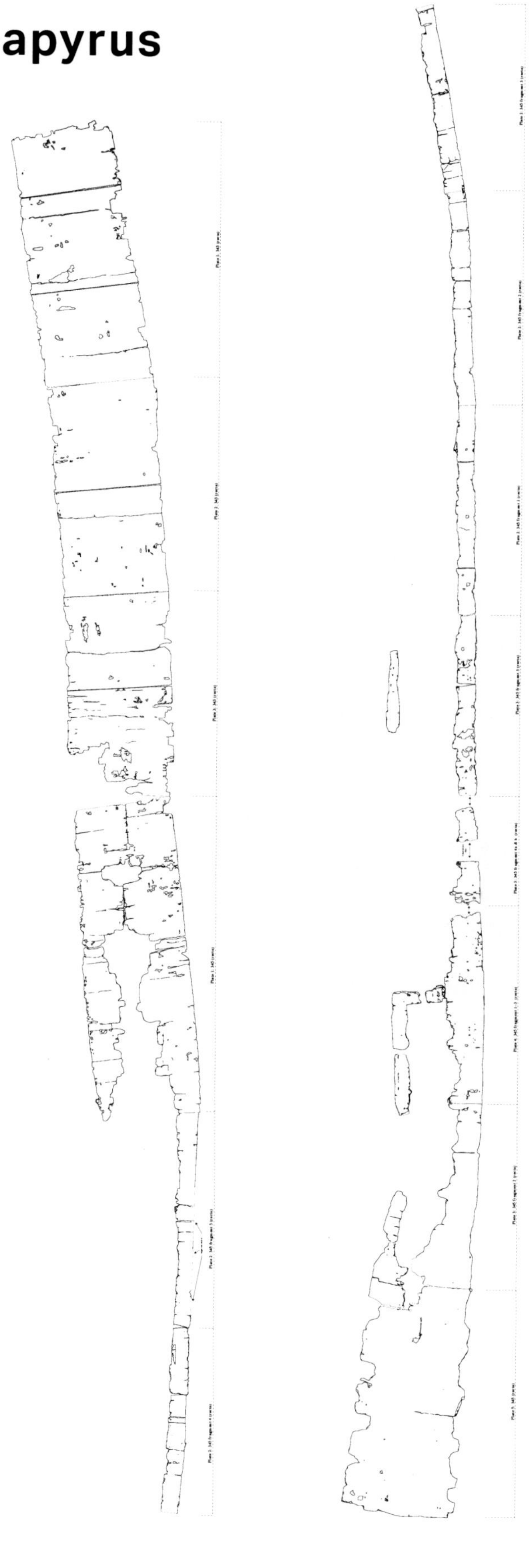

Sketch of Papyrus Leiden I 343 and I 345.

Plates

Pl. 1

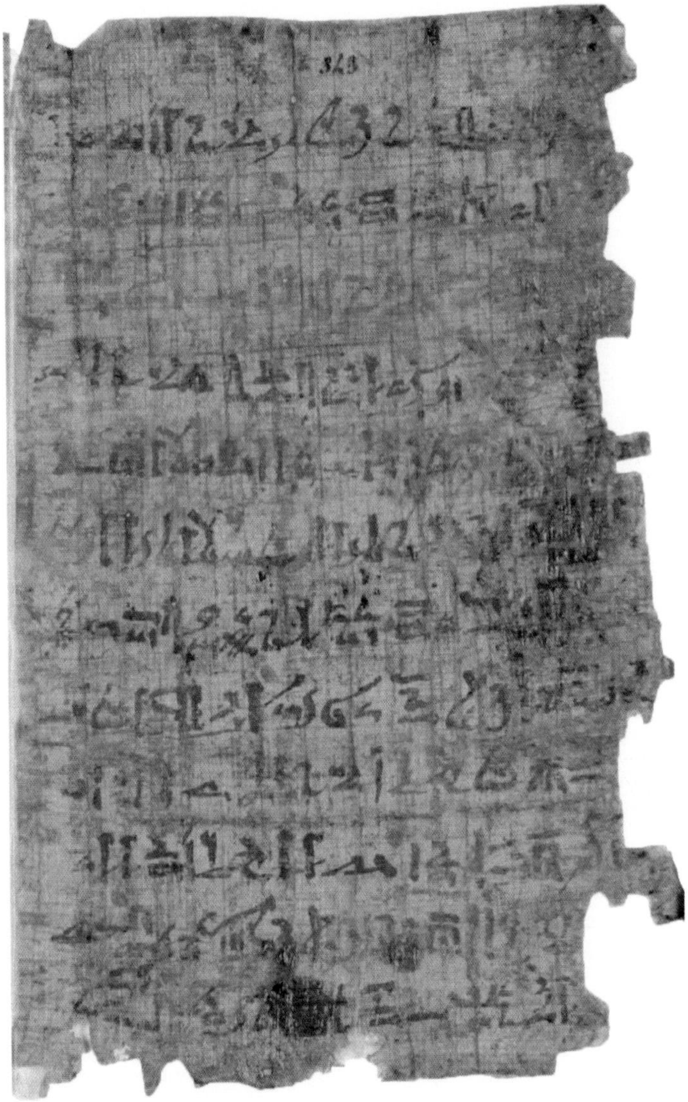

Papyrus Leiden I 343, recto column I (scale 1:1).

Pl. 2

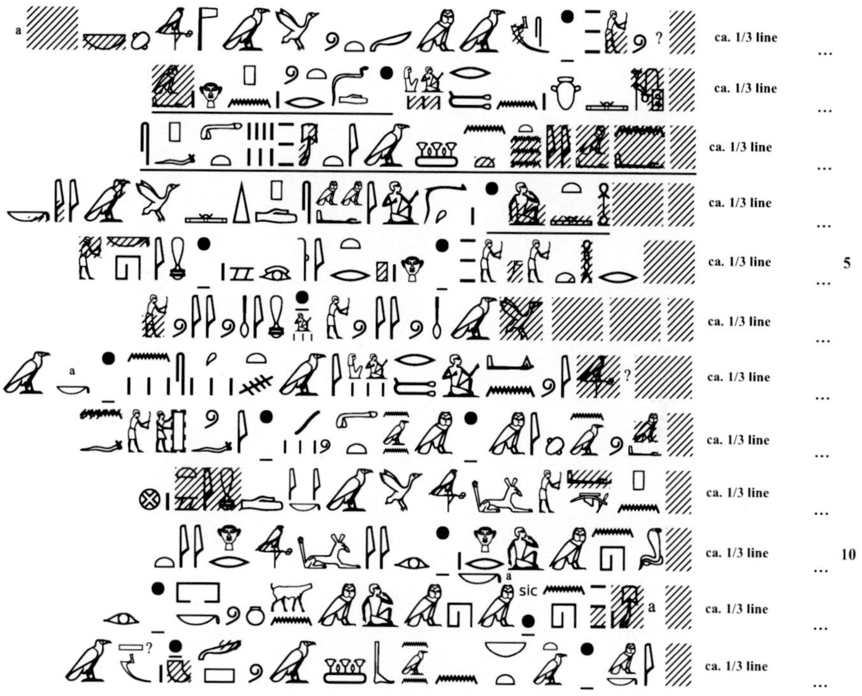

R:I1a *traces could fit mꜣꜥ.t* **7a** *traces are visible above* *and* *, remains of the palimpsest* **10a** *under the line* **11a** *Gardiner reads* **9**.

Papyrus Leiden I 343, recto column I, transcription.

Pl. 3

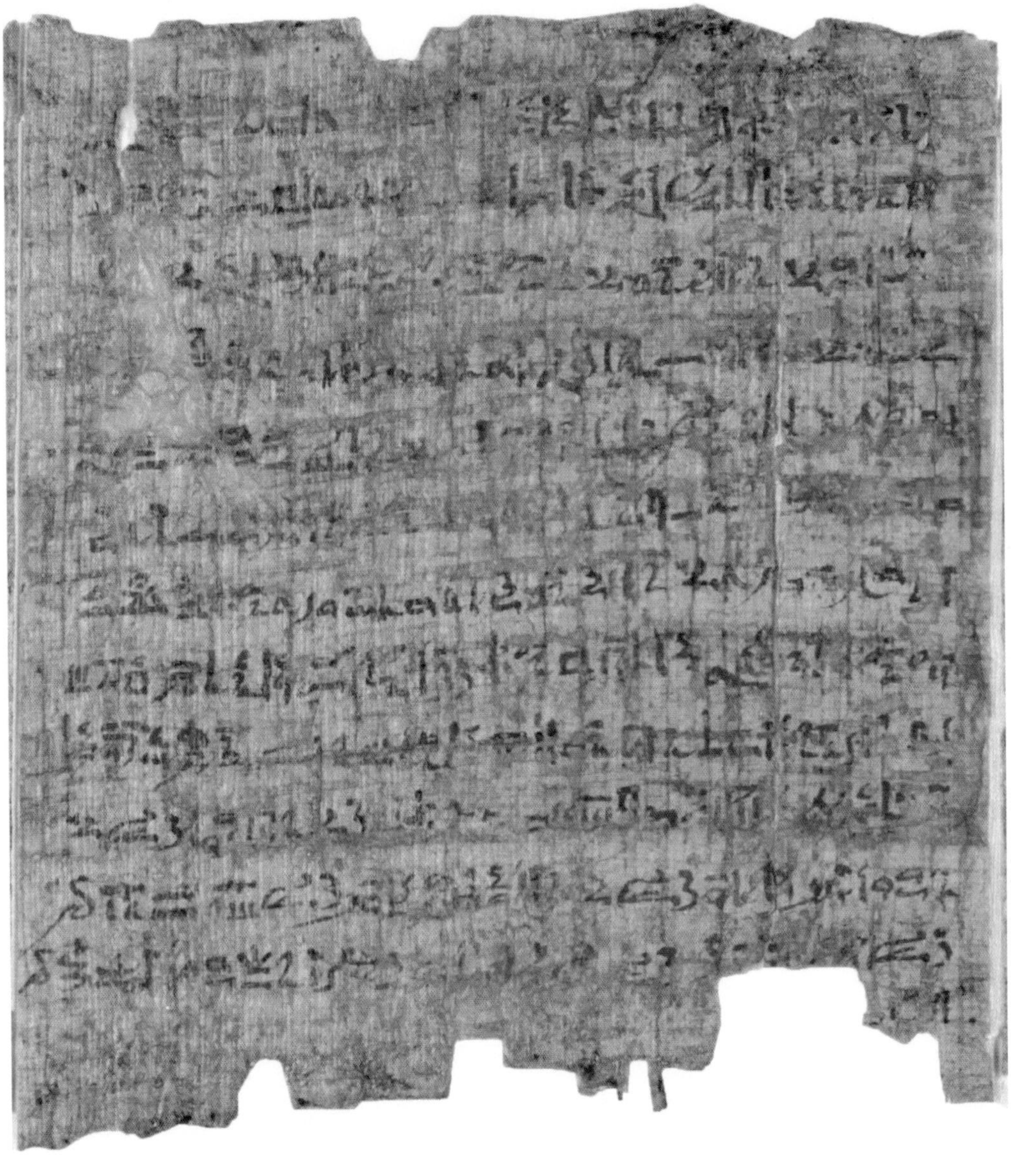

Papyrus Leiden I 343, recto column II (scale 1:1).

Pl. 4

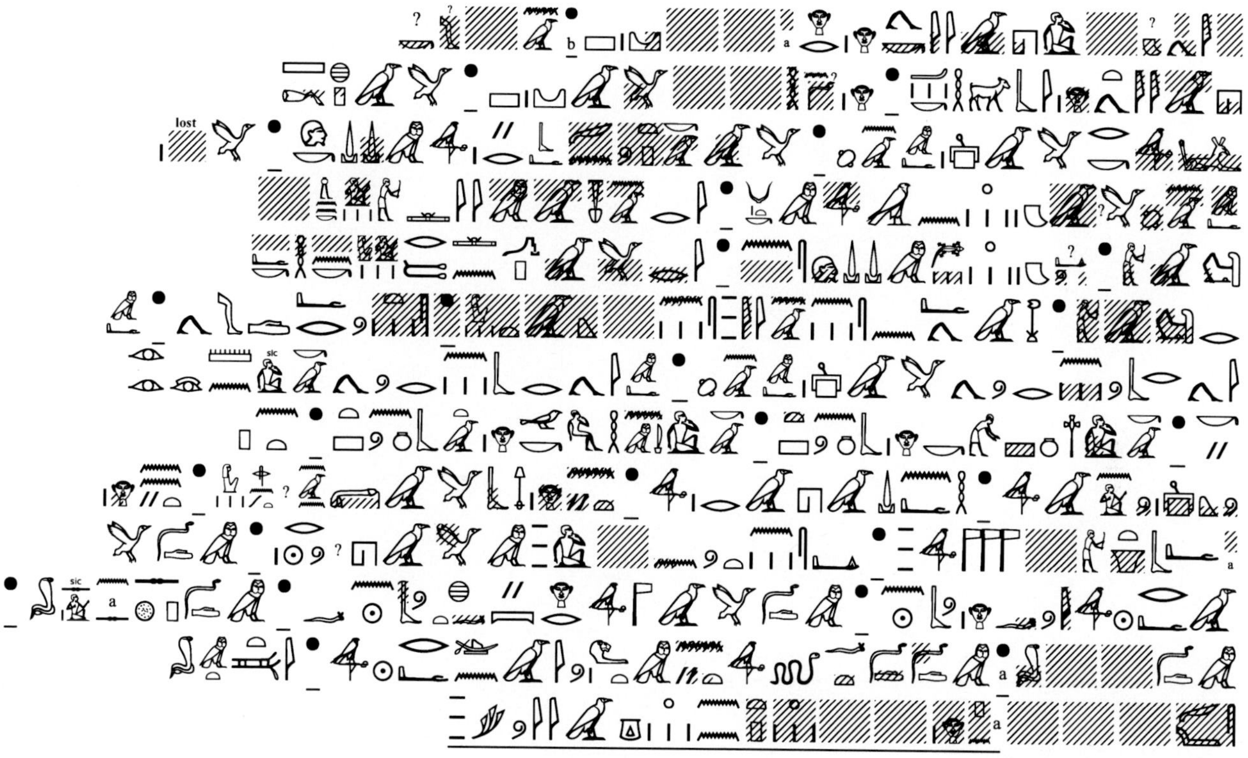

R:II1a *traces* **1b** *verse point and* *no longer visible* **10a** *if* ? **11a** *or* **12a** *verse point no longer visible*

13a *extremely faded.*

Papyrus Leiden I 343, recto column II, transcription.

Pl. 5

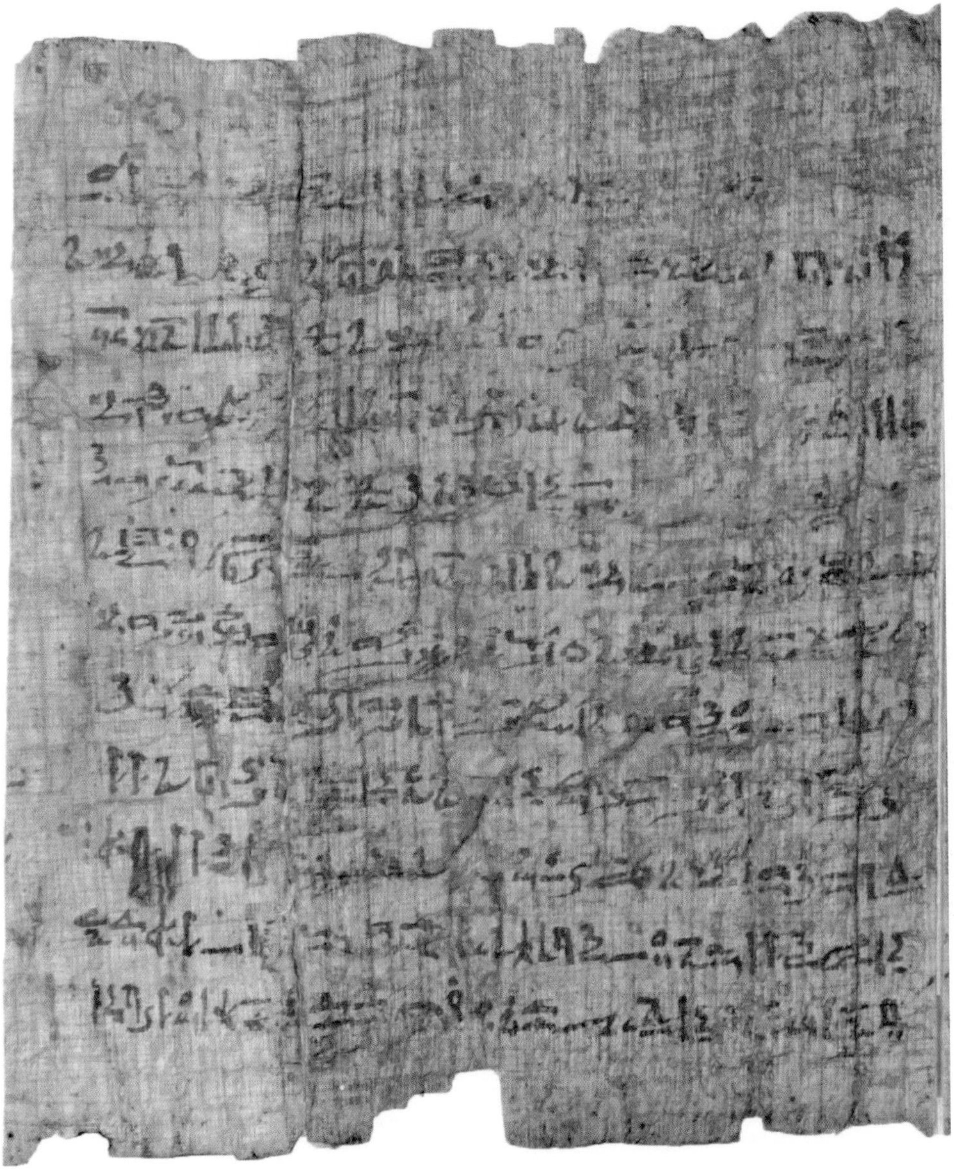

Papyrus Leiden I 343, recto column III (scale 1:1).

Pl. 6

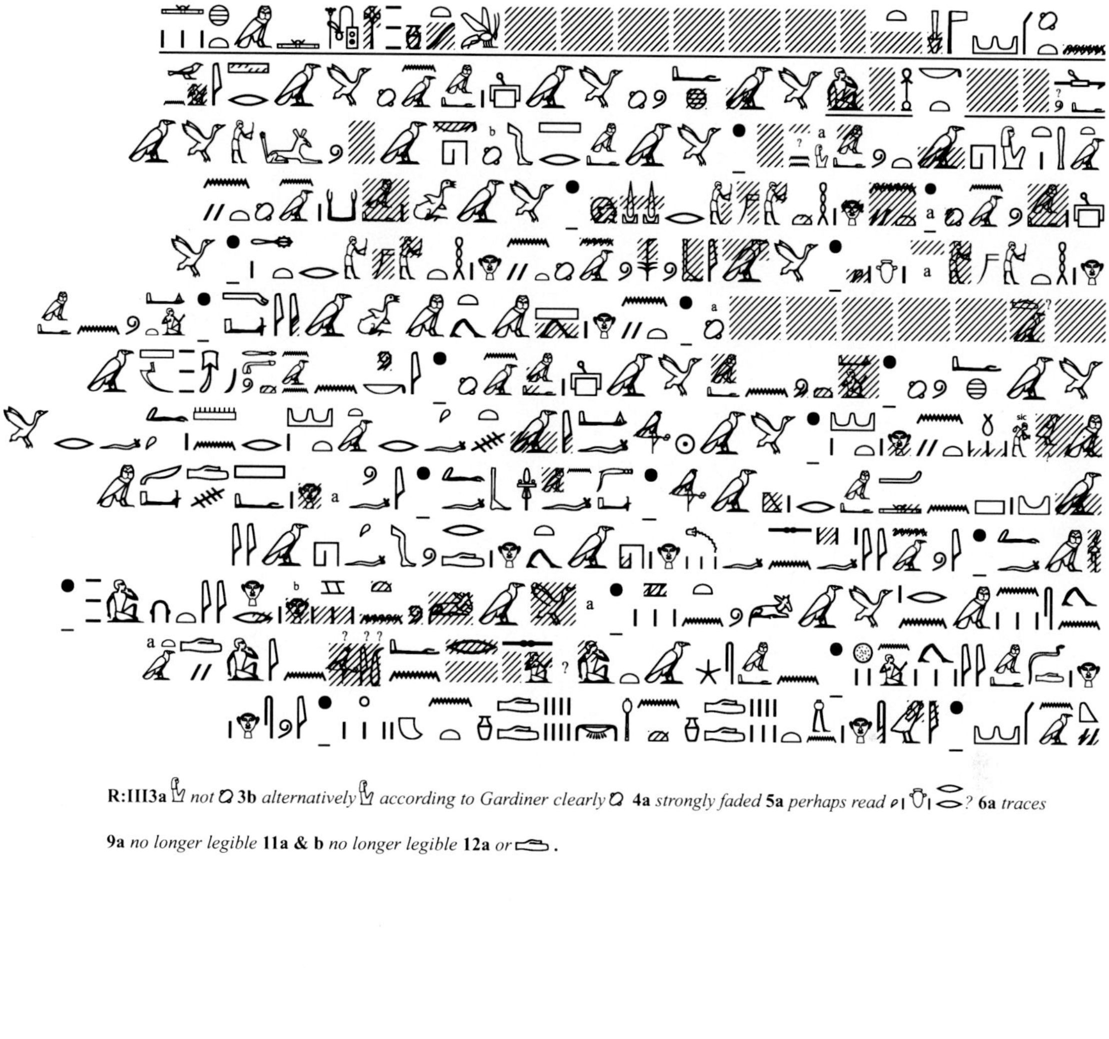

R:III3a *not* **3b** *alternatively* *according to Gardiner clearly* **4a** *strongly faded* **5a** *perhaps read* ? **6a** *traces*
9a *no longer legible* **11a & b** *no longer legible* **12a** *or* .

Papyrus Leiden I 343, recto column III, transcription.

Pl. 7

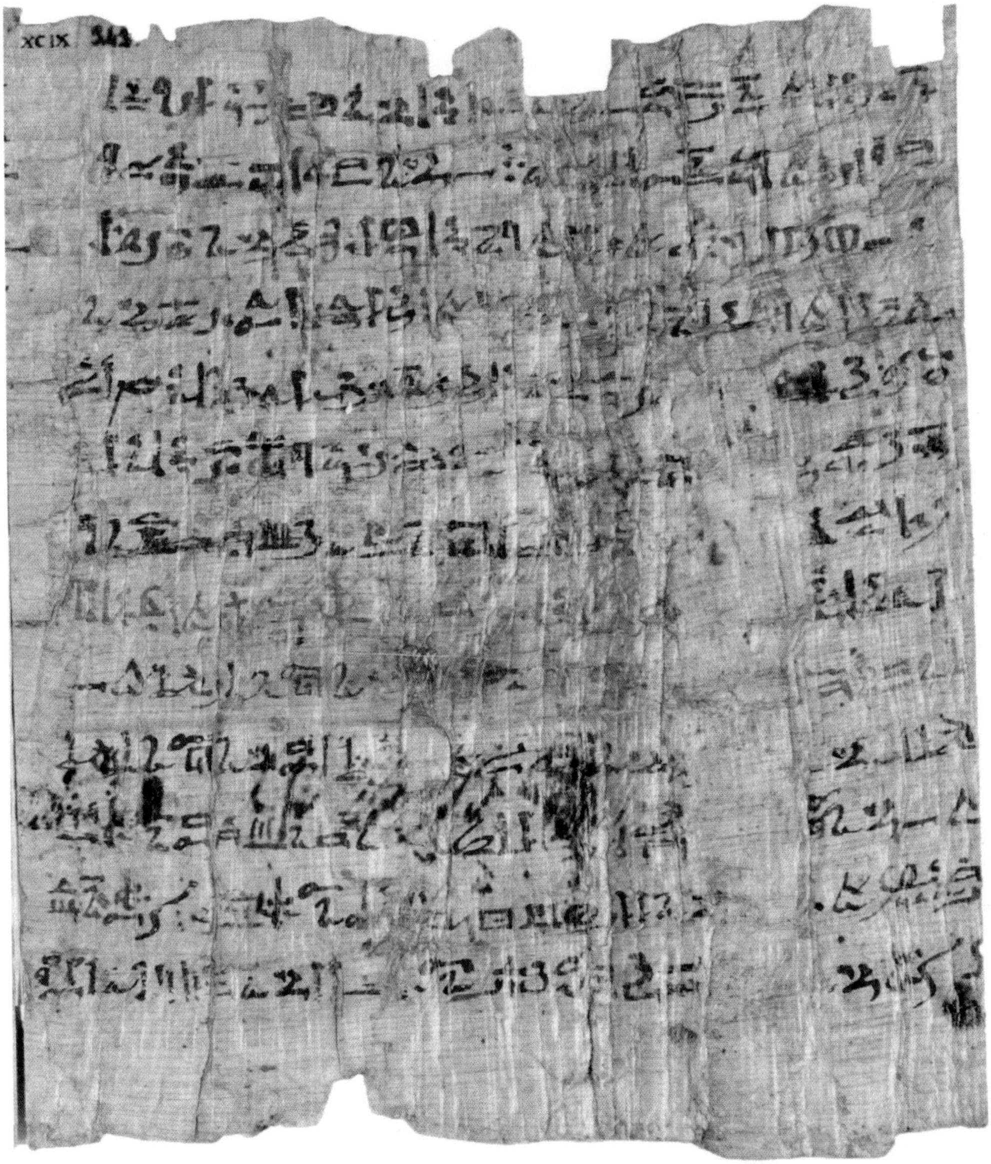

Papyrus Leiden I 343, recto column IV (scale 1:1).

Pl. 8

R:IV2a *or* [glyph] **2b** *traces above* [glyph], *perhaps palimpsest* **13a** *if* [glyph] *?* **b** *traces after* [glyph].

Papyrus Leiden I 343, recto column IV, transcription.

Pl. 9

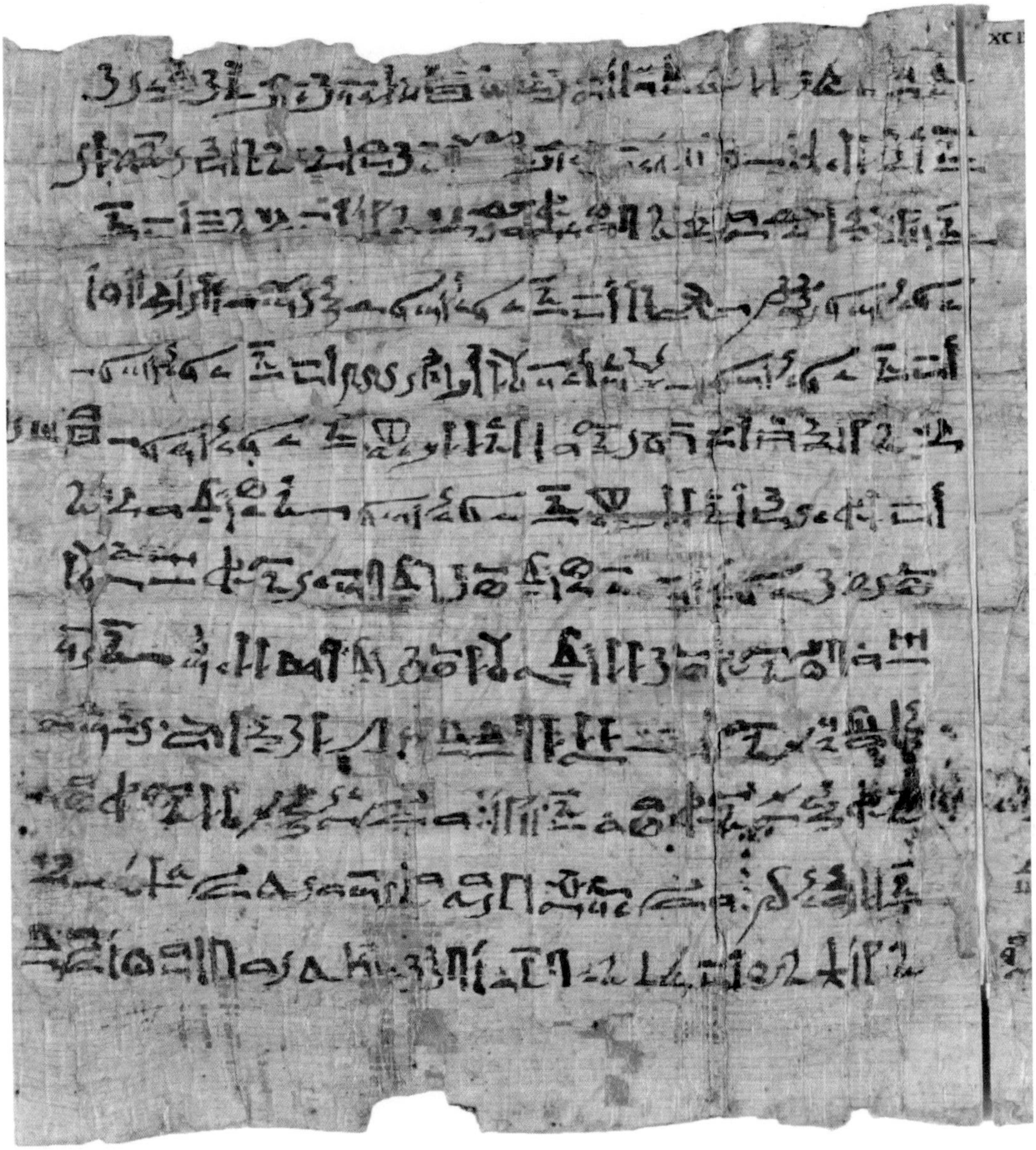

Papyrus Leiden I 343, recto column V (scale 1:1).

Pl. 10

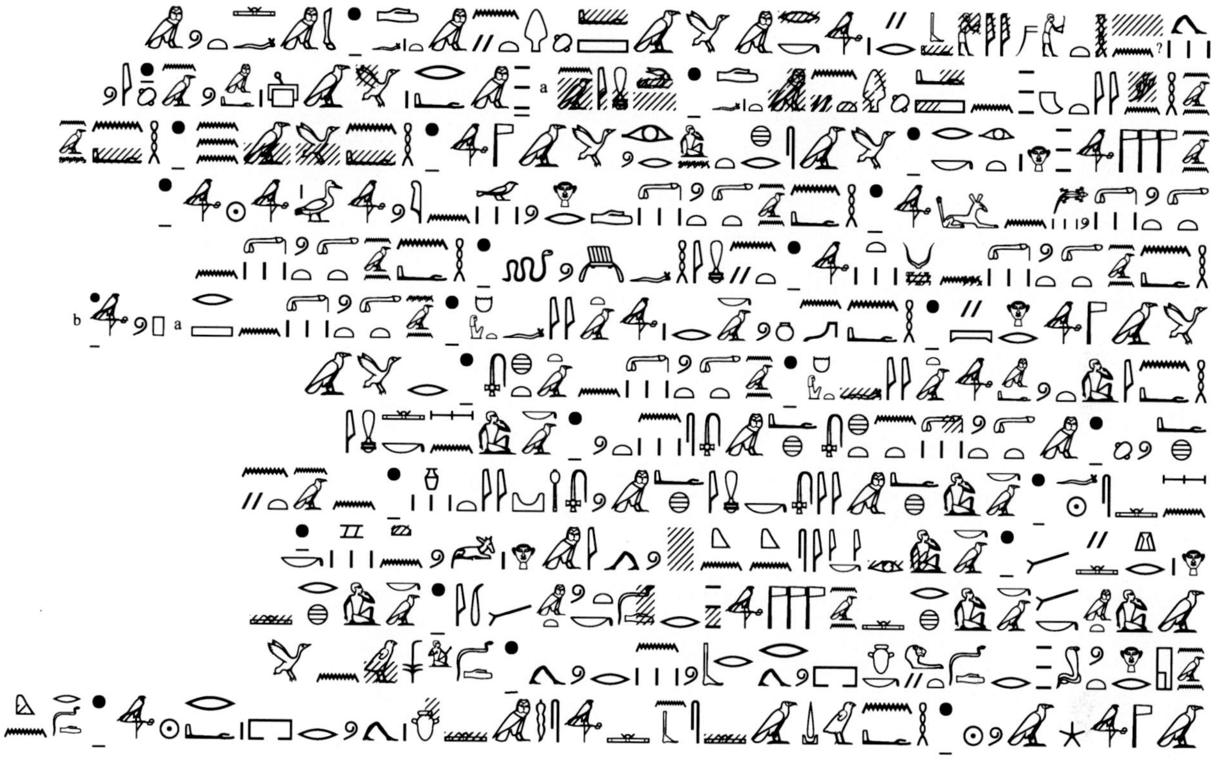

R:V2a ⁝ *added later in red* **6a–b** *written between the columns V and VI.*

Papyrus Leiden I 343, recto column V, transcription.

Pl. 11

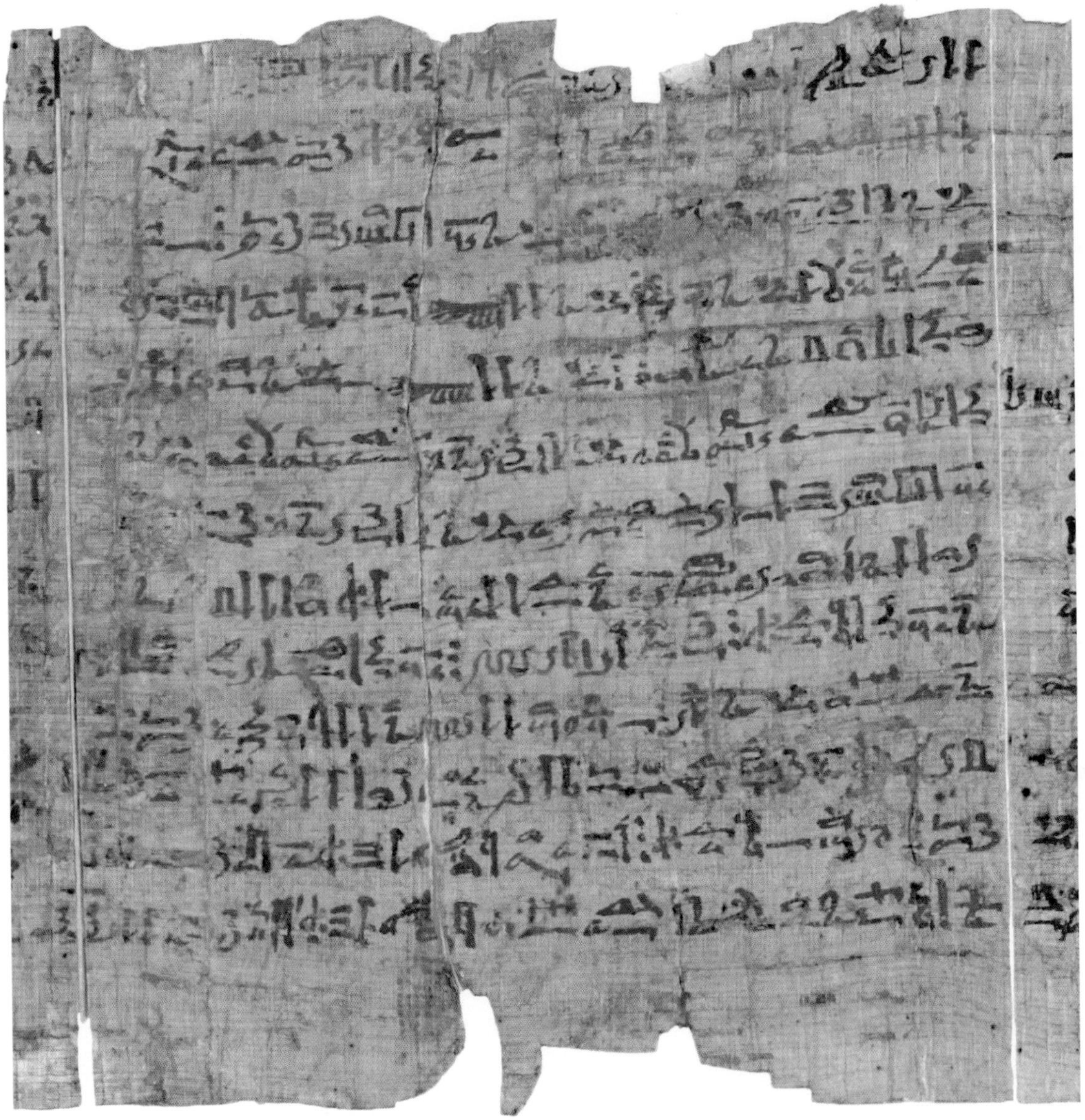

Papyrus Leiden I 343, recto column VI (scale 1:1).

Pl. 12

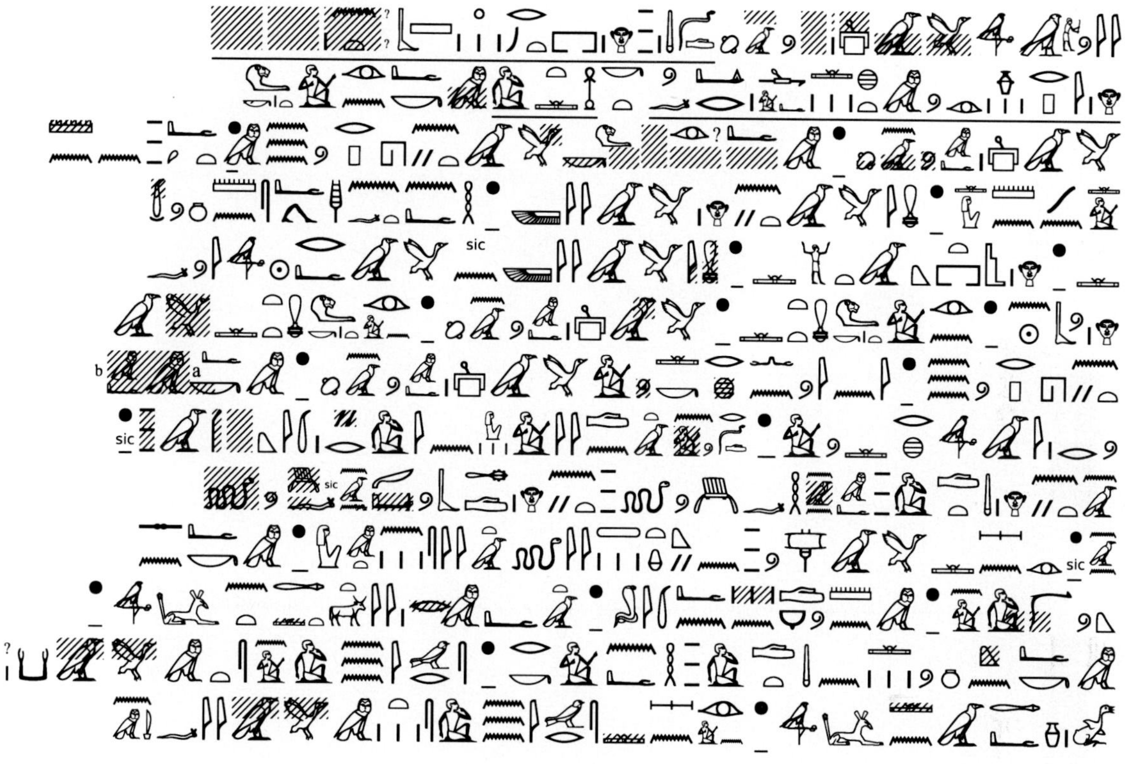

R:VI7a–b *no longer legible* **9** *<ḥ>fȝw, see ḥfȝw in the same line.*

Papyrus Leiden I 343, recto column VI, transcription.

Pl. 13

Papyrus Leiden I 343, recto column VII (scale 1:1).

Pl. 14

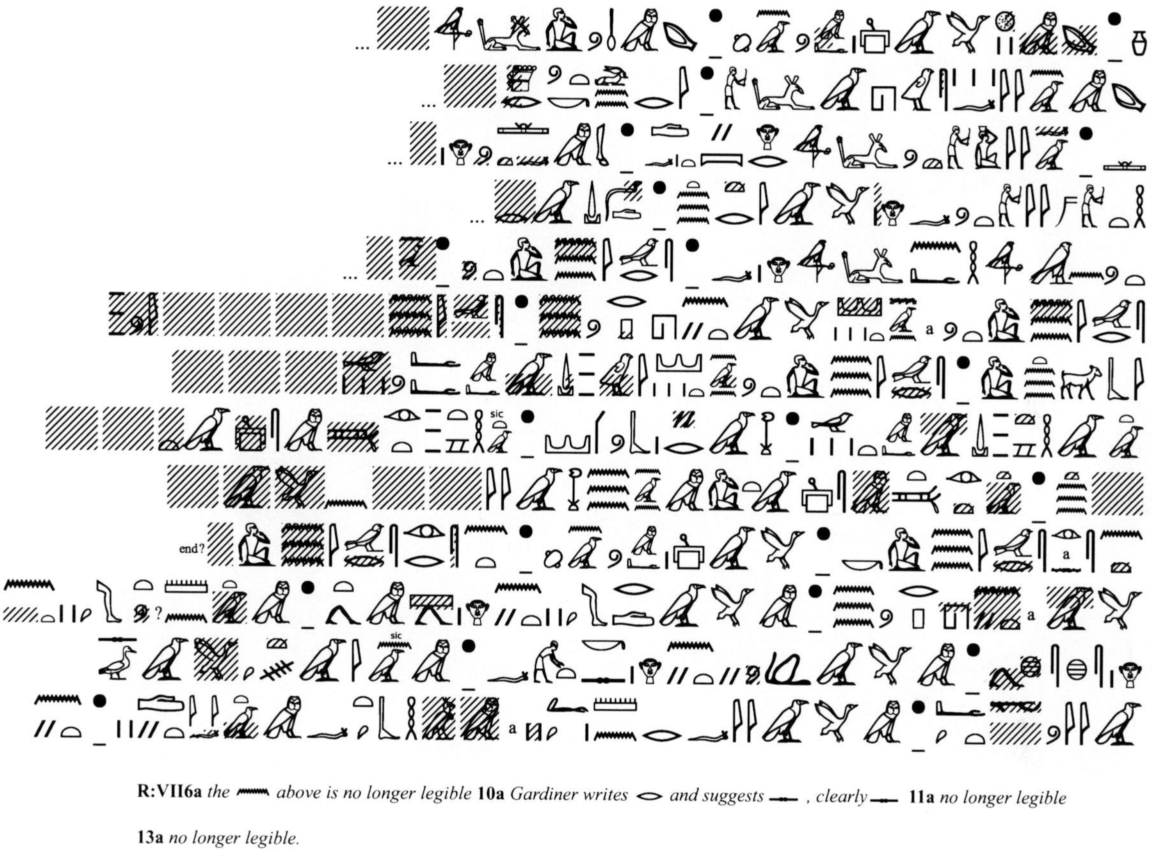

R:VII6a *the* *above is no longer legible* **10a** *Gardiner writes* *and suggests* *, clearly* **11a** *no longer legible*

13a *no longer legible.*

Papyrus Leiden I 343, recto column VII, transcription.

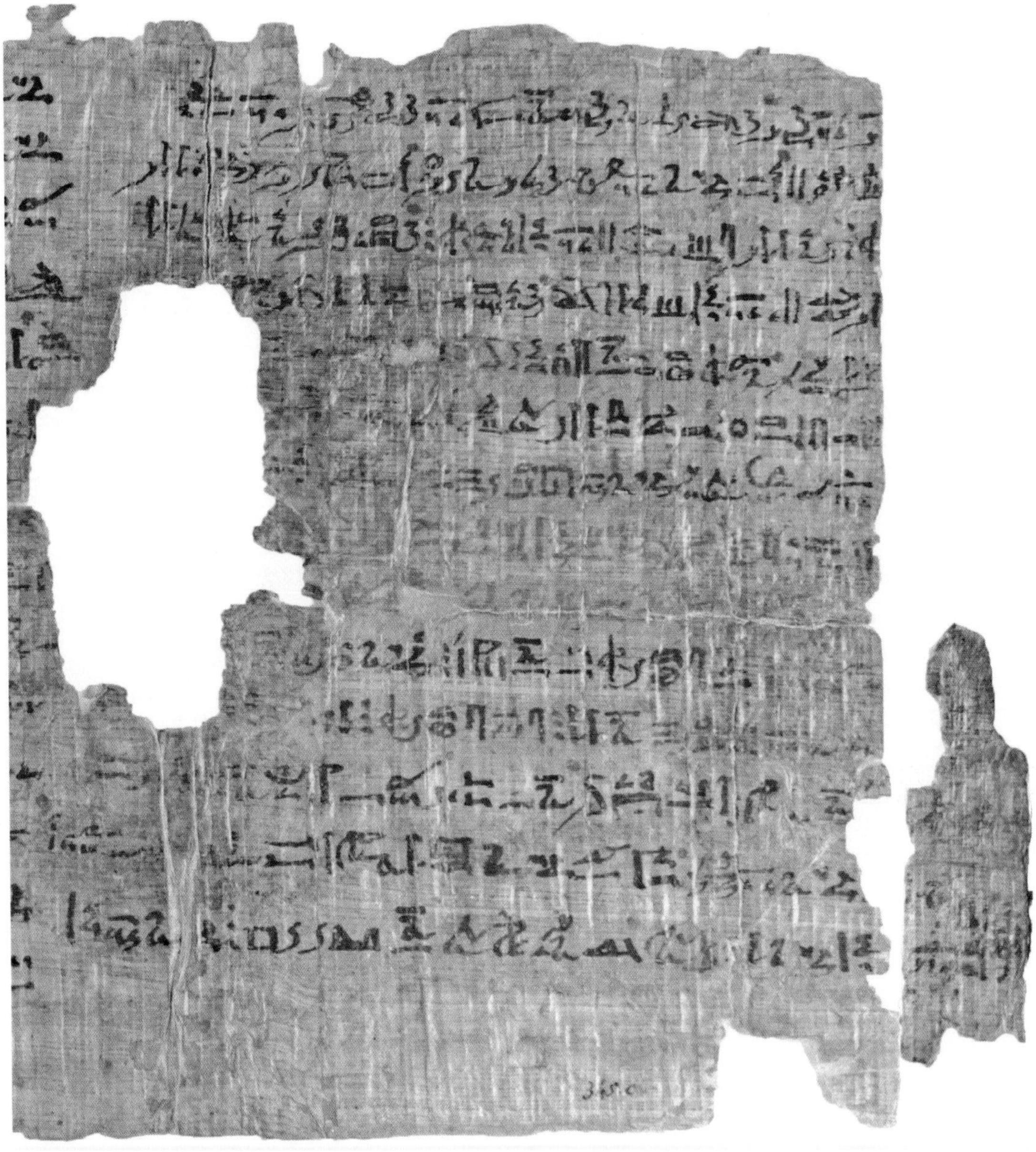

Papyrus Leiden I 343 + 345, recto column VIII (scale 1:1).

Pl. 16

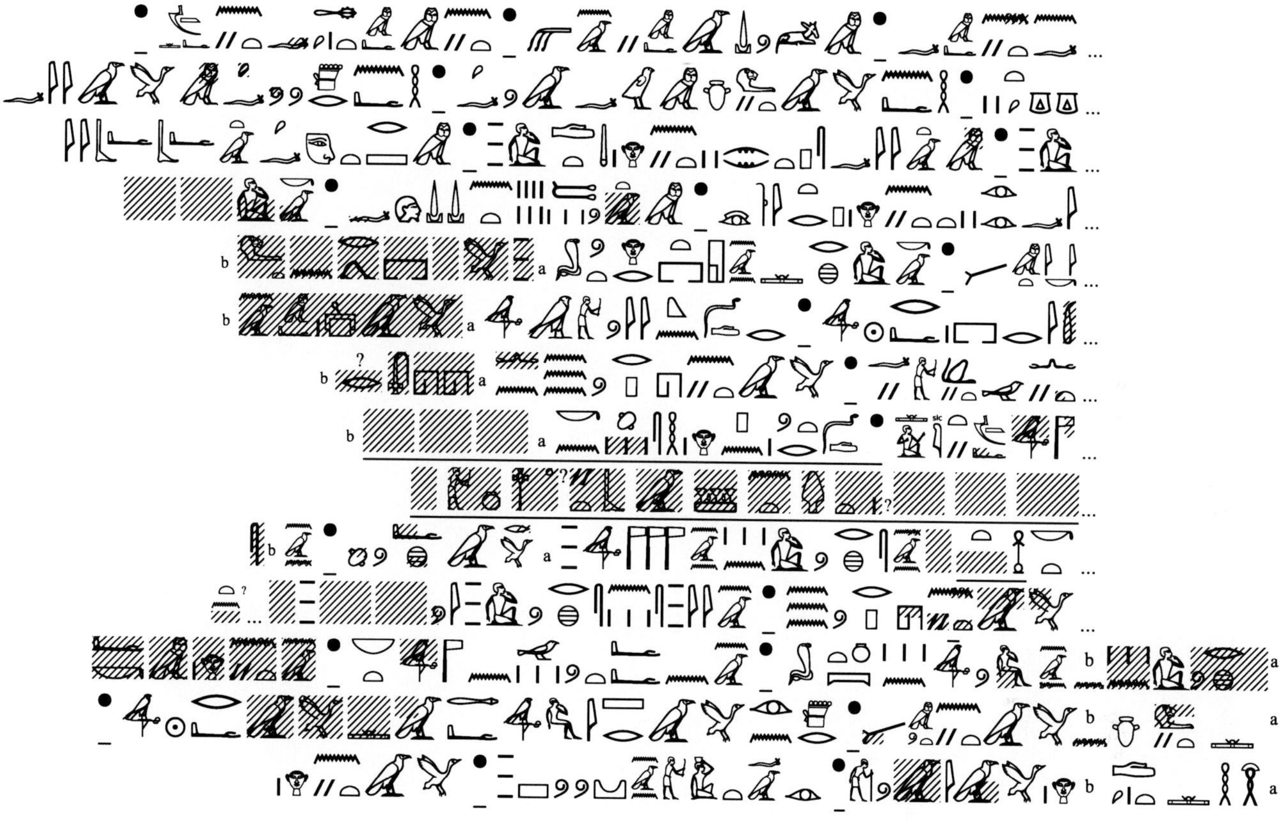

R:VIII5a–b *almost illegible* **6a–b** *only partially legible* **7a–b** *only partially legible* **8a–b** *traces of rubrum* **10a** *above the line* **10b** *no longer legible* **12–14a–b** *at the end of column R:VIII* **12b** *no longer legible.*

Papyrus Leiden I 343 + 345, recto column VIII, transcription.

Pl. 17

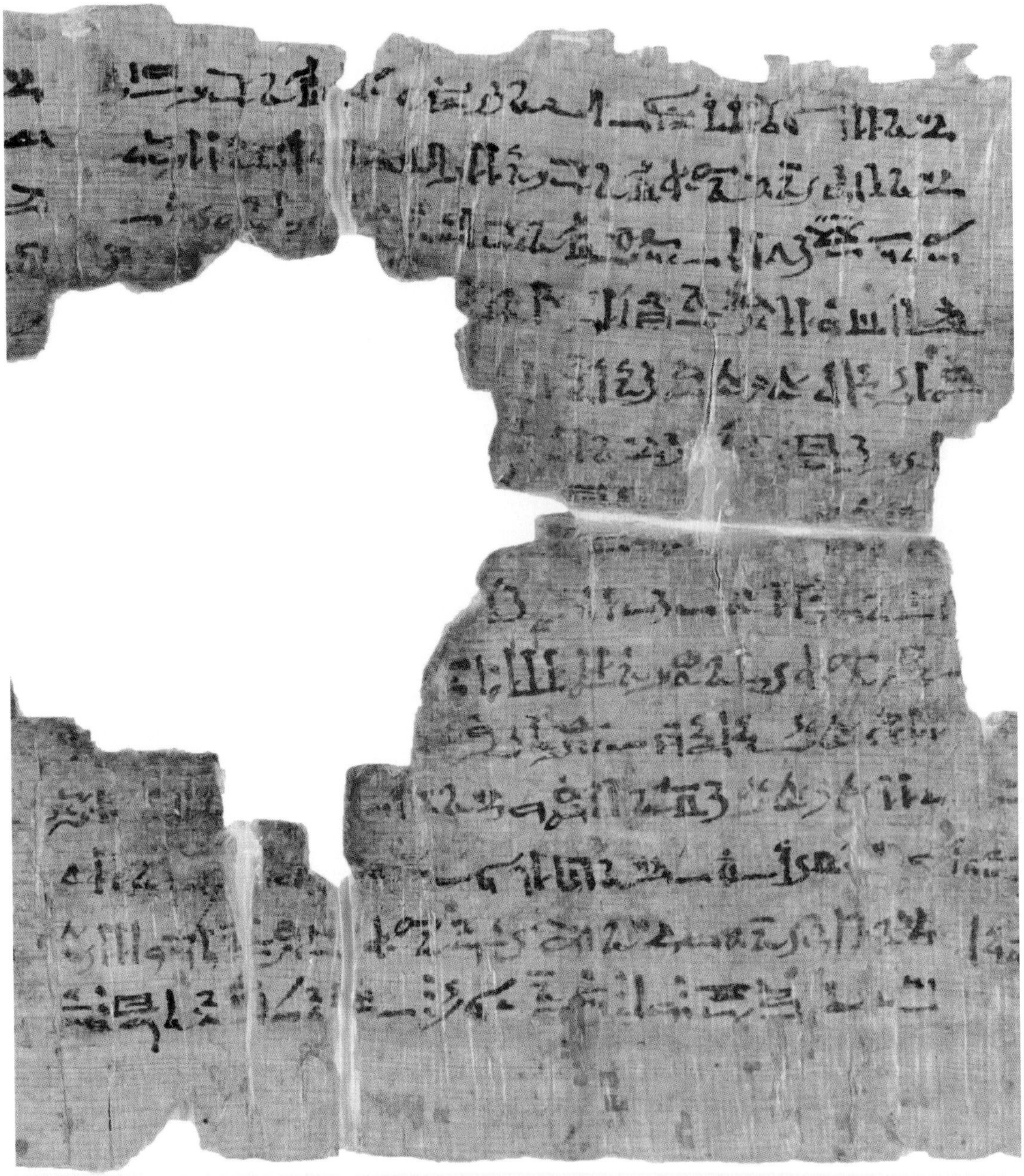

Papyrus Leiden I 345, recto column IX (scale 1:1).

Pl. 18

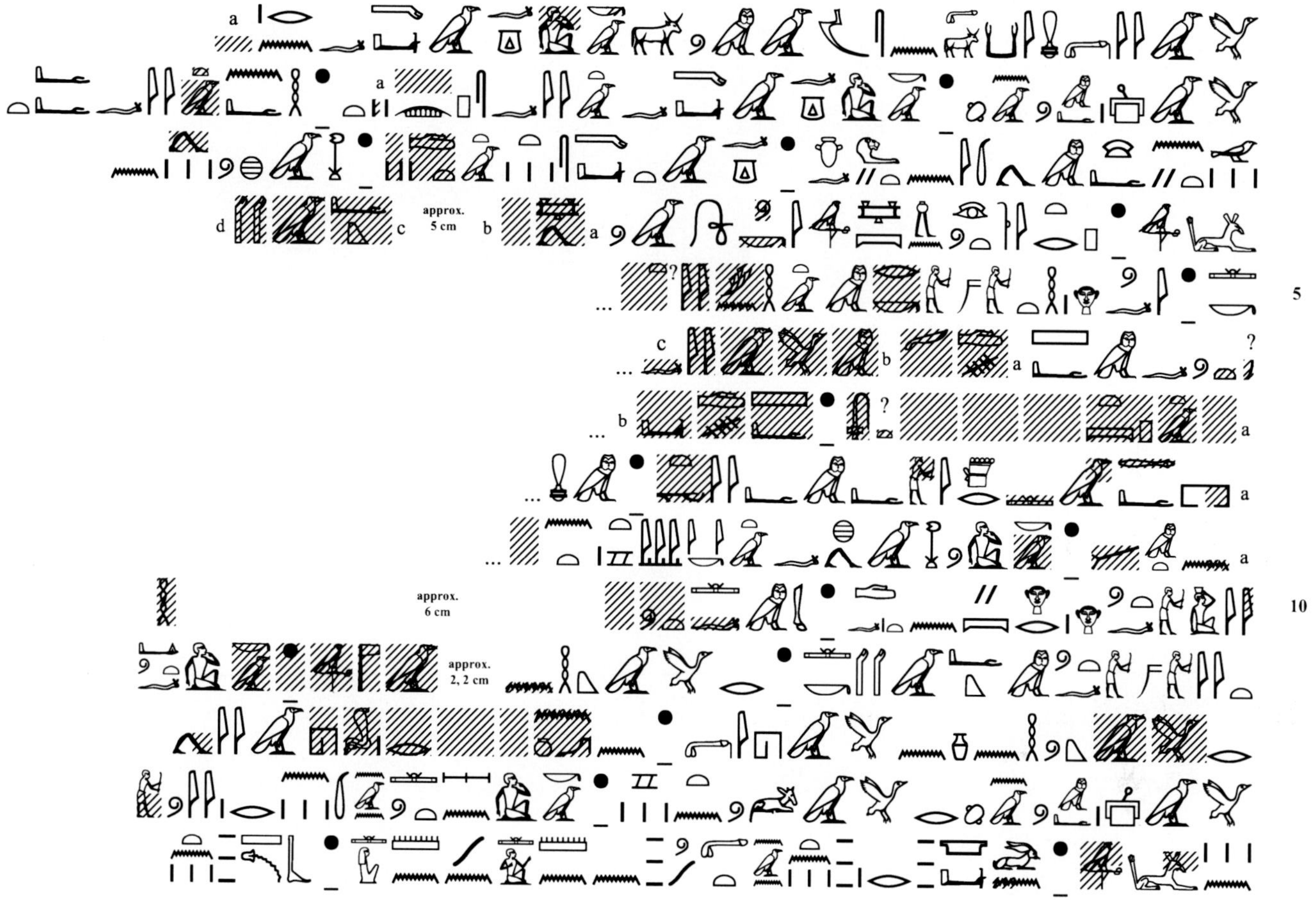

R:IX1a *traces of* **2a** II *on the edge of the rip* **4a–b** *almost faded* **4c–d** *partially legible* **6a–b** *almost faded* **6c** *almost faded* **7a–b** *difficult to read due to a rip in the papyrus, signs are faded* **8a & 9a** *perhaps nothing is missing.*

Papyrus Leiden I 345, recto column IX, transcription.

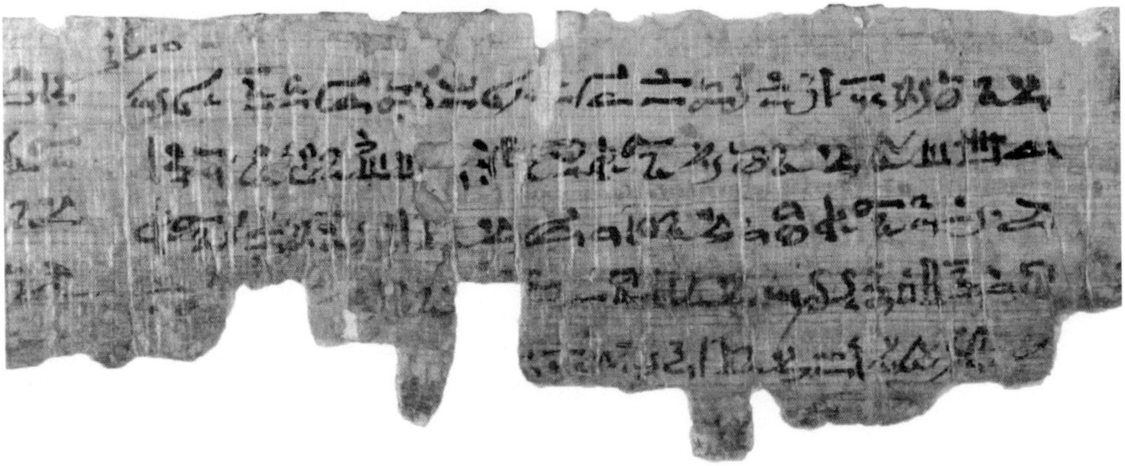

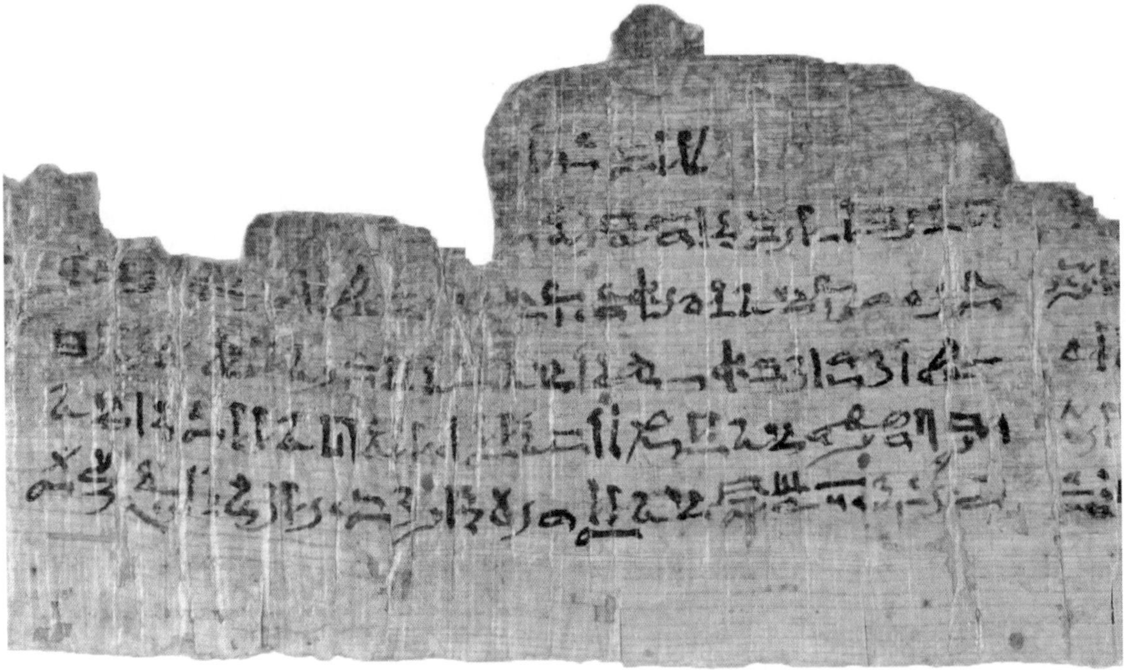

Papyrus Leiden I 345, recto column X (scale 1:1).

Pl. 20

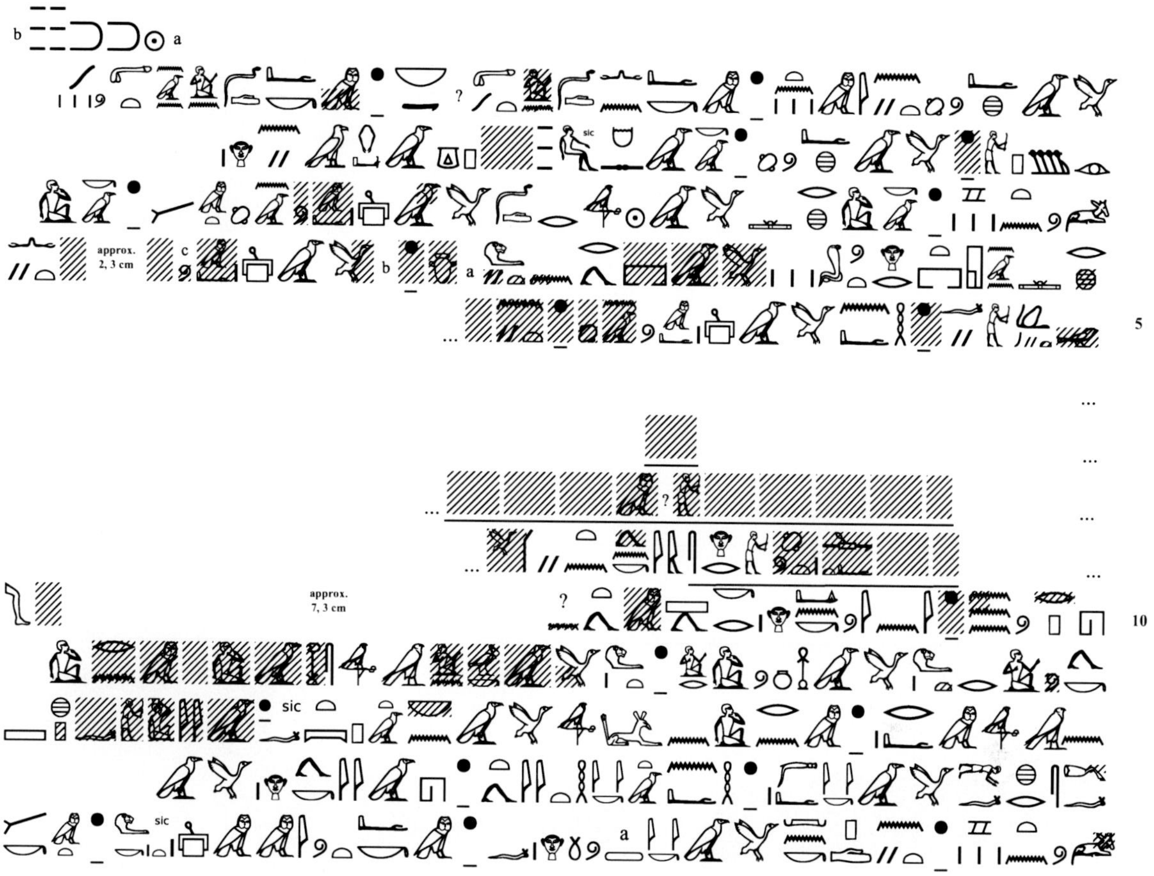

R:Xa–b *above the column* **4a–b** *almost faded, line is half broken off* **4c** *no longer legible* **14a** *at first glance the sign looks like* but it is actually (S130A).

Papyrus Leiden I 345, recto column X, transcription.

Pl. 21

Papyrus Leiden I 345, recto column XI (scale 1:1).

Pl. 22

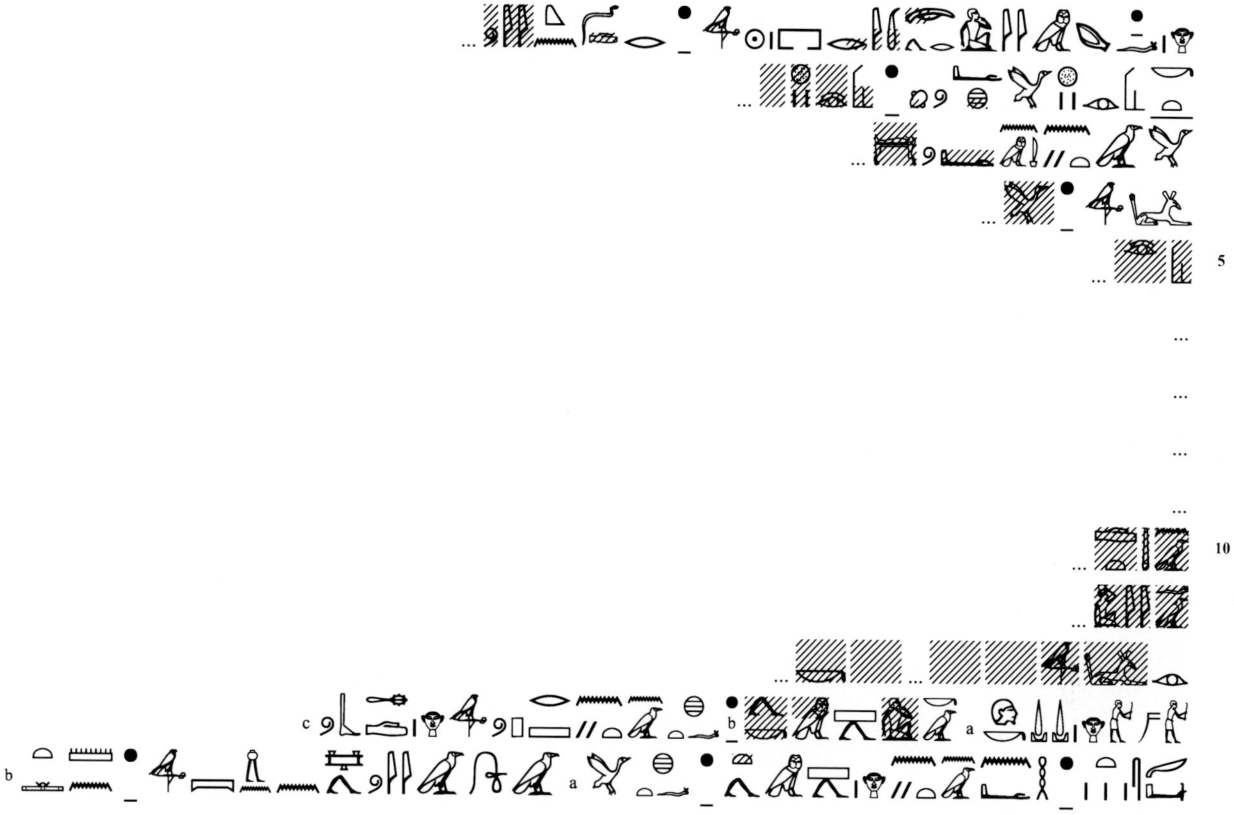

R:XI13a *Gardiner places a verse point* **13b** *now broken* **13b–c & 14a–b** *on Pl. 2 fragment 5 papyrus Leiden I 345.*

Papyrus Leiden I 345, recto column XI, transcription.

Pl. 23

Papyrus Leiden I 345, recto column XII (scale 1:1).

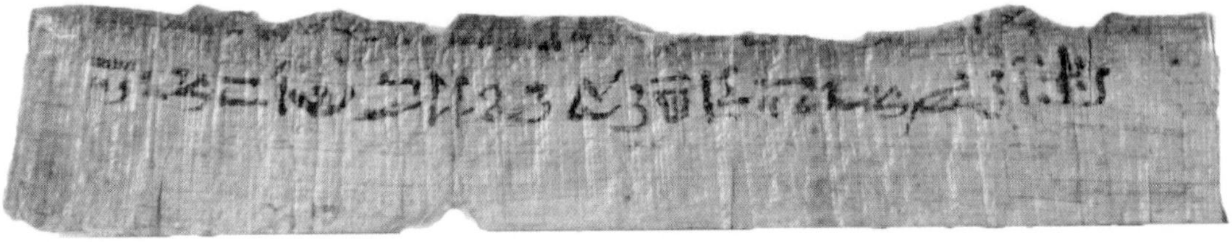

Papyrus Leiden I 345, recto column XIII (scale 1:1).

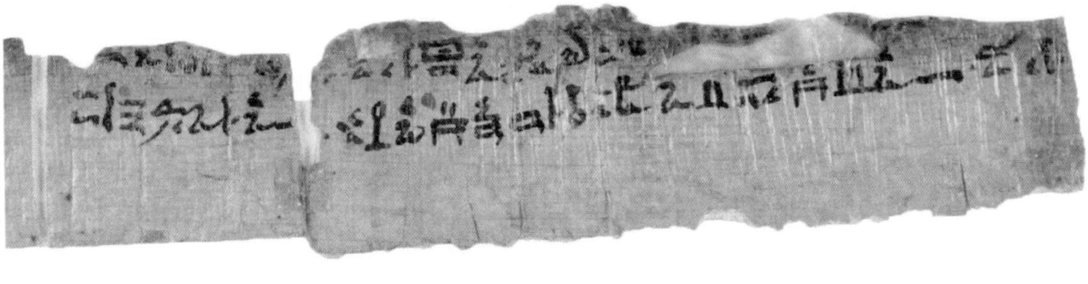

Papyrus Leiden I 345, recto column XIV (scale 1:1).

Papyrus Leiden I 345, recto column XV (scale 1:1).

Pl. 24

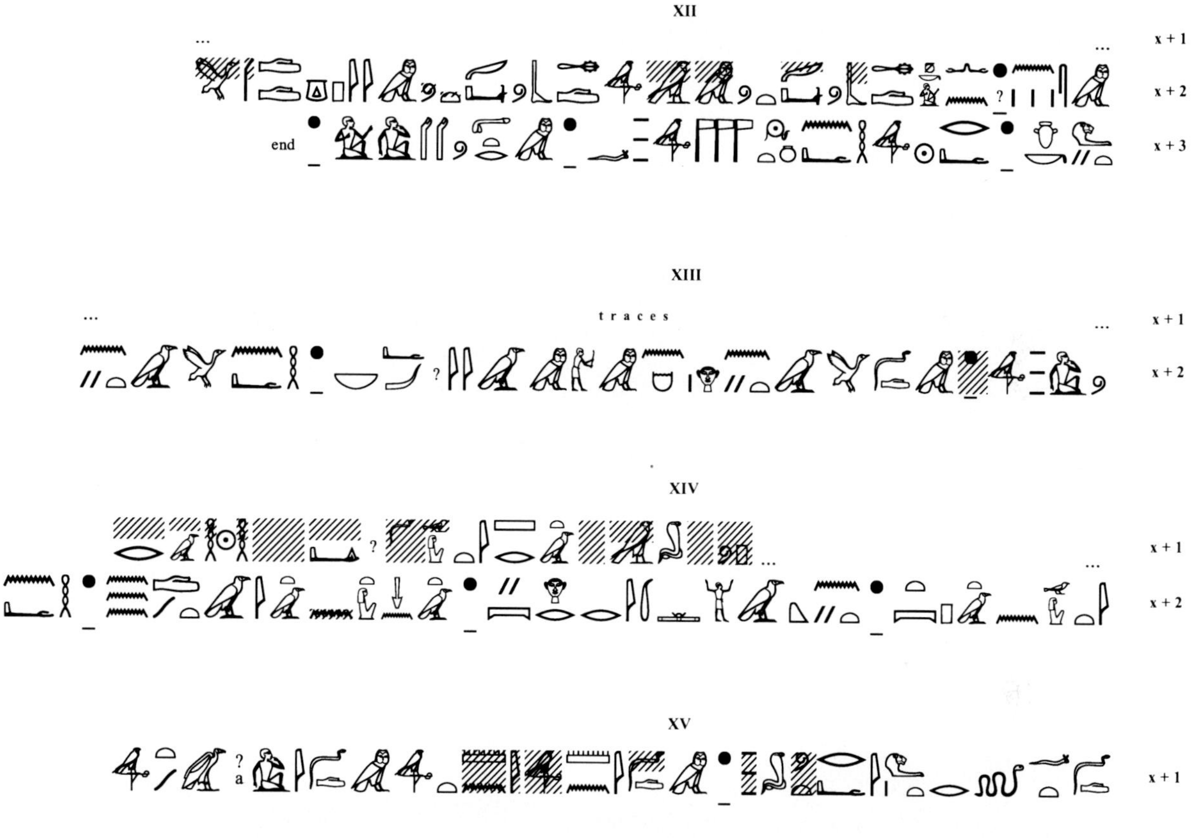

R:XII–XV: *Lower part of the column* **R:XVx+1a** *or* , *or* .

Papyrus Leiden I 345, recto columns XII-XV, transcription.

Pl. 25

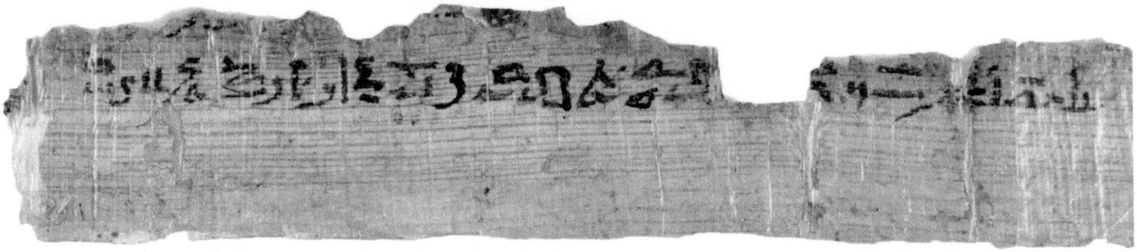

Papyrus Leiden I 345, recto column XVI (scale 1:1).

Papyrus Leiden I 345, recto column XVII (scale 1:1).

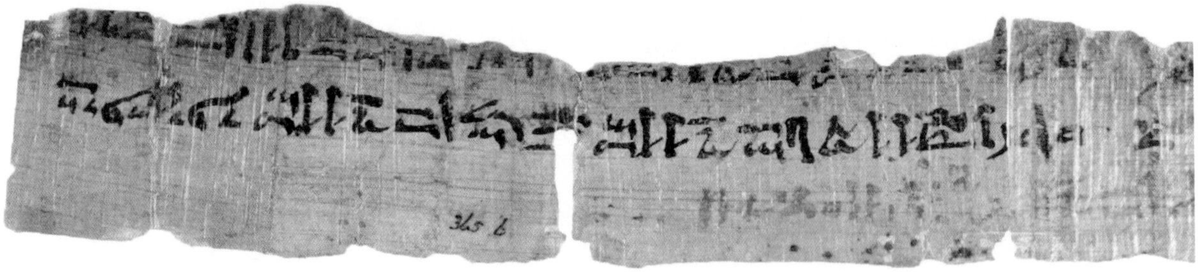

Papyrus Leiden I 345, recto column XVIII (scale 1:1).

Pl. 26

XVI

x + 1
x + 2

XVII

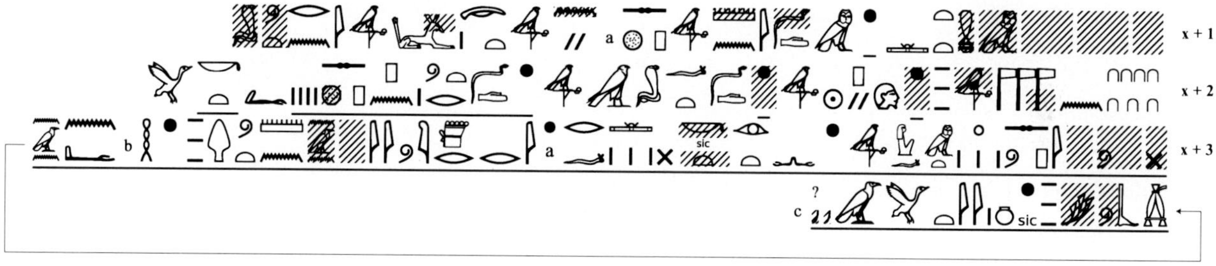

x + 1
x + 2
x + 3

XVIII

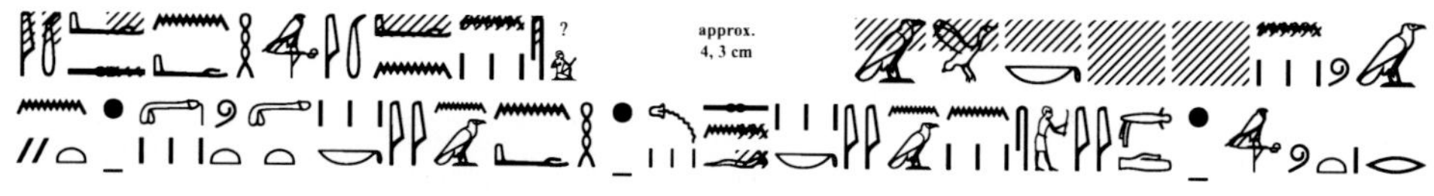

x + 1
x + 2

R:XV–XVIII: *Lower part of the column* **R:XVIx+1a** *or* [hieroglyph] **x+1b** *either* [hieroglyph] *or* [hieroglyph] **R:XVIIx+1a** *probably* [hieroglyph]

x+3a *perhaps only dots of ink* **x+3b–c** *below R:XVIIIx+2.*

Papyrus Leiden I 345, recto columns XVI-XVIII, transcription.

Pl. 27

Papyrus Leiden I 345, recto column XIX (scale 1:1).

Papyrus Leiden I 345, recto column XX (scale 1:1)

Papyrus Leiden I 345, recto column XXI (scale 1:1).

Pl. 28

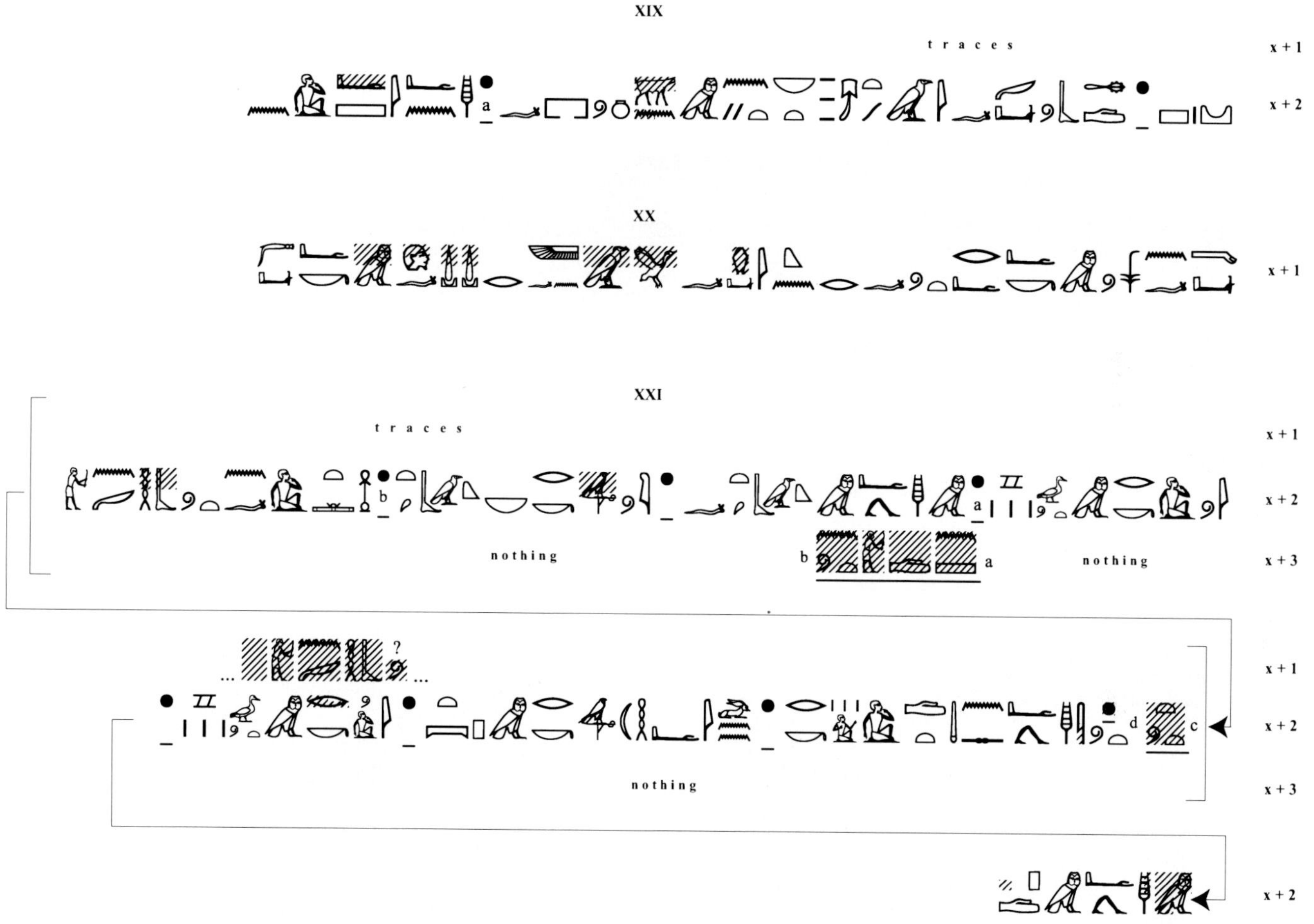

R:XIX–XXI: *Lower part of the column* **R:XIXx+2** *verse point no longer legible* **R:XXIx+2a** *-//-* **x+2b** *-//-*

x+2c–d *much faded, Gardiner writes ?* **x+3a–b** *much faded.*

Papyrus Leiden I 345, recto columns XIX-XXI, transcription.

Pl. 29

Papyrus Leiden I 345, recto column XXII (scale 1:1).

Papyrus Leiden I 345, recto column XXIII (scale 1:1).

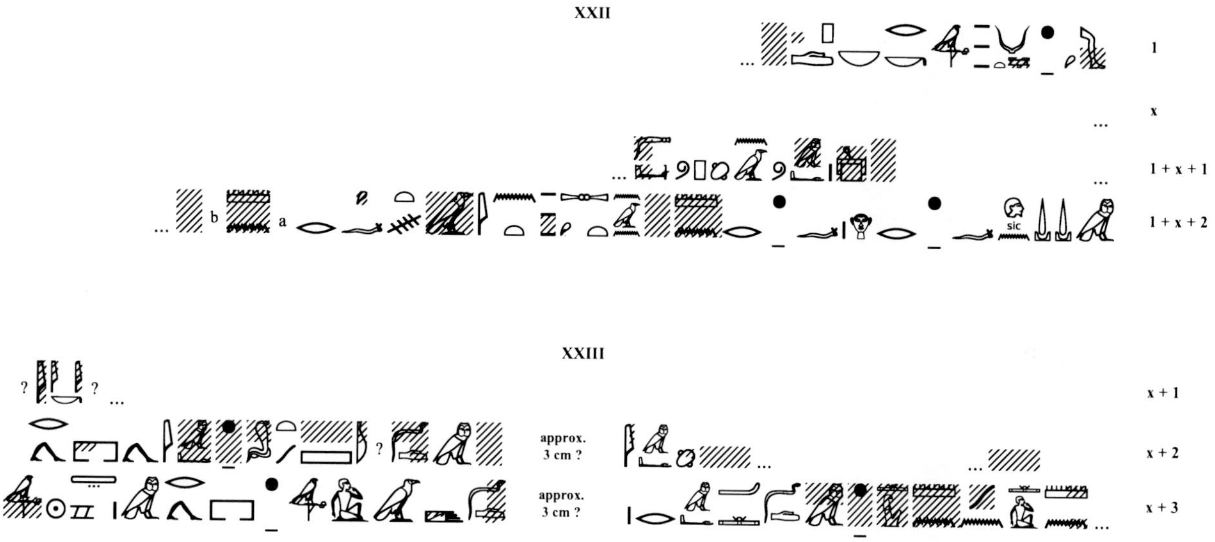

R:XXIII: *Lower part of the column* **R:XXII1** *perhaps parts of the column* **1+x+ 2a–b** *reading uncertain* **R:XXIII** *perhaps parts of the column.*

Papyrus Leiden I 345, recto columns XXII-XXIII, transcription.

Pl. 31

Papyrus Leiden I 345, recto column XXIV (scale 1:1).

Pl. 32

R:XXIV1a–b *much darkened and faded* **3 + x+2a–b** *much darkened.*

Papyrus Leiden I 345, recto columns XXIV, transcription.

Pl. 33

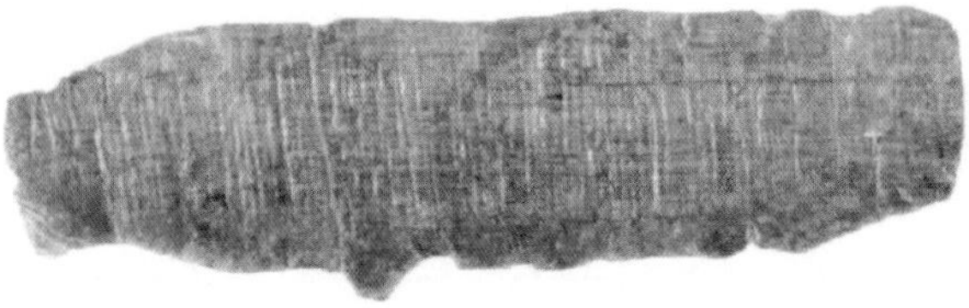

Papyrus Leiden I 345, recto column XXV (scale 1:1).

Pl. 34

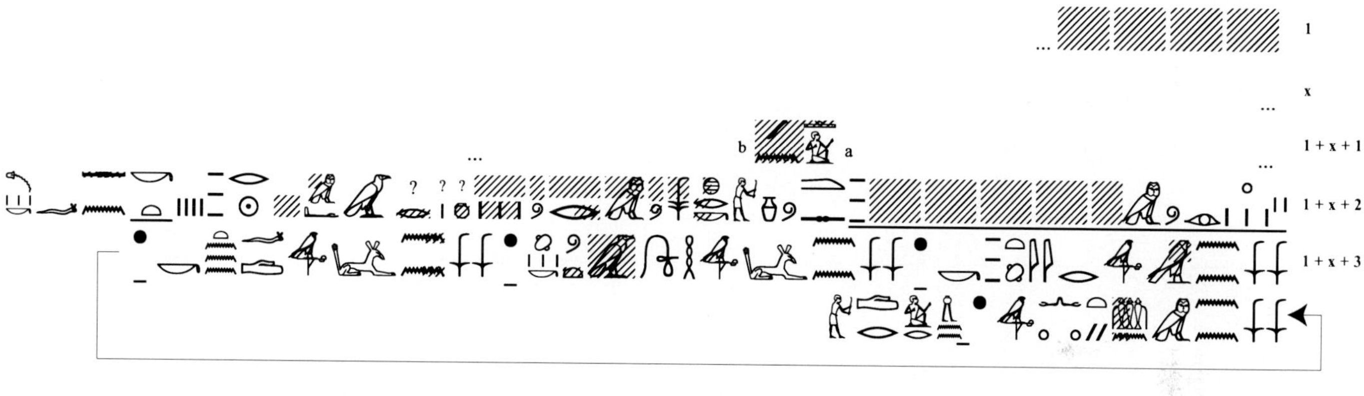

R:XXV1+x+1a–b *much darkened.*

Papyrus Leiden I 345, recto column XXV, transcription.

Pl. 35

Papyrus Leiden I 345, recto column XXVI (scale 1:1).

Pl. 36

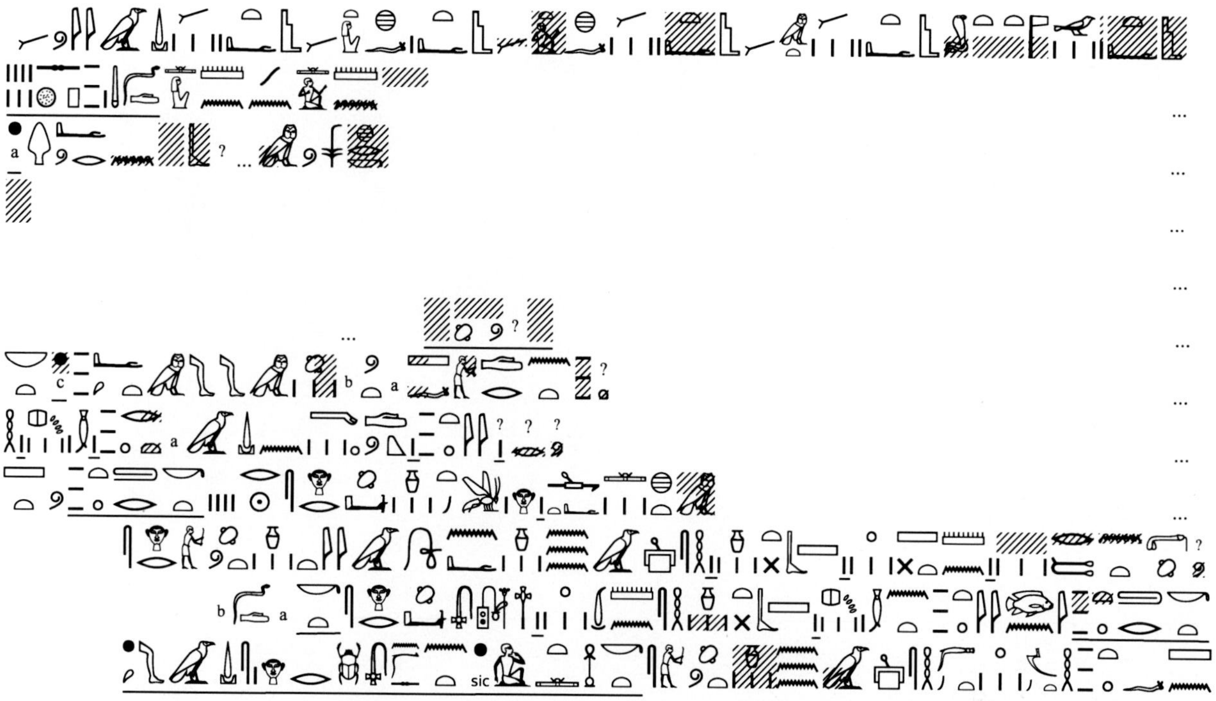

R:XXVI3a *verse point no longer legible* **7a–b** *this part of the papyrus does not exist anymore, the beginning and the ending of the previous and the following groups are missing too* **7c** *verse point almost illegible* **11a–b** *deleted.*

Papyrus Leiden I 345, recto column XXVI, transcription.

Pl. 37

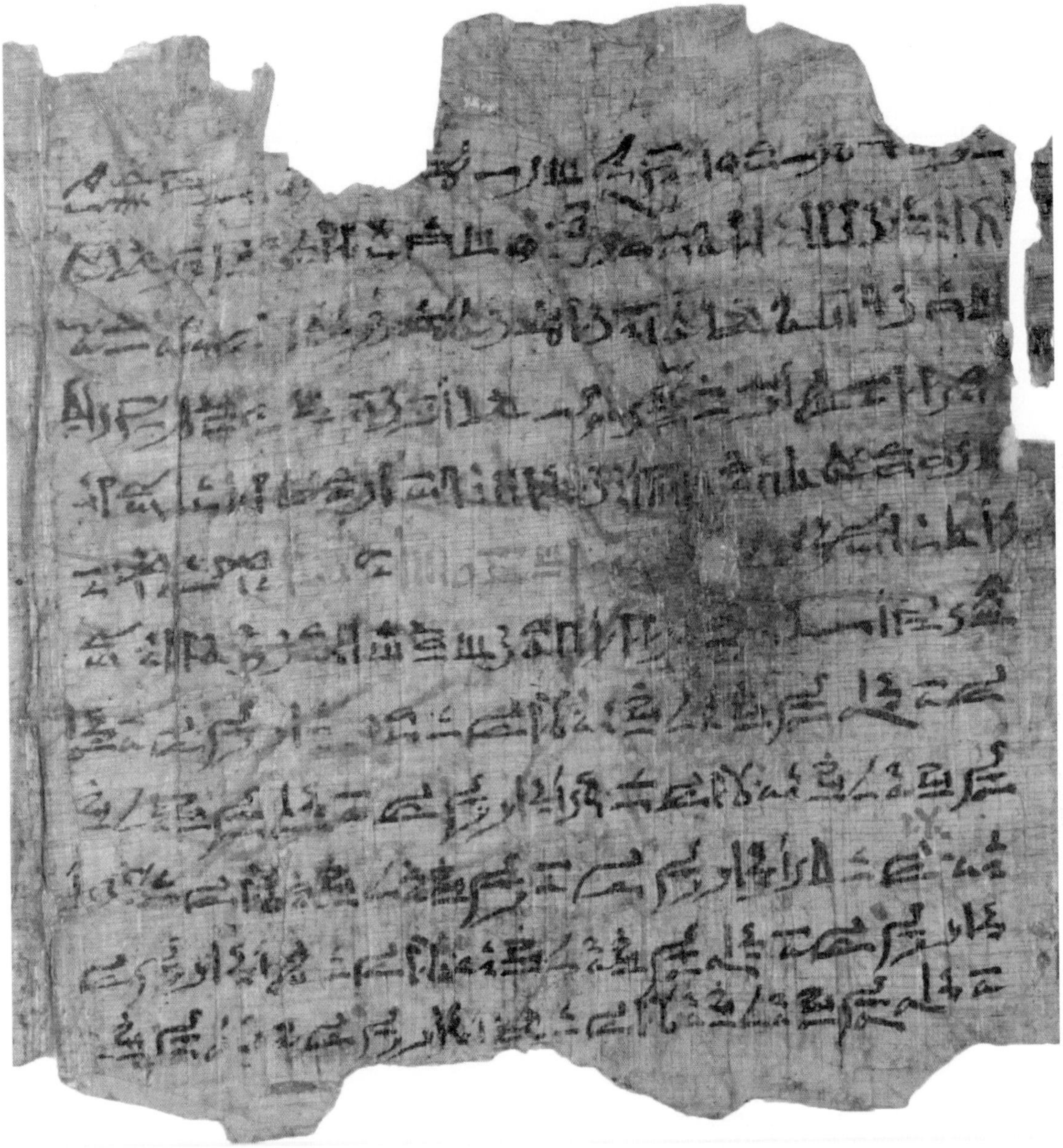

Papyrus Leiden I 345, recto column XXVII (scale 1:1).

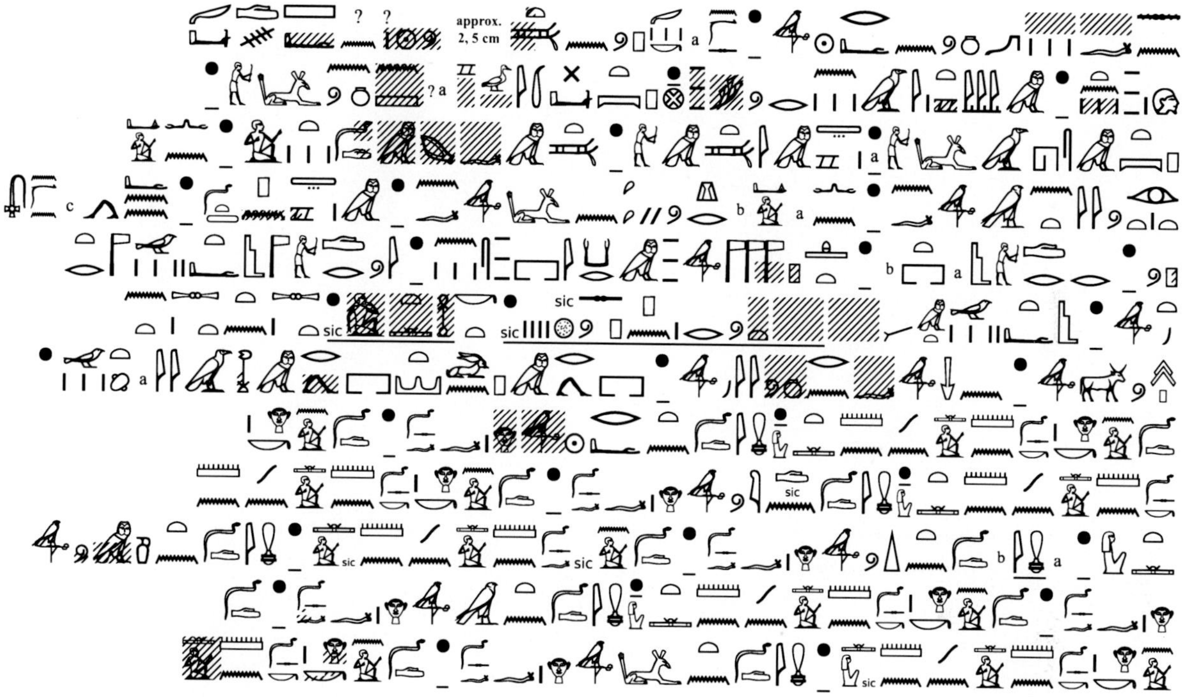

R:XXVII1a *under the line* **2a** *no verse point* **3a** *no verse point* **4a–b** *later added above the line* **4c** *read*

5a–b *read* **7a** *perhaps* **10a–b** *added later above the line.*

Papyrus Leiden I 345, recto column XXVII, transcription.

Pl. 39

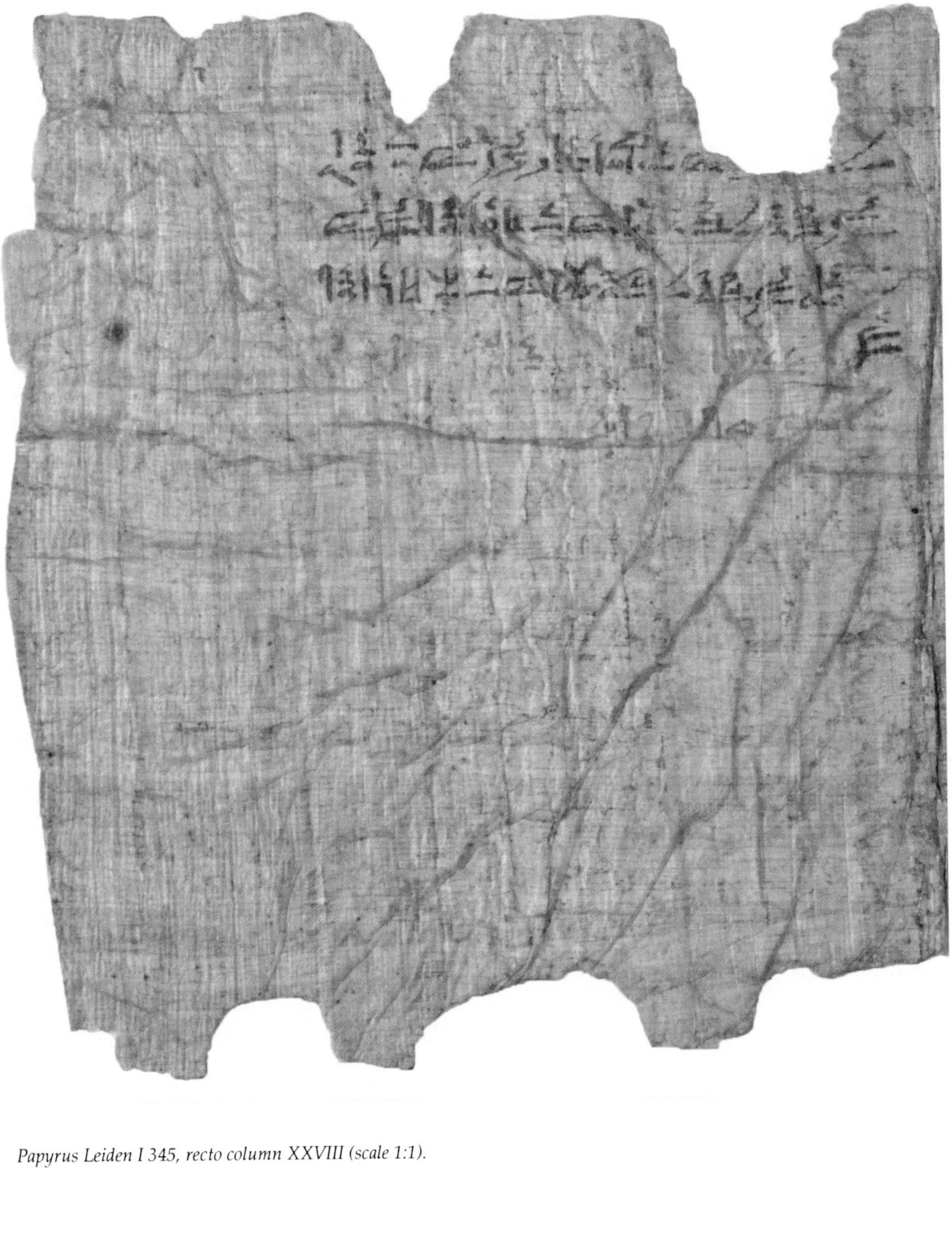

Papyrus Leiden I 345, recto column XXVIII (scale 1:1).

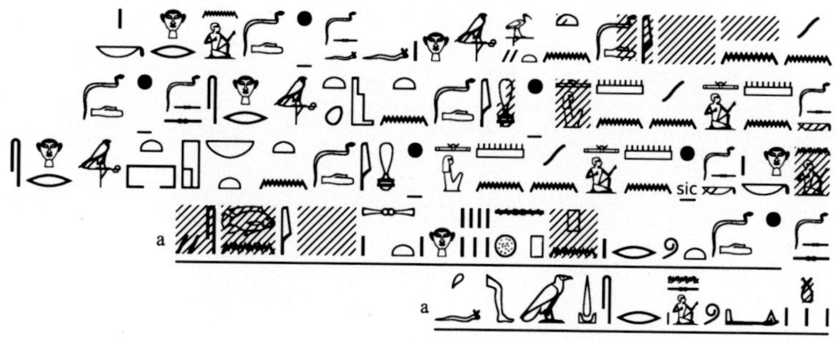

—

R:XXVIII4a *approx. 6 cm from the end of the line to the end of the papyrus* **5a** *approx. 11 cm from the end of the line to the end of the papyrus; the last part of the papyrus is blank.*

Papyrus Leiden I 345, recto column XXVIII, transcription.

Pl. 41

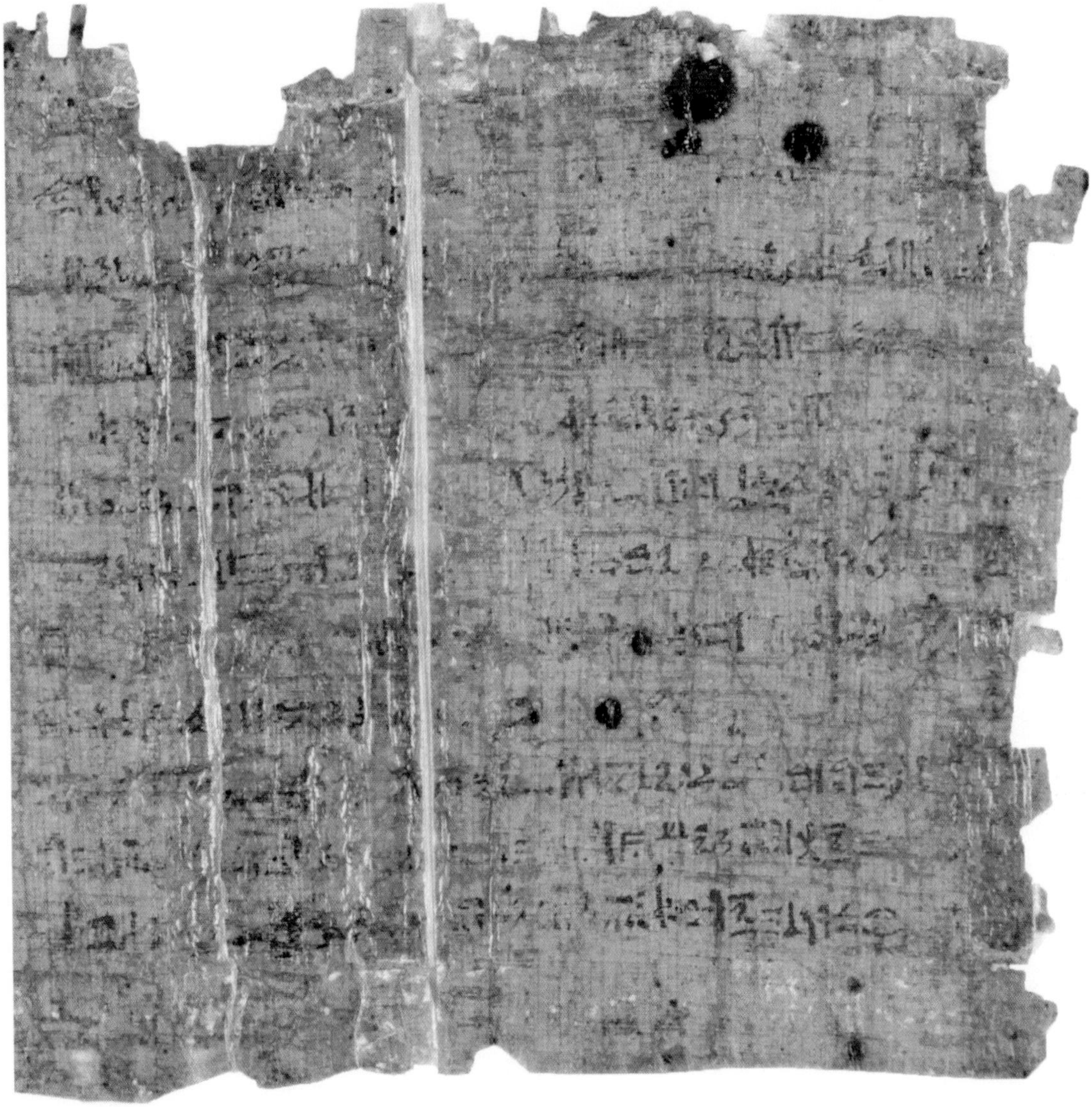

Papyrus Leiden I 343, verso column I (scale 1:1).

Pl. 42

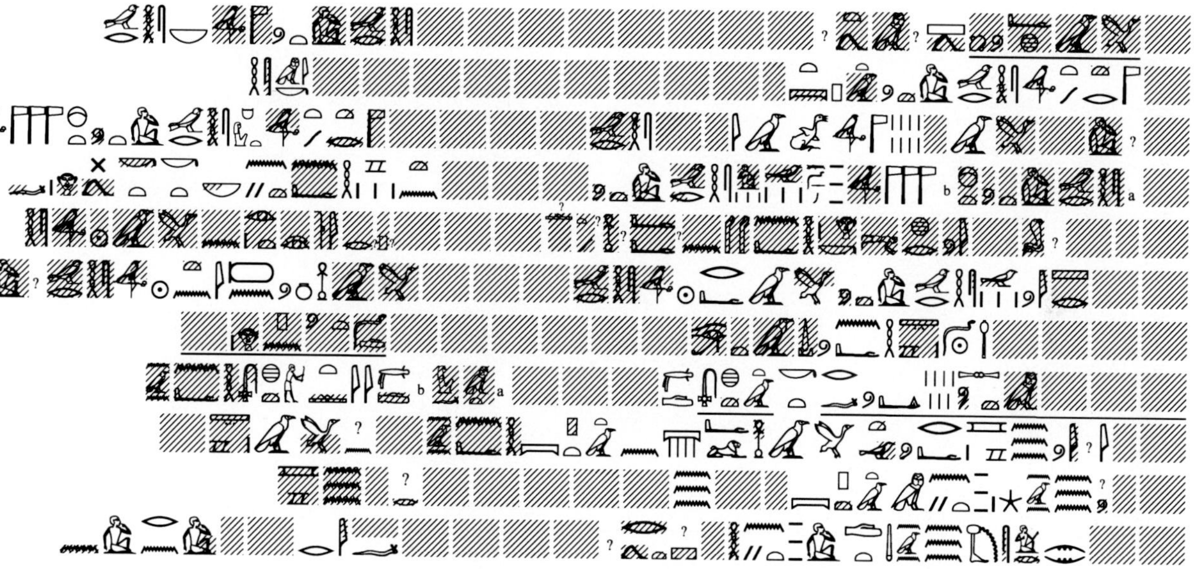

V:14a–b *traces, no longer legible* **8a–b** *traces fit* .

Papyrus Leiden I 343, verso column I, transcription.

Pl. 43

Papyrus Leiden I 343, verso column II (scale 1:1).

Pl. 44

V:II1a *traces of ink of the papyrus* **4a–b** *not visible any more* **4c–d** *according to Gardiner, a 'mere guess', traces match his suggestion* **5a–b** *group difficult to read due to sticky tape.*

Papyrus Leiden I 343, verso column II, transcription.

Pl. 45

Papyrus Leiden I 343, verso column III (scale 1:1).

Pl. 46

V:III1a–b *traces of palimpsest above the line* **3a** *or* **3b–c** *barely legible* **5a–b** *barely legible* **6a–b** *no longer legible*

7a *no longer legible* **7b** ıı *no longer legible* **7c–d** *no longer legible* **8a–b** *barely visible* **9a–b** *no longer legible*

10a *under the line* **10b** *no longer legible.*

Papyrus Leiden I 343, verso column III, transcription.

Pl. 47

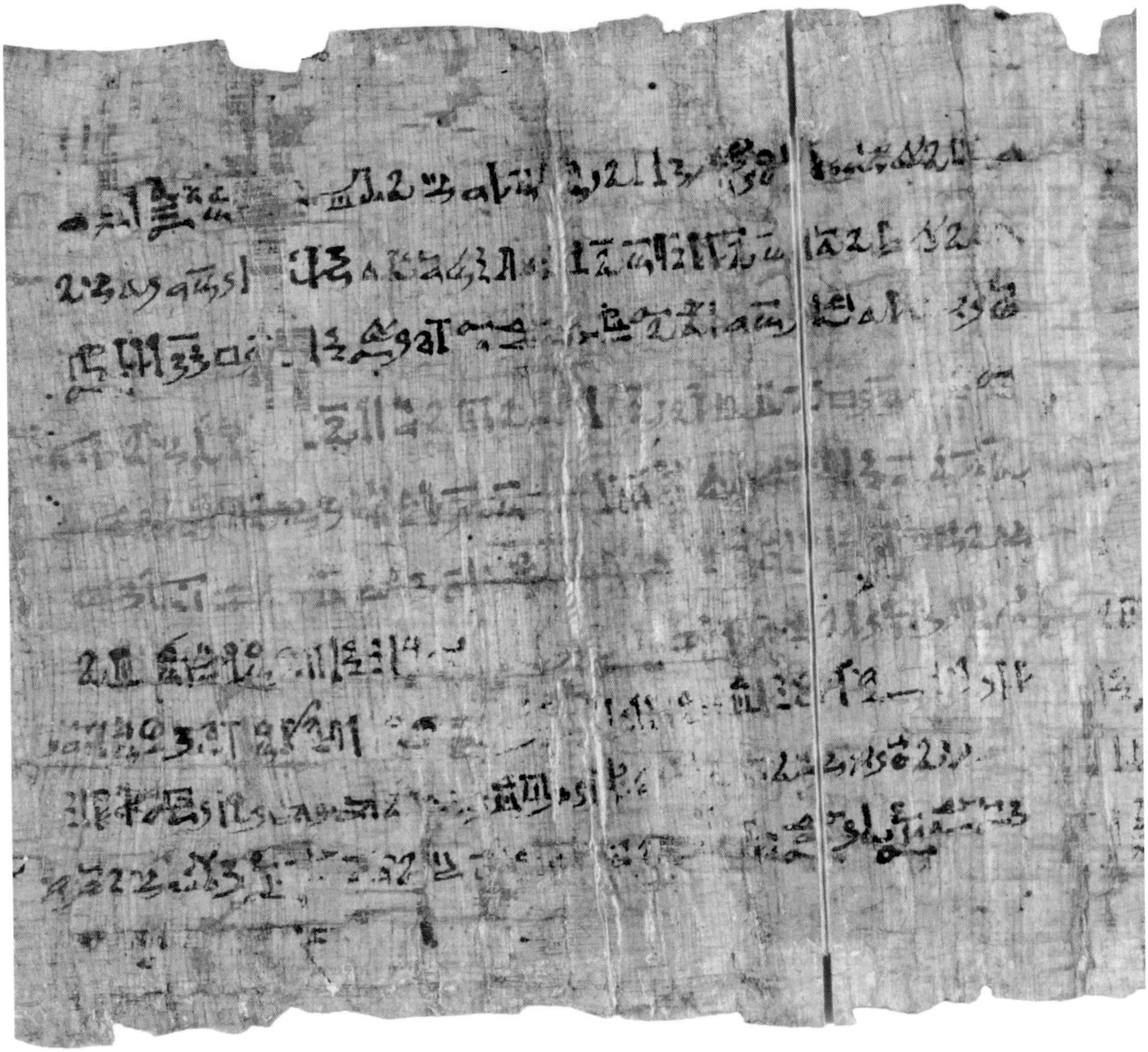

Papyrus Leiden I 343, verso column IV (scale 1:1).

Pl. 48

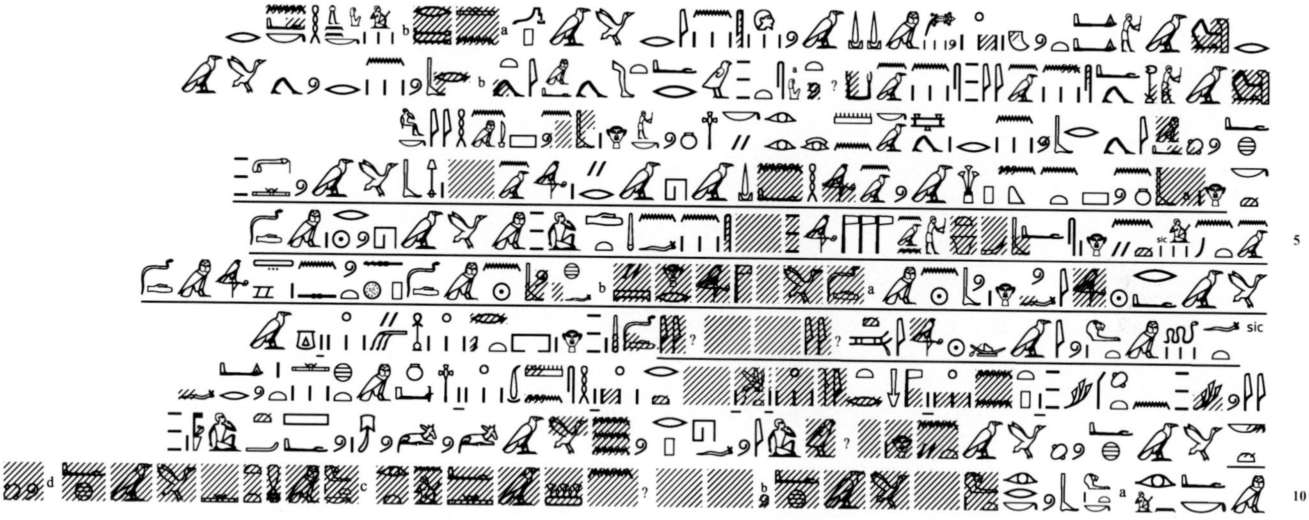

V:IV1a–b *traces* **2a** *or* **2b** *almost rubbed off* **4a** *almost rubbed off* **6a–b** *only traces are visible* **10a** *under the line* **10b** *no longer legible* **10c** *under the line* **10c–d** *traces of palimpsest under the line.*

Papyrus Leiden I 343, verso column IV, transcription.

Pl. 49

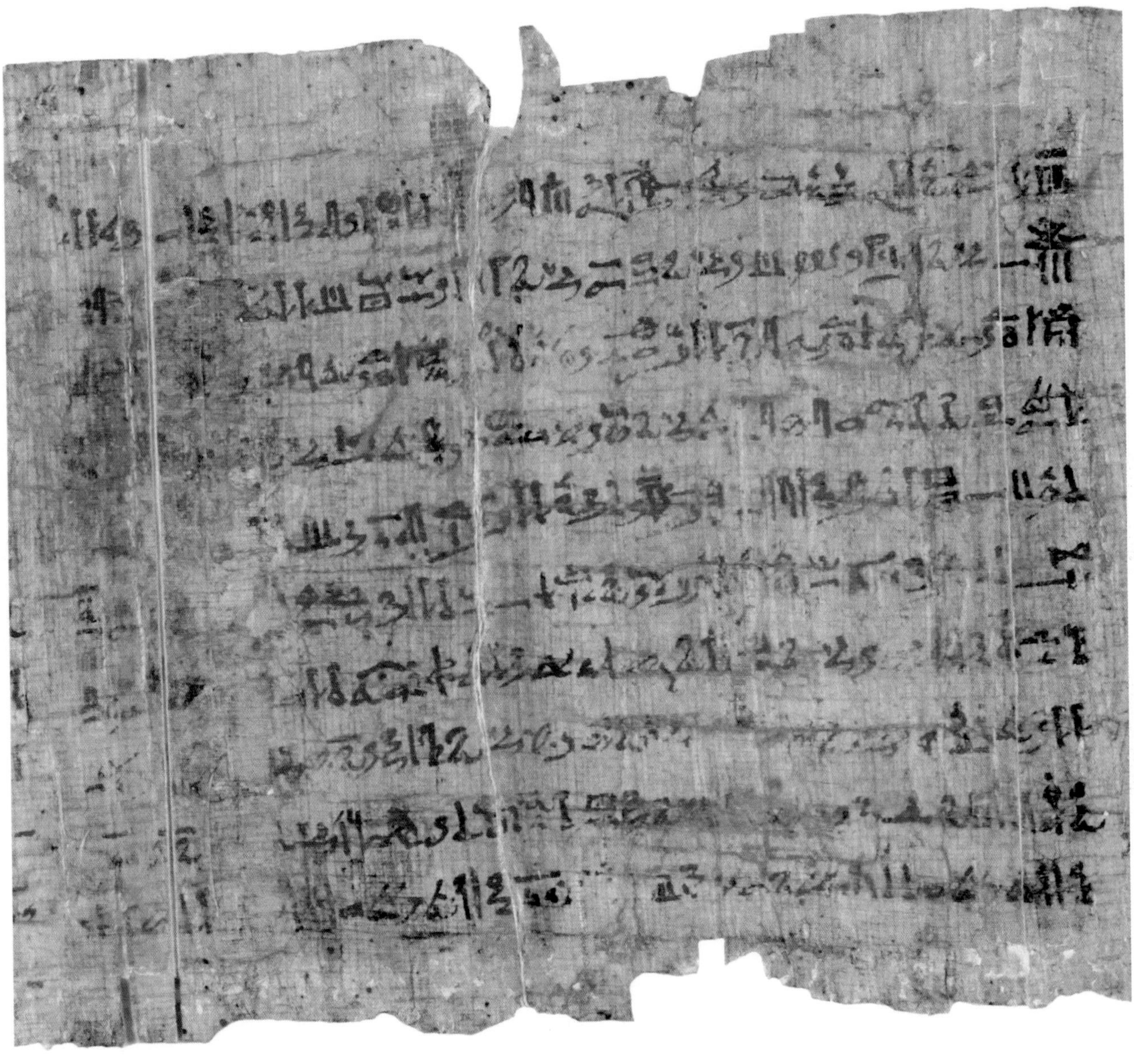

Papyrus Leiden I 343, verso column V (scale 1:1).

Pl. 50

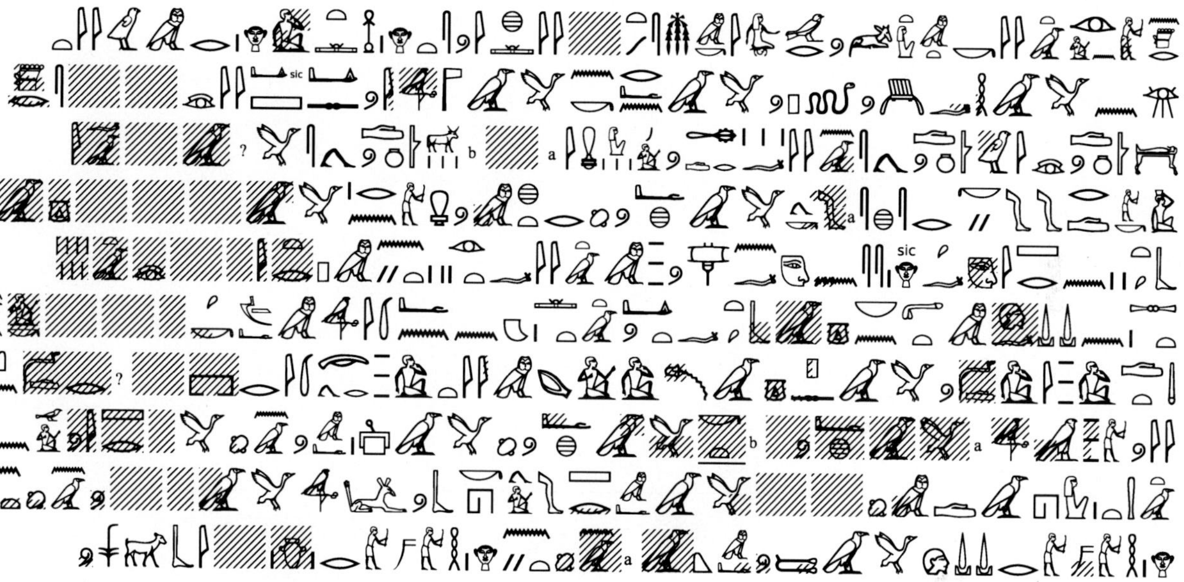

V:V3a–b *no longer legible* **4a** *traces of* **8a–b** *traces* **10a** *no longer legible.*

Papyrus Leiden I 343, verso column V, transcription.

Pl. 51

Papyrus Leiden I 343 + 345, verso column VI (scale 1:1).

Pl. 52

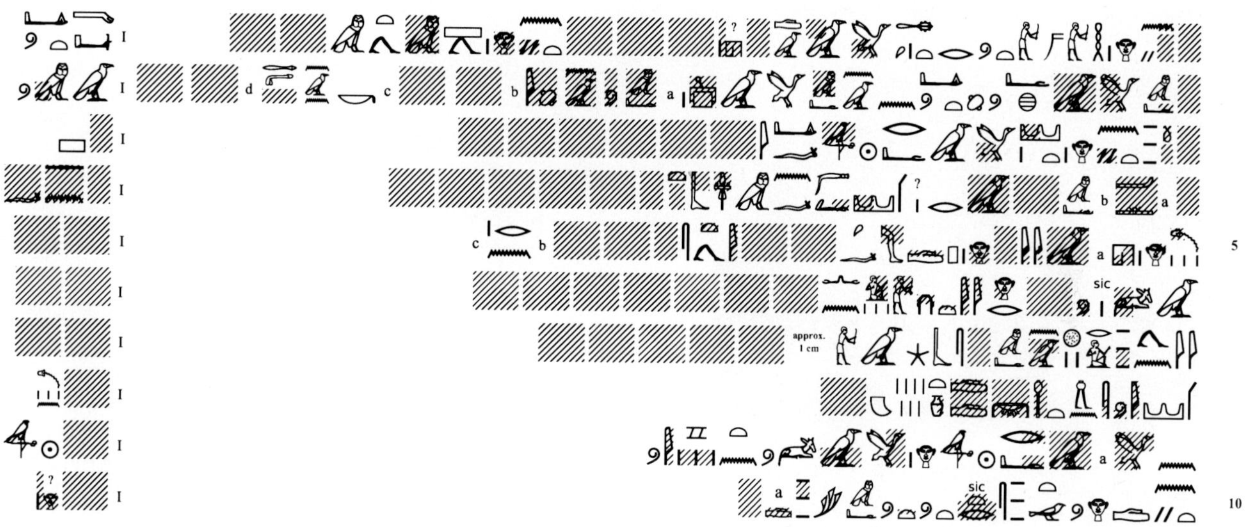

VI *from I onwards papyrus I 345, before that a gap* **2a–b** *traces* **2c–d** *traces* **4a–b** *no longer legible* **5a** *no longer legible* **5b–c** *barely legible* **9a** *no longer legible* **10a** *or* [sign].

Papyrus Leiden I 343 + 345, verso column VI, transcription.

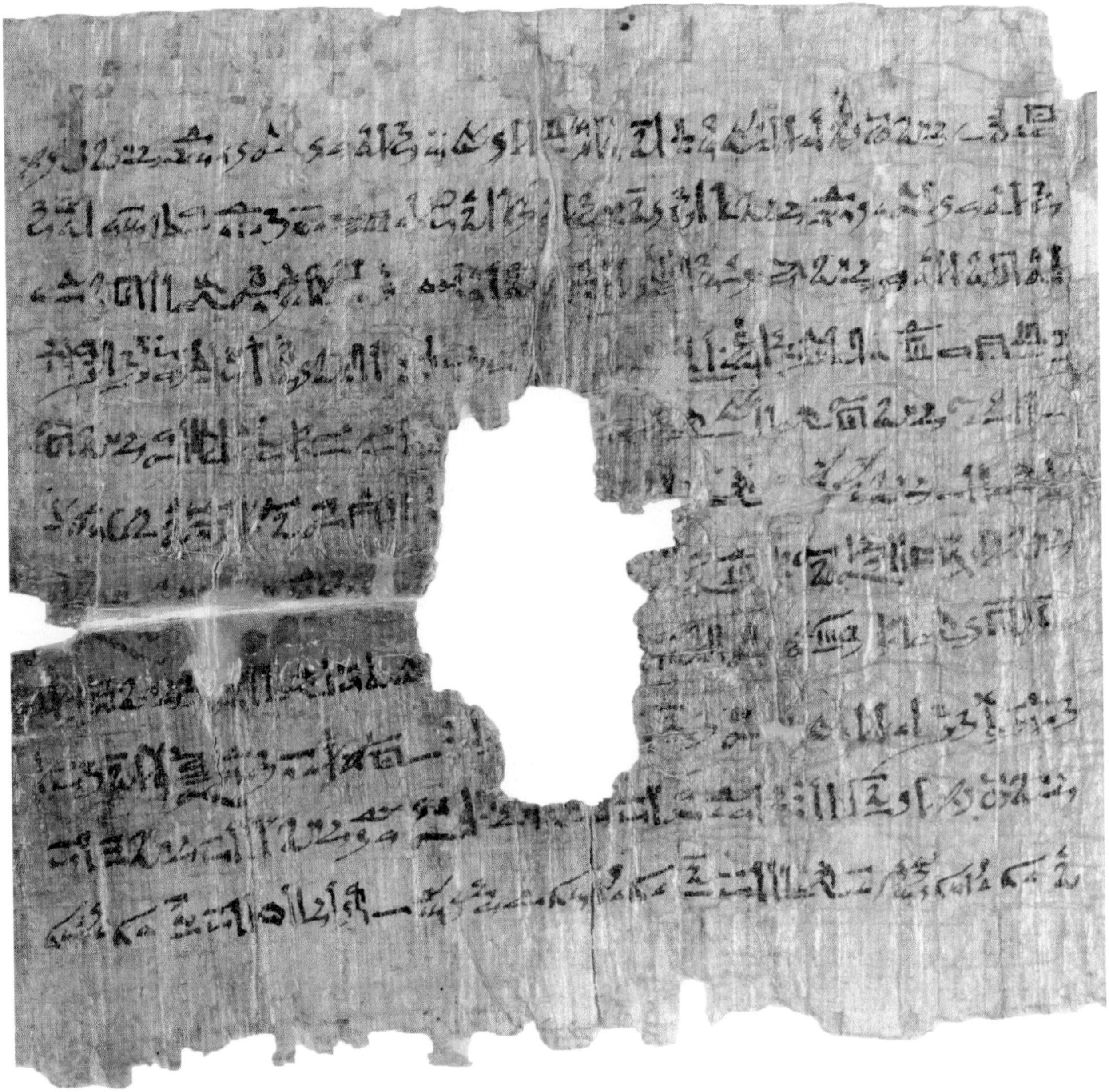

Papyrus Leiden I 345, verso columnVII (scale 1:1).

Pl. 54

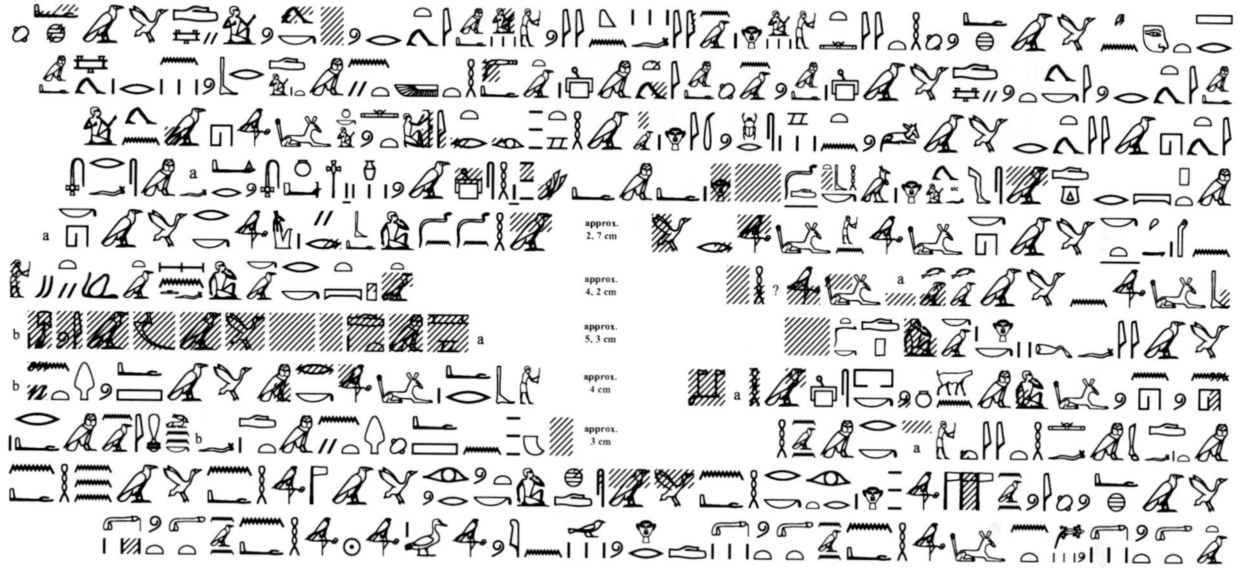

V:VII4a *traces above* [hieroglyph] **5a** *Gardiner reads* [hieroglyph] *but only palimpsest* **6a** *the upper fibres are missing* **7a–b** *rip in the line*
8a *half missing* **8b** *broken off at the end* **9a** *upper fibres are broken off* **9b** [hieroglyph] *under the line.*

Papyrus Leiden I 345, verso column VII, transcription.

Pl. 55

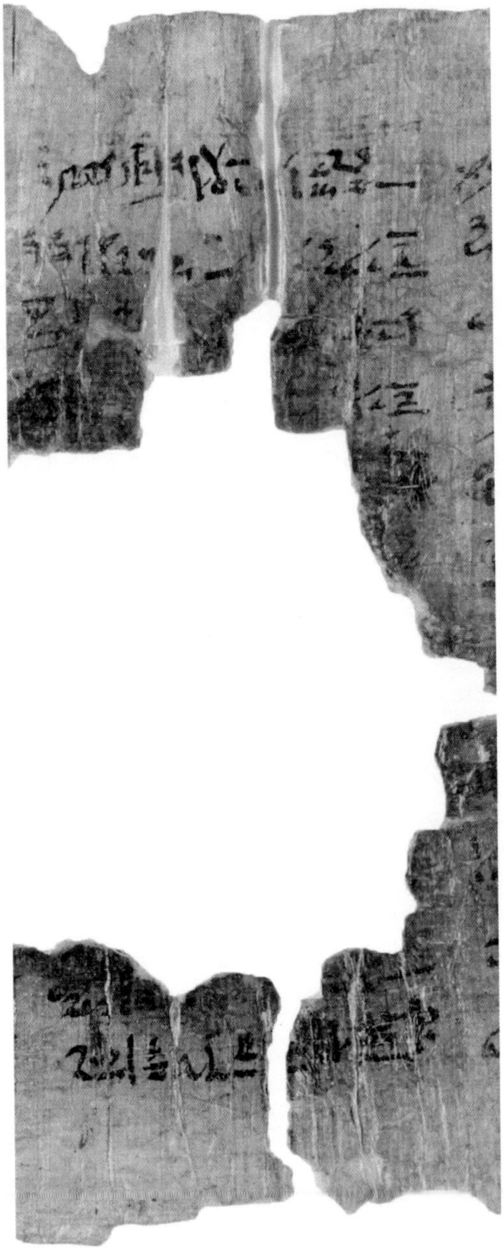

Papyrus Leiden I 345, verso column VIII (scale 1:1).

Pl. 56

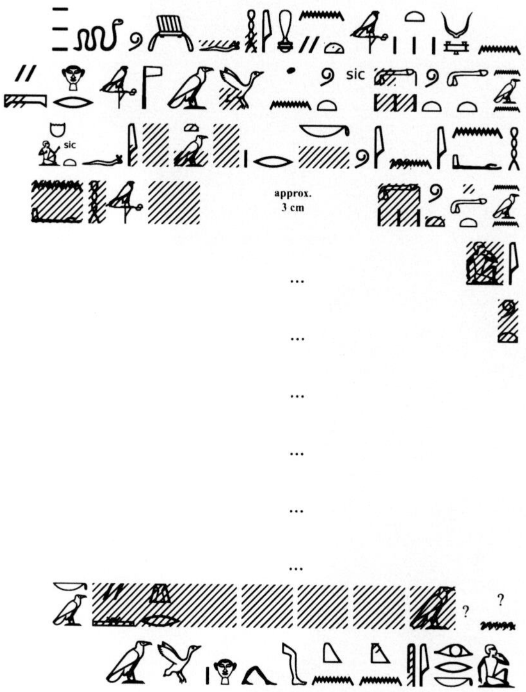

Papyrus Leiden I 345, verso column VIII, transcription.

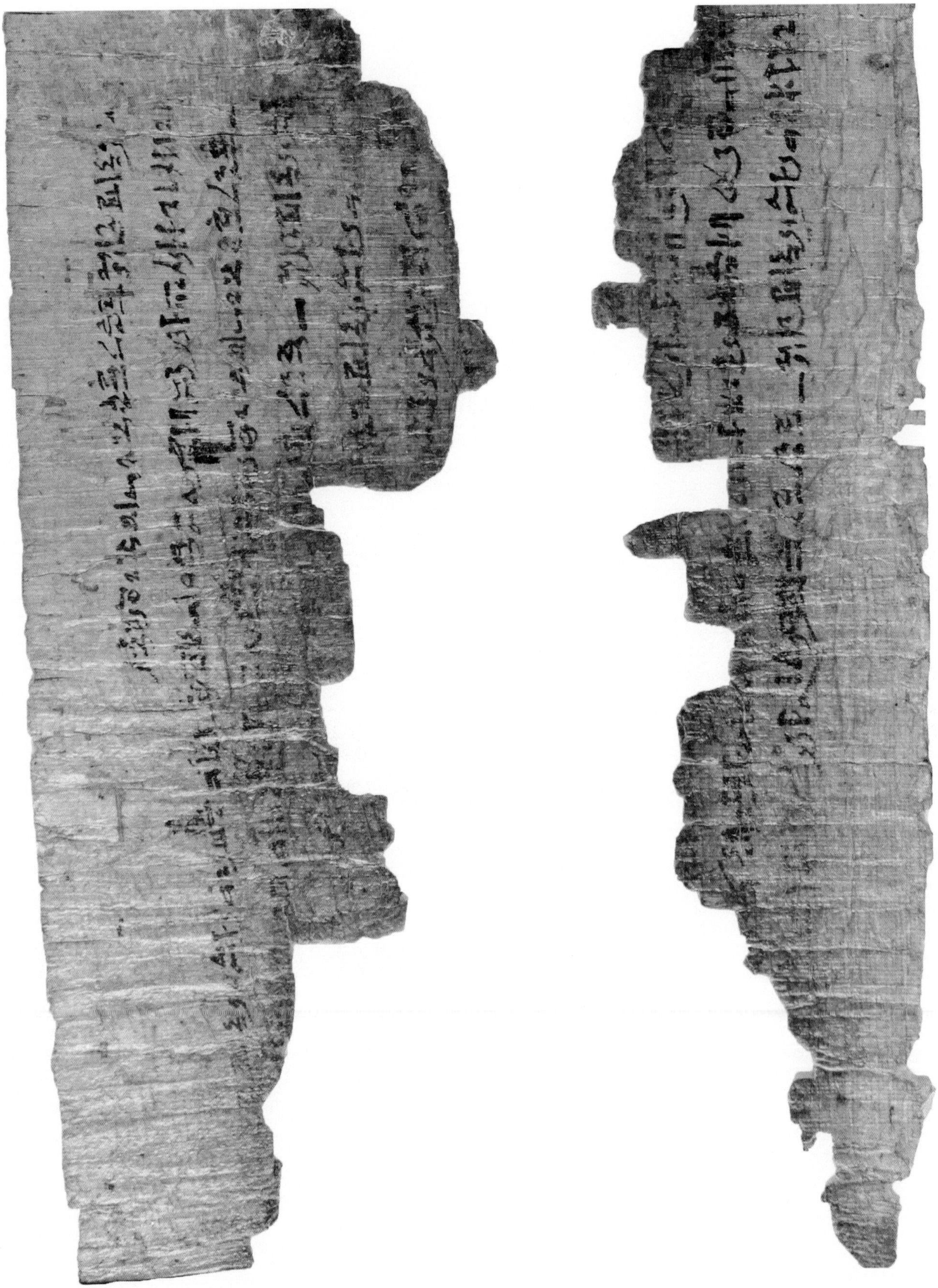

Papyrus Leiden I 345, verso column IX (scale 1:1).

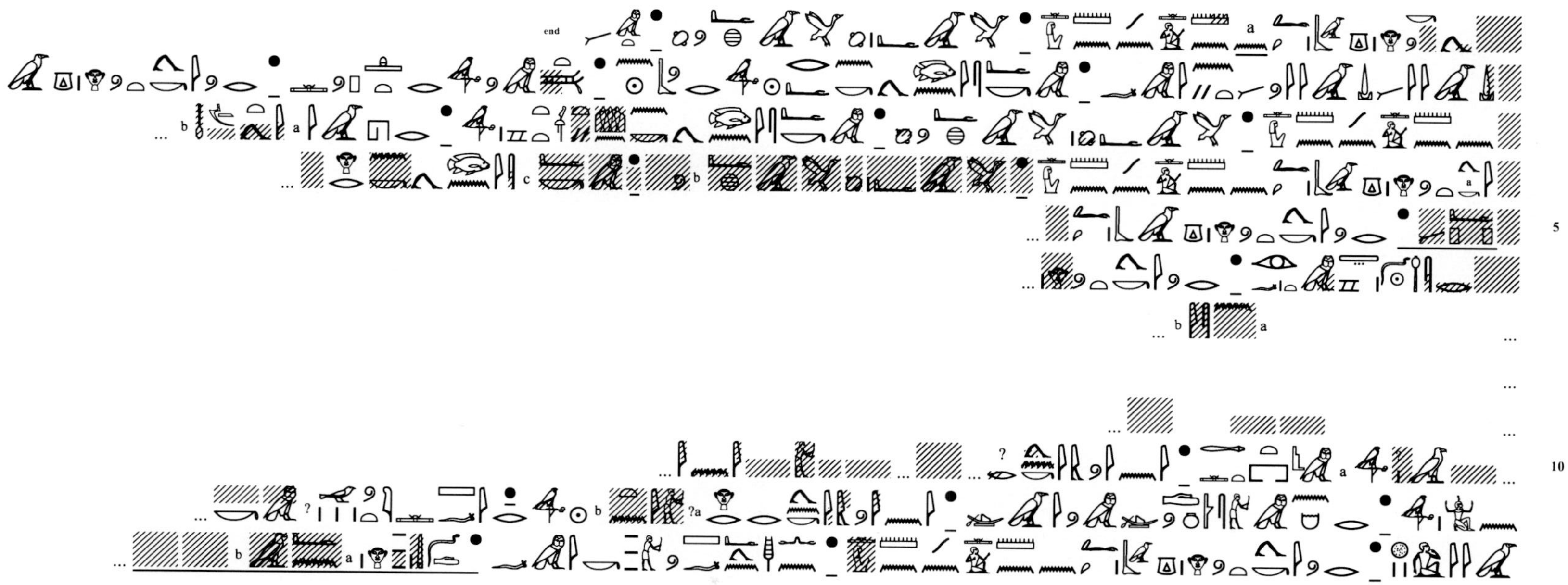

V:IX1a added above the line **3a–b** *line broken below* **4a** *strange* **4b–c** *line broken below* **7a–b** *reading uncertain*

10a *the curve of* *goes far under the line* **11a–b** *line broken above* **12a–b** *hardly visible.*

Papyrus Leiden I 345, verso column IX, transcription.

Pl. 59

Papyrus Leiden I 345, verso column X (scale 1:1).

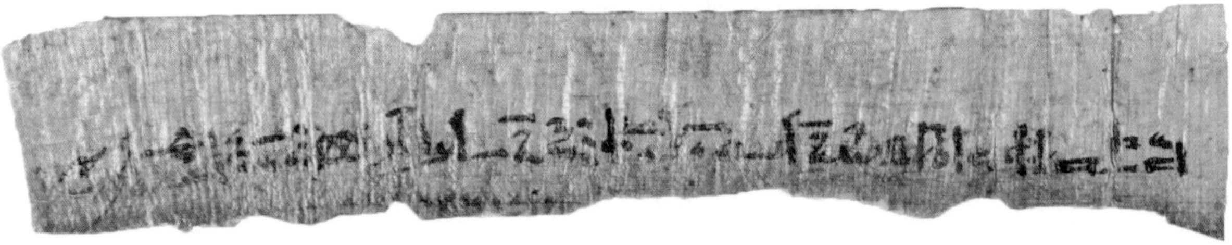

Papyrus Leiden I 345, verso column XI (scale 1:1).

Papyrus Leiden I 345, verso column XII (scale 1:1).

Papyrus Leiden I 345, verso column XIII (scale 1:1).

Pl. 60

X

XI

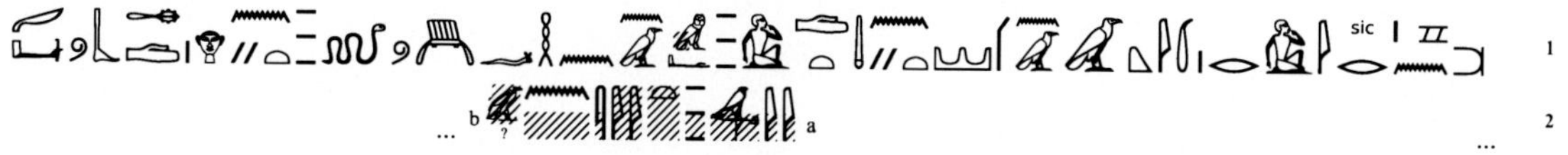

XII

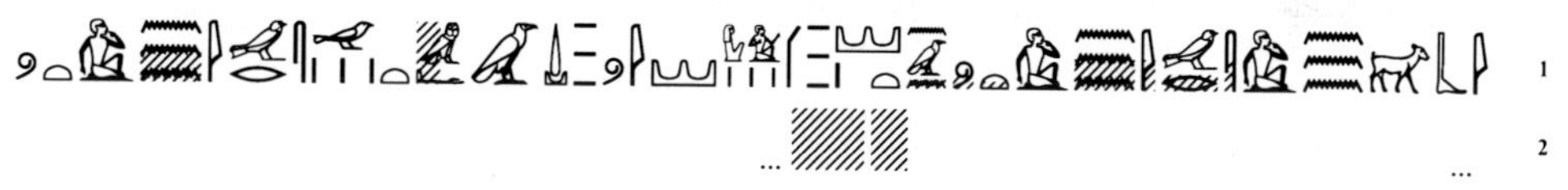

XIII

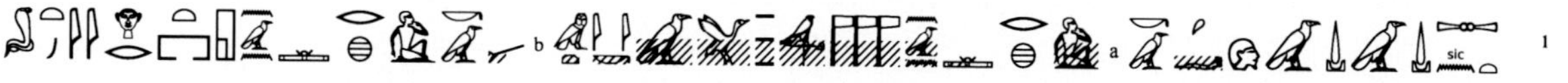

V:X–XIII *upper part of the column* **V:X2a–b** *much darkened* **V:XI2a–b** *lower part of the line is broken off, only traces partially visible* **V:XIII1a–b** *lower part of the line is broken off.*

Papyrus Leiden I 345, verso columns X-XIII, transcription.

Pl. 61

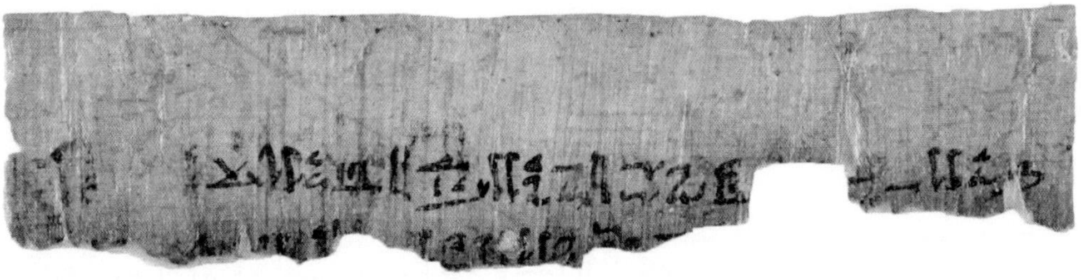

Papyrus Leiden I 345, verso column XIV (scale 1:1).

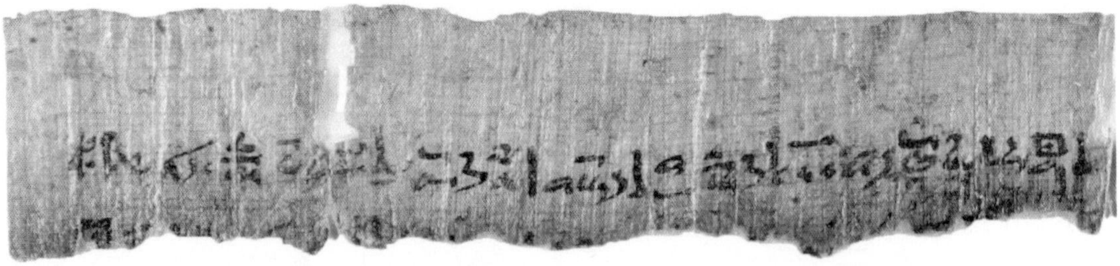

Papyrus Leiden I 345, verso column XV (scale 1:1).

Papyrus Leiden I 345, verso column XVI (scale 1:1).

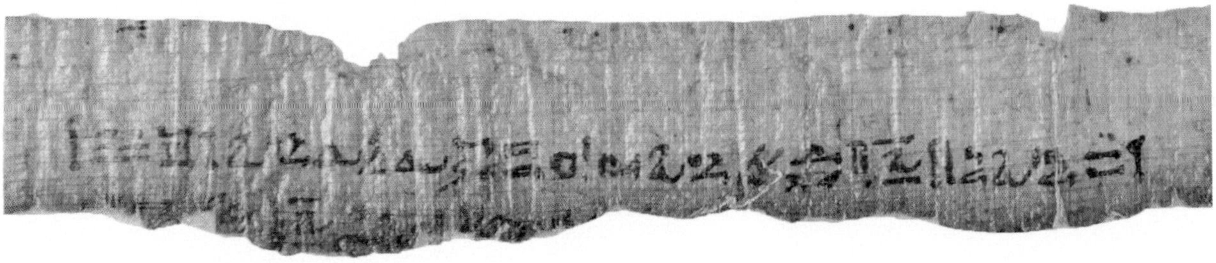

Papyrus Leiden I 345, verso column XVII (scale 1:1).

Pl. 62

XIV

XV

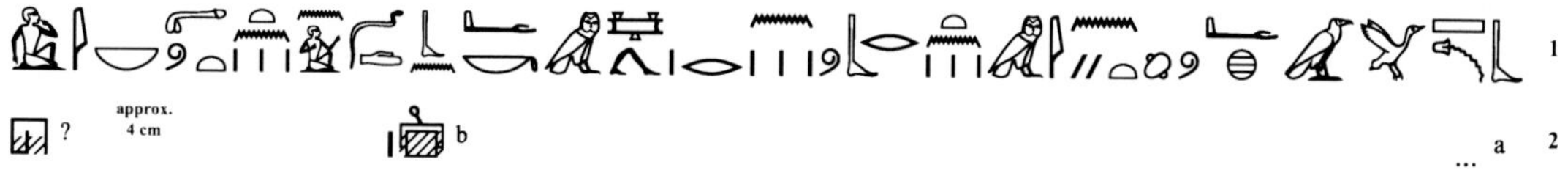

XVI

XVII

V:XIV–XVII *upper part of the column* **V:XIV1a** *traces* **2a–b** *lower part of the line is broken off* **V:XV2a–b** *traces*

V:XVII2a–b *lower part of the line is partially broken off.*

Papyrus Leiden I 345, verso columns XIV-XVII, transcription.

Pl. 63

Papyrus Leiden I 345, verso column XVIII (scale 1:1).

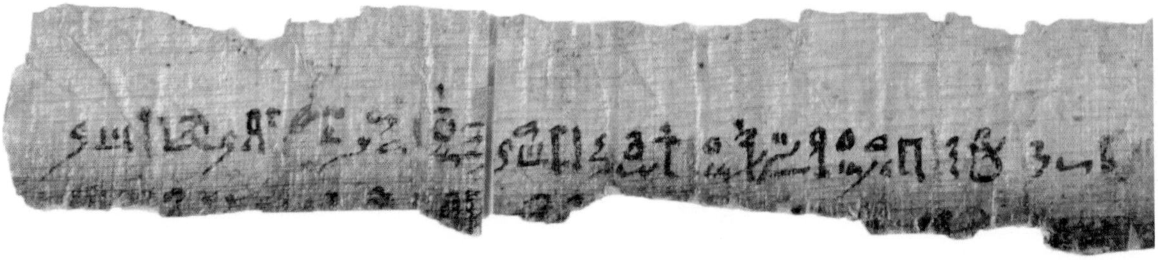

Papyrus Leiden I 345, verso column XIX (scale 1:1).

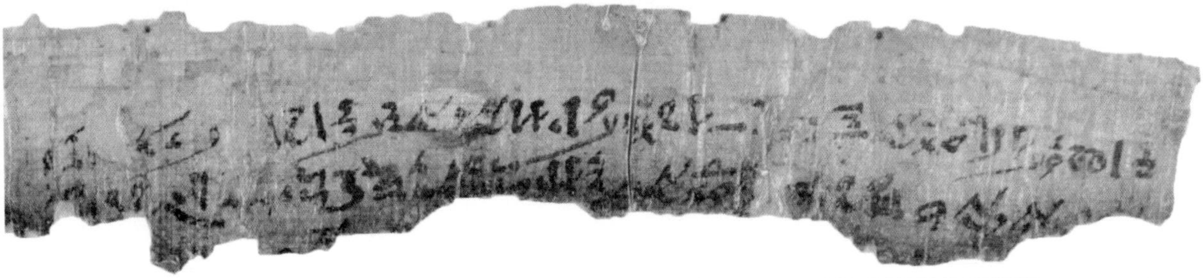

Papyrus Leiden I 345, verso column XX (scale 1:1).

Pl. 64

XVIII

XIX

XX

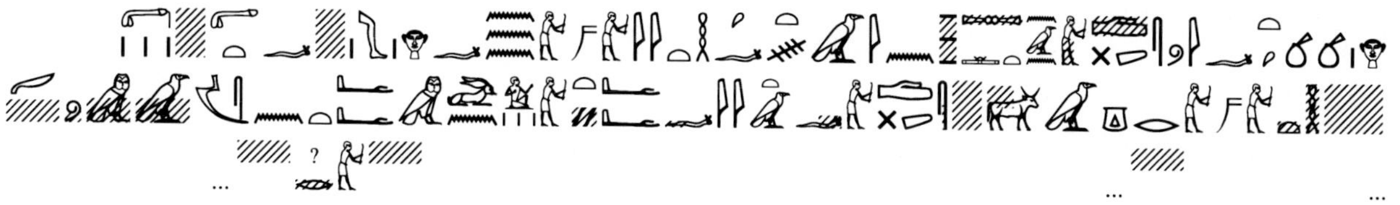

V:XVIII–XX *upper part of the column* **V:XVIII2a** *or* —.

Papyrus Leiden I 345, verso columns XVIII-XX, transcription.

Pl. 65

Papyrus Leiden I 345, verso column XXI (scale 1:1).

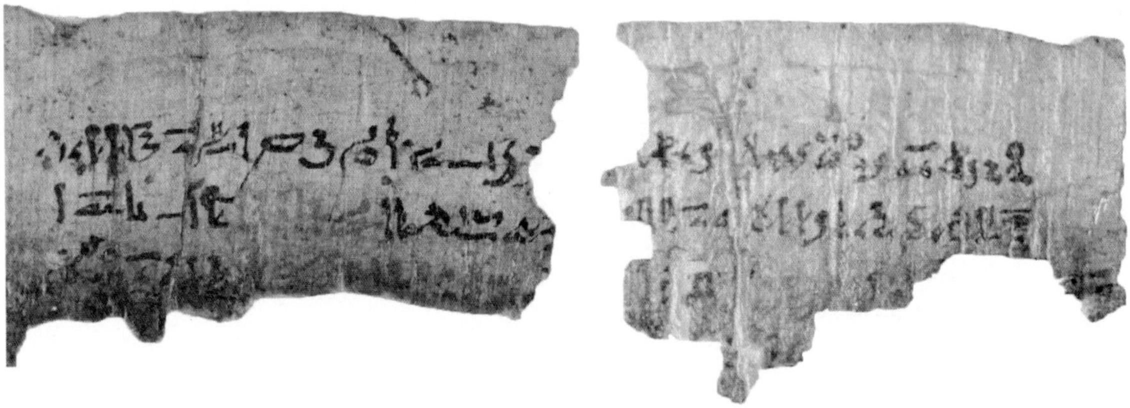

Papyrus Leiden I 345, verso column XXII (scale 1:1).

Pl. 66

XXI

XXII

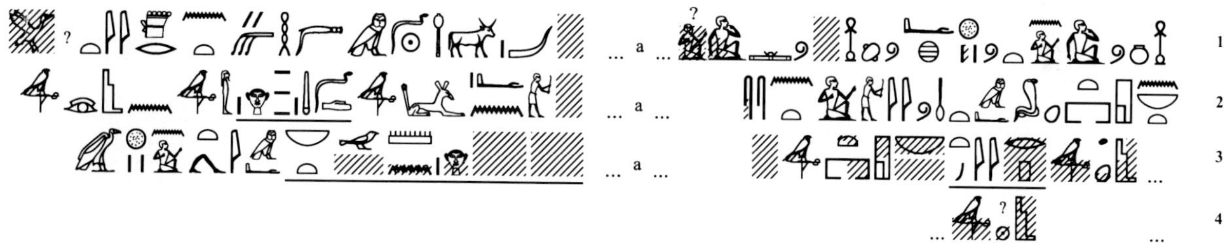

V:XXI *upper part of the column* **V:XXI1a** *space between the fragments not certain* **2a** *space not certain* **2a–b** *no longer exists* **2c–d** *lower part of the line almost completely broken off* **V:XXII1a, 2a and 3a** *the distance between the fragments is uncertain.*

Papyrus Leiden I 345, verso columns XXI-XXII, transcription.

Pl. 67

Papyrus Leiden I 345, verso column XXIII (scale 1:1).

Pl. 68

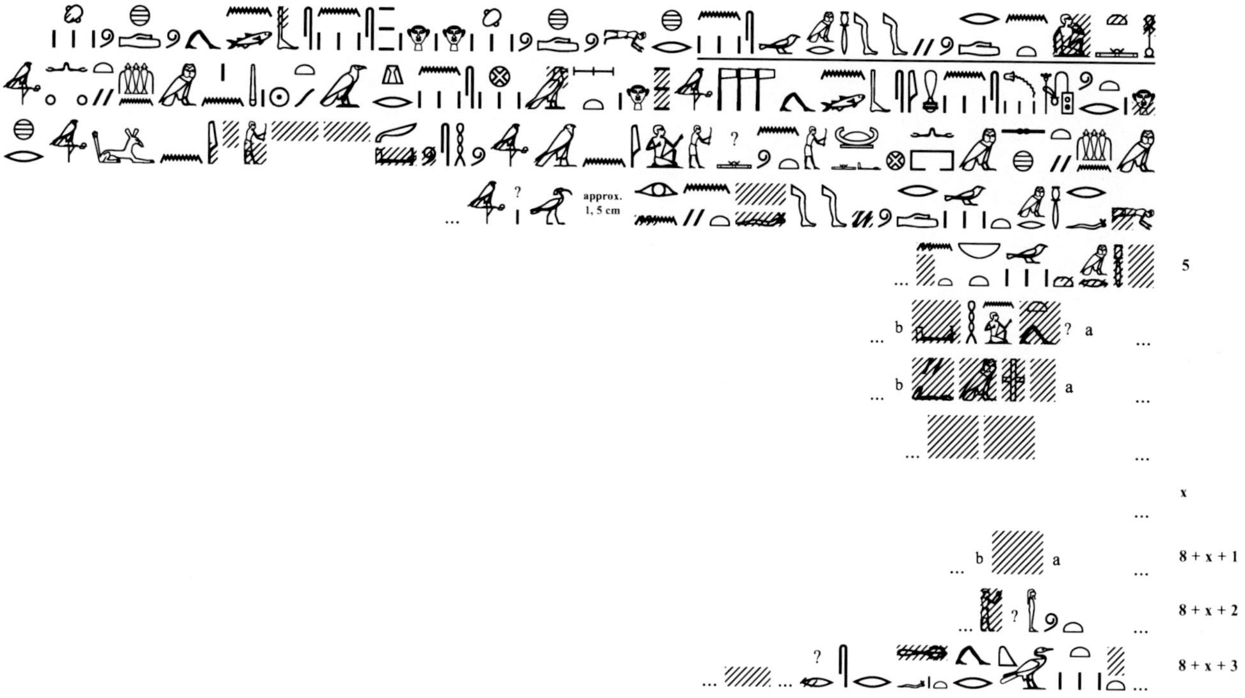

V:XXIII6a–b *partially only traces* **7a–b** *partially only traces* **8+x+1a–b** *traces in red.*

Papyrus Leiden I 345, verso column XXIII, transcription.

Pl. 69

Papyrus Leiden I 345, verso column XXIV (scale 1:1).

Pl. 70

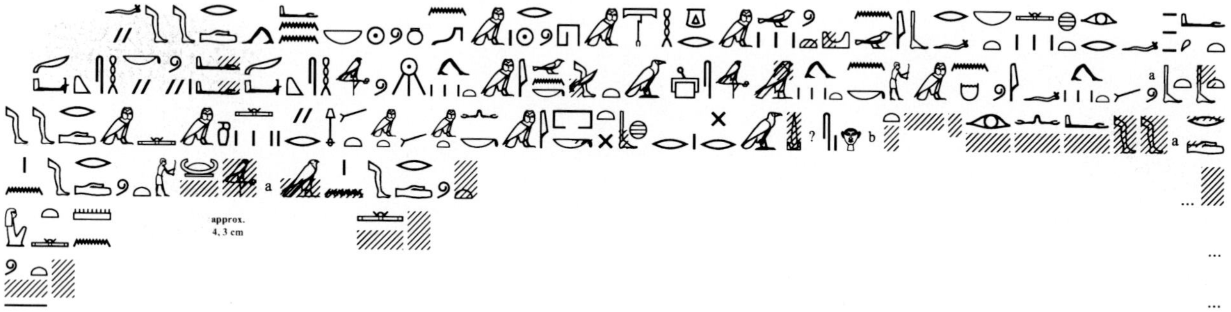

V:XXIV2a 9 *above the line* **3a–b** *lower part of the line is broken off* **4a** 4 *is no longer legible.*

Papyrus Leiden I 345, verso column XXIV, transcription.

Pl. 71

Papyrus Leiden I 345, verso column XXV (scale 1:1).

Pl. 72

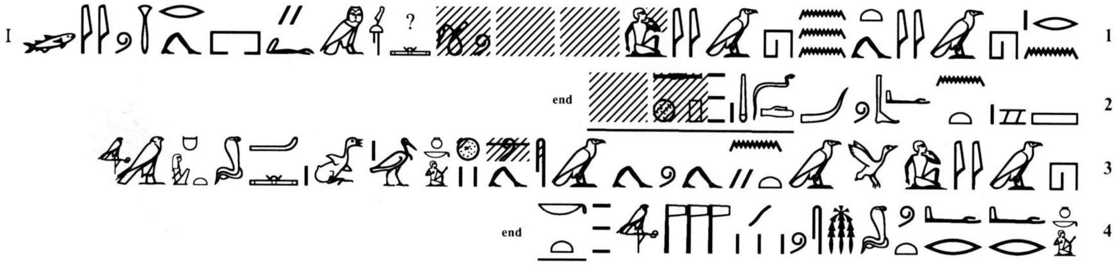

V:XXV 1 *From the end of this column to the end of the papyrus approx. 29 cm are blank.*

Papyrus Leiden I 345, verso column XXIV, transcription.